7----- Bells
Mine Safety & Accidents
at
Bisbee, Arizona
(Second Edition)

A reenacted safety photo showing a mine car tub that has
fallen backwards from a cotter key failure. C-1917

Richard W. Graeme IV

Dedicated to
Jack Schissler, Julian " Cat" Durazo, Julio Palomino, Toby Valdez, Al Hirales,
Bobby "Pete" Olier, Bennie Scott, Melvin Elkins, Henry Hernandez, Julian " Kelly"
Castillo, Sam " Silent Sam" Elkins, Neto Chavez, Blas "Sonny" Tovar, Douglas
"Whirlpool" Graeme, Richard Graeme III, A.T. "Snake" Huerena, Bill Acuna
Great Miners, but finer men!

Special thanks to the kind patience of the ladies at the
Polly Rosenbaum Archives and History building for their kindness, hard work and
patience.

Thanks to Annie Larkin and Deloris Reynolds for their hard work and research
skills.

All images are part of the Graeme-Larkin collection, except where noted.

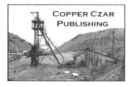

COPPER CZAR
PUBLISHING

Edited April 19, 2024

Table of Contents

Evergreen Cemetery with the Denn Mine in the background.

Introduction

When the mines in Bisbee began, accidents were relatively few. The number of men employed was small, and the technology was basic. This early mining was done by hand drilling and blasting shallow drill holes. Often only one or two holes were blasted at a time. New ground was opened at a tediously slow pace. The mine workings were still new and the timber was in good condition. Safety was largely a personal responsibility and was dependent on the skill of the miner. President of the Copper Queen Consolidated Mining Company, Dr. James Douglas was a paternal leader with a strong reputation of being concerned for the welfare of his employees and the Copper Queen was the only significant mining company in Bisbee. Although, his fatherly concern for his employees defined company policy, his son Walter Douglas the general manager for the Copper Queen decided that mine safety needed to be resolved with direct action.

At the end of the 19th century and beginning of the 20th other mining companies arrived. Soon many mines were open, these were small and often little more than a prospected claims. The Calumet and Arizona Mining Company soon developed into a substantial mine that rivaled the fabled mines of the Copper Queen. This was followed by the Lake Superior and Pittsburg Mining Company, Junction Development Company, Shattuck and Arizona Mining Company and others. These mines began to employ thousands of men, and the district became worth the investment of modern technology. The introduction of pneumatic rock drills started in the 1890s, and by 1900 was replacing hand drilling. Suddenly, the men could drill in minute's hole that would have taken hours hand drilling. Blast patterns became larger, although still relatively shallow. Large amounts of new workings were being created quickly. In 1912, 2,401 men were employed by the Copper Queen alone. A similar number would have been employed by the Calumet & Arizona Companies. Always in demand skilled miners, who could "read" the rock and timber had to be coaxed from their homes in Cornwall, Saxony, and Michigan to take the arduous trip into the Arizona Territory and then travel further to Bisbee along the Mexican Border. Desperate to fill positions. Less skilled men were hired, but the mechanization of mining allowed for this to be somewhat effective. Pneumatic drills are easy to operate. Also, the need for "reading the rock" for weaknesses to take advantage of in blasting was reduced. Holes could be placed anywhere with pneumatic drills and the brute strength of explosives broke the rock.

The mines were also aging by 1900, some of the drifts and stopes had been standing open for two decades. These stopes mined years before, even those carefully backfilled, were beginning to collapse. This caving destroyed or damaged workings nearby. Subsidence cracks began to form on the hillsides hinting at the destruction underneath the ground. Some of these cracks were twenty-feet across, hundreds of feet long and two-hundred-feet deep. Bridges were built to allow pedestrians to cross these crevices. There were so many cracks that when the Spray Change House was robbed, the thief ran out and disappeared. The men searching for him believed he had fallen to his death in one of the seemly bottomless crevices. The Copper Queen Hospital that was located above the Holbrook Mine workings had to be moved in 1909 because of mining subsidence. In 1906 the main hoisting shaft, the Holbrook No.1 collapsed from ground movement and was forcibly abandoned. Additionally, the increased number of mine workings that honey-combed the earth, structurally weakened the entire mining area.

Accidents began to increase and the local newspapers began reporting injuries nearly every day. Most were slight injuries, but a significant number were crippling or fatal. By 1907, a miner was being killed on average every 19 days. The reporters often spared little and discussed the events in gruesome details. It seems the population became blinded to the number of men being killed. On February 17, 1904, at least one reporter was bothered by the men being killed and injured. After W.G. McCall was killed in the Wolverine mine and Frank Tremain in the Holbrook Mine the front page of the Bisbee Daily Review told of their deaths. Unique in the newspaper articles about mine accidents, the writer expresses emotion. At first, the writing begins sympathetically and then focuses on the mechanical and routine nature of retrieving Tremain's body.

It is a pathetic and touching moment to stand at the mouth of the yawning shaft, awaiting from below which will be the means of causing grief and sorrow in some beloved home. There is the clang of bells and the cable tightens and commences to hoist. It was a double signal from the 400, and a miner standing near remarked: "They are hoisting the body from below now." The miners on top gather about the landing as the cable reels up from below, and as the cage jumps into view the limp form of the departed comrade is seen supported in the arms of his co-workers, who kneel about the deck of the cage. Tenderly they lift the still form from the cage and the stretcher that has served on similar occasions is brought out. The dead body is borne into the engine room and a kind hand places a newspaper over the face. The coroner is summoned and another mining incident is closed. The bells clang and signals again and other men are lowered into the black shaft. Another cage is lowering timbers and the great mine resumes its hum of industry.

As the writer continues his frustration with these deaths are revealed.

"It would seem that there is to be no cessation in the long trend of mine fatalities occurring at the various properties in the immediate vicinity of Bisbee, and on account of the sad and horrible accidents which have been occurring, one closed on the heels of the other, one becomes dread what the coming day will bring forth. Barely are the printed sheets giving particulars of a mine horror dry, than the cold types are again being hastily gathered for the purpose of printing the details of another fatality.

People here have not had sufficient time to recover from the awful shock produced by the Pittsburg and Duluth mine horror, in which two miners met death and another will be scarred and maimed for life as a result, when now they stand again called upon to with stand the news of still another occurrence which has been destructive of life."

It was not only fatal accidents that caused concern. Significant number of serious injuries occurred and a portion of these were crippling. Prominent citizens Dan Hankins and Judge Burdick, both had been crippled underground. Other injuries were insignificant when the man was young, but bothered them as the aged or as in the cases of silicosis finally killed them. Then also there were secondary accidents such as a lone cowboy who fell into a shaft and a young house wife was badly mutilated when she dropped hot ashes from a fire into a trash barrel. Someone earlier had discarded blasting caps in the barrel and they exploded instantly as the ashes touched them. Before a safety movement could be successfully started, human life had to be valued in a new way. The lethality of daily life in pre-antibiotic Bisbee was frightening. Sanitation and drinking water of the community were questionable. Disease was rampant. Typhoid, tuberculosis, pneumonia, nephritis and peritonitis killed far many more miners than accidents. These illnesses and traumatic accidents occurring on the railroads and farms overshadowed mine accidents. The idea that life in the West was hard and short had to give way to optimism. Slowly, the community evolved to accept that work related accidents could be reduced or eliminated. By 1912, Bisbee was ready for safety in the homes, at schools and in the mines.

Safety Movement

In 1912, the El Paso & Southwestern Railroad a company interrelated to the Copper Queen Consolidated Mining Company discovered that from June 30, 1911 to June 30, 1912 that one out of every eight employees and officials of the railroad was injured. They also learned one out of every 949 employees was killed. It was time for action. Edward L. Tinker was hired as the safety supervisor and the railroad joined part of the "Safety First" agenda. The Copper Queen's General Manager Walter Douglas, influenced by the railroad, decided the company would join the "Safety First" movement. Before 1912, the Copper Queen had made beginning steps towards safety and employee health by providing a hospital, modern change houses and equipment like candle sconces for fire prevention, pulmotors and a few Draeger mine rescue helmets. Basic first aid equipment, such as bandages, were available underground. On June 29, 1913 the Bisbee Daily Review announced that the Copper Queen was adopting the "Safety First" program. The first meeting of the Safety First Committee had actually been on March 21, 1913 and it had been decided that entire workforce needed to be part of the program. Representatives were going to be chosen and Mr. Tinker of the El Paso & Southwestern was going to be advising the development of the program. Within a few weeks Wallace E. McKeehan was chosen as safety inspector by representatives of the mine workers. McKeehan was sent to visit coal and iron mines as well as steel mills to learn the safety practices. A rescue building was also constructed to house the safety offices and the mine rescue equipment. He also traveled to the Red Cross Society and the U.S. Bureau of Mines. The critical element was the company's vision that all employees had a say in safety. It was understood that miners are often slow to accept new ideas, unless they were their own. It was to be a *get together program*" and McKeehan was a wise choice. He was passionate about safety and understood how to motivate not only the employees, but the entire community. Postcards were placed so employees could mail in their safety suggestions or if they preferred they could drop them into a locked suggestion box. The Copper Queen began issuing bulletins describing the nature of accidents in the Copper Queen's mines. The intent was to provide a quick interesting look at recent accidents in a quality document. These bulletins were posted widely through the town. Although, McKeehan was a motivator and leader of men. He could be hard. His bulletins often were blunt and called out the employees specifically. For example, when Ivan Klobucar was working in 8-25-9 raise in an unspecified Copper Queen mine. He found the previous round had failed to break and there remained about 18 inches of each hole. Ignoring the shift bosses' order, he decided to drill in one of the bootlegs and it detonated. Not only was his story published in the Copper Queen Bulletin and posted around Bisbee, it was distributed state wide in the April 1, 1916 issue of the State Safety News. There is little doubt that Klobucar's fellow miners teased him hard about his mistake, but that was the point. Klobucar was faced with peer pressure and now had to prove to the world that he was a good miner. McKeehan's policies made the miners vested in the success of the Safety Program. If the miners had made an excellent choice for a safety inspector, the company had made an equally brilliant choice by making Joseph P. Hodgson, mine superintendent. He was a believer in mine safety and brave. Soon, first aid cabinets and cans were made in the mine shops and delivered to all mine departments and locations underground. Even minor injuries were expected to receive first aid treatment. This was to prevent septicemia. Data was being collected. During the beginning fifteen days of August 1913, which only 13 were days worked, there were 45 accidents reported. Although, 44 were considered slight, one was considered serious. Of interest was the nature of the accidents.

Ran nail in hand: 1
Bruised hand on rock: 3
Falls of ground: 6
Hurt by cars: 16
By timbers: 6
Eyes cut while breaking boulder: 1
Stepping on nail: 1
Sliding on rope: 1
Cut wedge saw: 1
Hurt by tools: 9
Falls ordinary: 1

This information was used to guide the safety movement particularly when new equipment such as mucking machines and jackleg drills were introduced. The data collected from accidents was gathered until the end of mining in Bisbee. This knowledge was used to change policies and used as topics for discussion in safety meetings. Safety inspectors used the data to note that skilled miners had few accidents. New employees underground were at great risk. This was particularly noted when then had about six months experience. It was felt that they became over confident and were often injured. Although, brand new workers were killed or injured. Frank Billings was killed after spending less than 15 minutes underground.

Safety rallies were held at the Y.M.C.A. called "smokers" At one meeting participants were given free cigars with a "Safety First, Copper Queen" cigar band. These were later sold throughout the city and could be found on several different cigar brands. The "Smokers " included motion picture films of mine accidents, stereopticon cards, and magic lantern slides of the Copper Queen's mines. These meetings had a vaudeville influence with songs, and comedy and western drama films intermingled with the safety discussions. Over 700 men attended the first night. At a safety meeting in April 1914 Mine Superintendent Joseph P. Hodgson made his view point clear. *"Labor is the dearest commodity we have and human life is and always should be held sacred."*

A 1913 ad from The Bisbee Daily Review

The safety movement was infectious and businesses began to add the "Safety First" to their advertisements. The safety program began to focus on the wives and families of the employees. It was the families that suffered the long term consequences if an employee was injured or killed. To encourage attendance among the ladies of Bisbee, refreshments were served and the ladies were given boxes of candy. The Copper Queen was seeking cooperation of the women and friends in miner's lives to motivate them to safe work. Poems and letters from mothers were printed in the newspaper in support the program. At the end of 1913, the Copper Queen published their accidents report in the newspaper. This document revealed that following number accidents occurred by working with

Cages: 3
Chutes: 13
Dirt in eyes: 16
Explosives, carbide: 5
Electricity: 1
Fall in manway: 1
Fall through floors: 6
Falls ordinary: 21
Falling timber: 46
Falling ground: 150
Ladders: 3
Machinery, falling machines: 33
Mine cars: 41
Mine fires, gas: 2
Motors and motor: 11
Nails stepped on: 21
Pipe, Fitting: 2
Pockets, Conveyors: 10
Strains and Sprains: 61
Tools: 55

Between 1913 and May of 1914 the Copper Queen had spent $150,000 dollars in mine safety at Bisbee. Part of this money was spent giving a physical examination for all new employees. Although, most elements of the safety program that were introduced were generally accepted in 1914. This was less than popular and was an issue protested by the social organization, The International Workers of World in the 1917 strike. During 1918, 88 men were initially rejected for employment out of 2,342 that were given a physical. Twenty of the 88 men who failed the exam were passed on the condition that they would receive medical treatment. These men needed to undergo a hernia repair operation.

The reasons for the 88 failed physical exams.

acute hernia: 48 (20 these conditionally passed)
heart condition: 7
active tuberculosis: 7
eyesight: 6
drugs, alcohol, morphine: 4
fever: 3
hearing: 2
bad teeth: 1
measles: 1
Bright's disease: 1
unusable arm or leg: 1
acute venereal disease: 1
The final six men did not have a reason noted.

Phelps Dodge used these exams to place their employees in the best working conditions suited for them. For example, men with lung issues were hired for work on the surface. Older or disabled men could be given less intensive positions like powder monkey or put on a track crew. The program expanded rapidly and soon incorporated first aid techniques as well as developing safety rules and procedures. As part of the program, boulders hanging precariously from Queen Hill were blasted down. There was concern that these rocks would be loosened by the monsoon rains and roll down into Holbrook and Czar Buildings.

Edward Tinker began presenting Safety First programs to schools, first to 900 students in Tucson, then to 2,000 students in Bisbee. The company had recognized that these were not children, but rather their future work force. Many of these students would seek employment in the mines starting around the age of 14. Although, these young men were hired as light duty surface labor or tool nippers. Underground danger is everywhere and Frank Bowman was killed at 16 years of age and Charles Huber was killed soon after his 17th birthday. 16 year-old L.M. Strumm was crippled in an accident in the Czar Mine.

Tough, but enlightened Wallace McKeehan, felt it was essential that all employees be part of the safety process. The Copper Queen was particularly open to suggestions of workers and adopted inventions patented by Bisbee men, like the spitter board, Scott car, Frosco board and Saffold bar. Frosco boards and spitter boards were inventions to improve safety. Bert Frosco invented the Frosco board that prevented rocker dump mine cars from swinging back after being dumped. Spitter boards were invented by Thomas Spears and helped organize fuses for lighting. His invention reduced misfires, by reducing the chance of a miner forgetting to light a fuse. This was critical as expert ideas that seemed logical, failed in practice. As part of the "Safety First" program, all open holes were covered and extra landings were installed in manways. Unfortunately, this reduced the flow of air and working areas were becoming unbearably hot. Dependent on the practical knowledge of the employees, different designs were submitted by workers until one was found that allowed for safety and air movement. The Copper Queen continued to rely on employee participation in making the mine safer. During 1974, the last full year of mining, workers suggested 431 safety recommendations. By the end of the year 393 had been accepted and completed, 34 were rejected, and the remaining 14 were still under consideration or had not been finished.

A series of detailed photographs were taken showing common types of accidents and proper methods of working were taken in the mines. McKeehan felt it was essential that the images be of Bisbee mines and the participants in the photos be Copper Queen Employees and ideally popular ones. McKeehan recognized that miners would relate to this type of photographs and they would be kept engaged by realizing these were real miners that they knew. These included images showing situations "before and after" a recreated accident, safety rules being broken and areas where accidents had occurred. These images were not only used for safety training, but at times were shown to a coroner's jury to help them understand an accident. Normally, a coroner's jury visited the accident site themselves, but these images allowed them to see the location in detail rather than by the dim flickering light of a carbide lamp or candle.

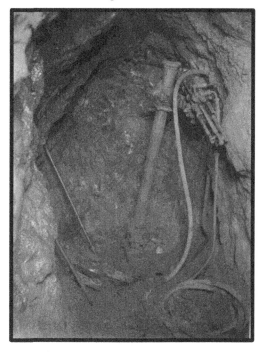

**A safety photo showing an where a miner
has drilled into a missed hole. C-1920**

The complexities of mining rules, quickly revealed the need for specialized training. A practical course in mining was developed in 1918, to train miners about their specific job and of those around them. These classes were taught at the Y.M.C.A. and miners were required to attend 35 meetings before they could take the final examination. This was required to become a shift boss or those with two years mining experience, a certificate of "Skilled Miner" was issued. The course was intense and covered timbering, blasting, haulage and even assaying. The complete text book used was over 850 pages and well-illustrated. Miners were generally given the chapters one at a time to be kept in a ringed binder. The course was updated as the mining changed. 44% of all miners and 39% of all muckers attended these course during the 1919-1920. The practical course was not static and continually evolved.

Around 1919, W.W. Gidley became the safety inspector and continued the aggressive safety policies. First aid classes were offered and each employee was give $1.00 per class they attended. Sanitation underground was one of his focus points. He encouraged the drifts be clean of loose debris on the ground, can were provided for the trash from lunches and toilet mine cars were provided. Gidley expected underground mule barns to be kept as clean as *As clean as the stables of a high priced dairy herd from the middle west.* "To improve sanitary conditions on the surface, modern change houses were constructed at the Czar, Lowell and Sacramento mines with others being renovated. Specially made toilet mine cars were made and place underground. The department place "Safety First" signs around the mine site in notable places. General warning signs were added as well as some more unusual signs with safety phrases. Examples are *"Be careful, there are no round trip tickets from the graveyard."* and *"The Bank of Safety pays 100 percent and never fails."*

A Copper Queen style, directional sign 7th level Southwest Mine

By the 1920s, a "School of Mines was started by the Copper Queen Branch using workings of the Southwest and upper levels of the Czar Mine. These were expansive, ore producing mines that included a variety of it stope and mining conditions. The concept of mine safety was gaining momentum. This school gave critical hands-on experience under the watchful eye of instructors and bosses. Although, these mines did lack the intensely hot or wet areas that could found in the deeper mines. They provided an excellent training ground. All underground employees regardless of their experience worked in the "School of Mines" for around three months to learn how to mine the Bisbee way. During this time the unexperienced learned the basics of safe mining and how to find their way around a mine. This was not make believe mining. These were major ore producing areas with all the hazards of the deeper mines. Once the three months of training were over the men were transferred to other mines or remained as part of the Czar/Southwest mine crew.

The Copper Queen Bulletin was being issued. It was a monthly, bulletin that addressed among other things safety concerns. A section addressed safety concerns brought up by employees and the safety department. Also around this time safety incentives, lapel pins, belt buckles and wallets were being given out for number of years without having a lost time accident. The number of mine accidents began to fall sharply. In 1912 the Copper

Queen Consolidated Mining Company had nine fatal accidents and in 1917 three fatal accidents had occurred. After a mine accident the injured person was taken to the company hospital. These hospitals provided free and modern medical care. At times an injured employees was given half their regular salary. If the injuries were fatal the mining company covered the cost of the funeral. No conclusive records give details on any financial settlements that were made with the surviving families, but Martin Carter's widow reportedly received a pension from the Copper Queen.

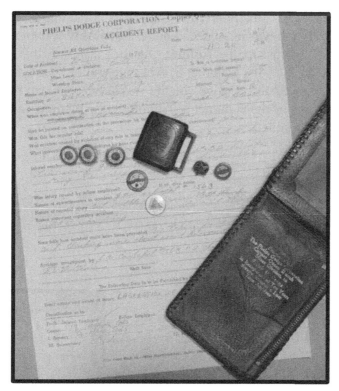

Examples of safety incentives given to Phelps Dodge employees.

Other mining companies became interested in the Safety First Program in August 1913. The Calumet & Arizona Mining Company and soon the Shattuck & Arizona Mining Company began teaching safety first to their employees. These programs seem to have faltered and did not become a driving force. The Shattuck's program was briefly mentioned and seems to have largely disappeared. It probably became dependent on hiring miners from its larger rivals and using the safety skills taught to them to teach other miners, in an on the job environment.

The Calumet & Arizona Safety Department was not formed until February 1915 under engineer Thomas Cowperthwaite. In contrast to the Copper Queen, his plan was designed to force the "Safety First" into effectiveness. His committee was formed of only mine bosses. He felt that the men and bosses felt safety was a joke. Cowperwaite knew the supervisors resented attending his mandatory safety meetings. Believing that only the bosses could enforce safety and should be absolutely responsible for mine safety, he proceeded in developing the program. Safety Supervisor Cowperthwaite used the data collected from accidents to discharge poor bosses. Furthermore, he told the workers that they should secretly tell him about any safety issues they knew about. In this way they could not be disciplined by a supervisor for the exposing unsafe conditions. Men found working unsafely could be laid-off from two days to two weeks. Instead of "Smokers" the C&A held a "Safety First" dance in Warren during 1916, but appears to not have the focus or appeal of the Copper Queen's rallies. By 1916, the safety movement had gained national appeal and was applied to automobiles, children and food products. The Calumet had genuinely committed to the safety movement after both the Copper Queen and nation. Signs were posted in and around the mines with bright red borders indicating they hazard warnings. The Calumet & Arizona Safety Program does not to appear to be as strong. Part of this is likely due to how it was managed. The responsibility was of safety was given to the bosses. This is in contrast to the Copper Queen's program that included even the families of the miners. In 1931 the Calumet & Arizona Mining Company merged with the Copper Queen Branch of Phelps Dodge. In the merger the Queen's safety philosophy replaced most components of the Calumet's. Although, the warning signs with the highly visible red borders were retained.

Calumet & Arizona style signs at a call bell
2700 level Junction Mine.

Calumet & Arizona style directional sign
770 level Junction Mine.

In 1917, another new technology arrived in Bisbee, open pit mining. The Sacramento Pit resulted in the number of accidents soaring. It was the second open pit mine in Arizona and was started shortly after the New Cornelia pit at Ajo. Lack of familiarity with heavy equipment and heavy open pit blasting resulted in the worst accidents that occurred in Bisbee. The Copper Queen had hired a number of experienced open pit employees from other pit mines such as Santa Rita, New Mexico. Both experienced bosses and workman came to Bisbee. But even with their experience, it was not until 1925 that the number of accidents returned to low numbers. The original safety building built in 1913 was located too close to the new pit and a new building was constructed near the Czar and Southwest Mines.

Safety building near the Czar & Southwest mines. c- 1928

In 1927, safety moved forward again when hard hats were required. Miners were given pocket first aid kits to be carried at all times. The "School of Mines" ceased around 1929, when the Southwest Mine was officially closed and the remaining ore reserves were turned over to lessees. The future of the safety education was moving towards the Standards of Practice Manuals. The Practical Mining Course eventually evolved into the Standards of Practice Manuals of the 1930s and the Procedure of Safe Practice Manual in the 1940s. Finally, in 1947 they became the Codes of Safe Practice that were used until operations ceased. These were also well-illustrated booklets that covered a broad number of topics, but were larger about 8.5" X 11" bound in a soft cover. The manuals were updated regularly into 1974 and the New Cornelia, United Verde & Morenci branches of Phelps Dodge also adopted their own versions. A miner would be loaned a copy of Code of Safe Practice he needed. During the mid-1950s-1960's a local artist named Bauer was assigned by the safety department to sketched safety cartoons for the local newspaper. These cartoons made fun poor choices made by miners and even included health issues like smoking. Monthly meetings were held underground. Recent accidents were discussed and men who had broken safety rules teased as part of the underground comradery. Other times the meetings were more serious such as when they discussed an accident where a piece of steel broke off a drill steel shank and blinded a J.S. Montoya in one eye. Meetings were not only focused on mine safety they would sometimes be oriented on making the home safer. One issue addressed was the electricity in houses. Many of the houses still retained the old-fashioned knob and tubing wiring which could be dangerous. Many miners did not like working with careless men. The term "Bonus Hound" was a nickname and a term used for a hard working productive miner. This phrase could also be used with a negative tone implying the miner took chances with safety. After 1925, the number of fatal accidents declined until the 1970s when fatal accidents were rare. When an employee was injured he filled out a blue card, a form printed on blue card stock. They would include information about the injury and the incident. At times miners would abuse this system and fill out a blue card to get a day off. Some old Bisbee miners feel the number of accidents in the later years is falsely high because of this practice.

Code of Safe Practice for three positions underground

During the last three decades of active mining, safety was the driving force. Breaking a safety rule was the fastest route to being dismissed from employment. Even 40 years after the suspension of active mining, the safety department for the Copper Queen Branch, now of Freeport-McMoRan still exists and works with the employees maintaining and reclaiming the mining area. The program has run 103 years continuously and is possibly the oldest safety program still working in Arizona.

The united safety program developed by Wallace McKeehan was successful. The key element was that he gave every employee ownership of safety. In the way the movement gathered the entire community it was more of a safety revolution than a program. Working safely was the first concern. He also gave the movement a driving force, which did not fade or falter. Never stagnant, the movement grew from rules and meetings to a full "School of Mines and later evolved into the Code of Safe Practice and safety trainings. In the 1970's many Bisbee miners proudly boasted that they worked in *"The safest mines in the world."* It would be difficult to prove this, but the men believed it. To think otherwise would be critical of themselves. *"Good miners are safe miners"* and these men were proud of their skills. No one was going to accuse them of otherwise.

Phelps Dodge the last major company to actively mine the Bisbee area had developed such a safety conscious work force that the research contradicted what the miners *"knew."* The over 375 fatal accidents came as such a distinct surprise that the number was highly questionable. In many cases the information was unbelievable to those who worked decades in the district both as management and as miners. Coroner's inquests, death certificates and mortuary records were used confirmed the accuracy of these numbers. Even with the seemingly high numbers it still might be considered *"The safest mines in the world."* Just ask a Bisbee a miner.

Significant Causes of Accidents

The greatest achievement of the safety departments in Bisbee is that there never was a mine disaster. All the conditions to create a mine disaster abundantly existed. The ground in areas was difficult to keep open even for a few days. The central magazine on the surface stored tons of explosives and numerous magazines underground kept hundreds of pounds readily available. Nearly 30 fires occurred underground. Developing an accurate comparison of safety conditions to other mining camps would be challenging. In 1910's the Copper Queen found it impossible, because many mining companies recorded only serious injuries, while the Copper Queen recorded, all accidents regardless of how minor. The other element is the mining conditions. Few metal mines were faced with the difficulties mining areas like the Dividend Fault Zone and the sheer size and variety of the other ore zones. Society today seems to need to find someone or a corporation to blame. This is not simple and would never accurately reflect the safety of the mines. After studying early inquests which assign a party at fault. It is clear that this was not even understood in the days following the accident. At times a fatal accident is listed in the inquest as "unavoidable" even though a company could have been logically at fault and other times a company is blamed even though it clearly appears the employee made the poor decision. Every employee underground is responsible for the safety of the entire crew. This their primary responsibility. Miners are proud of their skill as miners. They are passionately devoted to their art and do not take kindly to interference, even by mining engineers. The condition of their stope, drift or raise is a reflection of themselves. To question a miner's ability to work safely could easily be received as an insult. Many an old miner sitting at grassy park near the old P.D. offices or at the mine tour *"mucking a few tons."* (telling of their mining days) will tell you if they had to live their lives again that they would change a lot, but they would still be underground miners. Two miners at the Campbell, Toby

Valdez and Al Hirales described Heaven as *"a well timbered stope running high grade bornite."*

The four leading causes of fatal accidents were fall of ground, shaft accidents, blasting, and fall of person. As time progressed the hazards associated with these areas were never eliminated, but were dramatically reduced.

"Fall of Ground"

The mining ore does not generally occur in the "tunnels" which are called drifts or crosscuts. The ore is mined in great irregularly shaped chambers called stopes. These stopes can be 200 ft. or more tall and 2,000 ft. across. Under normal conditions a section is mined and timbered. Then the section is backfilled with waste rock to support the room and then another section is mined. This continues until the ore is mined out and all that remains is chamber completely filled with broken rock and possibly timber. Yet, while mining out these chambers or stopes, large open spaces can be created that are being worked. The ground will move seeking to reach a point of stability. Whether tunnel or stope, the ground will shift until it attains a stable condition.

The leading cause of mine injuries and deaths was "fall of ground." 137 men were killed in this manner. This is a rather broad and vague category. The accident could be caused by a five-pound rock falling from above a timber or a massive collapse of a 50-ton boulder. It does not include situations where a miner has been buried by rock from a chute or ore pass. This is where the true skill of a miner is discovered. Years of working in different rock types enables a good miner to read the language of the rock. From a safe area with a scaling bar a miner taps the walls and ceiling listening to changes of sound and feeling. The point of the bar is driven into cracks and the bar is pried on to see if it can be moved or "feels loose." They have learned how certain rock types or geologic features behave, the silica breccia is hard ground and breaks in massive boulders weight from a couple of tons to hundreds of tons. The Martin Limestone is often somewhat shaley and regularly breaks up in small pieces of a couple pounds, but occasionally boulders of hundreds of pounds become loose. Timber will likely be required to support drifts in the Martin. Generally sturdy and strong standing is the Escabrosa Limestone, but boulders particularly in freshly blasted areas can be problematic. The Dividend Fault Zone is a nightmare. The soft, heavy, clays moving and squeezing. Every inch will have to be strongly timbered and broken timber regularly changed. At times, it is impossible to keep these Dividend areas open. Each rock unit or feature has its personality which must be catered too. An individual miner may not know the geologic name of the rock unit or feature they are working, but they understand its characteristics. In general, smaller rocks under two tons are easier to detect if they are loose. One reason is that they are small enough that the force a man can apply with a well-placed scaling bar can be significant enough to move the boulder. When tapping the boulder with a bar it is small enough to give a hollow sound or punchy feeling. The disadvantage is that they are also small enough that trying to catch them up with timber can cause them to fall. Larger boulders that are loose can be difficult to find. They have such great mass that with a scaling bar a miner cannot possibly exert a force to even barely move the slab. They also are of such size it is challenging to see the cracks, fault lines and contacts that give clues to their stability.

19

Clearing ground to put in timber was the activity that injured the most miners by falling rock. In these cases, the men are dependent on the opinion of the rock condition by themselves and their shift. It is up to their skill. In the major mines at Bisbee timber was available for the asking and was delivered to the workplace with little or no questioning. The amount of timber used varied dependent on ground conditions. At times it was 33 board feet for each ton mined. In comparison for every 485 tons of ore mined the same amount of lumber was used to create 2,400 sq. ft. house. In 1910 the Copper Queen used 16,000,000 board feet of timber.

The timber yard at the Junction Mine c-1920

In difficult situations advice could be readily had from other miners and bosses. Experienced miners were expected to know when they needed to place in temporary timber. They were required not to move out beyond the protection of the cantilevered temporary timber known as booms. Miners are human. They can be lazy, tired, and ill-attentive to their work and make poor decisions. This is often when accidents happen. As a warning to younger men, the older guys would regularly remind them *"Miners are not killed in dangerous areas, they are killed in safe ones."* This is actually true according to the primary sources nearly all the men killed were working in areas they considered safe. Only a few were killed in dangerous areas. In dangerous areas miners are attentive, the air is thick with stress. Every pebble or handful of dust that falls is noted. Miners listen to the timbers and rocks talking with every crack or pop. In safe locations over confidence is problematic and miners need reminders that the *"goddess of all mud diggers"* is a fickle woman who is in complete control. Many miners suffered broken bones and bruises being reminded of seriousness of mining. One ton of rock is considered a three-foot by three-foot block or cubic yard. The two and three hundred pound rocks that killed many miners are not very large.

Mines are dynamic and part of an ever changing system. A change in ventilation will result in changes in the rock condition and timber decay. Caving of mine workings can begin to destroy nearby mine workings. It was essential that all stopes and openings such as natural caves be backfilled completely with waste rock. Normal mining operations failed to produce enough waste rock for backfill, so raises were driven at the Briggs and Gardner Mines transfer waste rock from the surface underground. At times drifts were driven just to provide backfill material. The Calyx raise was driven at the Cole Mine to transfer rock underground. Mill tailings mixed with cement were pumped underground for sand filling stopes. The sand filling technique was largely used to mine ores in the treacherous Abrigo Limestone. This limestone was so structurally weak they would fill a section with the sand fill and then mine underneath the fill. The tailings sand and cement mixture provided a strong back (ceiling) to work underneath. Checking the ground is a constant process and with miners is observing the ground is almost reflexive. This is done constantly where ever they may be working.

Closely timbered crosscut in heavy ground. C-1908

21

Shaft Accidents

Sixty-one men were killed in shaft accidents in Bisbee. As deep ores were exploited, both inclined and vertical shafts were sunk. As the shafts penetrate the earth, levels which are like floors branch out at regular intervals, normally every 100 feet. In Bisbee there are over 40 levels accessing over 2,200 miles of underground workings. Supplies and men are raised and lowered in elevator-like cages. Ore is brought out in mine cars on cages or skips by powerful hoists. Sinking buckets are used when the shaft is being deepened to remove broken rock. Modern mines are serviced with well-designed cages with limited access to the shaft and seem a particularly safe part of mining, but this was developed from hard lessons. Compared to other mining districts the shafts at Bisbee are shallow and small. The deepest shaft is the Campbell Mine at 3,333 ft. in depth and only the Junction and Sacramento shafts were 30' x 6' with five compartments for cages or skips.

The early cages were completely open to the shaft. They had no gates or doors. The shafts themselves were open and largely unprotected. Most cages in Bisbee could hold nine men on each deck although the cages at the Junction, Sunrise, and Cole shafts could hold 12 or more. These cages moved about 800 ft. per minute while moving men and 1,200 ft. per minute for ore or supplies. For most of the years of mining either candles or carbide lamps were used for illumination. To prevent miners from burning each other, the miner's trip into the mine was completed in darkness. The journey through the blackness was only broken by the flashes of light as the cage passed brightly lit level stations. It was in this eternal darkness that a man would make a mistake, a lunch box, lamp or limb would catch the shaft timber and he would be dragged from the cage. Instantly, he would be fatally crushed against the timber. The hoistman sometimes would see the cable on the massive hoist shake or feel a jar and suspect a problem. Often the cage was brought to the surface, and even the men on the cage were unsure of what had occurred. By the 1914, folding gates were added to the decks on most cages. Small mines like the Ivanhoe continued to use the small open cages to transport men into the mid-1920. Today, one of the cages from the Ivanhoe Shaft is on display at the Queen Mine Tour and is the last of this type of cage from Bisbee. The other major cause of shaft accidents was riding with tools or supplies. If any tool or mine car shifted during travel and became caught on the shaft wall or timber, the results were catastrophic. The objects would be thrown smashing anyone on the cage and likely knocking them into the shaft. Even if no person were on the cage, the shaft timber would be damaged, and the hoisting cable can be injured. It took decades for folding gates to be installed on cages in Bisbee. In contrast, shaft gates appear to have been introduced early on. These protected a person from stepping or falling into an open shaft. This safety device was probably added soon after shaft type mining was introduced in 1881. A few of the shaft accidents such as Casper Herr's appear to be intentional on part of the victim. The events are difficult to explain unless it was deliberate or an extremely poor decision was made. Accidents that where an individual was looking up or down a shaft are also possibly intentional. These accidents are difficult to understand. After the cages were gated and the rule of not riding with equipment was enforced, the number of shaft accidents declined sharply.

Cage with gates at the Dallas Mine.   Men being lowered on open cages at the Gardner Mine. C-1909

Blasting

The rock underground is hard and picks are almost never used to dig. Picks are typically used to loosen up previously blasted rock for shoveling or used to pry down loose rock that is below waist high. Miners would drill a pattern of blast holes and load them with explosives to blast out the rock. Underground miners in Bisbee were expected to complete their blasting. Only in the open pits was blasting completed by a specialized crew.

Dynamite, which is generally called powder was used for the majority of blasting until the late 1960s when ANFO (ammonium nitrate fuel oil) began to partially replace it. Dynamite is relatively shock resistant explosive and available in different strengths and such as types Straight, Low Freezing (freezes at 35° F), Gelatin (water resistant), Amogel (ammonium nitrate based). Unfortunately, some animals like dogs, cattle, and mine rats find dynamite tasty with often fatal results. Dynamite also readily burns, and for decades, burning powder was the preferred method of destroying old dynamite. Legend has that old dynamite is unstable and wickedly dangerous. In fact, old dynamite is not likely to detonate at all. Each case of powder is dated on one end and if stored in a cool, dry magazine and occasionally the case is turned over it is expected to remain reliable for one year. These ideal conditions are difficult to achieve at times in Bisbee. Humidity is the most problematic as dynamite contains sodium nitrate which is hygroscopic (absorbs water) to the point it becomes deliquescent. The liquid solution of water and sodium nitrate forces the nitroglycerin to settle out of the dynamite. This is one reason cases of powder are turned. Tiny white crystals of sodium nitrate are often found on sticks that have been left underground. These abandoned sticks have stained the dirt or the wood of the powder box they are sitting on with leached nitroglycerin. In 1915 typical 1 ¼" X 8"stick of 40% straight dynamite contained.

40% Nitroglycerin
15% Wood Pulp
44% Sodium Nitrate (donates oxygen to the explosion)
1% Calcium Carbonate

The insensitivity of dynamite to shock creates the need for a detonator to provide an initial explosion which results in the powder exploding. A typical detonator or as more commonly called a blasting cap is a copper tube slightly less than ¼" in diameter that is closed on one end. Then a small amount of the highly sensitive explosive, mercury fulminate is added. The remainder of the tube is left open so a fire or safety fuse can be carefully slid into the cap and contact the fulminate. When a fuse is lit, it burns until it reaches its end. Sparks and flame are emitted from the end detonating the mercury fulminate and in turn detonating the dynamite. Since the mines in Bisbee used trolley locomotives and stray currents were potential problems. Electric blasting caps were rarely used. Safety fuse dominated the mines until the end.

No. 3   1" copper tube 8.3 grains of mercury fulminate
No.4   1 1/16" copper tube 10.00 grains mercury fulminate
No.5   1 3/16" copper tube   12.30 grains of mercury fulminate
No. 6   1 ½" copper tube   15.4 grains mercury fulminate
No. 8   2 ½" copper tube   30.8 grains of mercury fulminate

From left: No.8, No.6 & No.3 Blasting caps.

After a pattern of drill holes was completed, a miner went to a magazine and would get from a powder monkey the necessary fuses, caps and dynamite. At the face and a miner would take a single stick of dynamite slightly twist it to loosen up the contents of the stick. He then would pierce a hole in the powder with a sharp wooden skewer at about 30° angle, about between 1" and 2 ½" depending on the size of the blasting cap. The detonator is placed into the dynamite. Often the fuse is tied to the powder with string. The stick is placed in the mouth of a blast hole and pushed to the back of the hole with a wooden tamping rod. At the end of the hole it is normal to apply pressure on the tamping rod slightly crushing the stick of dynamite. This is essential in vertical blast holes, or the dynamite will fall out. After the first stick is placed it is followed with more sticks of dynamite. Each stick is tamped or crushed with even pressure from the tamping rod to ensure all sticks of dynamite are in physical contact. Only one blasting cap is added in each hole. Care is taken not to damage the fuse.

After all the holes are loaded the fuses are lined up cut to the length for firing order. The first hole to detonate has the shortest fuse. These fuses are ignited (spit) in their firing order. After the fuses are burning, the miners leave to guard all entrances to the area being blasted. At their guarding points, the miners wait and count the holes as they detonate. If they suspect one or more of the holes misfired, it is reported to the shift boss as they leave work. Starting before 1910, the boss would mark it up on a misfire board so the next shift would expect to find a miss. If there is a louder than normal shot heard that the miners suspect is two shots detonating at the same time it is still reported as a misfire.

A leading cause of misfires was improperly cut fuse. It was important that a sharp knife be used to give a clean cut. The scissor-like jaws on a blasting cap crimper or a dull knife crushed the fuse and smears the tar-like waterproofing over the end of the fuse. This blocks the sparks from reaching the fulminate. Sharp bends, knots or cuts in the fuse can result in the fuse stopping to burning, or worse create a slow burning fuse, called a hang fire. Improper crimping of the blasting cap on the fuse can result in a misfire. A stationary crimper or a pair of hand blasting cap crimpers provides a reliable crimp. Also using too low strength of a blasting cap causes problems. The cap explodes but does not provide enough force to detonate the dynamite. A gap between sticks of powder in a hole can prevent the detonation from carrying to all the sticks of dynamite. Part of the hole will remain unblasted. This happens if the blast hole caves in while loading or even if a few rocks fall leaving a space between sticks. Not properly tamping the dynamite can also cause this type of misfire. Another, type of misfire is the result of a "cut-off" hole. This occurs when the detonation of one hole blasts out a nearby hole before it has exploded. This can be caused by unseen fractures or weaknesses in the rock, using the wrong firing order and by using too much explosive for the rock conditions. Using old dynamite where the nitroglycerine has leached causes misfires, because the blasting caps are not strong enough to cause detonation.

To prevent misfires the larger mining companies stopped using any blasting cap smaller than a No. 6 or No. 8 strengths The Copper Queen appears to have stopped using No.3 caps before 1900. To ensure all fuses were cut and capped correctly. This procedure was eventually completed on the surface by powder men. A standard method of priming a stick of dynamite was developed. Also, only a few days' supply of dynamite or caps were stored in the magazines underground. Even with this, powder monkeys distributed dynamite in order of oldest first. This ensured the miners were getting fresh product. These procedures could not eliminate, but did reduce the number of misfires underground.

Premature explosions underground are difficult to explain unless a blasting cap was accidently detonated while it was near dynamite. Smoking while working with explosives is suspected in at least two fatal accidents. Another chance for a premature explosion was how men carried small quantities of dynamite. If a miner needs 20 sticks of powder, he would make a bundle of dynamite and tie it together with the fuse to carry it. The fuses with blasting caps he would hang around his neck or put them around his hat. If the miner fell or crushed a cap an explosion would occur. In 1916, Wallace McKeehan developed the first powder sacks to eliminate this issue. The sacks could hold up to 70 sticks of powder.

A problem with dynamite is its tendency to burn. Sometimes the fuse can ignite the dynamite. The concern is when dynamite burns it releases toxic gasses this did result in injury and the deaths of men. In the Congdon Mine fire, a miner's candle ignited a case of powder killing two men with the gasses and injuring a third. To handle gasses and hang fires the companies, had the men blast at the end of the shift. The time it took for shift change allowed the gasses to clear and reduced the chances of someone being caught by a hang fire.

Fifty men were killed in blasting accidents, and the majority were preventable. Unfortunately, there is little excuse for drilling into a misfire. An experienced miner looks over his work area for safety issues the moment he arrives at his workplace. He checks for loose rock, timber that was knocked out of place by the blast and misfires. In raises, stopes and drifts, misfires are normally easy to detect. A mound of partially broken rock may remain. Often the bootlegs or remains of drill holes will still have the fuses leading out of them. In winzes and shafts misfired holes are more difficult to detect. The freshly blasted rock can disguise a misfired hole. It is wise to remember the miner is concerned about the blasting cap not the dynamite. Although, in the early days miners would sometimes pull on the fuse of a missed hole to try to retrieve the fuse and blasting cap. This is more difficult that it would appear. The hole itself is likely damaged by the blast and the sticks of dynamite were tamped into the hole and have been squeezed out of shape. The preferred method was to reshoot the hole. Get a new stick of dynamite with a cap and fuse. Then clear out the front of the missed hole and slid in the new charge and detonate it. Miners can be impatient to get on with their work and misfires typically were blasted at lunch time. This meant the miners would be delayed until they could shoot the misses. Hot-headed miners would begin to drill knowing the misfire was in the face. This sometimes resulted in accidently drilling into the missed hole. The moment the blasting cap was crushed it detonated along with any remaining dynamite in the hole. In the days of hand drilling or in hard ground that was difficult to start a drill hole. Miners would decide to save themselves trouble by drilling into a "bootleg" or the remains of a previous drill hole. There was always the chance the "bootleg" was actually a "cut-off" hole. A "cut-off" hole never detonated, but rather the surrounding holes blasted it out leaving the explosives in the muck pile or partially in the remains of the hole. Again if the blasting cap was crushed by the drill bit the hole, and any remaining explosive would detonate. This type of misfire also caused trouble for the men mucking out the area. If a pick or a shovel crushed a cap, it would explode. Pieces of dynamite wrappers and unburned fuse are signs of a miss in a muck pile, the muck would be searched carefully, and all pieces of wrappers and fuse are removed from the pile. This tells the bosses the muck was checked. Failure to remove powder wrappers was an immediate firing offense.

View into a misfired hole revealing a stick of dynamite and a fuse. This image was taken in the Georgia Tunnel.

Fall of Person

Large numbers of open holes are used in underground mines. They may be shallow and less than 12 feet in depth or be deeper than 3,000 feet deep. The deepest openings are main shafts accessing multiple levels, but numerous raises and winzes are used. These raises and winzes are normally 100 ft. in length and can be vertical or inclined. They are used to transport broken rock from one level to the next or from a stope to the level. Also, they are used to move men and supplies. A standard raises or winzes designed handle men, normally have a ladder way called a manway with a timber slide built in for lifting timber and tools up the raise. Next to the manway is a chute compartment that is separated by a timbered wall that is used for dropping broken rock from the top of the raise to the bottom. At the bottom a chute with a door is built to load the rock directly into mine cars. Stopes that have mined through a level are also found as open holes. There were plenty of opportunities for a miner to fall.

Thirty-three men were killed by falling. The early manways often consisted of a raise or winze with a single ladder extending 100 ft. or more above the level. As a result anyone who fell went to the bottom of the raise. After returning from a trip to visit European mines in 1912, Assistant Mine Manager Gerald Sherman adopted European style manways. The ladders in the raise or winze would extended upwards about 8 ft. and passed through a landing (small floor) and then the next ladder was offset and continued upwards to another landing. This continued until the top or bottom was reached. If a man fell in this type raise they typically could on fall less than 8 ft. onto a landing. The ladders were also installed inclined, when possible. This reduced the number of fatal falls. In 1913, these landings saved at least three shift bosses and mine superintendent Joseph P. Hodgson. These men were caught by gasses from a mine fire in the Holbrook Mine 600 level. Hodgson ordered a retreat up a raise to the 500 level. Two of the shift bosses collapsed while climbing the raise and collapsed onto landings and Hodgson lifted one boss up one landing. He used the remaining landings to rest on until he reached the top and help arrived. During the safety movement, guards and covers were placed over open holes. Falls continued to cause injuries, but fatal accidents were to become rare.

Above: A safety photo showing an open raise (foreground right)

Right top: A manway with landings, 3rd level Southwest Mine

Right Bottom: an early type of manway of ladders scabbed together with no landings, Hargis incline, Higgins Mine

Fires: Disaster Prevented

The thought of an underground fires brings out the horrors of the infamous mining disasters. Although, fires are believed to be more typical of coal mines, metal mine have catastrophic fires. The Granite Mountain Mine, a copper producer at Butte, Montana had a fire that killed 163 men in 1917. In 1972 a fire in the silver mine known as the Sunshine at Kellogg, Idaho killed 91.

It could be argued that the mine safety concept had begun in Bisbee with fire prevention. The leading cause of mine disasters is fires. A mine disaster is considered any accident that kills five or more people. Bisbee never had a mine disaster. This was likely to how they handled fires. To a layman, supporting timber was the obviously flammable material and candles and later carbide lights both with exposed flames were the source of light for miners. This was a source of concern, but to miners, the sulfur-rich copper and iron pyrites are worse. During mining, masses of sometimes, millions of tons of pyrite are exposed to an oxygen abundant environment. These pyrites begin to oxidize in a significantly exothermic chemical reaction. The temperature rises and the pyrites ignite. As these fires burn, tremendous amounts of corrosive and toxic sulfur dioxide is released into the ventilation path. The heavy ground condition required that much of the stoping had to be completed using the timber intensive square-set method and as mining was completed the square set was filled with waste rock. After the stope was mined out it was ideally filled to the ceiling with buried waste rock, leaving a strongly supported structure in place of the ore. Inside these filled stopes oxidation would begin and sometimes the pyrite and timber would ignite. In 1902, the first underground fire occurred in the Neptune Country of the Holbrook Mine. This fire was soon extinguished, but the district would have least 27 underground fires. One of these located was in the Brigg mine and continued to smolder for over a decade after the mining operations ceased in 1975.

One decision that limited the number of fires was keeping the mine clean. The Copper Queen and the Calumet & Arizona removed trash from their mines. In many mines, empty spike kegs, candle boxes, dynamite boxes and scrap timber was either dumped into a gobbed stope or an abandoned crosscut. This provided an excellent source of fuel for a fire. Only in the leased sections of the Bisbee mines is it common to find garbage, like empty dynamite boxes. W.G. Gidley was a significant proponent of keeping the mines trash free. Oddly, it is even rare to find underground where dynamite or candle boxes repurposed. Many mines dismantled wooden boxes to use for head boards and wedges for stulls. Repurposed boxes tend to only be found in leased sections of the mines. Before 1909, steps had been taken to reduce the hazard of miner's candles. Cast iron sconces were introduced and used at locations were a candle could unattended for a time. Chutes and shaft stations often had sconces hanging on the timbers. The advantage of sconces is that they were cheaply made from cast iron in the mine foundry and they controlled the wax by catching the liquid in a basin. Standard miner's candlesticks dripped wax over the timber and when the candle burned down to a snub. The tiny left over candle would fall out of the thimble, potentially igniting mine timber. Even timber that is damp will ignite when wax is present.

Copper Queen Sconce   **Mission mining candle box end**

Men known as "Fire Bugs" were employed and similar to watchman had rounds underground that they followed in search for signs of fire. In January of 1911 a fire broke out in the square-set stopes between the 1000 and 1200 levels of the Lowell Mine. This fire forced the temporary abandonment of the upper part of the Lowell Shaft. Also, Charles A. Mitke was brought from the Stag Canon Mine at Dawson, New Mexico to help fight the fire and repair the Lowell Shaft. It was Mitke who introduced and trained crews to use Draeger units. Theses oxygen helmets allowed the miners to work for 20 minutes in the hot toxic environment, then have a 50-minute break. The men would only work two hours per day. Importantly, after this time, the mines at Bisbee would now have trained helmet crews able to respond an underground fire quickly. This enabled the company to build bulkheads and seal off fires soon after they were detected. To further protect the mines from fires, sprinklers were installed in the main shafts Massive fire doors with concrete frames were built in all drifts leading off shaft stations in 1917.

Miraculously, fires resulted in only three fatal accidents and only one of these occurred after the implementation of the "Safety First" program. Although, the Copper Queen Rescue team never assisted in a mine disaster in Bisbee. They were called to one in Mexico. It was technically not a mine, but rather the El Cumbre Railroad Tunnel in the Sierra Madre Mountains of Mexico. This was a great underground disaster, and the Copper Queen Rescue team was called to assist. The tunnel was approximately 4,000 ft. long and heavily timbered On February 2, 1914, a Mexican revolutionary/bandit Maximo Castillo and his band captured a freight train at the south end of the tunnel. The train was looted, and then the men backed the last five cars into the tunnel, covered them with oil and set them ablaze. At the north end of the tunnel, a passenger train carrying 51 people including women and children entered the tunnel. Unable to see the burning train until too late the engineers on the passenger train collided with the inferno. Both trains were soon ablaze along with the tunnel's supporting timber. Everyone suffocated. Mexico was caught up in the revolution and the railway bridges had been destroyed, and telegraph wires had been cut. After two days railway officials discovered what had happened and contacted the Copper Queen Rescue team. The train had been burning six days by the time the Copper Queen men arrived. Captain Joseph P. Hodgson took charge of one team of three men, and Wallace McKeehan took charge of another team of three men. The north end of the tunnel

30

was still burning and caving in. So the crews took their equipment had hauled it over the peak 1,500 feet above them and over to the south entrance. After three days the crews had reached the end of the passenger train 2,200 feet inside. They soon determined they were no survivors, and they found only piles of ash and bones only identifiable by keys and watches. Once it was decided that all the remaining bodies could only be piles of ash. The rescue work was called off, and the men returned to Bisbee with horrid yet invaluable experience.

The next emergency call for the Copper Queen Helmet crews was to Cananea, Mexico on July 24, 1914. In what was either a revolutionary attack or one by strikers the Veta Grande and Oversight Mines were set ablaze with incendiaries. On arriving and seeing the fire, Wallace McKeehan notified Bisbee that he would need more men. One of the first actions undertook by McKeehan was to remove 37,000 lbs. of dynamite (740 cases) from a burning underground magazine. The smoke filled, and unfamiliar mine workings were treacherous with open raises and stopes. Another issue faced by the Copper Queen crews was that the miners in Mexico had a tendency to place unused blasting caps and dynamite hidden behind timber. This caused small, unexpected explosions. After two weeks the mine was reduced to a smolder and most of the crews returned to Bisbee. One crew remained in the case of an emergency. The experiences at Cananea would be applied to prepare for further fires.

Mine rescue crews would be maintained at Bisbee even after the closure of operations. The Campbell Fire in the 1940s resulted in significant loss of equipment and Frank Ham suffocated. About this time carefully designed emergency escapeways were built. These were well–marked with signs and maps and would allow miners to escape a potential disaster. The Whitetail Deer and later the Boras Shaft were used as escape shafts. At times miners would practice these routes. Originally, all the lights in the mine would flash nine times and then it would repeat. This was the signal to evacuate. Later, ethyl mercaptan, a chemical that has a strong rotten egg smell was added to the airline as a warning stench. When a miner smelled the stench, they would evacuate

During the 1950s and 1960s, the Queen Tunnel of the Southwest Mine was used for fire training. The first 150 ft. of the tunnel is blackened from the practice fires. Later, the 770 level adit in the Junction Mine was used for rescue training in the 1980s and finally for a short time the Shattuck Adit was used in the 1990s.

Fire door on the 6th level station of the Sunrise Shaft.

At least 369 men were killed in mine accidents at Bisbee. These accidents are examined in the following section in detail. A number remain to be uncovered, because unless the person was well-known or happened to die on a day slow for news their death may never have been recorded in the newspaper. Death certificates and funeral records have uncovered some of these incidents. Others like the accident of D.O. Chapman remain unclear. Chapman was transported on April 26, 1907, from the Gardner Mine to the Copper Queen Hospital under the admitting diagnosis of a cut right arm. He remained in hospital until his death on May, 20, 1907, from pneumonia. It is unknown whether the pneumonia was related to his accident or if it was contracted in the hospital. Thousands of less serious accidents occurred each most were minor cuts and bruises, but others resulted in amputations or crippled the man. Representative examples of these accidents are described in the following section. An effort was made to uncovered accidents of each time period, but the information available for 1930s- 1960s is less than ideal. The spelling of names is difficult the newspapers often published the wrong spelling and although rarely, even death certificates are incorrect, particularly with foreign names or with men who had been in Bisbee only a short time. Three people, including the only woman, have died in the mines since 1975. Out of respect to the surviving families, the decision was made to allow more years to pass before these accidents are addressed. The nicknames of the miners were added. Often miners, such as G.E. Ware were only known to others by their nicknames. Note, these nicknames can be offensive and are sometimes racial slurs. These were added for the sake of historical context and research and not to promote inequality. The second edition also includes accidents that occurred in the three Copper Queen smelters that were located in Bisbee, the two concentrators and the mine repair shops. The available information on these sites is limited and is not even close to complete. After 1904, all smelting occurred in Douglas, Arizona and has not been addressed.

Miners at the Gardner Mine c-1905. Note, one is wearing an eye patch.

Bisbee Queen Mine

This unsuccessful exploration shaft was started in 1903 by the Bisbee Queen Development Company. The mine operated until 1905. In 1926, the property was purchased by the United Verde Extension Mining Company. The shaft was eventually sunk to a depth of 825 ft. with two hoisting compartments and a pipe and manway compartment. The mine ceased operation in 1928 and failed to produce ore. This shaft is sometimes called the UVX shaft or the United Verde Extension shaft.

June 7, 1927, Bisbee Queen Mine

Oscar Lewis was working with Harry Tucker at the bottom of the shaft, timbering. The hoistman received two bells to lower timber. Along with the timber, two foot long bolts with washers and nuts were being sent down. They had been tied to a clevis with copper wire. These bolts were used to attach the cap to the wallplate. A bolt came loose and fell the shaft. On the bottom, Lewis was standing under the dividers between the compartments, when the bolt struck the wall. It bounced striking him in the head. He was rushed to the Copper Queen Hospital, but his skull was fractured by a falling bolt. He was seen by a physician at 12:35 pm and died around 4:30 pm. Lewis was 40-years-old and survived by a widow Mary Lewis.

"Original Certificate of Death." Arizona Department of Health http://genealogy.az.gov/azdeath/035/10350027.pdf (May 31, 2012)
Office of State Mine Inspector. *Sixteenth Annual Report of the State Mine Inspector State of Arizona for the Year Ending November 30, 1927.*
"Cochise County Coroner's Inquest No. 1657" Arizona State Archives. Phoenix

**Mechanical call bell
from the Czar hoist house**

November 8, 1927, Bisbee Queen Mine

Joe Winters broke both arms in an undescribed mine accident. He spent 52 days at the Copper Queen Hospital.

Copper Queen Hospital Patients Register November 8, 1927, Bisbee Mining and Historical Museum, Bisbee.

The Bisbee West Mine in the distance c-1903

Bisbee West Mine

Development of this group of four exploration shafts began on October 25, 1899. They operated off and on until 1907. During the final year, the equipment on the site was sold off. Although, the development failed to produce ore of value, the mines did discover considerable clean water. For a time there were plans to use the shafts to provide water to Bisbee. The Bisbee West Shaft #1 was sunk to a depth of 50 ft. Bisbee West Shaft #2 sunk to 750ft. with three levels, Bisbee West Shaft #3 descended 550ft. with one level and the Bisbee West Shaft #4 was completed at a depth of 650 ft.

December 13, 1901 Bisbee West Mine
At six o'clock in the evening, Frank Bowman and Alex Duder were killed when the crosshead of the sinking bucket they were riding broke. During the day, the bucket had been used to hoist (bail) water from the shaft. The hoisting rope and guide (s?) were wet and the cold temperatures froze the crosshead. After Bowman and Duder had begun descending down the shaft, the crosshead broke. The bucket with the two men plummeted over 600 ft. Superintendent Dwight went down and recovered the mangled bodies. Frank Bowman was a young man around 16 years old.* * Bowman is the youngest man recorded to have been killed in the mines at Bisbee. (No coroner's inquest could be located)
"Two Men killed at the Bisbee West Last Evening" Bisbee Daily Review 14 December 1901 page 1

Men riding a sinking bucket at the Dallas Shaft. C-1911

January- February 1902 Bisbee West Mine

A miner was killed after a timber fell on top of him. The family of the miner then sued the Bisbee West Copper Mining Company for $5000.00.

"For Big Damages" Bisbee Daily Review 8 January 1903 page 8

The Boras Mine. Although, it appears abandoned it actually being used for ventilation and as an escapeway. C-1963

Boras Mine

The Boras shaft was sunk in 1919 near the site of a small, incline, prospect, shaft. This shaft was sunk to a depth of 1,035ft. with three compartments. Two compartments for hoisting and the third was for a manway and pipes. Seven levels were developed and rich ore was mined from 1921-1926. The mine was closed in 1926, but reopened in 1938 and mined until 1944. During the 1950s the Boras was refitted as an escapeway and ventilation for the Cole Mine. It remained in this function until 1975.

September 1, 1920 Boras Mine

Manuel Enriquez injured himself pulling on a stuck stoper steel. He stayed at the Calumet & Arizona Hospital until September 13, 1920.

"Calumet & Arizona Hospital Records." My Cochise.
 http://www.mycochise.com/hospcalde 2fi.php (June 2, 2012)
Office of State Mine Inspector. *Ninth Annual Report of the State Mine Inspector State of Arizona for the Year Ending November 30, 1920.*

Briggs Mine c-1904

Briggs Mine

Started in 1902, the Briggs Mine was eventually sunk to a depth of 1630 ft. with four compartments including one massive compartment that was more than double the standard size. Eventually, eight levels were developed from this shaft. In 1904, water at a rate of 2,700 gallons a minute began flooding into the mine. This rapid influx of water,continued until 1906 when it was decided to shut down the Briggs shaft and drain the ground from the crosscuts from the Junction Mine.

The mine reopened in 1909 and operated continuously until March 27, 1920. A massive mine fire began on the 27th which continued to burn until after 1975. The Oakland Shaft was driven to ventilate the fire gasses. A sheave wheel was mounted at the 1000 level of the Briggs and the lower parts of the shaft were used. In 1925, the upper part of the Briggs shaft was restored and mining continued until 1929. After this the shaft was closed until 1935. It continued to mine until 1942, when the hoist was removed and sent to the Cuprite Shaft. Work continued underground until 1946. In the last years, it is likely mining was completed from the Junction Mine and credited the Briggs Mine as the ore was mined on the Bengal claim that was traditionally considered the Briggs mining ground. The Briggs was also called the C. & P. shaft and the Calumet & Pittsburg Mine.

October 4, 1906, Briggs Mine

Timberman, H.W. Powell was looking down the Briggs Shaft examining the condition of the shaft timbers. As he was investigating the timber, a cage came down and struck him on the head. Luckily, he pulled back in time and was not thrown into the shaft. He suffered only a serious cut on the head.

"Hit by Cage" Bisbee Daily Review 5 October 1906 page 3

November 3, 1906, Briggs Mine

During the morning, John Warren was timbering inside the shaft, when he fell twelve feet to the bottom of the shaft. He broke his right arm above the elbow. Ironically, earlier that morning Mrs. Warren had given birth to a baby boy. His injury was dressed at the Calumet & Arizona Hospital.

"Hurt in Mine" Bisbee Daily Review 4, November 1906 page 7

June 21, 1910, Briggs Mine

Peter Roquette had his hands smashed and cut by a falling boulder. He was treated at the Calumet & Arizona dispensary.

"Hands Badly Injured" Bisbee Daily Review 22 June 1910 page 5

July 2, 1910, Briggs Mine near 1200 level

Jacob C. Switzer, a day foreman at the Briggs Shaft was killed while transporting drill steel on a cage. Switzer had gone to the 1400 level station and had loaded the steel on the cage with the intent of delivering it to the 1100 level. Once the cage was loaded, he boarded the cage and headed up towards the 1100. Just below the 1200 level, the steel must have shifted and caught on the shaft wall plates. The steel thrashed about and nearly ground him into fragments. His body was knocked from the cage and he fell to the sump. Oddly, he landed in the same shaft compartment the cage, he was riding used. He was survived by his wife, Mrs. Kate Switzer. Jacob Switzer was thought to have been from Germany and was 39 years old. Around July 10th, John Sanders, shift boss at the Hoatson Shaft was transferred to the Briggs Shaft to replace Switzer as day foreman.* The hoistman on duty when Switzer was killed was Josiah Mank a good friend of Switzer. Regardless that he was not in any way responsible for the accident, the accident haunted him. Soon after when he contracted typhoid, it was felt that his stress over the accident weakened his resistance, and he died on July 19, 1910

"John Switzer Meets Awful Death in Mine" Bisbee Daily Review 3 July 1910 page 1

"The Briggs" Bisbee Daily Review 10 July 1910 page 9

"Joseph Mank Dies of Typhoid Fever" Bisbee Daily Review 20 July 1910 page 8

"In Probate Court" Bisbee Daily Review 24 July 1910 page 3

"Original Certificate of Death." Arizona Department of Health Services. http://genealogy.az.gov/azdeath/009/10090562.pdf (26 March 2011)

"Cochise County Coroner's Inquest No. 758" Arizona State Archives. Phoenix

July 16, 1910, Briggs Mine

H.J. Blowers was looking up the Briggs Shaft, and copper water fell into his eyes. He was treated at the Calumet and Arizona Dispensary for swollen and irritated eyes.

"Eyes Painfully Injured" Bisbee Daily Review 17 July 1910 page 5

September 9, 1913, Briggs Mine

Austrian, Nick Davidovich, a mucker, was assigned to clean out 138 crosscut on the 900 level. For some unknown reason, he was standing next to a switch in 142 crosscut holding his candlestick when John Prnyat a mule driver drove his train of six empty cars passed. Davidovich became caught on the fourth car and was crushed between the mine car and chute timber. Prnyat heard him holler and stopped his mule and went to help with a couple other men. They side tracked three of the empty cars to allow a timber truck to be brought in to carry him out. Then they turned the car he was trapped on and laid him onto the timber truck. Davidovich was taken to the Calumet & Arizona Hospital, where he died on September 10 from a perforated intestine. The young man was 28 years old and was buried in Evergreen Cemetery. He was survived by a brother Sam Davidovich, a miner at the Junction Mine and a wife in Castulatua, Austria.* *The name of the community was probably misspelled in the inquest, actual spelling is unknown.

"Original Certificate of Death." Arizona Department of Health Services. http://genealogy.az.gov/azdeath/011/10112479.pdf (March 11, 2012)

"Bisbee-Lowell Evergreen Cemetery." My Cochise. http://www.mycochise.com/cembisbeed.php (March 11, 2012)

"Legs Injured" Bisbee Daily Review 10 September 1913 page 1

Office of State Mine Inspector. Second Annual Report of the State Mine Inspector State of Arizona for the Year Ending November 30, 1913. Tombstone Epitaph.

"Cochise County Coroner's Inquest No. 1044" Arizona State Archives. Phoenix

December 12, 1913, Briggs Mine

Pat Hackett, a 50-year-old miner, was hit by a falling rock which broke a bone in his leg. He was taken to the Calumet & Arizona Hospital and released on January 25th.

"Broke Small Bone" Bisbee Daily Review 13 December 1913 page 8

"Calumet & Arizona Hospital Records" My Cochise. http://www.mycochise.com/hospcalgr2he.php (April 25 2011)

December 27, 1913, Briggs Mine

Swedish miner, Edward Johnson was working with a distressed mule and was trying to settle down the mule, when it overturned a mine car onto him. The impact of the care broke his pelvis and killed him. (No coroner's inquest could be located)

"Injuries are Found Fatal" Bisbee Daily Review 18 December 1913 page 3

January 12, 1914, Briggs Mine

Fred Legge, a 23-year-old mucker was working as a substitute cager. He rang the shaft bell and it "*registered wrong*" and the cage was swiftly hoisted. Legge's head became caught between the cage and the wall plate. In nothing less than a miracle, he was thrown through an opening in the shaft timber above the wall plate, instead of being decapitated. He landed on a small lagged platform above the station. Badly, but not mortally injured he crawled back into the shaft and onto the wall plate and slid down the rods back to the station. In extreme pain, he was later found and transported to the Calumet & Arizona Hospital. One side of his face was smashed from the lower jawbone to his temple, and it was possible that one eye would be lost. He was released from the hospital on February 15, 1914.

"His Call was a Close One" Bisbee Daily Review 14 January 1914 page 3

"Calumet & Arizona Hospital Records." My Cochise. http://www.mycochise.com/hospcalkr2man.php
(April 28, 2012)

January 29, 1914, Briggs Mine

I.H. Strickland needed to leave the mine early and asked Henry Howser, a mucker to spit twelve holes he had drilled and loaded at the end of shift. Howser had Steve Fallis hold the candles so, Howser could see to ignite the fuses. Fallis became concerned that Howser was taking too long to light the fuses and told him three times they need to leave. Finally, Fallis left and was knocked down by the first shot detonating. Then he got up and ran to the station and found a mucker and a mule driver to help him with Howser. The blast killed Howser instantly. His sister Mrs. R.L. Burris of Dayton, Washington was contacted, and she responded that her brother should be buried in Bisbee.

"Hawser Funeral" Bisbee Daily Review 31 January 1914 page 6

"Original Certificate of Death." Arizona Department of Health Services. http://genealogy.az.gov/azdeath/012/10120902.pdf (June 6, 2012)

"Cochise County Coroner's Inquest No. 1078" Arizona State Archives. Phoenix

September 15, 1914, Briggs Mine

Shift Boss, John Coughlan was caught between a chute and a mine car being pulled by a mule. Two of his ribs were broken, and he was bruised. A week later he was seen on the streets of Bisbee with his ribs bothering him, but ok.

"James Conway is Dead from Injuries Received in Mine" Bisbee Daily Review 17 September 1914 page4
"Back on the Streets" Bisbee Daily Review 23 September 1914 page 8

January 7, 1915,* Briggs Mine

On the graveyard shift at 2:30 pm, Stojan Sakota and the cager Wesley S. Arksey were ascending in a cage loaded with dull drill steel. The rope tying the bundle of drill steel together broke and it appears that a piece of steel fell and caught on the shaft timber. This steel became entangled with the rest of the steel and threw Sakota and Arksey out of the cage. Sakota's body was thrown onto the shaft timber. Arksey was thrown into another shaft compartment, and his body fell 1,000 ft. into the sump. Little is known about Arksey. It is known that a little more than a month before his death on December 1, 1914 the 27-year-old man married the 17-year-old Pearl Holman. He also was a well-known competitive bowler for the "*Sprays.*"**The unmarried Stojan Sakota*** was native to Herzegovina, Austria and was 27 years old. It is unusual to note that his funeral was paid for by the Society Nemanja and not by the Calumet and Arizona Mining Company. In most cases the mining company paid the funeral expenses for men killed. During the coroner's inquest, the other cagers were asked if they used the box designed for safely handling drill steel. They all said they did not and one stated he felt it was safer not to use the box. These men were also ask if they realized about the safety rules in the time keepers office and one man admitted, even if he knew they were there he could not read them.

*The date on Arksey's Headstone is January 6, 1915 while the date on Stojan's death certificate is the 7th
** Bowling teams were named after mines or job positions on January 9, 1911 Wesley Arksey of the team the Sprays help defeat the Irish Mags other teams that played that night were Time-Keepers, Lowell Miners, Dew Drops and Machinists
*** His name was reported as Sacota, Sokota and Sakota
"Thomas is Boss Pin" Bisbee Daily Review 10 January 1911 page 5
"Wedding Bells" Bisbee Daily Review 6 December1914 page 8
"Two Men Killed in the Briggs Shaft." Bisbee Daily Review 9 January 1915 page 6
"Funeral Today" Bisbee Daily Review 10 January 1915 page 8
"Original Certificate of Death." Arizona Department of Health Services. http://genealogy.az.gov/azdeath/011/10112479.pdf (May 14, 2012)
"Cochise County Marriages 1911 – 1920 Grooms A-B" My Cochise http://www.mycochise.com/groomsa2b.php_(May 14, 2012)
Dugan Mortuary Records 1914-1917 Accession 2010.10.8 Bisbee Mining and Historical Museum, Bisbee.
"Cochise County Coroner's Inquest No. 1135" Arizona State Archives. Phoenix

Men riding a cage at the Oliver Mine with timber, c-1914. After this time, riding a cage with any item that was not small and handheld such as carbide lamp was a serious safety violation. (Courtesy of the Bisbee Mining & Historical Museum)

July 11, 1916, Briggs Mine

John Rajhala and Oscar Nemie were working in a six-post raise known as No. 285. They had installed the top set, on the night of the 10th and were working two sets below. Without warning, the lagging broke on the upper set and it fell and broke through the floor of the second set and dropped onto Rajhala. His back was broken, and he died instantly. His partner Nemie was not believed to have been injured. He was 39 years old and from Finland and was buried in the Evergreen Cemetery.

Dugan Mortuary Records Aug. 26, 1914 – Dec 21, 1916 Accession 2010.10.9 Bisbee Mining and Historical Museum, Bisbee.

"Original Certificate of Death." Arizona Department of Health Services. http://genealogy.az.gov/azdeath/015/10150713.pdf (May 28, 2012)

Office of State Mine Inspector. *Fifth Annual Report of the State Mine Inspector State of Arizona for the Year Ending November 30, 1916.*

"Cochise County Coroner's Inquest No. 1224" Arizona State Archives

February 1, 1917, Briggs Mine

Charles C. Weed was caught in a cave-in and broke his pelvis. He remained in the Calumet & Arizona Hospital until May 18, 1917.

"Calumet & Arizona Hospital Records." My Cochise.
http://www.mycochise.com/hospcaltr2we.php (June 2, 2012)
Office of State Mine Inspector. *Sixth Annual Report of the State Mine Inspector State of Arizona for the Year Ending November 30, 1917.*

May 31, 1917, Briggs Mine

A splinter of wood penetrated and scratched the eye of John Bokarizas. He was released from the Calumet & Arizona Hospital on June 6, 1917.

"Calumet & Arizona Hospital Records." My Cochise.
http://www.mycochise.com/hospcalb.e 2br.php (June 2, 2012)
Office of State Mine Inspector. *Sixth Annual Report of the State Mine Inspector State of Arizona for the Year Ending November 30, 1917.*

January 3, 1918, Briggs Mine

James Clark was caught in a cave-in. He was treated at the Calumet and Arizona Hospital. Clark was released January 16.

"Is in Hospital" Bisbee Daily Review 6 January 1918 page 8
"Calumet & Arizona Hospital Records." My Cochise. http://www.mycochise.com/hospcalb.u2cl.php (May 28, 2012)

January 31, 1918, Briggs Mine

A mine car derailed and crushed Malek Smail against a timber. Two ribs were broken, and his left shoulder was bruised. The mule driver remained in the Calumet & Arizona Hospital until February 8, 1918.

"Calumet & Arizona Hospital Records." My Cochise.
http://www.mycochise.com/hospcals2sm.php (June 2, 2012)
Office of State Mine Inspector. *Seventh Annual Report of the State Mine Inspector State of Arizona for the Year Ending November 30, 1918.*

February 8, 1918, Briggs Mine

S.P. Roberts was caught in a blast. His right eye was scratched, and his left thigh was bruised. He stayed in the hospital until February 15.

"Calumet & Arizona Hospital Records." My Cochise. http://www.mycochise.com/hospcalpr2ry.php (June 2, 2012)
Office of State Mine Inspector. *Seventh Annual Report of the State Mine Inspector State of Arizona for the Year Ending November 30, 1918.*

May 15, 1918, Briggs Mine

While igniting a fuse, John Osborne stepped into a hole and fell bruising his back. He rested at the Calumet & Arizona Hospital until May 22.

"Calumet & Arizona Hospital Records." My Cochise. http://www.mycochise.com/hospcalo2 po.php (June 2, 2012)
Office of State Mine Inspector. *Seventh Annual Report of the State Mine Inspector State of Arizona for the Year Ending November 30, 1918.*

May 20, 1918, Briggs Mine

Jack Fisher drilled into a misfire. The resulting explosion cut his cornea, chest and arms. His initial treatment occurred at the Calumet & Arizona Hospital, but on May 22, 1918 he was sent to El Paso for treatment.

"Calumet & Arizona Hospital Records." My Cochise.
http://www.mycochise.com/hospcalde 2fi.php (June 2, 2012)
Office of State Mine Inspector. *Seventh Annual Report of the State Mine Inspector State of Arizona for the Year Ending November 30, 1918.*

June 21, 1918, Briggs Mine

Sam C. Duff broke his left leg after it became caught between a lagging and a heavy timber. He was released from the hospital on July 11.

"Calumet & Arizona Hospital Records." My Cochise.
http://www.mycochise.com/hospcalde 2fi.php (June 2, 2012)
Office of State Mine Inspector. *Seventh Annual Report of the State Mine Inspector State of Arizona for the Year Ending November 30, 1918.*

August 12, 1918, Briggs Mine

K.L. Hodgkin was raising lagging up a raise and knocked a rock into his right eye. His cornea was injured.

"Calumet & Arizona Hospital Records." My Cochise.
http://www.mycochise.com/hospcalhi2ja.php (June 2, 2012)
Office of State Mine Inspector. *Seventh Annual Report of the State Mine Inspector State of Arizona for the Year Ending November 30, 1918.*

February 21, 1919, Briggs Mine

Alfred Bednorz was struck by a rock falling from a stope and broke his leg.

"Calumet & Arizona Hospital Records." My Cochise. http://www.mycochise.com/hospcalb.e 2br.php (May 28, 2012)
Office of State Mine Inspector. *Eighth Annual Report of the State Mine Inspector State of Arizona for the Year Ending November 30, 1919.*

October 7, 1919, Briggs Mine

H.J. Crawford, a nipper broke his forearm while disengaging a mule train and he became caught between the train and the rib of the drift.

"Calumet & Arizona Hospital Records." My Cochise. http://www.mycochise.com/hospcalco2day.php (May 28, 2012)
Office of State Mine Inspector. *Eighth Annual Report of the State Mine Inspector State of Arizona for the Year Ending November 30, 1919.*

March 24, 1920, Briggs Mine

W.C. Gullifer suffered a hernia from pulling a plugger drill out. He stayed at the Calumet & Arizona Hospital until April 7, 1920.

"Calumet & Arizona Hospital Records." My Cochise. http://www.mycochise.com/hospcalgr2he.php (June 2, 2012)
Office of State Mine Inspector. *Ninth Annual Report of the State Mine Inspector State of Arizona for the Year Ending November 30, 1920.*

A Cochise model 36 plugger

April 24, 1922, Briggs Mine
Mucker, Charles T. Barrett drove his pick into a misfire. The explosion blew out both of his eyes, shattered his chest and broke both arms. He lived for over six hours before dying just before 7:00 pm. He was survived by a wife and small child. (No coroner's inquest could be located)
"C.T. Barrett dies from Explosion" Tombstone Epitaph 30 April 1922 page 2
"Original Certificate of Death." Arizona Department of Health Services. http://genealogy.az.gov/azdeath/025/10250634.pdf (July 23, 2015)

Campbell Mine.

Campbell Mine

This mine was started in 1916, with a combination of sinking from the surface and raising from the 1400 level. The shaft was intended to help with ventilation with the Junction and Briggs Mine. Even though the shaft was started in 1916, all work on the project temporarily ended with the miner's strike that ended with the Bisbee Deportation. In 1919, the Campbell Mine reopened and the sections being raised and sunk were connected on New Year's Eve 1919. During the summer of 1920, the development was again temporarily stopped to use the shaft for venting fire gasses from the fire gasses from the Briggs Mine Fire. In 1922, the mine again was shut down and development did not continue until ore was found south of the shaft in 1924. The mine operated largely continuously from 1925 until 1975. In the early 1980s, some sulfide ore was mined as smelter flux with gold-silver values, but this proved uneconomical.

The Campbell orebody was the largest underground in the district and contained over one million tons of ore. This shaft eventually reached of a final depth of 3,333 ft. with three compartments and is the deepest mine in Bisbee. Two interior shafts were also the part of the mine. One was located from the 1300 level to the 1200 level. The other extended from the 2966 level to the 3100 level.

June 17, 1919, Campbell Mine

V.M. Crawford had his hand cut up when it was caught between a sheave wheel and a cable. (He was later killed underground in the Junction Mine on January 8, 1928)

"Calumet & Arizona Hospital Records." My Cochise. http://www.mycochise.com/hospcalco2day.php (May 28, 2012)

Office of State Mine Inspector. *Eighth Annual Report of the State Mine Inspector State of Arizona for the Year Ending November 30, 1919.*

January 6, 1934, Campbell Mine
Henry Stewart and Steve Petrosia had barred down 478 stope, on the 1600 level. They wanted to knock down a slab so they could build a gob fence. They decided to drill a three-foot hole into the rock and blast it down. While Stewart was drilling, the boulder fell and missed him. A second boulder of high-grade ore hanging next to the one he was drilling, suddenly fell. The rock rolled over Stewart, killing him.

Original Certificate of Death." Arizona Department of Health Services http://genealogy.az.gov/azdeath/049/10490542.pdf (May 27, 2014)
"Cochise County Coroner's Inquest No.1728" Arizona State Archives Phoenix

September 6, 1935, Campbell Mine
James P. Monaghan Jr. went to the 1800 level to fill water kegs. The water tank mine cars were late being delivered from the 1800 level Junction Mine, but 32 kegs had been filled and were waiting to be delivered. Monaghan loaded five kegs to transfer to the 1600 level. As he moved to step on the cage the cage moved and he fell into the shaft and was rolled between the cage and fell into the skip. His body was found in the skip on the 2200 level.

"Cochise County Inquest No. 1740 Arizona State Archives Phoenix

December 12, 1936, Campbell Mine
Motorman, Shelby C. Brooks and his swamper R.L. Stewart were driving down 23 crosscut on the 1800 level. In 23 crosscut were two air doors 150 ft. apart. Brooks opened the first door without a problem. As they passed the lever for the second door, Brooks did not move the handle enough for the door to open. Stewart noticed the white target on the door and called to Brooks telling him the door was closed. Brooks stood up to brakes and the locomotive smashed into the door. Dragged off the motor, Brooks was crushed between the locomotive's sandbox and the heavy door. It took half an hour to cut away the door and pull the motor back to free Brooks, but he had already died. Sometime earlier Brooks had been injured in a mine accident, and had lost an eye. At the time of the accident he had a glass eye.

"Cochise County Inquest No. 1750Arizona State Archives Phoenix

September 1, 1939, Campbell Mine
Charles Whitney Pierce was working 70 ft. above the 2566 level concreting the shaft. While working, he knocked out the staging he was standing on and fell to the bulkhead on the 2566 level. When Thomas Ruff found him he was still alive, but he died soon afterward. His body was hoisted from the Junction Mine.

Original Certificate of Death." Arizona Department of Health Services http://genealogy.az.gov/azdeath/061/10611524.pdf (May 27, 2014)
"Cochise County Inquest No. 1775" Arizona State Archives Phoenix

November 3, 1939, Campbell Mine
Bill H. Greer was working with William Moore in 35 stope on the 2100 level. Moore was taking out a stull to put in a square set, when it caved. Greer jumped back into the chute

and was caught on the grizzlies by his jaw and shoulder. His neck was broken. (Note, the inquest was not clear if he was struck by falling rock.)

Original Certificate of Death." Arizona Department of Health Services. http://genealogy.az.gov/azdeath/059/10592478.pdf (May 27, 2014)

"Cochise County Inquest No. 1768" Arizona State Archives Phoenix

May 5, 1941, Campbell Mine

Oscar Evan Hairston had his chest crushed by a locomotive. He was taken to the Copper Queen Hospital, where he died. He was survived by his wife Ruby and three children. Oscar also had four brothers.

"Bisbee" Evening Courier 7 May 1941 page4, Prescott Az.

November 15, 1942, Campbell Mine

Howard T. Coon and 21-year-old William Melvin Garner were working in 526 stope on the 1500 level. Coon was barring down and Garner was about 9 ft. away. Garner, a mucker was asked to move a few more feet away and weighs about 14 ft. from Coon, when a one-ton slab fell and fractured his skull. He was killed instantly. His partner was uninjured. The accident occurred during night shift.

"Accident fatal to miner "unavoidable" Tucson Daily Citizen 17 November 1942 page 4
"Bisbee Miner Killed when struck by Rock" Tucson Daily Citizen 16 November 1942 page 2
"Cochise County Inquest No. 1813" Arizona State Archives Phoenix

February 1, 1944, Campbell Mine

John L. Baker age 26 was killed by a flying sliver of rock when the drill holes he and his partner were loading with explosives detonated. The fragment of rock punctured his throat. He was survived by his wife Rowena Baker and his two-year-old daughter Julia Ruth Baker.

"Flying Sliver of Rock Fatal to Bisbee Miner" Tucson Daily Citizen 1 February 1944
"John L. Baker, Copper Queen Miner is Killed" Bisbee Daily Review 1 February1944 page 8

January 2, 1945, Campbell Mine

S.D. Burks and Luke Luember Fling were driving a crosscut on the 2833 level. They had drilled out a round and only needed to move out the jumbo to begin loading the blast holes. According to the record at the magazine two sacks of powder, one containing 100 sticks of dynamite and another sack with 90 sticks, along with 27 fused blasting caps had been delivered. For some unknown reason, the dynamite detonated before they even had begun loading. The blast knocked out five to six sets of timber and the area had to be retimbered before the bodies could be removed. The explosion blew the men into pieces. Miners worked nine hours straight to recover the bodies.

"Two Workmen Perish in Copper Queen Mine" Tucson Daily Citizen 3 January 1945 page 3
"Cochise County Inquest No. 1824" Arizona State Archives Phoenix

March 1, 1947, Campbell Mine

Raymond Lee Richardson was killed on the 2566 level in 77 stope. Day shift had blasted and had knocked out three of the five stulls in the stope. E.C. Ramirez was cleaning out an area to set up a new stull, when suddenly, a boulder fell. A lagging fell and knocked

Ramirez out of the way, but the rock crushed Richardson. He was buried by 10 tons of broken rock.

Original Certificate of Death." http://genealogy.az.gov/azdeath/079/10791409.pdf (May 27, 2014)
"Cochise County Inquest No. 1835" Arizona State Archives Phoenix

August 28, 1947, Campbell Mine
Albert Frank Griffith was working in 229, a square set stope on the 1700 level and was well timbered. A boulder fell and killed him.

Original Certificate of Death." Arizona Department of Health Services. http://genealogy.az.gov/azdeath/080/10801789.pdf (May 27, 2014)
"Cochise County Inquest No. 1838" Arizona State Archives Phoenix

April 9, 1948, Campbell Mine
Fire Bugs, Bryden Milburn and Thomas B. Peters were burned at a bulkhead, sealing off a fire. Although, it is not stated the men were probably repairing the bulkhead when they were burned on their faces and hands.

"Two Men Injured in Campbell Shaft" Bisbee Daily Review 11 April 1948 page?

April 1, 1954, Campbell Mine
D.L. Shuck was struck by falling rock in 22 crosscut on the 2966 level.

D.L. Shuck Accident photo #p1095. 1 Apr. 1954.

The D.L. Shuck accident site. The original location of the fallen rock is marked in ink on the original image. 22 crosscut 2966 level Campbell Mine.

January 27, 1959 Campbell Mine
J.O. Guerrero was working in 6-P stope and copper water dripped into his right eye.

1959-1961 safety ledger p.2

January 27, 1959 Campbell Mine

A.F. Corona was moving timber in 6-A stope on the 2966 level. He cut the 1st and 2nd fingers on his left hand.
1959-1961 safety ledger p.2

January 29, 1959 Campbell Mine
J.C. Luna was working at the 103 stope chute on the 2700 level. Copper water dripped into his left eye.
1959-1961 safety ledger p.2

June 13, 1959 Campbell Mine
J.M. Cabello broke his nose in 10-B stope on the 2833 level in an undescribed accident. This was not a lost time accident. A few days later on the 20th he was injured again in the same stope, but on the 2700 level.
1959-1961 safety ledger p.42

June 22, 1959 Campbell Mine
A.E. Acuna broke a toe while loading the face of 143 stope on the 2700 level. This was not a lost time accident
1959-1961 safety ledger p.42

July 31, 1959 Campbell Mine
A.M. Morales broke his right thumb while drilling in 56-A stope on the 2833 level.
1959-1961 safety ledger p.50

July 31, 1959 Campbell Mine
E.L. *"Flat Top"* Montoya was struck by falling rock in 52 stope on the 2833 level. His right arm was broken.
1959-1961 safety ledger p.50

February 24, 1960 Campbell Mine
S. Soriano was in 9-A stope on the 2700 and broke his pelvis in an undescribed accident.
1959-1961 safety ledger p.82

March 17, 1960 Campbell Mine
I.A. Randolph broke the 4th finger on his left hand using a mine car. In 52 crosscut on the 2833 level.
1959-1961 safety ledger p.90

April 26, 1960 Campbell Mine
In 67 crosscut on the 2833 level, N.A. Hairston broke his right thumb with a mine car.
(Note, on August 2, 1960 he broke his left thumb)
1959-1961 safety ledger p.98

May 4, 1960 Campbell Mine
J.Y. Vasquez broke his third left finger handling timber in 86-A stope on the 2566 level.
1959-1961 safety ledger p.106

May 13, 1960 Campbell Mine
 L.E. Burkett broke his 4th right toe working at 110 chute on the 2700 level
1959-1961 safety ledger p.106

48

May 31, 1960 Campbell Mine
A.M. Cabbage broke his 5th left toe in 119 stope on the 2700 level

June 17, 1960 Campbell Mine
J.H. Proctor suffered a fractured chest bone while handling mine cars in 129 crosscut on the 2700 level.
1959-1961 safety ledger p.114

July 26, 1960 Campbell Mine
A.E. Acuna broke his 6th rib after falling in 3-A stope on the 2700 level.
1959-1961 safety ledger p.110

August 2, 1960 Campbell Mine
 In 67 crosscut on the 2833 level, falling ground broke the left thumb of N.A. Hairston.
(Note, on April 26, 1960 he broke his right thumb)
1959-1961 safety ledger p.130

August 30, 1960 Campbell Mine
A.E. Corona broke his right thumb working with 7-M chute on the 2433 level
1959-1961 safety ledger p.130

September 24, 1960 Campbell Mine
In 3-A stope on the 2700 level, T.R. Santillan fractured his left tibia when he was struck by falling rock.
1959-1961 safety ledger p.130

November 14, 1960 Campbell Mine
 C.W. Phillips broke his 2nd left finger in a cage on the surface.
1959-1961 safety ledger p.154

November 16, 1960 Campbell Mine
 Caving ground struck T.C. Chavez in 14 stope on the 2966 level. His face was cut and his right arm was broken.
1959-1961 safety ledger p.154

January 10, 1961 Campbell Mine
On the 2700 level in 126 stope. Al *"High Rails"* Hirales bruised his left hand in an undescribed accident.
(Note later he became a popular Queen Mine tour guide)

April 24, 1961 Campbell Mine
On the 2566 level in 34-B stope, J.Y. Elkins bruised his left foot working around chute.
1959-1961 safety ledger p.194

June 14, 1961 Campbell Mine

In 163 crosscut on the 2566 level, Toby *"Yongo"* Valdez bruised the left side of his face and cut his scalp while loading muck. (This was probably caused by a mucking machine. Note, later he became a popular Queen Mine tour guide.)
1959-1961 safety ledger p.210

September 9, 1961 Campbell Mine
On the 2833 level in 64-B stope I.A. Randolph had the end of his 4th finger amputated while working at a chute.
1959-1961 safety ledger p.234

December 15, 1961 Campbell Mine
On the 2966 level in 55 crosscut, S.B. McCormick broke his jaw and right 4th finger while drilling.
1959-1961 safety ledger p.258

April 26, 1965, Campbell Mine 2700 level
Lyle Floyd Means was killed by falling ground in a stope.
Office of State Mine Inspector. *Seventh Annual Report of the State Mine Inspector State of Arizona for the Year Ending November 30, 1965.*
Dugan Mortuary Records 6/65 – Nov 29 66 Accession 2010.10.? Bisbee Mining and Historical Museum, Bisbee

Before 1967 Campbell Mine
Richard W. Graeme III was working in a cut & fill stope on the 2700 level. A rock fell striking him in the side of the face chipping his teeth.
Richard W. Graeme III Personal communication July 19, 2016

February 28, 1967, Campbell Mine
J.C. Luna had boomed out in 62 crosscut on the 3100 level. His leg broken by falling rock. Luna was probably barring down when the rock fell.
J.C. Luna Accident photo # p1112. 28 Feb. 1967.

February 28, 1967 Campbell Mine
Frank R. Burgos was killed by falling rock on the 2700 level in 143 crosscut. He died at the Copper Queen Hospital on March 5th.Note, photographs from the site indicate the crosscut was part of a square set stope.
Dugan Mortuary Records 1966-1968 Accession 2010.10.51 Bisbee Mining and Historical Museum, Bisbee p. 97
Office of State Mine Inspector. *Seventh Annual Report of the State Mine Inspector State of Arizona for the Year Ending November 30, 1967.*
"Bisbee Miner's Death Probed" The Sun 4 March 7, 1967, page 2, Yuma
F.R. Burgos Accident Photo # p1087. 2 Feb. 1967.

The boulder that killed F.R. Burgos lying on the ground. 143 crosscut 2700 level Campbell Mine

March 14, 1967 Campbell Mine

On the 3100 level at the intersection of 24 crosscut and 45 crosscut a small fire broke out in a pile of scrap timber. The fire occurred between 3:00 pm and 4:00 pm. No one is believed to have been injured.

3100 level fire Accident Photo # p1083 14 March. 1967.

March 14, 1967, Campbell Mine

H. Orton was in 31-B stope on the 3100 level. The miners had boomed out and had used a slusher to muck out the face. Although, written records of the accident could not be located, photographs reveal he was extremely lucky. A couple tons of rock fell tearing off his wheat lamp and partially covered a scaling bar.

H. Orton Accident Photo # p1083 14 March. 1967.
H. Orton Accident Photo # p1100 14 March. 1967.

A view of the caved face in 31-B stope on the 3100 level. This is the site H. Orton was injured. In the foreground is a slusher rake. At the center and just above the end of the scaling bar is the head to Orton's wheat lamp among the fallen boulders. Hidden in the left corner is a gin pole with a paper tag hanging from it

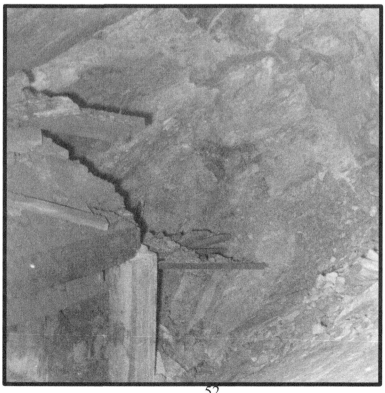

A view of the source of the caved rock from the previous picture (top center.) The point of the gin pole seen in the previous picture is located just above the standing square set post. 31-B stope 3100 level.

May 5, 1967 Campbell Mine

Mitchell Larned was killed by falling rock and timber on the 3100 level in 25 stope. It took twenty miners, 33 hours to recover his body. He was survived by his wife, Roberta and a 14 month old daughter named Michele.

Office of State Mine Inspector. *Seventh Annual Report of the State Mine Inspector State of Arizona for the Year Ending November 30, 1967.*

"Body Found After Cave-in at Bisbee" <u>Arizona Republic</u> May 7, 1967, page A-19

M. Larned Accident Photo # p1105. 5 May. 1967.

Miners working to recover the body of Mitchell Larned.
25 stope 3100 level Campbell Mine

November 11, 1968, Campbell Mine
C.G. Robeson and J.H. West were in 42-A stope on the 2966 level. This was a square set stope and a single 10"x10' post had broken from ground movement. West and Robeson needed to change out the post. First, they slushed about 12 tons of ore out of the way. After lunch they decided this was enough and began cutting the broken post to attach a slusher cable to yank it out. The miners were in a set out of line of sight of the broken post. The set was lagged about four feet high for protection, but the slusher block was directly in front of the slusher. West was watch over the lagging as Robeson operated the slusher. On Robeson's fifth attempt. The cable sling holding the slusher block broke. The block went flying and hit West on the hard hat and threw him against a 10"x10" post. West's collar bone was broken.
"Discussion of a lost time accident occurring in November 1968" 11-11-1968

March 24, 1969, Campbell Mine
Richard Carbajal, a 23-year-old was killed when he was buried in a cave in on the 3100 level. Richard started working in the mines after his discharge from the Marine Corps, three months before the accident. (Note, if I remember correctly, Toby Valdez was one of the first men to arrive on the scene. He helped removed Carbajal from a caved square set.)
"Bisbee P-D Miner Dies in Cave –In" Tucson Daily Citizen 25 March 1969 page 28
Toby Valdez, Personal Communication August 4, 1996

February, 1970 Campbell Mine
John "*The Rock*" Palomino was having lunch on the 2700 level at the intersection of two crosscuts. He had laid out a lagging to lie down on near a blower. A rock fell and struck him on the head. The other miners playfully gave him a hard time about this accident. He later worked at the Queen Mine tour as a popular guide for about 30 years. Note, his brother, Julio was injured at the Dallas Mine on March 13, 1974
J. Palomino Accident photo # p1108. Feb. 1970.
Richard W. Graeme III personal communication 2017

The accident location of John Palomino on the 2700 level Campbell Mine. The lagging lying relatively flat were used to lie down on at lunch time. Note, the coat hanging on the water line and the lunch box on the blower stand. These likely, belonged to Palomino.

March 29, 1971, Campbell Mine

On the 2566 level in 158 stope, L.A. *"Aunt Jemima"* Chavez was mucking out a on the sill level. His partner A.T. Bustamante was using a slusher to muck the ore to 181 crosscut, where Chavez was using a mucking machine to load the ore into H cars. Chavez was loading his fifth car when his foot slipped off the step and was caught between the Finlay and a 10"X10" post. His ankle was broken. (Note, his nickname today could be consider a racial slur and is given only for research and historical purposes.)

"Discussion of a Lost Time Accident Occurring in March 1971" 3-31-1971

March 31, 1970, Campbell Mine

G.L. Fletcher and L.Y. *"Chinaman"* Coronado were working in 96 crosscut on the 2966 level. After the previous blast had been mucked out, a large slab about 21"x23"x53" was exposed. The miners could not find a safe place to bar it down from. They decided to run out booms to use as a staging so they could crib up the boulder. Coronado handed Fletcher one 10"x10" block and a piece of another. Fletcher was on top of the booms in a 3 1/2' space. Coronado left to get a ruler that was several hundred feet away at the blower. While he was gone, Fletcher was installing a block on the booms and the rock fell. According to Fletcher the smaller rocks injured him not the larger one. After the collapse and still above the drift he was totally in the dark his lamp had been torn off him and the lamp knocked out. In the darkness, he felt and found a boom hangar. He lowered himself to the crosscut floor and crawled under the protection of the drift timber. When Coronado returned Fletcher was under the last set of timber on his stomach. The left boom had been knocked out and the end of the right boom had fallen to the muck pile. Fletcher suffered a fractured vertebrae, a broken rib, bruised kidney and dislocated right ankle. (Note, his nickname today could be consider a racial slur and is given only for research and historical purposes.)

"Discussion of a lost time accident occurring in March 1970" 3-31-1970

April 22, 1970, Campbell Mine

C.T. Martinez was in 149 stope on the 2700 level. A boulder fell and fractured his left ankle. It appears he may have been barring down when the accident occurred.

C.T. Martinez Accident Photo # p1092. 22 Apr. 1970.

September 21, 1970, Campbell Mine

C.G. Lopez and O.G. Allen had delivered H cars to a stope on the 3100 level. Then they hauled five timber trucks of timber to 64 crosscut between 31-E stope chute and 31-D stope chute. After they had unloaded three of the timber trucks, M.L. *"Spanky"* Mendez dropped out of 31-E stope to get timber. Lopez passed Mendez lagging over two empty trucks to load on the third. Lopez was then getting collar braces* from behind a stack of 10"x10". As he was getting the seventh collar brace he smashed his right index finger between the collar brace and a sharp rock. His finger was broken. * Collar braces are 4"X6" X5' pieces of timber used to keep drift sets apart.

"Discussion of a lost time accident occurring in September 1970" 9-21-1970

C.T. Martinez Accident site 149 stope 2700 level Campbell Mine

January 5, 1974, Campbell Mine
At 11:45 pm, J.A. Teran was headed to the station on the 2700 level. As he walked down 9 crosscut. Another miner began talking to him. Teran turned around and stepped on the rail spraining his left knee. He refused a blue card to go to the hospital. Teran stated, that he felt it was the result of an injury to his knee that occurred in May 1973 in 93 crosscut on the 2700 level.
Phelps Dodge Corporation Copper Queen Branch Accident Report 1-15-74

January 7, 1974, Campbell Mine
Machinist, J.P Camiano was on the 3233 level. He smashed his little finger while setting a pump on the ground.
Phelps Dodge Corporation Copper Queen Branch Accident Report 1-8-74

January 8, 1974, Campbell Mine
27 crosscut on the 3100 level was partially flooded by mine water. L.A. Hare "*Wild Hare*", a pipe and trackman was replacing rail that was underwater. As he pulled up an old rail, water splashed into his eyes. (Note, mine water was often acidic and charged with dissolved metals. This type of injury often was painful and the eyes could become seriously inflamed and swollen)
Phelps Dodge Corporation Copper Queen Branch Accident Report 1-9-74 2:45 pm

January 8, 1974, Campbell Mine
A.H. Austin was drilling the face in 60 stope on the 3100 level. A boulder fell from the wall and smashed his left foot.
Phelps Dodge Corporation Copper Queen Branch Accident Report 1-9-74 3:20 pm

January 9, 1974, Campbell Mine

In 10 stope on the 3233 level, J.H. Alexander needed to move a slusher rake. The slusher hoist was not blocked in so he quickly blocked the hoist in with a 2" lagging in the front and with a 4"x 6" in the back. Alexander then started to move the rake with the hoist. Suddenly, the 4"x 6" block securing the slusher hoist fell out. The slusher hoist moved back and pinned him against the back (ceiling) and then fell to the ground striking his leg. Luckily, he suffered only a bruised upper trunk, right leg and left shoulder.

Phelps Dodge Corporation Copper Queen Branch Accident Report 1-10-74

January 11, 1974, Campbell Mine

At 5:30 pm, J.M. McKinney was pulling the 101 chute on the 2833 level. McKinney was the motor swamper and Ralph Hastie was the motorman. As McKinney lifted the chute door the handle slipped out. The door fell bruising his right knee. (Note, this almost definitely was a Verde style chute)

Phelps Dodge Corporation Copper Queen Branch Accident Report 1-11-74

January 14, 1974, Campbell Mine

Buck Lynch and F.O. *"Figure Eight"* Figueroa were putting in air and water line in 100 stope on the 2833 level. The men turned off the air and water lines and extended them by a section. Then these miners installed a valve on the compressed air line and turned the main airline valve on. This was so that a diamond drill crew could continue drilling * Figueroa began to push another section of pipe into the new valve. The valve came off and the rust in the airline blasted out and injected rust into both his arms and gave him air burns.

*On a bonus system, diamond drill crews were paid a bonus on how many feet they drilled. Not having air would have cost them money on their paycheck.)

Phelps Dodge Corporation Copper Queen Branch Accident Report 1-15-74

February 5, 1974, Campbell Mine

At 10:00 am, D.N. *"Candy"* Mesa was drilling with a stoper in 171 raise on the 2700 level. He was drilling with the second drill steel.* A one pound rock fell off the timber and struck Mesa on the wrist. The rock was moved by the vibrations of the drilling. Although, Mesa reported the incident on the 5th he told J. Cross, the shift boss he felt he was ok. On the 13th the cut became infected and he reported to the doctor.*Miners changed out drill steels as they drilled. The first steel or starter steel was short and the second steel was longer and the third longer yet. In the early years the drill bits were often dulled by the time a steel needed to be changed and the steel changes were needed to provide a sharp and slightly narrower bit. The gauge of the bit was also important. The first bit was slightly larger than the second and the second was slightly larger than the third bit. This prevented drill steels from becoming stuck in the drill hole. By the time Mesa was injured, bits with carbide tungsten inserts were in use and changing steels was not as important in stopes or crosscuts where longer steels could be used to start drill holes. In raises, room was often limited and steel changes remained important.

Phelps Dodge Corporation Copper Queen Branch Accident Report 2-15-74

February 8, 1974, Campbell Mine

The sump of the Campbell Shaft was being cleaned out. An H car had been loaded with wet, sticky, mud from the sump and was hoisted to the 3233 level. At the trench for the hoisting pocket, H.C. Morgan and R.M Shenton dumped the H car. The tub came off the car and fell into the trench* taking Shenton who was still holding on. The force of the tub falling off the car broke the chain holding the mine car to the tracks**. Luckily, Shenton was only bruised and cut up in the chest, head and neck. Shenton was off work 219 days.

* On this level broken rock was dumped into a trench cut out on the level and then a slusher was used to drag the rock into a pocket

for hoisting to the surface.**Mine cars were attached to a short chain when dumping. This prevented the car from derailing while dumping or in worst case falling onto the grizzly.
Phelps Dodge Corporation Copper Queen Branch Accident Report 2-11-74
"January1-through December 31, 1974" Phelps Dodge Corporation Copper Queen Branch Annual Report Safety Department

February 14, 1974, Campbell Mine,
Although, the details are not known R.D. Reynolds suffered a hernia while handling materials. "January1-through December 31, 1974" Phelps Dodge Corporation Copper Queen Branch Annual Report Safety Department

February 16, 1974, Campbell Mine
At 9:30 am, T.E. Brady and J.A. Teran were dumping H cars. They were dumping one car that contain half sandy muck and ore. The men dumped the car part of the way over when Brady tried to get a hold of the bottom of the tub to turn it the rest of the way over. Brady's foot slipped and the tub of the car swung back bruising his chest
Phelps Dodge Corporation Copper Queen Branch Accident Report 2-19-74

February 19, 1974, Campbell Mine
A.M. Salaiz strained his back carrying a boom up a muck pile. He was injured on the 3233 level in 29 stope.
Phelps Dodge Corporation Copper Queen Branch Accident Report 2-22-74

February 27, 1974, Campbell Mine
On the 3100 level at 45 stope, J.P. Valenzuela was timbering a chute. He had attached the chute sides and was trying to nail the cleats to hold a secondary door. Valenzuela stepped on a nail protruding from a wedge. He was off work 11 days.
Phelps Dodge Corporation Copper Queen Branch Accident Report 2-28-74
"January1-through December 31, 1974" Phelps Dodge Corporation Copper Queen Branch Annual Report Safety Department

March 7, 1974, Campbell Mine
On the 3100 level, R.L. Waggoner was getting ready to hoist a gin pole up into No.65 raise. When he turned to get the chain off the tugger cable, the gin pole rolled off a stack of timber and bruised the instep of his right foot.
Phelps Dodge Corporation Copper Queen Branch Accident Report 3-8-74

March 13, 1974, Campbell Mine
Back in 171 raise on the 2833 level, D.M. *"Candy"* Mesa and C.L. Talbert were nailing down a bulkhead. They were running late and wanted to blast. Mesa was holding two nails in his hand and was driving a nail with an axe. He accidently hit the wrong nail and drove it into his palm.
Phelps Dodge Corporation Copper Queen Branch Accident Report 3-18-74

March 18, 1974, Campbell Mine
T.H. Vernagus jr. was pulling the chute at 64 stope. A 10"x10" timber came under the chute door Vernagus placed his left foot under the chute door while he tried to pull out the timber. When the 10"x10" came out the chute door fell on his foot. His foot was broken. This was a lost time accident. He was off work 27 days.
Phelps Dodge Corporation Copper Queen Branch Accident Report 3-20-74 2:15 pm
"January1-through December 31, 1974" Phelps Dodge Corporation Copper Queen Branch Annual Report Safety Department

March 19, 1974, Campbell Mine
Around 8:00 am, an evacuation drill was called. B.P. Salazar was assigned to 31 stope on the 3233 level. To evacuate he need to climb the 29-A stope manway and eventually reach the 2700 level station of the Junction Mine. As Salazar was climbing the 29-A stope manway, the man ahead of him knocked a piece of scrap timber loose. The man called *"Look out below!"* The piece of timber fell three or four ladder rungs and then hit Salazar's knee. He was only bruised.
Phelps Dodge Corporation Copper Queen Branch Accident Report 3-20-74 8:05

March 27, 1974, Campbell Mine
R.H. *"Ojos de Ostión"* Torres was drilling to install roof bolts in 168 stope on the 2700 level. A rock fell from the back (ceiling) and broke his right hand and cut up his wrist. He remained off work 18 days. (*Ojos de Ostión* translates to English from Spanish as Oyster Eyes)
Phelps Dodge Corporation Copper Queen Branch Accident Report 3-28-74
"January1-through December 31, 1974" Phelps Dodge Corporation Copper Queen Branch Annual Report Safety Department

April 1, 1974, Campbell Mine
F.A. Torres and E.W. Kangas were using a mucking machine to cleanup sand*in 174 stope on the 2700 level. The men uncovered a section of 12" x10' ventilation pipe. When it was free they picked it up and began to move it out of the way. As Kangas set the pipe down it turned and cut his middle finger.* This was probably residue from sand fill. Sand fill was a mixture of cement and tailings sand used to back fill stopes in the later years of mining. Many of the orebodies found in the Abrigo limestone had treacherous ground conditions and have been unmineable without this technique.
Phelps Dodge Corporation Copper Queen Branch Accident Report 4-2-74

April 3, 1974, Campbell Mine
J.E. *"Kimba"* Cordova was walking down a drift on the 3333 level when he tripped. His left hand impacted the head of a track spike. His hand was bruised.
Phelps Dodge Corporation Copper Queen Branch Accident Report 4-5-74

April 10, 1974, Campbell Mine
Although few details are known, L. Chavez was off work 165 days for a twisted knee. He was handling materials when the accident occurred.
"January1-through December 31, 1974" Phelps Dodge Corporation Copper Queen Branch Annual Report Safety Department

April 24, 1974, Campbell Mine
E.F. Carbajal was working in 25 stope on the 3233 level. He was holding the drill steel as his partner was collaring a hole with a jackleg. A boulder fell striking his left hand. Carbajal had two fingers and his hand bruised.
Phelps Dodge Corporation Copper Queen Branch Accident Report 4-29-74

April 24, 1974, Campbell Mine
At 10:05 am, Y.L. *"Korea"* Sorilla was working in 10 stope on the 3233 level. His partner had lowered a post down a floor to him. Sorilla was dropping the post down another floor. As he dropped the post his fingers were caught between the post and the floor. He broke two fingers. He was off work 117 days.
Phelps Dodge Corporation Copper Queen Branch Accident Report 4-26-74
"January1-through December 31, 1974" Phelps Dodge Corporation Copper Queen Branch Annual Report Safety Department

April 26, 1974, Campbell Mine
G. Gherna Jr. was carrying samples to the manway in 31 stope on the 3233 level. He
tripped on a slusher cable in the mucking scram and bruised his knee.
Phelps Dodge Corporation Copper Queen Branch Accident Report 4-29-74

May 7, 1974, Campbell Mine
Powderman, A.R. Masgrove was tramming his powder car. As he passed the battery station
on the 2966 level, he slipped and fell hitting his knee on a rail. His knee was bruised.
Phelps Dodge Corporation Copper Queen Branch Accident Report 5-10-74

May 7, 1974, Campbell Mine
On the 3333 level, LY. *"Chinaman"* Coronado was walking out of 6 stope. As he
walked by a mucking machine, he stepped on a jackleg lying on the ground. The jackleg
rolled over and smashed his left ankle.
Phelps Dodge Corporation Copper Queen Branch Accident Report 5-8-74

May 15, 1974, Campbell Mine
At 2:15pm, C.B. Talbert was walking to 103 raise on the 2833 level. The drift was
partially flooded and the water was above the rails. Talbert was walking on top of the rail
(to keep drier) and he slipped and sprained his right ankle. The timekeeper gave him a
blue card to fill out.
Phelps Dodge Corporation Copper Queen Branch Accident Report 5-16-74

May 16, 1974, Campbell Mine
C.J. Feltman and A. D. Draper were in 101 stope on the 2833 level. Feltman was drilling
and Draper was installing side lagging. As Draper was working, a 300 lb. boulder broke
free and landed on his left big toe. The boulder broke his toe. This accident resulted in 31
days lost time.
Phelps Dodge Corporation Copper Queen Branch Accident Report 5-18-74
"January 1-through December 31, 1974" Phelps Dodge Corporation Copper Queen Branch Annual Report Safety Department

May 22, 1974, Campbell Mine
O.J. Burton was drilling with a jackleg in 20 stope on the 3233 level. The jackleg had a
broken steel holder. As he attempted to wire the holder to keep it from moving back, he
punctured his left hand with the wire.
Phelps Dodge Corporation Copper Queen Branch Accident Report 5-23-74

May 24, 1974, Campbell Mine
Electrician, E.M. Downs was moving a 50 hp. Joy blower. He tried to stop the impeller
from slowly moving by using his foot. When Downs touched the impeller with his foot,
he fell off a short 12" blower stand. He cut his head and required five stitches. The
accident occurred on the 3233 level.
Phelps Dodge Corporation Copper Queen Branch Accident Report 5-24-74

May 28, 1974, Campbell Mine
R.R. Morales was opening an air door in 7 crosscut on the 2566 level. As he grabbed for
the air door to close* it he slipped and injured his back. It was noted that Morales had
injured his back two years earlier and this was suspected to have increased the chances of

injury. * Note that some air doors could be incredibly difficult to shut. This was because of the massive volume of air flowing past them. Other air doors could be shut easily. It is unknown how difficult the door was to close.
Phelps Dodge Corporation Copper Queen Branch Accident Report 5-29-74

An air door in the Campbell Mine.
The round circle is called a target and
was applied to make the door easier to see.
(left image)

A train passing through the same air door as in previous image.

May 29, 1974, Campbell Mine
Around midnight, J.G. *"3D"* Rodriguez and M.D. Montiel had returned from lunch to 62 stope on the 2966 level. They had blasted out room to install a boom as they went to lunch. When they returned Rodriguez was barring down. A 100 lb. boulder was barred down. The rock rolled and smashed Rodriguez's right ankle.
Phelps Dodge Corporation Copper Queen Branch Accident Report 5-30-74

May 30, 1974, Campbell Mine
G.M. *"Turkey George"* Alcantar was in 35 raise on the 3233 level. He was removing a bulkhead with R.L. Waggoner. As Alcantar removed a lagging and was handing it to Waggoner, a small rock fell and struck Alcantar in the mouth. He suffered a chipped tooth.
Phelps Dodge Corporation Copper Queen Branch Accident Report 5-31-74

May 30, 1974, Campbell Mine
D.C. *"Pigmy"* Estrada was climbing down from the loading stand at 5 stope on the 3333 level. His foot slipped off a ladder rung and his knee slammed into a rung.
Phelps Dodge Corporation Copper Queen Branch Accident Report 5-31-74

June 1, 1974, Campbell Mine
On the 1800 level in 296 stope, W.R. Jewell was getting ready to blast and a raise. As he was walking towards it, a small amount of muck caved from above and a boulder rolled down. This rock struck him on the left foot. It was noted that the stope had a reputation of sluffing down rock.
Phelps Dodge Corporation Copper Queen Branch Accident Report 6-1-74

June 6, 1974, Campbell Mine
Diamond Drill Helper, E.A. Torres was pushing a load of drill core in 154 crosscut on the 3233 level. The miner car tilted and a box of core fell smashing his left finger between the core box and the timber truck.

Phelps Dodge Corporation Copper Queen Branch Accident Report 6-4-74

June 5, 1974, Campbell Mine

In 118 crosscut on the 2966 level, H.R. Sherman was removing rail with H. *"Porkchop"* Guillen. They were removing rails to add curved rails for a new crosscut being driven off 118 crosscut. Sherman had raised the rails up with the bucket on a mucking machine. Guillen was knocking the ties free from the rails. Mud splattered into Sherman's left eye.

Phelps Dodge Corporation Copper Queen Branch Accident Report 6-7-74

June 12, 1974, Campbell Mine

At. 9:00 am, W.R. Jewell was placing a chute bomb to free up muck in a raise in 296 stope on the 1800 level. He slipped on a rock and cut up his left leg.

Phelps Dodge Corporation Copper Queen Branch Accident Report 6-13-74

June 14, 1974, Campbell Mine

Back in 62 stope on the 2966 level. R.M. Mesa and M.D. Montiel were working with a slusher. They needed to remove crib timber and attached a slusher cable to yank it out. When Mesa pulled out the timber it flung out and struck Montiel in the left knee.

Phelps Dodge Corporation Copper Queen Branch Accident Report 6-17-74

June 19, 1974, Campbell Mine

M. Urena was getting ready to install more roof bolts. He was in 63 stope on the 3100 level. Unknown to Urena the jackleg had not been completely shut off. His partner went and turned on the air valve and the jackleg jumped up. He fell against the rib (wall) and received a cut hand.

Phelps Dodge Corporation Copper Queen Branch Accident Report 6-20-74

July 2, 1974, Campbell Mine

On the 2833 level in 130 crosscut, E. G. Bryon was hooking a train of H cars to a motor. He was bent over lifting a drawhead and signaled Ralph Hastie to move the locomotive. The brakes on the locomotive were faulty and Bryon's head was caught between the cab of the locomotive and an H car. Luckily, he suffered only a bruised head.

Phelps Dodge Corporation Copper Queen Branch Accident Report 7-3-74 9:00 am

July 2, 1974, Campbell Mine

In 60 stope on the 2966, George Mayers had barred down. He then stood up a post and blocked it in the top. As he was bent over blocking the bottom, a rock fell striking him in the back. He suffered only a bruised back.

Phelps Dodge Corporation Copper Queen Branch Accident Report 7-3-74 11:05 am

July 10, 1974, Campbell Mine

On the 2700 level in 169 stope, F.A. Escarcega was drilling for eyebolts. He slipped and fell down a muck pile. He suffered a broken wrist, and two broken ribs. He was off work 46 days.

Phelps Dodge Corporation Copper Queen Branch Accident Report 7-12-74
"January 1-through December 31, 1974" Phelps Dodge Corporation Copper Queen Branch Annual Report Safety Department

August 27, 1974, Campbell Mine

Motor Swamper, J.J. Pomaski was on the 2966 level with motorman, M. *"Milo"** Prince. They intended to work pulling 55 chute, but they needed to drop off a single "H" car at

the 72 stope chute. About 9:45pm, Pomaski was riding on the tail car and as they pulled under the 72 stope chute, miners in the stope dropped two boulders. The chute must have basically empty as the boulders jumped over the door and into the crosscut. At least one struck Pomaski's left hand, breaking his middle finger. He was off work 110 days.*His nickname meant and he was sometimes called *"Mile O" Minute."*
Phelps Dodge Corporation Copper Queen Branch Accident Report 8-27-74 9:45
"January1-through December 31, 1974" Phelps Dodge Corporation Copper Queen Branch Annual Report Safety Department

August 27, 1974, Campbell Mine
At 11:00 pm, O. Huerena was pulling a 64 chute on the 3100 level with E. Yungaray. The chute was hung up and Huerena was trying to free it with a blow pipe. A boulder fell and struck the blowpipe causing the valve to turn, striking Huerena in the chin. His chin was cut and he bit his tongue.
Phelps Dodge Corporation Copper Queen Branch Accident Report 8-27-74 11:00

August 29, 1974, Campbell Mine
In 171 stope on the 2566 level, E. Jimenez was carrying burlap into the stope and strained his left leg.
Phelps Dodge Corporation Copper Queen Branch Accident Report 8-29-74

September 18, 1974, Campbell Mine
In 72 stope on the 2966 level, R.R. Abril was struck by a falling slab of rock. His left hip and leg were bruised. Abril was off work 26 days.
Phelps Dodge Corporation Copper Queen Branch Accident Report 9-23-74
"January1-through December 31, 1974" Phelps Dodge Corporation Copper Queen Branch Annual Report Safety Department

September 30, 1974, Campbell Mine
72 stope on the 2966 level was being mined by C.L. Cole and R.R. Tovar. The stope was sulphur* rich. After blasting a nail bag four sets back from the face was ignited and was found smoldering nearly two hours later. The potential of a mine fire from this blasted created concern. No one was injured. *Sulphur is a term indicating the presence of particularly flammable sulfide ores. Particle size, composition, (pyrite, chalcopyrite, bornite, etc.) along with state of oxidation can affect the flammability of the rock. Sulphide ores were regularly mined in Bisbee.
Phelps Dodge Corporation Copper Queen Branch Report of Accident 9-30-74

October 1, 1974, Campbell Mine
J.A. *"Never Ready"* Navarrete was walking from the shaft to 173 stope on the 2700 level. J.R. Franco was walking behind him. Navarrete slipped and attempted to catch himself. He strained his back. The accident was more serious than it sounds. It was a lost time accident. Navarrette was off 6 days.
Phelps Dodge Corporation Copper Queen Branch Accident Report 10-2-74
"January1-through December 31, 1974" Phelps Dodge Corporation Copper Queen Branch Annual Report Safety Department

October 4, 1974, Campbell Mine
W.J. *"KY"* Ferrell was drilling a lifter in 32 stope on the 3233 level. Mud fell off the face (wall) of the stope and struck the jackleg. This caused the leg of the machine to smash his foot.
Phelps Dodge Corporation Copper Queen Branch Accident Report 10-9-74

October 25, 1974, Campbell Mine
On the 2700 level in 193 crosscut, C.A. Lugo. Strong copper water was draining from the back (ceiling) of the diamond drill station. As he was drilling some of this copper water splashed into his eyes.
Phelps Dodge Corporation Copper Queen Branch Accident Report 10-28-74

November 7, 1974, Campbell Mine
On the 2966 level in 73 stope, F.C. Acosta* was drilling holes to blast out room for timber. He had finished drilling a hole and was moving his machine (jackleg), when a 30-40 lb. boulder fell and knocked off his left thumbnail. *Was also known as "Chino"
Phelps Dodge Corporation Copper Queen Branch Accident Report 11-8-74

November 9, 1974, Campbell Mine
Welder, T.P. Martin was working with J.E. Martinez on the 3233 ore pocket.
They were lifting out a ladder and Martin was standing on an angle iron with his right foot under the upper chute door. Martinez tried to shut the lower chute door, but mistakenly closed the upper chute door. The impact broke four of Martin's toes. Martin was off work 52 days.
Phelps Dodge Corporation Copper Queen Branch Accident Report 11-9-74

November 22, 1974, Campbell Mine
L.Y. *"Chinaman"* Coronado was going to pull the 32 stope chute in 2 crosscut on the 3233 level. As he drove the locomotive towards the chute, he was facing away from the chute. The hinge board at the chute was down. The board struck him in the head and he was thrown forward. Coronado's chest landed on the locomotive siren. He chipped and fractured his sternum. Coronado was off work 39 days. (Note, his nickname today could be consider a racial slur and is given only for research and historical purposes.)
Phelps Dodge Corporation Copper Queen Branch Accident Report 11-22-74
"January1-through December 31, 1974" Phelps Dodge Corporation Copper Queen Branch Annual Report Safety Department

January 13, 1975, Campbell Mine
J.C. Estrada was trying to put a 10"x 10" post into a timber slide. He dropped the post on his right foot, breaking a toe. The accident occurred in 31 stope on the 3233 level. This was a lost time accident.
Phelps Dodge Corporation Copper Queen Branch Accident Report 1-14-75

January 22, 1975, Campbell Mine
At 8:15 am, L.H. Romero and T.M. McKinney were mucking in 173 stope on the 2700 level. Romero was running a mucking machine. He backed the machine up and became caught between the chassis and a timber post. This caused the bucket to swing back and strike him on the shoulder. Luckily, Romero was only bruised.
Phelps Dodge Corporation Copper Queen Branch Accident Report 1-27-75

January 27, 1975, Campbell Mine
In 32 stope on the 3233 level, A.H. Austin and H.C. Fernandez were installing booms. They had set the end of one boom on the edge of a hanger. When Austin moved the boom it fell from the hanger and struck Fernandez in the chest. He suffered only a bruised chest.
Phelps Dodge Corporation Copper Queen Branch Accident Report 2-5-75

A miner in Bisbee operating a mucking machine. Notice, the narrow working conditions.

January 27, 1975, Campbell Mine
 At 4:30 pm, T.M. McKinney was with #37 locomotive on the 2700 level. As he threw a switch (rail) he smashed his finger between the switch throw and a steel plate.
Phelps Dodge Corporation Copper Queen Branch Accident Report 1-28-75

January 28, 1975, Campbell Mine
Timberman, T.C. Chavez strained his back on the 2866 level in 131 crosscut. He was replacing a post that was broken behind a vent pipe. Chavez was injured while lifting a new post into place.
Phelps Dodge Corporation Copper Queen Branch Accident Report 1-23-75

March 19, 1975, Campbell Mine
E.J. McDonald rode the bottom deck of a three deck cage to the surface at the end of his shift. The cager spotted the cage with the bottom deck of the cage still underground. As the cager stepped off he knocked dirt from the turnsheet down into the bottom deck of the cage. The dust went into McDonald's eyes
Phelps Dodge Corporation Copper Queen Branch Accident Report 3-21-75

March 20, 1975, Campbell Mine
On the 3100 level, P.N. Quinones was moving a mucking machine onto the main drift. He crushed his right hand between the machine's tram throttle and a corner post. He suffered a Toft fracture of his middle finger and bruising.
Phelps Dodge Corporation Copper Queen Branch Accident Report 3-27-74 (original document misdated?)

Two different types of switch throws, above and below

March 25, 1975, Campbell Mine
L.H. *"Wild Hare"* Hare was on the 3100 station getting a drink from the water cooler. His foot slipped into a drain hole and pulled a muscle.
Phelps Dodge Corporation Copper Queen Branch Accident Report 3-26-75

April 15, 1975, Campbell Mine
B.V. *"Chief"* Garcia was barring down a hung up 34 chute on the 3233 level. A boulder fell and struck the end of the bar. This knocked the bar into Garcia's chin. He suffered a bruised chin.
Phelps Dodge Corporation Copper Queen Branch Accident Report 4-16-75

Form 275-B

ACCIDENT ON DUTY

ACCIDENT CERTIFICATE FOR MEDICAL ATTENTION

PHELPS DODGE CORPORATION — Copper Queen Branch

Date.. Hour..........................

Copper Queen Dispensary (or Hospital),
  Bisbee, Arizona

The bearer.. No..

employed at .... is entitled to receive medical attention

on account of an alleged injury received at...

while working for the Company on the.................day of.................................., 19.........

at...P. M. or (A. M.)

Timekeeper, Foreman or Shift Boss

This card must be presented at the Dispensary or Hospital before the expiration of 24 hours from the time of accident and will be forwarded by them to the Accident Department.

Received C. Q. Dispensary (or Hospital), Date.........................Hour..................

  By ....

An example of a "Blue card". Printed on light blue paper were given to injured employees to present at the Copper Queen Hospital

May 21, 1975, Campbell Mine
At the Campbell loading dock, F. Wedzik were trying to center a 10"x10"x11' timber on a flat car. His partner pushed the timber towards Wedzik quickly. Wedzik's right hand was caught between the timber and the concrete loading dock. (Note, this accident occurred on the surface in the Campbell mine yard)
Phelps Dodge Corporation Copper Queen Branch Accident Report 5-21-75

June 5, 1975, Campbell Mine
Back in 10 stope on the 3233 level, Y.L. *"Korea"* Sorilla was dropping booms with C. Huerena. The boom turned in Huerena's hands and then he dropped the timber. Sorilla's end raised and smashed his hand.
Phelps Dodge Corporation Copper Queen Branch Accident Report 6-9-75

June 10, 1975, Campbell Mine
W.R. *"KY"* Ferrell was in 32 stope on the 3233 level. He was installing a gin pole and rocks fell and bruised his left ankle.
Phelps Dodge Corporation Copper Queen Branch Accident Report 6-11-75

After mining ended on June 12, 1975, the salvage of valuable equipment, such as mine cars, rails, blowers etc. continued. Also the pumps on the 2966 level were maintained for a time. The following accidents occurred after mining had ceased, but during the salvage period. Note, a small amount of mining occurred in the Campbell for precious metals and salvage under Lorenzo *"Cacho"* Gonzales for Bisbee Salvage & Equipment Company and Gilbert Construction Company between 1982-1986.

July 19, 1975, Campbell Mine
Eric Nelson was checking the starter on a pump located on the 2966 level. When he reached inside the starter to check voltage He touched the terminus of an amp meter and was electrically burned on the right forearm by 440 volts.
Phelps Dodge Corporation Copper Queen Branch Accident Report 7-21-75

Pumps at the 2200 level Junction Mine

September 25, 1975, Campbell Mine
G.E. Cornett had gone underground to check on the 2200 level pumps at the Junction shaft and the Campbell pumps on the 2966 level. As he was being hoisted to the surface, water was raining down the shaft. When he got off the cage on the surface he closed the shaft gates and copper water splashed into his eyes.
Phelps Dodge Corporation Copper Queen Branch Accident Report 9-25-75

September 28, 1975, Campbell Mine
On this Sunday around 10:00 am, Jim Hansen lowered on a cage, Larry French and a miner named Lugo* to the to the 2700 level to inspect the mine. When the men released the cage from the 2700 level, Hansen raised the cage about 10 feet above the level. The cage in the #3 compartment was stopped in a tight spot and the cage guides were not well oiled. When French and Lugo called for the cage the cage in the # 3 compartment became stuck in the shaft and the cage did not arrive. No one was injured in this incident.*There were two miners with the surname Lugo working around this time C.A. Lugo and R. Lugo
Phelps Dodge Corporation Copper Queen Branch Report of Accident 9-28-75

68

September 29, 1975, Campbell Mine
On the 3233 level at the 3 crosscut substation, Lorenzo *"Cacho"* Gonzales, Tom McKinney and J.H. Warne were using chain hoist to remove a 50KVA transformer onto a timber truck. While swinging the transformer onto the truck Warne's left had was smashed. He was bruised and cut up.
Phelps Dodge Corporation Copper Queen Branch Accident Report 9-29-75

Changing a post near a caved chute. The bottom of the post on the right has rotted out. 33-1 raise, 19 crosscut, 3rd level Southwest Mine.

A gin pole resting on the rib of the main drift, 3rd level Southwest Mine.

The small headframe in the foreground is the Charon.
The larger headframe is the Holbrook No.2 Mine.

Charon Mine

This mine was a small access shaft, lessees used to reach ores left in the Holbrook mine. The shaft was around 100ft. deep and used from about 1914 until the 1930s. It was also known as the Van Horn Mine.

October 9, 1920, Charon Mine

Tomas Garcia was drilling a boulder in the ceiling of a stope when it fell and crushed him. Two miners were nearby and felt that the rock should have been supported by a stull before it was drilled.

Original Certificate of Death." Arizona Department of Health Services. http://genealogy.az.gov/azdeath/022/10222233.pdf (May 28, 2014)

Office of State Mine Inspector. *Seventh Annual Report of the State Mine Inspector State of Arizona for the Year Ending November 30, 1920.*

"Cochise County Coroner's Inquest No.1431" Arizona State Archives Phoenix

Cochise Mine c-1901. The shaft has a simple "Montana" style headframe. A horse whim is used for hoisting

Cochise Mine

        This unsuccessful mine started sinking in March 1900. Exploration activities occurred off and on until 1907 when work at the mine ceased. Eventually, it consisted of a small, incline shaft sunk 57 ft. and the main three compartment vertical shaft was sunk 930 ft. The main shaft had four developed levels and a fifth shaft station cut. The Cochise was sometimes called the Pajaro Mine.

May 2, 1906, Cochise Mine
Pat Powers was injured in a cave-in at 1 o'clock in the morning. A rock broke free and carried a large amount of rock and dirt onto him. He was taken to the Calumet and Arizona Hospital. His injuries were severe bruises and flesh wounds. His partner suffered minor injuries.
"Rock Rolls on Miner in Cochise" Bisbee Daily Review 2 May 1906 page 1

March 22, 1902, Cochise Mine
Matt Washby loaded a mine car onto the cage and sent it up. After the cage came back down with the car, Washby got on the cage and rung the bells for the 600 level. As the cage left the station, the mine car caught on a bar mounted on the shaft timber to drive water away from the station. The mine car tipped over and knocked Washby out of the cage and onto a bulkhead. He was quickly found by the men on the station, lying on the bulkhead. Still alive, he was taken to the surface. After 15 minutes he died.
"Cochise County Coroner's Inquest No.425" Arizona State Archives Phoenix

Calumet & Cochise Shaft c-1903

Calumet & Cochise Mine

Sinking of this shaft began in April 1903 and development of the three compartment shaft continued until spring 1905. After no ore was located the operation was shut down. In 1917, Phelps Dodge needed a source of water for their new Sacramento Concentrator. The shaft was sunk to a depth of 1,835 ft. and with effort, significant clean water was discovered. The Calumet & Cochise became successful as a *"water"* mine. The headframe which had been original on the Spray Shaft was transferred to Shattuck Mine in 1973. Parts of the Calumet & Cochise were maintained until 1975. The mine is generally better known as the C&C Mine.

April 29, 1903, Calumet & Cochise Mine
Timberman, Godfrey Henderson was installing timber, when he slipped and fell. He dislocated his shoulder and was cared for by Dr. Caven.
"Dislocated Shoulder" Bisbee Daily Review 30 April 1903 page 8

August 20, 1903, Calumet & Cochise Mine
John Daley was working at the bottom of the C&C Shaft*. He had checked the ground and felt it was strong. Soon, after several tons of rock and dirt fell from the side of the shaft. The muck pinned him against the shaft wall bruising his shoulders and back. He was taken to the Calumet & Arizona Hospital.

*The shaft would have been around 340 ft. deep at this time. On June 27, 1903, the shaft. was 275 ft. deep.
"Caught by Fall of Rocks" Bisbee Daily Review 21 August 1903 page 5
"Calumet and Cochise" Bisbee Daily Review 28 June 1903 page 8
"Calumet & Arizona Hospital Records." My Cochise. http://www.mycochise.com/hospcalco2day.php (May 28, 2012)

September 29, 1903, Calumet & Cochise Mine
Victor Henrickson crushed his middle finger on a compressor. It was necessary to amputate the finger.
"Lost Middle Finger" Bisbee Daily Review 30 September 1903 page 5

September 11, 1918, Calumet & Cochise Mine

In an undescribed accident, Joe McNelis received a severe cut on the cheek.

"Is Badly Injured" Bisbee Daily Review 11 September 1918 page 6

June 7, 1921, Calumet & Cochise Mine

Claude William Narce was struck by fly-rock from a blast. He died a few minutes after being struck. He was 31 years-old and was buried in Oklahoma

"Original Certificate of Death." Arizona Department of Health Services. http://genealogy.az.gov/azdeath/023/10233046.pdf (May 30, 2012)

Office of State Mine Inspector. *Tenth Annual Report of the State Mine Inspector State of Arizona for the Year Ending November 30, 1921.*

June 30, 1927, Calumet & Cochise Mine

Dallas A. Harris, Walter C. Dexter and a man named White had mucked four cars out a crosscut and set up to drill. They began drilling and hit a missed hole. The detonation broke about two wheelbarrow loads of rock. White's jaw was broken but, Dexter and Harris were mortally injured. At the Copper Queen Hospital, Dexter requested *"that he was not to be put in the room where his wife had passed some time ago."* Harris was survived by a wife, Isabel Crowley Harris.

Certificate of Death." Arizona Department of Health Services. http://genealogy.az.gov/azdeath/035/10350054.pdf (May 28, 2012)

Dugan Mortuary Records Aug. 29, 1926 – Jan 4 1930 Accession 2010.10.20 Bisbee Mining and Historical Museum, Bisbee p. 69

Certificate of Death." Arizona Department of Health Services. http://genealogy.az.gov/azdeath/035/10350054.pdf (May 28, 2012)

Dugan Mortuary Records Aug. 29, 1926 – Jan 4 1930 Accession 2010.10.20 Bisbee Mining and Historical Museum, Bisbee p. 62

"Cochise County Inquest No. 1656" Arizona State Archives Phoenix

Fallen slab in No. 30 crosscut, 5th level Southwest Mine.

Cole Shaft circa 1990

Cole Mine

The South Bisbee Copper Mining and Town site Improvement Company, under the direction of John. P. Martin began sinking the double compartment South Bisbee No.2 Shaft (Cole) in 1898. Sinking continued and in June 1899, the shaft struck sulphide ore at 680 feet, but not mineable amounts. Then in January 1902, the Cole was abruptly shut down and the property was sold to the Lake Superior and Pittsburg Development Company. The exploration of the Cole Shaft continued. This shaft was 1,050 ft. deep and drifting was being completed. In November 1903, the first significant orebody was struck on the 1000 level. The ore was carbonate and assayed around 12%. The drifts determined the ore was 73 ft. wide and was dipping towards the 1100 level.

Infused with capital and understanding of mining methods, the L.S. & P. Co. decided to completely remodel the Cole Mine. The Cole shaft consisting of 1 ½ compartments was enlarged to four compartments. Three were designed for hoisting and a manway and pipe compartment. Mules were lowered underground to haul the ore to the #3 shaft. Then modern surface facilities were constructed including, a new change house, sawmill, blacksmith shop and a large store house. To encourage miners to seek employment, two new boarding house were built and construction of two rooming houses was started. The town site was laid out in lots for leasing to employees.

In 1906, the Lake Superior and Pittsburg Mining Company was consolidated with other small companies related to the Calumet & Arizona Mining Company and helped form the Superior & Pittsburg Copper Company. With the merger of the Calumet & Arizona Mining Company with Phelps Dodge in 1931, the Cole Mine again closed and was to remain inoperative until 1934. An interior shaft was raised from the 800 level to the 500 level and completed in 1941. The Cole closed again on October 31, 1944 and remained out of operation until 1948. Mining continued and in 1950 a series of 48" calyx raises were drilled to provide waste rock from the surface to fill in stopes underground. The Cole remained in operation until June 12, 1975. At the end of operations the shaft had four compartments and was 1,563 ft. deep. Bisbee Salvage & Equipment Company salvaged the equipment of value after the closure of the mine. In 1980-1981 a precious metal orebody was examined on the 800 level, but proved uneconomic. The Cole shaft was called the South Bisbee No.2, Lake Superior & Pittsburg No.2, and L.S. &P #2, depending on the period of operation.

October, 1902, Cole Mine
W.B. Brown was struck by a descending cage and knocked into the shaft. He landed on a mine loaded with muck. He was taken to his home on School Hill in an unconscious state, but was later interviewed by a newspaper reporter. The extent of the injuries are not known, but it appears he survived the ordeal.
"Accident at South Bisbee" The Arizona Republican 7 October 1902 page 4

December 3, 1902 Cole Mine
Shift boss, Ed McFarland was nearly killed when a cable began breaking while hoisting a water tank out of the mine. If the cable had broken off, McFarland would have fallen down the shaft.
"South Bisbee Accident" Bisbee Daily Review 5 December 1902 page 8

February 10, 1903 South Bisbee #2 Mine /Cole Mine
Henry Branbis was seriously injured when a misfire detonated and broke two bones in his upper leg. A rock was thrown by the detonation and hit his leg.
"Hurt in Mine" Bisbee Daily Review 11 February 1903 page 8

June 15, 1903, South Bisbee Shaft. (L.S. &P No. 2 or Cole Shaft.)
Sam Dickey entered a work area to relight a fuse that had not detonated. The hole detonated, catching him in the explosion. One eye was destroyed, his right arm was broken, and they were powder burns on his body. The other eye was thought could be saved. Dickey traveled to Phoenix to undergo an operation on his remaining eye in August 1903. He later died from his mine injuries in Phoenix, sometime before October 17, 1903. Dickey was a cousin to Albert McFarland who was later killed at the Cole Mine on October 17, 1903.
"Another Mine Accident" Bisbee Daily Review 17, June 1903 page 5
"Will Lose his Eye" Bisbee Daily Review 17, June 1903 page 5
"Mining Briefs" Bisbee Daily Review 21, June 1903 page 6
"Will have Eye Treated" Bisbee Daily Review 2, August 1903 page 5
"Death Follows Stabbing" Bisbee Daily Review 18 October 1903 page 5

October 17 1903, Cole Mine/ South Bisbee# 2/ L.S. &P. #2
The hoist at the Cole had broken down on the 16th and was not repaired until the evening of the 17th. Frank Obermiller was the operating hoistman. Jim Gresham a pipe-fitter had been working on the hoist. Obermiller asked, Gresham if he would run the hoist for the rest of his shift so he could go to a dance. Gresham explained, that he had been working 35 hours straight and it would not be safe for him to operate the hoist. Later, Obermiller asked Gresham to use his pocket knife to cut packing string for the engine valve, stem and piston. Again, Gresham declined because cutting packing was hard on a knife. Obermiller ended up rolling the packing around the piston. Frank Meyer and Albert Brown were there at the time operating a drill press. John Steinway and Charles Holmquist (Hultquist?) were trying to fix the drag on the signal bell. After, 7:00 pm the hoist was fixed and Gresham, Holmquist, Brown and Meyer left. While the larger hoist

75

was out of order, a smaller (dinkey) hoist had been attached to the cage. After the large hoist was back in order, Albert McFarland was attaching the cable from the large hoist to the cage again. He needed the cage lifted a couple feet and asked Obermiller to raise the cage. Obermiller responded, that he needed the hoist to warm up first. This seemed to irritate McFarland.

After the cage was attached, Obermiller lowered miners to the 900 level. Foreman, Albert McFarland and a shift boss named Miller got off on the 900 level. After this the signals were given to lower the cage to the 1000 level. Then signals were given to lower on the 1100 level. On the 1100 level a mine car loaded with muck was loaded on the cage and brought to the surface. As the cage was traveling, Obermiller received the bell signal 2-1 which indicated the cage was needed on the 900 level. At the 900 level the landing chairs* were set and a loaded mine car was put on the cage. The cager underground rang two bells to travel to the next station. It appears the cager had forgotten to release the landing chairs. As a result 100 ft. of cable and likely flat cable coiled on top of the cage. Obermiller suspected this had occurred, but he had received a two bell signal and was ethically required to respond**. When enough cable had been lowered for the cage to be at the 1000 level, Obermiller received a stop bell. This was followed by three bells that were rung slowly indicating to raise the cage slowly. After the slack cable was pulled in, a man rang a stop bell. This was soon followed by a signal to raise the cage to the surface. Once on the surface foreman Albert *"Bert"* Mc Farland went and told Obermiller to be more careful on the 900 level. Obermiller responded, *"What is the trouble?"* Mc Farland commented, that he had let down nearly 100ft. of cable. Obermiller mentioned, that he suspected that was happening. Mc Farland said, *"What did you do it for?"* Obermiller replied, *"I got two bells."* After this the situation degraded rapidly. McFarland *said, "Don't you call me a liar, you little son of a bitch!* Obermiller said, *"Mr. Mc Farland, I have the code of signals bells that I have been running by."* *"Well"* responded, McFarland and he continued, *"If you don't go away, I will can you and tie a big dam (sic) can to you."* Obermiller commented, that he was not sure that McFarland had the authority to fire him Mc Farland left the hoistroom stating, *"I will show you".* During the time McFarland was out of the hoist room, Obermiller received a blasting signal, four bells. The miners underground must have been getting ready to blast in the shaft or possibly on a shaft station not far from the shaft. Obermiller responded, to this signal by raising and lower the cage a couple feet. This told the miners that the hoistman had understood the signal and would be waiting for the signal to hoist them away from the blast*** Obermiller then raised the cage between two levels and was waiting for the signal of the men blasting. At this time McFarland reentered the hoist room holding a piece of paper. He came up to Obermiller and shoved the paper into his face and said, *"You little son of a bitch, I suppose this will do."* Then McFarland hit Obermiller in the temple with the fist. It appears he was holding his miner's candlestick. The wound was shaped like a candle socket on a miner's candlestick. The impact dazed Obermiller. He told McFarland, men were waiting to be hoisted away from a blast. McFarland knocked him down. A bell rang and Obermiller tried to get to the hoist, but was knocked down again. He continued to try get to the hoist and two more bells rang. Understanding that he could not get to the hoist and McFarland wanted to hurt him, Shoved McFarland. McFarland slipped and fell off a twelve inch platform.

Obermiller ran from the hoistroom to the home of Mr. Hoatson. He was chased by McFarland out of the hoist house to a turn sheet (probably near the shaft) Jerry Donnelly later told, Hoistman Harry Adams of the events underground. They were on the 1100 level getting ready to blast. They rang the blasting signal and the hoistman responded to them by raising and lowering the cage. The miners spit (ignited) their fuses. Then they rang the signal to be hoisted to the 1000 level and safety. Their call was never answered. Finally, they crawled over a pump and climbed up the manway ladders. E.M. Tong was on the 1000 level station and heard the bell signals for the blasting. J.W. Burnett saw Obermiller run down the hill being followed for a short distance by McFarland. McFarland returned to the hoist house and called for Burnett and told him Obermiller had cut him. He told Burnett to go to Mr. Hoatson's home. Alton M. Mills removed McFarland's pants and located the small wound with blood streaming from it. He place his finger over it to restrict the blood flow. At this time, Burnett realized the mine was without a hoistman. He ran to Lowell to find a replacement hoistman. Harry Adams took over the hoist at 10:30 pm. When Burnett returned the doctor had arrived.

After, Obermiller arrived at Jack Hoatson's house and explained the events. Hoatson said he did not allow men to beat up his employees. As they were talking a Burnett came to their home and told them McFarland was bleeding badly. Mr. Hoatson and his wife headed to the mine after telling Obermiller to make himself comfortable in their home. Dr. C.L. Caven was sent for and he found McFarlan extremely weak and saturated in blood. He could not find a pulse and the patient had bled out. The doctor gave McFarland strychnine stimulants and an injection of whiskey. After five minutes, McFarland's heart had stopped and breathing continued for at least ten minutes longer. McFarland was dead. A small ¼ inch puncture wound in his groin had cut into the femoral artery. The doctor felt it had been made by a dull instrument. Obermiller was arrested by Officer Biddy Doyle around midnight. He was later acquitted in the death of McFarland. At least publically, this was a popular decision. This was probably because McFarland had a reputation as an ill-tempered man. McFarland was survived by a brother Ed McFarland. He was also a cousin to Sam Dickey who was injured and later died from premature explosion on July 15, 1903 * Landing chairs are steel supports that are extended out into the shaft to support the cage when it receives a heavy load such as a mine car. If landing chairs were not used the cage would rapidly sink a few inches when a heavy load such as a loaded mine car was added. This typically would happen as soon as the front wheels of a car rolled onto the cage. This action could cause a loaded timber truck, steel car or mine car to turn over on the cage. ** Obermiller was on the surface and the events occurring were 900ft. below him underground. For safety reasons he was required to follow the instructions on the men underground as they were typically closer or part of events occurring.*** Blasting signal took precedence over all other signals including a danger signal. It is also interesting the code is slightly different from the Arizona State Code of Mine Bell signals adopted about a decade later. Also, two names may have been misspelled the newspaper has Hoatson's name spelled as Holtzen and Holmquist could actually be Hultquist who was later master mechanic for the Calumet & Arizona Mining Company , inventor of the Cochise rock drill and founder of Cochise Manufacturing Company in Los Angeles.

"Cochise County Coroner's Inquest No. 168" Arizona State Archives
"Death Follows Stabbing" Bisbee Daily Review 18 October 1903 page 5
"Obermuller Exonerated" Bisbee Daily Review 20 October 1903 page 5

January 17, 1906, Cole Mine/ L.S. & .P. #2 Mine
Cornish miner, James Lean was killed by a fall of ground. Lean was cleaning up the face of a drift. A boulder fell striking him on the side of the face. His skull was fractured. Lean died without regaining consciousness. He was 45-years-old and survived by a wife and son in Higher Terrace, Cornwall, England. It was reported that Lean intended to build a house and bring his family to Bisbee. James Lean is buried in Lowell. (No Inquest could be located.)

"Seriously Injured May Die" Bisbee Daily Review 17 January 1906 page 1

"Falling Stone Killed Miner" <u>Bisbee Daily Review</u> 18 January 1906 page 5
"Funeral Held" <u>Bisbee Daily Review</u> 19 January 1906 page 7

March 3, 1906, Cole Mine

At lunch time, 30 miners left No. 36 stope. While they were on break, several hundred tons caved, wiping out the top of the stope. Luckily, no one was injured. The collapse was unexpected and came without warning. This stope had been considered safe.

"Narrow Escape of Miners in L.S&P" <u>Bisbee Daily Review</u> 4 March 1908 page 8

August 12, 1907, Cole Mine

Around 8 o'clock in the evening, 23-year-old W.R. Gupton fell into No. 3 ore chute on the 1100 level. It is believed that he must have slipped and fallen into the chute while working at the top. The impact on the rock at the bottom of the chute appears to have broken his neck. His body was found by George Kovach a carman. When George opened the chute door to load his car, he discovered to his horror the body of Gupton inside the chute. He gathered some other men and removed the body from the chute and transported it to the surface, where it was identified as W.R. Gupton. The deceased had worked in Bisbee about six months. His body was escorted home to Swan, Kentucky, by his close friend H.B. Harding.

"Miner Falls to his Death in L.S&P" <u>Bisbee Daily Review</u> 13 August 1907 page 1
"Body is Sent Home" <u>Bisbee Daily Review</u> 16 August 1907 page 7
"Cochise County Inquest No. 586" Arizona State Archives

October 18, 1907, Cole Mine

Charles H. Smith was working in 34 stope on the 1100 level when a little before midnight the ground fell striking him. He was taken to the Calumet & Arizona Hospital where his injuries were determined to be minor. The 27-year-old, unmarried miner was released from hospital the next day.*

*The newspaper article refers to the mine as the Lake Superior and Pittsburg Shaft, which normally, could be one of two different shafts, the or the Lake Superior and Pittsburg No.2 (Cole), but the Lake Superior and Pittsburg No.3 did not have an 1100 level.

"Hurt in L.S. &P" <u>Bisbee Daily Review</u> 19 October 1907 page 5

November 14, 1907, Cole Mine

Albert. A. Griffin, a 24-year-old miner, was bent over working on the 1100 level, when a rock fell striking him on the back. He was taken by to the Calumet and Arizona Hospital, where it was determined that his back was broken. It was expected that he would be paralyzed for the remainder of his life. He was released from the Calumet & Arizona Hospital on July 29, 1908. His condition at this time was listed as *"unchanged"*.

"Miner Injured at Cole Shaft." <u>Bisbee Daily Review</u> 15 November 1907 page 3
"Calumet & Arizona Hospital Records." M<u>y Cochise.</u> http://www.mycochise.com/hospcalgr2he.php (June 17, 2012)

November 22, 1907 Cole Mine

G.W. Garner attacked Joe Williams at the L.S. & P. #2 Mine (Cole Mine). William was slashed three times under the right arm. Garner was arrested by Sherriff Bill White. He was arraigned before Judge Hogan.

"Cuts Three Gashes in Opponents Side" <u>Bisbee Daily Review</u> 23 November 1907 page 5

March 31, 1908, Cole Mine

Joseph Beers was moving machinery at the top of an incline on the 1000 level. While using a bar as a level, he slipped and fell 60 ft., fracturing his skull. He was taken to the Calumet & Arizona Hospital and died two hours later. Beers had been until just before his death, a hoist engineer for the dinky hoist. He was 23-years-old and his body was shipped to Calumet, Michigan. (No coroner's inquest could be located)

"Death Caused by Accident" Bisbee Daily Review 2 April 1908 page 3
"Body to Calumet" Bisbee Daily Review 3 April 1908 page 7
"Rolls Sixty Feet Dies Two Hours Later" Bisbee Daily Review 1 April 1908 page 5
"Calumet & Arizona Hospital Records." My Cochise. http://www.mycochise.com/hospcaldied.php (April 11, 2011)

November 1, 1909 Cole Mine

Nine-year-old, Paul Luke, Oliver Truelove and Hawley Garner were playing on the stacks of timber at the mine. Garner climbed to the top of the steep pile. The timber on the top was loose and the boys started to fall. Truelove jumped to safety. The other boys fell. A timber struck Luke on the nose fracturing his skull. The timber then hit Garner and knocked him unconscious. Luke died at the Calumet & Arizona Hospital and Garner recovered. Paul Luke was survived by his father, William Luke, his mother along with brothers and sisters.

"Cochise County Coroner's Inquest No. 698" Arizona State Archives
"Lad Dies as Result of Injuries" Bisbee Daily Review 4 November 1909 page 5
"Paul Luke Buried" Bisbee Daily Review 6 November 1909 page 5

January 1, 1910, Cole Mine

Nat Myers, a 45-year-old miner fell into a raise and broke his left arm. He was treated at the Calumet & Arizona Hospital and released.

"Suffers Broken Arm" Bisbee Daily Review 2 January 1910 page 7
"Calumet & Arizona Hospital Records." My Cochise. http://www.mycochise.com/hospcalme 2ny.php (April 22, 2011)

February 21, 1910, Cole Mine

John Boggs, a 41-year-old miner at the Cole was caught in a cave-in. He was severely smashed up and was taken to the Calumet & Arizona Hospital. Boggs was released from the hospital on March 1, 1910.

"Miner Hurt at Cole Shaft. by Cave-in" Bisbee Daily Review 22 February 1910 page 5
"Calumet & Arizona Hospital Records." My Cochise. http://www.mycochise.com/hospcalb.e 2br.php (April 5 2011)

February 27, 1910, Cole Mine

Joe Bahor was spitting his blast, (lighting fuses) and his candle blew out. Quickly, he began to fumble through the darkness to get away from his blast. In the blackness, he walked into another the blast of another miner. The explosion hit him in the back and knocked him over unconscious. He was not seriously hurt.

"Runs from One Blast into Another" Bisbee Daily Review 1 March 1910 page 8

March 7, 1910, Cole Mine

Joseph Graham was temporarily trapped by a cave-in. The fall of ground nearly caught other miners, but he luckily got away. Graham was able to free himself but sustained severe cuts on his right side and head. He was taken to the Calumet & Arizona Hospital.

"Graham Injured by Cole Shaft. Cave-in" Bisbee Daily Review 8 March 1910 page 4

July 1910, Cole Mine

A timber fell a crushed the left hand of W. Wildgrube.

"Arizona Custom Collections are Large" El Paso Herald 30 July 1910 page 11

July 1910, Cole Mine

Juste Barrazan dropped a nine-foot post on his left foot. His toes were smashed.

"Has Toes Crushed" Bisbee Daily Review 31 July 1910 page 7

July 1910, Cole Mine

W.P. Allen dropped a 50-pound can of powder* and smashed his right thumb. He was treated at the Calumet & Arizona Dispensary.

* The statement 50 lb. can of powder is confusing. Powder is normally a term for dynamite, but in this case, it implies that it was a blasting powder since dynamite was sold in a 50 lb. wooden case not a can like blasting powder. Blasting powder would be unusual since, it was not commonly used underground in Bisbee. It is possible that the article should have said a 50lb. case of powder.

"Has Thumb Crushed" Bisbee Daily Review 31 July 1912 page 5

July 8, 1910, Cole Mine

Oscar Zapf was securing timber onto a cage. The rope severed as he was pulling on it and he fell, injuring his back. He was expected to be off work several days. Zapf was treated at the Calumet & Arizona Dispensary.

"Accident at Cole Shaft." Bisbee Daily Review 8 July 1910 page 5

September 23, 1910 Cole Mine

John Brocbank and Richard Hopper were in a premature detonation. Both men were expected to survive, but were in agony. The men were peppered with small rocks from the blast. This incident occurred on the last night the Cole was operating before it was shutdown.* * Note, the Cole remained shut down from September 25, 1910 until November 1913. The ores in the Cole were mined through the Oliver Shaft during this time.

"Two Men Injured during Explosion" Bisbee Daily Review 24 September 1910 page 8

On September 25, 1910, the Cole Shaft. was shut down. The Cole workings continued to be mined but, the Oliver Shaft was used for hoisting. It was not until November 1913 did the Cole Shaft reenter operation. Men injured during this shutdown period would have been hoisted out through the Oliver Shaft.

August 16, 1911, Cole Mine

Tom Coppersmith* an engineer and M.W. Mitchell had descended the Oliver Shaft and head over to the workings of the Cole Shaft. In a stope at the Cole Mine, Mitchell was descending a ladder with Coppersmith above him. The ladder Coppersmith was climbing gave away, and he fell backward. As Coppersmith fell, he struck Mitchell and gave him minor injuries. Coppersmith fell around 50 feet. He was cut up around the pelvis. It was challenging to get the injured man back to the surface. They were 1,800 ft. from the Oliver Shaft and they had to drop 250 ft. before they could reach an Oliver Shaft station to be hoisted. It took three hours to get Coppersmith out of the mine. He was taken to the Calumet & Arizona Hospital where he stayed until September 18, 1911. *His name was possibly Copperwaite

"Falls 50 Feet in Mine Stope" Bisbee Daily Review 17 August 1911 page 3
"Calumet & Arizona Hospital Records." My Cochise. http://www.mycochise.com/hospcalco2day.php (April 3 2011)

May 26, 1912, Cole Mine

Finnish Miner, Gust Lailola Swanson was helping repair No.4 raise. This was an incline raise, and a stringer had worn out. They were to install a staging made of six 2" X 12" lagging to replace the stringer. He was working with John Maki, Matt Anderson and William Harris Martin. They had installed a lagging and Martin was standing on it while Swanson was cutting a hitch for another lagging with a pick. Suddenly, Swanson heard a noise and turned to see if it was something falling in the chute and fell. He dropped 56 ft. and Swanson was taken out the nearby Oliver Shaft. He died at the Calumet and Arizona Hospital from a fractured skull.

"Gus Swanson's Funeral" Bisbee Daily Review 30 May 1912 page 3
"Original Certificate of Death." Arizona Department of Health Services. http://genealogy.az.gov/azdeath/010/10100659.pdf (October 25, 2012)
"Calumet & Arizona Hospital Records." My Cochise. http://www.mycochise.com/hospcalsn2to.php (May 28, 2012)
"Cochise County Inquest No. 928" Arizona State Archives Phoenix

July 1, 1912, Cole Mine

John Cullen, Robert Ireland* and an unnamed Swedish miner were working at the top of a 35 ft. manway. The area they were working in began to cave-in, and Ireland and Cullen ran to escape. Ireland fell into the manway first and then Cullen plummeted down on top of him. Temporarily, they were trapped in the narrow manway. Then they were hit by caving muck falling into the raise. Two men were cut up and bruised. The Swede escaped the danger unharmed.

* Ireland was possibly, killed in the Shattuck on December 23, 1917.
"Flees Cave in Manhole Traps" Bisbee Daily Review 2 July 1912 page 6

July 1, 1912, Cole Mine

Bohemian Miner, John Wacek was told to crib up a section of the "new" 12 stope. The ground was heavy, particularly where the stope came close to the "old" 12 stope. Wacek began to work, but he was in the wrong part of the stope. A 150-pound limestone boulder fell and struck him. His back was broken between the 11th and 12th dorsal vertebrae and the spine severed. He was taken to the Calumet & Arizona Hospital. There he lingered until July 19, 1912, when he passed away. He was 38 years old when he died and the father of six daughters. His 11-year-old daughter Rella, was admitted to the same hospital her father had died in on October 29, 1912, for appendicitis. She was released on November 13, 1912, cured.

"Flees Cave-in Manhole Traps" Bisbee Daily Review 2 July 1912 page 6

81

"I'll of Appendicitis" <u>Bisbee Daily Review</u> 30 October 1912 page 8
"Original Certificate of Death." <u>Arizona Department of Health Services.</u>
 http://genealogy.az.gov/azdeath/010/10101204.pdf (April16 2011)
"Calumet & Arizona Hospital Records." <u>My Cochise.</u> hhttp://www.mycochise.com/hospcaldied.php (April 16 2011)
"Calumet & Arizona Hospital Records." <u>My Cochise.</u> http://www.mycochise.com/hospcaltr2we.php (April 16 2011)
"Cochise County Inquest No. 937" Arizona State Archives Phoenix

August 17, 1912, Cole Mine

Finnish Miner, Edward Johnson*, 24 was killed when a rock fell in 33 raise on the 1000 level. This raise went up through to the 900 level and was being used partly for hoisting timbers to the 900 level. A small hoist was at the bottom of the raise and a sheave wheel was mounted above the 900 level. Johnson was sent into the manway of this raise to free up a clog on the chute side. He was alone at the time, and the exact causes of death was presumed to be a rock falling. The falling rock crushed his skull. Sadly, Johnson was the only financial supporter of a widowed mother and blind sister who lived in Finland. Another Finlander, Leonard Lindras notified Johnson's mother. Lindras and Johnson had been neighbors in Finland and had come to Bisbee together. Edward also was survived by a sister in Minnesota. He was buried in Evergreen Cemetery. (Note, the newspaper description of the accident does not match well with the inquest.)
*Three Edward Johnsons died in Bisbee mine accidents in a one year period. The others were Edward Johnson from Sweden, Dec.27 1913 Briggs Shaft, and Edward Johnson also Swedish, June 17, 1912 in the Lowell Shaft.

"Killed at Oliver" <u>Bisbee Daily Review</u> 18 August 1912 page 6
"Johnson Funeral This Afternoon" <u>Bisbee Daily Review</u> 20 August 1912 page 3
"Original Certificate of Death." <u>Arizona Department of Health Services.</u>
http://genealogy.az.gov/azdeath/010/10101460.pdf (April2 2011)
"Cochise County Inquest No. 942" Arizona State Archives Phoenix

September 5, 1913, Cole Mine 900 level

Frank Sullivan was working on the 900 level of the Cole Shaft. Then about 10 o'clock at night, a large boulder fell on him breaking both of his legs. The boulder was of such a size that if it had hit him slightly, differently it would have crushed him. It took more than one hour to remove the boulder from his legs and bring him to the surface. He was hoisted out the Oliver Shaft and transported to the Calumet and Arizona Hospital. Both of his legs were badly bruised. His left leg was broken below the knee and the right leg just above the knee.

"Both Legs Broken" <u>Bisbee Daily Review</u> 6 September 1913 page 1

October 21, 1913, Cole Mine

Mucker, Martin Coyne was killed after he was pinned between two mine cars and one fell on top of him. He died at the Calumet & Arizona Hospital from a broken pelvis and ruptured bladder. He was 22 years old and from Ireland. (No coroner's inquest could be located)

"Injuries Prove Fatal- Martin Coyne Funeral" <u>Bisbee Daily Review</u> 30 September 1908 page 5

November 4, 1913, Cole Mine

W.R. Gibson received minor injuries when he caught by falling rock. He was taken to the Calumet & Arizona Hospital.

"Was Slightly Injured" <u>Bisbee Daily Review</u> 4 November 1913 page 8

**Miners in a square-set stope, circa 1908. Notice the man in the left foreground
and the right background have bandaged foreheads.
(Courtesy of Bisbee Mining & Historical Museum)**

November 8, 1913, Cole Mine
L. Olson, a mucker had boulder fall and break his leg. The 31-year-old single miner
remained in the Calumet & Arizona Hospital until February 1, 1914.

* Newspaper lists him as John Oleson
"Has Leg Broken" Bisbee Daily Review 9 November 1913 page 7
"Calumet & Arizona Hospital Records." My Cochise. http://www.mycochise.com/hospcalo2 po.php (April2 2011)

November 8, 1913, Cole Mine

Anton Sunn had his foot crushed by falling rock. He was taken home, where he was treated. At the time, there was a concern the foot may have to be amputated.

"Foot Mashed" Bisbee Daily Review 9 November 1913 page 7

November 21, 1913, Cole Mine

T. Thompson was injured by a fall of ground in the Cole Shaft. He was taken by ambulance to his home in Tombstone Canyon.

"Was Slightly Injured" Bisbee Daily Review 22 November 1913 page 8

November 26, 1913, Cole Mine

A fight broke out in the change room. Mlisov Radonavich attacked Mijuskovich with a miner's candleholder. Radonavich was arrested by Officer Walter Brooks.

"A Change House Assault – Deadly Intent" Bisbee Daily Review 27 November 1913 page 5

February 14, 1914, Cole Mine

Fedella Bottistena became ill and fell unconscious. He was transported by ambulance to the hospital. Weakness of his heart was suspected to be the problem. This does not appear to be a true mine accident.

"Miner Taken Ill" Bisbee Daily Review 15 February 1914 page 5

July 17, 1914, Cole Mine

Mike J. Midzor, a 30-year-old cager at the Cole Shaft. was pushing a steel car off the cage onto the 1000 level station with B.S. Hawes. The car held 298 pieces of drill steel, which weighed approximately three tons. After the first two wheels had touched the station, the landing chairs slipped and the cage dropped 18 inches, and the steel car fell onto Midzor, killing him. Although, he was a Serbian by birth he had become an American citizen. His largely attended funeral was held at the Pythian Castle, and he was buried at the Evergreen Cemetery. (He was survived by a brother Chris Midzor who was injured in the Hoatson Shaft on April 12, 1915)(Death certificate and newspaper page was missing).

"Inquest Held" Bisbee Daily Review 19 July 1914 page 6
"Midzor Funeral is Largely Attended Sunday Afternoon" Bisbee Daily Review 21 July 1914 page 5
"Card of Thanks" Bisbee Daily Review 21 July 1914 page 8
"Cochise County Inquest No. 1099" Arizona State Archives Phoenix

August 25, 1914, Cole Mine

A boulder dropped onto the leg of Leonard Lystila a 44-year-old miner. The rock broke and dislocated his right ankle.

"Broken Leg" Bisbee Daily Review 25 August 1914 page 6
Office of State Mine Inspector. *Fourteenth Annual Report of the State Mine Inspector State of Arizona for the Year Ending November 30, 1914.* Tombstone Epitaph.

September 23, 1914, Cole Mine

A 35-year-old Austrian Miner, named Andy Sterberg and Tobias Tiihanen were timbering a sub-crosscut between 9 and 10 crosscuts*. Tiihanen's lamp went out, and Sternberg did not have a light. When Tiihanen relit his lamp he saw Sternberg fall after being hit about 300 lbs. of loose rock and dirt. The newspaper reported that his actual surname was Sterbenz and he had changed it. He was survived by a wife, a ten-year-old daughter and twin daughters age eight in Warner, Idaho. His widow originally questioned the telegram sent by the Calumet & Arizona Mining Company informing her of her husband's death by sending a telegram in response reading *"Is it really true my husband is dead?"* Her late husband's landlady, Mrs. Widmer responded confirming his death. His body was shipped to Warner, Idaho for burial. (This accident is an example of the mining superstition that accidents occurred in groups of three. Thomas C. McBurney's death in the Czar Shaft on September 3, 1914 was considered the first, followed by an Irish Miner James F. Conway, who was killed in the Gardner Shaft. on September 15, 1914. Andy Sterberg's death in the Cole Shaft. was considered the third fatal accident.) * This was probably on the 1000 level.

"Miner in Cole is Instantly Killed When Rock Drops" Bisbee Daily Review 24 September 1914 page 6

"Couldn't Realize Her husband Have Been Taken Away" Bisbee Daily Review 25 September 1914 page 5

"Body to Idaho" Bisbee Daily Review 26 September 1914 page 6

"Original Certificate of Death." Arizona Department of Health Services. http://genealogy.az.gov/azdeath/012/10122717.pdf (April 28, 2012)

"Cochise County Inquest No. 1116" Arizona State Archives Phoenix

November 9, 1914, Cole Mine

Frank Thomas, a 29-year-old carman at the Cole Shaft lost three fingers in a mining accident. He was treated at the Calumet & Arizona Hospital and released on November 14.

"Loses Three Fingers" Bisbee Daily Review 10 November 1915 page 8

"Calumet & Arizona Hospital Records." My Cochise. http://www.mycochise.com/hospcalsn2to.php (April 25 2012)

November 17, 1914, Cole Mine

L.H. Martin strained his back in an accident.

"Mine accident" Bisbee Daily Review 18 November 1914 page 8

February 3, 1915, Cole Mine

A falling rock struck John Crelling inflicting minor injuries.

"Injured at Cole Shaft." Bisbee Daily Review 5 February 1915 page 8

May 6, 1915, Cole Mine

Albert Drew, a well-known local musician and secretary for the Calumet & Arizona Band was injured in a cave-in. He was taken to The Calumet & Arizona Hospital, where he died on the 9th from abdominal injuries. He was survived by a wife and five children in England. He also had Louis and Bert Pascoe his brothers-in-laws in Calumet, Michigan and a cousin Norman Pascoe in Bisbee (No coroner's inquest could be located)

"Last Tribute Paid Well Known Miner" Bisbee Daily Review 12 May 1915 page 8

"Well Known Miner Dies From Injuries" Bisbee Daily Review 11 May 1915 page 5

Certificate of Death." Arizona Department of Health Services. http://genealogy.az.gov/azdeath/013/10131767.pdf (May 28, 2012)

Office of State Mine Inspector. *Fifth Annual Report of the State Mine Inspector State of Arizona for the Year Ending November 30, 1915.*

March 3, 1916, Cole Mine

H.G. Albert drilled into a misfire and detonated it. Albert was taken to the Calumet & Arizona Hospital where he remained until April 7, 1916. He was reported to only have suffered bruises.

"Calumet & Arizona Hospital Records." My Cochise. http://www.mycochise.com/hospcala2ba.php (June 2, 2012)

Office of State Mine Inspector. *Fifth Annual Report of the State Mine Inspector State of Arizona for the Year Ending November 30, 1916.*

March 10, 1916, Cole Mine

Julian Najara had the end of a finger smashed off when it was caught between a mine car and a timber. He was taken to the Calumet & Arizona hospital and released the next day.

"Calumet & Arizona Hospital Records." My Cochise. http://www.mycochise.com/hospcalme2ny.php (June 2, 2012)

Office of State Mine Inspector. *Fifth Annual Report of the State Mine Inspector State of Arizona for the Year Ending November 30, 1916.*

March 24, 1916, Cole Mine

Henry Steele was struck by a boulder. He suffered a bruised left ear, and his skull was fractured. Steele was 31 years old and was released from the Calumet & Arizona Hospital on April 9, 1916.

"Calumet & Arizona Hospital Records." My Cochise. http://www.mycochise.com/hospcalsn2to.php (June 2, 2012)

Office of State Mine Inspector. *Fifth Annual Report of the State Mine Inspector State of Arizona for the Year Ending November 30, 1916.*

May 5, 1916, Cole Mine

26-year-old, Rene Vaernervijk, a miner from Belgium was working in a raise on the 1000 level. He blasted a missed hole and climbed back up the raise right away. In the smoke, he stepped or grabbed onto a loose timber and fell six sets down the chute side of the raise. The timber in the raise had been knocked loose by falling ore. The fall broke both his legs and damaged his spine. After a while, he was discovered unconscious. He died at 10 pm on May 6th at the Calumet & Arizona Hospital. (No coroner's inquest could be located)

"Sustains Serious Injuries in Accident" Bisbee Daily Review 6 May 1916

"Calumet & Arizona Hospital Records." My Cochise. http://www.mycochise.com/hospcaltr2we.php (May 28, 2012)

Dugan Mortuary Records Aug. 26, 1914 – Dec 21, 1916 Accession 2010.10.9 Bisbee Mining and Historical Museum, Bisbee. "Original Certificate of Death." Arizona Department of Health Services. http://genealogy.az.gov/azdeath/015/10150029.pdf (May 28, 2012)

Office of State Mine Inspector. *Fifth Annual Report of the State Mine Inspector State of Arizona for the Year Ending November 30, 1916.*

May 25, 1917, Cole Mine

L.E. McDonald, a 35-year-old timber was caught in a cave-in. He suffered a dislocated shoulder and bruises. He was admitted to the Calumet & Arizona Hospital and released on May 30.

"Miner is Injured" Bisbee Daily Review 26 May 1917 page 8

"Calumet & Arizona Hospital Records." My Cochise. http://www.mycochise.com/hospcalmar2mc.php (October 24, 2012)

July 20, 1917, Cole Mine

Mucker, F. Marvin Williams* was working with L.E. McDonald and had finished drilling out a round in 152 sub-cross cut on the 900 level. During the work, McDonald had lost the lava tip out of his carbide lamp and did not have a light. He told Williams to break down the drill, while he went and turned off the compressed air. As he bent down to release the air, a boulder fell and killed Williams. He was 30 years old and was buried in Blanket Cemetery in Brown County Texas.* Note a headstone in Blanket Cemetery reads F. Marvin Williams Not Marvin L. Williams

"Rock Falls out of Drift, Killing Man" Bisbee Daily Review 21 July 1917 page 3

"Original Certificate of Death." Arizona Department of Health Services. http://genealogy.az.gov/azdeath/016/10161788.pdf (May 28, 2012)

Office of State Mine Inspector. *Sixth Annual Report of the State Mine Inspector State of Arizona for the Year Ending November 30, 1917.*

"Blanket Cemetery." Find a Grave.

http://www.findagrave.com/cgi-bin/fg.cgi?page=gr&GSln=williams&GSiman=1&GScid=230249&GRid=18645431& (May 28, 2012)

"Cochise County Inquest No. 1285" Arizona State Archives Phoenix

October 8, 1918, Cole Mine

J.J. Dennis had his leg crushed while working at the Cole Mine.

"Leg Badly Crushed" Bisbee Daily Review 10 October 1918 page 6

October 3, 1921, Cole Mine

English Miner, Matthew C. Griggs struck a missed hole with a pick. He was killed subsequent explosion. Griggs was 36 years old, married and buried in the Evergreen Cemetery. (No coroner's inquest could be located)

"Bisbee Miner Drives Pick into Dud and Killed by Explosion" Tombstone Epitaph 9 October 1921 page 6

"Bisbee-Lowell Evergreen Cemetery." My Cochise.

http://www.mycochise.com/cembisbeeg.php (October 14, 2011)

"Original Certificate of Death." Arizona Department of Health Services. http://genealogy.az.gov/azdeath/024/10241222.pdf (October 14 2011)

September 27, 1939, Cole Mine

Barney Oscar Milam was working with Sep Bryer in 120 crosscut on the 1200 level. This was a new drift that was a dust-covered sulfide. They had disconnected the gunite machine and began to cut out for timber. Unexpectedly, a 300 lb. boulder fell from the center of the crosscut killing Milam.

Original Certificate of Death." Arizona Department of Health Services. http://genealogy.az.gov/azdeath/061/10611553.pdf (May 28, 2014)

"Cochise County Inquest No. 1776Arizona State Archives Phoenix

February 24, 1947, Cole Mine

Edward Stanley Carver was working in 56-B stope on the 800 level. He was replacing a post and had pulled out the old one and had hoisted up a new post. As he measured to cut the replacement post the area collapsed with fine dirt and broken rock. Carver was suffocated. Before working in the Cole Mine, Carver had been employed in both the Denn and Campbell Mines.

Original Certificate of Death." Arizona Department of Health Services. http://genealogy.az.gov/azdeath/079/10790791.pdf (May 27, 2014)

"Cochise County Inquest No. 1834" Arizona State Archives Phoenix

May 25, 1948, Cole Mine

Percy Miller was killed by falling rock. his pelvis and back were broken.

Original Certificate of Death." Arizona Department of Health Services. http://genealogy.az.gov/azdeath/083/10830079.pdf (May 28, 2014)

February-March 1950, Cole Mine

Herman F. Whitfield age 41 was killed while working in a crosscut on the 1200 level. A slab fell and caught him on the neck and head.

"Bisbee Miner Killed by Falling Slab" Arizona Daily Sun 7 March 1950

November 19, 1954, Cole Mine

Puerto Rican Miner, Peter Rivera was killed underground.

Original Certificate of Death." http://genealogy.az.gov/azdeath/216/02161685.pdf (May 27, 2014)

September 7, 1956, Cole Mine

Manuel A. Sandoval Jr. was killed when he was struck by falling rock. He was working in a square set stope

Original Certificate of Death." Arizona Department of Health Services. http://genealogy.az.gov/azdeath/017/10171258.pdf (May 28, 2014)
M.A. Sandoval Accident Photo # p1113 7 Sep. 1956.
M.A. Sandoval Accident Photo # p1116 7 Sep. 1956.

The boulder that killed M.A. Sandoval marked with an "X" resting between the booms. Sandoval's hard hat is in the right hand corner. Cole Mine

A view of the side of the area Sandoval was killed. His hard hat can be seen in the center of the picture partially covered by a small rock. One of the booms can be seen immediately behind the hat

March 9, 1959, Cole Mine
C.H. Hill was caught in a cave-in in 174 raise on the 900 level. He suffered bruises and cuts on neck head and shoulders. He was off work for a time.
1959-1961 safety ledger p.20

April 11, 1959 Cole Mine
N.K. Gill was caught by rock falling in 306 crosscut on the 1100 level. His right ankle and possibly fibula were broke. (Note, he was killed on November 15, 1968 in the Cole Mine)
1959-1961 safety ledger p.28

April 11, 1959 Cole Mine
At the 1440 level ore pocket a falling object knocked one of W.P. Marenez's teeth loose. This developed into a lost time accident
1959-1961 safety ledger p.28

April 15, 1959 Cole Mine
Falling rock caught E. Ladner in 70-C stope on the 800 level. His face was cut and right shoulder was bruised.
1959-1961 safety ledger p.28

May 20, 1959 Cole Mine
G.W. Crowley broke a rib while handling timber in 141-C stope on the 1200 level. This was a lost time accident.
1959-1961 safety ledger p.36

June 2, 1959 Cole Mine
M.L. *"Spanky"* Mendez had an object fly into his right eye while working in 203 stope on the 1000 level. This was a lost time accident.
1959-1961 safety ledger p.44

August 17, 1959 Cole Mine

A serious incident occurred on the 500 level at the interior shaft. A mine fire had broken out and at 7:30 am fire gasses poisoned Shift Boss, F. Madden along with diamond drillers F.E. "Gene" Bendixon , E.P. Gutierrrez, miner Andy Moravitz and cager B. Hancock. Soon after at 8:00 am two engineers E.E. Rounds and J.E. Johnston suffered gas poisoning. Luckily, all the men survived.
1959-1961 safety ledger p.60

August 15, 1959 Cole Mine

A.D. Randolph was in 71 crosscut on the 500 level. He suffered severe stomach pain that resulted in lost time. (Note that a mine fire was burning in the area of the interior shaft. Although, no details are given it appears this was possibly related to fire gas poisoning)
1959-1961 safety ledger p.60

August 17, 1959. Cole Mine

S.C. Rissio was in 64 crosscut on the 500 level of the interior shaft. He was poisoned by fire gasses. This was a lost time accident.
1959-1961 safety ledger p.60

1960-1970 Cole Mine

V.R. Rodriguez was injured when 129 general chute on the 1100 level overflowed. Rodiguez's injuries are unknown. The only source of information are two photographs. The crosscut was flooding with muck completely. At least one mine car was buried, trolley wire was torn down and the chute stand was cover with 100 lbs. of muck.
V.R. Rodriguez Photo # p1103 Date Unknown.
V.R. Rodriguez Photo # p1104 Date Unknown.

Two views of the V. Rodriguez accident at 129 gen chute on the 1100 level Cole Mine. Note the crosscut has been largely sealed by flowing mud

February 17, 1960 Cole Mine
G.A. Carrillo was loading rock in 62-J stope on the 1300 level. An undescribed accident occurred and he broke his 8th, 9th and 10th ribs.
1959-1961 safety ledger p.84

February 26, 1960 Cole Mine
D. Moreno was on the 1200 level at 200 general chute. An undescribed accident involving explosives and moving machinery left him with a cut forehead, and a bruised right arm and knee. This was a lost time accident. (Note, with explosives are listed as the cause which implies he was making or had shot a chute bomb. The moving machinery is confusing. It is possible the wrong accident codes were written down.)
1959-1961 safety ledger p.84

March 5, 1960 Cole Mine
In 118 stope on the 1300 level, H.J. Decker, had dust blown into his right. This resulted in a lost time accident and must have been rather serious.
1959-1961 safety ledger p.92

May 3, 1960 Cole Mine
At the mill ore pocket on the 1200 level, G.W. Stringer suffered bruises over his body and an injured left knee from working with mine cars.
1959-1961 safety ledger p.108

May 4, 1960 Cole Mine
On the 500 level in 15 crosscut B.S. Elkins broke the 1st finger on his right hand working with timber.
1959-1961 safety ledger p.108

May 13, 1960 Cole Mine
J. *"Mexican Joe"* Corral was caught in a cave-in in 11 stope on the 600 level and suffered broken 4th and 5th transverse processes. (He was a extremely well liked miner/ motorman on occasion my father Richard Graeme III swamped for him and thought highly of him as did many other miners)

June 20, 1960 Cole Mine
J. Wood broke his right hand working with a derailed mine car in 77 crosscut on the 600 level.
1959-1961 safety ledger p.116

August 3, 1960 Cole Mine
J. Sproule was caught in caving ground in 60-A stope on the 600 level. His left leg was broken.
1959-1961 safety ledger p.132

September 23, 1960 Cole Mine
In 141-F stope on the 1200 level L.D. Lewis fell and dislocated his left shoulder.
1959-1961 safety ledger p.140

September 30, 1960 Cole Mine W. Friend broke his right hand in 202 stope on the 1200 level.
1959-1961 safety ledger p.140

January 14, 1961 Cole Mine
At the Dallas pocket on the 1400 level, R. Bustamante suffered a broken nose in an undescribed accident
1959-1961 safety ledger p.173

January 25, 1961 Cole Mine
A collapse of ground broke the right foot of J.G. Rodriquez in 60-D stope on the 600 level.
1959-1961 safety ledger p.173

May 29, 1961 Cole Mine
In rather an unusual accident E. Macias was working on the 1200 level back in 68-F stope and was stung on the right hand by a scorpion. The scorpion was likely brought in with supplies.
1959-1961 safety ledger p.204

June 16, 1961, Cole Mine
On the 1300 level, motorman, Robert F. Beecroft was pulling 116 chute filled with wet muck. The chute began to run, and Beecroft jumped to get out of the way of the flowing muck. When jumped he contacted the trolley wire and was electrocuted when he fell on a power cable (trolley wire?)
Original Certificate of Death." Arizona Department of Health Services. http://genealogy.az.gov/azdeath/0246/2460183.pdf (May 28, 2014)
Pete Olier Personal communication May 27, 2014
1959-1961 safety ledger p.212

June 19, 1961 Cole Mine
In 206 stope on the 1000 level, G.R. Smith was caught in caving ground. He suffered broken ribs and internal injuries.
1959-1961 safety ledger p.212

November 2, 1961 Cole Mine
Collapsing ground caught H.L. Boomer in 310 crosscut on the 1100 level. He suffered two broken fingers on his left hand.
1959-1961 safety ledger p.252

November 15, 1961 Cole Mine
Luciano Perez was at the 700 level station of the Cole Interior Shaft. For an unknown reason* he was looking into the shaft, when a cage ridden by Cecil Cooke and an unidentified miner came down and stuck his head. Luciano was decapitated and his body was thrown onto the cage.

*Suicide was suspected by the other miners, but officially it was considered an accident.
Richard W. Graeme III personal communication May 27, 2014

"Original Certificate of Death." <u>Arizona Department of Health Services.</u> http://genealogy.az.gov/azdeath/0247/2472276.pdf (May 29, 2014)

November 25, 1961 Cole Mine

Falling rock struck W.A. Porter and broke his left hand. The accident occurred on the 800 level in 70-E stope.

1959-1961 safety ledger p.252

March 29, 1968 Cole Mine

Soon after the end of the 1967-68 strike, Kenneth Noble Gill was pulling waste for backfilling stopes out of the Calyx Raise on the 1100 with motorman R. Salazar. During the strike water had seeped into the chute and turned the waste material into a watery mud*. On the 1000 level, Leroy " Blue" Ballew and Bennie Scott discovered the calyx was flooded to the top and did not want to dump their "H" cars into the raise. Marty Benko gave them an order to dump the cars. As soon as Bennie had dumped a car, the raise cleared itself. The timber and chute doors on the 1100 were blown out. The watery mud poured out of the chute and buried Gill. Scott and Ballew were ordered to the 1100 level with their mucking machine. The loaded the "K" cars Gill was using and Scott uncovered Gill's hand. The rescuers followed the arm and found his body behind a post. It was felt that because of the position of the body, Gill had time to seek shelter but had no place to go. After this, the calyx chutes had their platforms (stands) extended to 15 feet long to provide an escape way.* This water may have been added intentionally to try to unclog the chute.

Richard W. Graeme III personal communication May 27, 2014

Bennie Scott personal communication April 23, 2016

June 6, 1968 Cole Mine

Motor Swamper, D.E. Altamirano and R. Salazar were pulling Granby car trains out of 69 general chute on the 800 level in 80 crosscut. They had pulled two train loads and were starting a third. Salazar pushed eight cars past the chute and spotted the car next to the motor under the chute. Altamirano had filled this car half full when Salazar told him that they would not have enough time to fill the train and dump it before the end of the shift. Altamirano cleaned up the loading stand, shut off the air cylinder and unhooked the first and second car to clean the track. While cleaning the track, Altamirano noticed the chute door was still open. He told Salazar he was going to up and shut it. After pounding it shut with a double jack Altamirano climbed into the drift and was squeezing between the posts and the car. At this time Salazar moved the train back catching Altamirano between the car and the timber. Salazar stopped the train and was unable to free Altamirano. So, he pulled the car away with the motor. D.E. Altamirano suffered a broken collarbone, four broken ribs, and a punctured right lung.

"Discussion of a lost time accident occurring in June 1968" 6-25-1968

December 20, 1968, Cole Mine

At 1:00 am J.R. Montoya drilling with a stoper starting168 raise in 1 crosscut on the 1300 level. Next to him and also drilling with a stoper was T *"Blackie"* Ladner. Montoya had put a lagging across the track and was drilling off the lagging. After Montoya changed to his 3rd steel the shank on the steel chipped. The steel flew by his eye shield and destroyed his left eye.

"Discussion of a lost time accident occurring in December 1968" 12-31-1968

After 1968 Cole Mine
Richard Graeme III and Pancho Yguado were loading cars on the 1300 level at the Calyx Raise. The chute was hung with sticky muck and Graeme loaded sevens cars by working the chute with a blow pipe. Pancho took over loading the cars when he saw shift boss Hiram Wright coming down the crosscut. After the boss left Pancho kept working the chute and suddenly mud poured out and flooded the crosscut. Yguado was completely buried and Graeme began digging and uncovered him. After ensuring Pancho was safe. He ran back to the shaft and rang the seven bell danger signal and the level code. He then phoned the cager and informed him there had been an accident and where it was located. Richard returned to the Calyx and moved out the train of cars to allow access to unbury Pancho. Yguado was uncovered and suffered a broken leg and bruises (Note, see full document in appendix.)

"Personnel communication with Richard W. Graeme, May 2014

January 28, 1970 Cole Mine
S. Lucero was injured in 78 stope on the 1400 level. Two photographs of the accident site exist, but do not reveal the nature of the accident. Unlike, most areas this area is relatively clean. The images reveal with a few handfuls of rock and the base of a scaling bar, but nothing else. Of course this accident could have been caused by a fall.

S. Lucero Accident Photo # p1091 16 Feb. 1970.

S. Lucero Accident site. 78 Stope, 1400 level Cole Mine

February 16, 1970, Cole Mine
O.L. Mengeso was injured in 60-A stope on the 1300 level. A series of four photographs of the accident site exist, but do not reveal the details of the accident. A scaling bar can be seen as well as a slusher rake. There is broken rock in the image, initially it appears to be the remains of the blast, but an unusual feature is that one boom is missing. The remaining

boom is blocked in as if the ground was moving in from the left side. Moving ground was problem at this site. Of course, this still could be a barring down or slusher accident. It is known that he broke five ribs and was off work 160 days

O.L. Menges Accident Photo # p1090 16 Feb. 1970.

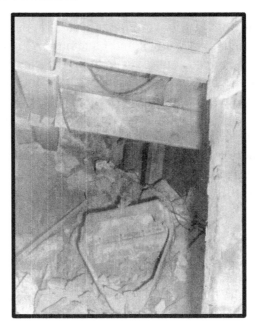

O.A. Menges accident site. 60-A stope 1300 level Cole Mine

April 22, 1970, Cole Mine

F. Duarte was caught in a fall of ground in 167-A stope on the 1300 level. The area had been roof bolted, but the boulders cracked around the bolts and fell.

F. Duarte Accident Photo # p1198 17 June. 1970.

Accident site of F. Duarte, 167-A stope 1300 level Cole Mine

June 17, 1970 Cole Mine

F.T. Nieta was caught in a fall of ground in 167-A stope on the 1300 level. His skull was fractured. No written documents could be located but two photographs exist. From the photographs it can be determine the rock fell out of a faulted area. Several slicken-sided layers are evident above the fallen rock. His skull was fractured and Nieto was off work 158 days.

F.T. Nieta Accident Photo # p1107 17 June. 1970.
1970-1971 safety ledger

167-A stope on the 1300 level of the Cole Mine. This is the location F.T. Nieta was injured. In the upper left 25% of the image slickened-siding from ancient movement along the fault is evident. More loose rock appears to be hanging by the blocking timber in the center of the photo.

December 7, 1973, Cole Mine

At 1:00 pm, B.C. *"Tongo"* Parra was driving a 30 penny nail attaching side lagging to a square set. As he was driving the nail with a bit hammer he struck the wall. A knuckle on his right hand was bruised. Parra did not report this to the shift boss, but later the safety department learned of the incident. Then and it was investigated under the direction of foreman K. *"Slim"* McCallister. The accident occurred in 104-A stope on the 800 level.

Phelps Dodge Corporation Copper Queen Branch Accident Report 1-11-74

January 2, 1974, Cole Mine

Mucker, E.A. Hopper was riding a man car in 102 crosscut on the 1100 level when the trolley pole jumped off the wire and hit the back (ceiling) of the drift. A rock was dislodged and fell bruising his left foot.

Phelps Dodge Corporation Copper Queen Branch Accident Report 1-3-74

Miners on a man car with locomotive in the Campbell Mine.

January 5, 1974, Cole Mine

J.R. Burgos was on the 1300 level getting ready to timber 188 raise. He was loading lagging onto a timber truck. When he lifted a lagging it knocked a used lagging off the pile and it struck him in the left ankle.

Phelps Dodge Corporation Copper Queen Branch Accident Report 1-7-74

January 7, 1974, Cole Mine

At the ore pocket on the 800 level, E F. Martinez was working boulders through the grizzlies with a boulder hook. A boulder hung to the hook and dragged Martinez onto the grizzly. The next day he reported to the hospital. (It was recommended in the safety report that he should have let the boulder hook fall. This was possible, but would have passed on a potentially dangerous and nightmarish of a job of pulling a chute with a grizzly hook inside for the men drawing ore from the bottom of the pocket.)

Phelps Dodge Corporation Copper Queen Branch Accident Report 1-12-74

January 9, 1974, Cole Mine

Motor Swamper, J. Barron was pulling 110 chute on the 800 level. He bent over and was struck in the hard hat and back by a rock falling out of the chute. Barron suffered a bruised back.

Phelps Dodge Corporation Copper Queen Branch Accident Report 1-11-74

January 17, 1974, Cole Mine

Motorman, E. *"Camel Jockey"* Baraky* had loaded a car from the 110 stope chute on the 800 level. He had spilled muck under a car wheel. When bent down to clear away the debris a boulder came out over the chute door and struck him in the back of the head. His head was bruised. He reported to the doctor on January 22. E.F. Martinez witnessed the accident.

(Baraky was from an Arabic country. Today, this would be considered a racial slur. Although, underground nicknames are often given as a sign of acceptance. It was likely not intended to be offensive)
Phelps Dodge Corporation Copper Queen Branch Accident Report 1-24-74

January 18, 1974, Cole Mine

H.R. *"Chato"* Miranda was in 188 raise on the 1300 level with J.R. Burgos. The raise had been blasted and they had removed the lagging from the bulkhead. Miranda was using an 8"x 8" cap to climb up a six foot post. He slipped and fell with his chest against a cap. Although, he reported the accident he thought he was fine. A few days later, he informed the boss his chest was hurting. ("Chato" means pug nose in Spanish)
Phelps Dodge Corporation Copper Queen Branch Accident Report 1-24-74

January 21, 1974, Cole Mine

J.C. Pomroy was operating a mucking machine in 229 crosscut on the 800 level. When he dumped the dipper, dust flew into his left eye.
Phelps Dodge Corporation Copper Queen Branch Accident Report 1-28-74

January 24, 1974

J. *"Cat"* Durazo and R. Lucero were in 64 stope on the 700 level. The stope had blasted through to a crosscut. Durazo went ahead to bar down and stepped on a nail. A scab (small board) had been knocked loose with the nail sticking up. He suffered a punctured left foot.
Phelps Dodge Corporation Copper Queen Branch Accident Report 1-28-74

January 29, 1974

In 12 crosscut on the 1300 level, F.F. Carbajal was walking to the shaft station. He twisted his knee on a track tie that was underwater. (It is not uncommon for sections of rail to be flooded over.)
Phelps Dodge Corporation Copper Queen Branch Accident Report 1-31-74

February 4, 1974, Cole Mine

On the 1100 level at 222 chute, J.R. Ratliff spotted (carefully placed) an empty E mine car under the chute to load. He climbed up to break a boulder in the chute with a double jack. He slipped and fell into the E car. His back was only scratched.
Phelps Dodge Corporation Copper Queen Branch Accident Report 2-5-74

February 6, 1974, Cole Mine

At 8:00 pm, in 110 stope on the 800 level, D.N. Cluff was getting ready to blast and needed to move a jackleg. As he was carrying in the drill, he hit his head on a cap (timber). He suffered pain in his neck.
Phelps Dodge Corporation Copper Queen Branch Accident Report 2-12-74 8:00 pm

February 8, 1974, Cole Mine
F. L. Farin was pulling 185 stope chute on the 1300 level. A rock jumped over the door and smashed his hand holding the chute door handle. His little finger was bruised.
Phelps Dodge Corporation Copper Queen Branch Accident Report 2-11-74

February 11, 1974, Cole Mine
Miner, G. Siltlala was pushing a loaded H car with a Finlay (mucking machine) on the 1400 level at 96 stope. Suddenly, he became caught between the Finlay and an empty H car in a side crosscut. The accident bruised his right hip and resulted in 6 days lost work time.
Phelps Dodge Corporation Copper Queen Branch Accident Report 2-12-74
Annual Report Safety Department January through December 31, 1974

February 11, 1974, Cole Mine
A.F. Romero was in 102-A stope on the 1400 level. He was walking through the lead set to a freshly blasted set. Romero stepped on a nail sticking out of lagging. The lagging was buried and difficult to see. He suffered a punctured left foot.
Phelps Dodge Corporation Copper Queen Branch Accident Report 2-12-74 10:00 am

February 13, 1974, Cole Mine
B.C. *"Tongo"* Parra and B.R. Robinson were in 104- A stope on the 800 level. Parra was barring down. He knocked a boulder down and it rolled down the muck pile. The boulder rolled over his right foot. He suffered bruising.
Phelps Dodge Corporation Copper Queen Branch Accident Report 2-13-74

February 25, 1974, Cole Mine
In 64 stope on the 700 level, R.L. Lucero was barring down. A boulder fell and struck the scaling bar. The impact caused the bar to jump and strike Lucero in the left knee. The knee was bruised.
Phelps Dodge Corporation Copper Queen Branch Accident Report 2-25-74

February 26, 1974, Cole Mine
L. *"Lurch"* Koscielniak was on the 1300 level. He wanted a drink, but a timber truck was in front of the water cooler. As he stepped over the truck he slipped. His right knee was bruised.
Phelps Dodge Corporation Copper Queen Branch Accident Report 3-1-74 4:20 pm

February 28, 1974, Cole Mine
C.A. Rhodes and G.P. Silva were mucking out 2 crosscut and retimbering the crosscut on the 1300 level. Silva was breaking a muddy boulder with a double jack. Mud flew by his eye shields and into his left eye.
Phelps Dodge Corporation Copper Queen Branch Accident Report 2-2?-74

March 1, 1974, Cole Mine
G.E. Lancaster was pulling 39-C chute on the 1400 level with R.J. Diaz. Lancaster had emptied the chute when the men in the stope dump a load of muck into the raise. A boulder went down the raise and bounced over the chute door striking Lancaster's left leg and foot. Luckily, it was only bruised.
Phelps Dodge Corporation Copper Queen Branch Accident Report 3-1-74 7:30 pm

March 1, 1974, Cole Mine
At 6:30 pm, M.I. Marusich was at 87 general chute on the 1400 level. He had loaded a train of G (Granby) mine cars. As he climbed down from the loading stand his foot slipped on a ladder rung. His left knee struck a rung and was bruised.
Phelps Dodge Corporation Copper Queen Branch Accident Report 3-5-74

March 4, 1974, Cole Mine
H.J. Irwin was installing booms in 60-A stope on the 700 level. While working off a ladder, he knocked a wedge loose from a block. The wedge flew and struck him in the mouth. His dentures were cracked and his upper lip was bruised. 60-A was a square set stope.
Phelps Dodge Corporation Copper Queen Branch Accident Report 3-7-74

March 8, 1974, Cole Mine
In 503 crosscut on the 1000 level, M.W. Lynch was holding for Carl N. *"Buck"* Hervey, the end of the ventilation pipe. The pipe slipped and cut Lynch's right wrist.
Phelps Dodge Corporation Copper Queen Branch Accident Report 3-11-74

March 12, 1974, Cole Mine
At 2:30 pm, L.G. Windsor was on the 1300 level dumping E mine cars into the top of 87 general chute. After, he finished dumping the cars he walked around the train. He stepped on a short piece of hardened wire. It pierced his boot and right foot.
Phelps Dodge Corporation Copper Queen Branch Accident Report 4-1-74

March 13, 1974
H. M. *"Stargazer"* Martin was mucking behind a drift post in 139 crosscut on the 800 level. A rock fell from the wall and pinned his shoulder against the drift post. His right shoulder was bruised.
Phelps Dodge Corporation Copper Queen Branch Accident Report 3-13-74

March 13, 1974, Cole Mine
Timberman, C. Davis was working in the sump of the Cole shaft. He was running a tugger hoist and the movement of the machine caused a saw to fall from above the hoist. The saw cut his left thumb.
Phelps Dodge Corporation Copper Queen Branch Accident Report 3-13-74

March 15, 1974, Cole Mine
On the 1300 level in 185 stope, C. Flores and L. *"Lurch"* Koscielniak had spit (ignited fuses) a round and Flores bent down to lift up a lagging. Flores fell one set. He broke seven ribs, his shoulder blade and a struck his head. It was suspected that Flores may have blacked out before he fell. Although, it is unknown what Koscielniak did once his partner fell, it must have been stressful. He had to get Flores to safety before the blast detonated. It is unlikely that he could prevented the detonation by cutting or removing fuses. Koscielniak probably had to carry Flores. Depending on the nature of the stope this could have been extremely challenging.
Phelps Dodge Corporation Copper Queen Branch Accident Report 3-18-74

March 18, 1974

R.R. *"Chichara"* Herrera and L.T. *"Snack Bar"* Garcia were in 99 stope on the 1400 level Herrera was building a slusher staging. He missed with a hammer and smashed his left thumb.
Phelps Dodge Corporation Copper Queen Branch Accident Report 3-19-74

March 22, 1974, Cole Mine
In 186 stope on the 1300 level, R.J. Orozco and J.G. Velarde were timbering. The previous shift and blasted into a section of old timber* Orozco barred down and was installing a cap (timber) to tie in (connect) to the old timber. About 60-70 lbs. of muck fell and knocked Orozco down one set. He received a twisted knee and a cut on the head.
* This likely from a stope mined parallel to 186 stope. They were intentionally blasting into this other stope to reach any ore that was between the stopes.
Phelps Dodge Corporation Copper Queen Branch Accident Report 4-1-74

March 22, 1974, Cole Mine
L.F. *"Honey"* Tschirhart was on the 1300 level in 222 crosscut pulling the rods from a diamond drill hole. As he was working copper water from the drill hole splashed in his eyes. Tschirhart was working with F. Archuleta at the time.
Phelps Dodge Corporation Copper Queen Branch Accident Report 3-26-74

March 24, 1974, Cole Mine
Roy Bradshaw and C.C. Oleary were working on Sunday to replace the shaft gates on the 1100 level. As he was working Oleary raised his head and struck a pipe. He *"liked to have drove his head between his shoulders."* The incident was reported on Monday, but Oleary did not feel he needed to report to the hospital.
Phelps Dodge Corporation Copper Queen Branch Accident Report 3-25-74

March 26, 1974, Cole Mine
At 1:45, H.R. *"Chato"* Miranda was installing a Verde chute at 189 raise on the 1300 level. As he was putting in the chute jaws he slipped on the bottom plate and twisted his right ankle.
Phelps Dodge Corporation Copper Queen Branch Accident Report 3-29-74

March 26, 1974, Cole Mine
At 4:15 pm, and on the 800 level in 111 crosscut, W.D. Windsor was unhooking a man car. The man car proceeded to roll over his foot. He was with J. Barron at the time. Windsor had his right foot bruised.
Phelps Dodge Corporation Copper Queen Branch Accident Report 3-27-74

March 28, 1974, Cole Mine
At 8:30 am, electricians, Don Barnett and A.W. Christo were climbing the manway at 186 stope on the 1300 level. Christo hit a cross brace while climbing. He knocked off his hard hat and dirt fell into his left eye.
Phelps Dodge Corporation Copper Queen Branch Accident Report 3-28-74

March 28, 1974, Cole Mine
At 5:45 pm, R.J. *"Turk"* Gardoni was to move the scrap timber from 129 crosscut with a mucking machine and stack it in 115 crosscut. He went to the 1400 level station to get a cable in which pull the timber. Gardoni arranged for the Cole motor crew the take the

cable back for him. In exchange for the favor, he began helping the crew clear boulders off the grizzlies at the 1400 level ore pocket. While standing between two E mine cars, he used a boulder hook to help turn over rocks so they would fall through the grizzly rails. As Gardoni was working the 6' boulder hook slipped and he smashed his right thumb against an E car.

(Gardoni was also injured at the Dallas Mine on July 8, 1974. He sometimes called by another nickname *"Gigolo"*)
Phelps Dodge Corporation Copper Queen Branch Accident Report 3-29-74

March 29, 1974, Cole Mine

Miner, G.S. *"Watermelon"* Renteria was loading an 8"x8" post onto a timber truck with his partner H. Soto, in 183 crosscut on the 1300 level. Renteria slipped and fell. The post landed on his right foot breaking it.

Phelps Dodge Corporation Copper Queen Branch Accident Report 3-24-74

April 4, 1974, Cole Mine

At 1:30 pm, H.R. *"Chato"* Miranda was drilling a round in 189 raise on the 1300 level with J.R. Burgos. While drilling a small boulder fell and struck Miranda on the right shoulder. At the end of the shift Burgos mentioned to the shift boss that Miranda had been hit by a rock. Miranda's shoulder was cut.

Phelps Dodge Corporation Copper Queen Branch Accident Report 4-5-74 1:30 pm

April 4, 1974, Cole Mine

At 2:15 pm, A.D. Vasquez was hoisting a stringer into 185 stope on the 1300 level. As he was *"landing"* the timber he struck the ventilation tubing. Dirt was blown out of the tubing into his right eye.

Phelps Dodge Corporation Copper Queen Branch Accident Report 4-5-74 2:15pm

April 8, 1974, Cole Mine

F.Q. Martinez and D.F. Hammett wanted to install an umbrella stull in 201 stope on the 800 level. As they were loading the second 10"x10" x 12'. stringer onto a timber truck, the stringer rolled off the truck. Martinez's left foot was smashed and bruised. The accident occurred at 9:00 am.

Phelps Dodge Corporation Copper Queen Branch Accident Report 4-9-74 9:00 am

April 8, 1974, Cole Mine

B.S. Stewart was helping R.F. Shields collar a lifter hole with a jackleg, at 9:30 am. The men were in 60-A stope on the 700 level. Mud was thrown into Stewart's left eye.

Phelps Dodge Corporation Copper Queen Branch Accident Report 4-10-74

April 9, 1974, Cole Mine

Miner, J.R. Burgos was drilling his fourth hole in 189 raise from the 1300 level. The hole penetrated an old flooded drift from the Lowell mine. Copper water (acidic) poured out of the holes into both of his eyes.

Phelps Dodge Corporation Copper Queen Branch Accident Report 4-10-74

An abandoned drift flooded with "copper water" on the 6th level Southwest mine.

April 10, 1974, Cole Mine

I. Woods and W. Morales were timbering in 338 crosscut on the 1300 level. Woods was standing by a post underneath a cap. A boulder broke free and struck him in the back and shoulder. He suffered only bruising.
Phelps Dodge Corporation Copper Queen Branch Accident Report 4-11-74

April 23, 1974, Cole Mine

R. Chavez jr was cleaning a water ditch in 142 crosscut on the 1300 level. Muddy copper water splashed around his eye shields and into his right eye.
Phelps Dodge Corporation Copper Queen Branch Accident Report 4-26-74

April 23, 1974, Cole Mine

On the 1400 level in 118 raise, R.K. Jimenez was drilling. A 5"x 6" rock broke free as he was collaring a drill hole. The rock struck his left wrist and cut through the top of the glove. Jimenez's left wrist was cut.
Phelps Dodge Corporation Copper Queen Branch Accident Report 4-24-74

April 24, 1974, Cole Mine

F.R. Abril and J.M. Jimenez, were in 102 stope on the 1400 level. Abril was lifting a 6"x 8" x 10' to hang and it slipped out of his hands. The timber fell against his left foot, leaving a bruise.
Phelps Dodge Corporation Copper Queen Branch Accident Report 4-25-74

April 30, 1974, Cole Mine

Sandfill operator, J.K. *"Jinx"* Livingston was dragging plastic pipe from the 1300 level station to 152 crosscut. As Livingston was moving the pipe, he entered 36 crosscut.

Behind him a short distance was the primary fan. The wind from the fan blew dust into his left eye.
Phelps Dodge Corporation Copper Queen Branch Accident Report 4-30-74

May 9, 1974, Cole Mine
In 39-C stope on the 1400 level, a boulder 5" thick and 4' long accidently fell into the stope chute. (through grizzlies) Miner, R.K. Jones went down to help get the rock out the chute door. Jones was barring the rock with the bar over the bump board. When the rock fell, it hit the bar. The bar bounced and smacked Jones on the right ear, cutting it.
Phelps Dodge Corporation Copper Queen Branch Accident Report 5-11-74

May 13, 1974, Cole Mine
At 106-A stope on the 800 level, Y.O. Garcia was breaking boulders on the grizzly. He slipped and fell. Garcia bruised his left side. The accident was reported after Garcia had showered at the end of shift. This was a square set stope.
Phelps Dodge Corporation Copper Queen Branch Accident Report 5-14-74

May 16, 1974, Cole Mine
At 9:45 am, G.V. *"Frijol"* Fraijo* was mucking with a Cavo loader in 200 stope on the 900 level. He wanted to clear a spot for an umbrella stull. As he was working the back (ceiling) caved-in and knocked out an existing umbrella stull. This umbrella stull fell on him and pinned him underneath it fracturing his pelvis and a rupturing urinal tube. This injury resulted in over 229 days lost time at the end of 1974 he was still off work This stull struck Fraijo and pinned him to the ground. Fellow miner, L. Windsor was nearby.

.* *"Frijol"* is Spanish for bean. He was also referred to as *"Free hole."*
Phelps Dodge Corporation Copper Queen Branch Accident Report 5-22-74
Annual Report Safety Department January through December 31, 1974

An umbrella stull in Bisbee. C. 1960

May 16, 1974, Cole Mine

On the 1100 station and at 10:30 am, M.P. Olvera and R.E. *"Bogger"* Brant were repairing the ore general chute. Olvera was lifting a bump block when it slipped. His wrist was sprained. He reported the injury 2:30 pm.

Phelps Dodge Corporation Copper Queen Branch Accident Report 5-17-74

May 17, 1974, Cole Mine

D. Crowley* was repairing a batwing in 83 crosscut on the 1300 level at the Calyx drift. He was with G.G. Chavez and H. *"Paladin"* Soto**. They were planning to install a doubler at the batwing. As Crowley lifted 10"x 10"x12' stringer he strained his right hip.

* D. Crowley built a fine collection of minerals during his years mining and in particular had collected a number of cuprite variety chalcotrictite off the 1100 level. **Paladin was a reference to a the 1957-1963 television & radio shows *"Have gun –Will travel"* The miners would refer to Soto a timberman, as Paladin and say *"Have saw-will travel"*. He was also known as *"Scarface"*

Phelps Dodge Corporation Copper Queen Branch Accident Report 5-20-74

May 22, 1974, Cole Mine

F.R. Abril was loading a round in 102 stope on the 1400 level. As he was loading the breast holes, Abril slipped on the wet ground. Abril broke his right ankle. He was off work 123 days.

Phelps Dodge Corporation Copper Queen Branch Accident Report 5-23-74
"January1-through December 31, 1974" Phelps Dodge Corporation Copper Queen Branch Annual Report Safety Department

May 28, 1974, Cole Mine

M.A. *"Bones"* Echave was in 102 stope on the 1400 level. He was with E.G. Shields. A temporary block had been installed to secure a post until the tenant block was placed. This was on a bulkhead that was going to be covered in burlap. This temporary block was in the way of the burlap work. When Echave knocked this block out, ground fell and knocked him down. He suffered a bruised head and a twisted ankle.

Phelps Dodge Corporation Copper Queen Branch Accident Report 6-4-74

May 30, 1974, Cole Mine

J. R. Burgos was walking by an E car in 90 crosscut on the 1300 level. As Burgos was passing the mine car, he slipped and twisted his ankle. He went to the hospital to have it examined.

Phelps Dodge Corporation Copper Queen Branch Accident Report 5-31-74

June 12, 1974, Cole Mine

On the 1400 level in 102 stope, M.A. *"Bones"* Echave was drilling a lifter with jackleg. As Echave was pulling out of the hole the gooseneck on the air hose broke. Dirt was thrown into his right eye. The safety chain on the gooseneck held and the hose did not wildly flop around.

Phelps Dodge Corporation Copper Queen Branch Accident Report 6-14-74

June 17, 1974, Cole Mine

In an undescribed accident, F.C. Luna strained his back while handling materials. He was off work 27 days

"January1-through December 31, 1974" Phelps Dodge Corporation Copper Queen Branch Annual Report Safety Department

June 24, 1974, Cole Mine

J.B. Vargas was helping cleanup a *"wreck"* or rather a derailed E car in 11 crosscut on the 1300 level. He was putting a drawhead pin and the E car rolled forward and smashed the third finger on his right hand.

Phelps Dodge Corporation Copper Queen Branch Accident Report 6-25-74

Safety photograph of a mine car drawhead.

June 25, 1974, Cole Mine
At 10: 20 pm, E. De Haven was running a Finlay in 183 stope on the 1300 level with
V.E. *"Bullwinkle"* Hare. The Finlay derailed and caught De Haven between the Finlay
and a drift post. His right hip was bruised.
Phelps Dodge Corporation Copper Queen Branch Accident Report 6-26-74 10:20 pm

June 25, 1974, Cole Mine
Electrician, D.J. Eiting was installing a safety switch on the 1000 level at the 257 general
bore holes. The switch was for the loading chute signal. As he was working a 4"x 6"x 4'
fell on his left foot. Eiting was only bruised.
Phelps Dodge Corporation Copper Queen Branch Accident Report 6-26-74 12:30 pm

June 26, 1974, Cole Mine
W.S. Acuna was breaking boulders in the 200 stope on the 900 level. Acuna needed to
break a number of hard sulfide boulders to get them through the grizzlies. As he was
pounding with a double jack a rock fragment flew off and chipped one of his upper front
teeth.
Phelps Dodge Corporation Copper Queen Branch Accident Report 6-27-74

June 28, 1974, Cole Mine
A.D. Vasquez was preparing to boom out and. He was barring down in 185 stope on the
1300 level. A rock fell and bounced off the timber and struck Vasquez over his right eye.
He was cut above the eye.
Phelps Dodge Corporation Copper Queen Branch Accident Report 7-1-74

July 1, 1974 Cole Mine
A.A. *"Million Dollar Man"* Vega was in 129 crosscut on the 800 level. He was
rehanging the air and water lines. Vega was using a 2" lagging to pry over the pipe when
the lagging slipped. His thumb was smashed between the lagging and the drift wall (rib).

106

July 3, 1974, Cole Mine
J. Lason was dumping H cars into the waste slot on the 1000 level station with E.C. Zepeda. A boulder became caught in the bottom of the car. The mine car tub swung back. Lason put up his hands to stop the tub and the impact of the tub sprained his wrist.
Phelps Dodge Corporation Copper Queen Branch Accident Report 7-5-74

July 9, 1974 Cole Mine
M. Hyatt was barring down over a spreader in 223 stope on the 1000 level. A boulder fell and hit the bar. The end of the bar and struck him in the right side of jaw.
Phelps Dodge Corporation Copper Queen Branch Accident Report 7-10-74

July 11, 1974, Cole Mine
E. J. *"Yaqui"* Chavez and J.A. Carbajal were in 116 stope on the 1400 level. Chavez was trimming a fuse when the knife slipped. He cut the middle finger on his left hand.
Phelps Dodge Corporation Copper Queen Branch Accident Report 7-12-74

July 12, 1974, Cole Mine
J.E. Figueroa was in 169 crosscut on the 1300 level. He was moving a 1/2 sack of plaster to work on a brattice. When he set down the sack dust went into his right eye.
Phelps Dodge Corporation Copper Queen Branch Accident Report 7-23-74

August 22, 1974, Cole Mine
In 219 stope on the 1100 level, E. Fisher was working boulders through a grizzly with a boulder hook. The hook lodged into the remains of a drill hole in a boulder. When the boulder fell through the grizzly, it twisted Fisher's left arm. His left arm was broken. This was a lost time accident. R. Hillard witnessed the accident.
Phelps Dodge Corporation Copper Queen Branch Accident Report 8-23-74

August 22, 1974, Cole Mine
The front car of a train of empty H cars derailed on the switch points of 502 crosscut on the 1000 level.* When the motorman tried to pull the train back to rerail the car, it turned over breaking, write-in motor swamper, P.L. Dunagan's right leg. The accident resulted in 75 days lost time.* Note, the empty cars were being pushed by the locomotive.
Phelps Dodge Corporation Copper Queen Branch Accident Report 8-26-74
Annual Report Safety Department January through December 31 1974

August 23, 1974, Cole Mine
A. Sullivan and J. *"Jinx"* Livingston, were working in the interior shaft at the 700 level. Sullivan was altering the sand line in the shaft and had a 24" ratchet wrench on a 4" clamp. He was leaning against a ¾" pipe union in a confined area. While working he bruised his a rib on his left side.
Phelps Dodge Corporation Copper Queen Branch Accident Report 8-27-74

August 25, 1974, Cole Mine

H.T. Millican was repairing the toplander's deck on the headframe (surface). F.L. Hallstead was operating the Austin-Western Crane to bring up a 200lb plate of steel. Due to overhead wires, the steel plate had to be "manhandled" by Millican into position. Millican strained his back.

Phelps Dodge Corporation Copper Queen Branch Accident Report 8-26-74

August 27, 1974, Cole Mine
In 36 crosscut on the 1300 level, G.R. White and J. *"Jinx"* Livingston were going to install a sand fill line to 44 crosscut. White was trimming the 3" plastic pipe with a knife and cut the inside of his left wrist.

Phelps Dodge Corporation Copper Queen Branch Accident Report 8-27-74

August 29, 1974, Cole Mine
M.P. Olvera was trying to disconnect a water hose in 338 crosscut on the 1100 level. The airline was in the way, so Olvera was using a drill steel to pry the airline away. The airline was not properly screwed together and broke. Rust in the line shot out and imbedded itself in his right forearm.

Phelps Dodge Corporation Copper Queen Branch Accident Report 8-30 -74

September 6, 1974, Cole Mine
C. *"Buck"* Hervey was with C. O' Malley in 504 crosscut on the 1000 level. Hervey was working boulders through the grizzly with a boulder hook. The hook slipped and he smashed his hand between the handle of the boulder hook and a blowpipe.

Phelps Dodge Corporation Copper Queen Branch Accident Report 9-7-74

September 9, 1974, Cole Mine
A.H. *"El Diablo"* Chenowith was in 164 crosscut on the 1400 level. He was putting in cribbing to catch up the back and a boulder fell. The rock struck him on top of the right shoulder. Chenowith was only bruised.

Phelps Dodge Corporation Copper Queen Branch Accident Report 9-9-74

September 13, 1974, Cole Mine
G.E. Morin and C.W. Morin were booming out for a corner set in 113 stope on the 800 level. The ground was blocky limestone. As G.E. Morin was placing a 2" lagging over the booms. Muck fell from the above the set next to him and stuck him in the back. He suffered only bruising. (One of the Morins was nicknamed *"Piggy"*, but it is not clear which one.)

Phelps Dodge Corporation Copper Queen Branch Accident Report 9-16-74

September 14, 1974, Cole Mine
D. E. Wainwright and E. Archuleta were in 112 stope on the 800 level. Archuleta was dragging a slusher with a tugger hoist. They wanted to remove the slusher staging to drill. As the slusher hoist was being dragged it became hung on a gob fence. Wainwright took a bar and to pry it free. The bar slipped and smashed Wainwright's left foot.

Phelps Dodge Corporation Copper Queen Branch Accident Report 9-23-74

September 19, 1974, Cole Mine

C.D. Marrujo was mucking with a Finlay in 121 stope on the 1400 level. A boulder fell from the Finlay's bucket and smashed his left foot.
Phelps Dodge Corporation Copper Queen Branch Accident Report 9-20-74

September 26, 1974, Cole Mine
In 91 crosscut on the 800 level, E. Macias was stepping off a staging. The staging was two feet above the track level. He fell and hit his back on a short 4"x 6" that was at the side of the drift.
Phelps Dodge Corporation Copper Queen Branch Accident Report 10-1-74

October 1, 1974, Cole Mine
In the change room, Miner, J.R. Burgos was changing into his diggers, when he went to pull up the rope on his locker. His arm caught a nail and was punctured. Burgos was also injured on April 9, 1974.
Phelps Dodge Corporation Copper Queen Branch Accident Report 10-2-74

October 8, 1974, Cole Mine
Sanitation Nipper, J. Manje was changing out the toilet cars in 6 crosscut on the 1400 level. As he was pushing the full toilet car to the station, he slipped in the mud and fell hitting his knee on the rail bruising it.
Phelps Dodge Corporation Copper Queen Branch Accident Report 10-9-74

October 9, 1974, Cole Mine
C.W. Morin was in 113 stope on the 800 level. He strained his back trying to move a slusher with a scaling bar. Morin was off work 11 days.
Phelps Dodge Corporation Copper Queen Branch Accident Report 10-9-74
"January1-through December 31, 1974" Phelps Dodge Corporation Copper Queen Branch Annual Report Safety Department

October 21, 1974, Cole Mine
R.D. *"Vent Tubing"* Montiel was in 206 crosscut on the 800 level with F.L. *"Changito"* Nieto. Sand and cement had spilled into the drift. Montiel was mucking out the spill and cement water leaked through a hole in his boot. He suffered cement burns on his right foot.
Phelps Dodge Corporation Copper Queen Branch Accident Report 10-23-74

October 22, 1974, Cole Mine
At 9:00 am, in 191 raise on the 1300 level J.R. Burgos was putting oil into an oiler when muck fell from the ceiling (back). He chipped a tooth and his hand was cut.
Phelps Dodge Corporation Copper Queen Branch Accident Report 10-25-74

October 22, 1974, Cole Mine
At 10:30 pm, J.D. Silva was mucking in 127 crosscut on the 1400 level. He was mucking sand spilled in the crosscut with a Finlay. As he was dumping the dipper (bucket) it caught on the pipe line. This caused the Finlay to tilt and pin Silva between the Finlay and the timber. His right arm and back were bruised.
Phelps Dodge Corporation Copper Queen Branch Accident Report 10-24-3-74

October 23, 1974, Cole Mine

R.S. Stewart was in 104 stope on the 800 level. The stope was being sand filled. Stewart walked through cement water in the mucking scram. The water leaked through a hole in his right boot. The cement water burned his foot.
Phelps Dodge Corporation Copper Queen Branch Accident Report 10-24-74

October 29, 1974, Cole Mine*
M.I. Marusich was pulling 87 General chute on the 1400 level. Then he was supposed to clean out the G mine cars at the Dallas ore pocket. As his partner was cleaning out the cars with a blow pipe. . Dirt was blown into Marusich's right eye. * This was the motor crew assigned to the Cole Mine, but technically the accident occurred in the Dallas Mine.
Phelps Dodge Corporation Copper Queen Branch Accident Report 10-30-74

November 1, 1974, Cole Mine
In 217 stope on the 1100 level, H. J. *"Fat Decker"* Decker was preparing to boom out. As he was standing at the end of the timber of the he heard the ground begin to move (cave-in.) He ran under the protection of the timber of the left lead set. Timber gave away in the right lead set. A boulder fell and rolled down the muck pile into the left set. Decker was struck on the knee and left leg. The boulder broke his knee cap and bruised his upper leg. Decker was off at least 60 days and was still not back to work in 1975.
Phelps Dodge Corporation Copper Queen Branch Accident Report 11-5-74
"January1-through December 31, 1974" Phelps Dodge Corporation Copper Queen Branch Annual Report Safety Department

November 5, 1974, Cole Mine
At 9:00 am, L.G. Windsor was in 200 stope on the 900 level. He was barring down to install a gob lagging. A boulder fell out and broke his left foot.
Phelps Dodge Corporation Copper Queen Branch Accident Report 11-6-74

November 7, 1974, Cole Mine
On the 900 level at the 204B chute, Motor Swamper, D. Harvey discovered that the chute was hung up 10-12 ft. above the door. So he prepared a chute bomb to blast it down. When he climbed to place the bomb, he stood in the chute door. Muck fell out of the chute and pinned his right foot against the chute door breaking it. The accident resulted in 38 days lost time.
 Phelps Dodge Corporation Copper Queen Branch Accident Report 11-8-74
Annual Report Safety Department January through December 31 1974

November 11, 1974, Cole Mine
J. Leon was moving an 8"x 8" boom out of the boom hangar and the boom fell on his head. He was off work 10 days.
Phelps Dodge Corporation Copper Queen Branch Accident Report 11-27-74
"January1-through December 31, 1974" Phelps Dodge Corporation Copper Queen Branch Annual Report Safety Department

November 21, 1974, Cole Mine
In 482 crosscut on the 1000 level, F. Solano and R. Oquita were drilling holes for roof bolts with a jackleg. They were changing drill steels and Solano was holding the machine near the chuck. When Oquita slid in the new steel and slammed the steel holder shut it smashed Solano's middle finger on his left hand.
Phelps Dodge Corporation Copper Queen Branch Accident Report 11-22-74

November 22, 1974, Cole Mine
Motorman, E.C. *"Neto"* Chavez was in 269 crosscut on the 1000 level. The motor went
"B.O." or stopped. He climbed out of the motor to see what was wrong. He struck his
hard hat on the airline. When he grabbed it with his hand it knocked off the eye shield.
The eye shield bracket ruptured his left eye. This was not a lost time accident.
Phelps Dodge Corporation Copper Queen Branch Accident Report 12-22-74

December 2, 1974, Cole Mine
At 9:30 am, C.N. *"Buck"* Hervey was in 225 crosscut on the 1300 level. He was mucking
with a Finlay. As he went by the ventilation pipe, dirt blew into his right eye.
Phelps Dodge Corporation Copper Queen Branch Accident Report 12-3-74 9:30 am

December 2, 1974, Cole Mine
At 2:30 pm, B.R. Orozco was walking off shift at quitting time in 83 crosscut on the 1300
level. He slipped and fell. His back landed on a rail. Orozco's back was bruised and
strained.
Phelps Dodge Corporation Copper Queen Branch Accident Report 12-3-74 2:30 pm

December 6, 1974, Cole Mine
On the 900 level in 200 stope, J.R. Burgos was mucking with a Cavo 310 mucking
machine. As he was working a boulder rolled down the muck pile smashing his left foot.
R. L. Lucero witnessed the accident.
Phelps Dodge Corporation Copper Queen Branch Accident Report 12-9-74

December 9, 1974, Cole Mine
G.G. *"Panseco"* Drybread and S.T. *"Silent Sam"* Elkins were removing a slusher from
219 stope on the 1100 level. As Drybread was removing the slusher rake from the chute
with pull-lift a ring on a chain swung and chipped one of his teeth.
Phelps Dodge Corporation Copper Queen Branch Accident Report 12-11-74

December 11, 1974, Cole Mine
E.F. Martinez was unloading 25 lb. rail in 202 crosscut on the 1300 level. As he was
taking the rails off a timber truck he dropped one and smashed his right foot.
Phelps Dodge Corporation Copper Queen Branch Accident Report 12-13-74

December 27, 1975, Cole Mine
F. Solano was using a Cavo 310 mucking machine in 200 stope on the 900 level. As he
was operating the machine he lost control and was pinned between the Cavo and a wall
(rib). Solano suffered a bruised chest.
Phelps Dodge Corporation Copper Queen Branch Accident Report 12-28-74

January 1, 1975, Cole Mine
"Write–in" Motor Swamper, M.S. Almander was told to service 225 crosscut then to begin
pulling 188 stope chute on the 1300 level. He and H. Torres had pulled one train from the
chute. When he returned to pull the second train a boulder was caught behind the No.188
chute door. As he lifted the door he strained his back.
Phelps Dodge Corporation Copper Queen Branch Accident Report 1-10-75

January 4, 1975, Cole Mine

F.V. *"Greyhound"* Morales was moving a grizzly rail* in 219 stope on the 1100 level. He slipped and fell. Morales strained his back * Note, grizzly rails were normally at least 90lb. rail or weighed 90 lbs. per yard. The rail weighed around 200lbs.
Phelps Dodge Corporation Copper Queen Branch Accident Report 1-5-75

January 8, 1975, Cole Mine
On the 1100 level in 315 crosscut, R.V. Encinas jr. was picking up a *"wreck"* or derailed H car. He slipped and strained his back.
Phelps Dodge Corporation Copper Queen Branch Accident Report 1-9-75

January 9, 1975, Cole Mine
R.D. *"Vent Tubing"* Montiel and Y.O. Garcia were to get the ventilation fittings from 12 crosscut and bring them to the station on the 1300 level. Coming through an air door on a locomotive in 1 crosscut, the door began to shut. Montiel tried to prevent the door from closing. He dislocated his left little finger.
Phelps Dodge Corporation Copper Queen Branch Accident Report 1-10-75

January 16, 1975, Cole Mine
In 339 crosscut on the 1100 level, J.D. Pursley and B.F. Stewart had blasted at lunch time. Returning to work Pursley, began barring down. At one point he reached his head out past the timber to look at the back. A small rock fell at that moment and struck him on the right side of the mouth chipping a tooth.
Phelps Dodge Corporation Copper Queen Branch Accident Report 1-18-75

January 17, 1975, Cole Mine
J. *"Mexican Joe"* Corral was in 219 crosscut on the 1300 level. He was pushing a timber truck loaded with 6' lagging. Corral slipped and strained his back.
Phelps Dodge Corporation Copper Queen Branch Accident Report 1-20-75

January 23, 1975, Cole Mine
C. *"Keyhole"* Quiroz was on the 1000 level in 210-B stope. At 10:30 am His partner, G. Shields was throwing 8"x 8" blocks. A blocked bounced and bruised Quiroz left foot.
Phelps Dodge Corporation Copper Queen Branch Accident Report 1-24-75 10:30 am

January 23, 1975, Cole Mine
At 10:30 pm, J.R. *"Cat"* Durazo was salvaging rail and 2" pipe in 153 crosscut right off the 1300 level station. Durazo slipped while lifting a 25 lb. rail. He strained his upper right leg.
Phelps Dodge Corporation Copper Queen Branch Accident Report 1-24-75 10:30 pm

February 4, 1975, Cole Mine
J.M. *"Leona"** Martinez and C. Flores were in 109 stope on the 1400 level. They needed to blast out room for timber. Martinez was pulling a jackleg out of a lifter drilled into finely broken ground. He strained his back trying to get the drill out. * Note, Leona is Spanish for lioness
Phelps Dodge Corporation Copper Queen Branch Accident Report 2-7-75

February 10, 1975, Cole Mine

112

L.W. *"Sonny Bono"* * Vian and F.T. *"Changito"* * Nieto were in the mucking the scram of 201 stope on the 900 level. As Vian stepped off the ladder into the scram, he fell and landed onto his side. His back was bruised. * Note, *Sonny Bono* was a reference to Sonny & Cher popular musical artists of the time. *Changito* is a Mexican/border Spanish term for little monkey. It possibly, should be spelled Changiuto. Phelps Dodge Corporation Copper Queen Branch Accident Report 2-11-75

February 12, 1975, Cole Mine
R. *"Lieutenant"* Leon was carrying an 8"x 8" post up a muck pile in 109 stope on the 1400 level. He fell and strained his back.
Phelps Dodge Corporation Copper Queen Branch Accident Report 2-13-75

February 17, 1975, Cole Mine
In 161 crosscut on the 1400 level, W.D. Windsor had cut the bands from a bundle of timber. As he was bending the band back it flew and cut him on his left wrist.
Phelps Dodge Corporation Copper Queen Branch Accident Report 2-21-75

February 20, 1975, Cole Mine
Mining engineer, Sam Christo climbed into 237 raise on the 1000 level. He took measurements and lagged over the chute side of the raise. Then he began sampling. Oxide ore on the chute side fell and struck him on the hard hat and down his right side. He suffered bruising and scratching.
Phelps Dodge Corporation Copper Queen Branch Accident Report 2-20-75

February 24, 1975, Cole Mine
In 129 crosscut on the 800 level, E. *"Camel Jockey"* Baraky was cutting a 2" lagging with a power saw. He reached down to pick up the saw and accidently turned the saw on. His left little finger was cut. (Baraky was from an Arabic country. Today, this would be considered a racial slur)
Phelps Dodge Corporation Copper Queen Branch Accident Report 2-25-75

February 24, 1975, Cole Mine
Timberman, E. Macias was removing the 25 lb. rails from 293 crosscut on the 900 level, to convert it into a powder magazine. He was helping R. Brandt load the rails onto a timber truck when he strained his upper leg.
Phelps Dodge Corporation Copper Queen Branch Accident Report 2-26-75

March 3, 1975, Cole Mine
Frank Chavez was on the 1000 level station. He was pulling up the dead end of the trolley wire with a pull-lift. The pull-lift was attached to the trolley dead end and a cap on a timber set. The cap pulled free and struck Chavez in the back and shoulders. He was bruised.
Phelps Dodge Corporation Copper Queen Branch Accident Report 3-4-75

March 12, 1975, Cole Mine
At 10:30 am, E.O. *"Curly"* Rojo was at the sump of the shaft working on a staging. He was mucking out the sump. A cable broke on a bucket (sinking bucket?). The bucket fell and broke through the staging. Rojo fell about six feet and bruised his left shoulder. He was working with C. Davis and F.V. Morales.
Phelps Dodge Corporation Copper Queen Branch Accident Report 3-13 -75 10:30 am

March 12, 1975, Cole Mine
At 1:00 pm, C. Davis was running a tugger hoist. The vibrations of the hoist caused a saw to fall and cut Davis' left thumb. He was working in the shaft sump with E.O. *"Curly"* Rojo and F.V. Morales.
Phelps Dodge Corporation Copper Queen Branch Accident Report 3-13-75 1:00 pm

March 20, 1975, Cole Mine
At 4:30 pm, W.B. *"Boomerang"* Irvin was climbing into 191 stope on the 1300 level. As he climbing a ladder he slipped on a rung. When he caught himself he strained his back.
Phelps Dodge Corporation Copper Queen Branch Accident Report 3-24-75 4:30 pm

March 20, 1975, Cole Mine
At 6:15 pm, K. Adams was re-nailing* ladders in 102-A stope on the 1400 level. As he was working copper water splashed and went past his eye shield into his eyes. * Note, the copper water would be chemically reacting with the steel nails. In what is known as a substitution reaction the iron in the nails are drawn into solution and would be replaced by elemental copper. The resulting copper is weak and often mud-like and would not be suitable for nails. In instances that ladders were expected to be exposed to copper water the ladders were built with copper nails to prevent the replacement.
Phelps Dodge Corporation Copper Queen Branch Accident Report 3-24-75 6:15 pm

March 20, 1975, Cole Mine
At 8:45 pm, G.S. *"Watermelon"* Renteria, H. *"Paladin"** Soto and R. *"Lieutenant"* Leon were in 183 crosscut on the 1300 level. They were planning to install a doubler in the crosscut. H. Soto was loading an 8"x 8" post onto a timber truck and slipped. The post fell onto Renteria's right foot. Initially, it was thought that the foot was broken. At the hospital it was determined to be only bruised. Even though, this accident was a lost time accident. *Paladin was a reference to a the 1957-1963 television & radio shows *"Have gun –Will travel"* The miners would refer to Soto a timberman, as Paladin and say *"Have saw-will travel"*. He was also known as *"Scarface"*
Phelps Dodge Corporation Copper Queen Branch Accident Report 3-24-75 8:45 pm

March 31, 1975, Cole Mine
A slusher and rake were going to be lowered into 118 stope on the 1300 level. J.M. Jimenez was helping the slusher man. As the slusher and rake were being bundled together. Jimenez smashed his finger between the rake and slusher. His finger was cut and bruised.
Phelps Dodge Corporation Copper Queen Branch Accident Report 4-1-75

April 2, 1975, Cole Mine
E.S. Lopez was barring down in 118 stope on the 1400 level with Henry *"Pelón"** Hernandez. A boulder rolled down the muck pile and hit Lopez on the left shin. He was cut and bruised. * Pelón is Mexican/border Spanish for bald. Like many, of the men called *"Pelón"* he was not bald.
Phelps Dodge Corporation Copper Queen Branch Accident Report 4-3-75

April 16, 1975, Cole Mine
At 5:30 am, J.M. *"Leona"* Martinez and V.E. *"Bullwinkle"* Hare were repairing 229 crosscut on the 800 level. As Martinez was changing a bottom lagging a boulder struck his left foot. His foot was broken.
Phelps Dodge Corporation Copper Queen Branch Accident Report 4-22-75

April 16, 1975, Cole Mine

At the collar of the shaft, W.P. Marinez was taking off a skip from a cage. He smashed a finger between the skip and a Jip (Jib?) crane. The accident occurred at 10:30 pm.
Phelps Dodge Corporation Copper Queen Branch Accident Report 4-16-75

May 22, 1975, Cole Mine
On the 1000 level station, slusher maintenance man, S.T. Elkins was pushing a timber truck loaded with part of a Cavo mucker. The part fell catching his leg between the timber truck and the rib of the drift. He suffered a bruised leg.
Phelps Dodge Corporation Copper Queen Branch Accident Report 6-6-75

May 29, 1975, Cole Mine
Cager, N.A. Harriston was hoisting equipment being salvaged from the 1000 level. He was loading a part of a Cavo loader onto the cage with a timber truck, when the part slipped bruising and cutting his left ring finger.
Phelps Dodge Corporation Copper Queen Branch Accident Report 6-2-75

June 5, 1975, Cole Mine
R. *"Lieutenant"* Leon and L.W. *"Sonny Bono"* Vian were salvaging sand pipe from 129 crosscut on the 800 level. A piece of pipe fell and bruised Leon's left knee.
Phelps Dodge Corporation Copper Queen Branch Accident Report 6-5-75

June 9, 1975, Cole Mine
J. Lopez and Al Vorin* were on the 800 station loading a blower onto the cage. The blower slipped and smashed Lopez's hand between the cage and blower. * Al Vorin was an active collector of minerals and had built one the better local mineral collections.
Phelps Dodge Corporation Copper Queen Branch Accident Report 6-10-75

After the closure of the mine on June 12, 1975. Equipment was salvaged from the mine, by Bisbee Salvage & Equipment Company. The company continued to salvage equipment until around 1985. The Cole Adit was salvaged of trolley wire and rail about 1985.

December 10, 1975, Cole Mine
Hoistman, W.M. Kasun was raising a cage with a locomotive. The locomotive batteries were on the cage and the actual locomotive was slung underneath the cage. As it was being raised the cage became hung on a broken shaft guide between the 1200 and 1300 levels. About 50 ft. of hoisting cable coiled* on top of the #2 cage and partly into the #1 shaft compartment. L. *"Cacho"* Gonzales and Larry Echave went down the #1 compartment on a cage, the cage pinched the hoisting cable for #2 cage. No men were injured, but the cable was damaged. * Note it is likely after the cage became stuck Kasun tried to lower the cage and see if the weight of the loaded cage would cause it to drop and free itself.
"Report of Accident" 12-11-1975

Miners leaving a cage in the Campbell Mine c-1940

Diamond Drilling in the Campbell Mine C.-1948

116

Congdon Mine c-1904

Congdon

      The Pittsburg & Duluth Mining Company started sinking the Congdon shaft in March of 1903. Work proceeded rapidly and by 1904 the shaft was 1,244ft. deep. The 1050 level was connected to 850 level Irish Mag/ Oliver mine workings with an agreement from the Copper Queen Consolidated Mining Company that allowed the company to drive 600ft. of drift through Copper Queen's Lucky Jack Claim. This and another connection to the 1000 level of the Oliver Mine to the 1250 Congdon provided essential air flow. Later, the #2 crosscut on the 1250 level was driven towards the Cole Shaft of the Lake Superior and Pittsburg Mining Company. It connected to the Cole's 1350 level with a raise. While driving this crosscut, ore was unexpectedly discovered. The main ores discovered were on the Sunnyside claim, which lies halfway between the Cole Shaft and the Congdon. Due the location, it was decided to shut down the Congdon in 1905. The Cole Mine was already built to handle ore and had a rail line to the mine site. The mine was still credited for producing 150 tons daily of ore in 1906, but the Congdon shaft itself remained inactive. This ore was removed through the Cole Shaft. In 1943, a drift driven from the Cole 800 level intercepted the 1250 level for ventilation. The Congdon served as a source of ventilation until the mines shut down in 1975. At the closure of the mines in 1975, the Congdon had two and one half compartments and was 1,244 ft. deep. The mine was also called the Pittsburg & Duluth mine and the P. & D. Mine.

February 13, 1904, Congdon Mine* (Pittsburg and Duluth)
Otto Molander, Frank Hollister, and Dominic Brunas were working sinking, the two and a half compartment, Congdon Shaft. They had brought powder down to the bottom of the

shaft to begin loading their drill holes. Hollister was using his candlestick to puncture a hole in the dynamite for a blasting cap. Suddenly, his candle set fire to the stick of dynamite in his hand, and he dropped it into a case of dynamite which ignited in a blaze and it did not explode. This fire spread rapidly to the clothes of the miners. The panicked men signaled for the cage, but they sent such a confused signal that the hoistman could not respond** When smoke was detected the men on the surface became aware of the problem and turned on the compressed air to clear the smoke and fumes. As Brunas climbed into the sinking bucket, Hollister, who had climbed the shaft fell and struck his head against the bucket. Confused but suspecting an accident he raised the sinking bucket and brought Brunas to the surface. He had a knife in his teeth and had been using it to cut away his burning clothes. The bucket was lowered again and Molander was brought to the surface. On the surface, he jumped into a barrel of water to extinguish his clothes. Hollister had been killed, when his head struck the bucket and men gathered lanterns and went and retrieved his body. The newspaper described recovering Hollister's body as *"It was half an hour before they got Hollister's body to the top, and awful sight it presented, the poor fellow's head being split open, the flesh hung on his body in ribbons, and came off as burnt paper crumbles at the touch of a feather."* Molander died from his injuries on the February 14 and Brunas recovered from his injuries. A double funeral was given to Hollister and Molander with Presbyterian pastor Reverend Harvey M. Shields performing the ceremony. Frank Hollister was married and 32 years old, Otto Molander was Finnish and 26 years old. They were both buried in Evergreen Cemetery. A year later, Dominic Brunas later sued the Pittsburg and Duluth Mining Company for $41,104.00. He stated that he had twice complained to the mine supervisor that he was working with a fellow employee that was careless using powder.

*The article refers to the Congdon shaft by its earlier name the Pittsburg and Duluth Shaft. The newer name is given to allow easier research for anyone examining this mine further.

** The hoistman could not safely respond a signal he did not understand. Because these men were working inside the shaft itself, any movement of the cage to the area could cause the death of a miner. The hoistman would need to wait until he received a signal he understood before moving a cage. This would let the hoistman know that the men below were safely positioned, and he would not injure anyone by moving the cage. Cages were one of the leading causes of deaths of miners.

"Horrible Accident on the P. &D." Bisbee Daily Review 14 February 1904 page 1

"Horrible Accident on the P. &D." Bisbee Daily Review 14 February 1904 page 5

"Injured Miner Dies from Injuries." Bisbee Daily Review 16 February 1904 page 5

"Double Funeral Yesterday" Bisbee Daily Review 17 February 1904 page 5

"Suit for Damages" Bisbee Daily Review 15 February 1905 page 4

"Injuries and Damages" Bisbee Daily Review 11 June 1905 page 9

"Original Certificate of Death." Arizona Department of Health Services.
 http://genealogy.az.gov/azdeath/002/10020466.pdf (April18 2011)

"Original Certificate of Death." Arizona Department of Health Services.
 http://genealogy.az.gov/azdeath/002/10020465.pdf (April18 2011)

"Cochise County Coroner's Inquest No. 186" Arizona State Archives Phoenix

July 14, 1904, Congdon Mine

Guy Whipple, a 23-year-old miner was working in the bottom of the shaft. The sinking bucket was lowered on top of him cutting his head and spraining his leg. He was carried to the surface in the sinking bucket. While, Whipple was being raised, Dr. Caven, misunderstood the situation and informed the coroner that a man had been killed at the Congdon mine. The coroner and a jury went to the mine before they discovered Whipple was alive and at the Calumet & Arizona Hospital. He was released from the hospital on July 22. Later, after March 1906, Guy Whipple stopped making contact with his parents and on November 15, 1906, they placed an advertisement in the Bisbee Daily Review for information on the whereabouts of their son.

"Struck by Bucket Head and Leg Hurt" Bisbee Daily Review 15 July 1904 page 5
"Guy Whipple Wanted" Bisbee Daily Review 15 November 1906 page 7
"Calumet & Arizona Hospital Records." My Cochise. http://www.mycochise.com/hospcalwh2z.php (April 19 2011)

May 5, 1905, Congdon Mine

F.A. Roberts was notching a fuse* and did not realize it had a blasting cap on the end he was cutting. The cap exploded removing two fingers and a thumb. * Fuses were notched to make them easier to light.

"Injured Yesterday" Bisbee Daily Review 6 May 1905 page 6

January 4, 1907, Congdon Mine

Sam Vukich was pushing a heavily loaded mine car on the 1350 level. After he reached the chute he struggled to unlatch and dump the car. When the car dumped he fell over the car to the bottom of the chute. The rock from the car landed on him. His back was broken and his skull was fractured. Fortunately, a carman behind him heard him yell and rescued him.

"Miner Narrowly Escapes Death" Bisbee Daily Review 4 January 1907 page 6

Miners spitting a round in the Campbell Mine c-1938

Copper Queen Mine

The Copper Queen was started in 1880 by the mining of a surface exposure of copper ore with an open cut. The ore in fact was discovered to be a substantial orebody and the open cut continued underground as a stope. During this time a shallow shaft was sunk and level developed. In 1881, The Copper Queen Incline Shaft was sunk at a 45° angle about 200 ft. east of the open cut. The shaft was small with two compartments, one for a manway and the other for hoisting one ton mine cars modified for hoisting and holding about a quarter ton of ore. Four levels were developed and the original orebody was mined down to the third level (300 Queen level.) After the Atlanta Shaft struck a major orebody, the Copper Queen Mining Company merged with the Atlanta Mining Company to form the Copper Queen Consolidated Mining Company. The Czar Shaft was sunk in 1885 to replace the inadequate Copper Queen Incline. In 1888, the Copper Queen mine closed. After the closure, the shaft was used as a manway to access areas and used for some exploration.

In 1913, the Copper Queen Incline stopes were remined for about a year. Although, surviving documents do not indicate significant activity at the mine after this time. Evidence underground indicates some work was completed in the 1920's and 1930s. During these years the Myers tunnel was driven from the open cut to the west and under stopes of the Southwest mine. Sections of the manway compartment were backfilled with waste as well. The Copper Queen Incline shaft and one small stope are part of the Queen Mine Tour today (Most of the tour is actually spent in the Southwest Mine) Note, that the *"Copper Queen Mine"* was used as a euphemism to represent any mine owned by Copper Queen Consolidated Mining Company. Due to the short period of operation, few men worked in the Copper Queen Mine. Most of the men said to have worked in the Copper Queen Mine actually worked in one of the larger mines such as the Czar, Holbrook or Sacramento Mines.

Date probably 1881, Copper Queen Mine

After, the workings of the Copper Queen Incline Shaft had reached "B" level the air was of such poor quality it became essential to sink an air shaft. Stephen Bradish* and Stewart Hunt were working in this air shaft. It had been sunk the air shaft roughly 60 ft.

They had blasted and Bradish down to inspect the blast. He signaled to Hunt to be pulled up, and the air was fouled with powder gasses. At the collar of the shaft, Bradish suddenly let go and fell. Hunt went down the shaft to recover the body of his friend. Miraculously, the last blast had broken a hole into the drift below. Bradish's head had landed in this hole and was protected from being smashed. He suffered only injured shoulders * Bradish was later a primary witness of the shooting of Frank Stable at the Gem Saloon in Bisbee on March 18, 1882.

Wentworth, Frank L. Bisbee with the Big B.: Unknown Publisher,
"Cochise County Inquest No. 195" Arizona State Archives Phoenix

May 2, 1882, Copper Queen Mine

Mark Shearer was injured when he was struck by a timber falling from a stope. His injuries were serious.

"Wednesday "The Weekly Arizona Miner 5 May 1882, page 3

November 23, 1882, Copper Queen Mine

24-year-old, Frank Salmon walked to the 300 level station with Thomas Johnson carrying a pick. It was 11:40 am and time for lunch. Salmon sat down and leaned his head against a water pipe to have lunch. Johnson ask him what was wrong and Salmon responded he had been *"up late. Last- night'* William Kelly saw Salmon, suddenly just fall and landed on his face. Wes Howell and Kelly turned him over on his back, but Salmon died within two minutes. He was taken to a room at the Jones boarding house where Dr. H.W. Fenner examined and determine he had died from natural causes, a heart failure. The coroner examined Salmon's possessions and found a small broken trunk with clothes and a brass trunk that was locked and sealed with wax *. The contents of this trunk were not described. Under protest of the coroner and without legal authority, J.W. Blair took $7.50 in U.S. silver coins belonging to Salmon from the coroner. The remaining items were placed in the custody of Thomas Jones. Salmon was from California and buried in Bisbee.* possibly sealed by coroner.

"Cochise County Inquest No. 194" Arizona State Archives Phoenix

August 1884, Copper Queen Mine

A rock fell on John McDonough and broke his thigh and ankle.

"Small Talk "Arizona Weekly Citizen 23 August 1884, page 3

The collapsed B level station of the Copper Queen Mine

121

The original cemetery in Old Bisbee c-1901
(Courtesy of the Bisbee Mining & Historical Museum)

November 7, 1890, Copper Queen Mine

Robert Cagle and A.E. Arnold were working in a No.2 crosscut on November 5 and had blasted five holes. One failed to detonate. Arnold went back and relit the fuse on the misfired hole, but left the mine before he heard the explosion. They climbed the incline shaft and at the surface met J.L. Jones the miner that was working night shift in the crosscut and told him about the misfire that was remaining. That night Jones worked on the upper part of the crosscut away from where the missed hole was supposed to be. The next day Cagle and Arnold looked for the missed hole and could not find and decided that it must have detonated. They out two mine car loads of rock from the No.2 crosscut. That night Jones with Fred Stone went to work. Stone was to work in the Burleigh Drift, instead of with Jones. He passed Jones as he was headed out to get water for the Burleigh drill and Jones asked him to bring back drinking water. About ten minutes later Stone returned with a mine car with water barrels and found Jones standing there with a hammer*. Stone began to unload the barrels onto a timber truck and told Jones to get a drink. Jones returned to his drift and Stone went to the Burleigh Drift. As Stone was leaving the Burleigh Drift, he heard a detonation and his candle was extinguished. Jones exploded the misfire by picking or drilling. Stone found No.2 crosscut filled with smoke. C.P. Nelson went into the crosscut and found the mortally wounded Jones lying across the track and told the other men to get a doctor. They took Jones to the surface, but he was mortally injured.* Single jack or double jack, not a carpenter's hammer

"Cochise County Inquest No. 235" Arizona State Archives Phoenix

Copper Queen Smelter

The original Copper Queen Smelter was located below the Copper Queen Open Cut (Gloryhole) and was shut down in August 1886. It was replaced by a smelter built near the Czar Mine. The new smelter was *"blown in"* in May 1887.This smelter had four 36" inch furnaces and could produce 1,000,000lbs. of copper per month. The new smelter was less than ideal and in 1892, Dr. James Douglas was sent to Europe to examine the Manhes- David (Manhes-Bessemer) smelters. These had barrel shaped converters compared to the vertical converters used in Bisbee. It was decided to adopt the Manhes- David system in Bisbee and the third smelter was started in the fall of 1894 with a production of 3,000,000 lbs. of copper a month. Soon advantages of the new system were revealed the purity of the copper bars produced was much higher and sulphide ores could now be smelted. The location of the smelter was favorable in the sense it was close to the Holbrook and Czar mines and the ore was transported at most a few hundred feet from the shafts. The geography of the site was challenging. The smoke stack was constructed running inclined up the slope of Queen Hill around 400 vertical feet. This was an attempt to disperse the smoke away from the community. This was not as successful as desired and Bisbee was encompassed with the sulfur-odor of the smelter smoke. As the company desired to increase production to excess of 4,000,000 lbs. a month, it was realized the Czar-Smelter area was too crowded.

The decision was made to build a new smelter (fourth) in the Sulphur Springs Valley near the border with Mexico. This was a bold choice as the old smelter still was estimated to have a value of over 1.2 million dollars. This investment would largely be relegated to scrap if a new smelter was constructed. For a time both the new smelter in Douglas and the smelter in Bisbee operated in conjunction. Finally, in July of 1904, the Copper Queen Smelter in Bisbee poured its last bar of copper. The site was cleared and a precipitation plant was built in 1906 to recover copper from mine water.

The old slag from the smelter in Bisbee still contained substantial copper and was being mined and resmelted at Douglas. In 1914, the precipitation plant was dismantled in preparation of improvements to the Czar Mine. During 1915, the Queen Tunnel of the 3rd level of the

Southwest Mine was driven from the western end of the area. A few years later a joint Czar-Southwest mine change house was constructed covering the area. Today, the Queen Mine Tour occupies the change house. Occasionally, pieces of coke and slag are found on the ground. The last remaining section of the smelter stack pipe lies on the hillside just above the Queen Tunnel Portal. Several hundred feet up Queen Hill is a limestone foundation that was used to support the smelter stack at the point it went vertical for a few feet. In the western wall of the Lavender Pit, a small part slag dump is exposed. The majority of the dump was remined and smelted in Douglas for its copper values.

June 1882

A 16- year-old Mexican boy with the name Orice (Orize?) was near the Copper Queen Smelter when a slag pot rolled down the dump. The pot landed in a pool of water and exploded. Molten slag splatter onto the boy and burned down to his bones. It was expected the incident would be fatal. It is unknown whether the incident proved fatal. (No, inquest or death certificate could be located, but this is not uncommon for years pre-1900)
"Untitled" Pioche Weekly Record 17 June 1882 page1

March 2, 1898 Copper Queen Smelter

John Pyatt a teamster from La Morita, Sonora Mexico was in Bisbee at the Fury Saloon.* At the saloon he met L.H. Perkins. The men talked and Perkins asked if he could head out of town with Pyatt. Perkins lived near La Morita. At 2:30pm, Pyatt picked up his four horse wagon and had it loaded with barley at the Copper Queen Store. The men then started out of town. As Pyatt passed the slag dump the horses became frightened of the hot slag. They became uncontrollable. Pyatt told Perkins and several young boys hitching a ride to get off the wagon. Perkins said, *"Let her go!"* Sam King, a U.S. Customs inspector witnessed the accident. As the running horses passed him, Perkins either fell or jumped from the wagon. He landed on his head and then his head or neck was run over by the wagon. The wagon went about 40 more feet and turned over. Pyatt was partially buried by the load. Pyatt got out from under the barley and then cut his horses loose. By this time Pyatt had been carried into the blacksmith shop of A. K. Waddell. King took his horse and rode to get a doctor, but Perkins had already died. * The inquest was hand written and beautifully written, but the transcriber added decorative curlicues to letters that make some letters difficult to discern it is possible it was the Jury Saloon. Also note, this was by the standards of the time not a smelter accident. Today, it would possibly would.
"Cochise County Coroner's Inquest No. 354" Arizona State Archives

January 14, 1901, Copper Queen Smelter

Francisco Gomez was cleaning slag out of a converter pit and Selso Alvalez and Alejo Ariola were working under a bridge. There was an explosion* in converter #1. A *"barrel full"* of molten copper matte dropped onto Ariola. He caught on fire. Gomez heard the explosion and saw Alvalez and other men putting out the flames on Ariola. He died from his burns. Note, the molten slag, matte and crude copper is between 1500° F and 2730° F (650° C -1500° C). Also, the inquest was completed with the use of a Spanish-English interpreter. * The explosion could have been caused by the ignition of powder sulfide ore, possibly trapped SO_2 gas or a cause I am not familiar with.
"Cochise County Coroner's Inquest No. 458" Arizona State Archives

February 17, 1902, Copper Queen Smelter

Santa Cruz was struck by material (slag?) that accumulated above him. It fell and broke his leg in two places and fractured his skull. He was treated by Dr. Sweet.
"Serious Accident" Bisbee Daily Review 19 February 1902 page1

March 2, 1902, Copper Queen Smelter
Walter Tellum, Jim Johnson, John Shutty* and Thomas Logan were trying to remove a copper-rich cinder that had formed in the smoke stack above converter #2. Cinders built up in the stacks regularly. The stacks needed to be cleaned regularly at least every three days. These men had been prying and pounding on bars trying to get it to move. John Shutty was hammering on the side of the stack. This cinder was being particularly difficult, it weighed over a ton and the two bars had become stuck. The men decided to take a break. After about four or five minutes, Tellum walked underneath the stack. Suddenly, the cinder fell. The cinder pinned Tellum to the ground face down killing him.*

John Shutty was "Slavonian" and needed a Slavic-English interpreter. His story is slightly different than the other witnesses. He stated, that Tellum was holding a bar when it fell. Part of this may have been a confused interpreter. In reading the testimony after Nick Nobile, an interpreter was sworn in it is evident the interpreter did not clearly understand some of the terms Shutty was using. Also, it appears that Shutty at least spoke some English as the first part of his testimony was completed without an interpreter. Shutty also appears to has been a witness to the similar accident that killed Joseph Valley on September 24, 1903.
"Cochise County Coroner's Inquest No. 431" Arizona State Archives

May 3, 1902, Copper Queen Smelter
Intoxicated with a river of mescal, an alcohol deranged, Guadalupe Lomali was near the smelter when he decided his clothes were filled with rattlesnakes. Quickly he tore off his garbs and ran around the smelter area. Employees of the smelter tried to capture him but he evaded them. Then Lomali discovered a tank holding hot water. He dove head first into the tank with the intent of family in the "*infernal regions*". The smelter men rescued him and the n he tried to throw himself into a smelter furnace. After he had sobered up Dr. Edmundson determined he was suffering with a slight heart condition from over use of mescal, but otherwise a rational man.
"Crazy Man Jumps into Tank near Depot" Bisbee Daily Review 4 May 1902 page1

May 28, 1902, Copper Queen Smelter
Elmer E. Miller was trying to fix a leak in a converter. It was leaking molten metal between the top and bottom joint. The converter was turned down while he was working on it. Above and behind him was a slag pot filled with molten slag. When John Gallagher the locomotive engineer started to move the train of slag pots out , the train jerked* and the hook holding the slag pot from dumping slipped. Miller saw the slag coming at him and tried to get under a converter. The slag caught him and burned him all the way up his back. His clothes were burned off except a small amount around his wrist. He was taken first to the company drugstore for immediate attention and then to the Copper Queen Hospital. Miller told the nurses, *"I was standing just below the car when it tipped, and saw the hot slag coming towards me. I tried to crawl under a converter, but the slag caught me about the back throwing me down. The hot slag poured over me, but at the time I did not feel any pain."* He died at the hospital in the morning hours. Miller was survived by a mother in Sacramento, California. * This jerking is caused when the slack is taken up in the couplings of rail cars. It is considered normal at least in the trains used underground.
"Cochise County Coroner's Inquest No. 37" Arizona State Archives
"Death Caused by Hot Slag" Bisbee Daily Review 30 May 1902 page 4

July 22, 1902, Copper Queen Smelter
Andrew Vucotich was struck by a falling cinder. His skull was fractured. Dr. Sweet preformed an operation to lift the bone away from the brain.
"Hurt in Smelter" <u>Bisbee Daily Review</u> 23 July 1902 page 4

Date unknown around September 1902, Copper Queen Smelter
Engineer Gallagher was hauling slag to the dump when some spilled on his foot. The burned foot was still causing him considerable trouble as of September 30
"Untitled" <u>Bisbee Daily Review</u> 30 September 1902 page 8

October 14, 1902, Copper Queen Smelter
At 1:30 am, Frenchman, Maxim Demers was caught between a bucket and a converter. Several of his ribs were broken. He was taken to his home located in Brewery Gulch to recover.
"Accident at Smelter" <u>Bisbee Daily Review</u> 14 October 1902 page 8

November 14, 1902, Copper Queen Smelter
Sam Popovich and George Dobovich had come from Montenegro together and were working at the smelter. The men had known each other twelve years, but had come to Bisbee 18 months prior to the accident. Popovich wanted to oil a car (railcar?) and did not want to walk to the locomotive to get the oil. He decided to go near a machine to get oil. His jumper became caught on the moving shaft and began wrapping him around the shaft. This shaft was connected to the mud mill. The motion threw his legs up against a tin roof. His legs were cut off. Above him at a crane stand at the railroad tracks M. Kirschwing saw Popovich get caught, but by the time he got down, Dobovich had shut off the machine. Mr. Douglas (James or Walter?) and gave them sheets to cover the body and to take him away. He was survived by a wife, three children and an aged mother. The next morning the Bisbee Daily Review reported, *"an innocent appearing belt wheel on the main shaft which operates the Copper Queen mud mill. The shaft and the wheel are still, but a tattered jumper covered with blood, a pool of red life fluid on the ground beneath the shaft, with now and then a morsel of human flesh and a fragment of human bone, bore mute testimony to the tragic affair."*
"Cochise County Coroner's Inquest No. 98" Arizona State Archives
"Smelterman is Killed" <u>Bisbee Daily Review</u> 15 November 1902 page 1

November 15, 1902 Copper Queen Smelter
Austro-Hungarian, Peter V. Cassanegra worked as a converter liner, but spent part of his time breaking off slag or sometimes mud that spilled on the top of the converters. Fred worked nearby also as a converter liner. As Cassanegra was pounding off slag with a sledge hammer, one of the four chains holding the converter broke. He fell about twelve feet and landed on his head. Cassanegra had landed on a turn table*. Joe Goden a puncher and Fred Lavargne both Canadians, saw Cassanegra fall. J.W. Mc Allister was nearby pounding out rivets on a converter being repaired. McAllister noticed that Cassanegra did

not know the proper method to use a sledge hammer and thought Cassanegra was making himself work harder than necessary. About that time, McAllister heard the chain break. Cassangra died at the Copper Queen Hospital on the 16th. * Note, the turntable was probably used for the small locomotive used to pull out slag cars.
"Cochise County Coroner's Inquest No. 102" Arizona State Archives
"Injured at Smelter" Bisbee Daily Review 16 November1902 page 5

November 25, 1902, Copper Queen Smelter
Peter Effrin was bruised on the left leg when a valve blew out.
"Slight Accident at Smelter" Bisbee Daily Review 26 November 1902 page 8

February 13, 1903, Copper Queen Smelter
Raphael Aguirre* and Manuel Silvas they had reported to work drunk. Silvas had also brought a bottle of liquor along with him. They were sharing drinks from the bottle and with Michol Rios. Rios observed Silvas loading his wheelbarrow on the feeding platform of no. 5 converter and then start to fall. Aguirre tried to grab him and both men fell approximately 20 feet. Silvas was taken to the Copper Queen Dispensary and was seen by Dr. Dysart who prescribed stimulant medication and sent him home for care. Dr. Dysart did note that Silvas was suffering paralysis of the lower extremities. The doctor went to the home three times to check on the patient's condition. He died at 7:30 am Sunday morning the 15th of February. Silvas was married with two children. * Interestingly, Aguirre was not able to write his name on the inquisition, but made his mark (an X)
"Cochise County Coroner's Inquest No. 98" Arizona State Archives

February 23, 1903, Copper Queen Smelter
An unnamed Mexican man had his big toe run over by a slag train. The company doctors dressed the injury. He was expected to be off work only a few days.
"Toe Smashed" Bisbee Daily Review 24 February1903 page5

May 2, 1903 Copper Queen Smelter
Carpenter, Mike Colgan was repairing the roof of the smelter. He stepped on a piece of corrugated metal and it gave way. Mike Cogan was hired by two contractors to help paint smoke stacks. He walked out onto the roof of the smelter and fell through the corrugated roof. He fell twenty feet and was seriously injured. His right shoulder was dislocated, the third rib was torn from the spine and a bruised head. He was treated and taken to his home at the Central Lodging House. The injuries were not considered life threatening. He was treated by Dr. Dysart. Too make matters worse the two men who hired him carried him back to the Central Lodging house and robbed him. They took a five dollar gold piece and his watch. The men then drew their money and left town. Due to the fact Cogan was a not an employee of the Copper Queen he was not eligible for free hospital care. Cogan had a wife and six children in Joplin Missouri. He was trying to get employment from the Copper Queen.
"Colgan Robbed Employers" Bisbee Daily Review 5 May 1903 page 8
"Olgan Fell from Top of Smelter" Bisbee Daily Review 2 May 1903 page 8

June 9, 1903, Copper Queen Smelter
Frank Clark slipped and fell off the top of a converter. He dropped 15ft. and was bruised up.
"Accident at Smelter" Bisbee Daily Review 10 June 1903 page 5

September 8, 1903, Copper Queen Smelter
Walter Hatley an engineer, crushed a finger and a nail was torn from his right hand.
"Crushed his Finger" Bisbee Daily Review 9 September 1903 page5

September 12, 1903, Copper Queen Smelter
At 2:30 am, Jose Vasquez and another workman had finished dumping the slag cars. They tried to jump on the moving train. Vasquez became hooked on the train and fell. Two wheels rolled over one leg. He suffered a deep cut above the knee and other bruises and scratches. He was taken to the Copper Queen Hospital after he was treated by a doctor.
"Mexican Smelter Laborer Run Over by Slag Car" Bisbee Daily Review 12 September 1903 page 1

September 22, 1903, Copper Queen Smelter
George Kirkland was caught between two slag pots. He was bruised on the back and chest. The large crane was operating and he could not move. It was considered lucky that he was not killed.
"Caught by Slag Pots" Bisbee Daily Review 24 September, 1903 page5

September 24, 1903, Copper Queen Smelter
French-Canadian, Joseph Valley was punching a converter when a large cinder of around 1,500lbs. fell out of the smoke stack. It landed on a protective sheet of steel held by four chains. The impact broke the chains. The sheet of steel and the cinder struck Valley killing him instantly. According to the Bisbee Daily Review, his head was crushed and part of him was charred from the heat of the cinder. Also, the intense heat emanating from the cinder made it difficult to get the cinder and steel plate off of him. He was survived by a young wife. J.S. White, Gab Anderson, William Dye and John Shutey witnessed the accident. Note, that spelling was an issue with Valley's last name and even after the smelter's timekeeper was brought before the inquest it was not completely resolved. The timekeeper stated he spelled employees names phonetically. John Shutey is likely the John Shutty who witnessed Walter Tellum's death on March 2, 1902 at the smelter
"Cochise County Coroner's Inquest No. 157" Arizona State Archives
"Frightful Death of Joe Vally at the Copper Queen Smelter" Bisbee Daily Review 25 September 1903 page 1

September 30, 1903, Copper Queen Smelter
C.F. Rubush was working at the machine shop at the smelter. His hand became caught in a pipe machine. He was only bruised and would be able to return to work.
"Caught Hand in Machine" Bisbee Daily Review 30 September 1903 page 5

October 3, 1903, Copper Queen Smelter
Margarito Aguilar and Ramon Ruiz were cleaning spilled slag off the rails at 3:45 am. 19 year-old, Pedro Savala was handling No.3 slag car. Aguilar was not well known by his fellow employees. According to Savala, He had working at the smelter the previous

August and had recently returned to work there. Ruiz stated, Aguilar had been there 15 days. John Lemon was operating the small locomotive and pulling No.3 Slag pot car* as the train climbed up a small rise, Lemon rang the locomotives bell**. Lemon noticed and object on the No.2 track to the right of him. Then he looked back to check on the pot behind him. After this, he looked ahead and then looked back at No.2 slag pot car to see if was ready to come out. He was looking ahead as he crossed a switch then he felt a jar like the locomotive had derailed. Lemon got off the train and Ramon Ruiz told him there was a man under the locomotive. Aguilar was caught between the first and second drive wheels and already dead. The men jacked up the locomotive and removed the body. It appeared that Aguilar had tried to jump on the *"bumper"* of the locomotive and had fallen onto the rails. Aguilar was 25 years-old and from Sonora, Mexico.

"Cochise County Coroner's Inquest No. 161" Arizona State Archives
"Smelter Man Killed" Bisbee Daily Review 4 October 1903 page5

The train used to haul slag away from the smelter c-1890

October 14(?), 1903 Copper Queen Smelter
Geronimo Germen broke his leg when it was run over by a slag pot. (slag pot car)He was expected to remain in the hospital several weeks.

"Broke his Leg" Bisbee Daily Review 15 October 1903 page 5

October 16, 1903, Copper Queen Smelter
Pedro Barrola was hit by a bar of copper bullion. The bar was being rolled over by another employee and it hit Barrola. His shin was broken. It was expected to be off work several weeks. The copper bars were being loaded on rail cars for shipment.

"Broke his Leg" Bisbee Daily Review 17 October 1903 page 4

October 25, 1903, Copper Queen Smelter
Garrett Moore dropped a flue on his fingers. He was treated by Dr. Dysart.

"Flue Dropped on His Fingers" Bisbee Daily Review 27 October 1903 page 1

December 4, 1903, Copper Queen Smelter
B. Medigovich had hot slag land on his foot. He was reported as recovering.

129

"Untitled" <u>Bisbee Daily Review</u> 6 December 1903 page 8

December 14, 1903, Copper Queen Smelter
Charles Strong was turning a car (mine car or a small slag car) on a turnsheet. He slipped and struck his neck against the edge of the car. He was expected to be off work two days.
"Injured in Mine" <u>Bisbee Daily Review</u> 15 December 1903 page 5

February 26, 1904, Copper Queen Smelter
John Jory was holding a hand steel and his partner was swinging a double jack (sledge hammer) in a converter. His partner missed and struck him in the groin with the hammer. Jory was taken to the hospital.
"Injured at Smelter" <u>Bisbee Daily Review</u> 27 February 1904 page5

March 2, 1904, Copper Queen Smelter
Oscar Anderson was struck on the head. He received a two inch cut that needed stitches.
"Injured at Smelter" <u>Bisbee Daily Review</u> 3 March 1904 page 5

March 3, 1904, Copper Queen Smelter
J.A. Welch cut the palm of his hand.
"Injured at Smelter" <u>Bisbee Daily Review</u> 4 March 1904 page 5

March 5, 1904, Copper Queen Smelter
James McCoy was burned by a piece of slag.
"Accident at Smelter" <u>Bisbee Daily Review</u> 5 March 1904 page 5

March 26, 1904, Copper Queen Smelter
V. Rodule had a large rock roll over his foot. Dr. Dysart the staff surgeon dressed his wound. He was expected to be unable to walk for a few days.
"Smelter Employee Injured" <u>Bisbee Daily Review</u> 27 March1904 page 5

The Cuprite Mine c-1930

Cuprite Mine

In late August- September 1905, sinking began on the shaft under contract with Pete Moon. During March 1906, the shaft was 460ft. deep and a crosscut was being driven towards the Uncle Sam Claim. A drift on the 200 level was driven to connect with the 800 level of the Shattuck mine on June 6, 1907. In 1921, it was proposed that the Cuprite Shaft be deepened first by raising up from the 400 level of the Czar Mine to the bottom of the shaft at the 300 level. The Cuprite Shaft was retimbered to the 300 level and then was finally sunk to the 600 level. In 1942, the hoist from the Briggs Mine was installed at the Cuprite for mining under contract. During World War II, a group of African-American soldier-miners worked for a short time in the Cuprite Mine. At the end of its operational life, the shaft was 912 ft. deep and had two compartments until the 400 level. From the 400 level to the bottom of the shaft it was enlarged to two and one half compartments.

April 16, 1907, Cuprite Mine

At about 3:30 pm, Dave Nichols was going off shift at the Cuprite. He was hoisted to the surface with the other men. Three men left the cage immediately and headed to the change house. Nichols walked about four feet from the collar of the shaft and paused as he began to talk to a friend. A hoistman lifted the cage a couple of feet so a timber could be placed across the shaft. The cage was then to be lowered onto the timber and it would rest on the timber until the shaft needed to be used again*. This was in case, there were problems with the hoist; the cage would not fall down the shaft. As the hoistman raised the cage and the hoist jarred and a timber holding the sheave wheel being used broke and fell. The sheave wheel fell and struck Nichols on the head fracturing his skull. A timber fell and knocked Steve Ennohute to the ground. Within, a few minutes Nichols died from his injuries.

* The Cuprite shaft was only used during day shift. Blocking up a cage would normally only be done if the cage was going to be left unused for an extended period of time.
"Miner is Killed at Cuprite Shaft." Bisbee Daily Review 17 April 1907 page 5
"Cochise County Inquest No. 443" Arizona State Archives Phoenix

October 10, 1924, Cuprite Mine

"Curly" John Edward Woodbury and *"Pete"* Charles Atkins were driving two headings at the same time. In 106-9 crosscut the shift boss had told them there was a missed hole. Woodbury found a hole with a double fuse sticking out of it and gently pulled it free. There was no blasting cap on the fuse, and he spent time investigating the hole and determined it was not a missed hole. After Atkins had the drift mucked out they decided that there was not enough room to install the next set of timber, but the only need a couple of more inches. They decided to break out the area with a pick and a double jack. Woodbury struck the area a couple times with a pick and an undiscovered missed hole detonated. Mortally wounded Atkins walked out of the drift and found C.E Thatcher and said, *"Oh, I am hurt bad."* He fell and was caught by Thatcher. Woodbury shouted at that time *"Come and get me; I am bleeding to death and can't see anything."* Thatcher laid Atkins down in a wide section of the drift and ran into George Parrish and told him to get the foreman, while he went to help Woodbury. Atkins died at the hospital from internal injuries caused by chest punctures on October 11 and Woodbury survived the accident. Rebecca Atkins had her 34-year-old husband buried in Wilburton, Oklahoma.

"Cochise County Coroner's Inquest No. 1577" Arizona State Archives Phoenix
"Original Certificate of Death." Arizona Department of Health Services. "Original Certificate of Death." Arizona Department of Health Services. http://genealogy.az.gov/azdeath/009/10091068.pdf (July 22, 2011)

Czar Shaft (Copper Queen)   BISBEE, Arizona.

Czar Mine c-1906

Czar Mine

In the 1884, annual report of the Copper Queen Consolidated Mining Company Ben Williams urged the development of a new hoisting shaft on the Copper Czar Claim. Sinking began on the Copper Czar Shaft in 1885. This shaft was to replace the inadequate Copper Queen Incline shaft. Soon the name was shortened to simply the Czar Shaft. In 1886, due to low copper prices the Copper Queen Consolidated Mining Company, began constructed a smelter next to the Czar Shaft. The tall enclosed headframe was quickly hidden among a myriad of mine buildings. Until 1910, exploration for new ore was focus on going deeper. Interest began to develop in examining Queen Hill. Raises were driven and converted into interior shafts and began to mine ores inside Queen Hill above the collar elevation of the Czar Shaft. Although, these shafts were originally part of the Czar Mine, by 1914 they were considered as the Southwest Mine and no longer part of the Czar.

During the 1920s, both the Southwest and Czar mines were used as a mining school. The men were taught basics skills, such as terminology, finding their way around and learning jobs. These mines were both active, producing mines at the time. After the men were proficient, many were transferred to other mines, but some did remain in the Czar-Southwest. Reserves were dwindling and the mine worked off and on until August 1930, when it was shut down.

In 1932, it reopened for lessees. Leases had been granted on sections of the Czar, since at least 1911. The early lessees worked alongside Copper Queen/Phelps Dodge miners working areas containing small or difficult to mine ore. After 1932 the Czar was mined exclusively by lease until 1942. During this year the Czar 300-400 levels were opened for exploration by Phelps Dodge. In 1944 all leases were canceled and mining ceased. The remainder of the year was spent salvaging trolley wire, rail, pipe and fittings. Although, not actively mining the shaft was maintained until the late 1940s or possibly early 1950s. This shaft had three and one half compartments and was 441 ft. deep.

November 1, 1888, Czar Mine

Cima Martino and Mike Greeley were cleaning up ore on the 200 level to make room for timber. Greeley walked up to the face of the drift with a pick to clear out an area when it caved-in. The falling rock covered Greeley's legs and Cima. Alack Aridano* was pushing a mine car by the area and Greeley called to him. Soon Greeley was rescued and the body of Martino was uncovered. Martino was 29 years old and Italian.

*Writing is very faint on document this could easily be misspelled
No title The Arizona Silver Belt 10 November 1888 page 1
"Cochise County Coroner's Inquest No. 57" Arizona State Archives Phoenix

January 18, 1890, Czar Mine*

A miner with the surname of Hall was being lowered on a cage arriving at a 200 level station he stepped off before the cage stopped. Realizing his mistake he tried to get back on the cage. His leg was caught between the cage and the shaft timber and he fell the shaft onto the descending cage. The leg was almost torn completely off. The leg was later amputated below the knee. * There is a slight possibility this accident occurred in the Holbrook Mine

"Territorial News" Arizona Weekly Citizen 18, 1890 January page 3
"Wholesale Accidents" Arizona Weekly Citizen 25, 1890 January page 4

December 14, 1896, Czar Mine

Domincio Romero was digging with a group of men into the waste dump, below the Czar Mine headframe. Foreman, Manuel Aguirre told the men to gather their tools and get out of the area, because it was undercut. When Romero didn't move, he called to Romero, and he said he was cold, and he wanted to shovel a while to warm up. The dump collapse and buried him up against the rails to the waste dump* Romero died on December 17th from internal injuries. * The photographs from the period indicate that it may have been the tracks from the smelter to the slag dump. These rails went below and in front of the Czar Headframe and were next to a steep section of dump that had been cut away.

"Cochise County Coroner's Inquest No. 326" Arizona State Archives Phoenix

June 24, 1902 Czar Mine

A Mexican miner working in the rock quarry above the Czar noticed smoke coming from the rope house. He alerted Charles Moore and Billy Hankins. They tried to fight the fire but the water pressure from the reserve tanks was not great enough for the water to reach the top of the building. A chemical fire engine was called. Several cans of pine tar began exploding, spraying burning tar. The change room ignited as well as a railway trestle. At this the firefighting efforts focused on preventing the hoist house and headframe from burning. Superintendent Walter Douglas held the nozzle of a fire hose and worked in the most dangerous areas with other men. He was recognized as one of the hardest working men fighting the fire. 200 ft. of track, part of the trestle, the rope hose and changeroom were destroyed. The company losses were estimated at $2,000.00 and the employees lost around $3,000.00 in personal possessions in the change room. B. Macphun had left the rope house a few minutes before the fire suspected that there could have been three reasons for the fire, small children smoking, a spark from a locomotive hauling slag, or the actions of a disgruntled miner.

"Fire Destroys Property Near Czar Shaft" <u>Bisbee Daily Review</u> 25 June 1902 page 1

August 23, 1902, Czar Mine

Robert Hansen and his partner W.A. Richards were working on the 200 level in the Southwest Country at the Clay raise. They were installing a grizzly about six and a half sets up (45 ft.) Richards had hoisted up a grizzly timber* and Hansen was placing it when he slipped and fell head first down the raise. Richards called down the raise and heard no response. He went to #27 stope on the 200 level and gather helped Robert Kneale was lowered down the raise and discovered Hansen was dead. The miners removed the chute lining and pulled Hansen's body out into the manway. Hansen had come from Colorado a few weeks before although, he had worked at the Lowell Mine in Bisbee sometime earlier. He was survived by a father in Salt Lake City. * Early grizzlies were made of timber and not rail.

"Plunged to His Death" <u>Bisbee Daily Review</u> 24 August 1902 page 1
"Cochise County Coroner's Inquest No. 84" Arizona State Archives Phoenix

January 19, 1903, Czar Mine

E.P Leyley, a miner working under foreman Jack Taylor had a narrow escape around noon when he was hit in the scalp by a falling rock. He was taken to the companies' physician's office. The injury required a few stitches.

"Miner Hurt" <u>Bisbee Daily Review</u> 20 January 1903 page 8

August 2, 1903, Czar Mine near 100 level

L.M. Strumm, a 16-year-old tool nipper was on the 200 level at a raise that had been fitted to serve as an interior shaft. He told the Tommy Woods, the hoistman that he wanted to take his tool car up to the 100 level. The hoistman stated that Strumm told him to go to the top of shaft. At 9:30 am, the cage slowed down as it passed the hundred level young man reached out to lift the landing chairs, but the cage continued up and Strumm, head struck the shaft timber. His scalp was peeled from his head and was left hanging over his face. The young man's nose was broken, and part of the bone was taken off. His eyes were also injured. Immediately, Strumm signaled the hoistman with the shaft bell to lower the cage to the 200 level. He was taken to the Copper Queen Hospital and his parents were notified. Miners told the newspaper that they had warned Strumm that he was taking too many chances and was reckless of the dangers underground. In January of 1906, the Copper Queen Consolidated Mining Company sent L.M. Strumm to New York to receive treatment for his eyes. After the accident, the happiness of the L.M. Strumm family declined. On a few days later the on August 11, L.M. Strumm's father Albert W. Strumm was arrested for discharging a firearm in city limits. On August 9th at 10:00 pm. A.W. Strumm fired five shots from his pistol in front of the Strumm restaurant on O.K. Street. He was discovered still holding the smoking pistol. He stated that he fired the shots in the air to scare off Mrs.

Strumm who was attacking him with a butcher knife. He was reported to be drunk at the time. Mr. Strumm, who had lived many years in Bisbee as a miner had a reputation for being a peaceful, quiet man, and this was felt to have influenced the legal proceedings, and he was only fined $10.00. The decline continued and on April 7, 1905, his parents Augusta and Albert W. Strumm filed for divorce. Albert was served the divorce papers when he traveled back from Cananea, Mexico where he was employed. The divorce must have been a difficult one as the newspaper announced that on May 19, 1905, a *"Restraining order as prayed for had been issued."* The divorce was finalized in November 3, 1905.

"Tool Nipper Strumm is Terribly Injured" <u>Bisbee Daily Review</u> 2 August 1903 page 8
"Strumm on Warpath" <u>Bisbee Daily Review</u> 11 August 1903 page 4
"Actions Brought for District Court" <u>Bisbee Daily Review</u> 8 April 1905 page 1
"Short Personal Notes" <u>Bisbee Daily Review</u> 13 April 1905 page 8
"Court Proceedings" <u>Bisbee Daily Review</u> 19 May 1905 page 3
"Didn't Make a Case" <u>Bisbee Daily Review</u> 3 November 1905 page 1
"Sent by Copper Queen" <u>Bisbee Daily Review</u> 24 January 1906 page 2

January 3, 1904, Czar Mine

Chas. Kinney was injured on the 300 level. A rock fell from a stope and struck him on the foot. The injury was not serious.

"Slight Accidents" <u>Bisbee Daily Review</u> 5 January 1904 page 5

March 13, 1905, Czar Mine

Theodore D. Burdick slipped and fell 20 ft. in the Southwest Stope on the 200 level. His back was broken and was initially questioned whether he would live. He remained at the Copper Queen Hospital for nearly two years and was released painfully crippled and weak for the rest of his life. Theodore was a man of many careers. He had graduated college and had worked as a pharmacist and doctor in Michigan, before taking a joining a theatrical group and taking it and a couple of others on tour. Later he returned to his medical profession and became a doctor in Albuquerque, New Mexico. From New Mexico, he came to Bisbee and became a miner for a time. Burdick left the mines for a time to run a saloon, before returning to the mines. It was soon after this second time in the mines, he was injured. After his fall and while he was still in the hospital, Burdick was nominated by the Republican Party as their candidate for Justice of the Peace. He won the 1906, election by a substantial margin and became a Justice of the Peace on January 1, 1907. The crippled miner became a successful, Justice of the Peace winning both the 1908 and 1911 elections and becoming more commonly known as Judge Burdick. Most of his cases were minor robberies, disturbing the peace, saloon fights, vagrancy and marriages. Such as when he fined "Trixy" Fawcett a lady of the red-light district $15.00 for drunkenness. Some of his cases drew the public spotlight, like the "famous" chicken coop case where two parties spent $300 fighting months over the possession of a $13.00 chicken coop. He was also the first Justice to try a deaf and mute person in the district. The young Mexican man was arrested for disturbing the peace and was found guilty and sentenced to seven days in jail. Police officers and lawyers attempted to tell the young man about his sentence, but the man was also illiterate. They gave up. Justice Burdick was able to use hand signs to inform the man of his sentence. In *"one of the strangest cases in the history of the district"* accused thief I.B. Calhoun skipped bail and bought a train ticket to El Paso rather than face Justice Theodore Burdick's court Calhoun was working on the 500 level of the Spray mine in a stope with jigger boss J.T. McCorkle. The boss had $55.00 in his overall pocket. As the stope was warm, McCorkle removed his overalls and set them near Calhoun. Later, he went down to the 600 level to work and returned to pick up his overalls as he went up to the surface. On the change house, he discovered the money was missing. Returning underground, McCorkle accused Calhoun of stealing the money. Calhoun denied this, so McCorkle decided to see a shift boss about the matter and ordered Calhoun to take a cage to the surface with him. While on the cage Calhoun took off a shoe to remove a *"nail."* In the process of aggressively removing the shoe he knocked other men around on the cage, some who nearly were thrown into the shaft. At this time, it was believed he kicked the money down the shaft. Although, no money was found on Calhoun he was arrested on $250.00 bond and ordered to appear before Judge Burdick two days later. While out on bond he purchased his train ticket and eventually forfeited his bond. Judge Burdick died on January 3, 1913, and was survived by his mother and brother Clinton A. Burdick of Douglas, Arizona.

"Perhaps Fatally Injured" Bisbee Daily Review 14 March 1905 page 1

"Personal Mention" Bisbee Daily Review 16 March 1905 page 5

"Shropshire Reelected" Bisbee Daily Review 9 November 1906 page 1

"New Officers will Begin Work" Bisbee Daily Review 2 January 1907 page 2

"Miner Arrested on Larceny Charge" Bisbee Daily Review 18 June 1907 page 1

"Accused Miner Will Forfeit His Bail" Bisbee Daily Review 20 June 1907 page 5

"Did Not Appear in Court" Bisbee Daily Review 21 June 1907 page 5

"Deaf and Dumb, yet Disturbs the Peace" Bisbee Daily Review 6 December 1907 page 8

"Trixy Fined $15" Bisbee Daily Review 6 December 1907 page 7

"Bartender is Under Arrest for Assault" Bisbee Daily Review 31 January 1908 page 5

"Own Troubles Took up Time of Witnesses" Bisbee Daily Review 5 February 1908 page 5

"Jury Frees Wilson of Assault Charge" Bisbee Daily Review 12 February 1908 page 8

"Chicken Coop Case goes to District Court" Bisbee Daily Review 10 July 1908 page 5

"Hen Coop Case near End" Bisbee Daily Review 29 November 1908 page 7

"Judge Burdick Passes Away" Bisbee Daily Review 4 January 1913 page 2

The headstone of Theodore Burdick.

September 15 1905, Czar Mine

German, Hugo Krahn* a carman at the Czar, was loading a mine car at a chute. It appears the muck became hung up in the chute, and Krahn was using a bar to free up the rock. Muck fell, and the bar was shot back at him. The bar struck him on the side of the head. He was found on the ground and was taken to the Copper Queen Hospital. Originally, it was thought his wounds were not serious, but at 9:00 that evening his injuries proved fatal. A letter was found in the deceased pocket by Walter Hubbard, the undertaker. This letter was given to Mrs. Jack Breeding, who translated the document, which revealed that Krahn was the son of a member of the staff of German Emperor Wilhelm II. The young man was 24 years old and buried in Evergreen Cemetery. (No coroner's inquest could be located)

*Listed as Frank Krahn and Frank Kahn in the Bisbee Daily Review articles
"Fred Kahn Killed in Mysterious Manner" Bisbee Daily Review 16 September 1905 page 5
"Of Kaiser Wilhelm's Staff" Bisbee Daily Review 17 September 1905 page 1
"Bisbee-Lowell Evergreen Cemetery." My Cochise.
http://www.mycochise.com/cembisbeek.php (March 29, 2011)

The funeral monument for Hugo Krahn.

April 9, 1906, Czar Mine

German Miner, William Grossklaus, Harry Palmer and George McMillan were getting ready to leave 100 level when sets of timber underneath them gave way. Grossklaus and Palmer fell while McMillan was able to hang onto a rail. Palmer was lifted out with a rope Grossklaus was still alive but buried. Rescuing miners covered his unburied face with lagging to protect him. Then a second cave-in occurred. This one killed him. His head was crushed, and several bones were broken. Miners were able to recover his body in about two hours by mining from underneath him. The deceased was a recent widower and had quit the Lowell Mine since he could not get work on Sundays and he needed the money. According to the Bisbee Daily Review, Three days before he was killed Grossklaus had a premonition of his death and mentioned it to several people in the town including Palmer and McMillan. He was survived by his children Albert William Grossklaus and Elizabeth Rose Grossklaus, a brother-in-law A.T. Rose in Bisbee, Two sisters in New York and a brother in Custer City, South Dakota. His parents were still living and in Germany at the time. His children were living in Valley Hills, Bosque County, Texas.

"Miner is Killed" Bisbee Daily Review 10 April 1906 page 6
"He Had a Warning" Bisbee Daily Review 12 April 1906 page 5
"In the Probate Court of the County of Cochise Territory of Arizona" Bisbee Daily Review 23 December 1909 page 6
"Cochise County Inquest No. 335" Arizona State Archives Phoenix

June 14, 1906, Czar Mine

While gobbing, Joe De Souza hit his foot with a pick. He was expected to be off work a few days.

"Young Joe De Souza Drove Pick in Foot" Bisbee Daily Review 15 June 1906 page 3

September 17, 1906, Czar Mine

Richard Cayberry had his leg broken while being hoisted to the surface at the Czar Shaft.

"Getting Better" Bisbee Daily Review 19 September 1906 page 3

November 2, 1906, Czar Mine

Victor Clawson was working on the 100 level* when a section of the roof (back) collapsed and a rock impacted his left foot. He was taken to the Copper Queen Hospital, where the doctors felt it was likely that part of the foot would need to be amputated.

"Hurt in Mine" Bisbee Daily Review 3 November1906 page 8

*Newspaper had misprint stating the 1000 level

November 9, 1906, Czar Mine

Albert Close was working in a drift on the 300 level when the back (roof) fell pinning to the ground. After he was uncovered, he again was knocked to the ground by a subsequent cave-in. He was taken to the Copper Queen Hospital where it was determined he had received a Colles' fracture on the right wrist. He was expected to be able to use his arm in three weeks.

"Has Arm Broken" Bisbee Daily Review 10 November 1906 page 7

November 14, 1906, Czar Mine

A half hour after starting his first shift underground, a mysterious individual named either William Newton or E. Ruegg was working with C.H. Lee cleaning track on the 200 level towards the Holbrook Mine. They were taking a second mine car filled with rock to dump and the door on the mine car stuck. Lee told Newton to watch out for a hole (raise). Newton said *"hole!"* and fell into it the raise. He fell 100 feet to the next level. Lee called for him but, received no answer. The name he gave for employment was William Newton, but he had the initials E.R. tattooed on his arm. A notebook in his pocket contained a message that *"in case of injury, please notify my parents, No.530 West Hoboken N.J. Mrs. Amelie Ruegg."* His actual name was not determined, but his body was shipped to Mrs. Ruegg for burial in New Jersey. This man was a newcomer to Bisbee had been in town only a few days.

"Falls to Death First Shift in Mine" Bisbee Daily Review 15 November 1906 page 8
"Will Ship Body" Bisbee Daily Review 16 November 1906 page 7
"Cochise County Coroner's Inquest No. 379" Arizona State Archives Phoenix

December 14, 1906 Czar Mine

Shift Boss, Edward N. Ruff was in a drift on a lower level, when the ground caved above him. It threw him face down on the ground, and the rock covered his legs. He was taken to the Copper Queen Hospital. An examination revealed that no bones were broken, but his legs were bruised.

"Is Slightly Injured" Bisbee Daily Review 15 December 1906 page 7

April 27, 1907, Czar Mine

Eighteen-year-old, newlywed, D' Arcy Trezise better known as "Jack" Trezise was injured at 8:30 pm on the 200 level. He had been working about an hour when he bent over using his pick and detonated a partially unexploded hole. The blast hurled him back knocking him unconscious. He received a severe cut on the right side of his face and lost his right eye. His right side and leg were bruised. Miners near him rushed him to the surface where he regained consciousness and was taken to the Copper Queen Hospital. At the hospital, he was cared for by Dr. Shine and Dr. Wall. After 43 days, Trezise was released on June 8 from the hospital. Trezise had been married to Miss Mabel Jeffries on April 13, 1907, just over two weeks prior. Mabel divorced him and married Albert Harris on March 21, 1908. Her new husband, Albert Harris was killed in a cave-in in the Gardner just over a year later on May 5, 1908. On May 12, 1909, D'Arcy gave a demonstration of his boxing skills, punching a bag with elaborate moves at the Y.M.C.A. open house. He had practiced this after his mine accident. (Last name was spelled both Trezias and Trezise in the paper.)

"Narrow Escape for Young Man at Czar Shaft." Bisbee Daily Review 28 April 1907 page 5
"Trezise-Jeffries" Bisbee Daily Review 14 April 1907 page 5
"Caught by Cave-In a Miner is Killed" Bisbee Daily Review 6 May 1908 page 1
"Funeral services Sunday" Bisbee Daily Review 8 May 1908 page 5
Copper Queen Hospital Patients Register Jan 1, 1907 – Jun 30, 1908, Bisbee Mining and Historical Museum, Bisbee.
"Married Saturday" Bisbee Daily Review 24 March 1908 page 7
"Pleased Crowd See Exhibit" Bisbee Daily Review 14 May 1909 page 5

July 6, 1907, Czar Mine

Miner, G.H. McCorken was struck in the shoulder by a timber. He was expected to be off work a few days.

"Is Struck by Timber" Bisbee Daily Review 9 July 1907 page 7

July 24, 1907, Czar Mine

W.F. Lemma was using a small air compressed drill (plugger?) on a lower level of the Czar Shaft when it slipped and tore of the first joint of his fingers and cut up his hand.

"Meets with Slight Accident" Bisbee Daily Review 25 July 1907 page 7

March 4, 1908, Czar Mine

Around 12:15, Sam Goodenstein was climbing down a manway between the 200 and 300 levels. He accidently stepped off a ladder and fell into the opening. Ed Hottopp was working in the manway turned and saw him fall past. Joe Costello and Thomas Cook climbed down the manway and found him on a lagging one set above the 300 level. Mr. Goodenstein fell 90-feet. He was taken to the surface and rushed him to the hospital. On arrival, his injuries appeared to be a broken jaw and a bruised shoulder. Goodenstein was still alive at the hospital, but the doctors had little hope. The 19-year-old miner died on March 5, 1908. His father Max Goodenstein lived in Dubacher Canyon.

"Falls 100 Feet Down Manway Fatally Hurt" Bisbee Daily Review 4 March 1908 page 1
"Goodenstein Funeral Today" Bisbee Daily Review 6 March 1908 page 7
Copper Queen Hospital Patients Register Jan 1, 1907 – Jun 30, 1908, Bisbee Mining and Historical Museum, Bisbee.
"Cochise County Inquest No. 539" Arizona State Archives Phoenix

March 12, 1908, Czar Mine

A.M. Richmond survived a close call. Around 12:00 pm. Richmond was working at the bottom of a manway when an ax fell close to seventy feet down the manway and struck him on the head. He was taken by ambulance to the Copper Queen Hospital. It was determined that his skull had a compound fractured. As of March 14, he was recovering well in the hospital. Finally, he was released from the hospital on March 25, 1908. (Note, Richmond is believed to have been a friend of Roy Gardner who was injured in the Lowell mine on March 26, 1908)
"Miner at Czar has Close Call" Bisbee Daily Review 13 March 1908 page 5
"Resting Well" Bisbee Daily Review 14 March 1908 page 7
Copper Queen Hospital Patients Register Jan, 1 1907 – Jun 30, 1908, Bisbee Mining and Historical Museum, Bisbee.

April 18, 1908 Czar Mine

Ed Pervins, a pipe repairman, was working on a cage when he was caught in the waist and crushed. Originally, it was believed the injuries would be fatal. By 9:00 that evening, it was determined he would recover. He was initially released from the hospital on April 25, 1908. On May 15, 1908, an operation was performed to mend his severed abdominal muscles. He had a wife, K. Pervins and two children and was a member of the Salvation Army Band. Pervins survived the accident.
"Ed Pervins Hurt" Bisbee Daily Review 19 April 1908 page 5
"Operation Performed" Bisbee Daily Review 16 May 1908 page 7
Copper Queen Hospital Patients Register Jan 1, 1907 – Jun 30, 1908, Bisbee Mining and Historical Museum, Bisbee.

July 17, 1908, Czar Mine

Robert H. "Bob" Campbell, a native of Goldenville, Guysboro, Nova Scotia and a former shift boss at the Shattuck Mine was crushed and killed by a boulder. Campbell, a timberman, was with a shift boss named Rogers. Rogers was making his first visit to the "Southwest Drift" stopes. They began climbing down a manway into a stope with Campbell in the lead; When Campbell looked down into the stope and called *"How is she looking?"* Suddenly, a boulder around 500 lbs. fell and smashed Campbell's head beyond recognition. Even though, he had already died the miners took him to the Copper Queen Hospital. He was 31 years old and had married Miss Josie Metz (Mrs. Campbell) His wife was devastated by the death of her husband and had to be cared for by Mrs. James Wood of Douglas, Arizona. Robert Campbell's brother James had been killed when he drilled into a misfire at the Pittsburg & Hecla Shaft on September 6, 1903. He was survived by two sisters, Sadie Campbell of Bangor Maine, Mrs. Albert Weber, two brothers, John Campbell and William Campbell of British Columbia. Also, his surviving cousins were Stewart Grant and Robert Grant of Bisbee, A.F. Grant of Lowell, Arizona and Mrs. John A. McKinnon of San Francisco. He was buried in Evergreen Cemetery next to his brother James.
"R.H. Campbell Popular Miner Killed by Rock" Bisbee Daily Review 18 July 1908 page 5
"One Miner Killed and Two Injured by Powder Explosion" Bisbee Daily Review 8 September 1903 page 4

Grave stones of James and Robert Campbell at Evergreen Cemetery.
The Junction mine is in the background. C-1908
(Courtesy of the Bisbee Mining & Historical Museum)

September-October 1909, Czar Mine
A large boulder began moving, and Edward Maddern stepped out of its way and was slightly struck on the side. He then jumped out of the boulders way. Maddern was only bruised.
"Miner Suffers Narrow Escape" <u>Bisbee Daily Review</u> 2 October 1909 page 8

October 8, 1909, Czar Mine
At 1:00 am. S. L. Brown and James Critchley Jr. were working at 51-3 chute on the 400 level.* The chute was hung up and they needed to free it. These men were working in the manway, and the muck broke through from the chute, injuring Brown and suffocating, Critchley. Elmer Hall, who was running, the locomotive on the level had pulled mine cars from a chute, but had stopped after it had hung up. When they heard the chute beginning to run, he headed back there to load cars and discovered the accident. His father James Critchley Sr. was at the Spray Shaft,* when the accident occurred. He arrived at the Czar and saw the "mangled" remains of his son brought to the surface. James Jr. was one of twelve children of the Critchley family. * Inquest indicates he may have been working in the Czar Mine also.
*The newspaper article states they were working between the 300 and 400 levels. Since the accident included locomotives, it must have occurred on a haulage level. The haulage levels in the Czar mine were the 200 and 400 levels
"James Critchley is Killed at Czar" <u>Bisbee Daily Review</u> 8 October 1909 page 8

"Unavoidable Accident Verdict of Jury" Bisbee Daily Review 8 October 1909 page 8
"Cochise County Coroner's Inquest No. 692" Arizona State Archives Phoenix

October 13, 1909, Czar Mine

Author, Lew Wilson sought employment in the Bisbee mines to help him write a series of magazine articles about working in mines. He was working on the 400 level at the same area James Critchley Jr. had been killed five days earlier. The ladder he was climbing gave way. Wilson fell 30 ft. and broke two ribs from hitting the timber as he fell. A trap door that had been shut in the manway prevented him from falling the full 100 ft. Before becoming a miner, Wilson was reported to have worked as a playwright, author, actor, and composer and telegraph operator. While recovering he worked at Western Union office, filling in for a vacationing telegraph operator.

"Wilson Has Narrow Escape from Death" Bisbee Daily Review 14 October 1909 page 2
"On His Old Job" Bisbee Daily Review 17 October 1909 page 7

March 13, 1910, Czar Mine

"Cousin Jack," T. H. Hocking and Frank Campbell, a Canadian were assigned to restart up a working in the *"Southwest Country"*. Unknown to the men, there was a misfire that had been left by the previous miners about 18 months before. While picking at soft ground, one of the miners struck the misfire. The force of the blast peppered their faces with small rocks and dirt. There was concern that Hocking would lose his eyesight. Hocking's wife was living in Cornwall, England at the time of the accident.

"Hocking may Lose Sight from Blast" Bisbee Daily Review 15 March 1910 page 8
"Remedy Suggested For the "Missed Hole" Tragedies" Bisbee Daily Review 20 March 1910 page 10
Copper Queen Hospital Patients Register Jan, 1 1910 – Aug. 30th 1911 Bisbee Mining and Historical Museum, Bisbee.

April –May 1910, Czar Mine

Hoistman, Ruben (Rube) A. Davidson was caught by his jumper when he leaned over the gears of the Czar hoist. He began yelling, and Mr. Moon was able to rescue him before he was killed by the gears. His chest was ripped up with muscles and tendons severed. He was taken to the Copper Queen Hospital. Later, Oscar Johnson donated skin and in late May early June, Davidson received the first skin grafting operation in the Warren Mining District. On June 28, a second skin graft was performed. An unnamed young man was the donor of the skin. He was released from the hospital on August 14, 1910, after 106 days. Ruben was 50 years old and from Nova Scotia.

"Bisbee Engineer has Narrow Escape from Horrible Death" El Paso Herald 4 May 1910 page 3
"Skin Grafting for Bisbee Miner" El Paso Herald 2 June 1910 page 7
"Skin Grafting is Proving a Success" Bisbee Daily Review 29 June 1910 page 4
Copper Queen Hospital Patients Register Jan 1, 1910 – Aug. 30th 1911 Bisbee Mining and Historical Museum, Bisbee.

June 1910 Czar Mine

R.M. Irish stepped on a large nail and was treated at the Copper Queen Hospital.

"Mexican Laborer Drops Dead of Heart Failure" El Paso Herald 13 June 1910 page 7

August 30, 1910, Czar Mine

A miner from the Isle of Man named William Henry Kewley was pulling No.1 chute on the 400 level. The chute was filled with dry, but sticky muck. He had loaded a car and pulled up another car when the chute suddenly began to run. Kewley was rapidly buried by about five tons of muck and smothered. His partner, H.W. Price heard the muck fall and found Kewley buried. Price heard two groans from Kewley and noticed the chute door was open. Sadly, his wife had died six months earlier and with his death, their infant child was orphaned. He was also survived by a widowed mother.

"Miner Meets Death under Tons of Ore" Bisbee Daily Review 31 August 1910 page 8
"Death Accidental is Jury's Verdict" Bisbee Daily Review 1 September 1910 page 8
"Cochise County Coroner's Inquest No. 778" Arizona State Archives Phoenix

September 3, 1910, Czar Mine

John Gallagher* was tamping dynamite into a blast hole, when it is believed a boulder of sulfide fell striking him in the face. Harold B. Mackintosh heard rocks fall and found Gallagher holding his face with his fingers working. Substantial blood was coming from his nose and head. Mackintosh left to get help to bring him down the manway. While he was gone, Gallagher revived for a time and climbed down the manway by himself. The rescuing men found him still alive at the bottom of the ladders and took him to the surface and the Copper Queen Hospital. Gallagher told the men that the machine bar had fallen and hit him in the face. This did not happen since, the machine bar was still mounted, and a loading stick was still in a partially loaded blast hole. Contrary to the newspaper report the blast hole had not detonated. The rock badly fractured Gallagher's skull. Originally, it was hoped he would survive, but his condition worsened, and he died. Twenty-six-year-old Gallagher was survived by a widow and nine month-old child.* The accident explained in the newspaper is dramatically different than the one described in the inquest.

"Man Injured at Copper Queen Properties Dies" Bisbee Daily Review 6 September 1910 page 8
"Original Certificate of Death." Arizona Department of Health Services. http://genealogy.az.gov/azdeath/009/10091068.pdf (July 22, 2011)
"Cochise County Coroner's Inquest No. 779" Arizona State Archives Phoenix

October 11, 1910, Czar Mine

English Miner, J. Weber was hit in the back by a falling timber. He was taken to the Copper Queen Hospital where he remained until the 18th with a bruised back.

"Injured in Mine" Bisbee Daily Review 13 October 1910 page 5
Copper Queen Hospital Patients Register Oct 11, 1910 Bisbee Mining and Historical Museum Bisbee

November 5, 1910, Czar Mine

W. McGraff was stuck by a falling boulder. His right arm suffered a compound fracture. His injuries were dressed, and he was sent home.

"Injured in Mine" Bisbee Daily Review 6 November 1910 page 5

January 4, 1911, Czar Mine

A cage gate became caught on an undetermined object while a cage with nine men was being lowered. The gate was torn off and the cage continued to descend another 50 ft. before it was stopped. John Morris was taken to the hospital with minor injuries.

"Accident at Czar Shaft." Bisbee Daily Review 4 January 1911 page 5

January 14, 1911, Czar Mine

About 3:00 pm, Mike Bello fell into a manway and injured his head and back. Remarkably, Shift Boss Smith, who weighed 200-pounds lifted 198-pound Bello's back up the manway ladders. After carrying Bello to the level, Smith was exhausted from the effort and had to be revived. Bello was Italian by birth and had been in Bisbee only eight months.

"Mike Bello is Hurt at the Czar Shaft." Bisbee Daily Review 15 January 1911 page 5
Copper Queen Hospital Patients Register Jan 1, 1910 – Aug. 30, 1911, Bisbee Mining and Historical Museum, Bisbee.

January 23, 1911, Czar Mine

Jack Greener was working at 2:00 am when a brace holding back gobbed waste rock was knocked out. Around five tons of muck fell and partly buried him. He was taken to the Copper Queen Hospital and released the same day. Confusion between this accident and the fatal accident of Santiago Ranteria at the Oliver Shaft on the same day led to the rumors that Greener had been killed.

"Miner is Killed Instantly at Oliver Shaft." Bisbee Daily Review 24 June 1911 page 8

February 18, 1911 Czar Mine

Dick Helberg, who is believed to have worked in Bisbee under the alias Frank Rinehart, was killed in an undescribed fall underground that punctured his small intestine. He was taken to the Copper Queen Hospital, where he died on February 21. The only paper found in his possession was a lapsed insurance policy made out to his brother Frank Helberg in Shellville, California. His brother Fred Helberg was contacted to pay for the burial, but he refused. Stating that he had loaned his brother money several times and had never received any back. He also noted that his brother had been in trouble a number of times. The paper felt that Dick Helberg was the *"black sheep"* of the family. Positive identification of the body was never made as the brother never came to Bisbee. (No coroner's inquest could be located)

"Body of Rinehart Still Held Here" Bisbee Daily Review 5 March 1911 page 4
"Refuses to Pay for Funeral of Brother" Bisbee Daily Review 24, February 1911 page 5
"County Will Bury Unidentified Body" Bisbee Daily Review 7 March 1911 page 8
"Original Certificate of Death" Arizona Department of Health Services http://genealogy.az.gov/azdeath/009/10092325.pdf (August 10, 2015)
Copper Queen Hospital Patients Register Feb.18, 1911 Bisbee Mining and Historical Museum Bisbee

July 17, 1911, Czar Mine

Sam Brown sprained his back in the Czar. He was taken to his home.

"Injured at Czar" Bisbee Daily Review 19 July 1911 page 8

August 15, 1911, Czar Mine
At 9 o'clock at night, George Murdock was caught in a cave-in on the 400 level. His right leg was broken and he complained of pains in the breast. It was feared he may have suffered internal injuries. He was transported to the Copper Queen Hospital where he remained 132 days.
"George Murdock is injured at Czar" Bisbee Daily Review 16 August 1911 page 1
Copper Queen Hospital Patients Register Aug 15, 1911 Bisbee Mining and Historical Museum Bisbee

October 7, 1911 Czar Mine
German, Harry Collings broke his leg in accident on a Saturday night. He was taken to the Copper Queen Hospital where it was reset. He had been in Bisbee only two months
"Leg Broken" Bisbee Daily Review 10 October 1911 page 2
Copper Queen Hospital Patients Register October 7, 1911 Bisbee Mining and Historical Museum, Bisbee.

November 8, 1911 Czar Mine
George Davis was struck in the back by a small rock, which injured his back. The injury was minor.
"Miner Injured" Bisbee Daily Review 9 November 1911 page 5

December 30, 1911 Czar Mine
Miner, Charles Tramp was caught in a cave-in. He was taken to the Copper Queen Hospital, where he died from a fractured pelvis on December 31. He was 31 years old and survived by a wife and four daughters of ages 9 and younger. (No coroner's inquest could be located)
"Miner is Injured" Bisbee Daily Review 31 December 1911 page 3
"Charles Tramp Funeral" Bisbee Daily Review 3 January 1912 page 6
"Original Certificate of Death" Arizona Department of Health Services http://genealogy.az.gov/azdeath/008/10082350.pdf (May 2, 2012)
Copper Queen Hospital Patients Register December 30, 1911 Bisbee Mining and Historical Museum, Bisbee.

April 12, 1912, Czar Mine
Italian Miner, Jerry Rolle* was injured in a cave-in. He received a cut on the head and bruises. He was treated at the Copper Queen Hospital for 16 days. His injuries were not severe.*Listed as Charles Rolly in the newspaper.
"Miner is Injured" Bisbee Daily Review 13 April 1912 page 2
Copper Queen Hospital Patients Register April 12, 1911 Bisbee Mining and Historical Museum, Bisbee.

June 17, 1912, Czar Mine
M. Cavanaugh had his arm broken when a boulder fell while he was fixing overhead lagging.
"Miner's Arm Broken" Bisbee Daily Review 18 June 1912 page 6

September 19, 1912, Czar Mine
A Spaniard named Felix Blanco was injured and taken home.
"Miner Injured" Bisbee Daily Review 20 September 1912 page 8

November 23, 1912, Czar Mine
Canadian, Simon Jacques was struck by a falling boulder. He was taken to the Copper Queen Hospital where he died from a fractured pelvis and internal injuries on December 4th. (No coroner's inquest could be located)

"Personal Mention" Bisbee Daily Review 25 November 1912 page 3
Copper Queen Hospital Patients Register November 23, 1912 Bisbee Mining and Historical Museum, Bisbee
"Original Certificate of Death." Arizona Department of Health Services. http://genealogy.az.gov/azdeath/010/10102417.pdf (July 30, 2011)

June 5, 1913, Czar Mine

Harry J. Kohlmeyer was descending on a cage. It began falling quickly and he realized it was falling uncontrolled. He grabbed onto the iron bars at the top of cage (probably the steel rods for the cage dogs) to cushion the force of the impact. This was felt to have possibly saved his life. The impact broke his scapula. Also, the cage did not fall into the sump. If the cage entered the sump it was felt Kohlmeyer would have drowned. He was at the Copper Queen Hospital seven days.

"Presence of Mind Saves Miner in Czar" Bisbee Daily Review 6 June1913 page 5
"Is Recovering" Bisbee Daily Review 12 June 1913 page 6
Copper Queen Hospital Patients Register December 5, June 1913 Bisbee Mining and Historical Museum

June 6, 1913, Czar Mine

Two miners, Albert Hodge an Australian and William T. Menear a "Cousin Jack' from Cornwall, England began working in a drift on the 200 level. They were pulling out the supporting timber to be reused. The men continued this work for most of the day. At noon, they ate lunch and at around 2:00, shift boss Cass Benton checked on the two men He left at 2:15 pm about 45 minutes before these men would head off shift. They stopped work 30 minutes before most crews because William helped gather man checks for the 200 level. This was the last time anyone saw the men alive. It is believed that between 2:15 and 3:00 pm the drift collapsed completely filling the opening from the track to the back. At 11:00 at night Mrs. Menear contacted her brother-in-law, Henry Menear a miner at the Holbrook mine to check up on her husband. He checked William's locker at the Czar Change House and discovered that his brother had not changed into his clean clothes. Henry informed the timekeeper, and it was also determined that William had not turned in his man check. Soon, the cave-in was discovered and rescue organized. Captain Hodgson, mine superintendent, took charge of the rescue. After working for one hour, the body of Albert Hodge was found. It appeared that he had suffocated as there were no broken bones. At the time, there was hope that William Menear might have been trapped alive, but after working nine hours, his body was also found. It appeared that he also had suffocated. William was 28 years old and survived by his wife, daughter, son, and brother. Albert Hodge was about 26 years old and unmarried. He had a mother and sister who were dependent on him. Although, Hodges was from Moonta, Australia, Fellow Bisbee miner, John Truscott had met him at Harteon Tower in South Queensland.

*This accident reinforced to Copper Queen Consolidated Mining Company the importance of man checks. Menear and Hodge went missing eight hours before the mining company recognized this. It was felt that part of the problem was that it was payday Friday and the crews of miners were in a rush to leave the mine. Since both of these men were considered good miners the coroner's jury had difficulty in assigning blame for the accident. Part of this was probably due to the nature of the work the men were doing, removing the supporting timber. To someone who is not familiar with underground could cause them to question the logic of this Removing timber can be done safely as the witnesses called to testify agreed. Not noticing missing man check is more problematic. Five man checks had not been turned in, and it was assumed because it was a payday Friday the men were in a hurry and had forgotten to turn in their checks.
"Two Killed under Cave in the Czar" Bisbee Daily Review 8 June 1913 page 1
"Inquest of Death of Menear and Hodge is Prolonged by Questions" Bisbee Daily Review 10 June 1913 page 1

"Inquest is Prolonged" <u>Bisbee Daily Review</u> 10 June 1913 page
"Original Certificate of Death." <u>Arizona Department of Health Services.</u> (http://genealogy.az.gov/azdeath/011/10111466.pdf (July 30,
2011)
"Original Certificate of Death." <u>Arizona Department of Health Services.</u> http://genealogy.az.gov/azdeath/011/10111464.pdf (July 30,
2011)
"Cochise County Coroner's Inquest No. 1015" Arizona State Archives Phoenix

Man checks from the Shattuck Mine.

Man Check Board from the Dallas Mine.

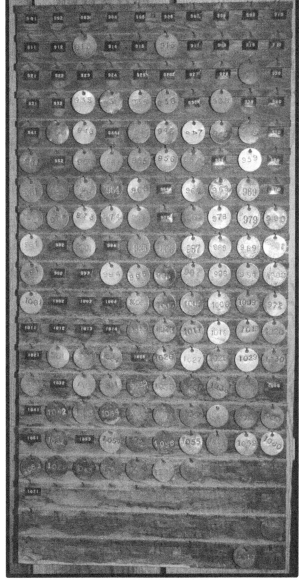

December 12, 1913, Czar Mine

A timber fell onto the ankle of Mike Keefe and sprained it. He was taken to the Copper Queen Hospital.

"Broken Ankle" <u>Bisbee Daily Review</u> 13 December page 8
Copper Queen Hospital Patients Register Dec 12, 1913, Bisbee Mining and Historical Museum Bisbee

December 18, 1913, Czar Mine

James Critchley* was pushing a mine car, when a timber fell smashing his right hand between the mine car and timber. His middle finger was amputated, and the others were badly smashed. After the accident, he went into town and found an automobile ride to the hospital. While talking to friends, he said *"It did not bother him much."* * believed to be the father of James Critchley Jr. who was killed in the Czar Mine on October 8, 1909
"Jim Critchley has the Grin" <u>Bisbee Daily Review</u> 19 December page 8

January 7, 1914 Czar Mine

Around 9:00 am, Edward A. Gidley was working in a raise about 30 feet above the 300 level. He was installing a *"Safety First"* lagging. The night shift had set up two posts and a cap, and he wanted to finish the timbering. Suddenly, a rock of about two tons fell rolled and crushed Gidley to death. Miners had to use jacks to remove the boulder from the body. After the accident, Will Gidley,* brother of the deceased and a shift boss in the Southwest mine was called. Edward Gidley had only worked as a miner for one year. He was survived by a wife and a son Edward who for a time was the leader of the orchestra at the Orpheum Theater until he took a position as an electrician for the Copper Queen Consolidated Mining Company. Gidley was also survived by his brother Will and sister Adina of Bisbee and two other brothers, one in New York and the other in Louisiana. * This may be the same Will Gidley that became the Safety inspector for the Copper Queen Consolidated Mining Company.
"Ed. Gidley Crushed to death When Boulder Fell in the Czar" <u>Bisbee Daily Review</u> 8 January 1914 page 5
"Cochise County Coroner's Inquest No. 1072" Arizona State Archives Phoenix

February 23, 1914, Czar Mine

February 1914, was not a good month for the Copper Queen Band. First, Dick Rich of the Czar Shaft and Dave Truscott of the Holbrook Mine were injured and unable to perform in a Valentine's Day Performance. Then on the 23rd, the band's leader Pat McCusker was crushed between timbers in the Czar Incline. He was taken to the Copper Queen Hospital began recovering. He was released, but later was readmitted. Around May 17, he began to be seen around the town of Bisbee. McCusker was able to resume his position as a band leader on June 20, 1914.

"McCusker Improving" <u>Bisbee Daily Review</u> 26 February 1914 page 8
"McCusker Again Out" <u>Bisbee Daily Review</u> 17 May 1914 page 8
"McCusker Comes Back" <u>Bisbee Daily Review</u> 21 June 1914 page 5
Copper Queen Hospital Patients Register Feb. 23, 1914 Bisbee Mining and Historical Museum Bisbee

Around April 1914, Czar Mine

Shift Boss, Tom Marshal had a foot badly smashed when it was run over by a mine car at a shaft station.

"Marshall Improving" <u>Bisbee Daily Review</u> 11 April 1914 page 8

July 6, 1914, Czar Mine

At 3:00 pm, George A. Love was cutting a hitch to install a timber near the ore chutes on the 400 level in the main haulage drift. While, he was working approximately a ton of broken rock fell carrying down the high voltage trolley line, a bare ½" copper wire. Love was pinned to the ground with the wire contacting his shoulder and electrocuted. He was 32 years old and survived by his wife Mrs. Marie J. Love, two small children and his mother Mary Love of Grand Rapids Michigan. George was buried in his wife's hometown of Grottoes, Virginia. Interestingly, his body was escorted from the Palace Undertakers to the Episcopal Church by both the Copper Queen Band and the Calumet and Arizona Band. He had worked for both companies during the three years he had lived in Bisbee.

*George Love was in the stope when the fatal accident of Arthur Poquette occurred on May 9, 1911, at the Oliver Shaft.

"Live Wire is Cause Death of Geo. Love" <u>Bisbee Daily Review</u> 7 July 1914 page 1
"Inquest Held over Body of George Love Yesterday Morning" <u>Bisbee Daily Review</u> 8 July 1914 page 2
"Love Internment is Awaiting Word from Mother of Deceased" <u>Bisbee Daily Review</u> 9 July 1914 page 5
"Love Funeral Sunday" <u>Bisbee Daily Review</u> 22 July 1914 page 8
"Funeral Services Held" <u>Bisbee Daily Review</u> 26 July 1914 page 6
"Original Certificate of Death." <u>Arizona Department of Health Services.</u> http://genealogy.az.gov/azdeath/012/10122118.pdf (May 15, 2012)
"Cochise County Inquest No. 1098" Arizona State Archives Phoenix

July 18, 1914, Czar Mine

George Paprika, a carman, working on the 400 level was injured when he was *"caught and squeezed"*. He was treated at the Copper Queen Hospital. (It is likely that he was either wedged between a timber and a mine car or caught between a two mine cars.)

"Carman Injured" <u>Bisbee Daily Review</u> 19 July 1914 page 6

August 21, 1914, Czar Mine

Avery Sheer was pinched between a loaded mine car and a timber. His injuries were felt to be minor, and he was expected to return to work after a day off.

"Between Timber and Car" <u>Bisbee Daily Review</u> 21 August 1914 page 6

August 26, 1914, Czar Mine

A carman, named Joe Miller broke his index finger on his left hand while dumping a mine car. When he lifted the car to dump into a chute, his finger was caught on the car, and his finger was bent towards the back of the hand. He was taken to the Copper Queen Hospital where the cut and fractured finger was treated. The Safety First man determined the accident had occurred at *"Eleven minutes of Eleven."*

"Joe Miller Breaks His Index Finger" <u>Bisbee Daily Review</u> 27 August 1914 page 3

September 3, 1914, Czar Mine

Canadian Miner, Thomas C. McBurney, was timbering on the 300 level. He was repairing a drift set that was taking weight. The set had dropped and was no longer the proper height of the drift. McBurney had removed muck from behind the back lagging of the lower end of the set and had blocked this timber. After this, he began to remove the side lagging. At this time, the back lagging slipped, and dirt rushed in and buried McBurney suffocating him. His partner, Howard Curnow was a few feet away and uninjured. Thomas was 51 years old and buried in Evergreen Cemetery. He was survived by a brother in Los Angeles and a wife (Agnes Manson McBurney ?)(This accident is an example of the mining superstition that accidents occurred in groups of three. McBurney's death in the Czar was considered the first, followed by an Irish Miner James F. Conway, who was killed in the Gardner Shaft on September 15, 1914. The third fatal accident occurred in the Cole Shaft when Andy Sterberg was killed by a falling rock on September 23, 1914)

"Berney Burried (sic) in Dirt When Lagging Slips and Opens Up" Bisbee Daily Review 5 September 1914 page 6
"Miner in Cole is Instantly Killed When Rock Drops" Bisbee Daily Review 24 September 1914 page 6
"Original Certificate of Death." Arizona Department of Health Services. http://genealogy.az.gov/azdeath/012/10122690.pdf (April 28, 2012)
"Bisbee-Lowell Evergreen Cemetery." My Cochise. http://www.mycochise.com/cembisbeem.php (April 28, 2012)
"Cochise County Coroner's Inquest No. 1108" Arizona State Archives Phoenix

September 18, 1914, Czar Mine
Shift Boss, John Cochlan broke two ribs when he was crushed between a mine car being pulled by a mule and a timber.
"Miner is Crushed in Mine Accident" El Paso Herald 18 September 1914 page 1

Around 1916, Czar Mine
Avery E. Shearer lost five teeth in an accident. He later tried to sue the Copper Queen Consolidated mining Company for $10,000. Shearer decided that he had been given bad advice in suing the mining company and settled for a job back in the mines, and the company would pay for his dental work.
"Shearer Suit" Bisbee Daily Review 12 January 1916 page 8

1917-1918 Czar Mine
Michael Sullivan had broken his shoulder at the mine. Later, he was able to return to work at the mine.
"Returns to Work" Bisbee Daily Review 15 August 1918, page 8

February 16, 1918, Czar Mine
A rock fell injuring Robert Burn's head. He was taken to the Copper Queen Hospital for treatment.
"Head Injured" Bisbee Daily Review 17 February 1918 page 8

September 16, 1918, Czar Mine
A. Bays was injured when rock fell on his right foot. He was expected to be off work a few days.
"Is Slightly Injured" Bisbee Daily Review 17 September 1918 page 6

December 7, 1918, Czar Mine
Joe Pycklick was fatally injured in a fight on the 400 level. Around 12:45 pm, Francisco Velardo, and Joe began arguing over a detail of their work. The argument became so fierce, they left the raise they were working and enter a drift that had several other men in it. Joe referred to Francisco with a term that upset him. Francisco challenged Pycklick to say it

again and he did. The Francisco struck Pycklick on the head with a short pipe that was used as a chute bar*. Francisco was arrested in the Czar Change Room and taken to the county jail. He was later found not guilty. * This pipe was likely placed over a chute door handle to give added leverage and distance from the chute.

"Quarrel Results in Fracture of Skull for Miner" Tombstone Epitaph 8 December 1918 page 1
"Alleged Slayer of Miner Freed" Bisbee Daily Review 13 February 1919 page 3

January 22, 1919, Czar Mine
A miner was barring down with shift boss, Harry L. Schofield a boulder fell and landed on a timber. The board shot up and struck Schofield in the face breaking his nose and giving him a black eye.
"Meets Peculiar Accident" Bisbee Daily Review 23 January 1919 page 6

August 14, 1919, Czar Mine
A little after 7:00 pm, new employee, Joe Romano a "one man car" (trammer?) was caught when the Rucker Slice (stope) caved in. Romano was protected under an arch of rock, and Superintendent Tollman had all available men work to get him out. Soon they were able to get an airline to him. After five hours he was rescued uninjured.
"Miner Buried under 5 Tons of Rock in Czar Shaft as Result Cave-in; Is Uninjured" Bisbee Daily Review 15 August 1919 page 1
"Southwest News" Casa Grande Valley Dispatch 29 August 1919

March 28, 1920, Czar Mine
James E. Whisand and Alex Blinman were working on the 400 level at 10:00 pm. The drift was in heavy ground, and the timber was crushing. The height of the drift had dropped 13 inches in three months from ground movement, and the trolley wire was only six feet and five inches above the track. A string of empty mine cars had been parked in the crosscut and Whisand need to walk by them. He reached a point where the space between the wall and the mine car was too tight for him to fit. He decided to crawl across the top of the mine car. While doing this, he contacted the live trolley wire and was electrocuted. He was survived by his widow, three daughter's ages seven, fourteen and a married daughter, Mrs. Hoff.
"Fall from Car Kills Worker" Bisbee Daily Review 30 March 1920 page 3
"Original Certificate of Death." Arizona Department of Health Services. http://genealogy.az.gov/azdeath/021/10211869.pdf (May 30, 2012)
Office of State Mine Inspector. *Ninth Annual Report of the State Mine Inspector State of Arizona for the Year Ending November 30, 1920.*
Dugan Mortuary Records 1920-1923 Accession 2010.10.13 Bisbee Mining and Historical Museum, Bisbee
"Cochise County Inquest No. 928" Arizona State Archives Phoenix

July 18, 1920, Czar Mine
Dell M. Dursham was loading from a chute when a boulder rolled out and struck him on the left thigh. He was treated at the Copper Queen Hospital.
"Miner Injured" Bisbee Daily Review 20 July1920 page 8

November 22, 1920, Czar Mine
Around 10:30 pm, motor swamper, R.P. Yarbrough and Scottish motorman, George Sutherland were hauling ore on the 400 level and had just dumped at the Sacramento shaft and were about 600 ft. from the Gardner shaft, when a timber holding up the trolley wire

fell. It hit Yarbrough and knocked Sutherland off the locomotive. The locomotive's light went out after the trolley wire broke and Sutherland's lamp was knocked out. Yarbrough struck a match and found that Sutherland had been crushed between the locomotive and the rib of the drift. He was critically injured and was taken to the Copper Queen Hospital, where he died.

"Original Certificate of Death." Arizona Department of Health Services. http://genealogy.az.gov/azdeath/022/10222653.pdf (May 30, 2012)

Office of State Mine Inspector. *Ninth Annual Report of the State Mine Inspector State of Arizona for the Year Ending November 30, 1920.*

"Cochise County Coroner's Inquest No. 1436" Arizona State Archives Phoenix

May 10, 1921, Czar Mine

Roy Smith was working on the 400 level and picked into a missed hole. He was cut up by the blast.

"Miner is Injured"" Bisbee Daily Review 11 May 1921 page 6

August 4, 1921, Czar Mine

A man with the surname Taylor and Dan Hearch were gassed, but survived. (They were most likely, exposed to powder smoke and not fire gasses.)

"Miners are Gassed"" Bisbee Daily Review 5 August 1921 page 5

December 16, 1921 Czar Mine

Joseph Besil and William Higgins were installing timber at the top of a chute on the 200 level. Higgins was giving tools to Besil who was above him on a platform when a boulder fell and knocked Besil into the 140 ft. raise. A hole was cut through the chute lagging and Besil's broken, and bruised body was recovered. He was survived by a widow and two children. (No coroner's inquest could be located)

"Miner is Killed at Czar Shaft." Bisbee Daily Review 17 December 1921 page 4

Office of State Mine Inspector. *Twelfth Annual Report of the State Mine Inspector State of Arizona for the Year Ending November 30, 1923.*

"Original Certificate of Death." Arizona Department of Health Services. http://genealogy.az.gov/azdeath/024/10241956.pdf (May 31, 2012)

April 5, 1922, Czar Mine

C.H. Horstmeyer had his foot struck by a boulder. He was taken to the hospital for treatment.

"Foot Injured" Bisbee Daily Review 6 April 1922 page 3

August 5, 1924, Czar Mine (Wheeler & Hargis Lease)

While working on the 100 level, a boulder fell and broke the leg of Harry C. Wheeler.

Office of State Mine Inspector. *Thirteenth Annual Report of the State Mine Inspector State of Arizona for the Year Ending November 30, 1924.*

August 14, 1952 Czar Mine

Charles William Teel was electrocuted in an undescribed accident. The mine had been shut down a few years before, but was maintained until the late 1940's. He was 27 years old and from Oklahoma. (Note, this accident is often attributed to have occurred in the Lavender Pit.)

"Original Certificate of Death." <u>Arizona Department of Health Services.</u> http://genealogy.az.gov/azdeath/0208/dc0009.pdf (July 27, 2015)

The Czar mine & Precipitation plant c-1913

Czar Precipitation Plant

Czar Precipitation Plant was planned in 1905, but completed in 1906. As rain water soaked through the broken ground of the Holbrook and Czar stopes a copper-rich mine water was created. This water was pumped to the surface. The copper water chemically reacted with the scrap iron and the iron was dissolved and copper was precipitated. ($Fe + CuSO_4$ ------ $FeSO_4 + Cu$)The mine water was slowly sent through a series of troughs filled with scrap "tin" cans. Each trough was three feet wide with two inch riffles every two and one half feet. The riffles caught denser particles much like gold dust in a sluice box. Finally, the water was sent to a precipitation tank. The resulting copper mud contained about 35% copper. Since the plant was dependent on rainfall, it operated at times intermittedly. Water from the plant was used to fill carts used sprinkle the roads to keep dust down. Bisbee welcomed a cold pre-winter day in 1908 with the precipitation plant was covered in icicles. As the day would warm up the icicles fell. Larger ones pieced the ground like spears, *"presenting quite an unusual spectacle as the bright rays of the sun shot off in all directions in a myriad of haloes."*

On August 5 1909, the plant collapsed injuring two men. The action of the copper rich water had destroyed the nails holding the plant together. Construction of a new plant was begun immediately. The new plant was finished on August 26, 1909. This time wooden pegs were used instead of nails. An unexpected effect of the precipitation plant was that it allowed for Bisbee to be a cleaner community. All scrap iron and tin cans were sold to the plant. In one city cleanup 12 tons of cans were collected and sold. This almost completely paid for the cleanup labor. During, 1912 the Czar plant was enlarged, but the following year a new precipitation plant began to be built in Lowell to replace the Czar Plant. In March 1914, the new plant was started and the Czar Plant began to be dismantled to prepare for improvements of the Czar Mine and the development of the Queen Tunnel.

August 5, 1909, Czar Precipitating Plant
The structure was beginning to move apart from an adjoining building. The copper-rich mine water had eaten away nails in the structure. Superintendent Parker Woodman decided that the plant needed to be braced. Initially, he wanted the work to begin immediately, but then decided to wait until the morning of the 6th before the crews would install the braces. Pedro Morales and another man was working on top of the plant. A

little after 12.00 pm the plant collapsed. Both men were injured, but only Morales was hospitalized. He received multiple scalp wounds and remained in the Copper Queen Hospital 23 days.

"Precipitating Plant Falls Suddenly" <u>Bisbee Daily Review</u> 6, August 1909, page 8
Copper Queen Hospital Patients Register August 5, 1909 Bisbee Mining and Historical Museum Bisbee

Dallas Mine c-2014

Dallas Mine

Sinking of this mine began on April 11, 1911 and was connected to a raise driven from the 1100 level (Lowell-Sacramento Mines.) After the connection, sinking continued towards the 1400 level and was completed to this level in 1912. 1912-1914 promising ground discovered, but no significant ore found. With the development of the Sacramento Open Pit Mine it was expected the Sacramento shaft was going to be lost to the open pit. The Dallas was developed to be the replacement of the Sacramento Shaft and become the main hoisting shaft for the Phelps Dodge Mines. During 1919, the shaft was enlarged shaft enlarged and a "subway" or an adit from the surface to the 77 ft. level was driven. Orders of mine cars and locomotives for Phelps Dodge became dependent on Dallas haulage scheme. In 1920, plans were made to mine the Lowell shaft pillar and fire zone from Dallas after abandonment of Lowell shaft. The following year the shaft was concreted from 1300 level to surface and the shaft was sunk 313ft. from 1400 level. The tunnel from conveyor to shaft completed with and skip pockets built. It was planned to continue work rapidly to complete project even though cost was 10 percent above estimates. The shaft was to be deepened to 2000 level to provide ore pockets for ore from 1800 level Sacramento Mine. During 1921, the main ore hoist from the Sacramento Mine was moved to the Dallas with the surface loading facilities. Also, 200 ft. of shaft needed sinking with 1600 & 1800 level pockets completed.

When the merger occurred between the Calumet and Arizona, the purpose of the Dallas Mine changed, it was no longer going to be needed as the main hoisting shaft. The Dallas was temporarily closed and the Campbell and Junction Mines were the only two mines to remain operational. When the Dallas reopened, many of the mines that it was intended to serve were either being mined by lessees under a small scale or like the massive block cave stopes were sending ore to the Junction Mine for hoisting. Yet in 1945, headframe was rebuilt between 1948-1950 the surface plant was rebuilt. It was planned to begin exploring the Powell and Congdon mine areas from the 900 level at this time. The Dallas continued to operate until June 1975 and hoisted ore from the Cole & Dallas Mine All remaining equipment was salvaged by Bisbee Salvage & Equipment Company in the years immediately following the closure. At the cessation of mining the Dallas shaft was completed at a depth of 2,031 ft. and four compartments. The massive 11' x 6' fourth compartment had a go devil rather than a traditional cage. Go devils do not have guides and rather bounce off the walls as they travel thru the shaft. This go devil had a reputation of a rather exciting ride.

March 1, 1913, Dallas Mine
H.B. McIntosh went down the shaft to get samples. It appeared that about 12 ft. about the 1300 level his head contacted the shaft timber, and he was killed. Initially, the hoistman reported to C.C. Finlayson that he had felt resistance on the cage and had stopped it. He was concerned that a guide was broken. Finlayson took another cage down, and when he approached the 1300 level, he found McIntosh lying dead on the bottom deck of the cage. A piece of confusing evidence was that McIntosh's candlestick was found on the top deck indicating he was riding there, but there were no signs that he was dragged to the bottom deck from the top deck. McIntosh was survived by a wife and child.
"Cochise County Coroner's Inquest No. 987" Arizona State Archives. Phoenix

November-October 1916, Dallas Mine
Harry Hellon suffered a bruised leg in an undescribed accident.
"Hellon is About" Bisbee Daily Review 5 October 1916 page 8

February 26, 1917, Dallas Mine
On the surface, a fight broke out between Barney Williams and Lee Hinkle. One man armed himself with an axe handle and the other a wrench. Soon these weapons were discarded, and the men were locked in combat. Unaware or not caring of their location the men fought themselves over the edge of the dump. Both men survived the fall, but were beat up from the descent.
"Narrow Escape" Bisbee Daily Review 27 February 1917 page 6

June 9, 1920, Dallas Mine
Paul H. McOsker was killed around 10:30 when he was hit by a cage coming to the surface. McOsker's profession was listed as an engineer. This was probably a hoisting engineer, not a mining engineer. His body was shipped to Lowell, Massachusetts. (No coroner's inquest could be located)
Dugan Mortuary Records 1918 – 1922 Accession 2010.10.12 Bisbee Mining and Historical Museum, Bisbee
"Original Certificate of Death." Arizona Department of Health Services. http://genealogy.az.gov/azdeath/022/10220496.pdf (May 30, 2012)
Office of State Mine Inspector. *Ninth Annual Report of the State Mine Inspector State of Arizona for the Year Ending November 30, 1920.*

October 13, 1921, Dallas Mine
P.J. Tucker stepped off the cage on the 1100. The cage suddenly was lowered *"virtually doubling him up like a jack-knife."* Men nearby rang the cage up and freed Tucker, who luckily, had not fallen into the shaft. He was taken to the Copper Queen Hospital where he was treated and had X-rays taken.
"One Killed Three Injured in Peculiar Series of Accidents in Bisbee District Yesterday" Bisbee Daily Review 14 October 1921 page 4

December 16, 1953, Dallas Mine
Motorman, J.L. Parten was working with Motor Swamper, Paul John Tonkyro loading mine cars at 193 raise located in 424 crosscut on the 1000 level. They were loading waste rock into a train. The chute was around a corner in the drift, and the motorman could not see Tonkyro as he was loading. Communication was done with a whistle. This was standard procedure. One whistle meant to stop, three whistles to move the train forward or backward. After the seventh car was loaded Parten was given the signal to move the train forward. He pulled the eighth car into place, but never got the stop signal. Quickly he suspected something was wrong, and he found Tonkyro crushed between a mine car and the timber. Tonkyro was killed instantly.
"Cochise County Coroner's Inquest No. 1881" Arizona State Archives. Phoenix

January 10, 1959 Dallas Mine
S.T. *"Silent Sam"* Elkins was working in 599 stope on the 1800 level when the caustic sodium hydroxide solution leaked from his Edison Miner's lamp and chemically burned him. Edison lamps often leaked and chemically burned miners. These burn could be severe. (Note, that it was likely a model P lamp, but the Cole did use the Edison R4 for a short time.)
1959-1961 safety ledger p.4

January 20, 1959 Dallas Mine
N.E. Sena dislocated his right shoulder while handling a mine car. He was working on the 1800 at 278 General chute. This was a lost time accident
1959-1961 safety ledger p.4

February 5, 1959 Dallas Mine
On the 1800 level, at 596-E stope R. Green fell from a staging and strained his left shoulder. This was a lost time accident.
1959-1961 safety ledger p.12

March 28, 1959 Dallas Mine*
C.S. Mendoza was in 463 crosscut on the 1800 level. He was bitten on right second finger by a mine rat. (Note, that mine rats had entered the mines with the introduction of mules. A large population grew and supported a few stray cats that lived deep underground, largely in the Sacramento Mine. The rats all died out during the strike of 1967. * The ledger indicates the accident was in the Cole Mine, but the Cole does not have an 1800 level, but the Dallas does. He was probably assigned to the Cole, but that day was working in the Dallas.)
1959-1961 safety ledger p.20

March? 1959 Dallas Mine
At #1 chute on the 1650 level a falling object broke the left 4th toe of A. Duarte.
1959-1961 safety ledger p.20

March 2, 1959 Dallas Mine
C.S. Chavez fell from a staging in 592-E stope on the 1800 level. He broke and
dislocated his left shoulder.
1959-1961 safety ledger p. 20

March 10, 1959 Dallas Mine
F.Q. Villa was struck by falling ground in 600 stope on the 1800 level. He suffered a
bruised left thigh
1959-1961 safety ledger p.20

February 17, 1960 Dallas Mine
B. Lee broke his left foot in 603 stope on the 1800 level. An undescribed object fell on
his foot.
1959-1961 safety ledger p.84

March 15, 1960 Dallas Mine
In 600 stope on the 1800level, J.D. Loper had a nail penetrate his boot and chipped the
bone on his right large toe.
1959-1961 safety ledger p.92

June 11, 1960 Dallas Mine
P. Marrujo was caught in caving ground in 345 crosscut on the 2000 level. He broke two
fingers, one on each hand.
1959-1961 safety ledger p.118

June 15, 1960 Dallas Mine
On the conveyor (surface) Julio M. Palomino fell on a stairway and twisted his right
ankle. (Note Julio had been badly disabled at the Battle of the Bulge as a member of the 82nd Airborne. A stair way would be
awkward for him to traverse. He later was a tour guide at the Queen Mine Tour)
1959-1961 safety ledger p.118

August 18, 1960 Dallas Mine
J.A. McMillan was drilling in 6 crosscut on the 1550 level. A flying object struck him in
the mouth. His dentures were broken and his upper lip was lacerated.
1959-1961 safety ledger p.130

November 3, 1960 Dallas Mine
In 8 crosscut on the 1550 level, W, P. Farley's mine lamp leaked and burned his right hip.
Edison lamps often leaked and chemically burned miners. These burn could be severe.
(Note, that it was likely a model P lamp, but the Cole did use the Edison R4 for a short time.)
1959-1961 safety ledger p.155

November 22, 1960 Dallas Mine
G.A. Shipley was injured at 278 general chute on the 2000 level. It appears that he may
have been buried when the chute overflowed. . He suffered bruising of the arms, back and
legs and dirt filled eyes.
1959-1961 safety ledger p.154

January 22, 1961 Dallas Mine
O.A. Sena broke his nose while drilling in in 349 crosscut on the 2000 level.
1959-1961 safety ledger p.170

October 13, 1961 Dallas Mine
In 611 stope on the 1800 level, J.F. Sullivan broke his right foot while drilling.
1959-1961 safety ledger p.244

November 4, 1961 Dallas Mine
A falling rock caught W.P. Farley in 19 crosscut on the 1550 level. He was seriously cut on the back of his left hand and a tendon was severed.
1959-1961 safety ledger p.250

Before 1967 Dallas Mine
Richard W. Graeme III was working with Pancho Yguado on the 1400 level hauling waste from the slusher scram with Granby cars. The muck was sticky and would hang inside the cars. At The 1400 level pocket, Graeme would stop a mine car on the camelback (dumping mechanism). This would leave the car's tub tilted with the door open and as he loosened the muck stuck in the car with an air hose, it would fall into the pocket. He then proceeded to blow out the muck stuck in the cars. After this was complete, Richard need to pass by the train and moved between a timber post and a Granby car. At this moment Pancho moved the train. Caught between the car and the post, the motion rolled Richard between the post and the car. His spine was crushed against the timber. At the time he reported to the Copper Queen Hospital and was X-rayed and released. Years later, it was determined the accident had fractured two vertebrae with a number of vertical cracks.
Richard W. Graeme III Personal communication July 19, 2016

October 25, 1968, Dallas Mine
T.A. Segovia and E.A. Silva were in 627 stope on the 1800 level. This was cut and fill stope that was mining sulfide ore a section between 7-9' high and 15' wide and 42' long. This area had been mined out on the 10th floor. The back (ceiling) was supported by roof bolts and umbrella stulls. They were done slushing one section and needed to move the slusher block. Segovia walked over and removed the slusher block from and eyebolt and handed it to Silva to re-hang it. As Segovia walked towards the slusher a boulder fell breaking his left leg. It was expected he would be out of work six to eight weeks.
"Discussion of a lost time accident occurring in October 1968" 10-25-1968

December 27, 1968, Dallas Mine
M.M. *"Nueva de Columpio"* Acedo was working with R.R. Smith in 34 stope on the 1550 level. Although this was a square set stope on the 11th floor it was decided to follow a stringer of ore without using square sets. The back (ceiling) was supported by 6"x 8" stringers that formed a "V" shape that were lagged over and blocked in. The stringers were supported by hitches cut in the walls. The miners had drilled 18 holes and Smith went to get powder (dynamite.) While Smith was gone Acedo noticed the right stringer moving downward. He tried to cut a new hitch below it and block it in. As he cut the new hitch the stringer and three tons of muck fell. Acedo was pushed down into a sitting position and partially buried. Initially, his injuries were identified as only cuts and bruising

April 9, 1970 Dallas Mine
J.E. *"Kimba"* Cordova was working at 24-A stope on the 1650 level. He broken his right ankle in a manway.
J.E. Cordova Accident Photo # p1093 9 Apr. 197

Manway in 24-A stope on the 1650 level of the Dallas Mine. J.E. Cordova accident site

June 7, 1971, Dallas Mine
Antonio Figeroa went down two ladders and passed underneath a boulder that was supported by an 8"X 8" timber. The boulder fell and killed him.
Dugan Mortuary Records 1969-1971 Accession 2010.10.52 Bisbee Mining and Historical Museum, Bisbee p. 168
Pete Olier Personal communication May 27, 2014

January 17, 1974, Dallas Mine
Slusher Maintenance Man, G.G. *"Panesco"* Drybread was on the 1400 level station. He needed to change the cutting blades on the slusher bucket in115 stope. On the station he pulled a tool sack off a timber. As he did this it dragged a cutting blade off. The blade struck him on the left foot. His foot was bruised. (*"Panesco"* is Spanish for Drybread)
Phelps Dodge Corporation Copper Queen Branch Accident Report 1-18-74

January 21, 1974, Dallas Mine
C.W. Morin was digging a water ditch in 108 crosscut on the 1400 level. He need to replace rail and wanted to drain the water out of the area. As Morin was digging the pick glanced off a rock and punctured his left boot. Morin received a cut on the foot. (Either G.E. Morin or C.W. Morin was nicknamed *"Piggy"*, but it is not clear which one.)
Phelps Dodge Corporation Copper Queen Branch Accident Report 1-23-74

February 1, 1974, Dallas Mine
C.M. Teran was on the 1550 level at the steel rack in 42 crosscut. He was walking by the locomotive to talk with the crosscut crew. As Teran passed the motor he cut his hand on a frayed timber truck cable . The cable was hanging on an oil drum.
Phelps Dodge Corporation Copper Queen Branch Accident Report 2-5-74

A timber truck cable with pigtails

February 6, 1974, Dallas Mine
In 117 stope on the 1400 level, G.M. Mosteller was cribbing the sill timber. He was working in an area of tight space. As Mosteller was tightening the wedges (probably driving them with an axe) he struck the ceiling. A rock fell and cut him on the left cheek.
Phelps Dodge Corporation Copper Queen Branch Accident Report 2-7-74

February 14, 1974, Dallas Mine
The earlier shift had left a loaded train of ore on the 1550 level. These cars contained a number of large boulders. After dumping the cars into the ore pocket, D. L. Havercamp was working the boulders through the grizzlies with a boulder hook. The hook slipped off a boulder and Havercamp strained his neck.
Phelps Dodge Corporation Copper Queen Branch Accident Report 2-16-74

February 18, 1974, Dallas Mine
On the 1550 level in 52 stope, G.J. Denagean was trying to saw off 10" block off 4"x 6"x 30" to use as a bridge block. As he was cutting with a Wright Saw* the handle turned and caused the saw to bounce off the 10"x 10" stringers he was using to cut on. Denagean tried to grab the handle, but caught the blades instead. He severed the tendons on the second and third left fingers and cut a third. He was off 153 days. *These look similar to a chain saw, but have reciprocating blades rather that a chain.
Phelps Dodge Corporation Copper Queen Branch Accident Report 2-19-74
"January1-through December 31, 1974" Phelps Dodge Corporation Copper Queen Branch Annual Report Safety Department

February 22, 1974, Dallas Mine
J. R. *"Wormy"* Ledford was drilling with a jumbo in 74 crosscut on the 1550 level. His partner, T.A. *"Mr. Dithers"* Murray was collaring a hole. A chip of rock flew off and struck Ledford in the right eye. Ledford went to the hospital on February 25th. (T.A. Murray was also known as *"Rosebud"*. This was likely a reference to the movie *"Citizen Kane"*. The name *"Mr. Dithers"* was derived from the newspaper comic strip *"Blonde"*.
Phelps Dodge Corporation Copper Queen Branch Accident Report 2-26-74

March 4, 1974, Dallas Mine
In 46-D stope on the 1000 level, J.S. Garcia had set up a mucking bar in the face to muck it out with a slusher. As he walked back towards the slusher a chunk of sand fill fell from two sets above him. He was hit on the left shoulder and bruised.
Phelps Dodge Corporation Copper Queen Branch Accident Report 3-5-74

March 11, 1974, Dallas Mine
In 74 crosscut on the 1000 level, Miner, T.A. Murray was helping the motor crew who had turned over an H car while pulling the train off the super switch. He assisted them in trying to upright the car with a block and cable. When he reached for the cable, a frayed wire punctured his left index finger.
Phelps Dodge Corporation Copper Queen Branch Accident Report 3-12-74

March 13, 1974, Dallas Mine
Julio Palomino was on the conveyor and wanted to talk to a truck driver. He leaned out the window and his left hand thumb was cut on the broken glass. Note, Julio had been with the 82nd Airborne Division at the Battle of the Bulge. During the battle, he was badly wounded by German mortar round and among other injuries, his hands were crippled. His left hand was seriously damaged and he used his thumb mainly to accomplish tasks. Later, he worked as a tour guide for the Queen Mine. Julio is the brother to John *"The Rock"* Palomino who was injured in the Campbell Mine in February 1970.
Phelps Dodge Corporation Copper Queen Branch Accident Report 3-14-74

April 1, 1974, Dallas Mine
R.E. Livingston was working the ore transfer on the 1650 level. The ore had been dumped into the transfer on March 28 and had compacted. Livingston was using a blowpipe to free up the muck and keep it flowing. A boulder hit the end of the blowpipe and bent his left wrist. He suffered a sprained wrist
Phelps Dodge Corporation Copper Queen Branch Accident Report 4-2-74

April 3, 1974, Dallas Mine
Timberman, O.A. Sena had timbered the frame for an air door in 85 crosscut on the 1400 level. Sena was loading left over and scrap timber onto a timber truck to haul it away. After loading a piece of a 10''x 10"x 8'. He began to push the timber truck. The 10''x 10"x 8' rolled and smashed his right middle finger.
Phelps Dodge Corporation Copper Queen Branch Accident Report 4-4-74

April 8, 1974, Dallas Mine
E.P. *"Blackie"* Gutierrez a diamond driller was pulling rods in 71 crosscut on the 1550 level. As he was removing the drill rods he pulled a muscle in his groin.
Phelps Dodge Corporation Copper Queen Branch Accident Report 5-9-74 (wrong date on form?)

162

April 9, 1974, Dallas Mine
On the 1550 level, in 57 stope G. E. Morin and J.R. Alvarez were laying gob wire and spreaders for concreting (sand fill.) Morin was using an axe and a bit hammer to cut the wire. A small piece flew up and struck him under the right eye, cutting him. (Either G.E. Morin or C.W. Morin was nicknamed "*Piggy*", but it is not clear which one.)
Phelps Dodge Corporation Copper Queen Branch Accident Report 4-10-74

April 17, 1974, Dallas Mine
R.S. Romero, a mucker was working shoveling up rock from behind the spill doors on the 1800 level station. He was pushing an H car and became caught between the mine car and a post. His chest was bruised. It was not until Romero was mucking out a water ditch on the 1400 level on April 24th that he began to have trouble breathing. He suspected that the injury on the 17th was the cause.
Phelps Dodge Corporation Copper Queen Branch Accident Report 5-1-74

May 3, 1974, Dallas Mine
In 96 stope on the 1400 level. M.F. Davenport was breaking boulders. A chip flew and cut a finger on his left hand.
Phelps Dodge Corporation Copper Queen Branch Accident Report 5-6-74

May 10, 1974, Dallas Mine
Electrician, G.R. Brown was "*skinning*" a parkway cable (heavy duty electrical cable) in 74 crosscut on the 1550 level. The knife slipped and Brown was cut on the palm of the left hand. He required five stitches.
Phelps Dodge Corporation Copper Queen Branch Accident Report 5-10-74

May 15, 1974, Dallas Mine
In 78 crosscut on the 1550 level, J.R. "*Wormy*" Ledford was mucking the waste rock out of 78 crosscut and into 24 crosscut. He intended to drill in 78 crosscut. As he was mucking, dirt flew into Ledford's right eye.
Phelps Dodge Corporation Copper Queen Branch Accident Report 5-16-74

May 31, 1974, Dallas Mine
J.R. "*Tater Digger*" Laird was working in 59 raise on the 1550 level. The raise had been blasted and Laird was opening up the bulkhead installed to protect the manway from the blast. As he was working boulders fell from the back of the raise and struck him on the head and shoulders. Laird suffered only bruising.
Phelps Dodge Corporation Copper Queen Branch Accident Report 6-1-74

Wheat Mark II Miner's Lamp, c-1974

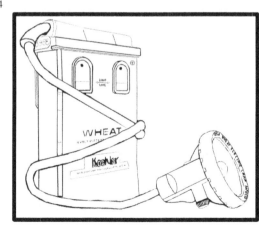

May 20, 1974 Dallas Mine
When Motorman, G.G. Chavez was coming off the cage at quitting time at the shaft collar. His lamp cord was attached to a chain. As a result, he strained his back. It was suspected that someone had hooked his lamp cord on the chain as horseplay.
Phelps Dodge Corporation Copper Queen Branch Accident Report 5-20-74

June 6, 1974, Dallas Mine
J.H. Conroy was cleaning up 4 crosscut on the 1400 level. As he was working his left foot contacted a 25lb. switch frog laying against the drift wall (rib). The frog punctured his foot.
Phelps Dodge Corporation Copper Queen Branch Accident Report 6-10-74

June 7, 1974, Dallas Mine
In 28 crosscut on the 1650 level, R.S. Romero and O.A. Sena were installing a 6"x 8" stull. A rock was knocked loose and left a puncture wound on Romero's right arm. The rock was small and only about 2"x 3" x ½".
Phelps Dodge Corporation Copper Queen Branch Accident Report 6-11-74

June 7, 1974, Dallas Mine
Cager, C. Sena was at the 1650 level station and was going to turn off the blower ventilating the 1650 ore pocket. Four 8"x 8" posts were stored in front of the blower. As Sena stepped on a post to turn off the blower, he slipped and fell. His back suffered a sprain.
Phelps Dodge Corporation Copper Queen Branch Accident Report 6-10-74

June 14, 1974, Dallas Mine
In 137 crosscut on the 1400 level, B.N. Blakely was operating a mucking machine. A boulder fell off the machine's dipper and struck Blakely on the inside of his left ankle. He was only bruised.
Phelps Dodge Corporation Copper Queen Branch Accident Report 6-17-74

June 20, 1974, Dallas Mine
C.L. Martinez and R.F. Jones were working in 92 crosscut on the 1400 level. The miners were planning to clean up the drift and drill to install ventilation brattice. In the crosscut was a loaded H mine car that had been sitting for a several months. Martinez took a 4"x 6" and was using it to pry the car forward and sprained his back. He was off work 48 days.
Phelps Dodge Corporation Copper Queen Branch Accident Report 6-21-74
"January1-through December 31, 1974" Phelps Dodge Corporation Copper Queen Branch Annual Report Safety Department
"Minutes of Meeting held on July 2,, 1974" Phelps Dodge Corporation Copper Queen Branch p.4

June 28, 1974, Dallas Mine
Miner, D.M. Morgan was installing a 4"x 6" spreader in a gob fence. As he was working he knock a boulder loose. The rock fell on his right thumb. His thumb was cut up. The accident occurred in 96 stope on the 1400 level.
Phelps Dodge Corporation Copper Queen Branch Accident Report 6-28-74

July 8, 1974, Dallas Mine

R.J. *"Turk"* Gardoni and W.D. Hare intended to boom out and muck in 119 stope on the 1400 level. As they were pushing the timber the mine car (timber truck?) split the super switch and re-injured Gardoni's back. Gardoni had injured his back approximately one week earlier in an undescribed incident. (This first injury, possibly did not occur at work. Also, Gardoni was sometimes called by another nickname *"Gigolo"*)
Phelps Dodge Corporation Copper Queen Branch Accident Report 7-9-74

August 19, 1974, Dallas Mine
O.A. Sena was mucking out a cave-in in 70 crosscut on the 1400 level. As he lifted a boulder into an H mine car, the rock broke. Part of it fell and cut him between this left thumb and forefinger.
Phelps Dodge Corporation Copper Queen Branch Accident Report 8-20-74

August 20, 1974, Dallas Mine
At 1:00 pm, W.H. Smith a miner, was installing an eyebolt to hang a blower in 1 crosscut on the 1650 level. As he was working he brushed the wall of the crosscut and a rock fell. The rock landed into the water ditch and splashed copper water into his left eye. Smith washed out his eyes, but it still bothered him. (Note, the following accident occurred at the same time and location.)
Phelps Dodge Corporation Copper Queen Branch Accident Report 8-20-74

August 20, 1974, Dallas Mine
Also, at 1:00 pm electricians Don Barnett and Frank Chavez were installing roof bolts to hang a "Joy" blower on the 1650 level. As Chavez was looking up a drop of copper water fell from the roof bolt passed his eye shields into his right eye. (Note, the preceding accident occurred at the same time and location.)
Phelps Dodge Corporation Copper Queen Branch Accident Report 8-20-74

August 27, 1974, Dallas Mine
F.B. Romo, a write-in motorswamper was riding the tail E mine car of a train in 73 crosscut on the 1400 level. His right hand was on the handle of the car. As the train moved through the crosscut the car tilted and smashed his hand against a drift post.
Phelps Dodge Corporation Copper Queen Branch Accident Report 9-5-74

September 12, 1974, Dallas Mine
R.S. Romero and G.J. Chavez were using #13 locomotive to haul ore from a stope. They were at the intersection of 58 crosscut and 66 crosscut on the 1400 level. Earlier they had used a small board to pound a fitting on the blower at 39-C stope. Chavez placed the board on the locomotive. Later, at the intersection Romero climbed onto the locomotive and sat on a slightly bent nail sticking out of the board. Romero's right buttock was punctured.
Phelps Dodge Corporation Copper Queen Branch Accident Report 9-16-74

September 15, 1974, Dallas Mine
Shaft repairman, J. Soldana was repairing the 1800 level shaft station and needed timber. He went to the 576 crosscut timber station to get a 10" x 10". In 576 crosscut a rock fell and struck him on the forehead and nose. He was only bruised.
Phelps Dodge Corporation Copper Queen Branch Accident Report 9-7-74

September 17, 1974, Dallas Mine
D.L. Havercamp was at the 1550 level ore pocket with C.R. Gamblin. Havercamp was prying on an H mine car with a chipper steel. The steel slipped and he smashed his hand between the steel and the dump rail*. * A dump rail is also called a camelback
Phelps Dodge Corporation Copper Queen Branch Accident Report 9-18-74

September 18, 1974, Dallas Mine
At 7:30 am, P.P. Torres was headed down the Dallas Shaft to repair mucking machine in 137 crosscut on the 1800 level. Torres was riding the cage when it struck the *"bottom"* at the 1800 level. His back and neck were injured .S.T. *"Silent Sam"* Elkins and C. Sena were witnesses to the accident and were possibly also riding the cage. Torres injured his back and neck. (It is possible if not likely, that this accident is actually part of the next accident.)
Phelps Dodge Corporation Copper Queen Branch Accident Report 9-19-74

September 18, 1974, Dallas Mine
At 7:45 am, Hoistman, Melvin Ray was lowering D. Abril to the 1800 level on the cage. The cage struck a muck pile lying in the bottom of the shaft and reaching two feet above the turnsheet at the 1800 level. Abril suffered an injured back and upset stomach. R. Silva, R.G. Brown and Joe Torres witnessed the accident and were possibly riding the cage but were uninjured. (It is possible that this accident is actually part of the previous accident.)
Phelps Dodge Corporation Copper Queen Branch Accident Report 9-20-74

September 23, 1974, Dallas Mine
Motorman, C.R. Gamblin was working in 15 crosscut on the 1550 level to bring to B.O. Koppel (K) cars to the shaft to be hoisted. After he had hooked up the K cars, he ran a cable from the drawhead on the K cars to two B.O. H cars that he wanted to move as well. While he was between the K cars and the H cars his partner D.L. Havercamp moved the train Gamblin was caught between a K car and H car. He suffered a bruised right shoulder from the accident. The accident resulted in 76 days lost time.
Phelps Dodge Corporation Copper Queen Branch Accident Report 9-24-74
Annual Report Safety Department January through December 31, 1974

October 28, 1974, Dallas Mine
B.E. Crabtree was on the 1650 level. He intended to haul muck out of 52 crosscut and then salvage the air and water lines from 28 crosscut. In1 crosscut Crabtree need to change the direction of the trolley pole on the locomotive. As he was doing this he strained his left side. E.G. Bryan witnessed the incident.
Phelps Dodge Corporation Copper Queen Branch Accident Report 10-28-74

October 29, 1974, Dallas Mine
M.I. Marusich, a motor swamper was working pulling 87 general chute. His partner began to blow out the G cars at the 1400 level ore pocket to clean them out. While Marusich was watching, dirt struck him in his right eye.
Phelps Dodge Corporation Copper Queen Branch Accident Report 10-30-74

November 1, 1974, Dallas Mine

F.E. Reynolds was barring down in 46-D stope on the 1550 level. A rock fell and struck his left eye.

Phelps Dodge Corporation Copper Queen Branch Accident Report 11-5-74

December 5, 1974, Dallas Mine

M.R. Burgos was barring down in 114 stope on the 1400 level with M.C. Dominquez. Burgos tried barring down a boulder and it would not fall so he left it and began barring down a different section. The boulder fell and rolled over Burgos' ankle. This resulted in a lost-time accident. The ankle may have been only seriously bruised

Phelps Dodge Corporation Copper Queen Branch Accident Report 12-6-74

December 12, 1974, Dallas Mine

G.L. Mosteller and R.E. Jones were working in 120 stope, a square set oxide stope on the 1400 level. Mosteller was picking down a four foot muck pile and a small rock rolled down left knee. He was surprised that such a small rock would injure him. His knee was bruised.

Phelps Dodge Corporation Copper Queen Branch Accident Report 12-6-74

January 7, 1975, Dallas Mine

At 2:00 pm, B. Rodriguez , a hoistman was walking between the rails between the headframe and the changeroom. He slipped and fell. His right elbow was dislocated. This was a lost time accident.

Phelps Dodge Corporation Copper Queen Branch Accident Report 1-7-74

January 15, 1975, Dallas Mine

John W. Sanders, a shift boss was walking down three crosscut on the 1550 level to collect water samples. At the time of the accident, he was wading in mud and water about 18 inches deep. Unknown to Sanders a roof bolt had fallen out of the back of the crosscut and was lying sharp point up about four inches above the plate. When Sanders stepped over a boulder in the mud, he landed on the bolt, which cut through the boot and about one inch in his right foot.

Phelps Dodge Corporation Copper Queen Branch Accident Report 1-16-75

January 27, 1975, Dallas Mine

At the waste pocket on the 1400 level, the motor crew was breaking boulders. As G.L. Mosteller was walking by a chip of rock flew and struck him in the eye. Initially, the eye did not bother him, but that night he went to the hospital and was examined.

Phelps Dodge Corporation Copper Queen Branch Accident Report 1-28-75

February 19, 1975, Dallas Mine

In 46-D stope on the 1550 level, J.S. Garcia was mucking with a Finlay (mucking machine) when he decided to pick a boulder by hand and lift it into a K mine car. As Garcia lifted the boulder it slipped and smashed his hand between the mine car and the rock. His ring finger was cut and the small finger of the left hand was broken.

Phelps Dodge Corporation Copper Queen Branch Accident Report 2-20-75

Eimco 12B "Finlay" Mucking machine.

February 21, 1975, Dallas Mine
At 7:30 pm, O.E. Padilla was on the Dallas Conveyor (on the surface) pulling off scrap timber. He opened a window to toss out wood. Heavy winds outside blew dust into Padilla's left eye. (Note, night had fallen outside and the conveyor was lit by incandescent lights.)
Phelps Dodge Corporation Copper Queen Branch Accident Report 2-24-75

February 26, 1975, Dallas Mine
B.F. Stewart was drilling with a jumbo in 83 crosscut on the 1550 level. He was changing drill steel when he cut his middle finger on the end of a cable.
Phelps Dodge Corporation Copper Queen Branch Accident Report 2-27-75

March 26, 1975, Dallas Mine
H.R. Miranda and G.J. Chavez were on the 1550 level and were getting ready to drill and blast for the sill timber for a new raise #61. Miranda was drilling with a stoper and a nine foot steel. The drill steel hung up and Miranda tried to loosen it up with the stoper. The stoper slipped off the drill steel and sprained his right arm.
Phelps Dodge Corporation Copper Queen Branch Accident Report 3-27-75

April 1, 1975, Dallas Mine
At 7:30 pm, C.A. Halstead was working in 51 sub-crosscut above the 1400 level. Halstead was hoisting timber with a tugger hoist up a timber slide. As the timber was raise he heard it strike something. When Halstead looked up the raise dirt fell into his left

168

eye. He refused to take a blue card from his shift boss, R. Rachilla. After showering, Halstead said his eye was better.
Phelps Dodge Corporation Copper Queen Branch Accident Report 4-2-75

April 14, 1975, Dallas Mine
R.C. Gonzales was going to muck up spilled sand and repair a crosscut at 60 stope. At the timber station in 74 crosscut he was going to get a *"stope"* post. When he was pulling off a post from a stack of 8"x8" posts they fell over and bruised his big toe.
Phelps Dodge Corporation Copper Queen Branch Accident Report 4-14-75

April 22, 1975, Dallas Mine
R.H. Jorgenson was with L.M. Carbajal on the 1400 level in 86 crosscut. The sand filling of 99 stope had been completed. Jorgenson was cleaning sand out of the water ditch and strained his back. He told the boss, C.W. Welles that his back *"bothers him quite a bit."*
Phelps Dodge Corporation Copper Queen Branch Accident Report 4-22-75

April 24, 1975, Dallas Mine
On the 1550 level at the bottom of 61 raise, H.R. Miranda was nailing a board onto the timber slide. A nail flew back and chipped one of his false teeth. C.G. Chavez witnessed the incident.
Phelps Dodge Corporation Copper Queen Branch Accident Report 4-25-75

April 29, 1975, Dallas Mine
In 86 crosscut on the 1400 level, E.G. Salmon was trying to put a derailed E mine car back on the track. He hooked a timber chain from the mine car to the guard rail on the locomotive. The chain came off and struck Salmon on the sternum. He suffered a bruise above the xiphoid process.
Phelps Dodge Corporation Copper Queen Branch Accident Report 4-30-75

May 27, 1975, Dallas Mine
R. J Fant was in 60-B stope on the 1550 level, was pulling on a slusher cable. When it freed he fell into the muck scram. Fant reported this to shift boss, R. Rachilla as he went off shift. And stated he was not seriously injured. He suffered a bruised back.
Phelps Dodge Corporation Copper Queen Branch Accident Report 5-28-75

May, 29, 1975, Dallas Mine
In 61 raise on the 1550 level, H.R. Miranda was drilling with a stoper. A boulder of sulfide peeled off the waste rock and struck him in the right shoulder. It was believed his right clavicle was broken. This was a lost time accident. It was suspected the drilling water had loosened the boulder.
Phelps Dodge Corporation Copper Queen Branch Accident Report 5-29-75

June 5, 1975, Dallas Mine
J.D. Pursley was on the 1550 level in 60-A stope. He was removing the skids off a slusher. The slusher was to be hauled out on a timber truck. When he lowered his knee onto the slusher staging a piece of slusher cable punctured his left knee.
Phelps Dodge Corporation Copper Queen Branch Accident Report 6-9-75

June 12, 1975, Dallas Mine
On the final day of active mining, a blower in 85 crosscut on the 1400 level was being moved. E.G. Salmon was the motor swamper. R.R. Smith and G. Chavez were helping move the blower. Salmon moved the locomotive the wrong direction and caught Smith's right knee between the locomotive and a timber truck. His knee was bruised.
Phelps Dodge Corporation Copper Queen Branch Accident Report 6-12-75

Interior of the Diesel Power Plant c-1920

Diesel Power Plant

Located in Don Luis near the Sacramento Concentrator, construction for this plant began in **1918. The plant began operation on December 15, 1921. It worked until mining ceased in 1975. The building and machinery remained intact until the Sacramento Mill site was reclaimed in 2014.**

August 15, 1959 Diesel Power Plant
W.R. Buford bruised his right toes.
1959-1961 safety ledger p. 62

April 11, 1960 Diesel Power Plant
J.H. Ledford was handling timber and bruised his right leg.
1959-1961 safety ledger p. 102

May 7, 1960 Diesel Power Plant
D. Vucurevich flash burned both eyes.
1959-1961 safety ledger p. 110

August 6, 1960 Diesel Power Plant
J.M. Stickel cut his nose.
1959-1961 safety ledger p. 134

August 12, 1960 Diesel Power Plant
T.A. Martin fell and bruised his nose and cut his scalp
1959-1961 safety ledger p. 134

March 27, 1961 Diesel Power Plant
R.L. Rojo sprained his ankle at the cooling pond.
1959-1961 safety ledger p. 190

May 1, 1974
Assistant engineer, J.R. McClain* was washing down the basement floor of the diesel power plant with K. Gambill. When he leaned against a hose on the wall a scorpion stung him on the right arm.* He also was injured on October 2, 1975
Phelps Dodge Corporation Copper Queen Branch Accident Report 5-1-74

October 2, 1975
J.R. McClain* was locking the front door to the power plant when the telephone rang. He ran to get the phone. As he passed the #1 engine he ran into the end of a guard rail. His chest was bruised. * He was also injured May 1, 1974
Phelps Dodge Corporation Copper Queen Branch Accident Report 10-2-75

Inside the diesel power plant

December 19, 1975
F.A. Chavez was clearing weeds with R.M. Flores. As Chavez was swinging a mattock it struck a rock and bounced off. The mattock hit his leg. Chavez suffered a cut on the lower leg
Phelps Dodge Corporation Copper Queen Branch Accident Report 12-19-75

The Denn Mine with the headframe of the Saginaw Shaft in the background.

Denn Mine

In April of 1905, Joe Colley and his crew of the Denn & Arizona Copper Company had prepared the site northwest of the cemetery for sinking of the Denn Shaft. On December 8th 1905 the shaft was already 740 ft. deep and fifteen sinking buckets of muck were being raised every ten hour shift. In March 1906, the shaft was equal to the 1000 level (983 Denn) of the Junction Mine. A station was going to be cut with drifting started towards a diamond drill hole that struck ore. The pumps were being installed. Then on December 10, 1906, the drift on the 1000 level struck ore near the drill hole. In July 1907, a drift on the 1100 intercepted the same orebody. With falling metal prices, the Denn was ordered closed in November 1907 with the exception of the diamond drilling crews. By April 1909, the 1250 level station was being cut and the shaft was being sunk at a rate of 15 ft. per week.

Trouble began in November, drill holes on the 1350 level were spouting jets of water up five feet and releasing 1,400 gallons per minute into the mine. Later, a large flow of water was struck in a drift on the 1600. Initially, the pumps held off the water, but then more water was struck. Soon the shaft was flooded to 35 ft. below the 1350 level. In December 1910, the pumps were pulled and Denn was shutdown. The mine remained closed until June 1917 when work resumed. By January 1918, dewatering the mine to the 1600 level was being worked on. February 1919 a fire broke out inside the Denn and after one week it was still not under control.

It was not until the controversial merger of the Shattuck & Arizona Copper Company with the Denn & Arizona Copper Company that the Denn became a consistent producer. Under the Shattuck Denn Mining Company the Denn was pumped out and the mine operated from 1925-1944. In 1947, the Denn was purchased by the Phelps Dodge Corporation. A waste pocket was built so waste could be hauled by dump trucks dumped into the pocket and lowered underground for back filling stopes was for backfilling. The Denn hoisted ore from the Campbell Mine. This made the shaft muddy as water seepage mixed with dirt falling out of skips and This mine remained in operation used until the end of mining in 1975. Although, the working condition were less than ideal being hot, wet and some areas had an unpleasant smell. Local legend tells that the scent was caused by the cemetery above the mine workings. The shaft was completed at a depth of 3,157 ft. deep and with

172

four compartment. The Denn was one of the more noticeable mines. Even after the closure in 1975, the loud, eerie, howl of the mine fan echoed across Evergreen Cemetery and into Lowell for years. This fan was providing ventilation for the Junction pump stations and parts of the Campbell Mine. The Denn Mine is sometimes referred to as the Denn & Arizona Mine, or Shattuck Denn Mine in period literature.

May 8, 1906, Denn Mine

Shift Boss, John Flannigan rang the cage on the 1000 level to go up. After the cage had ascended 100 ft. the hoist malfunctioned, and the cage fell to the bottom of the shaft. Originally, it was thought that Flannigan had suffered only a severe cut on his side. Later, he claimed that he was crippled by the accident and sued the Denn & Arizona Mining Company for $40,000.00. He felt that the company knew the hoist was defective. The case was heard on July 23, 1907. It was settled and Flannigan was rumored to receive a large settlement and a pension.

"Miner Falls Down Shaft and Lives" Bisbee Daily Review 10 May 1906 page 3
"Wants $40,000 in Damages from Denn-Arizona" Bisbee Daily Review 26 September 1906 page 2
"Court Cases are Given Dates for Trial" Bisbee Daily Review 3 July 1907 page 2
"Father Begs for Liberty of Son" Bisbee Daily Review 25 July 1907 page 3

January 4, 1907 Denn Mine

At 4:50 pm, 8,700 lbs. of dynamite stored in the main powder magazine exploded. Mine Foreman Collie had just returned to the surface when the explosion occurred the door of the change house was blown from its hinges and struck him on the head. Suffering a serious cut he went outside and gathered the men on the surface and began checking to see if the hoist was still operational. This was to determine if they could get the men out of the underground. During the explosion the hoist engineer was thrown against the wall of the hoist house and was bruised on the cut on the cheek, but able to operate the hoist. The blacksmith shop was completely destroyed, but the blacksmith, Ben Smith and his helper J.L. Adkinson suffered only minor injuries. Smith was working and the forge at the time of the blast and Adkinson was near the door. Adkinson received a cut on the head and a sprained wrist and Smith also a cut on the head along with bruises. W.E. Wallace was in the change house with Foreman Collie and was struck in the back by a flying door. Every window of Superintendent Patterson's house on the mine site was broken as were a large number of windows in Lowell. Lee Wyatt, a carpenter had his horse and buggy harnessed near the magazine and it was completely destroyed. (It is not clear, if the horse was killed or even injured.) The mine stables were located behind the change house and actually shared a wall. These stables were completely undamaged, but two of the three horses stable there ran for the surrounding hills after the explosion. The third horse remained in his stall and was uninjured. In Douglas, Arizona, people thought an earthquake had occurred. The men quickly removed broken wood and other debris from on top of the hoist. The hoist raised a cage from the dinkey compartment to the surface, but was unable to stop the cage and it was hoisted into the sheave wheel. It remained stuck in the sheave. Foreman Collie was sent by buggy to Bisbee to be treated for his injury after mine superintendent Patterson arrived. With the dinkey cage stuck it was decided to use a sinking bucket in the center compartment to retrieve the men underground. Shift Boss Sherman Ross was lowered down to gather the men underground. By this time a crowd of hundreds of people had gathered at the mine. It was

173

soon revealed that the underground part of the mine suffered no damage. To the relief of the crowd men were quickly hoisted to the surface unharmed. Underground the explosion was heard as a sound like a muffled rifle shot. The miners underground failed to realize anything was wrong, until they realized their call bells were going unanswered by the hoistman. At around 4:20 pm, Samuel Yeach was the last man to enter the magazine before it exploded. He had removed some dynamite and locked the door. He stated, that no light (open flame) was burning in the magazine and everything seemed alright. Within 24 hours work began to repair the mine facilities and work resumed underground. Although, for a time the underground miners had to change into their work clothes in the winter air. Sherman Ross was given five shares of Denn & Arizona stock for his brave act of entering the mine.

"Awful Explosion at Denn" Bisbee Daily Review 5, January1907 page 1
"Repair Work is Progressing at Denn" Bisbee Daily Review 6, January1907 page 5

A view soon after the explosion at the Denn Mine. The X marks the location of the powder magazine and the T indicates where the buggy was parked.

The blacksmith shop after the explosion

September 24, 1907, Denn Mine

A Mexican man named Maghacino (spelling?) was moving pieces of angle iron from the hoist house to near the oil tanks on a car (mine car?). He fell 25 ft. into a creek bottom. Maghacino was taken to the Shattuck-Denn Hospital. Initially, his injuries were thought to be somewhat minor, but he died at 1:30 pm. (Note, no inquest or death certificate could be located.)
"Fall of 25 ft. Kills Worker at Denn" Bisbee Daily Review 25 September 1907 page 3

July 5, 1908, Denn Mine

The night watchman, Joseph Collie had a .38 six-shooter sitting in his lap and was going to shoot at a couple dogs that had been bothersome. The gun accidently went off and a bullet entered his groin.
"Joseph Collie Accidently Shot Himself" Bisbee Daily Review 5 July 1908 page 9

May, 1910, Denn Mine

W.H. Jones had two ribs broken by a falling cage.
"Two ribs Broken" Bisbee Daily Review 28 May 1910 page 7

September 3, 1911, Denn Mine

The mine watchman, Sandy Sutton was at his home at the Denn Mine with his young daughter. An enraged Jim Sharp was searching for his wife that had left him. An unnamed man told him that he had seen Mrs. Sharp enter the home of Mr. Sutton. Sharp entered the home and shot Sutton through the right testis into his hip with a. 22 caliber rifle. Wounded, Sutton took the rifle away from Sharp. As it turned out Mrs. Sharp had taken the train to Douglas, Arizona to escape her husband. It is not clear whether Sutton was performing his duties as a watchman when he was shot.
"Went Gunning after his Wife" Bisbee Daily Review 5 September 1911 page 2

January 6, 1918, Denn Mine

Around 11:00 am, M.B. Davis and Jack Morgan drilled into a misfire. The blast struck the men in the face and arms. It was thought that each man would lose an eye. Morgan was released from the Calumet and Arizona Hospital on January 19th in *"good condition."* Davis wasn't let out until May 18th and was considered in *"improved condition."*
"Were Injured" Bisbee Daily Review 8 January 1918 page 8
"Calumet & Arizona Hospital Records." My Cochise.
http://www.mycochise.com/hospcalco2day.php (June 2, 2012)
Office of State Mine Inspector. *Seventh Annual Report of the State Mine Inspector State of Arizona for the Year Ending November 30, 1918.*

July 20, 1918, Denn Mine

Claud *"Curly"* Perris, a pumpman broke his arm in the mine.
"Suffers Broken Arm" Bisbee Daily Review 24, July 1918 page 8

July 24, 1918, Denn Mine

41-year-old John Lorang, was killed in a cave-in. The falling rock broke his sacrum and other pelvic bones in a compound fracture. He was buried in Evergreen Cemetery a few hundred feet from the headframe of the Denn Shaft, where he worked. Lorang had lived in a house located near the Denn Shaft. (No coroner's inquest could be located)
Dugan Mortuary Records July 19, 1918 – March 27, 19206 Accession 2010.10.14 Bisbee Mining and Historical Museum, Bisbee.

Office of State Mine Inspector. *Seventh Annual Report of the State Mine Inspector State of Arizona for the Year Ending November 30, 1918.*

"Calumet & Arizona Hospital Records." My Cochise. http://www.mycochise.com/hospcaldied.php (May 28, 2012)

"Bisbee-Lowell Evergreen Cemetery." My Cochise.
http://www.mycochise.com/cembisbeel.php (May 29, 2012)

October 29, 1918, Denn Mine

A mine car struck the foot of Frank Kren and injured his ankle.

Office of State Mine Inspector. *Seventh Annual Report of the State Mine Inspector State of Arizona for the Year Ending November 30, 1918.*

November 8, 1918, Denn Mine

Peter Popvich Badich, Andrew John Johnson and Theodore Mattson were working in a crosscut on the 1600 level. They loaded 14 holes with 40% Hercules Gelatin dynamite. Around 1:00 am, the partially spit (ignited) round detonated. The miners were having difficulty lighting the fuses because of the amount of water. Mattson warned the men it was time to leave, but they stayed cutting and spitting fuses. The holes exploded, and Badich and Johnson were killed. Mattson an 18-year-old miner went to the station with his face covered with blood to get help. His eyes were injured and suffered bruises. He was treated at the Calumet & Arizona Hospital and released on November 12, 1918. Both of the men killed were buried in Evergreen Cemetery a few hundred feet from the headframe of the Denn Shaft. Badich was 30 years old and was from Austria-Hungary. Johnson was 42 years old. The state mine inspector felt that a quick burning fuse was to blame. Only the two center holes and one hole in the upper right hand corner detonated. The others did not appear to have been lit.

"Two Dead and One Man is Injured" Bisbee Daily Review 8 November 1918 page 1

Dugan Mortuary Records July 19, 1918 – March 27, 1920 Accession 2010.10.14 Bisbee Mining and Historical Museum, Bisbee

"Calumet & Arizona Hospital Records." My Cochise.
http://www.mycochise.com/hospcalmar2mc.php (June 2, 2012)

"Bisbee-Lowell Evergreen Cemetery." My Cochise.
http://www.mycochise.com/cembisbeeij.php (May 29, 2012)

Office of State Mine Inspector. *Seventh Annual Report of the State Mine Inspector State of Arizona for the Year Ending November 30, 1918.*

"Cochise County Coroner's Inquest No. 1344" Arizona State Archives Phoenix

December 10, 1918, Denn Mine

Joe Meighan had his left hand broken and cut up after a rock fell on it while he was drilling.

Office of State Mine Inspector. *Eighth Annual Report of the State Mine Inspector State of Arizona for the Year Ending November 30, 1919.*

December 12, 1918, Denn Mine

George Tomlanovich was hit in the head by a falling rock.

Office of State Mine Inspector. *Eighth Annual Report of the State Mine Inspector State of Arizona for the Year Ending November 30, 1919.*

May 19, 1919, Denn Mine

Emil Haggblom picked up a lit fuse and seriously burned his hand. (Also, injured June 6, 1918, in Shattuck Mine)

Office of State Mine Inspector. *Eighth Annual Report of the State Mine Inspector State of Arizona for the Year Ending November 30, 1919.*

September 16, 1919, Denn Mine

William McCormick was struck by a boulder, which broke his leg.

Office of State Mine Inspector. *Eighth Annual Report of the State Mine Inspector State of Arizona for the Year Ending November 30, 1919.*

October 23, 1919, Denn Mine

Working on the surface, Earnest Miners caught his hand between two miner cars. He suffered a cut finger.

Office of State Mine Inspector. *Eighth Annual Report of the State Mine Inspector State of Arizona for the Year Ending November 30, 1919.*

March 11, 1920, Denn Mine

C.G. Tobakovich broke his foot when he dropped a lagging.

Office of State Mine Inspector. *Ninth Annual Report of the State Mine Inspector State of Arizona for the Year Ending November 30, 1920.*

March 20, 1920, Denn Mine

Taylor L. Perry had a drill fall against him cutting his leg.

Office of State Mine Inspector. *Ninth Annual Report of the State Mine Inspector State of Arizona for the Year Ending November 30, 1920.*

June 7, 1920, Denn Mine

Chauncie Hines, a mucker, was hit by a rock falling from the back of the drift, injuring his back and a finger. He was released from the Calumet & Arizona Hospital on June 13, 1920.

"Calumet & Arizona Hospital Records." M<u>y Cochise.</u>
 http://www.mycochise.com/hospcalhi2ja.php (June 2, 2012)

Office of State Mine Inspector. *Ninth Annual Report of the State Mine Inspector State of Arizona for the Year Ending November 30, 1920.*

September 9, 1920, Denn Mine

While, Pete Kraker was drilling and a piece of steel struck him in the left eye.

Office of State Mine Inspector. *Ninth Annual Report of the State Mine Inspector State of Arizona for the Year Ending November 30, 1920.*

January 17, 1927, Denn Mine

Richard La More was working on a Sullivan Compressor with Henry J. Finn. The compressor was new and was having problems. La More saw the safety valve lift and tried to close the intake valve. Finn tried to shut off the power. The compressor then exploded. La More's right arm was nearly amputated. The blast knocked him through the east wall of the compressor building. Parts of machine were scattered through the hoist house and compressor building. La More was killed

"Original Certificate of Death." http://genealogy.az.gov/azdeath/034/10340039.pdf Arizona Department of Health (August 8, 2015)
"Explosion of Air Compressor at Shattuck-Denn Plant" Engineering & Mining Journal, 1927 Vol 123 p. 255
"Cochise County Coroner's Inquest No.1265" Arizona State Archives

November 16, 1928, Denn Mine

William Matta and Ramon Veliz were working on retimbering the Denn Shaft at 30 ft. above the 1100 level station. They cut out a water-soaked 12-inch by 12-inch post, which was heavier than they could handle. This post fell into the shaft, passed through an opening in a bulkhead and landed on a hurricane deck on a cage. Robert S. Lampi was instantly killed and a miner named Kempton was injured. Lampi was helping retimber the shaft at the 1200 level when he was killed. (Note, a new kiln dried 12"x 12" x8' post weighs 256lbs. Underground the timber would absorb water and become substantially heavier. Also it would have been coated by a slippery mixture of mud and mold.)

"Original Certificate of Death." http://genealogy.az.gov/azdeath/038/10380038.pdf Arizona Department of Health (May 31, 2012)
Office of State Mine Inspector. *Seventeenth Annual Report of the State Mine Inspector State of Arizona for the Year Ending November 30, 1928.*
Dugan Mortuary Records Aug. 29, 1926 – Jun4 1930 Accession 2010.10.20 Bisbee Mining and Historical Museum, Bisbee.
"Cochise County Coroner's Inquest No. 1681" Arizona State Archives Phoenix

May 20, 1936, Denn Mine

Pete Lutich and Arthur Kaneaster were working concreting the Denn shaft. They had been working on this for approximately eight months. Above the 2565 ft. level (2566 level Campbell Mine) the men were installing a bulkhead to work on. The men were using safety lines. After completing the staging the men removed their safety lines and began moving concrete forms. The staging slipped and both men fell to a platform on the 2680 level. Lutich was 26 years-old and survived by his wife. Kaneaster 40 years-old was survived by his wife Ann, a child and his mother Lucy Lutich. Pete was buried in Evergreen cemetery. Kaneaster was buried at Whitewater in the Sulphur Springs Valley near Elfrida, Arizona.

Original Certificate of Death." Arizona Department of Health Services. http://genealogy.az.gov/azdeath/052/10521157.pdf (May 28, 2014)
"Kaneaster and Lutich Killed"n The Bisbee Evening Ore 21 May 1936 page 2
"Inquest Held This Morning In Fatal Mine Accident At Denn" The Bisbee Evening Ore 22 May 1936 page 1
"Victims Rites Sunday The Bisbee Evening Ore 23 May 1936 page 4
"Industrial Comission Planning Two Hearings "Arizona Daily Star 21 Jun 1936 page 3
"Personel Communications" Kim Sertich 2019-2020

July 10, 1935, Denn Mine

Timber was being lowered to Italian Miner, Thomas Benny when he fell into a raise and broke through a 2" X 12" lagged bulkhead. Benny landed in No. 21 drift on the 2100 level. The fall was fatal.

Original Certificate of Death." Arizona Department of Health Services. http://genealogy.az.gov/azdeath/052/10521157.pdf (May 28, 2014)
"Cochise County Coroner's Inquest No. 1737" Arizona State Archives Phoenix

December 29, 1940, Denn Mine

Electrician's Helper, Henry R. Gerdes was working on a tower 400 ft. from the Denn Shaft when he contacted a live wire and was electrocuted.

Original Certificate of Death." Arizona Department of Health Services. http://genealogy.az.gov/azdeath/064/10640562.pdf (May 28, 2014)

"Cochise County Coroner's Inquest No. 1790" Arizona State Archives Phoenix

January 13, 1942, Denn Mine
George Andrew Page and N.C. McDaniel had lowered a mucking machine from the 2100 level and pulled it off on the 2200 level. Then they put a locomotive on the middle deck of the cage to be lowered to the 2300 level. Page rang the cage down and boarded the top deck with McDaniel. After giving the bell signal 3-2, Page reached his head too far out into the shaft, and his head was crushed between the station floor and the cage. He died instantly. Chester Merrill was one of the witnesses to the accident. He was later killed on September 1, 1944 at the Denn Mine.
"Cochise County Coroner's Inquest No. 1807" Arizona State Archives Phoenix

September 1, 1944,* Denn Mine
James Watson and Chester Henry Merrill were driving No.3 raise on the 2800 level. They had loaded and began spitting the round, when a shot detonated. Merrill was knocked into the chute, but Watson was able to get under the bulkhead protecting the manway and down to the level. When the rest of the blast detonated it shot about 18 ft. of muck on top of Merrill. It took four hours to uncover his body by drawing muck out of the chute.
* The accident occurred around midnight and there was some question if the fatality happened actually on August 31.
"Cochise County Coroner's Inquest No. 1823" Arizona State Archives Phoenix

January 7, 1946, Denn Mine
Miners, David Soliz Flores and Manuel Serrano, were cleaning up the seventh floor of No. 10 stope on the 2800 level to install timber. Serrano climbed down to the sixth floor to get an axe, and the area caved on Flores. When Serrano found Flores, he had two 100- pound rocks on him and a 50 lb. boulder on his feet. Flores died soon after the accident.
"Cochise County Coroner's Inquest No. 1830" Arizona State Archives Phoenix

April 24, 1959 Denn Mine
At the skip pocket at the 1700 level skip pocket a miner bruised his lower jaw and chipped some teeth in a haulage accident.
1959-1961 safety ledger p.26

June 24, 1959 Denn Mine
In the Denn Mine Yard, R.O. Garcia, broke his left large toe in an undescribed accident.
1959-1961 safety ledger p.46

March 23, 1960 Denn Mine
On the 3100 level, C.E. Hamm suffered a cut right eyebrow.
1959-1961 safety ledger p.94

March 24, 1961 Denn Mine
A, C. Combel got debris in his left eye while working at the 3100 level pumps.
1959-1961 safety ledger p.190

October 2, 1961 Denn Mine
A.C. Boeckman was struck in the back by a falling object while he was in the shaft between the 2900 and 3100 levels.
1959-1961 safety ledger p.246

May 23, 1975, Denn Mine
At the pump station on the 3100 level, Ron Morrison was cleaning the electrodes for the sump. As he was *"crawling"** up the steps out of the sump he slipped and strained a muscle. * quoted from the report, this term implies the steps were in a confined area with restricted height.
Phelps Dodge Corporation Copper Queen Branch Accident Report 5-23-74

After the closure of the mine on June 12, 1975. Equipment was salvaged from the mine, by Bisbee Salvage & Equipment Company. The company continued to salvage equipment until around 1985. These following accidents are from the salvage period.

September 16, 1975, Denn Mine
At the collar of the shaft, B.B. Leiendecker was closing a door at the Denn Blower. He needed to close the door before starting the fan. Leiendecker pulled a muscle. Note, the blower/fan at the Denn was used to ventilate the mines for years after the official shutdown. Visitors to Evergreen Cemetery and much of Lowell could continuously hear the roar of the massive fan.
Phelps Dodge Corporation Copper Queen Branch Accident Report 8-24-75

November 24, 1975, Denn Mine
Pipe Riggerman, C.W. Amos along with L.E. Shafer, C.H. Giacomino, R.Nicolson and W.D. Blodgett were salvaging a transformer and a pump from the 3100 level Pump Station. The five men were carrying the pump over difficult terrain. Amos slipped and suffered bruising over sacral spine area. Interestingly, Dan Vucurivich investigated the accident and recommended to prevent the accident. These men should of cleaned up the drift including mucking up two cave-ins and laying 200 feet of rail. (It is interesting that the recommended repairs could have exceeded the value of the pump)
Phelps Dodge Corporation Copper Queen Branch Accident Report 11-24-75

December 29, 1975, Denn Mine
C.H. Giacomino was on the 2966 level walking between the Denn and Campbell Mines. He slipped on the wet ground and bruised his right hip.
Phelps Dodge Corporation Copper Queen Branch Accident Report 12-29-74

The Denn Mine C-1930

180

Gardner Shaft, c-1908

Gardner Mine

      The earliest mention of the Gardner property is the Tombstone Daily Prospector's report of November 22, 1890, a rich orebody was found in mine belonging to Gardner and West Howell. Soon after the Copper Queen Consolidated Mining Company purchased the property. This was considered a substantial risk since the extension of the ore to this area was considered doubtful.

      The starting date of the actual Gardner Shaft is unknown, but there was at least a small shaft on the property in 1895. In December 1901, the Gardner was already 626ft. deep and a connecting drift was being driven from the 400 level of the Holbrook #1 Shaft. At this time it was still considered an *"experiment"* and even when noted geologist Fredrick Ransome completed his field work in Bisbee for his U.S.G.S. Professional paper #21, it was considered a small prospect shaft. Ore bodies soon began to be developed, and the local newspaper commented that the waste dumps *"sparkled"* from sulfides.

      During 1903, it was decided to raise the third compartment from the 925ft. level to the surface. This additional compartment was added giving the shaft an unusual "L" shape. Eventually, this compartment was extended to the 1000 level. Extensive ore was discovered, and it became essential to purchase a new larger hoist. In 1904, a new steel headframe and hoist house was constructed. The new hoist was the largest in use in the southwestern United States. In August of 1906, it was decided to abandon the Holbrook # 1 Shaft. The Gardner and Czar Mines took over lowering men, supplies and hoisting ore for the Holbrook.

      The shaft was somewhat isolated and was not well connected with other mines and unlike in the Czar-Holbrook area, there were not numerous surface cracks that provided natural ventilation. The mine was hot and damp. Working temperatures were typically between 75° and 100°. This combined that the humidity levels ranged between 90% and 100% made working conditions challenging. Miners were rotated through the hot areas, working two-three days before being sent to a location with more agreeable conditions. Timber suffered as well the timber was damp and covered with abundant fungus growth. Wood deteriorated rapidly. New connections with other mine workings were tried, but only increased ventilation slightly and were ineffective. In 1912, ventilation plans were developed to install large fans, but took a few years to implement fully. During 1913, the first of the new fans arrived and were installed underground, and a winze was sunk from the 1000 level and began to develop an orebody. A 72,000 cu. Ft. fan was installed in 1914 on the 900 level. The mechanical ventilation plan was successful and not only reduced working temperatures it also dried up the mine and reduced timber decay.

The mine operated through the 1920's and was shut down for a few months in July 1930, but was operating again shortly until it closed on November 1, 1931, after Phelps Dodge merged with the Calumet & Arizona Mining Company. The Gardner remained closed until 1936, when it and the Sacramento Mine reopened as Division "E". In 1937, the shaft was repaired from the 1400 level to the surface. During this time leases were granted and continued the mining. Unused buildings were demolished in the 1940s on the site and in 1942, the change house was torn down. In 1944, with the cessation of lease mining, the Gardner was closed again. At the completion the shaft was 1,457 ft. deep with three compartments.

November 25, 1902, Gardner Mine

Edward. M. Norton & Fred Stone were 670 feet down at the bottom of the Gardner Shaft. They were working on sinking the shaft. Above, this shaft was being used as a hoisting shaft from the 600 ft. level to the surface. A cage was being lowered to the 600 level. The hoistman watched the cable looking for the indication tag* to appear. Suddenly, and unexpectedly, the cage struck the bottom of the shaft. Norton was bending over at the time, and his head and back was hit by the cage. Stone received lesser undescribed injuries since he was in a safer location when the cage hit. The hoistman was quoted as exclaiming *The cage has struck the bottom. I hope to God there is no one hurt.* It was later determined the indication tag for the 600 level had come off, and the hoistman had not known when to stop the cage. Fred Stone was helped to his home on School Hill by a friend, and Norton was taken to the Copper Queen Hospital. Eventually, Norton, his wife, and Stewart McGregor a steward at the Copper Queen Hospital went to Los Angeles to seek treatment for Norton's back injury. There his condition worsened, and he died in Los Angeles on March 30th. His body was taken to Texas and at his request, he was buried in his uniform for Redmen League. He was survived by his wife, Maggie and a sister in Bisbee. This was the first serious accident to occur in the Gardner, and it was eventually to become a fatal accident. (No coroner's inquest could be located)

*Normally, hoist have an indicator dial which has an arrow that pointed to marks or metal tags indicating which level the cage or bucket was located. Another method to determine the location of the cage was to tie on an indication tag of colored cloth to the cable. When the section of cable with the colored cloth tied became unwound and was free of the hoist drum the hoistman would know he had reached a level. This method was often used when sinking a shaft since the shaft depth was changing and with a smaller hoist that had temporary placements.

"Narrow Escape Gardner Shaft." Bisbee Daily Review 26 November 1902 page 5
"Norton Dies in Los Angeles" Bisbee Daily Review 3 April 1903 page 4
"Paid Insurance Bisbee Daily Review 7 June 1903 page 6

December 8, 1903, Gardner Mine

At 11:30 pm, William Cooper was turning a mine car on a turnsheet on the 900 level when it rolled over his left foot. He was expected to be off work four days.

"Had leg Crushed" Bisbee Daily Review 10 December 1903 page 5

October 26, 1906, Gardner Mine
A.B. Wyeth, a carman at the Gardner had his arm caught between mine cars. He was taken to the Copper Queen Dispensary, and they discovered that even though the wrist was badly bruised, no bones were broken. It was determined that he probably would not be able to use his arm for a couple of weeks.

"Hurt at Mine" Bisbee Daily Review 27 October 1906 page 6

October 28, 1906, Gardner Mine
A 22-year-old, pipe fitter named C.M. Putts*was told by the foreman to head to the 1000 level to repair pipes. Putts loaded his tools and pipe onto the cage. What happened next is not clear. C.M. Putts either mistakenly rang the signal* for the 900 level or the hoisting engineer misheard the signal and sent him to the 900 level. When Putts arrived at the station, he must have realized it was the wrong level. The hoist engineer was waiting to receive a single bell, which was the signal that the cage was released for other duties; instead, he received a signal to take the cage to the 1000 level. On the 1000 level, the hoisting engineer waited for an extended time and the cage was not released. Finally, a signal was given to raise the cage to the surface. At the collar, a group of miners carried the unconscious form of Putts off the cage. It was learned they had discovered Putts lying on the floor of the cage at the 1000 level. At the time of the investigation, C.M. Putts was in the hospital under opiates, recovering from a jaw broken on both sides and cuts around the left eye and scalp. A theory that was proposed was that Putts was leaning his head slightly out of the cage and looking down as it descended. His head struck the timbered station floor causing the injuries

*The name is spelled both Putts and Butts in the same article.
*In 1912 the bell signal for the 900 level was 4-1 and the signal for the 1000 level was 4-2. Since this accident occurred in 1906 before Arizona had adopted a state code of mine bell signals it cannot be assured that these were the signals in use at the time, but there was likely only one bell difference between these levels.

"Accident at the Gardner Shaft." Bisbee Daily Review 30 October 1906 page 8
"Warren District Mines" Bisbee Daily Review 23 June 1912 page 4

December 13, 1906, Gardner Mine
Nelson Gart was caught in a cave-in on the 700 level. The falling rock broke his right leg below the knee. He was taken to the hospital.

"Hurt at Gardner Shaft." Bisbee Daily Review 14 December 1906 page 5

December 13, 1906, Gardner Mine
Charles Nuquest broke his left foot when it was smashed by a 12" X 12" timber. This accident happened soon after Nelson Gart was injured.

"Hurt at Gardiner Shaft." Bisbee Daily Review 14 December 1906 page 5

November 16, 1907 Gardner Mine

Fred Bellisto had his head* in an undescribed accident. He suffered scalp wounds. It is noted in the Copper Queen Hospital records that he left the institution against advice.* The newspaper claimed he broke his leg, hospital records note head injuries.

"Miner Breaks Leg" Bisbee Daily Review 17 November 1907, page 3
"Copper Queen Hospital Records November 16, 1907" Bisbee Mining & Historical Museum

February 20, 1908, Gardner Mine

Ben Gerdes had just returned to work after recovering from a previous injury when timber fell on his foot. Then on his first day back to work in the Gardner, Ben was struck in the head by a cage and given a severe cut several inches long.

"Head Injured" Bisbee Daily Review 20 February 1908 page 3

May 5, 1908, Gardner Mine

Albert Harris and Alex Niglayson were in 3-1 stope on the 900 level. They had a boulder jammed up against the timber. At noon, they blasted and were working. Fred Benson was drilling on the set above them. They asked Benson to stop drilling, while they worked for about ten minutes. The men told Benson he could start drilling again. After about a minute of drilling, Benson heard the boulder fall. This slab fatally injured Harris and wounded Niglayson. Harris regained consciousness, but was unable to clearly communicate. Albert suffered a ruptured liver and bladder. Also, one of his legs was smashed. Harris was 30 years old and had married on March 21, 1908, a divorcee, Mabel Jeffries. She had divorced D' Arcy Trezise a miner who had lost his eyes in a mine accident on April 27, 1907. He was buried in the same plot with his father-in-law who had died in bed from a heart condition four months earlier.

"Caught by Cave-In a Miner is Killed" Bisbee Daily Review 6 May 1908 page 1
"Funeral services Sunday" Bisbee Daily Review 8 May 1908 page 5
"Narrow Escape for Young Man at Czar Shaft." Bisbee Daily Review 28 April 1907 page 5
"Trezise-Jeffries" Bisbee Daily Review 14 April 1907 page 5
"Married Saturday" Bisbee Daily Review 24 March 1908 page 7
"Original Certificate of Death." Arizona Department of Health Services. http://genealogy.az.gov/azdeath/002/10021406.pdf (November 5, 2011)
"Cochise County Coroner's Inquest No. 556" Arizona State Archives Phoenix

Headstone of Albert Harris and his father in law, John Jeffrey.

May 11, 1908, Gardner Mine

John Obertaxer was working on the 1000 level repairing an electric light wire that had been broken by blasting on the previous shift. The wire was too short for him to splice it directly together, so he spliced on a short piece of electric light wire onto the section he held in his hand. Then he asked M. Fitzpatrick to help him. Fitzpatrick held one end as Obertaxer tried to connect the wires together. Just as Obertaxer was about to make the connection, he shouted *"Wire! Wire!"* Fitzpatrick struck the wire with a shovel to break the circuit.

Obertaxer fell in a sitting position. The men with him tried to revive him by rubbing his face and hands. Obertaxer groaned twice and likely died. He was transported to the Copper Queen Hospital by four men and a stretcher. It was later, revealed that Obertaxer heart had been giving him trouble since at least November 1906. He was from Canton, Austria where his parents still lived. John Obertaxer was 34 years old. At the inquest, George Sabin a miner who was 50 ft. away, from the accident, translated a letter from Obertaxer's parents on March 11, 1906. He read, *"Dear Son I write to you today about news. Mother is sick. She is so sick the priest think she will die. We received your letter and you told us you would come about Easter. I wish you would come at once as so that you can see mother alive for I let you know that I have been sick for three weeks that he was watching the bed and now he has to attended mother and I wished if it is possible to come right away. My Regards Mother and Father."*

"Touches Live Wire is Killed Instantly" Bisbee Daily Review 12 May 1908 page 5
"Cochise County Coroner's Inquest No. 558" Arizona State Archives Phoenix

August 15, 1908, Gardner Mine
George Kiser was struck in the right knee by a timber. Kiser was carried to the Copper Queen Hospital. He was operated on and released on August 31.

"Hurt in Mine" Bisbee Daily Review 16 August 1908 page 7
"Copper Queen Hospital Records August 15, 1908" Bisbee Mining & Historical Museum

December 2, 1908, Gardner Mine
John Riley fell bruising his back and left arm. He was released from the Copper Queen Hospital on December 9th. His wife was Zella Riley.

"Copper Queen Hospital Records December 2, 1908" Bisbee Mining & Historical Museum
"Riley is Recovering" Bisbee Daily Review 12 December 1908 page 7

September 27, 1908, Gardner Mine
At 10:00 am, 23-year-old, William. T. Johnson was working with Mike Gerrity in 9-9 raise on the 800 level. He handed Gerrity some wedges then shouted *"Look out!"* and a rock fell from the side of the raise and crushed his head. His mother, Mrs. A.E. Cromer, reportedly had a premonition of his death she was quoted as telling her son *"My son, I have a premonition that you will be killed in the mines. Do be careful"* She told this to her son before she left on a trip to Findlay, Ohio. Johnson was survived by his parents Mr. & Mrs. A.E. Cromer and a brother and sister. He was buried in Evergreen Cemetery.

"Premonition Followed by Death" Bisbee Daily Review 28 September 1908 page 8
"Card of Thanks" Bisbee Daily Review 6 October 1908 page 6
"Original Certificate of Death." Arizona Department of Health Services. http://genealogy.az.gov/azdeath/007/10070718.pdf
   (May 15, 2012)
"Cochise County Coroner's Inquest No. 689" Arizona State Archives Phoenix

September 27, 1908, Gardner Mine
Two hours after W.T. Johnson was killed in a cave-in, Michael Welch was also killed in the Gardner. He died in a similar manner as Johnson. His skull was crushed in a cave-in.

He was survived by two sisters Mrs. H.A. Shuck of Oatman, Arizona and Mrs. Mary Griffin of Butte Montana. His brother Patrick Welch worked with the Heffern Mining Company in the Swisshelms. (No coroner's inquest could be located)
"Premonition Followed by Death" Bisbee Daily Review 28 September 1908 page 8

September 22, 1909, Gardner Mine
At 10.00 pm, Cornish Miner, Thomas H. Trengove* was working on the 700 level at the top of 8-11-10 stope. Trengove was going to lower timber down a manway. He told Ed R. Murtha, who was dumping wheelbarrow loads of muck into the chute to stop for a while. When reached for the timbers, Trengove uttered, "*Oh*", threw his arms up and fell into the chute. The young man died instantly. He was new to Bisbee and had arrived in the city on July 29th. Thomas was soon employed at the Gardner Mine. His brother Fred Trengove of Globe, Arizona was notified of the accident. His brother Fred and a good friend Fred Chinn attended the funeral. Thomas Trengove was buried in Evergreen Cemetery.(Note, the coroner's inquest for Trengove is misnumbered and has the same number as the Inquest for William T Johnson another miner killed in the Gardner Mine.)
*Name is spelled Trengrove in the newspaper articles.
"Bisbee-Lowell Evergreen Cemetery." My Cochise.
http://www.mycochise.com/cembisbeet.php (July 20, 2011)
"Brother is Coming" Bisbee Daily Review 24, September 1909 page 6
"Trengrove's Funeral Held" Bisbee Daily Review 28, September 1909 page 8
"Cochise County Coroner's Inquest No. 689" Arizona State Archives Phoenix

November 14, 1909, Gardner Mine
Urias W. Springer and Charles Jean were trying to free a hung up chute. They used a scaling bar and got it flowing. As Jean was cleaning up the area he looked and saw Springer had fallen and was holding the bar, which was touching the live wire. He told William Eldridge to knock the bar away from the wire, but Eldridge hesitated, and Jean struck the bar with his hand. Springer's body was shipped to Pecos, Texas for burial. He was 28 years old and unmarried.
"Miner Electrocuted at Gardner" Bisbee Daily Review 16 November 1909 page 1
"Remains go east" Bisbee Daily Review 17 November 1909 page 7
"Original Certificate of Death." Arizona Department of Health Services.
http://genealogy.az.gov/azdeath/007/10071192.pdf (April 22, 2011)
Gerald F. G. Sherman. "Tramming and Hoisting at the Copper Queen Mine." American Institute of Mining Engineers Transaction Volume LII 1916: Page 465.
"Cochise County Coroner's Inquest No. 701" Arizona State Archives Phoenix

January 28, 1910, Gardner Mine
Mining Engineer, C.W. Evans fell 100-feet down a raise* He was working at the top of the raise when he stumbled and fell. Evans landed on his feet and was relatively unhurt. The instruments he was using were destroyed by the fall. The engineer was expected to be able to return to work in a couple of days.
*The newspaper article states he fell into a new shaft, but this was a raise or winze
"Falls Hundred Feet and is Not Hurt" Bisbee Daily Review 29 July 1910 page 5

February 22, 1910, Gardner Mine

Abram Leise had his hand smashed by timber and was taken to the Copper Queen Dispensary. He was expected to return to work in about seven days.

"Hurt at Gardner" Bisbee Daily Review 24 February 1910 page 7

March 19, 1910, Gardner Mine

A.E. Cromer fell into a manway and was knocked unconscious. He was taken to the Copper Queen Hospital where he was revived. A medical examination revealed he had suffered only a few scratches and was suffering from shock. He remained in the hospital until March 29th.

"Injured by Fall Mine Shaft." Bisbee Daily Review 20 March 1910 page 5
"Copper Queen Hospital Records March 19, 1908" Bisbee Mining & Historical Museum

April 6, 1910, Gardner Mine

English Miner, Paul Arthur had his ankle broken by a falling rock. He was taken to the Copper Queen Hospital. On May 21, 1910, it was reported that had returned to England.

"Man Found Dead in Lowell; Bisbee Accidents" El Paso Herald 21 May 1910 page 17
"Injured in The Gardner" Bisbee Daily Review 7 April 1910 page 5

April 27, 1910, Gardner Mine

Frank Oliver was caught in a cave-in. He was cut and bruised. Treatment for Oliver was provided, and he was taken to the Copper Queen Hospital.

"Hurt by Cave-in" Bisbee Daily Review 29 April 1910 page 5

June 1910, Gardner Mine

A rock fell striking the head of A. Grim.

"Many Miners Injured; Local News" El Paso Herald 29 June 1910 page 9

June 26, 1910, Gardner Mine

A boulder struck the hip of W.R. Moss. He was taken to the Copper Queen Hospital where it was determined his back was only bruised. Moss was released three days later.

"Many Miners Injured; Local News" El Paso Herald 29 June 1910 page 9
"Copper Queen Hospital Records June 26, 1910" Bisbee mining & Historical Museum Bisbee

October 1910, Gardner Mine

An Italian, Charles Mosea was slightly injured when he was hit in the head by a falling rock.

"Slightly Injured" Bisbee Daily Review 29, October 1910 page 5

October 24, 1910, Gardner Mine

Charles Myers, brother of Edward Myers the foreman of the Gardner Shaft was caught between a *"motor car"** and a timber. His thumb was amputated during the accident. He stated that he did not hear the train coming towards him. Myers was taken to the Copper

Queen Hospital. There it was felt that he had not sustained any internal injuries. He was released from the hospital on December 12th. *The term "motor car" is used in a manner that it could mean a locomotive or a mine car being pulled by a locomotive.

"Workman is Badly Crushed in Mine" Bisbee Daily Review 25, October 1910 page 1
"Copper Queen Hospital Records October 24 1910" Bisbee Mining & Historical Museum

December 7, 1910, Gardner Mine

William Cooper was working on the 900 level turning a mine car on a turnsheet, when it ran over his left foot. He was put on disability for four days.

"Had Leg Crushed" Bisbee Daily Review 10 December 1910 page 5

July 14, 1911, Gardner Mine

William Bradley broke his wrist after falling. Bradley impressively withstood the pain. He asked the doctor *"Is it broken?"* After the doctor replied, *"Yes."* He responded, simply *"Fix it."*

"Suffers Broken Wrist" Bisbee Daily Review 15 July 1911 page 5

October 5, 1911, Gardner Mine

Frank *"Boswick"* Blozevich* a 40 -year-old single Austrian was working in 8-11-14 stope on the 800 level. He climbed 15 ft. to the 700 level drift to get an air hose. Two men were repairing the 700 level drift. This drift had settled from mining and was no longer large enough for a mine car to pass. Chris Gregovich and M.E. Fisher were cutting out and installing new timber and enlarging the drift. Fisher gave Blozevich the air hose and help him pull it down. Just as he was going to turn on the air for Blozevich he heard a crash as the stope collapsed. A mass of muddy earth and boulders buried his work area, trapping him. It was not clear whether he had been killed or was alive. Soon after the cave-in, Fisher crawled through a narrow opening to reach Blozevich, but falling dirt extinguished his candle, and he was never able to get to him. Three shifts of eight men spent forty-four hours trying to rescue him. The area continued to collapse hampering rescue attempts. At three o'clock, on October 7, his body was brought to the surface. Blozevich had been killed by the collapse. He was buried at Evergreen Cemetery and the Copper Queen Band played at his funeral. He was survived by his brothers, Anton and Gaspar. Anton lived in Calumet, Michigan.

* Sometimes referred to as Defwick in documents.

One Man is Buried in Gardner Shaft." Bisbee Daily Review 6 October 1911 page 1
"Buried Miner's Body Brought to Surface" Bisbee Daily Review 8 October 1911 page 1
"Funeral of Miner" Bisbee Daily Review 10 October 1911 page 2
"Cochise County Coroner's Inquest No. 869" Arizona State Archives Phoenix

A settling drift and chute.
Note, how a post has been
notched to allow a mine
car to pass through.
C-1917

A band playing for a funeral at Evergreen
Cemetery. The Denn Mine is in the background
(Courtesy of the Bisbee Mining & Historical
Museum)

October 24, 1911, Gardner Mine
Burt Hurst was struck by an unknown object falling down the shaft while he was working
on a cage. Three pieces of bone were embedded into his brain. He was taken to the Copper
Queen Hospital by ambulance, where an operation was performed. By November 15, 1911,

he had largely recovered and was able to travel to Phoenix with his mother, but he was still unable to completely use his left hand.*

*The newspaper article describing this accident stated it was the third mining injury of a fractured skull and completed the mining superstition that mining accidents occurred in sequences of threes. The others were Joe Hall on October 19, 1911 in the Uncle Sam Mine and a man named Dennis in the Sacramento Shaft on October 18, 1911.
"Skull Fractured by Falling Object" Bisbee Daily Review 25 October 1911 page 3
"Burt Hurst Leaves" Bisbee Daily Review 15 November 1911 page 5
"Miner Injured by Falling Timber" Bisbee Daily Review 20 October 1911 page 3

December 31, 1911, Gardner Mine

An Italian Miner, Antonio Buffone was lifting heavy timbers and stained his back. He was taken to the Copper Queen Hospital and was expected to be off work for several days.
"Suffers Injured Back" Bisbee Daily Review 1 January 1911 page 5

May 18, 1912, Gardner Mine
Perry Puckett was injured by a falling rock that fractured a rib.
"Stone Falls, Miner's Spine is Fractured" Bisbee Daily Review 19 May 1912 page 2

March 7, 1912, Gardner Mine

John Frodin, a miner recently from Komo, Colorado, was killed about 10 o'clock in the morning. He was trying to remove a loose sulfide slab. At first, he tried to pry it down with a bar when this failed he began to try to bring it down with a drill. After drilling a short distance, the slab fell striking Frodin on the head. The boulder crushed his head scattering his brains. The drill itself was broken in two by the impact of the rock.
"Caught in Cave-in Life Crushed Out" Bisbee Daily Review 8 March 1912 page 6
"Original Certificate of Death." Arizona Department of Health Services. http://genealogy.az.gov/azdeath/010/10100024.pdf (April 22, 2011)
"Cochise County Coroner's Inquest No. 902" Arizona State Archives Phoenix

August 22, 1912, Gardner Mine
Louis Grabes fell and injured his back in an undescribed accident.
Two Miners Hurt" Bisbee Daily Review 23 August 1912 page 8

August 24, 1912, Gardner Mine

E.W. Hallen was caught in a blast. He was taken to the Copper Queen Hospital where a "foreign body" was removed from his eye. Hallen remained in the hospital 28 days.
"Casualties in Mines 1912" Bisbee Daily Review 12 January 1913, page 7
Copper Queen Hospital Patients Register August 24, 1912, Bisbee Mining and Historical Museum, Bisbee.

October 29, 1912, Gardner Mine
Louis Anderson was injured in an undescribed accident.
"Miner Slightly Injured" Bisbee Daily Review 30 October 1912 page 8

December 15, 1912, Gardner Mine
Fred Laster had his hip dislocated in an undescribed accident. H.B. Green was likely with him, but only had minor injuries. Laster spent 53 days in the Copper Queen Hospital.
"Untitled" Bisbee Daily Review 17 December 1912 page 8
Copper Queen Hospital Patients Register December 15, 1912 Bisbee Mining and Historical Museum, Bisbee.

January 20, 1913, Gardner Mine

Meade A. Welty was injured his hip in the Gardner Mine and taken to the Copper Queen Hospital. On December 1, 1913, Welty left Bisbee to go to Chicago to have an operation for his injury.

"Injured in Mine" Bisbee Daily Review 21 January 1913 page 5
"Will Have Operation" Bisbee Daily Review 1 December 1913 page 8
"Copper Queen Hospital Records January 20, 1913" Bisbee Mining & Historical Museum

January 23, 1913, Gardner Mine

At 12:30 pm, William Vlacis, and John Strom were working on the 900 level in 8-23 stope. The men were cutting out room for a set of timber, when, a mass of rock fell. Vlacis was killed instantly, and Strom was trapped, but still alive. Miners were able to free Strom and recover Vlacis' body by cutting out the lagging and digging them out. William Vlacis was survived by his wife, Magdalena and his brother George. (Note the newspaper article describes the accident details different than the inquest.)

"Ground Caves One Life is Lost" Bisbee Daily Review 23 January 1913 page 2
"Vlacksis Funeral" Bisbee Daily Review 24 January 1913 page 6
"Cochise County Coroner's Inquest No. 974" Arizona State Archives Phoenix

January 23, 1913, Gardner Mine

J.J. Rowell had his left foot crushed and a fractured skull. He was taken to the Copper Queen Hospital, where he remained 321 days.

"Injured at Gardner" Bisbee Daily Review 24 January 1913 page 6
"Copper Queen Hospital Records January 23, 1913" Bisbee Mining & Historical Museum

February 12, 1913, Gardner Mine

Joe Gallagher was injured in the Gardner Mine. He was sent to the Copper Queen Hospital, then allowed to return home.

"Miner Injured" Bisbee Daily Review 13 February 1913 page 8

February 22, 1913, Gardner Mine

At 1 o'clock in the afternoon, Joseph Reibuffo, George Gregovich, and Fred Lasso were working on the 700 level loading a mine car in 771 drift. This drift was being driven to connect to 1110 stope. Reibuffo was working at the end of the drift behind the mine car which almost blocked the drift. Lasso and Gregovich were on the other side of the car in the part of the drift which connected to the rest of the mine. Without warning, the gob in 1110 stope underneath the drift began to cave in. This caused the drift to cave in as well. Gregovich and Lasso shouted to Reibuffo and ran out of the unhindered drift to safety. Reibuffo started to leave, but the mine car blocked his way out, and he was buried by tons of falling waste rock. Lasso and Gregovich alerted other miners and formed a rescue team. They were able to uncover Reibuffo, but he was already dead. It was determined at Palace Undertaking, that since he was only bruised and no bones were broken, Reibuffo must have died from suffocation. The cave-in was so severe that an old drift had to be opened to access abandoned stopes to reach Reibuffo. The serious nature of this collapse prevented the Coroner's Jury from visiting the site. He was 21 years old and a native of Italy. Before working at the Gardner, he was employed at the Spray Shaft. Mrs. John Caretto, his sister, was the only relative in Bisbee. He was buried in Evergreen Cemetery. In 1960, his sister was buried next to him. His close friend Dominic Papas was allowed to give his testimony to the Coroner's Jury early, so he could attend the funeral.

"Suffocated in Waste Slip" Bisbee Daily Review 23 February 1913 page 9
"Reibuffo Funeral Held Yesterday" Bisbee Daily Review 25 February 1913 page 8
"Cochise County Coroner's Inquest No. 986" Arizona State Archives Phoenix

March 10, 1913, Gardner Mine

A. Matzmacher slipped and fell while climbing a manway on the 200 level. He landed on the level and broke his arm both at the wrist and shoulder. Matzmacher was taken to the Copper Queen Hospital, where he remained 344 days.

"Injured" Bisbee Daily Review 11 March 1913 page 8
"Copper Queen Hospital Records March 10, 1913" Bisbee Mining & Historical Museum

June 5, 1913, Gardner Mine

Italian Miner, Martin De Fillippi broke his leg in an undescribed mine accident. During his recuperation at the Copper Queen Hospital he contracted pneumonia. He died on June 19, 1913 from pneumonia.

"Copper Queen Hospital Records June 5, 1913" Bisbee Mining & Historical Museum
"Original Certificate of Death." Arizona Department of Health Services. http://genealogy.az.gov/azdeath/011/10111504.pdf (August 15, 2015)
"Pneumonia Victim" Bisbee Daily Review 20 June 1913 page 8

November 18, 1913, Gardner Mine

Patrick Donnelly had his right leg broken and cut up in a cave-in. The wound became infected and he remained at the Copper Queen Hospital 41 days. He filed a lawsuit against the mining company, but this case was dismissed in December 1916 by the federal court in Tucson.

"Had Leg Broken" Bisbee Daily Review 19 November 1913 page 8
Case Dismissed" Bisbee Daily Review 19 December 1916 page 1
"Copper Queen Hospital Records November 18, 1913" Bisbee Mining & Historical Museum

Around 1913 Gardner Mine

An unnamed miner was seventy feet up a raise installing chute lining. He had taken a 2" X 12" lagging and placed it on a two 2" X 4" cleats nailed to the chute lining. The board was knocked out and the miner fell and only broke his ankle. This accident was brought up at a Safety First Meeting in January 1914. The company Safety Inspector Wallace McKeehan said *"Owing to the fact that the Goddess who watches over all mud diggers was right on the job had arranged a soft pile of muck for him to land on, he was not badly injured, otherwise he would have been killed. This accident was caused by carelessness on part of the bosses and the men and the poor method of doing work. Both the bosses and the men think that a mud digger can work on a shoestring if it is tied tight enough, no matter how high up in the air he may be. If you fellows intend to follows this practice you should get a bunch of toy balloons and tie them onto a miners back so that he will come down more slowly"*.

"Safety First Meetings Have Attendance of Wide Results" <u>Bisbee Daily Review</u> 20 January 1914 page 5

January 9, 1914, Gardner Mine

Around 11:00 am, Austin Scrimpsher was installing chute lining when he fell. Scrimpsher dropped 85 ft. and fractured ankle and sprained his back. He was expected to be in the hospital around three months.

"Miraculously Escapes Death" Bisbee Daily Review 10 January 1914 page 6
"Recovering Rapidly" Bisbee Daily Review 14 January 1914 page 8

February 28, 1914 Gardner Mine

J.B. Huff "Babe "was working on the 800 level when a small cave-in struck him and knocked him into chute. His arm, collar bone and ribs were broken. He died from internal injuries on March 6, 1914. Huff was survived by a brother J.A. Huff, a sister Mrs. C.A. Bennett and a half-brother J.R. Hill. (No coroner's inquest could be located)

"Injuries in Mine Fatal" <u>Bisbee Daily Review</u> 7 March 1914 page 3
Copper Queen Hospital Patients Register February 1914 Bisbee Mining and Historical Museum, Bisbee.
"Original Certificate of Death." <u>Arizona Department of Health Services.</u> http://genealogy.az.gov/azdeath/012/10121487.pdf (July 24 2011)

August 3, 1914 Gardner Mine

Frank Riley was injured by caught in collapsing rock. He was taken to the Copper Queen Hospital and recovered after 21 days.

"Is Improving" <u>Bisbee Daily Review</u> 5 August 1914 page 8
"Copper Queen Hospital Records August 3, 1914" Bisbee 4ining & Historical Museum

September 13? 1914, Gardner Mine

Ned White* had a block of timber fall onto his foot and broke his ankle. White was a well-known miner in the district. By September 12, he was able to get around town on crutches.

* This may be the local poet.
"Ned White Meets with Misfortune" <u>Tombstone Epitaph</u> 13 September 1914 page 4

September 14, 1914, Gardner Mine

Irish Miner, James F. Conway was working in 8-12-8 stope on the 800 level, cleaning up a corner set in a square set stope. This was a stope mining lead ore. When around 11:45 pm, a section of the hanging wall fell crushing him. The boulder broke and rolled off of him. But he was alone when the accident occurred. Later, Shift Boss, Harry L. Schofield discovered him and talked to him and had him taken to the Copper Queen Hospital. The 27-year-old died on September 15. Conway was from Ballyconelli County Slige, Ireland. He was survived by a brother Patrick from El Paso and a sister in Ireland. (This accident is an example of the mining superstition that accidents occurred in groups of three. Thomas C. McBurney's death in the Czar Shaft on September 3, 1914 was considered the first. The second was James F. Conway in the Gardner Shaft and Andy Sterberg was the third when he was killed in the Cole Shaft on September 23, 1914.)

"James Conway is Dead from Injuries Received in Mine" <u>Bisbee Daily Review</u> 17 September 1914 page4
"Original Certificate of Death." <u>Arizona Department of Health Services.</u> http://genealogy.az.gov/azdeath/012/10122706.pdf (April 28, 2012)
"Cochise County Coroner's Inquest No. 1112" Arizona State Archives Phoenix

October 22, 1914, Gardner Mine

At 8:00 am, Leopold P. Pavlicich and Elmer Birtulla were working at the top of a chute. Unbeknownst to Pavlicich the grizzly had been loosed by a previous blast. Approximately, five tons of ore, fell knocking him by the grizzly into the chute which was 20 ft. deep. Blas Sky found Shift Boss Harry Lyons and told him to get men together and when Lyons asked him why he responded, *"Good Bye Louie"* Lyons immediately went to the chute. Charles C. King went down to the chute and began emptying it until the men above shouted that he had been uncovered. His skull was reported to be crushed. He was 48 years old and survived by a wife and child. Interestingly, Pavlicich was Croatian/Austrian and was expected to become a U.S. citizen the day after his death. Curiously, in December 22, 1914, Pavlicich's mining man check No. 2057 was found on the body of Andy Neonan after he was struck by a street car and killed.

"Accident in Mine Cost Life" Bisbee Daily Review 23 October 1914 page 5

"Accidental Death is Verdict of Jurymen" Bisbee Daily Review 24 October 1914 page 5

"Finlander Killed When Street Car Runs over His Body" Bisbee Daily Review 23 December 1914 page 5

"Original Certificate of Death." Arizona Department of Health Services. http://genealogy.az.gov/azdeath/012/10122963.pdf (May 12, 2012)

"Cochise County Coroner's Inquest No. 1118" Arizona State Archives Phoenix

The grave monument for Leopold P. Pavlicich.

Late January, 1915, Gardner Mine
Michael Finnegan cut his wrist on a nail. He was off work about three weeks.
"Reports for Work" Bisbee Daily Review 14 February 1915 page 8

April 10, 1916, Gardner Mine
Motorman, Albert Hassen while heading into the mine, became caught between a mine car and the wall and smashed his back. It was a while before the accident was discovered. Hassen was alone at the time of the accident, so the details are unknown. He was expected to recover.
"Mine Motorman is Crushed at Bisbee is Recovering" El Paso Herald 18 April 1916 page 9

May 6, 1916, Gardner Mine
M.D. Manix was inside a chute* when a mine car of sulfide ore was dumped into the chute and buried him. His screams were heard and his partner unburied his head so he could breathe. It took over two hours to completely uncover him. He was cut up, but not seriously hurt. (The reason for this is not entirely clear. It was reported that he was either repairing the chute or trying to free the rock that was hung up. The latter would be extremely dangerous and does not make sense.)
"Escapes Serious Injury When Buried" Bisbee Daily Review 9 May 1916 page 5

January 28, 1917, Gardner Mine
A rock fell on the left leg of R.H. Rocky. He was transported to his home at the Lockie House by the Brown and Hubbard ambulance.
"Miner injured" Bisbee Daily Review 31 January 1917 page 8

March 19, 1917, Gardner Mine
On the 200 level, Michael McEnroe and his partner Herbert Hall were working in No.225 crosscut and were only about 320 ft. from the shaft station. These men worked on Friday night and nobody worked in the crosscut until Monday night when McEnroe and Hall returned. They pushed in a drill and hose on a timber truck and McEnroe began digging with a pick. He struck a misfire, and it detonated. Hall made is way towards the shaft and saw the station lights and realized he was not blinded by the blast. Although, injured he made his way to the shaft and rang the call bells several times. Concerned by the calls the hoistman sent Charles M. Pert to see if anything was wrong. Pert found the injured Hall lying in front of the shaft. He informed Pert that Mike was still back in the crosscut and there had been a missed hole. The injured man was taken to the surface. On the 1000 level, Pert asked, John Pickering to help him and that there had been an accident. They returned to the 200 level and walked back and found McEnroe. They took the drill and hose off the timber truck and placed lagging on the truck and then put McEnroe on the truck and took him to the surface. McEnroe asked Pert *"What happened?' "Who he was?"* and ask him to take off his shoes. He was taken to the Copper Queen Hospital where he died. He was survived by a wife and daughter living in Denver. Hall remained in the hospital for 35 days.
"Miner is Fatally Injured as Pick Hits Powder Pocket" Bisbee Daily Review 20 March 1917 page 5
Office of State Mine Inspector. *Sixth Annual Report of the State Mine Inspector State of Arizona for the Year Ending November 30, 1917.*

Copper Queen Hospital Patients Register March 19, 1917 Bisbee Mining and Historical Museum, Bisbee.
"Cochise County Coroner's Inquest No. 1263" Arizona State Archives Phoenix

July 11, 1917, Gardner Mine

Frank Hagen was drilling in 8-25-18 stope on the 800 level to install timber and had a heart attack. Before his partner, J.G. Lee could get to him he had died. Hagen had been suffering from trouble from his heart before his death. He died from natural causes and not a mine accident. Interestingly, Hagen's funeral had to be changed to 3:00 pm because of the funeral of Orson McRae. McRae was killed during the Bisbee Deportation, and his funeral was widely attended.

"Gardner Miner is victim of Sudden Seizure of Heart" Bisbee Daily Review 12 June 1917 page 2
"The Frank Hagen Funeral" Bisbee Daily Review 15 June 1917 page 5
"Cochise County Coroner's Inquest No. 1286" Arizona State Archives Phoenix

May 30, 1917 Gardner Mine

Joseph Pawlowski* and G.P. Maybry were working in 38-13 raise on the 600 level. This area was right up against the Irish Mag side line and the stope connected to the Irish Mag Mine. The Irish Mag Stope was being mined by leasers, and this sometimes made it difficult to count the shots from blasting. The misfire board on the surface indicated that there were three missed holes in the raise. Each hole had 18-20 inches of unburned fuse sticking out of it. Mabry and Pawlowski noted that they never had been burned and felt they may have never even been lit. Maybry suspected there was a fourth missed hole in the opposite corner because the rock had not blasted out of that section. He pointed this out to Pawlowski. Soon after, Maybry left the raise to get powder to shoot the misfires and about four small holes Pawlowski was going to drill. Against company rules, Pawlowski began drilling plug holes with a jackhammer *"plugger"* and he drilled into an unseen missed hole. The detonation broke an arm, a leg and destroyed one of his eyes. He died from shock and his injuries on May 31. Pawlowski was 28-years-old and from Austria Galicia. During the coroner's inquest, Night Foreman, James McGary mentioned that a year earlier, Pawlowski had climbed into a raise to soon after blasting, and the gasses knocked him out, and Pawlowski's partner had found him hanging head down from a foot caught on a ladder.

*The newspaper spelled his name Poliski
"Bisbee Miner Killed Picked into Missed Hole" Tombstone Weekly Epitaph 3 June 1917 page 8
"Original Certificate of Death." Arizona Department of Health Services. http://genealogy.az.gov/azdeath/016/10160920.pdf (August 1 2011)
"Cochise County Coroner's Inquest No. 1281" Arizona State Archives Phoenix

Joseph Pawlowski

August 14, 1918 Gardner Mine
J.H. Atchison (Atkinson?) was injured under the left eye with a pick.
"Receives Slight Injury" <u>Bisbee Daily Review</u> 15 August1918, page 8

October 8, 1918, Gardner Mine
Frank Smith was struck by falling rock. His shoulder was bruised
"Is Slightly Injured" <u>Bisbee Daily Review</u> 10 October 1918 page 6

October 10, 1918, Gardner Mine
William Woron suffered serious injuries to his back and shoulders when he was caught in a cave-in.
"Is Badly Injured" <u>Bisbee Daily Review</u> 11 October 1918 page 6

January 5, 1919, Gardner Mine
Gilberto Martinez broke his right leg and toe when a mine car loaded with steel overturned onto him. The car was probably loaded with drill steel.
"Leg is Injured" <u>Bisbee Daily Review</u> 5 January 1919 page 8

August 17, 1919, Gardner Mine
D. Galo was oiling a hoist when his foot became caught in the machinery. His foot was only severely bruised.
"Injures Foot" <u>Bisbee Daily Review</u> 17 August 1919 page 6

February 25, 1920, Gardner Mine

Motorman, Harry Gundy had his forefinger traumatically amputated while dumping a mine car.

"Loses Finger" Bisbee Daily Review 25 February 1920 page 6

Georgia Tunnel

This adit was driven by the Wolverine & Arizona Mining Company to explore the Georgia Claim in 1916. The adit was driven in barren limestone and failed to find any ore. This prospect is located south of the Powell Shaft at about 6,000 ft. in elevation.

July 18, 1916, Georgia Tunnel/Powell Mine

Austrian, Marco Sunara had his left eye destroyed and his right hand amputated after dynamite exploded in his hand. According to Sunara he had found a package on the road near the Powell Mine and when he opened it, the dynamite exploded. An investigation after revealed that Sunara had hired on as a miner to work at the nearby Georgia tunnel. Unfortunately, he was only a mucker and had had no experience with explosives. It is believed he went to the Powell Shaft to practice the use of explosives, so he would not be found out. After lighting the fuse in the Powell compressor and hoist house, it detonated. Blood and bone was found embedded in the wood of the building. A spent fuse was also found on the site.

"Miner Experimented with Dynamite, May Die" Bisbee Daily Review 20 July 1916 page 1

Hendricks Mine

Located in Hendricks Gulch at about 5,500ft.-5,600ft. in elevation these early workings were largely after silver rich cerussite and not copper. D.B. Rae, George Warren and Warner Buck worked these claims in 1878. They were able to build a small Mexican style furnace and refined 50lbs. of silver that was determined to be .947 fine at the U.S. Mint in San Francisco. Although, silver was their primary interests they did smelt enough ore to make 1,000lbs. of copper. During March 1881, some silver mineralization was explored on the Hendricks Claim then owned by Corbin company of Tombstone and had small, adobe, smelter with bellows which they refined ore at a rate of one ton per day. Frank Corbin with the Orion Silver Mining Company patented the Hendricks claim in 1882.

Before 1903, the Hendricks claim was purchased by the Copper Queen Consolidated Mining Company, who leased the property for mining. On February 9, 1904 John Kickham and Henry Tarr (1/2 of the Tarr brothers champion hand drilling team) reported to the Bisbee Daily Review that they had driven 200 ft. of drift and a raise into lead *"sand"* carbonates on the Tarr lease. The 200ft. of drift had cost them $1000, due to the hard ground. Worked continue on the property, but it was from workings deep underground that the value of the claim was determined. In 1911, raises were driven from the 200 level of the Czar Mine upward into Queen Hill. Upon finding ore, these raises were extended and eventually converted to interior shafts. These new interior shafts along with a number of adits and the Sunrise Shaft on the surface eventually became the Southwest Mine.

From examining photographs and maps of the area it appears that two of the adits, more commonly known as levels of the Southwest mine were likely original Hendricks Mine workings . The 5th level Southwest or Southwest Tunnel was likely part of the Hendricks, later it was renamed and a concrete façade added to the entrance. In these photographs, dumps are established around the 6th level Southwest area as well. The description of the mine accident that killed John Kickham fits well with mine workings, around 200 ft. from the entrance of the 6th level Southwest Mine there is a stope now day-lighted, in which cerussite was the primary ore. Also, one of the two 6th Level Southwest mine portals (the two portals are next to each other) matches a short adit that is found on the 1904 map of underground of the Copper Queen and was likely part of the Hendricks mine

workings. **Also there are the remains of a collapsed stope at about the 5640 ft. elevation just above the remains of the 6th level Southwest Mine portal. This stope could have been part of the original Hendricks workings. It appears the original Hendricks Mine became part of the Southwest Mine.**

February 9, 1904, Hendricks Mine
John Kickham, a leaser and a miner, C.F. Conrow entered the Hendricks Mine, and Kickham climbed a 15 ft. raise with a chute. The ground at the top of the raise was loose and probably was old gob from a stope they had accidently struck. Kickham knew the area was extremely dangerous and climbed to see how to proceed in mining. He intended to blast it down, while he was up there it is believed he poked at the loose ground with his candlestick, and it collapsed. The first cave-in partially buried him and he ordered Conrow to open the chute door, and let the muck out. When Conrow opened the chute door the rest of the rock caved-in, killing Kickham. His partner in the lease, Henry Kahrs was at the assay office when the accident occurred. He had a sister in Hampton, New York

"Cochise County Coroner's Inquest No. 869" Arizona State Archives
"A Sad Scene" Bisbee Daily Review 10 February 1904 page 3
"Will be Buried today" Bisbee Daily Review 11 February 1904 page 3

November 1, 1918, Hendricks Mine. Phelps Dodge Lease by Hunt & Zananoria
Aureliano Gomez was working in a stope when a half ton of dirt fell ten feet and buried him. Carletaho Raparous and Alfonso Guiterrez tried to unbury him, but could not, so they went to the home of one of the owners of the lease, Dominic Zananoria in Zacatecas Canyon. Zannoria had been at the mine most of the day, supervising the building of a corral and shed for the burros that hauled the ore down the hill. It was determined that Lee Hunt had wanted to install a 15 ft. stull, but they had to be special ordered, and the miner's said it was safe enough. The location for the stull caved, killing Gomez.

Office of State Mine Inspector. *Seventh Annual Report of the State Mine Inspector State of Arizona for the Year Ending November 30, 1918.*
"Cochise County Coroner's Inquest No.1359" Arizona State Archives Phoenix

The 5th & 6th levels of the Southwest mine high above Bisbee. The dark colored stables are at the 6th level & the long building is the changehouse for the 5th level. This is the area the Hendrick Mine was located. Before becoming part of the Southwest Mine.

The Higgins tunnel c-1904 (Courtesy of the Bisbee Mining & Historical Museum)

Higgins Mine

The Higgins Mine is located on the Webster Claim. This claim is a relocation of the early Copperopolis Claim. In the early years the Higgins Mine was actually considered part of the Twilight Mine. After some years the workings at the 5660 ft. elevation became known as the Higgins Mine and the workings at the upper elevations 5,800 ft. + retained the name Twilight Mine. The original Copperopolis property was developed around 1882 with an 85 ft. shaft. Thomas Higgins purchased the property from George Kline and Charles Anshultz (killed in Holbrook Mine November 9, 1899). It is reported that as the Twilight Company, Thomas Higgins working alone hand drilled the main Higgins Tunnel 650 ft. into the mountain

In 1903, Higgins sold the Twilight property including the Webster claim to the Higgins Development Company for $650,000. Thomas Higgins was a major stockholder of this new company. The tunnel was driven 1,600 ft. further. On May 28, 1903, a three compartment shaft was started south of the main tunnel. By June 5th a steam hoist and a headframe had been erected on the site and soon the shaft was completed to a depth of 298 ft. The Higgins Development Company had great property, but unfortunately the company was deprived of luck. They had come within 50 ft. of finding an orebody in the tunnel and a crosscut in the shaft was about 200 ft. from ore.

During April of 1907, the Wolverine & Arizona Mining Company approached Thomas Higgins about leasing the property. A diamond drill on the Warren Claim belonging to the W&A had intercepted an orebody of crystalline azurite and malachite. Unfortunately, the Warren claim was thousands of feet from the Wolverine Shaft. A lease was arranged and the W&A extended the Higgins Tunnel 300 ft. to the drill hole. Ore was hit on September 6th 1907 while the tunnel was still 125 ft. from the drill hole. Generally, this company only used the Higgins Tunnel as an access point to their own ores. The Wolverine Interior Shaft was developed to exploit their ores and along with extensive drifting.

A group of shrewd miners working in the nearby Southwest Mine, realized that the large New Southwest Orebody, likely continued onto Higgins ground. In 1918, Don Leedy, Edward Bergquist and G.M. Stole took out a lease on the Higgins. They drove the main Higgins Tunnel 50 ft. further and intercepted a 600 ft. X 200 ft. orebody. It was predicted that they would make about $700,000 before their lease expired. These men retired after the lease ended in 1919. This was considered the most profitable mine lease in Bisbee.

In July 1922, Phelps Dodge acquired an 18 month option on the Higgins Mine and eventually purchased the property. The Higgins was mined by lessees until 1930. In 1933, the Higgins Shaft burned, ending its possibilities of reopening. The tunnel continued to operate until 1944. The most well-known area of operation was the Hargis lease. It mined sulphide ores through an interior incline shaft that is popularly known as the Hargis incline. When operations ceased the Higgins Mine consisted of a three compartment 298 ft. vertical, Higgins Shaft, the Higgins "Hargis" Incline Shaft, the Wolverine Interior and two adits/tunnels. The old extensive main tunnel and a newer adit that were located near the Higgins Shaft.

May 30, 1903, Higgins Mine

During, blasting for the Higgins Shaft, a boulder was thrown into the air and crashed through the roof and floor of the home of the Black family. The boulder nearly hit the sister of Mrs. Black and her daughter. It was close enough to knock the hat off of one of the ladies. A four-foot square hole was left in the floor. Superintendent Parnell of the Higgins Mine made arrangements for the home to be repaired. The home was in Tombstone Canyon close to the road to the Twilight Mine*

*The Twilight Mine is a group workings mined for manganese on the hillside above the Higgins Shaft. They are considered part of the Higgins Mine.

"Dangerous Blasting" Bisbee Daily Review 31 May 1903 page 5

September 18, 1907, Higgins Mine

John C. Krumlin, Sam Briscoe and A. Earl Braund miners of the Wolverine and Arizona Mining Company were in the Higgins Tunnel. Sam and Earl arrived at the drift they were working in at 7:00 am. Krumlin who was Braund's partner arrived at 8:00 am. Briscoe started to push a mine car out of the drift and Braund informed Krumlin that he was going to set up the foundation for a small hoist. Krumlin began getting ready to start mucking and as he struck a rock with his pick it detonated a misfire. Braund was knocked to the ground. He got up and called to Krumlin who did not respond and ran to get Briscoe. He found Briscoe running back since he had heard the blast. They found Krumlin was still alive and Sam carried him 40 feet until they reached a mine car. Sam climbed into the car holding Krumlin, while Briscoe pushed the car to the surface. Krumlin died a few minutes after the explosion, but Braund was taken to the Calumet & Arizona Dispensary and treated for an injured right eye and other minor injuries. John C. Krumlin was 31 years old and was from California. His body was sent to San Miguel, California, the home of his family. He was survived by his father Charles Krumlin, brother J.H. Krumlin two sisters, Mrs.

Lizzie Olney Mrs. Nellie Compton, half-sisters Katie, Rose and Isabel Krumlin and a half-brother William E. Krumlin.

"Missed Hole is Responsible for Death" Bisbee Daily Review 19 September 1907 page 5
"Will Send Body Home" Bisbee Daily Review 20 September 1907 page 7
"Probate Court Orders" Bisbee Daily Review 4 August 1908 page 8
"Cochise County Coroner's Inquest No.492" Arizona State Archives Phoenix

February 14, 1908, Higgins Mine

Four miners of the Wolverine & Arizona Mining Company entered a winze 1,200 ft. from the portal. After 45 minutes George Jackson fainted from powder smoke. Two men began to take care of him and succumbed to the gasses. Joseph Cummings began to feel the effects of the smoke and climbed out of the winze and went for help. As he approached the mine entrance, the fresh air revived him a little, and he was able to reach the surface and get assistance. When Dr. N.C. Bledsoe arrived the men were being brought out, and he was able to revive them.

"Miners Have Narrow Escape at Wolverine" Bisbee Daily Review 15 February 1908 page 6

May 23, 1913, Higgins Mine

Jack McGregor was overcome by gasses (powder) and rendered unconscious. He was taken home to recover. He was a local insurance man and part of the Higgins Leasing Company.

"Jack McGregor Overcome" Bisbee Daily Review 24 May 1913 page5

December 16, 1913, Higgins Mine

Dan Hanley was pushing a mine car when a rock from a nearby blast smashed his right hand. He was taken to the hospital and released the same day.

"Struck by Rock" Bisbee Daily Review 17 December 1913 page 5

June 30, 1914, Higgins Mine

George Haigler, a miner, working on the Higgins Lease broke his foot when a boulder fell on it. The foot was later amputated below the ankle He was taken to the Calumet & Arizona Hospital and stayed there until July 25, 1914.

"Leg Broken" Bisbee Daily Review 1 July 1914 page 8
"Calumet & Arizona Hospital Records." My Cochise. http://www.mycochise.com/hospcalgr2he.php
(April 28, 2012)
Office of State Mine Inspector. Third Annual Report of the State Mine Inspector State of Arizona for the Year Ending November 30, 1914. Tombstone Epitaph.

May 21, 1914, Higgins Mine

A massive cave-in occurred in the main stope that was being mined by the Higgins Leasing Company. The miners had opened a large amount of ground and had little timber support. A foreman entered the stope and gave the order to evacuate the stope. Quickly, after the order was given, hundreds of tons of broken rock and ore fell. The ore fell and flooded a drift fifty feet below. The five men had sought safety against the far wall of the stope. Even there, some of the broken rock flowed over and buried some of the men up to their knees. The men only received scratches and bruises. James Letson, who was in charge of the

Higgins Leasing Company operations, stated later that none of the men were in danger during the collapse and the cave-in was "unavoidable." The Higgins Mine was small in 1914 and employed only nine men underground and produced around 200 tons of ore per month.

"Higgins Lease Men Narrowly Escape Death in Cave-in" Bisbee Daily Review 22 May 1914 page 5

"Minimize Accident" Bisbee Daily Review 23 May 1914 page 8

Office of State Mine Inspector. *Third Annual Report of the State Mine Inspector State of Arizona for the Year Ending November 30, 1914.* Tombstone Epitaph.

December 4, 1915, Higgins Mine

William H. Arnold had been told that the sinking bucket was hitting near the bottom of No. 2 winze and the foreman wanted him to blast it out. He began to drill and detonated a misfire. The subsequent blast killed the 23-year-old and mutilated him beyond recognition. Arnold had just returned to work after being off a couple of weeks. His body was taken by his brother Homan to Animas, New Mexico.

"Drills Missed Hole; Killed by Impact" Bisbee Daily Review 5 December 1915 page 1

"Inquest Held" Bisbee Daily Review 8 December 1915 page 8

Dugan Mortuary Records Aug. 26, 1914 – Dec 21, 1916 Accession 2010.10.9 Bisbee Mining and Historical Museum, Bisbee.

Office of State Mine Inspector. *Fifth Annual Report of the State Mine Inspector State of Arizona for the Year Ending November 30, 1916.*

"Original Certificate of Death." Arizona Department of Health Services. http://genealogy.az.gov/azdeath/014/10140814.pdf (May 28, 2012)

"Cochise County Coroner's Inquest No.1182" Arizona State Archives Phoenix

May 6, 1917, Higgins Mine

A fire broke out at the mine at 12:45 am the fire destroyed most buildings including the hoist house, change house and boiler room. Lack of water pressure prevented the miners from extinguishing the flames and the poor road to the mine block the city fire department from helping. The hoist was believed to be repairable, but the cable was ruined. Interestingly, the shift underground had no clue a there was a fire on the surface until, they left the tunnel and found the change house in ashes. The Higgins shaft had not been used for some time and work was focused on the main tunnel. No one was reported injured.

"Fire Destroys Higgins Mine Shaft House" Bisbee Daily Review 6 May 1917 page 1

November 28, 1919, Higgins Mine

Bert White picked into a misfire that exploded, puncturing his face shoulders and arms with small rocks.

Office of State Mine Inspector. *Eighth Annual Report of the State Mine Inspector State of Arizona for the Year Ending November 30, 1919.*

July 29, 1920, Higgins Mine

Elwin J. White was drilling in a *"bonus drift"* on the 200 level about 175 feet from the shaft station. He had set up his Leyner to drill down at an angle and when he started drilling, he detonated a misfire. Miners, Julius Wickman and John J. Brown at the shaft station heard the explosion and Wickman ran to discover the mutilated body of White. He was 33-years-old and the half-brother of M.F. Ryan the superintendent of the Higgins. White was survived by his half-brother a wife and three children. His family was living in Michigan. Elwin J. White was buried in Hancock Michigan.

"Explosion in District Mine Kills Worker." Bisbee Daily Review 20 July 1920 page 2
"Cochise County Coroner's Inquest No.1424" Arizona State Archives Phoenix

September 21, 1920, Higgins Mine

Guillermo Holguin (Alguien?) was struck by a cave-in. His skull was fractured, and the nose was broken. He died at the Calumet & Arizona Hospital on September 21. (No coroner's inquest could be located)

"Calumet & Arizona Hospital Records." My Cochise. http://www.mycochise.com/hospcaldied.php (May 30, 2012)
"Original Certificate of Death." Arizona Department of Health Services. http://genealogy.az.gov/azdeath/022/10221892.pdf (May 30, 2012)

Hoatson mine c-1910

Hoatson Mine

The Calumet & Pittsburg Mining Company started the Hoatson Shaft in April 1905. During the first week of the April, the shaft collar was set and the surface facilities were built. A temporary headframe and single drum hoist were installed. Also, a concrete tunnel was constructed from the shaft underneath the El Paso & Southwestern Railroad tracks to the waste dumping area. At the end of April, work focused on sinking the shaft. On May 22nd, a new double drum hoist was installed at the shaft and by June 22nd, a new wooden headframe was constructed over a period of two weeks. In the month of October, 157 ft. of shaft was sunk. This set a Warren Mining District shaft sinking record. The previous records of shaft sinking in one month were held by the Higgins shaft at 108ft. and the Denn Shaft at a 127ft. This was soon followed by a World's record set in December of 162ft. By the end of 1905 the shaft was 890.5ft. deep. During 1906, the Calumet & Pittsburg Mining Company merged with the Lake Superior & Pittsburg and Junction Development Companies and became the Superior and Pittsburg Copper Company.

205

Work continued and the shaft depth was increased by 418ft. and the ground was developed by 3,948ft. of crosscut. Pumps were installed on the 1200 level during 1907, but served only to raise the water to the 1000 level, where it was allowed to drain to the Junction Shaft for pumping to the surface. Most importantly, at this time the 1200 level had discovered important orebodies of both oxide and sulphide ores. Also, the shaft was sunk to a final depth of 1,680 ft. The following year was spent developing and discovering substantial ore on the 1300 and 1400 levels. The steel headframe planned years earlier, was completed in June and included a large toplander's deck, but the sheave wheels were taken off the old headframe and placed on the new. Mining focused on the 1200, 1300 and 1400 levels with minor ore being recovered from the 1000 and 1100 levels. In 1915 the Superior and Pittsburg Copper Company merged with the Calumet & Arizona Mining Company. During this year, a connection was made with the 1400 level Junction and trolley locomotives were installed to haul ore to the Junction Shaft for hoisting. After August 7th 1916, the Hoatson shaft was shut down and remaining ores were mined through the Briggs and Junction Shafts. By 1919, the Hoatson was entirely shutdown. In April 1921 the electric hoist was dismantled and reinstalled at the Lake Superior and Pittsburg #3 Shaft. At the end the shaft was 1,680 ft. deep with four compartments.

June 11, 1905, Hoatson Mine

William Pope was working in the bottom of the Hoatson Shaft. This shaft was only 133 ft. deep at the time. Angus Hector McDonald was working on the subway, a concrete tunnel from the shaft to the waste dumps about 20 ft. below the shaft collar. He was loading center pieces (timber) into a sinking bucket to be lowered. One fell, and McDonald was unable to catch it, and the timber fell the shaft. He yelled *"Look out below!"* and the men at the bottom of the shaft to get under what cover was available. Pope was under timber when the center piece struck him and threw him to the ground. Originally, it was thought he was only injured in the stomach and right hip. Later, it was discovered that he had internal injuries, and he died on June 16, 1905 from Peritonitis. Pope had just fixed up a home and sent for his wife in England. His wife arrived on June 17 and was met at the Lowell train station by a group of her late husband's friends and a few ladies of the town. Her first question to those that greeted her was whether her husband was working the night shift. The ladies present broke the news of her husband's death to her. The young bride was devastated and almost collapsed after she was told. William Pope was 23 years old and had been married seven months and had been in Bisbee five months. Mrs. Emmeline Pope was expected to return to England* shortly after her husband's funeral.

*She actually left Bisbee, but remained in Canada.

"Hurt by Falling Timber" Bisbee Daily Review 14 June 1905 page 3

"Wife Comes to Dead Husband" Bisbee Daily Review 17 June 1905 page 5

"Deeply Pathetic Incident Yesterday" Bisbee Daily Review 18 June 1905 page 1

"Bisbee-Lowell Evergreen Cemetery." My Cochise. http://www.mycochise.com/cembisbeepq.php (April 8 2011)

"Original Certificate of Death." Arizona Department of Health Services. http://genealogy.az.gov/azdeath/002/10020678.pdf (April8)

"Cochise County Inquest No. 277" Arizona State Archives Phoenix

Gravestone of William Pope.

July 17, 1908, Hoatson Mine

William B. Reed's candle went out while underground and in the darkness, he stepped into an open hole. He fell 40 feet and broke his back. Reed was taken to the Calumet & Arizona Hospital where he died on August 29, 1908, from his spinal injuries. He was 36 years old with a wife and daughter in England. (No coroner's inquest could be located)

"Has a Chance" Bisbee Daily Review 18 July 1908 page 7
"Died of His Injuries from Accident in Mine" Bisbee Daily Review 30 August 1908 page 7
"Calumet & Arizona Hospital Records" My Cochise http://www.mycochise.com/hospcalpr2ry.php (April 2, 2011)
"Original Certificate of Death" Arizona Department of Health Services
http://genealogy.az.gov/azdeath/002/10021509.pdf (April2 2011)

Timbermen c-1908

August 20, 1908, Hoatson Mine

James Shea and Jim Baughi were installing timber in No.21 stope about 32 ft. below the 1100 level. A post broke and hit Shea knocked him down and burying him under tons of broken rock. Miners were not able to uncover the 55-year-old's body until September 8 over two weeks after the fatal accident. Even though the cave-in was massive, miners expected to recover the body quickly. At one point rumors were spread that Shea's candlestick had been found indicating they were close. Those rumors were untrue. When Shea's body was found it was in such a state of decomposition that the palace undertakers took the body immediately to Evergreen Cemetery for burial. The deceased had no relatives outside of England.

"Body is Buried Neath Tons of Earth" <u>Bisbee Daily Review </u>21 August 1908 page 5
"Body Still Buried" <u>Bisbee Daily Review </u>27 August 1908 page 7
"Body Not Found" <u>Bisbee Daily Review </u>28 August 1908 page 7

"Body Not Found" <u>Bisbee Daily Review </u>29 August 1908 page 7
"Decomposed Body James Shea Found" <u>Bisbee Daily Review </u>9 September 1908 page 5
"Cochise County Coroner's Inquest No.591" Arizona State Archives Phoenix

November 9, 1908, Hoatson Mine

Watchman, Ben Johnson was caught by falling timber.* The timber broke his left foot and his left leg in three places, twice below the knee. He was a married man and 68 years old. Johnson was released from the Calumet and Arizona Hospital on March 15, 1909.

*This accident probably occurred on the surface, not underground.

"Sustains Severe Injuries" <u>Bisbee Daily Review </u>10 November 1908 page 7
"Calumet & Arizona Hospital Records." M<u>y Cochise.</u> http://www.mycochise.com/hospcalje 2ko.php (April2 2011)

December 11, 1908, Hoatson Mine

On the surface at the Hoatson, a man signaled the hoistman to lower the cage while the cage was still resting on landing chairs. With the cage not dropping the cable coiled on top of the cage. Then someone released the landing chairs and the cage fell until it reached the end of the cable. The resulting jerk on the cable damaged the top of the headframe. For several days Hoatson ore had to be hoisted out the Junction Mine.

"Gallows Frame Broken" <u>Bisbee Daily Review </u>13 December 1908 page 4

January 6, 1909 Hoatson Mine

Finnish miner, Charles Lane had come to Bisbee from British Columbia. Lane was working with John Salo a miner who he had worked with in British Columbia. The stope they were working in was on the 1200 level and 2,000-3,000 ft. from the Hoatson Shaft. Salo had dropped below and while he was down there, Lane began to clear out an area to install a stull. As he was working a boulder fell and rolled over him. He was then partly buried with small rocks and dirt. Salo heard the rocks fall and noticed Lane's light was extinguished. Back up with Lane, Salo uncovered him and called for help. John Hano, a timberman was first to arrive. Dr. N.C. Bledsoe examined the miner and found no broken bones, but Lane had bled from the nose and there was frothing from the mouth. Lane had brothers and sisters in Kotka, Wassa Finland.

"Cochise County Coroner's Inquest No. 615" Arizona State Archives
"Charles Lane Victim of Cave-in" <u>Bisbee Daily Review </u>7 January 1909 page 5

August 1909, Hoatson Mine

Ira A. Blalack was injured by falling rock. He suffered a 3-1/2 inch scalp wound.

"Falling Rock Injures" <u>Bisbee Daily Review</u> 11 August 1909 page 7

August 9, 1909, Hoatson Mine

Adolf Anderson was hit in the face by a bar from a rock drill column set up. He was struck on the head and face. It took 13 stitches to sew him up.

"Hurt in Mine" <u>Bisbee Daily Review </u>10 August 1909 page 7

August 16, 1909, Hoatson Mine

William Carlise had a finger crushed between two timbers. He was taken to the Calumet & Arizona Dispensary.

"Finger is Mangled" Bisbee Daily Review 17 August 1909 page 7

November 22, 1909, Hoatson Mine

Cager, Pat Sullivan was descending on the second deck of a cage. At about the 1100 level the clutch on the hoist broke. The cage began falling. Sullivan grabbed onto the steel bars at the top of the cage (probably the steel rods for the cage dogs.) At the 1500 level the cage hit the water filled sump. A crew of men descended immediately and expected to find only a body. To their surprise when they opened the cage bonnets the found Sullivan alive with an injured wrist. If Sullivan had been on the lower deck he would have drowned.

"Dropped 400 Feet Yet Lives" Bisbee Daily Review 24 November 1909 page8

November 27, 1909, Hoatson Mine

Twenty-year-old Tom Fisher was working in a drift when a rock fell from the back (roof) of the drift and smashed his left hand. His index finger was broken, and the thumb had to be amputated.

"Hand Badly Crushed" Bisbee Daily Review 30 November 1909 page 7
"Calumet & Arizona Hospital Records." My Cochise http://www.mycochise.com/hospcalde 2fi.php (April2 2011)

January 28, 1910, Hoatson Mine

Frank Emil Johnson a 31-year-old, Finnish Miner was laying track with William Mihelich and two other miners. The work needed to be completed. They had stayed after the shift to finish the job. Johnson and Mihelich were spiking down the rail when a boulder fell and struck them. Mihelich received minor injuries, but the impact resulted in a compound fracture of Johnson's left leg, along with internal injuries. He was taken to the Calumet & Arizona Hospital where he died on January 28 from shock and internal injuries. Johnson was survived by a Hilda, who lived on Youngblood Hill in Bisbee. He was from Vasa, Finland and had three sisters and a brother in Michigan, including Jenny Berg and Johan Perkiomaki.

"Johnson Dies from Injuries at Hoatson" Bisbee Daily Review 29 January 1910 page 8
"Calumet & Arizona Hospital Records." My Cochise. http://www.mycochise.com/hospcaldied.php (April 22, 2011)
"Original Certificate of Death." Arizona Department of Health Services.
 http://genealogy.az.gov/azdeath/007/10071670.pdf (April 22, 2011)
"Cochise County Coroner's Inquest No.719" Arizona State Archives Phoenix

June 8, 1910, Hoatson Mine

Albert Fassel, a mule driver, was raced through a drift by a mule. Fassel was driving the mule with a string of empty mine cars. The mule became startled began to gallop through the drift. The wind generated by the speed blew out his candle. Pulling the empty mine cars in an upgrade direction of the drift finally slowed the mule and it eventually stopped on its own. Luckily, he suffered only bruises on the right arm. Surprisingly, all of the cars the mule was pulling remained on the track during the mad race through the mine.

"Runaway in Mine Jars Alfred Fassel" Bisbee Daily Review 10 June 1910 page 5
"Mexican Laborer Drops Dead of Heart Failure" El Paso Herald 13 June 1910 page 7

June 21, 1910 Hoatson Mine

John Gilman was tramming with a mule. The mule became frightened and began kicking and tossing its head. Gilman was able to keep the mule from running away with the train, but was caught between the mule and the rib (wall) of the drift. The mule's wildly moving head caught Gilman in the head. He received a cut above the eye that required stitches.

"Miner in Sparring Match with Mule" Bisbee Daily Review 24 February 1910 page 5

August 2, 1910, Hoatson Mine

Mule Driver, Nick Jerosovich sprained his foot when it was caught between two mine cars. He was treated at the Calumet & Arizona Dispensary.

"Had Foot Sprained" Bisbee Daily Review 3 August 1910 page 5

August 3, 1910, Hoatson Mine

About 10 o'clock in the evening, James Hawthorn was working in a stope on the 1300 level of the Hoatson Shaft when he fell four sets, about 30 feet. He was taken to the Calumet and Arizona Hospital. Originally, it was thought he may have received internal injuries that may lead to his death, but by the following day he had recovered. The 24-year-old miner was released on August 10, 1910 in *"cured"* condition.

"Hawthorn is Injured at the Hoatson" Bisbee Daily Review 4 August 1910 page 1
"Injuries not Serious" Bisbee Daily Review 5 August 1910 page 5
"Calumet & Arizona Hospital Records." My Cochise. http://www.mycochise.com/hospcalgr2he.php (April 17, 2011)

August 6, 1910, Hoatson Mine

Victor Keckman was struck by falling rock. He suffered cuts on head and face. Treatment was provided at the Calumet & Arizona Dispensary.

"Injured at Hoatson" Bisbee Daily Review 7 August 1910 page 5

August 16, 1910 Hoatson Mine

M.D. Vanhulen fell 30 ft. and received several injuries including a broken foot. He was taken to the Calumet & Arizona Hospital. On August 28 the 46-year-old was sent home in a cast.

"Bisbee Mine Map being Prepared" El Paso Herald 23 August 1910 page 3
"Calumet & Arizona Hospital Records." My Cochise. http://www.mycochise.com/hospcaltr2we.php (June 22, 2011)

January 18, 1912 Hoatson Mine

A.C. Smith lost his right eye in an explosion. The eye was removed by doctors at the Calumet & Arizona Hospital.

"Eye Taken Out" Bisbee Daily Review 24 January 1912 page 5
"Calumet & Arizona Hospital Records." http://www.mycochise.com/hospcals2sm.php My Cochise. (March 8, 2015)

November 9, 1912, Hoatson Mine

John Hunt was installing timber when a boulder fell hitting his right leg below the knee. The leg suffered a compound fractured. Hunt, a 38-year-old mucker remained in the Calumet & Arizona Hospital until December 30, 1912.

"Fracture of Leg" Bisbee Daily Review 10 November 1912 page 8
"Calumet & Arizona Hospital Records." My Cochise. Http://www.mycochise.com/hospcalhi2ja.php (April 2, 2011)

June 24, 1914 Hoatson Mine

Alex Hemmaler, a 28-year-old mucker and Sam Vujacich* a 23-year-old miner were working in a stope on the 1200 level. Around 1:00 am the stope caved in. The collapse broke Hemmaler's collar bone and buried Vujacich completely. Ground conditions prevented the recovery of Vujacich's body until 5:30 pm the following day. The rescuing miners had to work from underneath the caved area to recover the body. Interestingly, the miners were mining on the property line with the Copper Queen's Sacramento Mine. The miners in the stope could hear the blasting in the Sacramento Mine. Joseph P. Hodgson Superintendent of the Copper Queen Consolidated Mining Company attended the Coroner's Inquest, to provide information on whether workings inside the Sacramento could have contributed to the cause of the accident. Vujacich was from Montenegro and was buried in Evergreen Cemetery. He was survived by his cousin, John Vujacich. Hemmaler was released from the Calumet & Arizona Hospital on July 14, 1914. * Vujacich name was spelled multiple was in the documents Sam Vuich State Mine Inspectors report, Sam Vukavich Bisbee Daily Review and Spiro R. Vijagich Evergreen Cemetery Records

"Accident in Hoatson is Fatal to One" Bisbee Daily Review 25 June 1914 page 1
"Calumet & Arizona Hospital Records." My Cochise http://www.mycochise.com/hospcalgr2he.php. (May 21, 2012)
"Original Certificate of Death." Arizona Department of Health Services. http://genealogy.az.gov/azdeath/085/10850381.pdf (May 21, 2012)
Office of State Mine Inspector. Third Annual Report of the State Mine Inspector State of Arizona for the Year Ending November 30, 1914. Tombstone Epitaph.
"Bisbee-Lowell Evergreen Cemetery." My Cochise.
http://www.mycochise.com/cembisbeeuv.php (May 21, 2012)
"Cochise County Coroner's Inquest No.1097" Arizona State Archives Phoenix

February 15, 1915, Hoatson Mine

Charles Fairclough was making repairs on an idler pulley at the Hoatson Shaft hoist. When the cable was being raised from the 1400 level it had a tendency to bunch up on the drum rather than wind straight. A pulley had been added to help the cable wind properly at the request of the hoistmen. Fairclough had been asked to repair this pulley. At the shaft, he had waited for an hour and was becoming impatient with the hoistman, William J. Cocking, and he tried to remove the pulley while the hoist was running. He became entangled with the hoisting cable and was crushed as he was wrapped around the hoist drum. He was survived by a brother Allen, a wife and two children.

"Twisted around Hoatson Hoist to Death" Bisbee Daily Review 16 February 1915 page 1
"Cochise County Coroner's Inquest No.1141" Arizona State Archives Phoenix

April 16, 1915, Hoatson Mine

Michael *"Micky"* Breen was working in a raise that had just holed through into a stope. The survey was five feet off, and the raise had unexpectedly struck a crosscut below the stope. Inside this crosscut, he started to dig with a pick and a post in a crosscut slipped out. Muck on top of the set fell and buried him completely in soft dirt. Shift Boss, J.A. Swanson, and Mucker, A.J. Phillips were next to him. Swanson immediately went for help, and they were able to unbury him. Dr. N.C. Bledsoe soon arrived underground and administered morphine. The doctor wanted to perform surgery because he suspected a punctured bladder. Breen refused the operation and died the next day.

"Injuries to Miner Cause His Death" Bisbee Daily Review 17 April 1915 page 3
"Injured in Cave-In" Bisbee Daily Review 16 April 1915 page 8
"Cochise County Coroner's Inquest No. 1150" Arizona State Archives Phoenix

April 12, 1915, Hoatson Mine

Chris Midzor was digging into a misfire with his candlestick. The hole detonated and mangled his hand to the extent that it was felt the hand would need to be amputated. He was taken to the Calumet & Arizona Hospital and released on April 17th. (Note, that this is a late year for candlesticks to be used underground in Bisbee)

"Hand Blown Off" Bisbee Daily Review 13 April 1915 page 8
"Calumet & Arizona Hospital Records." My Cochise. http://www.mycochise.com/hospcalme 2ny.php (April 24 2012)

**The Holbrook No.1 Shaft with an enclosed headframe (left) and the Holbrook No. 2
with an open headframe (right) c-1906**

Holbrook Mine

This mine's recorded history begins on March 6th 1881 when F.M. Adams and J.W. Harter of Visalia, California purchased both the Holbrook and Cave Claims. These claims had three shafts of 45ft., 20ft. and 12ft. depths at this time. A year later, Joe Russell was developing the property. In 1883, Walker Williams and Russell struck a large oxidation cave while working 30 ft. down on the Cave Claim. After enlarging the hole, a man was lowered down 50ft. and explored the cave by candle light. He discovered a classic Bisbee oxidation cave with stalactites and stalagmites stained green by copper. The walls were covered by velvety *"copper carbonate"* This cave was about two acres in size and about 50ft. tall.

The Holbrook Claim was patented in 1884 by Alphonse Larzard and Horace Jones. Before the end of the year J.W. Goddard of New York had purchased the property and began developing the property and had exposed 200 tons of ore. It is undetermined how much development occurred on the property under the ownership of Goddard, before William E. Dodge and D. Willis James of Phelps, Dodge and Company purchased the property in 1888. The work must have been considerable, as the new company known as the Holbrook & Cave Mining Company was able to produce 3,060,000lbs of copper that year. The production was sold to the French Copper Syndicate, which was controlling the world copper market. Early documents state that the Copper Queen Consolidated Mining Company was paid to hoist ore mined from the Holbrook and Cave workings. During November 1902, the first mine fire broke out in a stope in the Neptune Country. It was extinguished by pouring in water. Sulfide mine fires were to continue to plague this mine. The mine began to develop into the main hoisting shaft for the Copper Queen Consolidated Mining Company and the Holbrook became interconnected with the Spray, Gardner , Czar, Hayes and Copper Queen(incline) mines In August of 1904, plans were announced, to enlarge the Holbrook Shaft from four compartments to six. A new, towering, enclosed, headframe, was built next to and attached to the short, original, enclosed, headframe giving it an unusual shape. Expansion continued during the first half of 1906, a massive two story change house was constructed It had a total of 450 lockers each with their own key on both floors. Sinks and showers were on the bottom floor. Difficulties began around July 10th. The Holbrook Shaft had been heavily mined around and the shaft began to collapse. Soon the shaft could no longer hoist double deck cages. On July 16th the shaft caved-in from the 200 level to the surface. Engineers felt that the moisture from the monsoon rains had caused the collapse and planned to reopen the shaft after the end of the rainy season. A hoist was installed on the 200 level to service the lower levels of the shaft and the Czar and Gardner Mines handled all ore being mined as well as men and materials. The shaft was bulkheaded at 200 level to keep debris falling from the caving section, out of the shaft. Stopes around the shaft were backfilled. On August 3 it was announced that a new shaft would be raised 150ft. away, rather than repair the Holbrook Shaft. Raising the new Holbrook shaft took only 75 days. The stations were heavily timbered and were 18ft. X 24ft. in size. Each station had a floor of steel turnsheets and was electrically lit.

In 1907, a massive stope 600ft. wide and 800ft. long was developed from this steady producer. Around this time the headframe from the Holbrook #1 shaft was dismantled and the shaft was hidden under the floor of a new blacksmith shop. The new change house and mine shops remained in use for the #2 shaft.

In preparation for the Sacramento Shaft becoming the main hoisting shaft, crosscuts were widened and chutes raised to accept the new trolley locomotives and new, larger, gable-bottomed, Koppel and later rocker dump mine cars. Connections were made to the distant Uncle Sam Mine and the 600 level Spray was driven under the Holbrook #2 shaft. Once under the #2 shaft was deepened by raising from the 600 level to the bottom of the shaft on the 500 level. On May 15, 1910 the connection was completed to the 500 level and impressively the engineers surveys were off only 1 3/16 inches off in length and 3/8 inches of on width. A pump station had been cut on the 600 level and pumps taken from the 500 level were installed at the new station.

After the Spray Mine was shut down in 1914, it was mined from both the Holbrook #2 and the Gardner Mine. By 1917, the ore reserves in the Holbrook were badly depleted and little new ore was discovered. During 1919, The Holbrook #2 shaft was sharing the same fate of the #1. The shaft was several feet out of alignment from caving ground. In 1920, the Holbrook Mine was closed temporarily, but reopened the next year. The mine continued to operate until around 1926, when the headframe and hoist house for the Holbrook #2 shaft were torn down and the shaft was covered with a small shed. The other buildings at the site remained intact. Confusingly, the mine continued to operate without a distinctive hoisting shaft and continued to be an important producer. It is likely that the Charon, the Young and possibly the Czar shafts served to mine the Holbrook ground. The mine workings in the Holbrook were notoriously hot and were badly caving. Particularly, those areas near the Dividend Fault. Small shafts and raises like the Young and Charon shafts were driven to bypass dangerous or caved ground and provide much needed ventilation. Mining continued and in 1930 the Holbrook change house was enlarged. Mining, which was at least partially done be by lease continued until 1942, when Phelps Dodge drove 1,829ft. of crosscuts on the 300, 400 and 600 levels. This was the last major development project. In January1944, the Holbrook mine was closed with the cancellation of all leases.

In 1948, few signs of the Holbrook mine existed on the surface other than a few concrete foundations. All the headframes, including those on the Young and Charon Shaft were gone except for a single wooden headframe on an undetermined shaft located between the Charon and the Czar Shafts. The Holbrook mine consisted of two hoisting shafts the #1 which was 537 ft. deep with six compartments and the #2 shaft that was three and one half compartments and 645 feet. Deep. Sometimes the mine was called the *"Brook"* for short and it is likely, the shaft was originally called the Goddard Shaft.

March 1892, (around the 10th) Holbrook Mine
Will Munch* a *"tool boy"* was injured after being struck in the arm by a falling tool. * He is likely the Willie Munch, who attended Bisbee's first school in 1881, with Clara Stillman as the teacher.
"Bisbee Column" Tombstone Epitaph 27 March 1892 page 4

February 4, 1898, Holbrook Mine
E.C. Clark and W.S. Young were getting ready to blast two holes at around 5:30 pm. They lit the first fuse which began to burn, but the second fuse proved difficult to ignite. While they continued trying to light the second fuse, the first hole detonated. Clark was instantly killed by the blast, and one of Young's legs was broken. With his fractured leg and other wounds he crawled out of the drift. He was found about an hour later by Charles Warner* who was taking a visitor, Harry Brown, on a tour of the mine. Warner could not recognize Young, but he was able to speak and told him who he was. Quickly, Warner asked Brown to stay with the injured man and returned to the Dividend Stope and called, John Belle, Bill Pritchett, Henry Kahrs and Jack Wickstrom to help him. As they moved Young, he said, *"Boys if I die send me back to my dear old mother, in Lynn, Massachusetts."* Young was lowered down the 400 level and taken out the Holbrook Shaft. He was taken to the hospital, but died later. The body of Ed Clark was also lowered to the 400 level but was taken out the Czar Shaft. The area of the accident appears to have been midway between the Czar and Holbrook Mines.
*Charles Warner was later killed in the Holbrook No.1 Shaft on June 15, 1904
"Fatal Accident" The Arizona Republican 10 February 1898 page 5
"Cochise County Coroner's Inquest No. 352" Arizona State Archives. Phoenix

April 5, 1898, Holbrook Mine
John Dolan was walking with William P. Scott into the South Drift on the 400 level. After walking 1,200 ft., Dolan stopped to light candles and climb down a winze to an intermediate level. Shift Boss, Charles Warner saw Dolan start to descend and slip. Dolan fell 36 ft. to a landing. Warner climbed down while Scott went for help. James Harrington and Martin Nolan assisted raise Dolan out of the winze. At the Copper Queen Hospital a

steward ask Dolan if he was hungry. Dolan responded *"Yes"*. This was the only word he spoke after falling. He died three hours after the accident from shock and internal injuries.

"Bisbee Miner Killed" The San Francisco Call 6 April 1898 page 8

"Standard Certificate of Death." Arizona Department of Health Services. http://genealogy.az.gov/azdeath/001/10012195.pdf (May 28, 2012)

"Coroner's Register No. 2" MyCochise.com http://www.mycochise.com/1881-1901%20Coroner's%20Register%20(A-Z).pdf (May 28, 2014)

"Cochise County Coroner's Inquest No.359" Arizona State Archives Phoenix

December 11, 1898, Holbrook Mine

J.B. Benton fell 100 ft. down a stope and landed on E.H. Wittig. Benton suffered two broken ribs and an elbow. Wittig received minor injuries.

"Town Tattle" The Weekly Orb 11 December 1898 page 4

December 14, 1898 Holbrook Mine

Price Farrier called the north cage to the 400 level and boarded a cage with a mine car and tools. He rang the bells to be hoisted then 40 ft. below the 200 level, it appears Farrier fell from the cage and caused the cage to crash when he was caught between the cage and timber. Immediately, hoistman F.J. Bailey stopped the North cage. He received a signal from S.W. Clawson on the south cage, who took the cage to the site of the accident. Clawson found tools and a smashed mine car on the cage, but no persons. After investigating he rang the cage to the surface and talked to the hoistman, who told him, he thought someone had been on the north cage. Clawson with Ed Scott, John Ambrose, Albert Watkins* and Fred Davies continued the investigation and found Farrier's body on the 500 level possibly in the shaft sump.

*Watkins was later killed in the Southwest Mine on December 29, 1915

"Cochise County Coroner's Inquest No. 385" Arizona State Archives. Phoenix

May 22, 1899, Holbrook Mine

Usaii Daoust and R. Polglaze were working in Stope No. 29. They had set up timber and Daoust wanted to put in a tenant block and tighten it up with a wedge. Polglaze cut a six-inch block and gave him a wedge. As Daoust was driving the wedge between the rock wall and the block, a 300 lb. rock fell and landed on his face. Still alive, Polglaze, Aug Wetterau and an Italian nicknamed "Joe" helped get Daoust to the surface. He was still breathing and was taken to the Copper Queen Hospital. Polglaze did not go immediately to the surface but, returned to the accident scene to gather Daoust's belongings. Daoust died from a compound fracture of the skull.

"Original Certificate of Death." Arizona Department of Health Services. http://genealogy.az.gov/azdeath/001/10012236.pdf (June 6, 2012)

"Coroner's Register No. 2" MyCochise.com http://www.mycochise.com/1881-1901%20Coroner's%20Register%20(A-Z).pdf (May 28, 2014)

"Cochise County Coroner's Inquest No.402" Arizona State Archives Phoenix

June 28, 1899, Holbrook Mine

Close to 3:00 pm, P.A. "Paddy" Cunningham loaded an empty mine car on the cage at the 100 level. He forgot to put down with the bar designed to hold the car in place. Right after he gave the three bell signal to hoist the car rolled and pinned Cunningham between the mine car and the side of the shaft. When the hoisting cable began to tighten D.R. Hancock the hoist engineer stopped the hoist and sent R. Stewart Hunt, John Ambrose and Foreman Scott Turner down to investigate. They found him crushed up against the timbers, but alive. The men returned to the surface for lanterns and an axe. At the accident site, they constructed a platform and then had the cage lowered six inches and removed Cunningham to the surface. Still alive, Cunningham asked to see his wife and baby. He was taken to the hospital, where he remained conscious until right up until he died. "Paddy" died twenty minutes after reaching the hospital. Unfortunately, he died before being able to see his family. Cunningham had been a partner with Martin Costello in the purchase of a group of mining claims including the Irish Mag Claim. After the death of Martin Costello, the Patricia Julia Cunningham and Mary Aileen Cunningham, daughters of Cunningham filed a lawsuit against the estate of Costello to recover their late father's share of the profits. This suit was settled in favor for the daughters in 1915.

"Fatally Injured" The Weekly Orb July 2 1899 page 4
"Copperings" Tombstone Epitaph 9 July 1899 page 2
"Cochise County Coroner's Inquest No. 404" Arizona State Archives. Phoenix

August 7, 1899, Holbrook Mine
Near the end of his shift, Louis Junney* fell while trying to cross a stope. He fell almost sixty feet and hit his vertebrae and received a cut on the scalp. Junney was found unconscious and taken to the Copper Queen Hospital. The cut was closed up with ten stitches, but he has been unable to move the lower part of his body. It was feared that he was paralyzed. A week later the sense of feeling and circulation had returned to his legs. It is unknown whether he regained use of his legs.

*Spelled Gunney in August 15 article
"Sad Accident" The Weekly Orb 13 May 1899 page 2
 "Untitled" The Arizona Daily Orb 15 August 1899 page 4

November 9, 1899, Holbrook Mine
Charles Anshutz was killed on "B" level at 3 o' clock, when a box of Giant powder exploded. He was *"blown to atoms"*. His partner John Hughes was not with him at the time of the explosion, and what caused the detonation is unknown. He was last seen by Ed Alexander climbing a manway to "B" level. After about four minutes Alexander heard an explosion and then the blasting smoke flowed into the work area and Alexander, Tom Constable and James Rogers climbed to the 100 level to get away from the smoke and then by a different route back to "B" level to see what happened. The drift was filled with smoke, timber and debris. Constable stated that " *I noticed lots of dark pieces of dark colored stuff that looked like flesh, and I saw a piece of it hanging over on the wall over above where the powder stood."* Samuel Grant helped recover the remains from the drift. Little was left. He found a miner's candlestick, part of a watch, one ear, part of a foot and two-inch piece of the scalp. These were the only recognisable remains found. It was never determined what caused the explosion and the coroner's jury was interested to know if foul play or suicide could have been the cause. Charles was survived by a wife and two children. (Note, Anshutz was one of the earliest residents of Bisbee and had owned parts of several important mining claims in the district.)

   "Copperings" Tombstone Epitaph 12 November 1899 page 1
   "Bisbee News" Tombstone Prospector 9 November 1899 page 3
   "Cochise County Coroner's Inquest No. 417" Arizona State Archives. Phoenix

A Giant Powder Box.

Grave marker for Charles Anshutz.

November 25, 1899, Holbrook Mine
Ed. Stiffler was climbing the manway to No. 32 raise with a canteen of water into 32 stope on the 300 level. As he was climbing, he thought he heard someone dump a wheelbarrow load of rock down the chute side. When he got to the top, he found his partner Frank Littlejohn calling for timberman, William P. Long. They found Long's candle burning at the top of the raise and decided he must have fallen in it. Littlejohn took a piece of paper and set it on fire and dropped it down the chute. The paper went out before they could see anything, so they tried it again. This time, the flames illuminated a pair of legs sticking up. The men climbed down and opened the chute door and removed Long's body. It was felt that he had accidently walked into the raise.
"Cochise County Coroner's Inquest No. 418" Arizona State Archives. Phoenix

January 5, 1900, Holbrook Mine
Norwegian, George Stone was on the 400 level, clearing the ground to place a post for a drift set. He was standing a post, when suddenly, a boulder fell from three feet above and struck him in the right temple. He was killed instantly. His partner, Peter Johnson Bruseth was working on installing the opposite post. Bruseth heard the ground fall from the rib of the drift, and then George groaned. Quickly, Bruseth found J.C. Carpenter and Robert Caywood and they began to take him out on a mine car, but he died before reaching the surface. It was a relatively small amount of muck that killed Stone, as it would barely even fill a wheelbarrow.
"Accidently Killed" The Arizona Daily Orb 6 January1900 page 4
"Cochise County Coroner's Inquest No. 424" Arizona State Archives. Phoenix

May 8, 1900, Holbrook
Jack Oder was caught in a cave-in. He received contusion on his head and shoulders, and one arm was fractured in two places.
"May 9, 1900 Copperings" Tombstone Epitaph 13 May 1900 page 1

January 16, 1901, Holbrook Mine
Harry Holland and Patrick Spillane had blasted seven holes in a stope off No. 5 raise between the 200 and 300 levels and Holland and Spillane noticed that the seventh had not detonated. Ignoring words of caution, Holland entered the blast area to relight the fuse. Soon after he arrived at the blast area, the remaining hole detonated killing him. Spillane told H.L. Cameron to get help while he went back and found Holland. He was survived by a wife, two young children and a grown son in Rivervleet, Michigan.
"Killed in the Mine" Cochise Review 19 January 1901 page 2
"Cochise County Coroner's Inquest No. 463" Arizona State Archives. Phoenix

February 2, 1901, Holbrook

Ed Megs and John Huoit received injuries in 27 stope. At the end of the shift, they were bringing lagging into the stope when boulders fell striking Ed Megs on the side of the head and hitting Huoit's left shoulder.

"Copperings" Tombstone Epitaph 3 February 1901 page 1

March 7, 1901, Holbrook Mine

U. Conklin was in 21 stope on the 500 level in the Spray Country, hauling ore with a wheelbarrow and dumping it into the chute. After, he emptied his wheelbarrow he walked in front of it and fell into the manway. Conklin fell 50 ft. and fractured the base of his skull killing him. A man following him with another load found Conklin's wheelbarrow lying in the passageway. He started to take Conklin's wheelbarrow back, when he learned that Conklin had been killed. Initially, it was suspected that he had reached into the manway to get a canteen. Miners would hang canteens in the manway to keep the water cool.* This was later proven not to be true. Conklin was around 50 years old and was a widower. He was survived by a daughter going to school in Honolulu in the Hawaiian Islands. (Note the Coroner's Inquest gave little information.)

 * Greater airflow would be expected in a manway and by wetting the canvas or burlap wrapping around the canteen, evaporation would cool the water.
"Killed in the Mine" Cochise Review 9 March 1901 page 1
"Cochise County Coroner's Inquest No. 1" Arizona State Archives. Phoenix

March 10, 1901, Holbrook Mine

R. Coughran and John Keiler were working 50-feet up a raise in No.21 stope on the 500 level. A cave-in occurred, and Keiler was injured, but Coughran was knocked into the raise and fell the 50-feet to his death. (No coroner's inquest could be located)

"Bisbee Joitings" Tombstone Epitaph 17 March 1901 page 2

October 3, 1901, Holbrook Mine

J.S. Stewart was installing timber on the 500 level when dirt and rock fell injuring his back.

"Stewart Injured his Back" Bisbee Daily Review 6 October 1901 page 5

May, 1902, Holbrook Mine

Jack Harris was injured while using a saw. It was thought he may lose at least one finger.

"Hand Hurt" Bisbee Daily Review 9 May 1902 page 4

May 12, 1902, Holbrook Mine

At 10:30 in the morning, a Slavonian miner named Anton Koff drove a pick into a misfire. Anton had been informed of the misfire before he began work on the 500 level. He intentionally walked up and drove his pick into the misfire, which instantly exploded throwing him onto his back. Fine dust particles penetrated his eyes and flying small rocks cut up his face. His eyes were severely damaged. There were several miners working twenty feet away, they were uninjured. Later, Anton Koff headed to Los Angles to see if one of his eyes could be saved.

"Sticks His Pick in Dead Blast" Bisbee Daily Review 13 May 1902 page 1
"Koff in Los Angles" Bisbee Daily Review 20 May 1902 page 8

July 6, 1902, Holbrook Mine
N. M. Askel was working on the 200 level installing timber. A blood vessel ruptured in his lung and he was taken to the surface where he died. It was determined he died of natural causes.
"Miner Dies" Bisbee Daily Review 7 July 1902

October 6, 1902, Holbrook Mine
Jay Stolenberger was helping handle a turnsheet in "Block" 31 on the 200 level. Suddenly, the turnsheet fell against the wall of the drift. This tore Jay's ear, broke his jaw and knocked out a few teeth. He was taken to the Copper Queen Hospital.
"Hospital Notes" Bisbee Daily Review 7 October 1902 page 5

December 8, 1902, Holbrook Mine
Jay Wilmuth was working in the Neptune Stope on the 300 level. A boulder fell, striking and dislocating his shoulder. He walked to the Copper Queen Hospital. Jay was expected to be off work a few days.
"Shoulder Hurt" Bisbee Daily Review 9 December 1902 page 8

June 7, 1903, Holbrook Mine
John McDonald was injured when he fell 10 feet. He was taken to the hospital, and it was determined that he had no serious injuries, but was badly bruised.
"Miner Injured" Bisbee Daily Review 7 June 1903 page 6

August 19(?), 1903, Holbrook Mine
James Harris was moving a windlass to another stope when a timber slipped. He fell twenty feet and was knocked unconscious. His lip and nose were stitched by Dr. Baum.
"Miner is Injured" Bisbee Daily Review 20 August 1903 page 5

September 22, 1903, Holbrook Mine
A rock fell and struck William Huley on his Achilles' tendon. He was taken to the hospital.
"Rock Fell on Huley Bisbee Daily Review 24 September 1903 page 5

September 23, 1903, Holbrook Mine
George Stewart had his hand caught between a mine car and a shaft timber. His hand was cut and bruised.
"Crushed his Hand" Bisbee Daily Review 24 September 1903 page 5

September 23, 1903, Holbrook Mine
A.M. Johnson was loading a mine car onto a cage on the 300 level. He smashed his middle finger between the car and the cage. It was determined the finger was not broken.
"Crushed his Finger" Bisbee Daily Review 24 September 1903 page 5

October 6, 1903, Holbrook Mine

Around 7:00 am, M.J. Nolan was being lowered on the cage down from the 400 level. A rock fell the shaft from the 400 level and struck him on the head. He was taken to the Copper Queen Dispensary and treated by Dr. Dysart.

"Rock Fell on Him" Bisbee Daily Review 7 October 1903 page 5

October 6, 1903, Holbrook Mine

James Cowling was expected to be off work four or five days, after he was injured on the 400 level station. A rock fell from the 300 level station and struck him on the right hand causing two deep cuts.

"Cut Hand with Falling Rock" Bisbee Daily Review 7 October 1903 page 5

October 7 (?), 1903, Holbrook Mine

A rock fell into the eye of N.S. Peck while he was drilling in a raise on the 400 level. The small rock was broken free during the drilling. His cornea was cut and was expected to cause him considerable pain.

"Rock Cut his Eye" Bisbee Daily Review 7 October 1903 page 5

October 22, 1903, Holbrook Mine

Between the 300 and 400 levels men were working on a cage finishing a new shaft compartment. A scaling bar was protruding from the stationary cage into the next compartment. As Bob Campbell was descending on a cage in the adjoining compartment the bar hit him tear a gash into his back. He was expected to be able to return to work after a few days.

"Bob Campbell Injured" Bisbee Daily Review 23 October 1903 page 5

January 5, 1903, Holbrook Mine

Around 3 o'clock in the afternoon, Martin Eiting had loaded a hole with Giant powder and then decided that he needed to drill it deeper. He removed the powder from the hole. Unknown to Eiting, he had left a small amount of dynamite in the hole. As soon as began drilling in the hole again, it exploded, spraying him with a small amount of dirt and rock. Luckily, his face was hit, but his hands were severely cut and minor cuts on his arms and chest.

"Three Miners injured" Bisbee Daily Review 7 January 1903 page 1

January 6, 1903, Holbrook Mine

Reuben Davidson was climbing a ladder out of a stope. As he reached the fourth set, he missed a rung and fell 30-feet and landed on his back. He was taken immediately to the Copper Queen Hospital. He suffered a sprained back and a severe scalp wound.

"Three Miners injured" Bisbee Daily Review 6 January 1903 page 1

The Copper Queen Hospital with the Holbrook No. 1 Mine in the background, c-1904

January 6, 1903, Holbrook Mine

H.L. Fenner and his partner M.A. Stewart had blasted on the 500 level of the Holbrook Mine. They returned to their work area, and Fenner tapped on rock overhead to check if it was loose. As he was checking a boulder broke free and fell on top of him. It hit him in the left shoulder breaking his clavicle and landed on his knees pinning him to the wall. A cut on his scalp resulted in blood pouring onto the boulder. Stewart with the help of two other miners removed the rock, but had thought Fenner had been killed. They actually, told the superintendent that he had been killed. When water was splashed on Fenner's face, he revived.

"Three Miners injured" Bisbee Daily Review 7 January 1903 page 1

June 7, 1903, Holbrook Mine

John McDonald fell ten-feet and suffered bruising.

"Miner Injured" Bisbee Daily Review 7 June 1903 page 6

June 9, 1903, Holbrook Mine

T.R. Campbell, reportedly, had his hand blown off. Campbell started to fall and reached out to stop himself. The dynamite in his hand struck the timber or wall and detonated*. Later, it was determined that he would not lose his hand and the thumb could be saved. Originally, it was suspected he had been smoking, but this was disproven. *It is difficult to imagine a full stick of dynamite detonating and not taking off at least the entire hand. There must be more to this story that was not recorded. The explosion injuries results sound more typically like a blasting cap detonation.

"Was not Smoking" Bisbee Daily Review 10 June 1903 page 5
"Untitled" Bisbee Daily Review 11 June 1903 page 5

July 31, 1903, Holbrook Mine

A miner with the surname of Brown was barring down a loose boulder when it unexpectedly fell. The rock struck Brown, bruising him and scraping his knee.

"Miner Hurt his Knee" Bisbee Daily Review 2, August 1903 page 5

September 22, 1903, Holbrook Mine

William Huley was struck by a rock on the Achille's tendon. He went to the hospital and was expected to be off work a few days.

"Rock Fell on Huley" Bisbee Daily Review 24 September 1903 page5

September 23, 1903, Holbrook Mine

A.H. Johnson was putting a mine car on the cage at the 300 level. He smashed his middle finger between the mine car and the cage. His finger was determined not to be broken.

"Crushed his Finger" Bisbee Daily Review 24 September, 1903 page5

September 23, 1903, Holbrook Mine

On the 400 level, George Stewart caught his hand between a mine car and the shaft timber. His left hand was bruised and cut. He was treated by Dr. Dysart at the Copper Queen Dispensary and was expected to be off work a couple weeks.

"Crushed his Hand" Bisbee Daily Review 24 September, 1903 page5

September 29, 1903, Holbrook Mine

William Strawn was loading timbers at the Holbrook Shaft when another miner dropped a timber off the cage. This timber struck Strawn's left foot, cutting it. He was treated Copper Queen Dispensary and was released home. Strawn was expected to be off work a couple of weeks

"Timber Fell on Him" Bisbee Daily Review 2 October 1903 page 5

October 29, 1903, Holbrook Mine

J.W. Isom was struck by a rock falling out of a chute. The resulting cut on the forehead required four stitches.

"Local Personal" Bisbee Daily Review 30 October 1903 page 5

December 6, 1903, Holbrook Mine

James Sutherland was repairing the shaft between the 200 and 300 levels when he placed his feet on the wall plates of the shaft compartment. A cage being lowered in the next compartment struck his right leg breaking it. The accident occurred around 1:30 am. He was transported to the hospital.

"Miner is Injured" Bisbee Daily Review 8 December 1903 page 5

January 30, 1904, Holbrook Mine

Irishman, Michael Thomas O'Neill* was working with J. H. Q. Dye in a drift in the Hayes Country. They were mucking out the drift and Dye pushed up, an empty car and O'Neill moved to the side of the car to reach for a candlestick. This candleholder had a wire attached to it to hook to the side of the car. As Dye was handing the candlestick to him, a 1,000 lbs. of rock fell from the rib of the drift and smashed him into the mine car. Dye uncovered him and used a bar to free one of his feet that was caught between the fallen rock and the car. He laid him down and went to the 200 level station for help. O'Neill was survived by a brother Patrick J. O'Neill, also a miner in the Holbrook Mine. * There working two

Michael O'Neills working in the Holbrook Mine in 1904. They were given the nicknames Michael O'Neill No. 1 and Michael O'Neill No. 2 It is not clear if No.1 or No.2 was killed.
"Cochise County Coroner's Inquest No. 187" Arizona State Archives Phoenix.

January 30, 1904, Holbrook Mine
Charles Gustofson had his back bruised and his knee injured by a falling rock.
"Knee Badly Injured" Bisbee Daily Review 31 January 1904 page 5

February 4, 1904, Holbrook Mine
Miner, John True was working on the 500 level when a timber fell smashing his foot.
"Had Foot Crushed" Bisbee Daily Review 5 February 1904 page 5

Febuary 17, 1904, Holbrook Mine
Frank Tremain a native of Cornwall, England had begun to work his third shift in Bisbee inside the Neptune Stope between the 300 and 400 levels. Tremain was clearing an area to install timber in a stope with treacherous ground. Sterling J. Shaw was next to him when the area caved. He was covered with 75-100 tons of fine sulfide. The ore poured out like sand. This accident occurred soon after the shift started The shift began at 6 o'clock in the evening and by 6:15 the area caved-in. It had been reported to the surface at 6:15 that stope had collapsed and that a miner was buried. Men were brought from all parts of the mine in an attempt to rescue. A little after 8 o'clock his body was uncovered and taken to the surface. His death was determined to be caused by suffocation.
"Two Miners Killed Accident Last Night" Bisbee Daily Review 18 February 1904 page 1
"Results of Inquests" Bisbee Daily Review 19 February 1904 page 5
"Cochise County Coroner's Inquest No. 189" Arizona State Archives Phoenix.

March 30, 1904, Holbrook Mine
J.W. Beam was struck in the back by a boulder. He was expected to be off work a significant amount of time.
"Hurt at the Holbrook" Bisbee Daily Review 2 April 1904 page8

May 30, 1904, Holbrook Mine
John Rule was injured in 37 stope when a square set timber fell on his foot and mashed off two toes.
"Injured at Holbrook" Bisbee Daily Review 31 May 1904 page 5

June 15, 1904, Holbrook Mine
An empty cage arrived on the surface and Assistant Mine Superintendent Charles C. Warner wanted to go down to the 400 level. He had Richard Todd put a mine car full of wedges on the cage then Jack Taylor, John Metcalf, Richard Todd and Charles Warner rode the cage to the 100 level. On this level Metcalf got off the cage. They proceeded to the 200 level, and then rang the bells to the 300 level. On the 300, Warner got off the cage thinking it was the 400 level. When he realized he was on the wrong level he tried to get back on. Todd cried out a warning, but Warner fell and was caught between the side plates and hood (bonnets) the cage continued to the 400 level dragging Warner along was caught by the cage. Taylor tried to ring a stop bell, but the hoistman, William Campbell never received the bell. The cage continued to the 400 level and stopped. Warner was on and dying. At the 400 level the cage was stopped and then he was discovered top of the cage

and alive, but mortally injured and was hoisted to the surface where he died a little over half hour later. Some believed he fainted on the cage. Charles Warner had been suffering from pleurisy which had chest pains dizziness and fainting spells. James Jones testified at the inquest that when the bell ropes were pulled too hard, they would not ring the signal bell. He believed this was why the cage was not stopped.

"Caught in the Shaft in the Copper Queen mine" The Arizona Republican 16 June 1904
"Cochise County Inquest No. 206" Arizona State Archives Phoenix

July 8, 1904, Holbrook Mine

W.T. Reynolds was cut up by debris flying from a blast. He was taken to the Copper Queen Hospital.

"Hurt by Blast" Bisbee Daily Review 9 July 1904 page 5

July 20, 1904, Holbrook Mine

Emmett Gannon was working in a drift placing timbers when a boulder fell, breaking his back. He was immediately raised to the surface. Dr. Dysart examined him and determined his lower body was paralyzed. On July 26 an operation was performed to remove bone that was putting pressure on the spinal cord. The spinal cord was discovered to be severely damaged. He recovered from the operation, but remained paralyzed, but generally healthy.

"Two Men Injured Perhaps Fatally" Bisbee Daily Review 21 July 1904 page 1
"Emmitt Gannon Undergoes Operation" Bisbee Daily Review 27 July 1904 page 8
"Is Doing Well" Bisbee Daily Review 29 July 1904 page 5
"Continues Helpless" Bisbee Daily Review 8 February 1905 page 6

August 16, 1904, Holbrook Mine

In a briefly described, accident an empty cage fell to the bottom of the shaft. The hoist and the cage were damaged. Luckily, no one was injured in the accident.

"Yesterday an Accident" Bisbee Daily Review 17 August 1904 page 5

September 16, 1904, Holbrook Mine

E.H. Wittig was working in No. 48 stope on the 400 level. He began to help dump a mine car when it overturned and landed on top of him. He suffered bruises on the head and body.

"E.H. Wittig Hurt" Bisbee Daily Review 17 September 1904 page 5

November 6, 1904, Holbrook Mine

James Matson was working in No. 45 stope on the 300 level. He was bent over using a pick, when boulders fell from the ceiling and striking him. The nearby miners found him up against a post with his head near his feet and one foot caught in a wheelbarrow. He was quickly unburied by other miners. It was determined that he suffered a severe spinal injury and was paralyzed from the waist down. Matson died at the Copper Queen Hospital on November 20, 1904. His body was shipped to San Francisco.

"Miner is Injured at Holbrook Mine" Bisbee Daily Review 8 November 1904 page 1
"Bisbee-Lowell Evergreen Cemetery." My Cochise.
http://www.mycochise.com/cembisbeem.php (May 25, 2012)
"Cochise County Inquest No. 231" Arizona State Archives Phoenix

January 13, 1905, Holbrook Mine

Thomas Walton had his right leg broken when rock fell on in it. He had just recovered from another broken leg that had laid him up for several weeks. Both accidents occurred underground.

"Leg Broken" Bisbee Daily Review 14 January 1905 page 5

February 10, 1905, Holbrook Mine

John Deck was the eighth man to board the cage on the 200 level. Near the 100 level. H.E. Cornish felt a jerk that knocked his lunch bucket and candlestick out of his hand. The lunch boxes of the men rattled.* As the cage reached the surface a miner stated that they had lost a man. Deck was killed instantly. Although, it was reported that not a single bone in his head had not been broken. His left arm leg and foot were. Broken. His left side was torn open exposing his heart, liver and intestines. He was survived by a wife children and a brother.

Note, that the cage trip to the surface would have been done in darkness. The miner's candles would have been extinguished to prevent them burning each other. Only the electric lights at shaft stations would have illuminated the cage for a second as they were passed.
"Stolen Horse Recovered" Bisbee Daily Review 14 February 1905 page 5
"Cochise County Inquest No. 250" Arizona State Archives Phoenix

April 16, 1905, Holbrook Mine

At 2:30 am, Joe Williams and W.H. Sexton were working preparing six holes for blasting. Close to blasting time and before the last hole was completely drilled an explosion occurred injuring them with flying rock. Both men were taken to the Copper Queen Hospital. Sexton was expected to be able to return to work the next day, and Williams was likely to remain in the hospital for nine days.

. "Short Personal Notes" Bisbee Daily Review 18 April 1905 page 5

June 13, 1905, Holbrook Mine

E.D. Johnson was struck by a cave-in and was seriously injured. A few days earlier he had fixed up his house and sent for his wife to live with him in Bisbee. She was expected to arrive on the June 14th. He was cared for at the Copper Queen Hospital.

"Miner Seriously Hurt." Bisbee Daily Review 14 June 1905 page 8

Loading blasting holes in the Campbell Mine C-1938

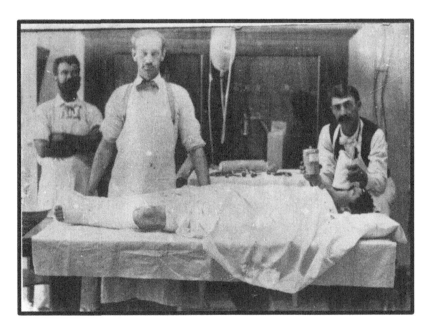
Interior view of the Copper Queen Hospital, c-1908 (Courtesy of the Bisbee Mining & Historical Museum)

July 6, 1905, Holbrook Mine

Steam-Fitter, J.W. Kelly was headed underground to work a stope. He boarded a cage loaded with timber. When the cage began to drop, a timber slipped and fell on Kelly. One of his legs was knocked out of the cage. This leg was crushed between the cage and the wall plates. Fortunately, the accident occurred near the shaft collar, and they were able to remove him quickly. Kelly's thigh was broken, and he was badly bruised. His broken bone

228

was set at the hospital, and the doctors were not able to determine the extent of any internal injuries.

"Possibly Dangerous Injuries Sustained" <u>Bisbee Daily Review</u> 7 July 1905 page 5

December 24, 1905, Holbrook Mine

Albert A. Branson, a miner, who was reported to be sick and was dizzy and faint. He had taken medication frequently during the shift. Following the tradition of the Copper Queen Company, the shift had ended three hours early on Christmas Eve. When he boarded a cage at 11 o'clock the station tender, Wm. A. Beaton noticed that Branson appeared to be acting near-sighted and made sure he was given a secure position on the cage. While, the cage was being hoisted to the surface Branson collapsed and fell out of the cage. He was crushed between the cage and the shaft timbers. His mangled body fell 330 feet to the bottom of the shaft. The signal was given to stop the cage immediately. When a cage was lowered to the shaft bottom, Beaton had already recovered Branson's body. He placed it on the cage for hoisting. Albert Branson had worked in Bisbee for only ten days. A letter from a lady in Hornitos, California was found in his pocket, who is believed to be his cousin and $102.35. The rumor that the cage had hit a crooked passage* which, caused him to fall was dispelled by the other men riding the cage.

*The Holbrook No.1 Shaft was caving by this time and the shaft had several times become twisted out of alignment. This caused difficultly in hoisting cages and rough spots when riding cages. On July 17, 1906 the decision was made to stop using the shaft for ore hoisting and the shaft had become so "crooked" that double-deck cages could no longer be hoisted. Then on August 3, 1906 the decision was made to raise a new shaft which would be later known as the Holbrook No.2 Shaft.

"Crushed and Killed" <u>Bisbee Daily Review</u> 26 December 1905 page 1
"Cause Unknown is Jury Verdict" <u>Bisbee Daily Review</u> 27 December 1905 page 5
"Holbrook to be given up by C.Q." <u>Bisbee Daily Review</u> 17 July 1906 page 1
"Will Raise New Shaft at Holbrook Mine Of C.Q. Co." <u>Bisbee Daily Review</u> 3 August 1906 page 1
"Cochise County Inquest No. 311" Arizona State Archives Phoenix

March 21, 1906, Holbrook Mine

Robert Cagel boarded the cage on the 200 level. Just as the cage reached the 100 level, he fainted. Miners quickly came to help him. Later that day he was able to walk home. He was extremely lucky. The newspaper reported that if he had fainted moments sooner, he would have suffered the gruesome fate that others in Bisbee mines had. He would have been dragged out of the cage, crushed against the timber and his body would have fallen 400 feet to the bottom of the shaft.

"Narrow Escape of Robt. Cagel" <u>Bisbee Daily Review</u> 4 December 1909 page 7

July 6, 1906, Holbrook Mine

Jack Nelson was pinned to the ground by caving rock and dirt in a stope. Nelson tried to continue working, but the pain became too great, and he was taken to the hospital. The majority of the rock and dirt hit his left knee.

"Jack Nelson Injured in Holbrook Shaft." <u>Bisbee Daily Review</u> 6 July 1906 page 3

Holbrook No. 2 Shaft

On July 8, 1906, the Holbrook No.1 Shaft began caving in between the 100 and 200 levels. On July 16th another cave-in occurred and the No.1 Shaft was abandoned. On August 3, 1906, work began on raising the new Holbrook No.2 Shaft. The No.1 Shaft had been had been caving for a couple of years previously. Close to three years before the shaft had caved blocking access to two levels and actually trapping three miners that had to be rescued. The No.2 Shaft was completed by December 8th 1906,

and was ready to put into service late January-Early February. Lack of timber may have prevented the shaft from going into service earlier. In February 14, 1907, all major Copper Queen mines were shut down because of a timber shortage.

August 20, 1906, Holbrook Mine
Ellis Miller was injured when a rock fell from the top (back) of a drift fracturing his skull. He was taken to the Copper Queen Hospital.
"Hurt at Holbrook" Bisbee Daily Review 22 August 1906 page 3

September 1906, Holbrook Mine
James Fulmare had his feet pinned under a turnsheet. He suffered severe bruising of both feet and was expected to be better in about ten days.
"Improving Steadily" Bisbee Daily Review 5 September 1906 page 3

April 25, 1906, Holbrook Mine
George C. Hall died at 7:00 pm of heart failure in a stope. This was his first shift in the mine and the only natural death to have occurred in this mine. According to Mrs. Geary, he ate a hearty supper at 4:30 pm at the Black Hills Café, where he boarded. He left for the mine a little later with a full dinner pail and high spirits about his new job. Letters found in his trunk failed to reveal the addresses of his relatives.
"Hall Well Known and Claimed Many Friends" Bisbee Daily Review 27 April 1906 page 3
"Hall Inquest has to be postponed" Bisbee Daily Review 27 April 1906 page 3
"First Shift Fatal for George C. Hall" Bisbee Daily Review 26 April 1906 page 4

July 26, 1906 Holbrook Mine
"Kid" Nash attacked Charles Wittig as he was leaving shift. Nash blamed Wittig for being fired and struck him on the body with a section of gas pipe. Nash was arrested in Lowell by Officer Humm after being discovered by Officer Jay Wilmoth and fined $10.
"Nash id Fined for Assault on Wittig" Bisbee Daily Review 27 July 1906 page 5

December 14, 1906, Holbrook Mine
At 2:30 in the morning, Timberman Jacob Curtain was caught by the cage and pressed up against the shaft timber. He was taken to the Copper Queen Hospital with internal injuries. That night the hospital reported he was doing well and was expected to be released soon.
"Hurt at the Holbrook Shaft." Bisbee Daily Review 15 December 1906 page 7

December 18, 1906 Holbrook Mine
William Foreman was walking along a drift on one of the lower levels of the Holbrook Mine when he fell into a manway. He was taken to the Copper Queen Hospital where it was learned that his right hip was bruised. Foreman was expected to be able to return to work in a few days.
"Hurt at Holbrook" Bisbee Daily Review 19 December 1906 page 7

April 12(?), 1906, Holbrook Mine
John L. Stanger was pushing a mine car, which rolled back at him knocking him down. He received a four-inch cut on the thigh. Stanger was expected to be off work several days.

"Leg is Injured" Bisbee Daily Review 13 April 1906 page 3

March 11, 1907, Holbrook Mine

Herbert Taylor was working on a deeper lever when a boulder fell bruising his foot.
"Sustains Slight Injury" Bisbee Daily Review 12 March 1905 page 7

May 13, 1907, Holbrook Mine

John L. Mauser, a German was caught in a cave-in. His head was cut, and his legs and arms were bruised. Luckily, the majority of the rock falling from the ceiling missed him.
"Was Caught in Cave-in" Bisbee Daily Review 15 May 1907 page 7
Copper Queen Hospital Patients Register Jan 1, 1907 – Jun. 30, 1908 Bisbee Mining and Historical Museum, Bisbee.

June 11, 1907, Holbrook Mine

J.A. Reyburn was working on the 500 level when a rock struck him after rolling down a muck pile. The rock punctured a varicose vein He was taken to the hospital and was released on June 13.
"Hurt in Mine" Bisbee Daily Review 12 June 1907 page 7
Copper Queen Hospital Patients Register Jan 1, 1907 – Jun. 30, 1908 Bisbee Mining and Historical Museum, Bisbee.

June 12, 1907, Holbrook Mine

Charles Huber, son of Ella and Joseph H. Huber was killed 2 days after his seventeenth birthday. Even though he was a junior in high school, who was an honor student and captain of the track team, he asked his father if he could get a job underground. Huber began working in the Holbrook Mine about a week before he was killed. At 9:00 am, the young man was working on a deeper level placing lagging over a manway raise. He placed one lagging then Huber proceeded to set in the next lagging he stood on the first one he had placed. The lagging he was standing on turned and Huber fell head first into the raise. Huber fell 100 ft. to the next level and his head impacted the side of a mine car sitting at the bottom of the raise. Miners soon found him. Huber was brought to the surface and carried him to the Copper Queen Hospital. He lived for two hours in the hospital before dying from a broken back and skull fracture. His father Joseph Huber was a blacksmith at the Holbrook Mine. (No coroner's inquest could be located) (Joseph Huber died just two years after his son from a gunshot wound in a hunting accident.) (A photograph of Charles Huber on the track team can be found in the Bisbee Daily Review June 17, 1906, on page 9)
"Boy Falls to His Death in Mine Man Hole" Bisbee Daily Review 13 June 1907 page 5
"Huber Victim of Accident is the Belief" Bisbee Daily Review 26 January 1910 page 8
Copper Queen Hospital Patients Register Jan 1, 1907 – Jun. 30, 1908 Bisbee Mining and Historical Museum, Bisbee.
"Standard Certificate of Death." Arizona Department of Health Services. http://genealogy.az.gov/azdeath/002/10021157.pdf (May 6, 2012) (this death certificate seems to be a typed copy from the 1930's)

June 13, 1907, Holbrook Mine

Alvin Heebee, a miner from Shafter, Texas was starting his shift with J.R. Briggs a school-mate. Briggs had helped Heebee get a job as a miner in Bisbee. Heebee had come to Bisbee on May 31, and Briggs had introduced him to Foreman Temby. They were working in a drift on the 300 level when a shift boss sent Briggs to work on an upper level and went to look for another partner for Heebee. In the meantime, Foreman Temby checked in on Heebee and learned that 30 feet of the drift was sloughing off rock. Temby inspected the area and told Heebee not to work at the face of the drift, but rather work around the opening and when his partner arrived to install a set of timber. Later, Thomas Rogers and W.W. Dexter came to talk to Heebee and found him working about ten feet beyond the protection of the timber. They talked a couple of minutes when a boulder fell at Heebee's feet. The miners yelled for him to jump, but instead Heebee looked up to examine the area where the rock fell from. At that instant, two tons of rock fell on top of him burying all but one of his feet. Quickly, Dexter began to uncover him and discovered Heebee was unconscious. Two other miners, H.N. Bunel and John Hughes, arrived about the same time. Heebee opened his eyes, asked for water and told them he was severely injured and that he needed to be placed on a timber truck and taken to the surface. He was brought to the Copper Queen Hospital, where Dr. F. E. Shine tried to save him. His injuries consisted of a fractured skull and internal injuries. These wounds were too great, and he died a half hour after reaching the hospital. J.R. Briggs contacted Heebee's adopted mother, and his body was shipped to his former home of Marfa, Texas. (No coroner's inquest could be located

"Hesitates and Loses his Life" Bisbee Daily Review 14 June 1907 page 1
"Body will be Sent" Bisbee Daily Review 15 June 1907 page 7

June 14, 1907 Holbrook Mine

Hiram E. Klinger* and Charles McGinty gathered timber and lowered it to the 300 level, where they were repairing timber in a drift. They had installed a false set so they could replace a damaged drift set. Around 5:00 pm, Klinger was driving a wedge under a lagging. The lagging fell and fine, loose muck began pouring out. Earlier, while he was working Klinger had placed his tools near his feet so they could be conveniently reached. It was believed that these buried tools became entangled with his feet and prevented his escape. When the muck reached his knees, he tried to get away and fell. The flowing earth rapidly buried him. McGinty, who was three feet away when this occurred, immediately, realized that he could not help Klinger until the running muck was caught up. He shouted for help. Foreman Temby was notified by telephone of the accident and quickly arrived at the scene. The area was timbered up in twenty-five minutes, and Klinger unburied in a couple of minutes, but he had already suffocated. Klinger had no sign of injuries except that his face was purple from being suffocated by the earth.** He was 40 years old and was survived by a brother A.R. Klinger and an elderly father in Los Angeles, Ca. Hiram Klinger was buried in the Elks section of Evergreen Cemetery. The inquest mentions a sister in California, Missouri.

*Spelled Hirman Clinger in June 15 Bisbee Daily Review article
**There was a superstition that mining accidents always occurred in groups of three. The newspaper reported Hiram's was the third consecutive accident in this completing this superstition J.A. Reyburn was injured in the Holbrook Shaft on June 11, Charles Huber was killed in the Holbrook Shaft on June 12, and Hiram Klinger was killed, also in the Holbrook on June 14.
"Old Time Miner Loses Life in Holbrook" Bisbee Daily Review 15 June 1907 page 8
"Coroner's Jury Investigates Accident" Bisbee Daily Review 16 June 1907 page 5
"Klinger is Buried" Bisbee Daily Review 18 June 1907 page 7

"Cochise County Inquest No. 464" Arizona State Archives Phoenix

June 21, 1907, Holbrook Mine

M. Grimes tried to lift and carry a large boulder. A blood vessel burst in his right arm. He was taken to the Copper Queen Hospital and was released on June 24.

"Bursts Blood Vessel" Bisbee Daily Review 21 June 1907 page 7

"Hurt in Mine" Bisbee Daily Review 12 June 1907 page 7

Copper Queen Hospital Patients Register Jan 1, 1907 – Jun. 30, 1908 Bisbee Mining and Historical Museum, Bisbee.

July 10, 1907, Holbrook Mine

Orlando Robbins, a miner from the Spray Shaft was unloading timber from the cage at the Holbrook Shaft when he slipped on a turnsheet and injured his hip. After spending a few hours at the Copper Queen Hospital, he was released to go home.

"Miner Injured" Bisbee Daily Review 11 July 1907 page 5

Copper Queen Hospital Patients Register Jan 1, 1907 – Jun. 30, 1908 Bisbee Mining and Historical Museum, Bisbee.

July 12, 1907, Holbrook Mine

Stope No. 75 caved-in, It was located between the 300 and 400 levels. Men working in the stope notified the Night Foreman Ernest Hughes, that the ground was moving. After examing the area, the foreman evacuated the five men from the stope. Soon after reaching the drift the entire stope collapsed, and the air blast hit the men with such force it knocked everyman in the drift off his feet. Foreman Hughes was thrown against the side of the drift and badly contused. A miner named John Sanderson had his leg broken an his kneecap torn off. The other men were bruised.

"Cave-in Occurs with Serious Results" Bisbee Daily Review 12 July 1907 page 5

"Cave-in Occurs In Bisbee Mine" Tombstone Epitaph 13 February 1907 page 1

August 8, 1907, Holbrook Mine

Charles A. Miller died at 1:30 in the afternoon at the Copper Queen Hospital. Miller had been installing lagging inside the shaft with John J. Jeffries. He had a lagging standing on end and was bent over. A descending cage caught the end of the board and threw him up. The accident signal was rung on the call bell (7- bells) and Jeffries removed the side lagging from the shaft to get Miller onto the dinkey cage. On the surface, he was carried by stretcher to the hospital. He arrived at the hospital unconscious with a broken sternum, nose and a scalp wound.* He was survived by a son, a daughter and his wife Mrs. Mary Miller, who was the proprietress of the Grandview house on School Hill.

*The newspaper claimed that he had walked to the hospital from the mine ignorant of how seriously he was hurt. Hospital records show he was comatose when he arrived.

"C.A. Miller Dies" Bisbee Daily Review 10 August 1907 page 7

"Miller laid to Rest" Bisbee Daily Review 11 August 1907 page 7

Copper Queen Hospital Patients Register Jan 1, 1907 – Jun 30, 1908 Bisbee Mining and Historical Museum, Bisbee.

"Cochise County Inquest No. 478" Arizona State Archives Phoenix

The Grandview Boarding House c-1907

August 9, 1907, Holbrook Mine

Matt Comsso had the main artery in his right arm cut open by a falling rock. They were unable to stop the bleeding at the mine. Fortunately, he was taken quickly to the Copper Queen Hospital. The bleeding was stopped, and he was released to return home later that day.

"Nearly Bleeds to Death" <u>Bisbee Daily Review</u> 10 August 1907 page 8

August 10, 1907, Holbrook Mine

Francis Thomas was working on a pump column. He was lifting an iron pipe that slipped and caught his small finger on the rim of the pipe. His finger was cut almost completely through. He was taken to the hospital where the finger was amputated. Thomas was released after his wound was dressed.

"Loses Finger" <u>Bisbee Daily Review</u> 11 August 1907 page 7

November 20 , 1907, Holbrook Mine

F.W. Wood was killed at 8 o'clock in the morning. Wood and his partner Paul Sampson were working on a drift on the 400 level. Sampson saw a mass a dirt break free and shouted, *"Look out!"* When Wood's stepped back a mass of about 100 lbs. of dirt hit him on the thigh and leg. He called out *" For God's sake get me out of here!"* The dirt mass had crumpled when it hit Wood and it was easy to extricate him. L. Downs arrived at the site immediately, discovering Wood, had a compound fracture. Part of a leg bone was sticking out of his leg and bleeding profusely. Downs used a handkerchief to make a tourniquet F.W. Wood was rushed to the hospital, where he died four minutes after arriving.

"Miners life is Ended by Fall of Earth" <u>Bisbee Daily Review</u> 21 November 1907 page 1

"Cochise County Coroner's Inquest No. 508" Arizona State Archives. Phoenix

February 5, 1908, Holbrook Mine

John Wood had been taking timber down into the mine. On a return trip to the surface, he stopped on the 100 foot level to put a timber truck onto the cage. As he ascended to the surface he became caught between the timber truck and the wall plates. This crushed his leg severely enough it was thought it may need to be amputated. He was released from the Copper Queen Hospital on February 17. His leg and knee were only severely bruised.

"Man is Crushed in Shaft of Holbrook" <u>Bisbee Daily Review</u> 6 February 1908 page 5

Copper Queen Hospital Patients Register Jan 1 1907 – Jun 30 1908 Bisbee Mining and Historical Museum, Bisbee.

March 1908, Holbrook Mine

Joseph Winsley, a cager, caught his head on the wall plate while riding a cage loaded with timber. His nose was broken, and his face was cut.

"Cager is Better" <u>Bisbee Daily Review</u> 21 March 1908 page 7

June 10, 1908, Holbrook Mine

Around 2:30 am, a man was struck in the head with a boulder. After reaching the hospital, the newspaper reported that he knew his last name was Jenkins but had no clue what his first name was. Hospital records reveal his name was in fact, E.C. Andrews and was released on June 11.

"Couldn't Remember His First Name" <u>Bisbee Daily Review</u> 11 June 1908 page 5

Copper Queen Hospital Patients Register June 1908 Bisbee Mining and Historical Museum, Bisbee.

April 1, 1908, Holbrook Mine

Tom Hargis was taking a load of timber down the dinky compartment of the shaft, when the ends of timber jutted out of the cage and caught the wall plate. His feet were caught between the wall and the timber. Luckily, the timber jammed the cage in the compartment its descent was halted. The cage in the adjacent compartment was lowered with workman and Hargis was freed.

"Had Narrow Escape from Death in Mine" <u>Bisbee Daily Review</u> 3 April 1908 page 7

August 15, 1908, Holbrook Mine

John O'Donald fell in a manway several sets on the 300 level. He was bruised. His fellow miners helped him to the hospital.

"Falls Down Manway" <u>Bisbee Daily Review</u> 16 August 1908 page 7

September 3, 1908, Holbrook Mine /Holbrook No.1 Shaft. *

Pipefitter, George Boyd was working on the 400 level at the "Old Holbrook Station" with Stewart Grant. Boyd leaned a ladder up against a timber to thread on a pipe. He slipped when Grant handed him a wrench and fell. One foot touched the trolley wire. The electric current held him about ten seconds and violently thrashed his head back and forth. Grant helped him down in a sitting position. Boyd groaned and was not able to speak, then died. Immediately, Grant rang the emergency signal (7-bells). Sam Boyd, brother to George, was killed in the Junction Shaft on February 2, 1906.

*The use of the term "Old Holbrook Station" in the September 4th newspaper indicates they were working 400 level station of the HolbrookNo.1 Shaft. The Holbrook No.2 Shaft. was barely two years old at the time of the accident.
"George Boyd Meets Death in Holbrook" Bisbee Daily Review 4 September 1908 page 1
"Electric Bolt Caused Death Jury's Verdict" Bisbee Daily Review 5 September 1908 page 1
"Miner Killed at Junction" Bisbee Daily Review 4 February 1906 page 1
Gerald F. G. Sherman. "Tramming and Hoisting at the Copper Queen Mine." American Institute of Mining Engineers Transaction Volume LII 1916: Page 465.
"Cochise County Coroner's Inquest No. 589" Arizona State Archives. Phoenix

September 15, 1908 Holbrook Mine

At 6:00 pm, C.L. Knucky was climbing down a manway to the 500 level. After he was about half way down, it is believed he fainted, losing hold of the ladder and fell between 6 and 7 sets (forty-fifty feet.) He was hoisted to the surface, but died before he reached the Copper Queen Hospital. His back was broken in two places, his skull was fractured, and he suffered other minor injuries. Knucky was an older miner about sixty years old. He was survived by a wife, and stepchildren, who live on Youngblood Hill. This older miner had experienced fainting spells at work before the accident. He was born in Cornwall, England.

"Falls to Death in Holbrook" Bisbee Daily Review 15 September 1908 page 5
"Funeral Services Knucky Today" Bisbee Daily Review 17 September 1908 page 7
"Cochise County Coroner's Inquest No. 595" Arizona State Archives. Phoenix

November 28, 1908, Holbrook Mine

At 1:00 pm, a cave-in inside a raise* suffocated Joe Vershay**. The raise continued to collapse, and it was not until 2:45 pm that miners were able to recover his body. According to Shift Boss C.W. Moon, Vershay was Austrian and spoke English well. He was 22 years old and had a cousin living in Bisbee. The young man's sister resided in Joliet, Illinois and his mother still lived in Austria-Hungary. His mother was the beneficiary of his accident insurance.

*The location of the raise was stated as 50 No.3 This likely means the accident occurred in 50 stope, but No.3 could refer to a crosscut or raise
**Was spelled both as Vershay and Vershea in the Bisbee Daily Review.
"Cave-in Smothers Man at Holbrook" Bisbee Daily Review 29 November 1908 page 7
"Inquest Held" Bisbee Daily Review 1 December 1908 page 7
"Cochise County Coroner's Inquest No. 606" Arizona State Archives. Phoenix

July 4, 1909, Holbrook Mine

Percy Robinson was run over by a mine car and trapped under the car for about five minutes. The car broke his leg between the knee and ankle. He was taken to the Copper Queen Hospital. On July 25, he went home against the advice of Dr. Miner.

"Injured Man Improves" Bisbee Daily Review 10 July 1909 page 7
Copper Queen Hospital Patients Register Jan 1, 1907 – Jun 30, 1908, Bisbee Mining and Historical Museum, Bisbee.

August 6, 1909, Holbrook Mine

At 3:00 pm, John Keton and W.C. Hurlbut were installing a blower on the 500 level. Hurlbut was standing on a timber truck when Keton called him a couple of times. He noticed Keton holding an electrical switch being shocked. Quickly, Hurlbut knocked Keton down but, he was already dead. He was 48 years old Texan. Keton is survived by a brother Matt Keton and a sister Mrs. Cowsert of Bisbee.

"Territorial Items of Interest Condensed" Tombstone Epitaph 15 August 1909 page 3
"Electric Shock Kills John Keton" Bisbee Daily Review 7 August 1909 page 8
"Cochise County Coroner's Inquest No. 671" Arizona State Archives. Phoenix

November 19, 1909, Holbrook Mine

Canadian, Frank L. Mankin was blowing out a blast hole when sulfide dust was blown into his eyes. Originally, it was thought that he would be blinded by the accident, but it later appeared that his eye sight would recover after several weeks. Quite a commotion was created when he was transported to the hospital by ambulance. The rumor circulated Main Street that a miner had been seriously injured in an explosion.

"Eyes are Damaged by Sulfide Dust" Bisbee Daily Review 20 November 1909 page 2
Copper Queen Hospital Patients Register Jan 1, 1907 – Jun 30, 1908, Bisbee Mining and Historical Museum, Bisbee.

September 21, 1909, Holbrook Mine

Around 2:30 am, an electric wire came in contacted with the A.E. (Ernest) Palmer's head leaving him a serious burn and temporarily insane. He fell to the ground and when the miners tried to help him he fought them off *"with the fury of a demon"*. It took seven men to bring Palmer to the surface, and he had to be strapped down to the stretcher to be taken to the Copper Queen Hospital. On September 24 he was released from the hospital recovered except that he had spells of dizziness. Saturday, September 26, Palmer was walking on the Brewery Gulch, when he sat down in front of B. Blunt's Cleaners. He sat there for a while, then as he got up fell and started into a fit. He was carried into the cleaners and the Palace Ambulance was called. While waiting, Palmer began an insane outburst and had to be calmed by about six men. He was taken back to the Copper Queen Hospital. After he was released again on October 5, 1909, Palmer found he was unable to work. On February 3, 1910, A.E. Palmer and his attorney W.P. Miller sued the Copper Queen Consolidated Mining Company for $30,000. They stated the electric wire had not been properly insulated. This was the first time the Copper Queen had been sued by an employee in 25 years they had operated in Bisbee. The case was heard in Tombstone, Arizona on July 25, 1910. Fifteen Employees of the Copper Queen were subpoenaed to appear in Court. These included, the Holbrook mine foreman Harry Barkdoll, Shift Boss James Hilaman, Timberman Ed. Dickerson, Carman George Phillips, John Dye, James Farrish and nine other employees. The jury quickly, decided on a verdict and rejected Palmer's claims for the Copper Queen Consolidated Mining Company.

*The hospital records initially registered him as Richard Parmer on September 21 when he was readmitted on September 25th they listed him as A.E. Palmer and made a note of the mistake.

**Palmer was 23 years old and had lived in Bisbee 7 years. Mrs. Bessie Sullivan, who lived in the back of the Broadway Rooming House, was related to him.

"Unbalanced by Shock in Mine" Bisbee Daily Review 23 September 1909 page 8

"Palmer Fully Recovered" <u>Bisbee Daily Review</u> 25 September 1909 page 6
"Palmer Becomes Maniac Once Again" <u>Bisbee Daily Review</u> 28 September 1909 page 8
"Advertisement" <u>Bisbee Daily Review</u> 19 August 1909 page 7
"Miner Sues Copper Queen for $30,000" <u>Bisbee Daily Review</u> 4 February 1910 page 1
"Witness Summoned in Damage Action" <u>Bisbee Daily Review</u> 24 July 1910 page 5
"Jury Finds for Company Shortly" <u>Bisbee Daily Review</u> 25 July 1910 page 1
Copper Queen Hospital Patients Register July 1, 1908 – Dec. 31, 1909 Bisbee Mining and Historical Museum, Bisbee.

January 12, 1910, Holbrook Mine

John Moore and his partner were sitting eating lunch at noon. Above in a stope, a miner lit the fuses on two blast holes. The first hole detonated and blasted out the dynamite in the second hole, scattering it. The stick containing the blasting cap fell several sets and with a sputtering fuse landed between Moore and his partner and detonated. Even though the powder landed closer to his partner, Moore was bent over and took the force of the blast. His partner was uninjured, but Moore was taken to the Copper Queen Hospital, where Dr. Downs from Douglas, Arizona, an eye specialist examined him. It was of Dr. Down's opinion that he would lose one if not both eyes. Later, it was reported that he was likely to regain the sight in one eye.

"Dynamite Accident May Blind Moore" <u>Bisbee Daily Review</u> 13 January 1910 page 5
"Moore Improves" <u>Bisbee Daily Review</u> 15 January 1910 page 7

January 26, 1910 Holbrook Mine

A falling boulder hit Scottish Miner, Robert Fergus on the head, then broke his ankle in two places. He was expected to be off work three months and as a member of the Bisbee Reds Football Team, he was out for the season.

"Ankle Broken in Two Places" <u>Bisbee Daily Review</u> 30 January 1910 page 7
"Today" <u>Bisbee Daily Review</u> 26 January 1910 page 1
Copper Queen Hospital Patients Register Jan 26, 1910 Bisbee Mining and Historical Museum, Bisbee.

January 29, 1910, Holbrook Mine

Mike Sullivan was hit by a falling rock that left a two-inch cut on his head. He was taken to the Copper Queen Hospital.

"Struck by Rock" <u>Bisbee Daily Review</u> 30 January 1910 page 7

January 29, 1910, Holbrook Mine

W.T. Bunch slipped while dumping mine cars, causing him to fall through the grizzly bars and into the raise. He continued to fall a distance of four sets. The grizzly bars were set eight inches apart how he fit through was quite a matter for contemplation. When men arrived to rescue him, they asked if he was injured he responded, *"Don't know whether I'm hurt or not." "But I know I've seen several kinds of comets in the last few minutes."* He was reported to have suffered the loss of one eyebrow and a few bruises. He was off work until February 14. The Bisbee Daily Review stated, *"W.T. Bunch who holds the record for falling through chutes without sustaining injury returned to work at the Holbrook shaft yesterday."*

"Falls Four Sets and Sees Only Stars" <u>Bisbee Daily Review</u> 30 January 1910 page 5
"Goes to Work" <u>Bisbee Daily Review</u> 15 February 1910 page 7

March 1910, Holbrook Mine
Foreman, James Temby was badly bruised when he fell two sets. Quickly, miners were able to help him, and he was able to walk home where he stayed under a doctor's care until healed.
"Timby's Narrow Escape" <u>Bisbee Daily Review</u> 30, March 1910 page 5

Dumping an E car into the top of a chute in the Campbell Mine C-1948

March 24, 1910, Holbrook Mine
John Quill, a carman, was loading a mine car at a chute, when another mine car came and crushed him between itself and the chute. He was knocked unconscious and severely bruised.
"Injured at Holbrook" <u>Bisbee Daily Review</u> 26, March 1910 page 5

April 3, 1910 Holbrook Mine
Finnish Miner, Oscar Kytola fell and broke his collar bone. He was released on April 6.
"Fall Breaks Collar Bone" <u>Bisbee Daily Review</u> 5 April 1910 page 5
Copper Queen Hospital Patients Register April 4, 1910, Bisbee Mining and Historical Museum, Bisbee

Chutes in the Higgins Mine on the tunnel level.

April 5, 1910, Holbrook Mine

After working the Copper Queen Consolidated Mining Company for nearly 20 years, James Rogers a Cornish miner 43 years old was killed in a cave-in. He was working on the 300 level in 54-12 stope, three sets above the level with Ernest Henry Waters. Rogers saw a sulfide boulder hanging and told Waters that he probably could pry it down with a scaling bar. After they had cleaned up the area and were getting ready to measure for timber, Rogers stooped down with his candlestick. The rock fell pinning him to the ground. Two boulders landed on Rogers, quickly Waters removed the smaller rock from Waters foot, but the larger boulder weighed about 600 lbs. and he couldn't move it. He went and got help. Three men were able to roll it off. Rogers asked his brother Thomas be notified. He was transported to the hospital by ambulance with his brother and Dr. L.L. Miner. During the trip, Dr. Miner mercifully administered anesthetic and told his brother that James would

240

die soon. He died at 3:00 pm, about ten minutes after reaching the hospital. Rogers's body was covered in cuts and bruises. His back, pelvis and six ribs were broken. His funeral was delayed a few days so his children, daughter Annie May age 18 and son James Rogers Jr. age 16 could arrive from their home in San Jose, California. They stayed with their Uncle *"Tommie"* Rogers. Mrs. Rogers had predeceased her husband by several years. Rogers parents were Thomas Rogers who was born in England and his mother Elizabeth May, who was born on a ship three miles out of New York. Annie May Rogers, James Rogers Jr. and Thomas Rogers, his children and siblings attended his funeral at the Palace Undertaking Parlor.

"James Rogers is Crushed to Death in Mine" Bisbee Daily Review 6 April 1910 page 8
"Funeral Date Undecided" Bisbee Daily Review 7 April 1910 page 5
"Accidental Death" Bisbee Daily Review 7 April 1910 page 5
"Rogers Funeral Tomorrow" Bisbee Daily Review 9 April 1910 page 5
"Rogers Funeral" Bisbee Daily Review 10 April 1910 page 11
"Big Events of a Year in El Paso and Vicinity" El Paso Herald 2 January 1911 page 10
"Original Certificate of Death." Arizona Department of Health Services. http://genealogy.az.gov/azdeath/007/10072429.pdf (July 22, 2011)
"Card of Thanks" Bisbee Daily Review 13 April 1910 page 3
"Cochise County Coroner's Inquest No. 734" Arizona State Archives. Phoenix

April 14, 1910, Holbrook Mine

English Miner, Dick Liddicote was stuck in the ankle by a large boulder on the 400 level. He was taken to the Copper Queen Hospital, where it was determined it was broken.

"Miner is Mangled by Buried Shot" Bisbee Daily Review 15 April 1910 page 5
Copper Queen Hospital Patients Register April 14, 1910 Bisbee Mining and Historical Museum, Bisbee.

June 20, 1910, Holbrook Mine

Chester Moon lost a finger on his right hand. He had placed his hand on the edge of a mine car when a rock fell out of a chute and struck his hand cutting off the finger.

"Moon loses Finger" Bisbee Daily Review 21 June 1910 page 4
"Three accidents at Bisbee; Notes from the Arizona Town" El Paso Herald 23 June 1910 page 4

Safety photo showing a miner risking his fingers by placing them over the edge of a mine car tub. C-1917

July 1910 Holbrook Mine

Thomas Keenan was struck by a falling rock.

"Several Miners Slightly Injured in Bisbee Shafts" El Paso Herald 16 July 1910 page 3

July 24, 1910, Holbrook Mine

A Cornish Miner, Henry Warmington was working under loose rock, when part of the rock fell and hit his leg. The leg received a compound fracture below the knee. He was transported to the Copper Queen Hospital by ambulance. He was released on October 8, 1910.

"Receives Serious Injury" Bisbee Daily Review 26 July 1910 page 5

Copper Queen Hospital Patients Register July 24, 1910 Bisbee Mining and Historical Museum, Bisbee.

July 24, 1910, Holbrook Mine

T.H. Cochrane * slipped and fell a distance of five or six sets. He did not break any bones, but was bruised. Cochrane was taken to the Copper Queen Hospital and was released around July 28, 1910, and was expected to return to work a few days later.

"Incident at Holbrook" Bisbee Daily Review 26 July 1910 page 5

"Discharged from Hospital" Bisbee Daily Review 28 July 1910 page 7

*His name was originally stated in The Bisbee Daily Review as Crockett and later as John Cochran. The hospital records state the name as Temprence (?)H. Cochrane .Which name has not been determined definitely.

October, 1910, Holbrook Mine

Angelo Bertol was working on the 300 level when a falling boulder broke one of his ribs.

"Bertol Getting Better" Bisbee Daily Review 20 October 1910 page 5

"Cochise County School Enrollment" El Paso Herald 22 October 1910 page 17

October 10, 1910, Holbrook Mine

Flying rock from a blast severely injured the left elbow of Charles Keller. He was taken to the Copper Queen Hospital and treated for a bruised back and arm.

"Two Miners Injured in Mine Accidents" Bisbee Daily Review 11 October 1910 page 1

Copper Queen Hospital Patients Register October 10, 1910 Bisbee Mining and Historical Museum, Bisbee.

November 18, 1910, Holbrook Mine

J.H. Hart was running a drill press and his glove became caught on a set screw. The machine dragged his hand in. He was seriously cut. Note, this accident happened on the surface and most likely in the machine shop.

"Injures Hand" Bisbee Daily Review 19 November 1910 page 5

June 6, 1911, Holbrook Mine

Irishman, W.E. Morgan's arm was injured from a fall of earth. He was taken to the Copper Queen Hospital. His wife was living near Burnley Lancashire, England

"Injured at Holbrook" Bisbee Daily Review 7 June 1911 page 5

Copper Queen Hospital Patients Register June 6, 1911 Bisbee Mining and Historical Museum, Bisbee.

September 11, 1911, Holbrook Mine

B. A Henderson received a bruised left hip and a cut on the scalp in a cave-in.

"Miner is Injured" Bisbee Daily Review 11 September 1911 page 8

October 30, 1911, Holbrook Mine

Ed Mitcherson dislocated his shoulder on night shift. He was transported to the Copper Queen Hospital.

"Miner Injured" Bisbee Daily Review 1 November 1911 page 5

November 30, 1911, Holbrook Mine

At 3:00 pm, John Alexander Green was killed in the cave-in of a stope between the 200 and 300 levels. He was working with William Smitham and W.H. Labell. They had measured for a new post and were cutting it. The gob underneath them suddenly dropped, and Smitham jumped clear but, Green fell with it. Green was buried under 22 feet of muck, and it took 11 ½ hours to recover his body. No bones were broken, and it appeared that he died from suffocation. Miners on the rescue team claimed to have heard him groaning, but doctors rejected this notion and believed he died within a few minutes of being buried. The coroner's jury found in a rare decision against the Copper Queen Consolidated Mining Company that he was killed *"in an accident due to the negligence of the company."* Green was a 41-year-old, native of Tennessee and was survived by a wife, Mary and four children. He was buried in Evergreen Cemetery.

"Miner Buried at Holbrook Shaft." Bisbee Daily Review 1 October 1911 page 3
"Miners Yet Live" Bisbee Daily Review 1 October 1911 page 2
"Green Funeral" Bisbee Daily Review 4 October 1911 page 4
"Cochise County Coroner's Inquest No. 866" Arizona State Archives. Phoenix

January 3, 1912, Holbrook Mine

Mine Repairman, John Warne was timbering 30 ft. off the 300 level station. He was putting in lagging and repairing timber, when at about 2:00 pm a small section of dirt, rock and timber fell. He was caught between timber and fallen rock. The rescuing miners had to install stringers before they could get Warne out. A crippled miner, Charles Henderson helped out by handing lagging to the rescuing miners. Dirt and rock continued to flow as they tried to free him. The trapped miner talked while the men dug him out, but he died soon after reaching the surface. It is believed, Warne must have died from internal injuries and not suffocation. Albert Reynolds, Warne's partner, had been sent away to get timber out of 54-15 crosscut and was a long distance from the accident. This likely saved his life. Angus W. Gillis was the first person to reach Warne. The deceased had been in Bisbee four years and lived on School Hill. He was survived by a wife and two young sons and a brother Sam Warne.

"Timbering Gives way Warne Meets Death" Bisbee Daily Review 4 January 1912 page 7
"Warne Funeral Today" Bisbee Daily Review 7 January 1912 page 6
"Cochise County Coroner's Inquest No. 887" Arizona State Archives. Phoenix

January 6, 1912, Holbrook Mine

Austin "Boston" Henderson was working in a stope on the 500 level. After lunch, he planned to install a blower pipe that had arrived a day earlier. He was last seen alive heading to a mule barn to retrieve bailing wire to hang the blower pipe. His body was discovered in the stope, by John Campbell. Campbell was working one set above him and about 50 ft. way. He climbed down to get a hammer and found Henderson lying on a turnsheet. After getting slightly shocked himself, Campbell shut off the blower and went to get help. It appears that even though the electrical wires were too far apart for Henderson to have touched them both, he may have contacted them with the bailing wire he was using to secure the blower pipe. Henderson was supposed to have had a sister living in a camp near Bisbee. His body was sent to Henry Henderson in Kittanning, Pennsylvania.

"Found Lying Dead in Holbrook Shaft." Bisbee Daily Review 7 January 1912 page 8
"Body Sent East" Bisbee Daily Review 10 January 1912 page 3
"Cochise County Coroner's Inquest No. 888" Arizona State Archives

February 8, 1912, Holbrook Mine

Robert Sanderson was overcome gas and taken to the hospital and released the same day.

"Slight Mine Accident" Bisbee Daily Review 9 February 1912 page 6
Copper Queen Hospital Patients Register Feb 8, 1912 Bisbee Mining and Historical Museum, Bisbee.

May 4, 1912, Holbrook Mine

Irishman, Patsy Leacey fractured his skull around 3:00 pm. He was taken to the Copper Queen Hospital by ambulance and released after 24 days.

"Miner's Skull Fractured" Bisbee Daily Review 5 May 1912 page 6
Copper Queen Hospital Patients Register May 4, 1912 Bisbee Mining and Historical Museum, Bisbee.

May 4, 1912, Holbrook Mine

Finnish Miner, John Maak was on the 200 level and was carrying a steel over his shoulder. He came across a stopped train with a motorman putting a new wheel on the trolley pole and a miner Angus Gillis. As he went by Gillis told him *"Be careful, Don't strike the wire with the steel you've got there."* Maak just looked at Gillis and went on. After he passed along and needed to cross over a train of mine cars and began to climb over the couplings between two cars. When he did this, the steel bar he was carrying contacted the trolley wire. He was stuck to the wire three to four seconds and *"The fire was flying from the wire all the time."* F.E. Barnes a miner, who also had just passed through cars, heard a holler. Barnes ran back through the cars and found Maak crawling. Barnes gave him first aid, but he died after five or six minutes He was a member of the Western Federation of Miners, a union. Maak's brother had been blinded in a mine accident in Colorado and returned to Finland. John Maak had come to Bisbee from Park City, Utah. 1,050 shares of Utah mining stock was found among his possessions. The coroner's jury found the mining company was at fault for his death.

"John Mack Killed in Holbrook Mine" Bisbee Daily Review 5 May 1912 page 1
"Company is Blamed for Miner's Death" Bisbee Daily Review 7 May 1912 page 8
"No Relatives of John Maak Found" Bisbee Daily Review 8 May 1912 page 8
"Funeral of John Maak Found" Bisbee Daily Review 9 May 1912 page 8
Gerald F. G. Sherman. "Tramming and Hoisting at the Copper Queen Mine." American Institute of Mining Engineers Transaction Volume LII 1916: Page 465.
"Cochise County Coroner's Inquest No. 919" Arizona State Archives.

May 18, 1912, Holbrook Mine

At 10:30 pm, J.M. Byrns was stuck in the back by a falling rock. It fractured a vertebra but, the spinal cord was not severed, and he was able to move the muscles in the lower part of his body. He was released from the hospital after 533 days in "improved" condition.

"Stone Falls, Miner's Spine is Fractured" Bisbee Daily Review 19 May 1912 page 2
Copper Queen Hospital Patients Register May 18, 1912 Bisbee Mining and Historical Museum, Bisbee.

October 5, 1912, Holbrook Mine

Robert Black was hit by a flying rock from a blast. The impact gave Black a compound fracture of the right leg. He was a key member of the Tombstone Canyon Stars Soccer Team and his loss from the team was attributed to having been an element in the team's defeat by the Lowell United Team on October 6th. He remained at the Copper Queen Hospital 156 days.

"Mexican's Leg is Broken" Bisbee Daily Review 6 October 1912 page 6
"Canyon Stars Lose to Lowell Soccers" Bisbee Daily Review 8 October 1912 page 8
"Annual Report of the State Mine Inspector" (Arizona) Board of Control 1913 p. 23
Copper Queen Hospital Patients Register Oct. 5 1912 Bisbee Mining and Historical Museum, Bisbee.

November 24, 1912, Holbrook Mine

Joe Baines was severely bruised at the Holbrook Mine. He was taken to the Copper Queen Hospital, where he remained 15 days.

"Personal Mention" Bisbee Daily Review 25 November 1912 page 3
Copper Queen Hospital Patients Register Nov. 24 1912 Bisbee Mining and Historical Museum, Bisbee.

August 22, 1913, Holbrook Mine

Franklin Silas Simpson was working with Martin Mitchell catching the back (ceiling) of 3-81stope on the 200 level when at 11:30 at night. A hidden rock slipped dropped a few feet and knocked out a supporting stull. The stull fell and continued to knock out the surrounding stulls. This collapse killed him. The fatality was one of the early accidents examined by the Safety First Organization of the Copper Queen Mine Workers. Silas had worked in western mines for about 20 years. He was 40 years old and left a wife and three children ages 3, 6 and 10.

"Silas Simpson Killed in Cave-In at Holbrook" Bisbee Daily Review 23 August 1913 page 1
"Found Death Due to an Accident" Bisbee Daily Review 24 August 1913 page 3
"Simpson Funeral" Bisbee Daily Review 26 August 1913 page 8
"Care Is to Be Ever Taken" Bisbee Daily Review 2 September 1913 page 3
"Cochise County Coroner's Inquest No. 1041" Arizona State Archives. Phoenix

October 13, 1913, Holbrook Mine

At 11:00 am, Charles Pelot was caught in a cave-in. The area collapsed without warning. Pelot suffered a bruised side and a smashed left foot. His fellow miners did not understand how he survived the accident. He was treated at the Copper Queen Hospital for ten days.

"Miner Severely Hurt When Ground Caved" Bisbee Daily Review 14 October 1913 page 3
Copper Queen Hospital Patients Register Oct. 13, 1913, Bisbee Mining and Historical Museum, Bisbee.

The freshly retimber 3rd SW Station of the Copper Queen Mine

**A safety incentive belt buckle awarded
for five years without having an accident.**

December 9, 1913, Holbrook Mine
John Madigan was preparing to blast when the blasting caps he intended to use, detonated.
The explosion cut his legs and face severely.
"Caps Explode; Madigan Hurt" <u>Bisbee Daily Review</u> 10 December 1913 page 4

February 14, 1914, Holbrook Mine
Dick Rich was bruised on the arm and side when he was struck by a falling rock He was
off work for several days. Rich and Dave Truscott members of the Copper Queen Band
were unable to play at the February 14 concert (St. Valentine's Day) because of injuries
from accidents underground. Truscott was injured in the Holbrook. The newspaper
reported that Rich was to be seen around the town of Bisbee on February 19.
"Band Members Hurt" <u>Bisbee Daily Review</u> 15 February 1914 page 8
"Able to Be Out" <u>Bisbee Daily Review</u> 20 February 1914 page 8

February 1914, Holbrook Mine
Dave Truscott was struck in the back by falling rock and was bruised. He was a member
of the Copper Queen Band and was unable to play at the St. Valentine's Day concert. His
fellow band member Dick Rich also could not perform as he was injured in Czar Mine on
February 14th.
"Band Members Hurt" <u>Bisbee Daily Review</u> 15 February 1914 page 8

September 24, 1914 Holbrook Mine

H.E. Henderson was working in a raise that continued to the surface near the supply house when a guide* being lowered fell and struck him on the head. He remained at the Copper Queen Hospital for ten days.

*It interesting to note that this raise was going to be used at least for some hoisting, probably for timber and materials. Ironically, this shaft later would be known as the Henderson Shaft on the Sanborn maps.
"Henderson Injured at Holbrook Shaft." Bisbee Daily Review 25 September 1914 page 5
Copper Queen Hospital Patients Register Sept. 24 1914 Bisbee Mining and Historical Museum, Bisbee.

August 7, 1914, Holbrook Mine

D.C. Williams was driving a small locomotive on the 400 level between the Sacramento Shaft and the Holbrook Shaft. As he crossed a switch on the main haulage drift a larger locomotive crashed into his, throwing him 15 feet.
"Man Injured When Cars Bump Together" Bisbee Daily Review 8 August 1914 page 6

May 17, 1917, Holbrook Mine

Joe Frank was struck by a locomotive. It was believed that his injuries were minor.
"Miner Injured" Bisbee Daily Review 18 May1917 page 8

October 20, 1917, Holbrook Mine

Around 11:00 pm, Edward Dickerson was working in a raise between the 200 and 300 levels when a boulder broke free and struck him in the head. Dickerson suffered a deep cut.
"Slightly Injured" Bisbee Daily Review 21 October 1917 page 6

October 7, 1918, Holbrook Mine

P.M. McCool was struck in the back by falling rock. He suffered bruises.
"Is Slightly Injured" Bisbee Daily Review 8 October 1918 page 6

October 29, 1918, Holbrook Mine

George Tokic, a miner from Austria-Hungary, was caught in a cave-in. One leg was injured. He was taken to the hospital, where his wife was being treated for pneumonia,
"Leg Badly Injured" Bisbee Daily Review 30 October 1918 page 8

November 14, 1923, Holbrook Mine / Hughes, Shields Merrill & Sharon Lease

Four men were injured when one of the picked into a misfire. The two most seriously injured were William Hughes and Jed Prater whom both had an injured eye along with other injuries. Bentero Valence and Jose McAguire both had only minor injuries, consisting of bruises and cuts.
Office of State Mine Inspector. *Twelfth Annual Report of the State Mine Inspector State of Arizona for the Year Ending November 30, 1923*

The Irish Mag Mine, c-1908

Irish Mag Mine

Irish Mag, a small dark haired woman of the ill-famed profession was one of Bisbee's earliest residents. A prospector/miner decided to name a mining claim to honor this charming lady. Later, James Daly a half-crazed tough character was owner the Irish Mag group of claims. This disagreeable man had been in a shooting with Dan Simmons and threatened to kill Ben Williams of the Copper Queen Consolidated. Daly was unhappy with the Copper Queen over a railroad right of way issue and felt the company was trying to force him to leave Bisbee. On April 11, 1890, Constable W.W. Lowther a popular man, needed to serve Daly for beating a young Mexican boy. As Lowther arrived at his house, he hitched his horse to a tree and opened up the gate. Then Daly fired a double barreled shotgun from the door of the house, killing the constable. Daly was last seen running up the side of Sacramento Hill. This left the ownership of the valuable property in question.

After a number of lawsuits, Martin Costello was determined to be the rightful owner with his partner Paddy Cunningham. After Paddy was killed in at the Holbrook Mine, Costello sold the Irish Mag and 10 other claims were sold to Lake Superior and Western Development Company in October 1899. This company began sinking the Irish Mag Shaft on the Irish Mag Claim on the morning of November 4, 1899. Initially, a windlass was used for hoisting. In 15 months the shaft was 850ft. deep and was developing the 750 and 850 levels. On March 1, 1901 the Lake Superior and Western Development Company became the Calumet & Arizona Mining Company. Mining continued and ore was first encountered on the 850 level. By June 6, 1901, a new hoist and headframe had been installed. Stoping began in November of 1902. In 1903, the Irish Mag shaft was deepened to 1,298ft. and the 1050 level was widened to hold double tracks to increase the tonnages from the northeast end of the mine. The following years saw massive changes on the site. A new drill press and lathes were added to the machine shops and a new change house was built. The old change house was remodeled, two-story engineering building and a new blacksmiths shop were constructed. Underground, a station was cut on the 1250 level and a pump was installed. Connections were made to the Oliver Mine in a great curving drift that avoided Copper Queen property. On the 850 level a connection was made to the Congdon Mine. Oxide ores and native copper were discovered on the 850 and 950 levels with sulphide ores being discovered on the 1050 and 1150 levels.

Even after *"religious"* backfilling, subsidence cracks began to develop on the surface from collapsing stopes in 1906. By January 1907 the land had moved 3-4ft. southeasterly and the surface cracks ranged from a few inches to two feet across. This subsidence resulted in the planning of an electric haulage level in preparation for a time when the Irish Mag shaft was no longer useable. On November 15, 1907, fire gasses began to seep into the 950 and 1050 levels. The fire was located in an inaccessible stope along the Copper Queen property line and gasses and also flooded the 600 and 700 levels of the Spray and Gardiner mines. Bulkheads were installed to stop the spread of the gasses. In 1908, in was decided that the main hoist was so badly out of line from subsidence that it would soon become inoperable. The company considered shutting down the shaft and tearing out the hoist and foundations and rebuilding it on new foundations, but since this would take at least six weeks. A new electric hoist was ordered to be installed in the summer of 1909 instead.

Exploration was focused on the area north east of the shaft. This area was heavily moving ground from collapsing Irish Mag and Gardner stopes and for a few years was considered inaccessible. Stations were cut on the 450, 550, and 650 levels and ore was developed in the area. Just above the 550 level a natural cave filled with oxide ore was hit. Around 50' x 100' in size, the treacherous ground conditions surrounding it, delayed its development.

For a time during 1910, the Irish Mag again became the main hoisting shaft as the Oliver was shut down for retimbering. The shaft was sunk 96ft. to a final depth of 1393ft. By 1911, the Irish Mag was beginning to show its age. All levels above the 750 level were abandoned and little new ore was discovered. In November, hoisting from the shaft was discontinued and all ore was hauled out the Oliver Mine. Underground drifts were driven on the 950 and 1050 levels out towards the fire zone in an attempt to recover ore lost by the fire. Exploration continued around old orebodies for searching extensions of ore. On May 6, 1912, it was decided to reactivate the Irish Mag shaft as the Oliver Shaft had difficulty handling all the ore. This lasted until May of 1913 the Irish Mag Shaft was closed and the remaining work on the 1350 level was completed from the Oliver Mine.

On February 18, 1915, the Irish Mag Mine reopened under a lease with Tom Stafford. This lease included all ground above the 1050 level. The shaft was retimbered from the 900 ft. level to the surface, in 1917. During 1918, 608ft. of crosscuts and raises were completed in Irish Mag ground from the Oliver Mine. Under the Irish Mag Leasing Company, the mine worked to around 1928. In 1929, the hoist and headframe were removed and installed at the Saginaw Mine.

1901, Irish Mag Mine

J.P. Shea was blinded when he was caught when a blast detonated early. He remained blind until February 1913. He was operated on by a Dr. Carpenter at Rawston Hospital in El Paso. By June 1913, he was released to return to Bisbee. After his sight returned, he planned to get a job back underground.

"Sight Restored Shea is Happy" Bisbee Daily Review 11 June 1913 page 2

August 5, 1902, Irish Mag Mine

E. Dickinson was struck in the area of the kidneys by a falling rock.

"Injured at Mine" Bisbee Daily Review 6 August 1902 page 8

October 1902, Irish Mag Mine

McFarland and W.B. Brown were installing landing chairs on the 950 level station. Brown looked up, and the cage stuck him and knocked him out. Unconscious, he fell into the shaft and miraculously landed on top of the same cage that hit him. This cage had dropped only a short distance. Luckily, Brown survived this accident.

"Recovering from Accident" Bisbee Daily Review 7 October 1902 page 5

January, 1903 Irish Mag Mine
At 8:15 am. Joseph Walker was working cutting out the 1100 level station. He had left his tools in the bottom of the shaft to be out of his way. As he reached for a tool a descending cage struck him on the head. He suffered a crescent shaped cut, but his skull was not fractured.
"Copper Queen Accidents" Arizona Republican 21, January 1903 page 3

July 29, 1903 Irish Mag Mine
Manuel Paco put his hand inside the chute at an ore bin. A boulder smashed a finger on his right hand. The Dr. Edmondson determined it would not need to be amputated.
"Crushed his Finger" Bisbee Daily Review 30 July 1903 page5

July 29, 1903 Irish Mag Mine
Jack Coyne was caught in a cave-in of ore on the 850 level. The rock broke his left leg twice above the ankle.
"Miner's Leg Broken" Bisbee Daily Review 30 July 1903 page5

August 8, 1903, Irish Mag Mine
Gabriel Palebro was helping unload a railroad car of timber on the surface. A 6"x*' timber slipped out of the hands of another worker. This timber struck him on the side of the head. Luckily, the doctors determined that he was only seriously cut up and no bones were broken.
"Falling Timber Hit Man" Bisbee Daily Review 9 August 1903 page 5

October 20, 1903 Irish Mag Mine
L.T. Beachman was caught in a cave-in. two ribs were broken and his scalp was cut.
"Caved on in Mine" Bisbee Daily Review 9 August 1903 page 5

October 22, 1903, Irish Mag Mine
Joe Johnson was struck by a boulder falling from a stope. He was knocked unconscious and suffered a scalp wound.
"Rock Fell on Him" Bisbee Daily Review 24 October 1903 page 5

January 17, 1903, Irish Mag Mine
Joseph Walker narrowly escaped death. He was about 1,100 ft. below the shaft collar and was reaching for tools lying on the bottom of the shaft. A descending cage hit him on the head.
"Narrow Escape" Bisbee Daily Review 18 January 1903 page 8

June 2, 1903, Irish Mag Mine
Charles Williams was working in 14 drift on the 1050 level when he was pinned to the ground by falling rock he suffered a broken right foot.
"Cave-in at C&A Crushes Miner" Bisbee Daily Review 3 June 1903 page 1

December 1, 1903, Irish Mag Mine
C.A. Roberts had his foot crushed by a falling sack of sand. Dr. Caven treated his injury.
"His Foot Crushed" Bisbee Daily Review 2 December 1903 page 5

April 5, 1904 Irish Mag Mine

John R. Kelly was struck by a falling rock. His knee and head were injured.

"C&A Miner Injured" Bisbee Daily Review 6 April 1904 page 5

July 1, 1905, Irish Mag Mine

Australian Miner, Louis Eppich had his back broken in an accident at the Irish Mag Mine. Around July 11, 1905, an operation was performed on Eppich to relieve pressure on his spine. It was expected that he would regain the ability to walk. (Eppich died on May 12, 1909, of Bright's disease.)

"Eppich Successfully Operated On" Bisbee Daily Review 11 July 1905 page 8
"Louis Eppich Dead" Bisbee Daily Review 13 May 1909 page 7
"Original Certificate of Death." Arizona Department of Health Services. http://genealogy.az.gov/azdeath/006/10061284.pdf (October 25, 2012)
"Calumet & Arizona Hospital Records." My Cochise. http://www.mycochise.com/hospcalde 2fi.php (May 28, 2012)

July 9, 1905, Irish Mag Mine

A mine car smashed the ankle of E. L. Jones, as he was unloading the car off a cage. It was expected that he would be unable to work for a few weeks.

"Severely Injured" Bisbee Daily Review 11 July 1905 page 8

October 20, 1905, Irish Mag Mine

On the 950 level, Sam Malcovich (Malovich?) began arguing with Mike Stefano. Stefano picked up a lagging and smashed, Malcovich in the side of the head. He left the mine ahead of Malcovich and went to hide in his house on Chihuahua Hill. Malcovich pressed charges against Stefano. The Bisbee Daily Review initially reported this as a mine accident in which the victim had been struck by a mine timber.

"Attempted Murder" Bisbee Daily Review 22 October 1905 page 1
"Struck on Head" Bisbee Daily Review 21 October 1905 page 8

October 27, 1905, Irish Mag Mine

20-year-old Basil Baslcanoff was caught in a cave-in. At the Calumet & Arizona Hospital, it was determined his back was broken. His wife distraught over her husband's injuries and believing they were mortal, she attempted to commit suicide, by drinking carbolic acid. Her neighbors, Mr. & Mrs. W.J. Slack, heard Mrs. Baslcanoff's screams as the chemical burned her throat and lips. Doctor Edmundson was called, and he pumped her stomach. On October 31, the Bisbee Daily Review reported that Mrs. Baslcanoff regretted her decision and that both were doing well. Her husband was released from the hospital on November 25, 1905.

"Woman Attempts Taking Her Own Life" Bisbee Daily Review 29 October 1905 page 5
"Both Man and Wife Better" Bisbee Daily Review 31 October 1905 page 5
"Calumet & Arizona Hospital Records" http://www.mycochise.com/hospcala2ba.php. My Cochise. (April 17, 2011)

January 3, 1906, Irish Mag Mine

Nicholas Vulich was working on the 1050 level when boulders fell striking him on the head. The 30-year-old miner spent the night at the Calumet & Arizona Hospital and was released on January 4, 1906.

"Mine Accidents" Bisbee Daily Review 5 January 1906 page 2

"Calumet & Arizona Hospital Records." My Cochise. http://www.mycochise.com/hospcaltr2we.php (April 17, 2011)

June 11, 1906, Irish Mag Mine

John Aglish and Tom Bristol were caught in a cave-in. Both men received minor injuries and were expected to be at home a few days.

"Two Miners Hurt at Irish Mag Shaft." Bisbee Daily Review 12 June 1906 page 3

August 14, 1906, Irish Mag Mine

James Cain was climbing a ladder when he slipped and fell into a chute. The 20 ft. fall bruised the 29-year-olds back and arms. He was taken to the Calumet & Arizona Hospital and released on September 5, 1906.

"Hurt in Mine" Bisbee Daily Review 15 August 1906 page 5

"Calumet & Arizona Hospital Records." My Cochise. http://www.mycochise.com/hospcalb.u2cl.php (May 19, 2012)

November 1906, Irish Mag Mine

Timberman, Jerry McNeil's was loading timber onto a timber truck, when a timber slipped and amputated the first joint of the index finger on the right hand.

"Sustains Severe Injuries" Bisbee Daily Review 10 November 1906 page 7

December 21, 1906, Irish Mag Mine

Peter Popovich boarded the cage and began to descend to his workplace. Just above the 650 level, the hoisting cable jerked, and the hoistman stopped the cage. A man was sent down to investigate using another cage. The man discovered Popovich crushed into the shaft timbers, his head was smashed, and his body was terribly disfigured. It appeared that Peter's lunch bucket had snagged on a timber and was dragged out of the cage, taking Popovich with it. The deceased was 21-years-old and from Montenegro, Austria-Hungary.

"Miner is Killed at Irish Mag Shaft" Bisbee Daily Review 21 December 1906 page 1

"Cochise County Coroner's Inquest No.408" Arizona State Archives Phoenix

January 19, 1907, Irish Mag Mine

At 4:00 pm, Fred L. Johnson a 25-year-old mining engineer was going up on a cage after spending the greater part of the day working on a deeper level. Right after he rang the shaft bells to be hoisted to the surface he screamed. His foot had become caught between the shaft timber and the cage. Doctors at the Calumet & Arizona Hospital operated on him to repair a compound fracture of the left leg. He was released from the C& A Hospital on August 2, 1907.

"Engineer Hurt at Mine" Bisbee Daily Review 20 January 1907 page 7

"Is Improving Steadily" Bisbee Daily Review 1 February 1907 page 7

"Calumet & Arizona Hospital Records." My Cochise. http://www.mycochise.com/hospcalje 2ko.php (May 19, 2012)

January 22, 1907, Irish Mag Mine
Edward Ryan was hand drilling in a stope when he missed the hand steel and struck his left knee. He was treated at the Calumet & Arizona Hospital and released to go home.
"Strikes Himself with Hammer" Bisbee Daily Review 23 January1907 page 7

May 16, 1907, Irish Mag Mine
Chris Miller a "Slavonian" whose surname was actually Millkervich or Millervich was working in a stope No.53 on the 1050 level. Chris and his partner were going to install timber, and Chris inspected the area for loose ground. When he believed it was ok, he and his partner began to timber. While his partner held up a timber, Chris bent over to pick up a tool and was struck by a boulder on the shoulders and was pinned to the ground. He died instantly. His remains were buried in Evergreen Cemetery.
"Miner Killed Instantly While at Work" Bisbee Daily Review 17 May 1907 page 1
"Arrangements for Funeral" Bisbee Daily Review 18 May 1907 page 7
"Bisbee-Lowell Evergreen Cemetery." My Cochise. http://www.mycochise.com/cembisbeem.php (March 31, 2011)
"Cochise County Coroner's Inquest No.448" Arizona State Archives Phoenix

June 6, 1907, Irish Mag Mine
A.M. Thompson was loading a mine car at a chute when a rock fell and smashed his hand against the car. His hand was not broken.
"Hurt in C&A Mine" Bisbee Daily Review June 1907 page 7

August 12, 1907, Irish Mag Mine
John Harnick was working in a drift on the 950 level when a rock fell and struck him in the head. He was not hospitalized.
"Is slightly Injured" Bisbee Daily Review 13 August 1907 page 7

October 6, 1908, Irish Mag Shaft
Two men were repairing the shaft and were using the dinkey cage as staging when the cable broke. The cage fell and became jammed between the 750 and 850 levels. No one was injured.
"Narrowly Escaped Death" Bisbee Daily Review 7 October 1908 page 7

June 15, 1909, Irish Mag Mine
At 10:00 pm, faulty wiring set the saw mill on fire. It quickly spread and engulfed the blacksmiths shop and part of the machine shop. Water from the Irish Mag and Gardner mines allowed for seven hoses to be sprayed onto the blaze. The flames were driven back after approaching within forty feet of a timber pile worth $50,000 and within 30ft. of the hoist house. At about 11:00 pm the fire was under control and by 11:30 largely out. No one was injured, but the men underground were in considerable danger. The concern was the shaft, headframe or hoist would begin burning.
"Fire Destroys C and A Mill at "Irish Mag"" Bisbee Daily Review 16 June 1909 page 1

The Calumet & Arizona Hospital in Lowell, c-1910

July 9, 1909, Irish Mag Mine

Murdock McKenzie was struck by a falling boulder that broke his leg. He was taken to the Calumet & Arizona Hospital and released July 27, 1909.

"Leg Badly Injured" <u>Bisbee Daily Review</u> 10 July 1909 page 7

"Calumet & Arizona Hospital Records." <u>My Cochise.</u> http://www.mycochise.com/hospcalmar2mc.php (April 3, 2011)

September 3, 1909, Irish Mag mine

Francis Segen was a riding on top of a mine car when he was knocked off by a timber. There was concern his injuries were life threatening, but it does not appear he was admitted to a hospital.

"Hurt at the Mag Shaft." <u>Bisbee Daily Review</u> September 1909 page 6

November 1, 1909, Irish Mag Mine

Charlie Kankaala, a Finnish miner, was on the 850 level when he fell in manway. He hit his head and shoulders. Kankaala was believed to have a suffered concussion and was cut up on the head. He was treated at the Calumet & Arizona Hospital and released on November 3, 1909. (Kankaala died from pneumonia at the C&A Hospital on November 1, 1918. Exactly nine years from the date of his accident underground.)

"Is Seriously Injured" <u>Bisbee Daily Review</u> 3 November 1909 page 5

"Calumet & Arizona Hospital Records." <u>My Cochise.</u> http://www.mycochise.com/hospcalje 2ko.php (May18, 2012)

April 5, 1910, Irish Mag Mine

Fifty-three-year-old, Charles Stevens broke his shoulder in the Irish Mag Shaft. He was taken to the Calumet & Arizona Hospital and was released on May 6, 1912.

"Has Fractured Shoulder" <u>Bisbee Daily Review</u>6 April 1910 page 5

"Calumet & Arizona Hospital Records." <u>My Cochise.</u> http://www.mycochise.com/hospcalsn2to.php (March 30, 2011)

May 28, 1910, Irish Mag Mine

John Charon, a 43-year-old miner had his jaw cut, and several teeth knocked out in a mine accident. He was taken to the Calumet & Arizona Hospital and remained there until June 8, 1910.

"Jaw Lacerated" Bisbee Daily Review 29 May 1912 page 7
"Calumet & Arizona Hospital Records." My Cochise. http://www.mycochise.com/hospcalb.u2cl.php (May 19, 2012)

August 1910, Irish Mag Mine

Henry Watson was caught in a fall of ground. He received cuts on head and shoulders. Watson was treated at the Calumet & Arizona Dispensary.

"Had Head Cut" Bisbee Daily Review 7 August 1910 page 5

September 24, 1910, Irish Mag Mine

Finnish Miner, Tovio Pasnenan* was timbering inside the Irish Mag Shaft near the 650 level. He leaned out into the shaft from behind the lagging to locate the cage, just as the cage passed. The cage cleanly decapitated him. His head plummeted to the bottom of the shaft while his body remained in position behind the lagging. Pasnenan's body was removed and taken to the surface as soon as the cage was available. The water filled sump had to be pumped out before the head could be recovered. This took around an hour and a half. Pasnenan was 26 years old and buried in Evergreen Cemetery. He was survived by his parents and his betrothed in Finland. Tovio had been saving his money and had over $4,000.00 in bank accounts. Remarkably, this was the first fatal accident to occur in the Irish Mag Mine in three years.

*The newspaper articles list him as Tovio Caanenan
"Miner Meets Awful Death at Irish Mag" Bisbee Daily Review 25 September 1910 page 1
"Original Certificate of Death." Arizona Department of Health Services. http://genealogy.az.gov/azdeath/009/10091098.pdf (March 27, 2011)
"Cochise County Coroner's Inquest No.787" Arizona State Archives Phoenix

November 19, 1910, Irish Mag Mine

Angelo Delgado was unloading a railroad car of timber. The side supports failed and buried him with timber. He was taken to the Calumet & Arizona Hospital. His injuries were considered serious.

"Buried Under Lumber" Bisbee Daily Review 20 November 1910 page 5

January 12, 1911, Irish Mag Mine

Adolph Anderson fell and broke his leg. He was taken to the hospital by ambulance.

"Has Leg Broken" Bisbee Daily Review 13 January 1911 page 5

March 3, 1911, Irish Mag Mine

Miner, R. Greenwood was taken to the Calumet & Arizona Dispensary after he received a cut on the head injury while laying track. He was treated by then, Mayor of Bisbee, Dr. C. L. Edmundson.

"Miner And Fireman Injured at Bisbee" El Paso Herald 7 March 1911 page 10
"Accident at Irish Mag" Bisbee Daily Review 4 March 1911 page 5

March 23, 1911 Irish Mag Mine

At 9:00 pm, a 31-year-old, Finnish Miner, Tsak "Isaac" Yokinen* was crushed in a cave-in. He was working on the 850 level in 25 raise. The ground was heavy and moving. Shift boss, John K. McRae wanted to put a stull in to hold the ground. Dust was falling, and McRae told the men to leave, but Yokinen said *"Oh, catch the stull."* They took a wedge and a two inch board and drove in the wedge to "catch" the stull. McRae heard the area start to crack and said *"Isaac, better get out!"* Then the area collapsed burying Yokinen under rock and a mass of fallen timber. The timber caused difficulty in recovering his body. The rescuing miners were forced to retimber the area before the collapsed timber and the rock could be removed. Yokinen was known as an excellent and contentious miner, after 18 hours his body was recovered. He was buried in Evergreen Cemetery.

*This man's name was listed as Isaac Yokinen in the Bisbee Daily Review. The death certificate has his names as both Tsak Jokinen and Tsak Yokinen
"Finnish is Victim of Cave-in" Bisbee Daily Review 24 March 1911 page 5
"Life Extinct When Miners Find Comrade" Bisbee Daily Review 25 March 1911 page 7
"Miners Funeral" Bisbee Daily Review 26 March 1911 page 5
"Original Certificate of Death." Arizona Department of Health Services.
 http://genealogy.az.gov/azdeath/008/10080047.pdf (April 8, 2011)
"Bisbee-Lowell Evergreen Cemetery." My Cochise.
http://www.mycochise.com/cembisbeexz.php (April 20, 2011)
"Cochise County Coroner's Inquest No.820" Arizona State Archives Phoenix

September 29, 1911, Irish Mag Mine

L.S. Davenport injured his leg in a mine accident. He was taken to the Calumet & Arizona Hospital and released September 30, 1911.

"Miner Injured" Bisbee Daily Review 30 September 1911 page 3
"Calumet & Arizona Hospital Records." My Cochise. http://www.mycochise.com/hospcalco2day.php (April 8, 2011)

February 7, 1912, Irish Mag Mine

Twenty-seven-year-old Mule Driver, John Fox, broke his leg in an accident at the Irish Mag Shaft. He was taken to the Calumet & Arizona Hospital and was released on February 26, 1912.

"Gets Leg Broken" Bisbee Daily Review 9 February 1912 page 6
"Calumet & Arizona Hospital Records." My Cochise. http://www.mycochise.com/hospcalfl2go.php(March 29, 2011)

October 30, 1912 Irish Mag Mine

Ben Hogarth was injured in an undescribed accident.

"Miner Slightly Injured" Bisbee Daily Review 30 October 1912 page 8

January 30, 1925, Irish Mag Mine

While working for Irish Mag Leasing Company, Antonio M. Cota fell off the mine dump and was killed. He was about 39 years-old and survived by a wife, Anita CotaWatkins.

"Original Certificate of Death." Arizona Department of Health Services http://genealogy.az.gov/azdeath/030/10300071.pdf (May 31, 2012)
Office of State Mine Inspector. *Fourteenth Annual Report of the State Mine Inspector State of Arizona for the Year Ending November 30, 1925.* Tombstone Epitaph.

The Junction Shaft. C-1910

Junction Mine

On July 15, 1903, the four compartment Junction Shaft was started by the Junction Development Company. The shaft was sunk rapidly making about 85ft. of depth per month. Diamond drill holes were used to guide the development of the shaft. One drill hole was even drilled from the bottom of the shaft in an effort to locate the limestones. At a depth of 850ft. enough water was entering the shaft that it was uneconomical to continue sinking. On July 31, 1904, 45 sinking buckets filled with water were being raise during day out of the shaft. Pumps were installed to handle the water, but being steam operated the temperatures underground were unbearable at the pump stations, exceeding 120° F. A fifth compartment was raised to handle the steam pipes for the pumps and reduce the temperature. A drift was also being driven on the 910 level to the Briggs Mine for ventilations. The inflow of water directed exploration for a time. The company wanted to ideally keep the water inflow at under 1,500 gallons per minute and no more than 2,000 gallons a minute. Thus sinking was stopped at the 1,006 ft. level and development work consisted of drifting on the 850, 910, 975 and 1006 ft. levels.

During 1905, the Junction Development Company became the short-lived, Junction Mining Company. This new company became part of the Superior and Pittsburg Copper Company in 1906. A steel headframe and double drum hoist were installed. The 1000 level became the main pumping station. In July 1907, massive pumps were installed with fly wheels weighing 12 tons on 1000 level. A total of nine rail cars were needed to hold pumps and parts. The stations to be cut underground were expected to be huge. To hold one pump, an area big enough for *"A six-horse team could turn on a trot without any trouble whatever."* was needed. This brought the 1000 level pump station to 5000 gpm capacity. Fortunately, as the ground was drained, the levels dried up and by 1909 only the bottom or 1500 level was producing significant water. It became necessary in early 1908 to install three deck cages to handle the ore being mined. Both oxide and sulphide ores were being produced.

A timbered shaft is a fire hazard and in 1912. It became apparent if a fire even shut down the pumping of water at the Junction for a single hour all the operating levels in the Junction, Hoatson and Briggs Mines would be lost. The Junction Shaft needed to be concrete lined for fire safety. Ore hoisted was diverted to the Hoatson and the tedious work concreting the shaft began. During the concreting project the shaft was flooded from the 1800 level to the 1500. When the upper portions of the shaft were finished the shaft was pumped out and the last 300 ft. was concrete lined. During the concrete work the shaft was being converted to use five-ton skips with a large pocket built

258

on the 1400 level. The 1400 level was built has a haulage level with electric locomotives. The idea was the Junction would hoist the majority of ore produced by the Calumet & Arizona Mines.

Natural ventilation no longer provided adequate air flow for the Calumet and Arizona mines. At the Junction four blowers were installed with a system of air doors, in 1915. The Campbell shaft was began in 1916 with the original intent that it would be used as a ventilating shaft for the Junction. After years of remaining 1,800 feet deep, in 1920 sinking of the Junction resumed and it was lowered to the 2200 level. The following year compartments 4 and 5 were sunk to the 2300 level. Then the remaining compartments were raised from the 2300 level up to the 1800 level. The well-known pump station on the 2200 level was built in 1924 and all the steam pumps were shut down. The following year one billion, one hundred million, gallons of water were pumped at Junction Shaft. A cast-steel water door in a concrete frame was built 600 ft. from the shaft on the 2200 level to protect the shaft from sudden flooding.

In 1931, the Calumet & Arizona Mining Company merged with Phelps Dodge Copper Queen Branch. Almost immediately, the Copper Queen's mines of were shut down and the Junction began to be modified to mine ore that traditionally been part of the Sacramento Mine. A shaft station was cut on the 960 level and the 1200 level was fitted to serve as a haulage level. These were to provide access to the Sacramento Mine's block cave and Southeast Extension stopes. The 2200 level pumping capacity was double in preparation for continued sinking of the Junction Shaft in 1933. By the end of 1934, the Junction was sunk to the 2710 ft. level with stations cut on the 2566 and 2700 levels. On August 30, 1941, water was struck in 12 crosscut on the 2700 level. The massive amount of water flooded the mines to above the 2566 level of the Campbell. Deep well pumps were borrowed from the Phelps Dodge mines at Morenci, Arizona and before 1942, the 2700 level had been recovered and restored.

In 1958, mining officially ended in the Junction mine, but the shaft and a limited amount of workings were maintained. During 1963, a vast amount of acidic water was released from the Czar-Holbrook mine area. The pumps on the 1800 struggled to hold it back. Miners diverted the water down raises and sent it to the 2200 level. It was treated with lime to de-acidify the water, so it could be pumped from the 2200 level. The pumps on the 2200 level and the 2700 continued to be used until 1985. In 1982, severe flooding occurred with acidic mine waters from the abandoned workings. The water came from a storm in Mule Gulch. These waters drained into the mine workings and overcame the pumps on the 1800 level and water poured directly down the shaft to the 2700 level.

In 1985, after the cessation of the precious metal mining in the Campbell Mine and salvage work, the pumps on the 2700 level Junction and 3200 level Campbell Mine were simply turned off on. The 2200 level pump was operated on a one shift basis to provide leach water. Water rose rapidly at 4 ft. a day a massive amount considering the hundreds of miles of mine workings being flooded. Slowing down, it began to rise about 2 ft. a day when it reached the 2200 level With water rising , on May 7th,1986 the power to the 2200 level shaft station was turned off in preparation of the flooding a few days later at 3:00 am May 11, *"Mother's Day"* water began flooding the station. During the 1990's, the 770 adit from the Lavender Pit to the Junction shaft was completely retimbered. The 770 station was retimbered as well and the shaft to at least this level was useable. This section of the mine was used for mine safety training. The shaft was completed at a depth of 2,727ft and five compartments.

December 29, 1904, Junction Mine
Bernard Lee was working on the pump station level when a rock smashed his foot. No bones were broken.
"Foot Crushed" <u>Bisbee Daily Review</u> 30 December 1904 page 5

February 14, 1905, Junction Mine
H.B. Mabry and William. Whitford were working on the pumps when rocks fell from about 30 feet above them. The men were knocked down and received cuts on the scalp about two

inches in length. The injuries were minor. Interestingly, the men were both struck down at the same moment and received identical injuries as to type and location.

"Hurt at Same Instant" Bisbee Daily Review 15 February 1905 page 5
*May 21, 1905, Wm Whitford died from fractured skull this may be related to his mine accident.

May 18, 1905, Junction Mine
William Mass was riding up on a cage when at the 770 level a spray of steam hot water from the pump column hit him burning his back and shoulders. He was expected to be off work a few days.

"Miner Severely Burned" Bisbee Daily Review 19 May 1905 page 1

July 8, 1905, Junction Mine
Wilson Percy Grier a pipe-fitter was being hoisted on a cage when the hoist malfunctioned at the 1000 level. Grier thought he had arrived at his station and stepped out of the cage. At the same moment, the hoist was fixed, and the cage moved to continue its journey. After the cage moved it cut him in half. Men nearby ran to help him but it was all over. The parents of the deceased had recently moved to California from Bisbee returned on July 11. When their train arrived in Lowell, Grier's grief-stricken mother had to be carried away from the train. The deceased was 28 years old and was buried in Evergreen Cemetery. This was considered one of the most *"horrible"* accidents in Bisbee at the time.

"Pipe-Fitter Loses Life at Junction" Bisbee Daily Review 9 July 1905 page 5
"Prostrated with Grief" Bisbee Daily Review 12 July 1905 page 1
"Parents of Percy Grier Coming" Bisbee Daily Review 11 July 1905 page 8
"Notice of Hearing Petition" Bisbee Daily Review 22 July 1905 page 6
"Bisbee-Lowell Evergreen Cemetery" My Cochise
http://www.mycochise.com/cembisbeeg.php (April 7, 2011)

December 9, 1905, Junction Mine
John Krieger was working on the 1000 level when he was struck in the head by falling rocks. He was sent home with a cut on the head.

"Hurt by Falling Rock" Bisbee Daily Review 10 December 1905 page 7

January 1906, Junction Mine
C.E. Gerry had his hand smashed between two mine cars. His hand was only bruised.

"Mine Accidents" Bisbee Daily Review 5 January 1906 page 2

March 3, 1906, Junction Mine
John Caine was working on the 900 level. At around 9:30 am, he was on his knees digging with a pick when a 250 lb. boulder fell and hit him in the neck. Nearby, miners quickly put him on a cage and hoisted him to the shaft collar. On the surface, he was still alive, but he had died before Dr. Elliot arrived. He was 23 years old and native to England. Caine was survived by a wife and a baby living in Cleator Moor, Cumberland, England*"Cochise County Coroner's Inquest No.408" Arizona State Archives Phoenix
*It was spelled Clearormoore in the Newspaper
"Miner is Killed by Falling Rock" Bisbee Daily Review 6 March 1906 page 5
"Funeral Yesterday" Bisbee Daily Review 7 March 1906 page 6

October 10, 1906, Junction Mine

George Daniel Earthal, a jigger boss/ timberman who was commonly known as "Tom" was working to timber the 1100 level station. He called for a double deck cage to be lowered so he could use it as a staging to work on. Earthal gave orders to the men on the station that the cage should not be moved. As he was working two men boarded the cage and did not realize Earthal was working on the top deck of the cage. They signaled the cage to go up to the 1000 level, and the engineer responded to the signal and moved the cage. The timberman was crushed between the cage and the shaft timber and as the cage continue to move his body was freed and fell to the bottom of the shaft. In a rare decision the inquest jury found that G.D. Earthal's death was caused by the negligence of the Superior & Pittsburg Mining Company. George's brother, Albert Earthal, an employee of the Copper Queen Consolidated Mining Company accompanied his brother's body to Winchester, Ohio, the home of their mother and father.

"Miner Killed at Junction Shaft." Bisbee Daily Review 11 October 1906 page 5
"Cochise County Coroner's Inquest No.373" Arizona State Archives Phoenix

February 2, 1906, Junction Mine

At 9:20 in the evening, Spencer B. Boyd, a cager, was killed. Denver D. Legget, the hoist engineer, said that he received a signal from Boyd to hoist the cage. He raised the cage to the 200 level when he realized something was wrong and stopped the cage. Denver waited for a signal from cage to either raise or lower it when this did not come he sent a man down to investigate. The exact circumstances of Boyd's are unknown since he was alone on the cage. Somewhere between the 300 and 200 levels, Boyd either slipped or fainted. His head was caught between the cage and the shaft. timbers and he was jerked out of the cage. Skull fragments and one leg was found at the 300 level. The rest of the body was found at the 1000 level, the bottom of the shaft. All his clothes had been torn off except a leather belt, one arm was gone, the other was broken in multiple places and both legs were gone below the knees. Spencer was known as an excellent cager, one of the best in the district. On September 3, 1908, his brother George was killed in the Holbrook No.1 Shaft. Another brother; J.J. Boyd was employed at the C&A shaft. (Irish Mag) at the time of Spencer's death.

"Miner Killed at Junction" Bisbee Daily Review 4 February 1906 page 1
"Body sent Away" Bisbee Daily Review 7 February 1906 page 7
"George Boyd Meets Death in Holbrook" Bisbee Daily Review 4 September 1908 page 1
"Electric Bolt Caused Death Jury's Verdict" Bisbee Daily Review 5 September 1908 page 1
"Miner Killed at Junction" Bisbee Daily Review 4 February 1906 page 1
"Cochise County Coroner's Inquest No.323" Arizona State Archives Phoenix

**A view of the upper deck on a pair of
double deck cages at the Shattuck Mine.**

February 8, 1906, Junction Mine
A large derrick being used to place parts of the massive new hoist fell over. Luckily, no one was injured Twelve men had been endangered by the falling derrick.
"Falling Derrick Threatened Life" Bisbee Daily Review 9 February 1906, page 8

January 27, 1907, Junction Mine
J.C. Farrell, a 38-year-old shift boss was riding a sinking bucket down the shaft when the bucket began swinging. His left leg was smashed between the bucket and the shaft timber. The leg suffered a compound fracture. Farrell quickly grabbed the bell rope and signaled

the hoistman to bring him to the surface. He was taken to the Calumet & Arizona Hospital and remained there until March 11, 1907.

"Suffers Painful Injury" <u>Bisbee Daily Review</u> 28 January 1907 page 7

"Calumet & Arizona Hospital Records" <u>My Cochise</u> http://www.mycochise.com/hospcalde 2fi.php (April 4 2011)

May 10, 1907 Junction Mine

Water was being pumped from the shaft into a retaining pond before being allowed to flow down a flume to the Warren Ranch. Several boys including, Clem Hall, Charlie Cash, Lee Westfield, Randolph Logan and Davey Brice were playing on a raft. Clem Hall became trapped under the raft. The other kids went for help. Clem was taken to the hospital, but he did not recover. He was ten-years old (The inquest gives limited information)

"Boy is Drowned While Playing in Pond" <u>Bisbee Daily Review</u> 11 May 1907 page 1

"Cochise County Coroner's Inquest No.447" Arizona State Archives Phoenix

July 1907, Junction Mine

Chris Lowell dislocated his foot in an undescribed accident.

"Dislocated Foot" <u>Bisbee Daily Review</u> 20 July 1907, page 7

November? 1907, Junction Mine

J.D. Harker and George Klag were on the 1200 level. A disagreement broke out. Harker wanted to use a pick that Klag was using to muck out. A fight broke out and Harker was charged with assault and fined $10. Harker then filed a complaint against Klag. The results of this complaint are unknown, but the trial had to be delayed because the witnesses failed to show up.

"An Underground Mix-up" <u>Bisbee Daily Review</u> 26 November 1907 page 3

"Trial Postponed" <u>Bisbee Daily Review</u> 27 November 1907 page 3

November 29, 1907 Junction Mine

A smoke stack was being raised for the new boiler. The gin pole broke and the stack plummeted to the ground. Luckily, no one was injured.

"Stack Falls at Junction" <u>Bisbee Daily Review</u> 30 November 1907 page 3

December 19, 1907, Junction Mine

David Hunt cut his finger with a circular saw. It was not expected that he would lose his finger.

"Finger Cut" <u>Bisbee Daily Review</u> 19 December 1907 page 3

December 19, 1907, Junction Mine

James Ralliman, Shift boss was struck in the head by falling rock. Although, painful the wound was not considered dangerous.

"Struck with Rock" <u>Bisbee Daily Review</u> 19 December 1907 page 3

January 20, 1908 Junction Mine
Robert White fell into a chute (raise) on the 900 level. He dropped forty feet and landed on soft ore. The ore cushioned his impact and he was taken to the Calumet & Arizona Hospital to be examined for internal injuries.
"Miner Narrowly Escapes Death" Bisbee Daily Review 21 January 1908 page 3

February 10, 1908, Junction Mine
Louis Burkovich, a miner who was called Louis Novick at the mine, was lighting fuses to blast on the 1200 level. To ignite the fuses he lit a short piece of fuse and began using this to ignite the rest of the fuses. He did not realize a blasting cap was attached to the short fuse. The cap detonated blowing off part of the index finger and his middle finger and thumb completely. He was taken to the Calumet & Arizona Dispensary for treatment.
"Cap Explodes Miner Loses Part of Hand" Bisbee Daily Review 11 February 1908 page 3

Febuary 17, 1908, Junction Mine
James McLay broke his thumb in an undescribed accident.
"Thumb broken" Bisbee Daily Review 18 February 1908 page 3

February 27, 1908, Junction Mine
Joseph Miller was hit by falling lagging. The lagging had slipped free from a rope that was being used to help place it. His injuries were minor, and he was seen around town later that day.

February 28, 1908, Junction Mine
About 6:00 am, Frank Slater was hit by rocks falling from a stope. He was taken to his home by livery rig. His wounds were minor.
"Hurt at Junction" Bisbee Daily Review 28 February 1908 page 3

March 1908, Junction Mine
J.W. Bledsoe was on the surface about to be lowered on a cage. As the cage dropped his leg became caught between the cage and the shaft. Luckily, the cage only moved a few inches.Bledsoe's leg was badly bruised and he was taken to the Calumet & Arizona Hospital.
"Narrowly Escapes Death" Bisbee Daily Review 4 March 1908, page 7

March 10, 1908, Junction Mine
J.P. Mahan was struck by rocks falling from the back (ceiling) of a stope. He was taken home to recover from bruises.
"Injured at Junction" Bisbee Daily Review 11 March 1908 page 2

March 16, 1908, Junction Mine
Forty-year-old Peter Gates was working below the 1400 level in the bottom* of the Junction shaft when a sinking bucket was lowered on top of him. The bucket stuck his head and dislocated his hip. The newspaper reported that he nearly "*kicked the bucket*" He spent four days in the Calumet & Arizona Hospital.

"Struck on Head by Falling Bucket" <u>Bisbee Daily Review</u> 17 March 1908 page 1
"Injured Man Better" <u>Bisbee Daily Review</u> 18 March 1908 page 3
"Calumet & Arizona Hospital Records." <u>My Cochise.</u> http://www.mycochise.com/hospcalfl2go.php (April 14 2011)

March 31, 1908, Junction Mine

John Spikes (Spiks?) a *"Slavonian"* miner had his finger smashed under a bucket. He was taken to the Calumet & Arizona Hospital where the finger was amputated.

"Loses Finger" <u>Bisbee Daily Review</u> 3 April 1908 page 7

April 23, 1908, Junction Shaft

A jack* fell and smashed the hand of Charles Miller. He was taken to the Calumet & Arizona Hospital, where his wounds were treated.

*This was probably a timber jack.
"Miner Injured" <u>Bisbee Daily Review</u> 23, April 1908 page 3
"Calumet & Arizona Hospital Records." <u>My Cochise.</u> http://www.mycochise.com/hospcalde 2fi.php (June 20, 2011)

Pre-1909, Junction Mine

M.H. Hardy entered an osteopathic sanitarium in Los Angeles to receive treatment for injuries from an accident at the Junction Mine

"Enters Sanitarium" <u>Bisbee Daily Review</u> 21 May 1909, page 7

June 4, 1909, Junction Mine

The cable broke on a cage. The cage plummeted 60 feet into the sump. No one was injured.

"Cage Drops" <u>Bisbee Daily Review</u> 22 March 1906 page 8

November 26, 1909, Junction Mine

Three repairmen from the Junction machine shop, William P. Wycoff*, William McDougal and Thomas H. Lindsey boarded a cage loaded with three turnsheets. (Plates of steel ¼ inch thick and 60 by 28 inches.) The turnsheets were believed to be firmly secured to the cage. As the cage rapidly descended, the turnsheets broke free and fell on Wycoff and McDougal crushing them both against the side of the cage. The Lindsey was uninjured. When the cage stopped on the 1000 level, the injured men were lying unconscious on the bottom of the cage bleeding. The accident was reported to the surface by a telephone underground, and the men were transported to the Calumet & Arizona Hospital. All of the turnsheets were dragged from the cage. Two fell and landed on the cage bonnets. One turnsheet was found hanging on the shaft timber, about 200 feet from the surface. Also found in the shaft timber were the men's lunch buckets, hats a shoe belonging to Wycoff and part of McDougal's hand. William P. Wycoff died two hours later from internal injuries, a broken right ankle, crushed left leg and broken right shoulder. McDougal died that night from a compound fractured skull and an amputated left hand. Wycoff's remains were sent to Kansas City, Missouri by his widow and a nephew Earl Wycoff for burial. Mc Dougal was taken to Humbolt, Nebraska for burial.

*Spelled Wykoff in the newspaper articles
*"Death Claims 2 in Mine Crash" <u>Bisbee Daily Review</u> 27 November 1909 page 8

"Accidental Deaths" <u>Bisbee Daily Review</u> 28 November 1909 page 7

"Wykoff to Kansas City" <u>Bisbee Daily Review</u> 30 November 1909 page 7

"Original Certificate of Death." <u>Arizona Department of Health Services.</u> http://genealogy.az.gov/azdeath/007/10071208.pdf (2 April 2011

"Original Certificate of Death." <u>Arizona Department of Health Services.</u> http://genealogy.az.gov/azdeath/007/10071207.pdf (April 2 2011

"Calumet & Arizona Hospital Records." <u>My Cochise.</u> http://www.mycochise.com/hospcaldied.php (April 2, 2011)

June 21, 1910, Junction Mine

John Illen and three other unnamed miners on the 1500 level entered a sulfide stope soon after a round had been blasted. The powder gasses had filled the stope. Illen was the first of the men to collapse. He was soon followed by two of the other miners. The fourth man was able to reach the shaft station and muster help. It was originally, thought that the men would quickly recover, but later Illen had to be admitted to the Calumet & Arizona Hospital. He remained there until June 26.

"Miner Overcome by Powder Fumes" <u>Bisbee Daily Review</u> 22 June 1910 page 5

"Calumet & Arizona Hospital Records." <u>My Cochise.</u> http://www.mycochise.com/hospcalhi2ja.php (April 2, 2011)

July 10, 1910, Junction Mine

Robert Blum was on the 1300 level and caught in a cave-in and was *"literally flayed alive"* by the falling rocks and dirt. Much of his skin from his back, arms, hands and face was peeled away.

"Blum Suffers Flaying" <u>Bisbee Daily Review</u> 12 July 1910 page 5

July 1910 Junction Mine

A rock drill fell on the left hand of David Mitchell. His hand was so badly smashed the small finger was amputated.

"Machine Injures Man" <u>Bisbee Daily Review</u> 5 July 1910 page 5

August 6, 1910, Junction Mine

John Takask was struck in the head by the bar falling on a rock drill bar and column setup. He was treated at the Calumet & Arizona Dispensary.

"Struck by Falling Bar" <u>Bisbee Daily Review</u> 7 August 1910 page 5

December 8, 1910, Junction Mine

Charles Salo, a 39-year-old miner had three fingers amputated when a blasting cap exploded. He was taken to the Calumet & Arizona Hospital. Salo was released from the hospital on December 19, 1910.

"Supposed Slayers of Two are Caught" <u>El Paso Herald</u> 14 December 1910 page 13

"Calumet & Arizona Hospital Records." <u>My Cochise.</u> http://www.mycochise.com/hospcals2sm.php (July 22, 2011)

February 4, 1911, Junction Mine

During construction, Harry F. Cook was installing a roof over the trusses on the new compressor building. Cook needed to move the scaffolding over to the next set of trusses, and he slipped and fell head first to the floor and then "flopped" onto a flywheel. He died from a fractured skull.

"Accidental Death is Coroner's Verdict" Bisbee Daily Review 7 February 1911 page 8
"Cochise County Inquest No. 808Arizona State Archives Phoenix

July 27, 1911, Junction Mine
J.W. Gordam, a 26-year-old, mule driver broke his leg at the mine. He was taken to the Calumet & Arizona Hospital and kept there until September 15, 1911.

"Miner Injured" Bisbee Daily Review 28 July 1911 page 6
"Calumet & Arizona Hospital Records." My Cochise. http://www.mycochise.com/hospcalfl2go.php (April 3, 2011)

October 17, 1911, Junction Mine
Eli Chupeck fell 20 feet down a manway. He was taken to the Calumet & Arizona Hospital and released the next day.

"Injured at Mine" Bisbee Daily Review 17 October 1911 page 5
"Calumet & Arizona Hospital Records." My Cochise. http://www.mycochise.com/hospcalb.u2cl.php (March 29, 2011)

April 1, 1912, Junction Mine
Mike Mellon received minor injuries at the Junction Shaft.

"Miners Injured" Bisbee Daily Review 2 April 1912 page 6

May 24, 1912, Junction Mine
John Houston, a 37-year-old miner lost two toes in an undescribed mine accident. He was taken to the Calumet & Arizona Hospital and remained there until June 13, 1912.

"Miner Loses Toes" Bisbee Daily Review 25 May 1912 page 6
"Calumet & Arizona Hospital Records." My Cochise. http://www.mycochise.com/hospcalhi2ja.php (April 3, 2011)

August 17, 1912, Junction Mine
Peter Hozich, a mucker fell into a chute. He was taken to the Calumet & Arizona Hospital by buggy. Surgery was performed on him and he was released from the hospital ten days later.

"Injured in Mine" Bisbee Daily Review 18 August 1912 page 6
"Calumet & Arizona Hospital Records." My Cochise. http://www.mycochise.com/hospcalhi2ja.php (April 2, 2011)

October 18 1913 Junction Mine
Clifford Ware, a 22-year-old mucker. He slipped and fell on to of a pick. The sharp point penetrated his leg. He was taken to the Calumet & Arizona Hospital, where he stayed until November 13, 1913.

"Was Injured" Bisbee Daily Review 19 October 1913 page 8
"Calumet & Arizona Hospital Records." My Cochise. http://www.mycochise.com/hospcaltr2we.php (April 3, 2011)

June 26, 1914, Junction Mine
Cousin Jack and Mine Foreman Frank Melville Juliff and Shift Foreman William Drury entered No. 19 stope on the 1500 level. The stope was caving, and they were trying to

determine whether the stope could safely mined. Unlike many of the stopes in Bisbee it was not a square set, but rather was mined supported by "T" stulls*. At 10:30 am, when they were in the north end the stope caved. Both men were instantly crushed to death by the same *"immense boulder."* It was not originally, understood that men had been caught in the collapse. The miners on the level had been accounted for, but one miner had stated that he had noticed lights** in that part of the stope. It was later determined that the two foremen were likely in the stope when it caved. The bodies of the two men were found next to each other under the boulder that killed them at 7:30 pm. Juliff was 49 years old and sent on the Golden State Limited Train for burial in Los Angeles, California. His widow returned after his burial to live in Bisbee. He was survived by his wife and daughter, Mrs. Compton of Bisbee. Drury was 39 years old and was buried in Evergreen Cemetery next to his eight -year-old daughter Audry May Drury who had died ten months earlier. He was survived by his widow Mary M. Drury. *** The funerals of these men were the largest Bisbee had seen and the coroners' report was supposed to be a largest written up to that time 36 pages.

* Probably, mined by cut and fill or a top-slicing method.

** In the darkness the mine, lights would have been distinctly noticeable even at a distance.

*** Maiden name was Alexander.

"Side by Side, Frank Juliff and William Drury Killed Instantly in the Junction" <u>Bisbee Daily Review</u> 27 June 1914 page 1

"Throngs Attended the Funerals of Frank Juliff and W. Drury" <u>Bisbee Daily Review</u> 30 June 1914 page 2

"Much Evidence Compiled" <u>Bisbee Daily Review</u> 7 July 1914 page 8

"Mrs. Juliff Returns" <u>Bisbee Daily Review</u> 10 July 1914 page 8

Office of State Mine Inspector. *Third Annual Report of the State Mine Inspector State of Arizona for the Year Ending November 30, 1914*. Tombstone Epitaph.

"Original Certificate of Death." <u>Arizona Department of Health Services.</u> http://genealogy.az.gov/azdeath/085/10850387.pdf (May 25, 2012)

"Original Certificate of Death." <u>Arizona Department of Health Services.</u> http://genealogy.az.gov/azdeath/011/10112522.pdf (May 25, 2012) "Standard Certificate of Birth." <u>Arizona Department of Health Services.</u> http://genealogy.az.gov/azbirth/401/401-2570.pdf (May 25, 2012

The gravestones of William Drury and daughter.

July 25, 1914, Junction Mine

Finnish Miner, Erick Hoffman and his partner Blozo Somozich were drilling on the 1500 level Junction They took a lunch break in 66 crosscut and ate their lunches then laid back on a lagging to nap until it was time to work. Six to eight tons of sandy sulfide fell and broke through the timber above Hoffman and killed him. Somozich was received only minor scratches. Hoffman was 33 years old, and his only relative in the U.S. was his brother John Hoffman a miner at Superior Arizona. His parents were living and in Finland.

"One Killed When Rock Falls from Roof of Working" Bisbee Daily Review 26 July 1914 page 3
"Air Slaked Ground Causes Hoffman's Death is the Verdict" Bisbee Daily Review 28 July 1914 page 3
"Funeral Occurs Today" Bisbee Daily Review 31 July 1914 page 8
"Original Certificate of Death." Arizona Department of Health Services. http://genealogy.az.gov/azdeath/012/10122147.pdf (May 4, 2012)
"Cochise County Inquest No. 1104" Arizona State Archives Phoenix

November 20, 1914, Junction Mine

John Tylke and Thomas Lerwell were working in the Junction Mine. Lerwell was mucking into a shallow inclined chute, when he fell nine feet to the bottom and was killed by fracturing his skull. His partner Tylke initially thought Lerwell was playing a practical joke on him. Lerwell had been seen by Tylke and a couple of minutes later had disappeared. Yet, his candle was still burning in its place. Tylke called out to his partner and began searching with other miners, until his body was found in the chute. Shift Boss, E. J. Williams stated, that he felt that a fall of rock likely knocked Lerwell into the chute. James Lerwell, brother of the deceased traveled to Bisbee to escort his brother's remains to Ishpeming, Michigan. Thomas Lerwell was 28-years-old and survived by his brother James and an unnamed sister who lived in Michigan. (Note, the late use of candles for illumination.)

"Thomas Lerwell a Mucker, is Killed in Fall Shute at Junction Shaft of C&A" Bisbee Daily Review 20 November 1914 page 1
"Death of Lerwell was Sad Accident" Bisbee Daily Review 21 November 1914 page 5
"To Escort Remains" Bisbee Daily Review 24 November 1914 page 8
"Lerwell Remains Shipped" Bisbee Daily Review 25 November 1914 page 5
"Original Certificate of Death." Arizona Department of Health Services. http://genealogy.az.gov/azdeath/013/10130044.pdf (May 4, 2012)

November 27, 1915, Junction Mine

At 3:00 pm, Cager J.J. Dennis brought the cage to the 1300 level, opened the cage bar and called "Going up!" William Roberts, a mule skinner, started to get on, and the cage moved crushing his head and nearly decapitating him when he tried to board cage. The Hoist Engineer W.A. White and an Oiler, J.W. Earhart were painting the marks on the cable for each deck position. They had painted the 1400 level marks, when the call came to raise the cage to the 1300 level. The 1300 level mark for the bottom deck on the cable was faint, and the oiler who was running the hoist missed the mark by about 18 inches and White told him he was off about 18 inches. Earhart moved the cage and Roberts was killed. He was 37 years old and from Texas. His mother and three brothers lived in Houston and one brother lived in San Antonio, Texas.

"William Roberts is Killed at Junction" Bisbee Daily Review 28 November 1914 page 8
"Coroner's Jury" Bisbee Daily Review 30 November 1914 page 8

"Original Certificate of Death." Arizona Department of Health Services. http://genealogy.az.gov/azdeath/014/10140567.pdf (May 4, 2012)

Office of State Mine Inspector. *Fourth Annual Report of the State Mine Inspector State of Arizona for the Year Ending November 30, 1915.* Tombstone Epitaph.

"Cochise County Inquest No. 1180" Arizona State Archives Phoenix

April 7, 1916, Junction Mine

Michael Denne, a 30-year-old miner was killed when he fell into a chute. It was thought that he was pushing a loaded mine car to a chute on the 1300 level. After reaching the chute, he removed the lagging covering the hole and somehow fell. His remains were sent to Portage, Pennsylvania. (No coroner's inquest could be located)

"Carman is Killed at Junction; First Since January One" Bisbee Daily Review 8 April 1916

Dugan Mortuary Records 1914 – 1917 Accession 2010.10.8 Bisbee Mining and Historical Museum, Bisbee.

"Original Certificate of Death." Arizona Department of Health Services. http://genealogy.az.gov/azdeath/014/10142769.pdf (May 28, 2012)

Office of State Mine Inspector. *Fifth Annual Report of the State Mine Inspector State of Arizona for the Year Ending November 30, 1916.*

June 5, 1916, Junction Mine

A mine car derailed and bruised and cut the left leg Phillip Munch, a mucker. He was allowed to go home after a six day stay in the hospital.

"Calumet & Arizona Hospital Records." My Cochise. http://www.mycochise.com/hospcalme 2ny.php (June 2, 2012)

Office of State Mine Inspector. *Fifth Annual Report of the State Mine Inspector State of Arizona for the Year Ending November 30, 1916.*

August 17, 1916 Junction Mine

Assistant Chief Engineer and Harvard graduate, James A. Lewis Jr. was on the 1300 level with two assistants. He stopped to fill out a sample card on top of a pile of broken muck and a 50 lb. boulder fell crushing his vertebrae. His assistants quickly removed the rock and he was transported to the Calumet and Arizona Hospital. He survived but was paralyzed.

"C&A official is Mortally Injured by Cave-In" Bisbee Daily Review 18 August 1916 pages 1 & 2

August 26, 1916, Junction Mine

Jack Hawkens was standing on a staging in a raise on the 1300 level. The staging slipped and Hawkens fell smashing his ankle. He also suffered bruising about the face.

"Ankle Crushed" Bisbee Daily Review 27, August, 1916 page 8

October 14, 1916, Junction Mine

Eli Atelovich fell and broke his arm after being "overcome" by gasses. He was allowed to return home after a 13 day stay at the hospital.

"Calumet & Arizona Hospital Records." My Cochise. http://www.mycochise.com/hospcala2ba.php (June 2, 2012)

Office of State Mine Inspector. *Fifth Annual Report of the State Mine Inspector State of Arizona for the Year Ending November 30, 1916.*

October 23, 1916, Junction Mine

Jack Hill, a 26-year-old mucker was hit in the head by a falling rock. Several stitches were needed to close the wound. He was released from the Calumet & Arizona Hospital on the same day he was admitted.

"Miner injured" Bisbee Daily Review October 24, 1916 page 8

February 10, 1917, Junction Mine

On the 1300 level, a miner with the surname of Fox (first name unknown) fell eighty-feet down a chute. The chute had both inclined and vertical sections. The largest part of the raise was vertical. Miraculously, he received only a scratch the head. He stayed at work and completed his shift against advice of his fellow workers.

"Bisbee Miner Falls Eighty Feet; Works out Shift." Tombstone Epitaph 11 February 1917 page 1

March 8, 1917, Junction Mine

Mule Driver, James Murray was crushed when he became trapped between a mine car and a timber. He was taken to the Calumet & Arizona Hospital where he died from a ruptured spleen on April 6, 1916. The Irish miner was buried in Evergreen Cemetery. (No coroner's inquest could be located)

"Calumet & Arizona Hospital Records." My Cochise. http://www.mycochise.com/hospcalme 2ny.php (May 28, 2012)
"Bisbee-Lowell Evergreen Cemetery." My Cochise.
http://www.mycochise.com/cembisbeem.php (May 28, 2012)
"Original Certificate of Death." Arizona Department of Health Services. http://genealogy.az.gov/azdeath/016/10160466.pdf (May 28, 2012)
Office of State Mine Inspector. Sixth Annual Report of the State Mine Inspector State of Arizona for the Year Ending November 30, 1917.

May 24, 1917, Junction Mine

Leonard B. Cary detonated a misfire while digging with a pick. He was cut up, bruised and temporarily blinded by dirt in his eyes. He was sent to the Calumet and Arizona Hospital, where he was expected to recover.

"Miner is Injured" Bisbee Daily Review 25 May 1917 page 8
"Miner is Injured" Tombstone Weekly Epitaph 27 May 1917 page 8
"Calumet & Arizona Hospital Records." My Cochise. http://www.mycochise.com/hospcalb.u2cl.php (August 2, 2011)

July 18, 1917, Junction Mine

Cager, William "Buck "Liggett was riding a cage with Charles Massey and Howard Dillaway. These men were electricians. For an unknown reason, the skip attachment came unlatched and caught on 1200 level station. Liggett was thrown to the cage floor, and his neck was broken. He died on July 20. The cager was 30 years old and buried in Evergreen Cemetery. William was survived by three children and his wife. The electricians were only bruised up.

"Buck Leggett Dies from Broken Neck" Bisbee Daily Review 19 July 1917 page 3
"Original Certificate of Death." Arizona Department of Health Services. http://genealogy.az.gov/azdeath/016/10161788.pdf (May 28, 2012)
Office of State Mine Inspector. Sixth Annual Report of the State Mine Inspector State of Arizona for the Year Ending November 30, 1917.
"Cochise County Inquest No. 1284" Arizona State Archives Phoenix

August 4, 1917, Junction Mine

It appeared that someone dropped a 140 lb. boulder down the shaft from the 1400 level. The rock bounced against the sides of the shaft barely missing a cage holding eight men riding the cage up from the 1800 level.

"No Clue to Criminal Who Dropped Rock down Junction Shaft." Bisbee Daily Review 7 August 1917 page 5

October 26, 1917, Junction Mine

Percy Anstess and Sidney Halverson got on the cage on the 1300 level. Buck Anderson was in the middle of the cage full of men. Around 70 ft. from the surface, the men on the cage heard what sounded like a carbide lamp being dropped then followed by a smashing sound. When the cage arrived on the surface, Anderson discovered Antess scrunched up dead, in the corner of the cage with his scalp hanging from a piece of steel. He was 24 years old and born in Michigan. Antess was the son of Cornish parents. Note that the cage ride was in total darkness. The miners would have extinguished their carbide lamps to prevent burning each other on the crowded cage. Only when shaft stations were passed with electric lights would the total darkness been broken.

"Original Certificate of Death." Arizona Department of Health Services. http://genealogy.az.gov/azdeath/016/10162875.pdf (May 28, 2012)

Office of State Mine Inspector. *Sixth Annual Report of the State Mine Inspector State of Arizona for the Year Ending November 30, 1917.*

"Cochise County Inquest No. 1296" Arizona State Archives

December 30, 1917, Junction Mine

Matt Sloutz was pinned between a mine car and timber. This resulted in a compound fracture of the sternum and four broken ribs he died at the Calumet & Arizona Hospital.

"Dies from Injuries" Bisbee Daily Review 1 January 1918 page 8

The Calumet & Arizona Hospital in Bakerville, c-1917

February 6, 1918, Junction Mine

Timberman, Edwin Elwood Gillaspy was repairing a chute on the 1600 level. He was standing on top of a locomotive and contacted the trolley wire. After the initial shock he was revived, but he died after reaching the surface. Gillaspy was 44-years-old and survived by a wife and a son named Grover C. Gillaspy.

(No inquest could be located)
"Electrocuted" Bisbee Daily Review 7 February 1918 page 1
"Original Certificate of Death." Arizona Department of Health Services. http://genealogy.az.gov/azdeath/017/10171244.pdf (March 8, 2019)

February 28, 1918, Junction Mine

G.M. Patterson fell more than forty feet down a raise. Patterson had been cleaning track, but the raise was over three hundred feet from the area he had been assigned to work. He suffered a broken right leg and a compound fracture of the lower jaw. He stayed at the Calumet & Arizona Hospital until March 25, 1918, when he left in the same condition he had entered it. Patterson had only recently returned to work. Earlier he had lost two fingers while dumping a mine car.

"Junction Miner has Jaw and Leg Broken" Bisbee Daily Review 1 March 1918 page 6
"Calumet & Arizona Hospital Records." My Cochise. http://www.mycochise.com/hospcalo2 po.php (June 2, 2012)
Office of State Mine Inspector. *Seventh Annual Report of the State Mine Inspector State of Arizona for the Year Ending November 30, 1918.*

March 19, 1918, Junction Mine

A timber fell and broke one of George Bronson's ribs. He was taken to the Calumet & Arizona Hospital.

"Is in Hospital" Bisbee Daily Review 20 March 1918 page 8

May 2, 1918, Junction Mine

Patrick James was working in 21 crosscut on the 1600 level with Mike Braon. It was getting close to lunch time and the crews nearby were getting ready to blast and then head to the shaft station to eat lunch. James came to see Earl Crawford and wanted to know if he was going to blast. Crawford replied, he wasn't, but they were going to blast in 40 crosscut. Rod McCloud lit the fuses in 40 crosscut and headed to the station. On the station, he asked where Pat James was. Nobody knew, so they went to look for him. They found him lying on the track in a smoke filled crosscut. Shift Boss, C.W. McHenry suspected that James had been heading to the station and accidently took a wrong turn and went into 17 crosscut. In this crosscut his carbide light went out and James took out matches and relit his lamp. What happened next is not clear in the inquest. Pat James walked into a blast from either 21 crosscut or 40 crosscut and killed.

"James Killed by Shot at Junction" Bisbee Daily Review 2 May 1918 page 1
"Cochise County Coroner's Inquest No. 1327" Arizona State Archives
"Original Certificate of Death." Arizona Department of Health Services. http://genealogy.az.gov/azdeath/017/10172624.pdf (March 8, 2019)

"Original Certificate of Death." Arizona Department of Health Services. http://genealogy.az.gov/azdeath/017/10172650.pdf (March 8, 2019)

August 7, 1918, Junction Mine

Motorman, Daniel T. Thayer had been employed running a motor at a smelter in Douglas, Arizona. After he was hired at the Junction Mine, he was made a motorman on the 1600 level. He was assigned Phillip R. Schumacher as a motor swamper. The locomotives underground were different than those at the smelter and Thayer did not understand the controls. They had loaded nine cars of low-grade ore at No. 25 chute and were headed towards the station. Along the route were a pair of air doors. At the first Thayer tried to trip the lever and missed, but Schumacher was able to pull the lever. About the time they reached the second the train being pushed by the heavy load it was carrying was moving quickly. Thayer again missed the lever and, this time, Schumacher was unable to trip the lever, because of the speed. Schumacher yelled at Thayer to stop, but Thayer turned the brake wheel the wrong direction and loosened the brake. The motor crashed part way through the door. Blood frothed at Thayer lips as Schumacher tried to free him, but after realizing Thayer was lifeless he went to the station for help. Thayer was 39 years old, and his body was shipped to Evansville, Indiana. He was survived by a wife and married daughter, Mrs. E.D. Maher.

Dugan Mortuary Records July 19, 1918 – March 27, 19206 Accession 2010.10.14 Bisbee Mining and Historical Museum, Bisbee.
"Original Certificate of Death." Arizona Department of Health Services. http://genealogy.az.gov/azdeath/018/10180872.pdf (May 29, 2012)
Office of State Mine Inspector. *Seventh Annual Report of the State Mine Inspector State of Arizona for the Year Ending November 30, 1918.*
"Cochise County Coroner's Inquest No. 1342" Arizona State Archives

August 30, 1918, Junction Mine

Muckers, Ralph Elliott and H.T. Cobb, were working together, and Cobb picked into a misfire. Elliott's left eye and left arm were shot-full of fine rocks. His partner took the brunt of the blast. Cobb's left eye was ruined his right eye filled with rock. Also, his collar bone was dislocated, and his right lung was damaged.

"Calumet & Arizona Hospital Records." My Cochise.
http://www.mycochise.com/hospcalco2day.php (June 2, 2012)
"Calumet & Arizona Hospital Records." My Cochise.
http://www.mycochise.com/hospcalde 2fi.php (June 2, 2012)
Office of State Mine Inspector. *Seventh Annual Report of the State Mine Inspector State of Arizona for the Year Ending November 30, 1918.*

October 10, 1918, Junction Mine

George C. Fulton derailed while driving a mule train. He was cut on his left heel. The 34-year-old was a shift boss and stayed in the hospital until November 8, 1918.

"Calumet & Arizona Hospital Records." My Cochise.
http://www.mycochise.com/hospcalfl2go.php (June 2, 2012)
Office of State Mine Inspector. *Seventh Annual Report of the State Mine Inspector State of Arizona for the Year Ending November 30, 1918.*

January 9, 1919, Junction Mine

Charles R. Brandon had a boulder smash his right foot.

"Is Resting Easily" Bisbee Daily Review 11 January 1919 page 6

April 27, 1919, Junction Mine

Italian Miner, Frank Balma was working on the 1500 level in No.127 stope, which was commonly, called the "Box" stope. Sulfides were being mined at this location. He was a timberman and had gone with L.C. Price to get some timber from a pile. They had retrieved four 2" X 12" lagging and were getting a fifth when a boulder fell crushing Balma's head against the ground. Samuel Horlick tried to stop the bleeding from Balma's ear, but this only caused his nose to bleed. He died from a fractured skull at the Calumet & Arizona Hospital. Balma was survived by a wife and three children living on Opera Drive.

"Original Certificate of Death." Arizona Department of Health Services. http://genealogy.az.gov/azdeath/020/10200627.pdf (May 28, 2012)

Office of State Mine Inspector. *Eighth Annual Report of the State Mine Inspector State of Arizona for the Year Ending November 30, 1919.*

"Cochise County Coroner's Inquest No. 1375" Arizona State Archives

May 27, 1919, Junction Mine

At 5:45 pm, Theodore Pesikan was killed in a by a rock falling in No. 211 stope on the 1500 level. He was working with G.E. Williams and was barring down. Pesikan was checking a boulder. Suddenly, a shaley slab weighing about one ton fell and crushed Pesikan. At the time of his death, he was 36-years-old and from Herzegovina. His cousin, Roy. M. Paken lived in Bisbee.

"Miner Killed by Falling Boulder." Bisbee Daily Review 29 May 1919 page 8

"Cochise County Coroner's Inquest No. 1387" Arizona State Archives

Dugan Mortuary Records July 19, 1918 – March 27, 1920 Accession 2010.10.14 Bisbee Mining and Historical Museum, Bisbee

"Original Certificate of Death." Arizona Department of Health Services. http://genealogy.az.gov/azdeath/020/10201061.pdf (May 28, 2012)

Office of State Mine Inspector. *Eighth Annual Report of the State Mine Inspector State of Arizona for the Year Ending November 30, 1919.*

July 7, 1919, Junction Mine

Eugene Allen was struck by a rock falling and breaking his leg. Later on July 13, he died at the Calumet & Arizona from a fat embolism that traveled to the brain. He was buried in Memphis, Tennessee.

"Original Certificate of Death." Arizona Department of Health Services. http://genealogy.az.gov/azdeath/020/10201926.pdf (May 28, 2012)

Office of State Mine Inspector. *Eighth Annual Report of the State Mine Inspector State of Arizona for the Year Ending November 30, 1919.*

July 19, 1919, Junction Mine

Mine Foreman, Thomas Wade Wright, was killed by a falling rock. Inspecting the work in No.16 stope on the 1600 level. The miners had blasted out a corner to install a post and had three post standing. The miners were lifting a cap into place, Wright came in and said *"Boys, you are doing fine."* At that moment, the sulfide ground collapsed catching miner,

Tony Bolen, Timberman, William Whitehead and Wright. Tony received a cut to the head, and Whitehead was taken to the Calumet & Arizona Hospital. Wright was killed. He was survived by a wife and three-year-old girl. The man was 30 years old and buried in Los Angles, California.

Dugan Mortuary Records July 19, 1918 – March 27, 1920 Accession 2010.10.14 Bisbee Mining and Historical Museum, Bisbee

"Original Certificate of Death." Arizona Department of Health Services. http://genealogy.az.gov/azdeath/020/10201935.pdf (May 30, 2012)

Office of State Mine Inspector. *Eighth Annual Report of the State Mine Inspector State of Arizona for the Year Ending November 30, 1919.*

"Cochise County Coroner's Inquest No.1386" Arizona State Archives

September 13, 1919, Junction Mine

Lester R. Moyer, a 21-year-old miner was struck by falling rock. His pelvis was broken, and one ankle was dislocated. He died at the Calumet & Arizona Hospital on September 14. Moyers remains were taken to Three Rivers, Michigan. (No coroner's inquest could be located)

Dugan Mortuary Records July 19, 1918 – March 27, 1920 Accession 2010.10.14 Bisbee Mining and Historical Museum, Bisbee

"Calumet & Arizona Hospital Records." My Cochise. http://www.mycochise.com/hospcaldied.php (May 30, 2012)

"Original Certificate of Death." Arizona Department of Health Services. http://genealogy.az.gov/azdeath/020/10202601.pdf (May 30, 2012)

Office of State Mine Inspector. *Eighth Annual Report of the State Mine Inspector State of Arizona for the Year Ending November 30, 1919.*

June 14, 1920, Junction Mine

Tom Dillaha was drilling with a stoper, and the drill steel broke. His hand was cut up when it became caught between the broken steel and the stoper.

Office of State Mine Inspector. *Ninth Annual Report of the State Mine Inspector State of Arizona for the Year Ending November 30, 1920.*

August 7, 1920, Junction Mine

Tom Foley fell down a timber slide. Foley and his partner had ridden up the timber slide from the 1800 level to the 1600. When his partner got off the slide the eyebolt broken and the timber slide and Foley fell back to the 1800 level. Foley broke a leg. Riding a timber slide was against company safety regulations.

"Miner Breaks Leg" Bisbee Daily Review 11 August, 1920 page 5

"Foley Will Live" Bisbee Daily Review 18 August, 1920 page 6

September 11, 1920, Junction Mine

The partner of Al Garland accidently struck him in the back with a pick and injured his spine. He was released from the Calumet & Arizona Hospital on September 14, 1920.

"Calumet & Arizona Hospital Records." My Cochise. http://www.mycochise.com/hospcalfl2go.php (June 2, 2012)

Office of State Mine Inspector. *Ninth Annual Report of the State Mine Inspector State of Arizona for the Year Ending November 30, 1920.*

October 26, 1920, Junction Mine

At 8:30 pm, English Miner, John H. James and J.P. Carlisle were removing lagging to allow gob to flow into other parts of the 556 stope on the 1400 level. E. M. Stephens was nearby drilling three holes under a stringer. Stephens went to get a drink of water and then a boulder fell and broke a stringer above James and Carlisle. Carlisle was knocked backward, and his light went out. He called for James, who did not answer. Confused that James would leave him in the dark, he called again, and James responded. He had been buried. Stephens returned and the two men tried to unbury James by following the sound of his voice. As the men dug to rescue James, the gob kept pouring in. Finally, they had to go below James and chop out the lagging and let the loose rock drain out. And then after 30 minutes they were able to pull him out from above, but he had already died.

Dugan Mortuary Records 1918 – 1922 Accession 2010.10.12 Bisbee Mining and Historical Museum, Bisbee

"Original Certificate of Death." Arizona Department of Health Services. http://genealogy.az.gov/azdeath/022/10222253.pdf (May 30, 2012)

Office of State Mine Inspector. *Ninth Annual Report of the State Mine Inspector State of Arizona for the Year Ending November 30, 1920.*

"Cochise County Coroner's Inquest No. 1433" Arizona State Archives Phoenix

January 5, 1925, Junction Mine

Around 10:00 pm, T.R. Davis was struck in the face with a chute bar. His nose was broken and his face was cut.

"Miner is Injured" Bisbee Daily Review 6, January 1921 page 3

January 31, 1921, Junction Mine

Tom Dillaha was caught an explosion and was injured on the face neck and throat. The 45-year-old miner was taken to the Calumet and Arizona Hospital, but on February 1 he was sent to El Paso for treatment. (Note: Dillaha was in another accident on June 14, 1920.)

"Calumet & Arizona Hospital Records." My Cochise.

http://www.mycochise.com/hospcalde 2fi.php (June 2, 2012)

Office of State Mine Inspector. *Tenth Annual Report of the State Mine Inspector State of Arizona for the Year Ending November 30, 1921.*

February 2, 1921, Junction Mine

J.J. Dennis was injured in an undescribed mine accident.

"Foley Will Live" Bisbee Daily Review 5 February 1921 page 6

May 1921, Junction Mine

Frank Huckleby had his leg broken by a falling timber.

"Broken Bone" Bisbee Daily Review 22 May 1921, page 8

October 13, 1921, Junction Mine

August Schlant, and William Rhoades were welding a casting, unknown to them a defect in the casting had trapped moisture and the casting exploded. The explosion threw Rhoades 30 ft. and out the doorway of the shop building. Schlant was struck in the head by a fragment of the casting, and three men outside were barely missed by a flying piece. (Note, this did not occur underground.)

"One Killed, Three Injured in Peculiar Series of Accidents in Bisbee District Yesterday" Bisbee Daily Review 14 October page4

April 5, 1922, Junction Mine

J.C. Tucker fell in a small stope He was treated for head and back injuries at the Calumet & Arizona Hospital. Tucker lived on Mason Hill.

"Injured at Junction" Bisbee Daily Review 6 April 1922 page 3

May 9, 1922, Junction Mine

On the 1800 level, C. Ralph Youtz an engineer was making an inspection tour with group of miners. They had lit a fuse on a single hole. Youtz returned to the area and was caught in the detonation a rock 1.5 inches long by. 75 inches wide and .5 inches thick was shot into his skull above his right eye. The rock which penetrated his brain was surgically removed at the Calumet & Arizona Hospital. The skull was shattered but the right eye was intact.

"Popular Young Engineer Hurt in Mine Blast" Bisbee Daily Review 10 May 1922, page 6
"Is Improving" Bisbee Daily Review 13 May 1922, page 3

May 28, 1922, Junction Mine

Edward Jusswald was putting in new reel posts on the ore hoist. The hoist parts were being raised with a chain and block. . Suddenly the chain broke and Jusswald was struck in the side by the parts. His arm was *"tore out"* and his side injured. He was taken to the Calumet & Arizona Hospital for treatment. Jusswald was weak from blood loss, but survived with the loss of an arm. (Note, his name is also spelled Jerswald and Jerold in an articles)

"C& A Machinist Injured by Falling Machinery"" Bisbee Daily Review 30 May 1922, page 6
"Doing Nicely"" Bisbee Daily Review 1 June 1922, page 6

July 8, 1922, Junction Mine

Max Schnieder was taken to the Calumet & Arizona Hospital suffering after being gassed. (powder gas?)

"Personnal" Bisbee Daily Review 9 July 1922, page 6

July 14, 1922, Junction Mine

Around 6:30 pm, W.R. Hall was riding on a train when he contacted the trolley wire. He was knocked off the locomotive and was dragged between two mine cars for a substantial distance. His injuries were considered slight.

"Slightly Injured" Bisbee Daily Review 15 July 1922, page 6

August 26, 1922, Junction Mine

Belbert Johnson was struck by a falling boulder. His side and leg were bruised.

"Was Slightly Injured" Bisbee Daily Review 27 August 1922, page 8

September 22, 1922, Junction Mine

Charles Vucovitch and A.L. Wise were injured when they fell down a raise.

"Were Slightly Injured" Bisbee Daily Review 24 September 1922, page 3

June 23, 1923, Junction Mine

Around 8:30 pm and on the 2500 level, James H. McDonald was moving a steel beam into place when it touched high voltage wire. All the men were knocked down, and McDonald fell 15 ft. At the time, it was felt he may have broken his neck, but his death certificate states electrocution as the cause of death. He was 42 years old and buried in Denver, Colorado.

"Original Certificate of Death." Arizona Department of Health Services. http://genealogy.az.gov/azdeath/027/10270534.pdf (May 30, 2012)

Office of State Mine Inspector. *Twelfth Annual Report of the State Mine Inspector State of Arizona for the Year Ending November 30, 1923.*

"Body of McDonald Will Be Shipped to Denver Colo." Bisbee Ore 27 June 1923 page 1

September 8, 1923, Junction Mine

Motorman, Frank Campbell with swamper Freeman Crouch had loaded their train with ore at No.15 chute and were hauling it to the ore pocket. Campbell mentioned to Crouch that the brake on the locomotive was not working. As they approached an air door on the 1800 level, Campbell pulled the lever, but the door did not open. Campbell threw the motor into reverse to slow down and the trolley pole jumped off the wire. The locomotive crashed into the door killing Campbell. His was survived by his wife Lottie and his remains were shipped to El Paso, Texas.

Dugan Mortuary Records February 9, 1923 – Aug. 16, 1926 Accession 2010.10.17 Bisbee Mining and Historical Museum, Bisbee. "

Office of State Mine Inspector. *Twelfth Annual Report of the State Mine Inspector State of Arizona for the Year Ending November 30, 1923.*

"Original Certificate of Death." Arizona Department of Health Services. http://genealogy.az.gov/azdeath/027/10271765.pdf (May 30, 2012)

"Cochise County Coroner's Inquest No. 1526" Arizona State Archives Phoenix

January 19, 1926, Junction Mine

John E. Williamson and Newton J. Velarde were installing a 16 ft. six by eight inch stringer along broken muck pile in a stope right on the level. The stope was heavy and caving and they were trying to catch up the caving ground. This would have made the drift that cut through the stope safe. Velarde considered the stope too dangerous to bar down. As the men began moving the stringer up the 45 degree muck pile a 400 lb. boulder broke free and hit the stringer broke it and impacted Williamson. Later Velarde said, *"looked as if he had his arms around the boulder, that is the boulder come down and he was rolling with the boulder"*. Williamson fatally ruptured his colon. He was survived by T. Williamson a brother in the Sulphur Springs Valley, Arizona, a sister and his mother and father.

"Workman Hit by Timber Dies this Morning" Bisbee Ore 20 January 1926 page 1

"Original Certificate of Death." Arizona Department of Health Services http://genealogy.az.gov/azdeath/032/10320052.pdf (May 31, 2012)

Office of State Mine Inspector. *Fifteenth Annual Report of the State Mine Inspector State of Arizona for the Year Ending November 30, 1926.*

"Cochise County Coroner's Inquest No. 1433" Arizona State Archives Phoenix

September 27, 1926, Junction Mine

Casper Herr, a sampler was going off shift and at the1600 level station, when told the men he was with that he had forgotten to shut a door. He went back to do this while the other men took a cage to the surface. Shift Boss William Sharpe was on the 1700 level and saw something fall the shaft that he did not believe was a block of wood, but he still did not think initially it was important. After the day shift was completely out it was discovered Casper was missing. His body was not located until around 8:00 on the morning of the 28th. His body was found in a 100 ft. of water at the bottom of the Junction Shaft with both arms and legs broken. The miners made a hook and fished for his body in the water filled sump. The sump was flooded to four feet below the 2200 level. After a weight was added to the hook, the miners were able to locate and retrieve Herr's body. Rumors in town told that Casper had sampled one row of mine cars parked on the shaft station then when he went to sample the second row of mine cars he slipped on a turnsheet, fell into the shaft and drowned. Shift Boss, Walter B. Haile felt it may have been a suicide and disagreed with the idea he may have slipped. Other men underground were concerned because Herr and seemed very nervous during the shift.

"Man Drowns in Junction Shaft today" Bisbee Ore 28 September 1926 page 1

"Original Certificate of Death." Arizona Department of Health Serviceshttp://genealogy.az.gov/azdeath/033/10331491.pdf (May 31, 2012)

Office of State Mine Inspector. *Fourteenth Annual Report of the State Mine Inspector State of Arizona for the Year Ending November 30, 1926.*

"Cochise County Coroner's Inquest No. 1636" Arizona State Archives Phoenix

October 13, 1926, Junction Mine

Charles N. Smith and Edward A. Miller were working in 317 stope on the 1600 level. Smith climbed to the 1500 level and gathered a pick and a shovel. He wanted to drill with a plugger and needed to pick down a rock. As he was picking the boulder fell smashing his head and killed him. The boulder had fallen from about two inches from his hanging carbide lamp. It was felt he had been able to move about 12 inches, the boulder would have not killed him.

Dugan Mortuary Records Aug. 29, 1926 – Jun4 1930 Accession 2010.10.20 Bisbee Mining and Historical Museum, Bisbee.

"Original Certificate of Death." Arizona Department of Health http://genealogy.az.gov/azdeath/033/10331879.pdf (May 31, 2012)

Office of State Mine Inspector. *Fifteenth Annual Report of the State Mine Inspector State of Arizona for the Year Ending November 30, 1926.*

"Cochise County Coroner's Inquest No. 1640" Arizona State Archives Phoenix

February 28, 1927, Junction Mine

On the 1600 level, Alfred Ramsen and August Orton built a bulkhead in a raise and blasted. The dynamite exploded poorly, filling the raise with carbon monoxide gas. A group of men entered the soon after they blasted and were overpowered by powder gasses Alfred Ramsen was the only man not to be revived. Four shift. bosses, Basil Wollman *, Lee Lambert, Earl Skinner and Thomas Mathews were caught in the powder gasses along with miners, Dan Seed, Tom Mason and Harry Hoover. * Basil later died in the Sacramento Mine in 1939.

"Original Certificate of Death." Arizona Department of Health http://genealogy.az.gov/azdeath/034/10340606.pdf (May 31, 2012)

Office of State Mine Inspector. *Sixteenth Annual Report of the State Mine Inspector State of Arizona for the Year Ending November 30, 1927.*

"Gas Takes One Miner's Life; Others Suffer" Bisbee Ore 1 March 1927 page 1

"Cochise County Coroner's Inquest No. 1652" Arizona State Archives Phoenix

January 8, 1928, Junction Mine

Vere Monroe "Tex" Crawford was asphyxiated by gas from a blast on the 2000 level. Crawford and his partner Thomas F. Hudson had spit the fuses for a round. When they around 50 ft. away a hole detonated and threw the men to the ground. Hudson got up and got out of the area. Crawford remained in the area about 15 minutes before he was recovered. Doctors determined that he was suffocated by the gasses and not fatally injured by the blast. He was survived by his father A.E. Crawford. He was one of the early miners at the Campbell Mine. There are records he was working there by 1919. Interestingly, Hudson only knew his partner as "Tex Rickerson" and did not learn his real name until after he was killed.

"Blast Gas Kills Man at Junction" Bisbee Ore 9 January 1928 page 1

"Original Certificate of Death." http://genealogy.az.gov/azdeath/036/10360589.pdf Arizona Department of Health (May 31, 2012)

Office of State Mine Inspector. *Seventeenth Annual Report of the State Mine Inspector State of Arizona for the Year Ending November 30, 1928.*

Dugan Mortuary Records Aug. 29, 1926 – Jun4 1930 Accession 2010.10.20 Bisbee Mining and Historical Museum, Bisbee.

"Cochise County Coroner's Inquest No.1665" Arizona State Archives Phoenix

April 5, 1928, Junction Mine

Riley Lawrence and John Henry Dean were breaking boulders over two grizzlies that were not far apart. A three foot by four foot boulder of ore rolled from above the grizzly and smashed his leg. For the first 15 minutes, Dean told the men instructed the miners on how to free him. They drove wedges under the boulder to lift it. It took 45 minutes to get the boulder off. Dr. Darragh, who had arrived by this time, stated the leg had been reduced to pulp, and he had never seen anything like it. Dean's leg. Dean a 50-year-old widower died from blood loss and shock.

"Original Certificate of Death." http://genealogy.az.gov/azdeath/036/10362480.pdf Arizona Department of Health (May 31, 2012)

Office of State Mine Inspector. *Seventeenth Annual Report of the State Mine Inspector State of Arizona for the Year Ending November 30, 1928.*

Dugan Mortuary Records Aug. 29, 1926 – Jun4 1930 Accession 2010.10.20 Bisbee Mining and Historical Museum, Bisbee. "Cochise County Coroner's Inquest No.1671" Arizona State Archives Phoenix

April 30, 1928, Junction Mine

Patrick Murphy was working in a square set stope on the 1600 level using a pick to clean an area for a set of timber. A 1,000-pound boulder fell and broke his back. His injuries were fatal.

"Original Certificate of Death." http://genealogy.az.gov/azdeath/036/10362480.pdf Arizona Department of Health (May 31, 2012)

Office of State Mine Inspector. *Seventeenth Annual Report of the State Mine Inspector State of Arizona for the Year Ending November 30, 1928.*

"Junction Shaft. Miner Killed By Fall from Rock" Bisbee Ore 27 October 1928 page 1

"Cochise County Coroner's Inquest No. 1679" Arizona State Archives Phoenix

May 27, 1929, Junction Mine

Armando Di Paolo was killed when he has caught between a locomotive and a timber. The accident broke his neck. He was only 17 years old and was one of the youngest men killed underground in Bisbee.

"Original Certificate of Death http://genealogy.az.gov/azdeath/039/10391380.pdf Arizona Department of Health (May 31, 2012)

Office of State Mine Inspector. *Annual Report of the State Mine Inspector State of Arizona for the Year Ending November 30, 1929.*

July 14, 1929, Junction Mine

Reyes, Valdez and Phillip Arthur Short were working in a cut and fill stope on the 1800 level. Short was drilling a boulder to cut out for a new set, when the rock fell. Reyes ran over to help him and turned off the air to the drill. He was spitting up blood from his lungs and a leg was broken. Short died soon after arriving at the Calumet and Arizona Hospital. He was buried in nearby Rucker Canyon.

"Post Mortem to Locate Cause of Miner's Death" Bisbee Ore 16 July 1923 page 1
Office of State Mine Inspector. *Fourteenth Annual Report of the State Mine Inspector State of Arizona for the Year Ending November 30, 1929*. Tombstone Epitaph.
"Cochise County Coroner's Inquest No.1688" Arizona State Archives Phoenix

July 12, 1929, Junction Mine

Finnish Miner, Fred Lifman, and J.L. Bradshaw were working in 21 stope on the 2000 level. This was a square-set stope, but it had a few stulls placed. The miners were measuring to put in a new stull when another ten by ten-inch stull fell hitting Lifman. He was also buried with about one foot of muck except for one hand and his head. He was wearing a hard hat, but it was buried under the muck. Lifman died from a fractured skull, but it was never determined whether the falling stull or rock had killed him. Lifman was 48 years old and buried in Evergreen Cemetery.

"Original Certificate of Death http://genealogy.az.gov/azdeath/039/10392632.pdf Arizona Department of Health (May 31, 2012)
Office of State Mine Inspector. *Annual Report of the State Mine Inspector State of Arizona for the Year Ending November 30, 1929*.
Dugan Mortuary Records Aug. 29, 1926 – Jun4 1930 Accession 2010.10.20 Bisbee Mining and Historical Museum, Bisbee
"Cochise County Coroner's Inquest No.1690Arizona State Archives Phoenix

October 8, 1931, Junction Mine

Watchman, John Woosley was on duty when at around midnight he was jumped by two men. The men grabbed Woosley by the throat and held him at knife point. During the struggle Woosley was cut on the face by the knife. The robbers took his watch and meal ticket.

"Veteran Miner of District is Victim of Holdup." Bisbee Daily Review 8 October 1931 page 8

March 27, 1933, Junction Mine

George Poole and Y.W. Buchanen were installing an electrical box on the 2200 level. Poole was not pleased how the box was hanging and was trying to fix it. They were using a mine car loaded with sacks of lime that were covered with paper as an insulated staging with a ladder. Poole asked for a rule and stood up on the ladder and contacted a live wire. He fell the ladder onto the car dead.

"Cochise County Coroner's Inquest No.1723Arizona State Archives Phoenix

January 29, 1934, Junction Mine

At 11:30 am, Manuel Garcia ate his lunch. Then close to 12:00 he filled his carbide lamp and told the other men he had about eight or nine cars to muck out. Garcia brought a mine car into his work area and just as he hung his lamp on a limestone boulder, the 500 lb. rock fell and crushed him.

"Cochise County Coroner's Inquest No.1729Arizona State Archives Phoenix

The Justrite, Copper Queen carbide lamp, c-1917

April 18, 1936 Junction Mine

Robert Rawley, W. Norman Harris and Charles A. Hamilton were in 231 crosscut on the 1800 level. Harris was working in 197 raise and had come down to help Rawley spit the holes. Hamilton was a mucker and not allowed to light fuses. They had drilled 60 holes and were using carbide lamps to spit the fuses. These men were going to detonate the first blast of what was going to become 196 raise. Rawley and Harris each decided to light 30 fuses after Harris ignited his he told Rawley he was going to ignite seven holes in his 197 raise. Harris climbed down and did not see Rawley and Hamilton, so he called for them, and Rawley answered from the smoke filled drift. Then the first hole detonated from the 196 raise and knocked down Rawley and extinguished Harris' carbide lamp. Harris began running, but slowed down because he was soaked, and his boots were filled with water. He slipped fell and had to relight his lamp. Near the station Harris had to work his way by two man cars parked in the drift. One of which was loaded with automatic drifters (rock drills). At the station, he was able to give the accident signal. Rawley was rescued, but Hamilton had been killed by the blast. On April 22, 1936, Robert Rawley died from his injuries.
"Original Certificate of Death http://genealogy.az.gov/azdeath/054/10540053.pdf<u>Arizona Department of Health</u> (July 27, 2015)
"Cochise County Coroner's Inquest No.1749" Arizona State Archives Phoenix

1939-1940 Junction Mine

Richard W. Graeme II was caught in a cave-in. The broken timber punctured his lung and he was sent to the Copper Queen Hospital. At the hospital one of his nurses was Josephine Keeler. The two later married. (Note, there is a possibility that this accident occurred at the Cole Mine.)

February 27, 1948, Junction Mine

The water pressure was low on the 2200 level and a pipe and trackman, Frank Alfred Ham wanted to check the valve in No. 4 crosscut close to the Campbell Mine. Sometime later, Mining Engineer, Jack Schissler found a hard hat in No. 4 crosscut and noticed some smoke. Then as he walked about 50-feet further, he found the body of Ham lying on the track of 96 crosscut who had been asphyxiated by gasses coming from a mine fire in the Campbell mine. Schissler stopped a train, and they opened the air doors to ventilate the 96 crosscut. After breathing the fire gasses, Schissler was overcome and passed out. He was taken out of the mine and recovered.

Original Certificate of Death." <u>Arizona Department of Health Services.</u> http://genealogy.az.gov/azdeath/082/10820898.pdf (May 27, 2014)

Schissler, Jack Personal Communication 1985

"Cochise County Coroner's Inquest No.1848" Arizona State Archives Phoenix

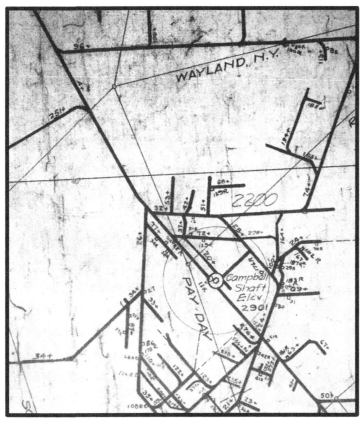

A 2200 level map, showing No.96 and No. 4 crosscuts in the upper left corner. This is the area that Frank Alfred Ham was asphyxiated.

1950's Junction Mine

G. Yavor was working on surface with the conveyor. His arm was torn off in an accident. Only a single photograph taken by W.P. Crawford provided the information.

G.Yavor Accident Photo #p1122. 1950's.

Accident site of G. Yavor Junction Conveyor

April 7, 1952, Junction Mine

B.W. Childress was injured on the 2433 level in a stope at the grizzlies. The photographs of the site indicate he was probably injured by a falling stringer.

B.W. Childress Accident photo # p1095. 7 Apr. 1952.

A fallen stringer at the top of grizzlies in a stope. This is the location B.W. Childress was injured. 2400 level Junction

October 6, 1952, Junction Mine

Floyd Elmo Hatten was killed when he was crushed between a locomotive and a timber.

Original Certificate of Death." <u>Arizona Department of Health Services</u>http://genealogy.az.gov/azdeath/0208/dc1140.pdf (May 28, 2012)

October 6, 1955, Junction Mine

Lester Hiram Henry Fogelson was transporting a bundle of wedges on the surface with a forklift. The forklift overturned on top of him and fatally fractured his skull.

Original Certificate of Death." Arizona Department of Health Services. http://genealogy.az.gov/azdeath/0224/02241083.pdf (May 28, 2012)
Graeme, Richard W. III Personal Communication May 22, 2013

May 29, 1958, Junction Mine

Motorman, Timothy Stanley Dugie sr was electrocuted when a trolley wire fell and landed on him. The wire's hanger had been eaten away by copper water.

Original Certificate of Death." Arizona Department of Health Services. http://genealogy.az.gov/azdeath/0231/02311411.pdf (May 28, 2012)
Graeme, Richard W. III Personal Communication May 22, 2013

March 31, 1960. Junction Mine

J.J. "Piggybank" Machain was working at the precipitation plant on the 1800 level and suffered a puncture wound on his right foot.

1959-1961 safety ledger p.92

May 4, 1960 Junction Mine

At the 2200 level pump station, R.E. Hopson was burned on his left hip. This appears to be from leakage of the Edison Mine lamp he was wearing. These lamps often leaked sodium hydroxide solution, a strong base. This was common source of injury. (Note, it was most likely a model P lamp)

1959-1961 safety ledger p.110

May 21, 1960 Junction Mine

W.L. Humphries suffered pain in his chest at the 2200 level pump station.

1959-1961 safety ledger p.110

May 25, 1961, Junction mine

On the 1600 level in 6 crosscut, T.M. Castillo cut his left palm on rail or pipe.

1959-1961 safety ledger p.202

January 4, 1974, Junction Mine

Pipe Riggerman, J.O. Garcia was on the 2700 level between the Junction and Campbell mines. He was hanging a CM Puller (lever hoist) and he knocked the eyebolts above him. Dust fell into his eyes. Dr. Mora checked his eyes.

Phelps Dodge Corporation Copper Queen Branch Accident Report 1-5-74

January 8, 1974, Junction Mine

On the 2700 level, M.E. Kalastro was hanging a chain hoist. He knocked sawdust in his eyes. Kalastro was a machinist helper.

Phelps Dodge Corporation Copper Queen Branch Accident Report 1-9-74

February 8, 1974, Junction Mine

Machinist, J.L. Figueroa and A.L. Murray were pushing a blower motor on a timber truck. As Figueroa was pushing the truck into the blower station on the 2700 he strained a groin muscle.
Phelps Dodge Corporation Copper Queen Branch Accident Report 2-10-74

March 12, 1974, Junction Mine
On the 2700 level, electrical sub-foreman, P.M. Silva was walking down No. 3 crosscut and slipped in the mud and twisted his right ankle.
Phelps Dodge Corporation Copper Queen Branch Accident Report 3-12-74

July 10, 1974, Junction Mine
Pump Repairman, Roy J. Brucks was at the 2200 level pump station. He was examining the overhead sump lines. It appears that when he climbed into the overhead sump he stepped on a screen. When he stepped forward his foot caved a hole in the screen. This caught his foot and he fell. His side and arm were cut up and bruised.
Phelps Dodge Corporation Copper Queen Branch Accident Report 7-11-74

September 27, 1974, Junction Mine
J.E. Martinez was working with an air impact wrench at the pump station on the 2700 level. The exhaust from the wrench blew dust around his eye shields into his eyes.
Phelps Dodge Corporation Copper Queen Branch Accident Report 9-30-74

December 11, 1974, Junction Mine,
J. *"Cat"* Durazo was constructing a brattice which is a wooden frame covered in a coated cloth to control ventilation. As he was walking through an air door on the 1600 level he bruised his hand. Initially, he did not want a blue card, but visited the doctor the following day. (Note, Durazo was normally assigned to work at the Cole Mine at this time.)
Phelps Dodge Corporation Copper Queen Branch Accident Report 1-2-75

April 23, 1975, Junction Mine
Pipe & Riggerman Gang Boss, C.E. Ham was trying to unclog a four inch drain line in the drain line. He was working in the #5 compartment of the shaft on the 2566 level. An object falling down the shaft struck him on the left knuckle. Luckily, his finger was only bruised. Note, that the object could have fallen as much as 2500 feet before it hit him. Rocks, bolts and pieces of would regularly fall down these shafts making shaft working a little unnerving. Sometimes, these objects actually whistle as they fall making you want to crawl under your hard hat. Most of the time a falling object bounces against the walls of the shaft and it can be heard knocking the walls above before it passes you.
Phelps Dodge Corporation Copper Queen Branch Accident Report 4-23-75

Active mining ceased in the Junction Mine in 1958 and for the entire district in June 12, 1975, but men still worked underground salvaging any equipment of value. They also maintained the pumps in the Junction Mine. The following accidents occurred during the mine salvage period

July 16, 1975, Junction Mine
 C.W. Amos a pipe riggerman was working on the stainless steel pipe line from the 1770 level to the 2700 level pump station. As he filled the line with water to check for leaks a factory* made 45° elbow blew out of Victaulic coupling. Although, details of how he was injury whether by a fall afterword or if he was struck by the coupling is unknown, He suffered cuts on face, back abdomen, left shoulder and two possible broken ribs. * Note, it

was felt that the groove on the elbow was not deep enough to hold. It was decided the mine shops would manufacture the elbow out of heavy 40 gauge stainless steel pipe. Also the use of stainless steel indicates that acidic mine water was to be pumped through the line.
Phelps Dodge Corporation Copper Queen Branch Accident Report 7-17-74

Junction Mine Boiler Shop

       Originally, called the "Plate" Shop the first boiler shop was constructed in 1907. The shop was originally 40'X128" and directly attached to the machine shop. In the boiler shop, heavy steel work such as repair and building cages and mine cars was completed. Chute doors were also built in this shop. The shop also repaired the liners for the haulage trucks for the Lavender Pit. The boiler shop remained in use until after the major operations ceased in 1975. The building and much of the equipment still remains on site as of 2020.

July 2, 1959 Boiler Shop
M.G. Reynolds was welding and flash burned his right eye. This was a lost time accident.
1959-1961 safety ledger p.54

June 29, 1960 Boiler Shop
G. Genko broke fell and broke his left leg.
1959-1961 safety ledger p.118

October 28, 1960 Boiler Shop
A.L. Corrin broke his left thumb in an undescribed accident.
1959-1961 safety ledger p.150

August 30, 1961 Boiler Shop
In an undescribed accident both A.E. Niemi and E.R. Moore were injured by a falling object. Niemi suffered a bruised right shoulder and left elbow. Moore broke three toes.
1959-1961 safety ledger p.230

April 10, 1961 Boiler Shop
E.M. Elliot bruised his right knee.
1959-1961 safety ledger p. 198

May 17, 191 Boiler Shop
W.J. Watkins punctured his right shin.
1959-1961 safety ledger p. 206

January 7, 1974, Boiler Shop
Welder, C.N. Phillips was cutting a hole into a 2" inch pipe post. As he was cutting the hole a hose broke where it connected to the torch. Flames shot out of the break and burned his stomach
Phelps Dodge Corporation Copper Queen Branch Accident Report 1-7-74

February 13, 1974, Boiler Shop
C.J. Riggs a boiler maker's apprentice was installing rubber molding at the Junction fire station. He jerked the rolling door and it fell. The nail on his small toe was smashed off.
Phelps Dodge Corporation Copper Queen Branch Accident Report 2-13-74

April 15, 1974, Boiler Shop

T.P. Martin was using a cutting torch on an 824 Caterpillar bulldozer blade. He was wearing welding goggles and he needed more hose. When he pulled on the hose the torch passed over Jack I. Rives. Rives shirt and skin were burned.
Phelps Dodge Corporation Copper Queen Branch Accident Report 4-16-74

April 30, 1974, Boiler Shop
In the boiler shop, H.E. Shork and T.P. Martin were repairing a 7 yard AMSCO electric shovel bucket. Martin was welding all the cracks and welding in the liner plates*. Shork must have been working above him and molten metal dripped from the area Shork was working and fell onto Martin's backside. Martin suffered a *"burn on the rump"*.
Phelps Dodge Corporation Copper Queen Branch Accident Report 4-30-74

May 17, 1974, Boiler Shop
Harold Norris was working on a loader bucket in the boiler shop. While he was welding a piece of hot metal fell onto his pants. It burned the pants and became stuck in his boot. He was unable to remove the boot before he became burned on the lower left leg.
Phelps Dodge Corporation Copper Queen Branch Accident Report 5-17-74

May 28, 1974, Boiler Shop
Roy Bradshaw was stretch fencing wire at the Junction parking lot. He was working near the gate and pulling the wire around the post. A pair of pliers slipped off and struck him in the mouth. He suffered a loosened and cracked tooth.
Phelps Dodge Corporation Copper Queen Branch Accident Report 5-28-74

December 18, 1974, Boiler Shop
William Harris was using a punch to make heavy washers. As he stepped on the control he failed to get his left index finger out of the way. The punch came down and amputated one quarter of his left index distal bone.
Phelps Dodge Corporation Copper Queen Branch Accident Report 12-18-74

The Junction Power Plant

Junction Power Plant

Originally, steam was the source of power for the mines, but as more efficient electrical equipment became available, the mines demand for inexpensive electricity increased. As early as 1909, electric generators were being installed at the Junction Mine. These served as additional power supply to the smelters. There were heat plants at both the Copper Queen and Calumet & Arizona mining companies smelters that produced large quantities of electricity.

Yet at times, the smelters did not produced an adequate amount. At night, the Junction and other mines primarily hoisted ore this heavy strain on the hoist motors dramatically increased power consumption. In the mills, soft ore required a larger number of ball mills to run adding to the drain on the power. The use of pumps, such as those on the 2200 was not entirely consistent, during times of increased water flow, extra pumps were turned on. The draw of power to start these pumps was so significant. That the pumpman were required to call the power house before starting a pump. It was challenging to balance power generation to the power demands. In 1930, the main Junction powerhouse was constructed with the intent to eliminate the use of steam power. The plaster steel building was constructed to hold two 725 H.P. boilers and one 3750 K.V.A. turbo generator and exciter.

The three air compressor were also in the building. During the last decades of mining the Junction Power plant was the third option for power production. The smelter was the primary and followed by the Diesel Power plant near Don Luis at the Sacramento Concentrator site. The Junction Power plant was used until mining was completed in 1975. The building suffered major structural damage from subsidence of the east wall of the Lavender Pit. The building was demolished a few years after major mining ceased in 1975.

May 14, 1918, Junction Power Plant

Around 10:00pm, Electrician, Lewis B. Naylor was installing switching boards in the Junction Power house with Andy Bijohn, William R. Gibson, R.G. Nichols and Alfred Frame. Gibson and Naylor were bending a wire to connect two switchboards. Naylor lifted his arm and contacted a steel rod that was shorted. A bright flash occurred burning Bijohn on his face and arm. Naylor fell causing a blinding flash. As quickly as the power could be shut off Naylor's body was taken out of the power house, but he was already dead. Dr. Bledsoe tried for forty minutes to revive him. Bijohn was taken to the Calumet & Arizona Hospital and treated. R.H. Frazier and Lewis Naylor had come to Bisbee on November 17, 1917. They shared a room above the Lowell Fire Hall. Deputy Sheriff A.E. Howe wrote the following telegrams to Naylor's mother and wife.

"It is with the feelings of deepest sympathy that I am called upon in the course of my duty to let you know that your son, Lewis B. Naylor, was accidentally electrocuted tonight while working at the Junction line, of the Calumet & Arizona Mining Company. Body now being held at the Henessey Undertaking parlors. Wire me or them what instructions you wish to make regarding burial. Have wired his wife at Pasadena.
A. E. Howe,
Deputy Sheriff."

and I sent the following telegram to his wife:

"I am sorry to inform you that your husband, Lewis B. Naylor, was accidentally electrocuted tonight at ten o'clock while employed Junction line in employ of Calumet & Arizona Mining Company. Body is now held at Hennessey Undertaking parlors here. Have wired his mother at San Luis Obispo."
A. E. Howe,
Deputy Sheriff."

In reply to the telegram from his wife I received this answer:

"Pasadena, Calif., May 15, 1918.
A. E. Howe,
Deputy Sheriff,
Bisbee, Arizona,

Please hold body until further instructions from me.
Mrs. Lewis B. Naylor."

Copy of telegrams from the Naylor Inquest

Lewis Naylor was survived by two children, his parents, his wife and two brothers. One brother was in France with the U.S. Army. Frazier noted that Naylor's possessions included several suits of clothes and a newly purchased rifle.

"Naylor Killed by Electric Shock at Junction Mine" Bisbee Daily Review 15 May 1918 page 2

"Pittman Sweet" Hitter" <u>Bisbee Daily Review</u> 19 May 1918 page 5
"Cochise County Coroner's Inquest No. 1323" Arizona State Archives

February 20, 1961 Junction Power Plant
E.M. Jimenez bruised his left second finger wen an unidentified object fell.
1959-1961 safety ledger p. 182

March 28, 1961 Junction Power Plant
J.J. Taylor cut is left thumb.
1959-1961 safety ledger p. 190

April 6, 1961 Junction Power Plant
B.R. Johnson punctured his right shoulder.
1959-1961 safety ledger p. 198

July 12, 1961 Junction Power Plant
J.J. Taylor fell and bruised his back.
1959-1961 safety ledger p. 223

October 17, 1974 Junction Power Plant
Chief Electrician, Lindsay A. Ferguson was examining an electrical tie-bus in the switch gear room in the Junction Power Plant. He touched the taped bus and was burned by an electrical shock. His right middle finger was burned and his right wrist was scraped.
Phelps Dodge Corporation Copper Queen Branch Accident Report 10-17-74

December 17, 1974 Junction Power Plant
Electrical Sub-Foreman, Pete Silva was removing a bearing from a storage bin. Dust fell into his right eye.
Phelps Dodge Corporation Copper Queen Branch Accident Report 12-17-74

Junction Mine Machine Shop

This shop was originally constructed in 1907 and remained in use until after major mining operations ceased in 1975. The massive machine shop in some ways was a holdover from the earlier days of Bisbee when parts for machines were difficult at best and slow to acquire. The shop was outfitted to build almost any part. Repairing rock drills and pumps were common tasks. Importantly, they kept the pumps on the 2200 level Junction Mine running. The parts for these massive pumps had not been produced for decades by the time the pumps ceased operating. The men who worked in this shop were true artists in metal. The shop remains relatively intact with equipment as of March 2020, but has not been used for several years.

February 15 1908 Junction Mine
Jack Neenan damaged his right eye when a blasting cap exploded. He was expected to be able to return to work and he would not lose the eye. Fred Kominsky was nearby but only injured in the legs.
"Cap Injures Eye" <u>Bisbee Daily Review</u> 16 February 1908 page 7
"Will Not Lose Eye" <u>Bisbee Daily Review</u> 1 March 1908 page 7

March 12, 1959, Junction Machine Shop
W.G. Henwood bruised his left shin.
1959-1961 safety ledger p. 22

July1, 1959, Junction Machine Shop
W.G. Henwood bruised his right leg.
1959-1961 safety ledger p. 54

December 12, 1960 Junction Machine Shop
R.L. McCormick was cut on the right hand by a falling object.
1959-1961 safety ledger p. 166

January 9, 1974, Junction Mine Machine Shop
Machinist's Apprentice, R.G. Green smashed his little finger while placing a pump on a stand.
Phelps Dodge Corporation Copper Queen Branch Accident Report 1-10-74

January 24, 1974, Junction Mine Machine Shop
Machine Repairman, W.E. Perkins was repairing a jackleg. He was putting the valve chest back onto a jackleg drill. Perkins was using his left index finger to align the pin while he was striking the valve chest with a hammer. The hammer handle caught on a belt loop on his pants. This caused him to smash his index
Phelps Dodge Corporation Copper Queen Branch Accident Report 1-24-74

September 4, 1974, Junction Mine Machine Shop
Machinist helper, T.H. Jewell was loosening the bolts on an underground locomotive. As Jewell was using the ratchet wrench he tore off a wart on his right middle finger knuckle.

June 6, 1975, Junction Mine Machine Shop
Machine Repairman, W.E. Perkins was repairing a stoper. He had finished repairing the cylinder and was walking back to the rest of the drill. He tripped on a floor mat and fell. He suffered a back strain and possible injury to a disk.
Phelps Dodge Corporation Copper Queen Branch Accident Report 6-10-75

A Gardner-Denver Model 63 jack leg drill being repaired at the Queen Mine

Cutting 8"X 8" timber in the Junction Mine Saw Mill c-1960

Junction Mine Saw Mill

The beginning of the saw mill is not recorded, but a small saw mill was likely constructed at the same time the Junction Mine was started. In 1915, the saw mill machinery at the Hoatson mine was moved to the Junction mine site. Originally, the main saw mills were located at the Oliver Mine then later at the Cole Mine. Then on Dec 12, 1918, the Cole Saw Mill burned. After this time, the Junction Saw Mill framed all regular mine timber sets with the special timbers cut at the individual mines. After the Calumet & Arizona Mining Company merged with Phelps Dodge, the Copper Queen Sawmill was shutdown. The Junction saw mill remained in use until well after mining ceased in 1975 and as of 2020 the saw mill is largely intact with equipment, but unused.

March 19, 1959 Junction Saw Mill
J. Barboa had debris enter his right eye.
1959-1961 safety ledger p. 22

June 12, 1959 Junction Saw Mill
J.M. Luna was bruised in the left leg by a falling timber.
1959-1961 safety ledger p. 46

November 17, 1960 Junction Saw Mill
C.L. Applegate fell and bruised his right shoulder and cheek.
1959-1961 safety ledger p. 1 58

January 22, 1974 Junction Saw Mill
Saw Mill Hand, R.O. Garcia cut his hand while painting the #1 conveyor
Phelps Dodge Corporation Copper Queen Branch Accident Report 1-22-74

March 19, 1974 Junction Saw Mill
Saw Mill Laborer, R.M. Huerrera and K.W. Phillips were stacking girts. These are 8"X10"X 5'6" timbers used in square sets. As they were stacking the timbers a girt slipped out of Phillips causing Huerrera to loose hold of his section. Huerrera's thumb was cut and bruised by the moving timber.
Phelps Dodge Corporation Copper Queen Branch Accident Report 3-19-74

September 11, 1974 Junction Saw Mill
A.R. Nunez a saw mill laborers was banding a bundle of wedges. Something blew into his eye. It continued to bothered him and get worse and finally he requested a blue card.
Phelps Dodge Corporation Copper Queen Branch Accident Report 9-11-74

April 1, 1975 Junction Saw Mill
G. Tyra was emptying the sawdust bin and something possibly saw dust blew into his left eye.
Phelps Dodge Corporation Copper Queen Branch Accident Report 4-1-75

Lake Superior and Pittsburg No. 3 Mine

  The South Bisbee Mining and Town site Company gave a contract to Maurice Denn and Peter Johnson to develop a 600ft. shaft on the Uncle Sam claim on May 31, 1900. Although, this claim had interesting surface out croppings it was largely undeveloped at the time. During the course of the next three years the shaft was sunk to the depth of 800ft. and small amounts of ore were mined. Three levels were advanced, the 100, 130 and 600. In 1902, the property was purchased by the newly formed Lake Superior & Pittsburg Development Company. At this time the shaft was renamed as the Lake Superior & Pittsburg #3 shaft .This Development Company was short lived and became the Lake Superior and Pittsburg Mining Company in 1904. At this time the shaft was deepened to the 1000 level.

  The new company was more interested in improving the nearby Cole shaft. During the year a 2,300 ft. drift was driven between the two mines to make a connection on the 1000 level for ventilation. It was decided to enlarge the Cole shaft to four compartments and it became necessary to handle all men and materials for the Cole shaft through the L.S.P. #3 shaft. To accomplish this a hoist was removed from the Cole and installed at the L.S. &P. #3. On October 8, 1904, mules arrived at the mine to haul cars from the Cole to the L.S. &P. #3 shaft. The haulage distance was too great for hand pushing of cars to be effective. Also, the #1 winze on the 1000 level was modified to serve as a temporary interior shaft by lowering cars and supplies with a small hoist. Work continued in1905 supporting the overhaul of the Cole Shaft and facilities.

  In 1906, the Lake Superior and Pittsburg Mining Company merged with the Calumet & Pittsburg Mining Company and the Junction Development Company and became the Superior and Pittsburg Copper Company. After the completion of the work at the Cole shaft, the use of the L.S.&P.#3 shaft declined and little or no work occurred during 1906- 1919 . During the period of inactivity the property became part of the Calumet & Arizona Mining Company.

  Excited by developments in Boras and Nighthawk mines, on April 15th 1920, the L.S. &P. #3 shaft was reactivated for development on the 500 and 600 levels. A hoist was moved over from the Hoatson mine and a new wooden headframe was built. 1,368 ft. of drifting was done during the first year along with shaft stations being cut. The following year exploration continued with 4,411ft of drifting on 500, 600 & 750 levels and mining small amounts of lead-silver ore. During 1923, 4,531ft of drifting was completed on the 600,700, 850 and 1000 levels with a modest 60 tons of ore shipped. Development work was stopped on the 600 level in 1924, but continued on 700, 850, 1000 levels with

5,200ft. of drifting and 746 tons shipped. 1925 was the last year the L.S. &P. #3 was operated with a small amount of drifting and raising.

In March 14 1925, all equipment underground and surface were removed, except on 1000 which connected to Cole. During the remaining years of mining in Bisbee the mine was allowed to ventilate, but it was not used specifically as a ventilation shaft. Later, the South Bisbee dump of the Lavender Pit avoided covering the shaft to allow for continuing air flow. Although, the waste dumps came reasonably close. The shaft was downcast and its neighboring shaft the Boras was an important up cast ventilation shaft. Parts of the L.S. &P. #3 mine workings were accessible through the Cole shaft during the 1960s and 70s. When the mine finally closed it was 913 ft. deep. It had 1 ½ compartments down to the 600 level. From the 600 level to the 1000 level, the shaft had two full compartments. The mine was also called the South Bisbee #3 mine and the Cole #3 mine.

December 26, 1904, Lake Superior & Pittsburg No. 3 Mine*
Mark Bulich was struck by a drill (steel) falling 15 ft. out of a raise. He was expected to be off work a few days. * This accident could have occurred at the Cole mine instead.
"Drill Struck Him" Bisbee Daily Review 27 December 1904 page 5

January, 1905, Lake Superior & Pittsburg No.3 Mine
Jack Staples was working unloading timber and a rock fell from a skip hit him. His arm was broken. The accisdent could have been more serious if the rock did not bounce off a wall before striking him.He was expected to be off work sometime.
"Broken Arm" Bisbee Daily Review 29, January1905 page 6
"From Broken Arm" Bisbee Daily Review 15 February1905 page 6

July 26, 1907, Lake Superior & Pittsburg No.3 Mine *
George Petrovich, a 22 -year-old was working in 73 stope on the 1000 level, with a miner named Ojang. The miners had inspected the stope and found it to be in good condition. Around 11:00 am, two tons of rock fell, crushing and instantly killing Petrovich. He was buried in Evergreen Cemetery.
*It is possible that he was actually killed in the Cole Shaft which at times was called the Lake Superior & Pittsburg No. 2 Shaft.
"Big Rock falls Crushes a Miner" Bisbee Daily Review 28, July 1907 page 2
"Bisbee-Lowell Evergreen Cemetery." My Cochise.
http://www.mycochise.com/cembisbeepq.php (July 20, 2011)
"Cochise County Coroner's Inquest No.471" Arizona State Archives Phoenix

May 17, 1923, Lake Superior and Pittsburg No. 3 Mine (Cole No.3)
George L. Stalley was killed around 11:30 pm. The information about this accident is confusing. It appears that he probably knocked out of a cage and crushed against the wall plate.
Office of State Mine Inspector. *Twelfth Annual Report of the State Mine Inspector State of Arizona for the Year Ending November 30, 1923.*
"Original Certificate of Death." Arizona Department of Health Services http://genealogy.az.gov/azdeath/025/10251109.pdf. (May 31, 2012)

Lavender Pit, c-1952

Lavender Pit*

In 1909, the two intrusive porphyry units began to be explored for ore potential. It was learned that two sections one called the West Orebody and the other the East Orebody lent themselves to mining. The West orebody was mined by the Sacramento Open Pit and the East Orebody was to be mined underground largely with the block- cave method and a few top slicing stopes. Unfortunately, the block-cave stopes failed to adequately collapse and the ore remained in situ. Also, the ore itself, also proved somewhat problematic as it was films of chalcocite (Cu_2S) coating pyrite (FeS_2.) It was difficult to separate the valueless pyrite from the desirable chalcocite. In March 1950, planning began on a new open pit mine. To start mining it was essential that the communities of Jiggerville, Upper Lowell and Johnson Addition were moved. Highway 80 would also be moved north. The topography eliminated the use of trains in the pit and 25-ton haul trucks were chosen to haul rock from the pit. P&H 9 yd. electric shovels loaded the trucks. The haul to the waste dumps initially exceeded the economic limits for a 25 ton truck and the waste was dumped into rail cars and transported to No.7 dump by rail. Stripping of the waste rock began in 1951.

After the death, of Phelps Dodge vice-president Harrison Lavender in 1952, the new pit was christened the Lavender Pit. In 1954, the Lavender Pit began producing ore. Following advances in technology, the first 35-ton dump trucks were introduced in 1960. Plans were beginning for the first expansion of the pit. This new area was to mine the southeastern side near the abandoned Hoatson Mine. The first of the 65-ton trucks were purchased in 1963. With these new larger trucks the rail line to No.7 dump ceased and the waste was hauled by truck. In the constant search for ore, exploration began in the Holbrook mine region. An air raise into the Holbrook mine was reconditioned and a diamond drill was placed underground. Also, drift was driven from the Lavender pit toward the 400 level Gardner. Enough ore was discovered and in 1965, the Holbrook Extension was announced. Most of the Holbrook Extension ore mined was oxides (azurite, malachite, and cuprite) and was sent directly to the smelter. The Lavender Pit continued to mine until December 14, 1974. Note, the accident information available for study is limited on this mine. *Note, William Teel was electrocuted at the Czar Mine, but in the State Mine Inspector reports it is attributed to the Lavender Pit

October 22, 1954, Lavender Pit Mine

Eugene Donald Stringer was working on 52-50 bench near the top bench on Sacramento Hill. R.B. Hodges was operating a shovel on the bench and stated the bench was hard rock on the bottom but was broken up and loose and at the top. A one-ton boulder broke free and rolled over Stringer. Truck driver, Francis Beach witnessed this accident in the mirror of his truck. Stringer was killed by the rock.

Office of State Mine Inspector. *Seventh Annual Report of the State Mine Inspector State of Arizona for the Year Ending November 30, 1954.*

"Cochise County Coroner's Inquest No.1886" Arizona State Archives Phoenix

1958 Lavender Pit Mine
The east wall in the pit began to fail (move). Cracks began to appear in the roads above the section of the wall in the Glance conglomerate (rock type). The movement of the rock was generally slow and carefully monitored. No one was injured from this movement, but the potential was there for serious problems. The bakery in Lowell and the Junction Powerhouse buildings were eventually badly damaged by the movement. They were torn down, in the 1990s.

"Personal Communication" Richard W. Graeme III March 18, 2020

February 11, 1959 Lavender Pit Mine
At 2:00 am, F, C, Dabovich bruised his left shin on #5 Shovel

1959-1961 safety ledger p.15

February 27, 1959 Lavender Pit Mine
 At the 4950 bench and on #2 Shovel, R.L. Tucker sprained his right wrist.

1959-1961 safety ledger p.15

April 11, 1959 Lavender Pit Mine
I.A. Scalp injured his back on # 3 Shovel in an undescribed Accident. This was a lost time accident.

1959-1961 safety ledger p.32

May 8, 1959 Lavender Pit Mine
W.L. Pomroy bruised his right shoulder while working at #5 Shovel on the 5000 Bench.

1959-1961 safety ledger p. 40

May 29, 1959 Lavender Pit Mine
C.N. Attaway cut his right knee working at the pit crane.

1959-1961 safety ledger p. 40

June 6, 1959 Lavender Pit Mine
P. Carreto broke his left third finger while working on # 18 Drill.

1959-1961 safety ledger p.48

July 13, 1959 Lavender Pit Mine
At 2:30 pm, D.L. Bohen and L.C. Windsor were both chemically burned on #7 Dump. Bohen was burned on the face and Windsor the arms (?)

1959-1961 safety ledger p. 56

August 10, 1959 Lavender Pit Mine

J.M. Doyle burned his right hand working on the Jiggerville Dump.
1959-1961 safety ledger p. 64

March 4, 1960 Lavender Pit
B.J. Shafer punctured his left hand working at # 15 Joy Drill.

April 9, 1960 Lavender Pit Mine
L.W. Brasher broke an upper tooth on #4 Shovel.
1959-1961 safety ledger p. 104

April 26, 1960 Lavender Pit Mine
Truck driver, M.E. Hendricks suffered an extremely serious but undescribed accident. He was on the a truck road at the 5300 level (elevation) and both his legs were broken along with his pelvis and his left hip was dislocated.
1959-1961 safety ledger p.104

May 8, 1960 Lavender Pit
On #7 dump, D.A. Matthews suffered a concussion in an undescribed accident.
1959-1961 safety ledger p.112

June 1, 1960 Lavender Pit
A.E. Petty bruised his right first finger working with #3 Bulldozer
1959-1961 safety ledger p. 110

August 15, 1960 Lavender Pit
R, D. Mills broke his right third finger on the #7 Railroad dump.
1959-1961 safety ledger p.136

August 30, 1960 Lavender Pit.
On the #7 Railroad dump, D. Mortenson was struck by a falling object. He suffered a concussion and bruised back
1959-1961 safety ledger p.136

September 16, 1960 Lavender Pit
In an undescribed accident, S.E. Hockstead broke his left leg on the South Bisbee dump.
1959-1961 safety ledger p.144

December 28, 1960 Lavender Pit
R.D. Spivey broke a rib after falling on or near #5 Shovel.
1959-1961 safety ledger p.168

April 13, 1961 Lavender Pit
On the 5100 bench (also elevation) J.H. Ray fell on #6 Shovel and broke his heel.
This was a lost time accident.
1959-1961 safety ledger p.200

May 5, 1961 Lavender Pit
J.W. Adams was bruised up and possibly had broken bones from an undescribed accident that occurred on #5 Shovel.
1959-1961 safety ledger p.208

May 24, 1961 Lavender Pit
On bench 4900 at #18 Drill, V. Damron was hit by a falling object that broke his denture plate.
1959-1961 safety ledger p. 207

June 7, 1961 Lavender Pit
L.D. Brown fell on #1 shovel at bench 4950. He fell and suffered a bruised chest, left leg and right hand.
1959-1961 safety ledger p. 216

July 6, 1961 Lavender Pit
On #4 Mack truck, V.R. Giacoletti sprained his right wrist.
1959-1961 safety ledger p. 224

July 28, 1961 Lavender Pit
On #1 Shovel, W.R. Crowley bruised his lower lip and chipped two teeth.
1959-1961 safety ledger p. 224

August 30, 1961 Lavender Pit
H.L. Reese broke his right wrist on #4 shovel at the 4850 bench (also elevation)
1959-1961 safety ledger p.232

October 27, 1961 Lavender Pit
On #16 Mack Truck, J. Scofield sprained his right ankle.
1959-1961 safety ledger p. 248

1962, Lavender Pit Mine
The northeast wall near the concentrator began to fail. In the area of the Dividend fault. This is noticeable as a person dives along the Highway 80 the road distinctly dips towards the Pit. As of 2019 the present owners of the pit have dumped rock inside the pit directly below this area to support the wall. As with the east wall failure this movement has been gradual and no one has been injured by this wall failure, but it has had the potential at times .
"Personal Communication" Richard W. Graeme III March 18, 2020

A truck that has gone over the berm on the east wall of the Lavender Pit c. 1959

1970 Lavender Pit Mine
A massive wall failure occurred on the southwestern wall of the Holbrook Extension
near the abandoned Spray Mine. In an unfortunate decision, waste dumps were placed
above this section of the wall increasing the weight. The toe (bottom of the wall) was a
large gobbed stope. This gob significantly weakened the wall. Monitors were placed
along the southwestern to the western walls of the pit. Incredibly, the sudden failure of
this wall was predicted to under 10 minutes. Within moments 300,000 yards of rock fell
filling a portion of the Holbrook Extension. The collapse of the wall was captured in a
series of photographs. The debris from the failure was used to build a berm at the toe of
the western wall to support this wall. It is evident still today (March 2020). Some of the
safety monitors still remained on western edge of the pit during the 1990's. They were
simple with a pull bottle (electrical switch) like those used for mine bells signals with
cables running down the wall of the pit. When the wall moved it pulled the switch and
the engineers would be warned of impending trouble. No one was injured in this collapse.
"Personal Communication" Richard W. Graeme III March 18, 2020

The wall failure in the Holbrook Extension as it was falling in 1970

January 17, 1974, Lavender Pit Mine
V. Damion was with R. Dinwiddie working on drill #20 on #7 dump. As he stepped off the drill he slipped on a rock and twisted his left ankle.
Phelps Dodge Corporation Copper Queen Branch Accident Report 1-18-74

February 5, 1974, Lavender Pit Mine
E.L. Henning was using a bulldozer to push the crusher dump. He climbed out of the dozer to clean the dozer's windshield. He slipped and skinned his leg.
Phelps Dodge Corporation Copper Queen Branch Accident Report 2-6-74

April 5, 1974, Lavender Pit Mine
Ron Mattingly was working on a power pole that was located on the haulage road to #7 dump. He had climbed a wooden pole with gaff climbers. As he was descending a gaff went into a bad spot in the pole. Mattingly slide ten feet down the pole. A wooden splinter was driven into his right breast. Steve Reardon was with him at the time. (Note, long after mining had ceased, Mattingly was electrocuted in the Junction Mine Yard.)
Phelps Dodge Corporation Copper Queen Branch Accident Report 4-5-74

April 29, 1974, Lavender Pit Mine
D.M. Wright was cutting scrap metal on the South Bisbee Dump*. It appears he was cutting a piece off a shovel or crane boom. When the piece came off he was thrown up and landed straddling a pry bar. He bruised his right groin area. * Scrap equipment was stored on top of this dump.
Phelps Dodge Corporation Copper Queen Branch Accident Report 5-1-74

June 17, 1974, Lavender Pit Mine
C.F. Dugie was changing a radiator cap on truck #142. As he was tapping* the cap off, it blew off. His right forearm and face were burned with steam. * Note , he was lightly striking the wings on the cap with a wrench, hammer or other tool.
Phelps Dodge Corporation Copper Queen Branch Accident Report 6-17-74

July 12, 1974, Lavender Pit Mine
D. B. Pelz was going to drill boulders* at # 8 shovel located at bench 4850. The carriage cable broke and the boom rolled down quickly. His back was sprained. * The boulders likely were set aside by the shovel as too large to load into the haul trucks. They were being prepared for secondary blasting.
Phelps Dodge Corporation Copper Queen Branch Accident Report 7-12-74

December 6, 1974 Lavender Pit Mine
J.M. Vargas was driving the #2 sand truck. He was disconnecting a pressurized hose and forgot to turn off the valve. The hose smacked him in the chest. Vargas was bruised.
Phelps Dodge Corporation Copper Queen Branch Accident Report 12-6-74

Lavender Pit Concentrator c-1958

Lavender Pit Concentrator

     The low grade ore containing 1.14 % copper in the Lavender Pit, largely consisted of thin veneers of chalcocite (Cu2S) coating pyrite(FeS2). To be profitably smelted the copper contented would need to be concentrated. In a simplified version, The ore was first crushed three times in a graduated series of crushers until the particles were small enough to be sent to a ball mill. Inside the ball mills, the ore was ground to a fine powder. This powder was mixed with water and chemicals and sent to the flotation tanks. The various chemicals caused the copper sulfide particles to cling to air bubbles created by agitating the solution in the tanks. As a result a the copper sulfide particles became concentrated in the floating solution. This floating mud was scrapped off and dried before being sent to the smelter. The concentrator was able to provide a 16-18% copper concentrate, not ideal but profitable. The underground mines also sent hundreds of thousands of tons of ore to the concentrator as well as the Lavender Pit. Note, all oxide ores were directly smelted and not sent to the concentrator. The waste rock particles that remained towards the bottom of the flotation tanks was pumped as a slurry to the tailings dam or in later years sometimes transported to an underground mine to be pumped underground to sandfill stopes. Site preparation began in 1951.

304

During the initial construct much used structural steel and equipment was used. Most of the steel came from the Montezuma mine at Nacozari, Sonora, but some came from Clarkdale, Arizona and a crusher was brought from Ajo, Arizona . During July of 1954, the mill was being tested and on August 7, 1954 it officially opened and operated until December 14, 1975. After the closure the mill was salvaged some parts were sent to Ajo, Arizona, others including two ball mills and a secondary crusher were sent to the Western Nuclear Mine in Spokane, Washington. Note, the amount of information availble to researchers is limited on accidents in the Lavender Pit Concentrator.

February 24, 1959 Lavender Pit Concentrator
T. Chavez broke a finger on the tailings dam.
1959-1961 safety ledger p.14

March 9, 1959 Lavender Pit Concentrator
E.L. Holley was at the primary crusher when he was struck in the back by a falling timber. He suffered bruising.
1959-1961 safety ledger p. 22

June 9, 1959 Lavender Pit Concentrator
R.A. Anderson was working at the tripper car and suffered a cut right eye lid and nose.
1959-1961 safety ledger p. 46

July 29, 1959 Lavender Pit Concentrator
F. Supanich strained his back at #3 Ball Mill.
1959-1961 safety ledger p. 56

August 10, 1959 Lavender Pit Concentrator
At the secondary crusher, J.G. Pilarczyk strained his left side.
1959-1961 safety ledger p. 62

August 17, 1959 Lavender Pit Concentrator
At the secondary crusher, A. Skinner sprained his left wrist moving timber (Note, he was probably removing old underground mine timber from the ore being crushed)

February 24, 1960 Lavender Pit Concentrator
In the assay room A.B. Hansen had his face, hands and arms burned. This was a lost time accident.
1959 -1961 safety ledger p.86

April 23, 1960 Lavender Pit Concentrator
V. Scott strained his back working in the flotation department.
1959-1961 safety ledger p. 102

October 4, 1960 Lavender Pit Concentrator
E.C. Vinson was struck by a falling object at the #5 dust collector. He was cut on the head. This was a lost time accident.
1959-1961 safety ledger p.150

February 4, 1961 Lavender Pit Concentrator
In the repair bay, an object fell and broke the large toe of E.M. Chavez.
1959-1961 safety ledger p. 182

March 1, 1960 Lavender Pit Concentrator. C. Dugie was in the Pit Change room and was struck in the side of the face by a falling object. He was bruised.
1959-1961 safety ledger p. 94

June 16, 1961 Lavender Pit Concentrator
B. Ratliff bruised his right side at a concentrate trip car.
1959-1961 safety ledger p. 214

July 24, 1961 Lavender Pit Concentrator
N. Norris crushed his left first finger and bruised his left arm at #11 Conveyor.
1959-1961 safety ledger p. 222

September 11, 1961 Lavender Pit Concentrator
Under the fine ore bin, M.H. Higgins was stung by a scorpion on the right and left arms.
1959-1961 safety ledger p. 240

January 9, 1970 Lavender Pit Concentrator
C.M. Boyles was injured in an undescribed accident. He suffered a depressed skull fracture and was not expected to be able to return to work.
1970-1971 safety ledger p.2

October 6, 1971 Lavender Pit Concentrator
K. McKinney broke his left leg below the knee. He was off work 342 days.
1970-1971 safety ledger p.122

May 18, 1972 Lavender Pit Concentrator
A ripper tooth came off a D-9 Caterpiller bulldozer. It was loaded into a truck sent through the primary crusher without a problem. In the secondary crusher it caused a sheave wheel to break on the secondary crusher. (Note, a concerted effort was made to prevent scrap steel and timber from entering the mill. A significant amount of timber and pieces of steel were discovered when the pit mined through abandoned underground mine workings. In the case of the top sliced stopes the masses of broken timber were sent directly to the waste dump.)
D-9 Ripper tooth Accident Photo # p1120. 18, May 1972.
D-9 Ripper tooth Accident Photo # p1121. 18, May 1972.

D-9 ripper tooth that was sent into the mill. tooth

Men examining the sheave broken by the ripper

January 12, 1974, Lavender Pit Concentrator
R.L. Rosenquist was a water hose to unplug the grizzlies on the primary crusher. Rosenquist was standing on a stack of crusher liners and slipped. He sprained his left ankle.
Phelps Dodge Corporation Copper Queen Branch Accident Report 1-13

February 1, 1974 Lavender Pit Concentrator
C.O. Malley and A. Gherna were laying out ball mill shell liners to install into the # 6 ball mill. They were using a crane and matching the liners before trying to install the liners. Rust went into O'Malley's right eye.
Phelps Dodge Corporation Copper Queen Branch Accident Report 2-6-74

February 9, 1974, Lavender Pit Concentrator
At 3:00 am, J.F. Herrera was removing pieces of steel and timber off #2-A conveyor. This was from when the pit mined through underground mine workings. The timber and pieces of steel could damage the mill equipment. Herrera was taking a large timber off the conveyor while it was running. He smashed his hand between the timber and the guard rail. R.J. Bernard witnessed the accident.
Phelps Dodge Corporation Copper Queen Branch Accident Report 2-9-74

February 12, 1974, Lavender Pit Concentrator
B.A. Rollins was picking rocks that had spilled off a conveyor at the primary crusher. As he was working another rock bounced off the belt and crushed his right index finger. This was a lost time accident.
Phelps Dodge Corporation Copper Queen Branch Accident Report 2-14-74

March 1, 1974, Lavender Pit Concentrator
F.C. Parrish was removing an old mine timber from # 3 pan feeder. A rock struck the timber. The timber moved and smashed his thumb against the side of the feeder.
Phelps Dodge Corporation Copper Queen Branch Accident Report 3-1-74

March 11, 1974, Lavender Pit Concentrator
F.C. Parrish was unplugging # 2 pan feeder under the coarse ore bin with a bar. He smashed a finger against the pan feeder.
Phelps Dodge Corporation Copper Queen Branch Accident Report 3-13-74

April 25, 1974, Lavender Pit Concentrator
J. C. Hargis was using a blow pipe (air lance) to clean out no. 1 pan feeder at the primary crusher. A rock fell and hit the blow pipe. The pipe bounced up and struck him in the jaw. He was bruised.
Phelps Dodge Corporation Copper Queen Branch Accident Report 4-25-74

May 4, 1974, Lavender Pit Concentrator
R.H. Hoffman had been working on oil pumps and his shoes became covered in oil and grease. Later, when he was climbing down the steps from # 1 ball mill, Hoffman slipped and fell. He twisted his left foot.
Phelps Dodge Corporation Copper Queen Branch Accident Report 5-6-74

June 3, 1974 Lavender Pit Concentrator
Kim Mauzy was barring down boulders hung in #1 pan feeder. The rocks fell striking the bar. The bar bounced up and struck him above the right eye. He suffered a cut above the right eye and a bruise on the side of the head.
Phelps Dodge Corporation Copper Queen Branch Accident Report 6-3-74

June 4, 1974, Lavender Pit Concentrator
G.E. Brooks was barring boulders in a pan feeder. The rocks fell and the bar bounced up and struck him behind the right ear.
Phelps Dodge Corporation Copper Queen Branch Accident Report 6-4-74

June 30, 1974, Lavender Pit Concentrator
D.R. Bowden was using a hose to drain the filter. The agitator caught the hose and pulled his hand into the filter drain. His right middle finger was bruised.
Phelps Dodge Corporation Copper Queen Branch Accident Report 6-30-74

July 17, 1974 Lavender Pit Concentrator
W.L. Atwood was going to sweep copper water off the floor. As he reached to pick up the broom he slipped and fell. He suffered copper water in both eyes.
Phelps Dodge Corporation Copper Queen Branch Accident Report 7-17-74

August 24, 1974 Lavender Pit Concentrator
W.N. Welch was repairing the chain driver on the # 3 pan feeder. Copper water was dripping down. He looked up to see where it was coming from and copper water dripped behind his glasses into his left eye.
Phelps Dodge Corporation Copper Queen Branch Accident Report 8-24-74

August 29, 1974, Lavender Pit Concentrator
B. Ray, J.E. Peeler, G. A. Mason, R.N. Munsey and W. Barcelo were eating lunch near the scrap bin. W. Barcelo threw an empty soda bottle at the bin. The bottle missed and hit Ray on the side of the head. Ray required six stitches for the cut on the right side of his head.
Phelps Dodge Corporation Copper Queen Branch Accident Report 8-29-74 6:00pm

August 29, 1974, Lavender Pit Concentrator
At the tailings dam, Kim Mauzy was dumping a sack of lime into a hopper. Lime entered his left eye.
Phelps Dodge Corporation Copper Queen Branch Accident Report 2-20-74 8:30 pm

September 11, 1974, Lavender Pit Concentrator
R.F. Cota was blowing out a junction box on a pan feeder with a blow pipe. Dust blew into his eyes.
Phelps Dodge Corporation Copper Queen Branch Accident Report 9-11-74

September 18, 1974, Lavender Pit Concentrator
J.E. Peeler was blowing the junction box on # 2 pan feeder. The blow pipe slipped and he bashed his elbow into the pan feeder. He was bruised.
Phelps Dodge Corporation Copper Queen Branch Accident Report 9-19-74

October 11, 1974, Lavender Pit Concentrator
B. Ray was going down the steps by #1 crushing unit at the secondary crusher. He slipped and twisted his right ankle.
Phelps Dodge Corporation Copper Queen Branch Accident Report 10-11-74

October 17, 1974, Lavender Pit Concentrator
H.M. Rogers was using a 988 Caterpillar loader to clean up muck. The muck was from a new fence around the day shift parking lot. The area was congested and when he was leaving he backed the loader into a pole. The pole was broken off at the ground. No one was injured.
Phelps Dodge Corporation Report of Accident 10-17-74

December 12, 1974 Lavender Pit Concentrator
Electricians and there apprentices were eating lunch in the mill electronics building. Unknown to the men the building was filled with a low concentration of carbon monoxide. At the end of lunch Bob Gaynor and Joe Montoya stood up and then passed out. As Gaynor fell he hit his head on a work bench. The other two men Tom Cornett and Henry A. Petsche felt nauseated with a headache. Luckily, all of the men survived the accident. Beyond nausea and headaches, Gaynor also suffered a cut over his right eyebrow.
Phelps Dodge Corporation Copper Queen Branch Accident Report 12-10-74, Tom Cornett
Phelps Dodge Corporation Copper Queen Branch Accident Report 12-10-74, Henry A. Petsche
Phelps Dodge Corporation Copper Queen Branch Accident Report 12-10-74, Joe Montoya
Phelps Dodge Corporation Copper Queen Branch Accident Report 12-10-74, Bob Gaynor

February 20, 1975, Lavender Pit Concentrator
A.L. Murray was flipping over ball mill liners with a bar. The bar became stuck in a bolt hole in the liner. When the liner flipped, the bar smashed Murray in the face.
Phelps Dodge Corporation Copper Queen Branch Accident Report 2-20-74

Timber from old underground mine workings in the wall of the Lavender Pit below the Gardner Mine

Lavender Pit Precipitation Plant c-1960

Lavender Pit Precipitation Plant

This plant was constructed to handle the leach solutions from no.7 dump and those being pumped from the 1800 Junction mine. Acidic mine water was pumped from the 1800 level of the Junction into sections of the dump containing copper sulfide bearing rock. The water percolated through the dump reacting with the sulfides with the help of certain bacteria species and releases an impure copper sulfate solution. This solution was captured at the base of the dump and pumped to the Lavender Pit Precipitation Plant located near the Campbell Mine headframe.

This plant consisted of about 20 concrete cells. The copper rich leach solution first entered cells filled with light scrap steel such as detained cans or sponge iron produced at the smelter at Douglas, Arizona. The replacement redox reaction occurred and much of the copper was deposited. Part of the scrap cans were removed in solution. Ideally, the chemistry is $Fe + CuSO_4 \longrightarrow FeSO_4 + Cu$. In reality, some iron remains and bits of plastic, cloth, chrome and other garbage does leave some contamination. the solutions continued to travel through cells until it reach the last stage with cell filled with heavy scrap steel such as automobile bodies and old mining equipment. Later, the copper mud was removed from the cells and dried. This concentrated copper mud could run up to 80% copper and was sent directly to the smelter in Douglas, Arizona. The water was then originally released into the creek bed from the Campbell Mine Yard. This creek travel through Warren and as a result was bright orange in colored from the deposition of iron hydroxides. During the 1970s this practice was stopped, but it is not clear what occurred with the iron sulfate charged water. It was possibly sent back underground into the Junction-Campbell Mine area. This plant is sometimes called the Campbell Precipitation Plant. It was typical for the operation to recover between 3,900 - 4,500 tons of copper per year from the dumps. Leaching continued, until 2013.

January 20, 1959 Lavender Pit Precipitation Plant
M. Panovich suffered a punctured left thigh from a flying object.
1959-1961 safety ledger p.6

April 10, 1959 Lavender Pit Precipitation Plant
G.L. Crowley suffered a puncture wound in his left hand.
1959-1961 safety ledger p. 30

March 23, 1960. Lavender Pit Precipitation Plant
R.W. Earnest suffered a puncture wound in his right foot. This resulted a in lost time
accident
1959-1961 safety ledger p.94

March 5, 1974, Lavender Pit Precipitation Plant.
R, R, Alvarez was cleaning trash out of cell #13 in the precipitation plant. He scratch his
left wrist on a piece of tin.
Phelps Dodge Corporation Copper Queen Branch Accident Report 3-3-74

May 4, 1974, Lavender Pit Precipitation Plant
J.H. Bonham was cleaning trash out of cell #1. There were pieces of cable in the cell.
When Bonham pushed a rail into the cell with his foot the cable rose up and scratched his
face.
Phelps Dodge Corporation Copper Queen Branch Accident Report 5-14-74

June 17, 1974, Lavender Pit Precipitation Plant
M.P. McConnell was cleaning trash out of the scrap steel on the heavy iron pad. He
found a piece of brass. When he went to pick it up a piece of copper wire pierced the
through his boot into his foot.
Phelps Dodge Corporation Copper Queen Branch Accident Report 6-17-74

June 26, 1974, Lavender Pit Precipitation Plant
J.K. Greenwood was cleaning trash out cell #17. He tried to pick up mass of hay and
bailing wire. The wire sliced through his glove and penetrated his thumb.
Phelps Dodge Corporation Copper Queen Branch Accident Report 6-26-74

November 11, 1974, Lavender Pit Precipitation Plant
R.W. Earnest and J.W. Huff were carrying a 6"x8"x8' timber into cell no. 9. When they
set the timber down, it rolled. Earnest's left thumb was smashed.
Phelps Dodge Corporation Copper Queen Branch Accident Report 12-2-74

March 23, 1975 Lavender Pit Precipitation Plant
R. W. Earnest was cleaning out copper mud from cell no. 29. He slipped and fell onto his
left thumb.
Phelps Dodge Corporation Copper Queen Branch Accident Report 3-3-75

April 14, 1975 Lavender Pit Precipitation Plant
R. W. Earnest was washing out cell no. 17. He lost hold of the hose and fell into the
copper sludge at the bottom of the cell. He struck a timber used as a spreader as he fell.
Earnest suffered a bruised side and hip.

Lavender Pit Repair Shop

Located in the Junction Mine Yard, this is where the heavy equipment for the Lavender Pit was repaired. The second floor was designated for repairing radiators. The lower floor is where dump truck engines, transmissions and rear-ends were rebuilt. Later, engines were changed with *"swing"* motors or previously rebuilt engines. Having a ready rebuilt engine waiting reduced   equipment downtime. Originally, Phelps Dodge rebuilt some of their own motors later, Bill Goar provided this service and the pit repair shop removed and installed the engines. A section was designated for generator and electric starter repair, but after the 65-ton Dart dump trucks with air starters were introduced, mainly generators were worked on. Some equipment such as, electric shovels and drills were typically repaired in the pit, but a heavy lowboy trailer could haul large equipment out of the pit to the shop. The lowboy was able to carry even a D-8 Caterpillar Dozer. This was typically done for rear end or transmission work which was easier in a cleaner less dusty environment. Outside of the pit repair shop, the beds of the dump trucks were rebuilt.

April 14, 1959 Lavender Pit Repair Shop
J.L. Gilliam had a flying sliver of steel embed itself in his left arm.
1959-1961 safety ledger p. 32.

June 29, 1959 Lavender Pit Repair Shop
C.L. Seller tore the finger nail off his left middle finger.
1959-1961 safety ledger p. 48

May 27, 1960 Lavender Pit Repair Shop
T.L. Gutierrez cut his left arm.
1959-1961 safety ledger p. 112

February 15, 1962 Lavender Pit Repair Shop
G.J. White punctured his right wrist.
1959-1961 safety ledger p. 184

January 13, 1974, Lavender Pit Repair Shop
J.H. Daniels was repairing the steering booster on a 65 ton dump truck. He had cleaned the parts in solvent. Daniels then went to turn off the bearing heating oven. The solvent on his shirt ignited. His left arm was burned. M.J. Benko witnessed the accident.
Phelps Dodge Corporation <u>Copper Queen Branch Accident Report</u> 1-13-74

February 2, 1974, Lavender Pit Repair Shop
E.G. Mendez was coming down from the upper dock at the service station. He fell and twisted his left ankle.
Phelps Dodge Corporation <u>Copper Queen Branch Accident Report</u> 2-5-74

May 8, 1974 Lavender Pit Repair Shop
E.J. Stukel was installing tracks on # 2 Caterpillar bulldozer at the Truck repair shop. He was installing the track on the left side. A come-along handle hit him in the nose. Stukel was cut under the nose. M.J. Benko and J.W. Finn witnesses the accident.
Phelps Dodge Corporation <u>Copper Queen Branch Accident Report</u> 5-8-74

Lowell Shaft. C-1908

Lowell Mine

The claims which eventually made up the Lowell Mine were located by W.S. Salmon in 1879. Salmon completed no work upon the claims other than the basic assessment. In February 1899, Frank Hanchett of Lowell Massachusetts purchased the property and started the Lowell & Arizona Copper Mining and Smelting Company. At this time Hanchett ordered a large amount of timber to construct buildings and a headframe. During March 1899, sinking began on the double compartment shaft that became known as the Lowell Mine. Work continued on rapidly and the two compartment shaft was 900 ft. deep. Water became problematic beyond the 1100 level. Originally, it was bailed by sinking bucket, but after W.L Clark of Butte, Montana, (not Senator W.A. Clark) took an option on the property he tried to acquire a pump. It did not arrive by the end of Clark's option. A newspaper reporter stated, *"As I came to the Lowell Shaft a bunch of miners came up so wet that moss was beginning to grow on their boots. They were wet on the outside and dry on the inside, but I could do nothing for them as I was dry on both sides. Judging from the size of the dump, I concluded that the shaft must be half way to China."* (A creative way of phrasing that the miners needed an alcoholic drink and the reporter had neither a bottle nor flask)

By October 1902, the Lowell Mine had come into possession of the Copper Queen Consolidated Mining Company. The new owners sank the shaft 30 ft. more and discovered an important orebody assuring the success of the mine. In 1903 a pump station was cut on the 1000 level and a third compartment was added to the shaft. A steel headframe was added in 1905 and a hoist taken from the Old Dominion mine at Globe, Arizona was installed. Soon after the Lowell Mine began to develop a tent community formed near the mine. This began to turn into the established town of Lowell. The Copper Queen Company decided that in 1906 that it would forfeit the $.50 land rent for homes and use the money to install a garbage collection and fire protection systems for the

313

town. The town would soon have a railroad depot, saloons, banks, stores, trolley cars and at least one brothel. In late 1909, the presence of a headless ghost began to be reported as haunting the mine. It was reported by a miner who found a man lying on a pile of timber. When he checked on him he discovered he was missing his head. Legends of this ghost were told decades later and even by the guides at the Queen Mine Tour. In 1910, the Sacramento Shaft replaced the Lowell as an ore hoisting shaft. At this time an incident occurred that reveals the difficulty in find ore in Bisbee. On the 800 level of the Lowell, lessees drove a drift searching for ore. They worked 35 days in the drift before they abandoned the area. Soon after, the drift began caving in and the collapse exposed a significant orebody just a short distance out of sight

A massive mine fire began during 1911. 1200-3 abandoned and gobbed stopes began burning in January causing initially little problems until drifts to the air raise to the surface venting the fire gasses caved. This forced fire gasses first to the 400 level and then to the 800 level. These gasses then vented through the main shaft. Originally, the sulfur dioxide levels were low and men were slowly hoisted through the gas flooded area of the shaft. Then the sulfur dioxide began destroying all steel components of the shaft such as the air and pump lines, hoisting cables and bolts for the guides. In October, the shaft became impassable from the 800 level to the surface and C.A. Mitzke was sent from Stag Canyon Fuel Company at Dawson New Mexico with Draeger helmets. These helmets allowed the shaft to be repaired and was operational by the end of December. At this time an underground precipitation plan was installed on the 1300 level. Water was sprayed into the fire zone on the 1100 and the copper rich water was collected on the 1300 in tubs of scrap iron and tin cans. Mine fires continued to be troublesome for years at the Lowell. Lessees focused on mining lead-silver-gold ores that could not be profitably smelted at Douglas were shipped by lessees to El Paso, Texas. One boulder of galena was broken up and filled one and one half mine cars.

With the start of the Sacramento Pit it became necessary for the Copper Queen Mine shops and warehouse to be moved. An area was cleared and the buildings constructed. A new change house was constructed in 1919 and a La France fire truck was purchased and station at the Lowell in 1921. Even with these improvements the end of the Lowell mine was insight. In 1926, the steel headframe was removed and installed at the Warren Shaft. Even without a headframe and the main shaft abandoned, mining continued in the Lowell Mine territory, but all materials and men were hoisted from the Sacramento Shaft and other mines. In 1929, the Lowell shaft pillar was mined. This action condemned the shaft from effectively being ever used as a hoisting shaft again. With the merger of the Calumet & Arizona Mining Company and Phelps Dodge, the Lowell Mine was closed and the change house was moved to the Campbell Mine. From 1935-1940, parts of the Lowell mined were leased and mined. After this point, any ore remaining in the former ground of the Lowell mine were mined through the Dallas Mine. In 1969, the dumps of the Lavender Pit covered the mine site. During the early years the Lowell shaft was sometimes called the Galena Shaft (not to be confused with the much newer Galena Shaft) or the Lowell and Arizona Mine. The mine reached a final depth of 1,603 ft. with three and one half compartments.

January 1, 1902, Lowell Mine

Charles Bolton and Frank Bandenberg were hit by a boulder of sulfide ore. Both men were taken to the hospital.

"Local Happenings in Brief" Bisbee Daily Review 4 January 1902 page 4

December 6, 1902, Lowell Mine

Loose rock caved-in on top of R.C. Coler inside a drift. The rock impacted his head and shoulders. He was dazed for a short time. After recovering, he walked to the shaft station and was taken to the surface. Coler reported to the physician's office. He was seen later the same day walking in town. It was felt he was fortunate, since if more of the rock had hit him, it could have given him a more significant injury.

"Painful Accident" Bisbee Daily Review 6 December 1902 page 6

January 9, 1903, Lowell Mine

Oscar Johnson and his brother Frank Johnson were working to enlarge the 1000 level station of the Lowell Shaft. They had completed about eighteen inches of digging when Frank left for a few minutes. When he returned, Oscar was covered by a couple of hundred pounds of dirt and a small boulder, except his head. Foreman Parker Woodman heard the collapse and came immediately to assist Frank. In minutes, they had uncovered Oscar, who told them he was alright, but his back was causing great pain. Oscar soon lost consciousness and was taken to the surface, where he regained his senses. At the Copper Queen Hospital, Dr. Sweet determined that he had suffered a broken back and collar bone. His skull was thought to be fractured. Foreman Woodman felt that Oscar must have been stooping over when the dirt hit him. The force of the impact threw him into a nearby post. The small boulder was believed to have caused the skull fracture and falling rock or impacting the post, broke his collar bone. A few days later he was recovering well. His nurse was impressed with him and stated *"He was one of the grittiest patients to have ever been brought to the hospital"* Both of the Johnson brothers were experienced miners and the accident was not to been caused by carelessness.

"Miner is Badly Injured" Bisbee Daily Review 10 January 1903 page 1
"Has Much Grit" Bisbee Daily Review 13 January 1903 page 8

October 2, 1903, Lowell Mine

On the 100 level, Joe Daily smashed his thumb on the drawhead of the cage. Dr. Baum at the Copper Queen Hospital amputated the damaged thumb.

"Joe Daily Lost Thumb" Bisbee Daily Review 3 October 1903 page 5

February, 1905, Lowell Mine

A miner with the surname McEthan boarded a cage to be lowered into the mine. The brake slipped on the hoist and the cage fell. The cage shot down the shaft 1,200 ft., passing all the levels and smashed through a bulkhead before landing in a water filled sump. In nothing less than a miracle, McEthan climbed out of the cage completely unharmed. Mine Superintendent Parker Woodman felt the hoistman had been able to slow the cage enough by carefully applying the brake on hoist. The cage was undamaged as well.

"Miner's Miraculous Escape" Arizona Silver Belt 9 February 1905 page 6

June 14, 1905, Lowell Mine

Two miners with the surnames of Miller and Carnell were caught in an explosion. The nature of the blast was not understood as both men were not able to discuss the events. Miller's thigh had a compound fracture as did Carnell's arm.

"Two Men Badly Hurt in the Lowell" Bisbee Daily Review 15 June 1905 page 5

October 6, 1906, Lowell Mine

Timberman, G.J. Perry was on the surface using a planer on a piece of timber. The machine threw the timber back and broke his nose and bruised his face.

"Hurt at Mine" Bisbee Daily Review 7, October 1906 page 35

December 1, 1906, Lowell Mine

Roy Dummond strain his back while lifting a boulder in a lower level. It was initially, thought Drummond needed an operation, but this was later dismissed.

"Injures Himself in Mine" <u>Bisbee Daily Review</u> 2 December 1906 page 5

December 18, 1906, Lowell Mine
Frank E. Billing was starting his first shift underground. He took the cage to the 1200 level, which was the wrong level. Billing got onto the cage for the dinky hoist with Mike Hannon and headed up to the 1100 level. At the 1100 level Hannon rung the bell for the 1000 level and told Billing that the men were waiting for him and asked him to release the cage after he got off. Somewhere on his journey up he was caught on the shaft timber and killed. The actual details are unknown as Billing was alone on the cage when he was killed. His right leg was broken multiple times and the bone had been splintered, and there were signs that he had received a strong blow over the heart. The accident occurred an hour after the shift had started and Billing had been underground around 15 minutes. He was initially reported to the newspaper as an unknown man as the timekeeper had several new men starting that shift and his paperwork had not been delivered to the mine. His body was shipped to Denver Colorado.
"Miner Killed at Lowell Shaft." <u>Bisbee Daily Review </u>19 December 1906 page 1
"Frank Billing was Name of Dead Miner" <u>Bisbee Daily Review </u>20 December 1906 page 8
"Two Funerals Held" <u>Bisbee Daily Review </u>22 December 1906 page 7

December 27, 1906, Lowell Mine
Frank Dorsey was on a lower level when he detected a small cave-in. As he turned to see what was happening when a rock struck him in the face. He was taken to the Copper Queen Hospital where he was treated for cuts on the chin and face. Dorsey was expected to return to work in a few days.
"Caught in Slight Cave-in" Bisbee Daily Review 28 December 1906 page 7

May 24, 1907, Lowell Mine
K.E. Stogdill was walking a drift and was not paying attention and fell into a manway. He dropped 50 ft. The miners nearby called for a cage and expected to recover only a body. Fortunately, Stogdhill only broke his left kneecap.
"Falls 50 Feet; Slightly Hurt" Bisbee Daily Review 25 May 1907 page 5

March 26, 1908, Lowell Mine
Roy G. Gardner was setting up a drill on his first shift underground and a small rock struck him on the head. The rock fractured his skull. He remained at the Copper Queen Hospital until April 6th, 1908. Gardner reported to work at the Lowell for one day. Then remained off work until April 14th. He quit on April 20th. After leaving the mines, he built himself a reputation as the *"Smiling Bandit"*. Eventually, he was caught and sent to prison. Gardner was represented by the media as a daring, handsome fellow. While in prison, he received hundreds of notes from admiring women. On September 5, 1921, he escaped from the McNeil Island Prison in Washington State. To escape, he ran away during a prison baseball game, but was hit in each leg by gunshots fired by the guards. His two accomplices were shot and fell. Wounded he hid in a barn and drank milk from a nearby herd of cows. After

five days he swam to the mainland. During his 23 days of freedom he called one of the women who sent him a letter in prison and met her, but said he was one of Gardner's friends. He had been serving a sentence for mail robbery. On November 16, 1921, Gardner learned that $15,000 was going to be sent by mail and tried robbing a mail car on Phoenix-Los Angles run of the Santa Fe Railroad, but was overpowered by a mail clerk. Earlier on November 3, he had taken sacks of mail from an Arizona Eastern Railroad mail car at Maricopa, Arizona. The money had in fact had been sent a night earlier than the robbery. Several girls attempted to visit Gardner in at the Maricopa County Jail, but only his wife, Florence was admitted. Marshall J.P. Dillion was surprised by her appearance, which was described as *"Mrs. Gardner is an unusually attractive and pretty blonde, but her features are regular and her complexion is of the real peaches-and-cream type. Her 24 years-five of which have been spent with Gardner-rest easily on her."* A cake, flowers and a fine meal were sent to the jail by admirers. During an interview, his wife stated that Gardner was *"a little over- balanced mentally."* Soon even the newspapers began to question his mental state. He filed an insanity plea stating that his insanity was a result of the mine accident. X-rays were taken of his head, and Copper Queen Hospital records were examined. The actual records note that a R.G. Gardner was carried from the Lowell mine suffering from a compressed fracture of the skull. He was released from the hospital on April 6, 1908. The X-rays taken by Dr. L.H. Goss of Phoenix revealed a bone scar that could be pressing on the brain. A well respected neurologist, Dr. Mary L. Neff agreed that Gardner suffered from insanity, but could not positive that the thickening of the healed bone had prevented him from differentiating between *"right and wrong."* On December 12, he withdrew his insanity plea and was sentence to 25 years and taken to Leavenworth, Kansas. In 1922, his wife wanted to pay for an operation on her husband to relieve the pressure of the bone on the brain. She had earned the money as a motion-picture actress "Dolly" Gardner. It is unknown whether the operation was ever completed. During his criminal career he stole $350,000 in cash and securities. Also he successfully escaped, four times and attempted two other times. In one attempted escape, he was digging a tunnel out of the Atlanta Prison. Gardner built an infamous reputation as a hardened criminal and a dangerous inmate. In 1934, he was moved to Alcatraz Prison. Where he remained until he was released in 1938. He tried to earn a living from his infamous exploits and wrote the book *"Helcatraz".* Two movies were made about his crimes, *"You Can't Beat the Rap".* and *"I Stole A Million"* in 1939. Gardner died in 1940.

Copper Queen Hospital Patients Register Jan 1, 1907 – Jun 30, 1908 Bisbee Mining and Historical Museum, Bisbee.
"Notorious Bandit Captured at Phoenix" Bisbee Daily Review 17 November 1921 page 1
"Roy Gardner" Bisbee Daily Review 17 November 1921 page 4
"Big Crowds Throng About Jail to See Noted Highwayman" Arizona Republican 17 November 1921 page 1
"Gardner Tells of His Travels since Escape" Arizona Republican 17 November 1921 page 8
"Gardner Declared a Fanatic Who Glories in Creating Sensations" Arizona Republican 18 November 1921 page 16
"Roy Gardner's Wife Here Says She Will "Stick"" Arizona Republican 20 November 1921 page 12
"Few Visitors Call on Bandit as Public Curiosity Dwindles"" Arizona Republican 20 November 1921 page 12
"Court Rebukes Famous Bandit for Insolence" Bisbee Daily Review 8 December 1921 page 4
"Alienists Tell Jury Gardner is Unbalanced" Arizona Republican 9 December 1921 page 2
"Gardner Changes Plea to Guilty; Given 25 Years Bisbee Daily Review 13December 1921 page 1

**Roy G. Gardner at San Quentin Prison c-1911 and Dolly Gardner in the
Washington Times, November 18, 1921**

September 9, 1908, Lowell Mine

John Morgan fell five sets and was seriously bruised. He was taken to the Copper Queen
Hospital.

"Hurt by Fall" Bisbee Daily Review 10 September 1908 page 5

March 14, 1909, Lowell Mine

Walter F. Dykeman was being raised on a cage with a few pieces of lagging from the 1200
level. Near the 800 level, the lagging became caught on the shaft timber. When the cage
reached the surface, Dykeman was discovered to be horribly mutilated. His right foot had
been torn off and the bones in the leg crushed, and his side was smashed in. Dykeman was
rushed to the hospital, but he died soon after arriving. Only one two foot piece of lagging
was found caught in the shaft. The rest must have fallen into the sump. When Albert Wittig
went down the shaft the next day, he found only two marks on the shaft timber six sets and
the one short lagging. There was timber floating in the sump, but it was impossible to tell
how old it was. The 29-year-old's parents* lived in Nova Scotia, he was related to A.M.
Colwell of Lowell, Arizona. * The inquest stated that his parents were dead, but inquest are sometimes not as accurate as
newspapers in these details.

"Caught in Cage Miner is Killed" Bisbee Daily Review 16 March 1909 page 5

"Bisbee-Lowell Evergreen Cemetery." My Cochise.

http://www.mycochise.com/cembisbeepq.php (April 16 2011)

"Cochise County Coroner's Inquest No.629 Arizona State Archives Phoenix

June 1, 1909 Lowell Mine

A rock fell on the left leg and foot of W.E. Mullen. He was treated at the Copper Queen Hospital and released on June 29th. Mullen was original from New Orleans.

"Rock Crushed Foot" Bisbee Daily Review 2 June 1909 page 7
Copper Queen Hospital Patients Register June 1, 1909 Bisbee Mining and Historical Museum, Bisbee.

December 1, 1909, Lowell Mine

A.L. Annis was caught in a cave-in and the falling rock and fractured vertebrae. He was taken to the Copper Queen Hospital by the Palace Ambulance. He remained in the hospital until January 7, 1910.

"Slightly Injured" Bisbee Daily Review 2 December 1909 page 8
"Injured by Cave in" Bisbee Daily Review 2 December 1909 page 8
(Both articles are on the same newspaper page)
Copper Queen Hospital Patients Register July 1, 1908 – Dec. 31, 1909 Bisbee Mining and Historical Museum, Bisbee.

March 19, 1910, Lowell Mine

Finlander, Peter Hirgo was knocked unconscious by gasses* He was taken to the hospital where he was revived and later sent home.

 *Probably it was powder gasses which are produced by blasting, less likely, but possible it could have been gasses from a mine fire.
"Injured by Fall Mine Shaft." Bisbee Daily Review 20 March 1910 page 5
Copper Queen Hospital Patients Register March 19, 1910 Bisbee Mining and Historical Museum, Bisbee.

April 13, 1910, Lowell Mine

On a lower level in the Lowell shaft, a misfired charge was buried and forgotten. Frank Edwards (Gordeau*) began digging with a pick when the powder detonated. The flying rock cut him and partially buried him. One eye was damaged, and it was felt that it might be lost. Also one leg was cut up and broken. There was a concern, whether the leg would need to be amputated. The leg was saved, and he was released from the Copper Queen Hospital on May 20.

"Miner is Mangled by Buried Shot" Bisbee Daily Review 15 April 1910 page 5
Copper Queen Hospital Patients Register April 13, 1910 Bisbee Mining and Historical Museum, Bisbee.

June 4, 1910, Lowell Mine

Hugh Jones* was killed in a premature explosion. Jones had drilled five holes in a drift and had loaded most of them. He was tamping the dynamite in one of the lifters. A hole detonated. Only one hole exploded, and that detonated with enough force to break the ten-inch by ten-inch post next to him in half. This also gave evidence that he must have been stooping down as the miners believe he would have been cut in half if he was standing. He was so badly mutilated by the blast it was challenging to identify the 24 -year-old. Foreman Mike Hannon, had the drift cleaned up carefully after the accident. The miner doing this work suspected there could be blasting caps in the debris from the explosion. The pieces of unburned fuse that were found, were tested to see if the burned normally. They did, and a *"fast fuse"* was eliminated as being a cause of the explosion. Hannon felt that maybe Jones had caused the explosion with his candle. According to the newspaper Jones had written to his mother stating that he intended to return to his home in Missouri. * The name on the Inquest is Evart Jones, but later refers to him as H. Jones.

"Explosion Kills Miner at Bisbee" El Paso Herald 7 June 1910 page 4
"Original Certificate of Death." Arizona Department of Health Services. http://genealogy.az.gov/azdeath/009/10090295.pdf (July 24, 2011)
"Cochise County Coroner's Inquest No.751Arizona State Archives Phoenix

June 17, 1910, Lowell Mine

On his first shift at the Lowell Mine, Joseph Kultanen*, a 25 -year-old Finnish miner was working with John Richards, Bob Lucas, George Hunn, Ben Matson, William Whalen, Robert Mallory and George Simpson in a 13-1-3 stope on the 1300 level. Around 1:00 am, he needed to remove one boulder, to install timber. After lunch, he tried to remove the rock with a pick and the slab fell and smashed him to the ground. Death was nearly immediate. He was a recent resident to Arizona and had been there about three months. The deceased was survived by a wife and child in Finland. His wife's address in Finland was Uusi Kirkko, Asema. Pamppala, Finland. *It was noted in the inquest that Kultanen had and extremely limited knowledge of English.

"Accident Verdict Kultanen" Bisbee Daily Review 18 June 1910 page 4
"Miner Killed at Lowell at One' Clock" Bisbee Daily Review 17 June 1910 page 1
"Funeral Held Today" Bisbee Daily Review 19 June 1910 page 5
"Original Certificate of Death." Arizona Department of Health Services http://genealogy.az.gov/azdeath/009/10090316.pdf (April 2, 2011)
"Cochise County Coroner's Inquest No.754Arizona State Archives Phoenix

July 1910, Lowell Mine

Joe Eldon was injured by a cave-in and taken to the hospital.

"Several Miners Slightly Injured in Bisbee Shafts" El Paso Herald 16 July 1910 page 3

July 1, 1910, Lowell Mine

J.E. Lockwood had his foot badly smashed. By July 17th he was seen around Bisbee on crutches.

"Around on Crutches" Bisbee Daily Review 17 July 1910 page 5

September 3, 1910, Lowell Mine *

English Miner, Thomas Taylor was crushed by a falling rock. John Rainey thought that Taylor was trying to knock down a boulder with a pick. The rock fell striking him and breaking the lagging he was standing on. When the lagging broke, Taylor fell four feet to the set below. It initially appeared that a foot was his most critical injury. By September 9, Taylor's condition worsened and on the 11th he died from broken ribs and internal bleeding. The 35-year-old miner was buried in Evergreen Cemetery. He was survived by a wife and two boy's one ten and the other 14 years old in Pennington, England.

*The Bisbee Daily review states the mine was the Holbrook Shaft.

"Injured by Cave-in" Bisbee Daily Review 4 September 1910 page 5
"Jealousy Causes Killing" El Paso Herald 14 September 1910 page 2
"Original Certificate of Death." Arizona Department of Health Services. http://genealogy.az.gov/azdeath/009/10091070.pdf (July 24, 2011
Copper Queen Hospital Patients Register Sept. 10, 1910 Bisbee Mining and Historical Museum, Bisbee.
"Cochise County Coroner's Inquest No.780 Arizona State Archives Phoenix

November 7, 1910, Lowell Mine

Irishman, James Jennings was caught in a collapse of ground. The falling rock exposed the bone of his skull in a small area, tore off part of his nose and fractured his frontal bone. The right eye had been punctured by rock particles. He was transported to the Copper Queen Hospital in an unconscious state. He recovered at the hospital. It was felt he may lose sight in his right eye.

"Miner is Injured by Falling Rocks" Bisbee Daily Review 8 November 1910 page 8
Copper Queen Hospital Patients Register Nov. 7, 1910, Bisbee Mining and Historical Museum, Bisbee.

January 12, 1911 Lowell Mine

Thirty-four-year-old, Irish Miner John P. Boyle was working with his partner Matthews in a stope on the 1200 level.   A previous round that had been shot had destroyed a cap (timber). Boyle's partner climbed to the level to get a new timber. Around 1:00 pm, just before sending down the new cap Matthews called down notifying Boyle's the timber was coming down. *"All right."* replied Boyle *"I am ready." "Those were the last words which Boyle uttered before he was killed. Almost at the same instant, it must have been, he was called into eternity and the answer so closely did his death follow his words" "I am ready."* Matthews climbed down after the timber and found his partner sitting on a block with his head in his hands. He soon discovered his partner was dead. The cause of death was a matter of debate. He had a minor wound on the top of his head and bruising on his right shoulder, right leg and forehead. This gave the impression that he had been thrown to the ground. The wound that killed him was triangular and continued into the skull and was located at the base of his nose. A pick with a bloody point was found in the area. This developed into the theory that he had accidently killed himself while using a pick. It was felt by others that a falling rock had caused the fatal wound. His death certificate hints that there were still people not convinced of the manner of Boyle's death. Justice of the Peace, Owen Murphy held the inquest for the accident and wrote on the death certificate *"Killed accidently supposed by fall of rock in Lowell shaft of C.Q.C.M.C Lowell A.T."* Before coming to Bisbee, Boyle had left Ireland to become a miner in the Transvaal. He was in South Africa when the Boer war broke out, and Boyle joined the Dutch to fight against the British under General Piet Cronje. After the Boer's had lost the war, he left for America and eventual made his way to Bisbee, where he was for a time before his death a foreman at the Lowell Mine. When the belongings of the deceased were examined letters to his mother in Ireland and a brother, Peter Boyle in Philadelphia were found. His brother was notified by telegram, and it was arranged that Boyle would be buried in Evergreen Cemetery. Peter Boyle requested that a letter be sent to him giving the full details of his brother's death.

"Meets Death far from His Loved Irish Home" Bisbee Daily Review 13 January 1911 page 1
"Boyle, Dead Miner is to Rest Here" Bisbee Daily Review 14 January 1911 page 5
"Original Certificate of Death." Arizona Department of Health Services. http://genealogy.az.gov/azdeath/009/10091983.pdf (June 6, 2012)

February 1911, Lowell Mine

S.S. White, a cousin of Captain John Greenway Manager of the Calumet & Arizona Mining Company, was injured when his leg was smashed. He was cared for at the Greenway residence.

"Will Stop Night Work" <u>El Paso Herald</u> 3 February 1911 page 3

February 19, 1911, Lowell Mine

An argument began underground the Lowell mine between Tom Carter and A. Oddo* over the placement of a set of timber. Oddo a large German ended up holding down the Carter, a relatively small man. At this point, Carter took his miner's candlestick and stabbed Oddo twice. One puncture penetrated just below Oddo's heart and the other pierced right above it. Oddo was taken to the Copper Queen Hospital. Initially, Tom Carter was arrested and was eventually charged with *"assault with intent to murder."* On February 21, Tom Carter posted a $1000.00 bond and was released. Around February 25 in the court of Judge Owen Murphy, the charges against Carter were dropped. It was decided that the assault was self-defense. Oddo was released from the hospital after three days. * Also spelled as Otto

"Candlestick used with Serious Effect" <u>Bisbee Daily Review</u> 21 February 1911 page 8

"Carter is Released on Bond of $1000. 00" <u>Bisbee Daily Review</u> 22 February 1911 page 5

"Carter is Acquitted" <u>Bisbee Daily Review</u> 26 February 1911 page 5

Copper Queen Hospital Patients Register Feb. 19, 1911, Bisbee Mining and Historical Museum, Bisbee.

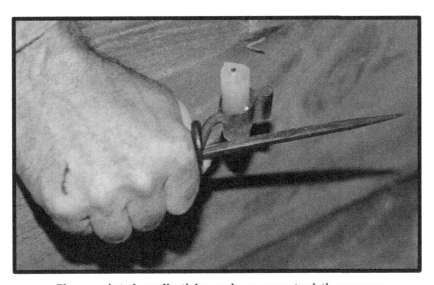

Sharp-pointed candlesticks made an opportunistic weapons.

February 20, 1911, Lowell Mine

A miner was carrying a case of dynamite and accidently dropped it down the Lowell Shaft. The case fell 259 ft. It landed on a station where the wooden case burst part near men waiting for the cage. The dynamite did not explode.* No one was injured or killed only startled.

*Actually, dynamite is difficult to detonate without a blasting cap and these men would have likely known this. But it still would have been unsettling.

"Dynamite Fails and Men Escape" El Paso Herald 20 February 1911 page 6

April 8, 1911, Lowell Mine

Pat O'Donnelly was taken to the Copper Queen Hospital around 2:00 pm after his leg suffered a compound fracture.

"Miner Injured" Bisbee Daily Review 9 April 1909 page 7

November 20, 1911, Lowell Mine

Austrian Miner, John Mukavoc* was going off shift and had been hoisted up to the 1000 level of the Lowell Shaft, from there he was with a group of men without lights ** headed to the 1000 level Gardner shaft. At the Gardner, these men were to be hoisted to the surface. About, 100 ft. from the 1000 level Lowell station Mukavoc was seen contacting a 220 volt wire***then falling. This wire must have had a section of wire exposed through the insulation. Mukavoc died as he was rushed to the surface. He was 36 years old when he died with a wife and three children in Austria. A few days after his death it was learned he had taken out three insurance policies a $800.00 policy with a group in Calumet Michigan, $ 1,000.00 with the Austrian Society of Philadelphia and $2,000.00 with miner's insurance association in Bisbee. These totaled a value of 19,000 Austrian Krones a small fortune. He was buried in Evergreen Cemetery.

*His name was spelled Mukavac, Mukavov, Vukavec, Mukayec and Mukavec in The Bisbee Daily Review articles.

**The 1000 level was a haulage level and would have likely been illuminated by electric light bulbs hanging every couple hundred feet. The distance between the Lowell and Gardner shafts was around 2,000 ft. along the haulage drift. It would have been difficult keep their candles lit while traveling in this drift and walk quickly.

***The wire was not a trolley wire, which are bare copper. Fatal Accidents involving trolley wire from 1908-1914 were published in Gerald Sherman's "Tramming and Hoisting at The Copper Queen Mine"

A fire had broken out in abandoned square set stope between the 1000 and 1200 levels of the mine. The Lowell shaft at this time was exhausting fire gasses from the 800 level to the surface. For a time, the shaft was used to service levels below the 800 level. Later an air shaft was driven to ventilate the fire gasses, and the entire length of the Lowell shaft was used again.

"Touches Power Wire and Dies of Shock" Bisbee Daily Review 21 November 1911 page 5

"He Left a Fortune to Austrian Family" Bisbee Daily Review 26 November 1911 page 2

"Working for Safety" Bisbee Daily Review 22 November 1911 page4

Gerald F. G. Sherman. "Tramming and Hoisting at the Copper Queen Mine." American Institute of Mining Engineers Transaction Volume LII 1916: Page 465.

"Cochise County Inquest No. 877" Arizona State Archives

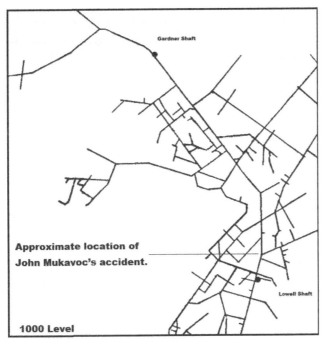

Map of the 1000 level

The electrically lit, Queen Tunnel. This amount of illumination is about the same amount Mukovac would have had during his walk from the Lowell to the Gardner Shaft.

November 30, 1911, Lowell Mine

John Regnier boarded the middle deck of a cage on the 1200 level. As the cage approached the 1100 level, he became caught on the shaft timber. When the cage stopped on the 1100 level, he fell dead onto the station. It is possible that Regnier fainted.

"Regnier Funeral Today" Bisbee Daily Review 2 December 1912 page 8
"Original Certificate of Death." Arizona Department of Health Services.
http://genealogy.az.gov/azdeath/007/10071212.pdf (June 22, 2015)
"Cochise County Coroner's Inquest No. 707" Arizona State Archives Phoenix

June 17, 1912, Lowell Mine

A 19-year-old Swede named Edward Johnson* and Andrew Beckman were working in 14-9 stope on the 1400 level. The ground was soft and heavy. Regular drills could not be used and augers were used, to drill blast holes. The stope was strongly and closely timbered. Johnson was caught in a cave-in in at 8:30 pm. Initially, it was not believed he was seriously injured, but Johnson asked that his brothers in Wilkerson, Washington be informed. It was later learned that one brother, Richard Johnson was in Alaska. He was taken by ambulance to the Copper Queen Hospital, but he died before he could be taken into the accident ward at the hospital. It is believed he died from internal injuries from a crushed chest, since the external injuries bruising and a broken right leg were not severe enough to kill him. He was an unmarried man was buried in Evergreen Cemetery.

*Three Edward Johnsons died in Bisbee mine accidents in a one year period. The others were Edward Johnson also Swedish, Dec.27 1913 Briggs Shaft and Edward Johnson from Finland, August 17, 1912 in the Oliver Shaft.
"Miner Dies from Hurts at Cave-in" Bisbee Daily Review 18 June 1912 page 3
"Johnson Funeral Today" Bisbee Daily Review 20 June 1912 page 6
"Original Certificate of Death." Arizona Department of Health Services.
http://genealogy.az.gov/azdeath/010/10100927.pdf (April 22, 2011)
"Cochise County Coroner's Inquest No. 931 Arizona State Archives Phoenix

June 19, 1912, Lowell Mine

At 1 o'clock in the morning, E.R. Miller received a scalp wound and a sprained ankle in a cave-in. He was taken to the Copper Queen Hospital

"Miner is Injured" Bisbee Daily Review 20 June 1912 page 6
Hospital Patients Copper Queen Register June 19 1912 Bisbee Mining and Historical Museum, Bisbee.

August 22, 1912 Lowell Mine

August Kauffman had his foot crushed when a mine car overturned and landed on it.

Two Miners Hurt" Bisbee Daily Review 23 August 1912 page 8

September 24, 1912 Lowell Mine

W.E. Cason received a bruised back while working. He remained at the Copper Queen Hospital five days.

"Personal Mention" Bisbee Daily Review 25 September 1912 page 8
Hospital Patients Copper Queen Register Sept. 24, 1912 Bisbee Mining and Historical Museum, Bisbee.

October 10, 1912, Lowell Mine

At 11:00 pm, Chris Marshall was injured, when he fell in the Lowell Mine. Marshall was the half-brother of the mine superintendent for the Copper Queen, Captain Joseph P. Hodgson.

"Chris Marshall Injured" Bisbee Daily Review 11 October 1912 page 3

February, 12, 1913, Lowell Mine

Belgian Miner, Oscar Rufflager attacked Willard Robinson with a miner's candlestick. Robinson then struck Rufflager with a shovel possibly breaking ribs. Rufflager was released from the Copper Queen Hospital after six days.

"Injured in Fight" Bisbee Daily Review 15 February 1913 page 6
Hospital Patients Copper Queen Register Feb. 12, 1913, Bisbee Mining and Historical Museum, Bisbee.

March 6, 1913, Lowell Mine

At 7:00 pm, Ruford Powell fell 35 feet off a ladder. He was taken to the Copper Queen Hospital and released the next day.

"Miner Hurt" Bisbee Daily Review 8 March 1913 page 6

April 19, 1913 Lowell Mine

Stanley Hunter was taken to the Copper Queen Hospital after receiving powder burns from a blast. He remained at the hospital five days and was released in "improved" condition.

(Note, this is likely the same person as Mark Stanley Hunter, who was killed in the Southwest Mine on October 26, 1923.)
Hospital Patients Copper Queen Register Apr 19, 1913 Bisbee Mining and Historical Museum, Bisbee.

February 5, 1914, Lowell Mine

Bohemian Miner, Dan Radix broke his right leg in an undescribed mine accident. He remained in the hospital until April 6.

"Miner Injured" Bisbee Daily Review 6 February 1914 page 6
Hospital Patients Copper Queen Register Feb. 5, 1914 Bisbee Mining and Historical Museum, Bisbee.

June 8, 1914, Lowell Mine

John Cone broke his leg in an undescribed accident. Records indicate that he spent 198 days in the Copper Queen Hospital and was released in improved condition. (Note, the hospital records indicate he was an employee in the Sacramento Mine, but he could have been working in the Lowell Mine at the time of the accident)

"Has Leg Broken" Bisbee Daily Review 9 June 1914 page 8
Hospital Patients Copper Queen Register June 8, 1914 Bisbee Mining and Historical Museum, Bisbee.

July 17, 1915, Lowell Mine

Mule Driver, James Hudnell broke a finger when it was caught between the timber and a mine car. (Note, he was also injured on December 26, 1916 at the Lowell Mine.)

"Hudnell Breaks Finger" Bisbee Daily Review 18, July 1915 page 6

August 17, 1915, Lowell Mine

Pipefitter, Burt Purnell and his partner Albert Des Sulles* were severely burned when hot oil exploded. Both men were treated at a hospital and released home.

*Des Sulles is likely the author of "An Arizona Ranger" published in 1906
"Burned in Mine" <u>Bisbee Daily Review</u> 18, August 1915 page 6

February?, 1916, Lowell Mine

J.G. Sutherland had a piece of steel imbedded in his eye from an undescribed accident. The steel was removed at a hospital in Phoenix.

"Prompt Recovery" <u>Bisbee Daily Review</u> 17, February 1916 page 8

February 15, 1916, Lowell Mine

Norman *"Heavy"* Craig a motor swamper had his foot run over by a mine car. Suffered a bruised foot and remained at the Copper Queen Hospital until March 5th.

"Has Foot Injured" <u>Bisbee Daily Review</u> 16 February 1916 page 6
Hospital Patients Copper Queen Register February 15, 1916 Bisbee Mining and Historical Museum, Bisbee

May 10, 1916, Lowell Mine

Hamilton E. Sellers was caught in a cave-in. Sellers was treated at the Copper Queen Hospital until May 29. He suffered only a bruised back.

"Injured in Mine" <u>Bisbee Daily Review</u> 11, May 1916 page 8
Hospital Patients Copper Queen Register May 10, 1916 Bisbee Mining and Historical Museum, Bisbee.

December 26, 1916, Lowell Mine

Mule driver, James Hudnell nearly tore the nail off his big toe in an undescribed accident.

Note, James Hudnell and his cousin "Blondy" Wilson represented Bisbee at the "Mule Skinner's" contest and the 1915. Panama –Pacific International Exposition in San Francisco They did not win, but enjoyed themselves. Later, the newspaper described him as the *"underground traffic expert and social lion of the Lowell Mine force."*
"Hudnell Hurt" <u>Bisbee Daily Review</u> 27, December1916 page 8
"Hudnell in Mule Skinners Contest" <u>Bisbee Daily Review</u> 10, August 1915 page 3
"Jimmie Hudnell Back" <u>Bisbee Daily Review</u> 26, July 1917 page 8

June-July? 1917, Lowell Mine

George Ordonyon was injured at the mine

"Weekly News Letter Young Men's Christian Association of Warren Mining District" <u>Bisbee Daily Review</u> 1 May1917 Mining Section, page 3

September 8, 1918, Lowell Mine

At 10:00 am, Thomas J. Compton was caught in a collapse on a lower level. He died from internal injuries. Compton had recently arrived in Bisbee from Whitehead, Texas. He was survived by a wife, four small children and a cousin, Reverend Compton. (No inquest could be located)

"Injuries (sic) are probably (sic) Fatal" <u>Bisbee Daily Review</u> 9 September 1918 page 8
Office of State Mine Inspector. *Seventh Annual Report of the State Mine Inspector State of Arizona for the Year Ending November 30, 1918.*
"Original Certificate of Death." <u>Arizona Department of Health Services.</u> http://genealogy.az.gov/azdeath/018/10181238.pdf (May 28, 2012)

November 6, 1918, Lowell Mine

B.P. Andrews had his leg crushed in a collapse. He was taken to the Copper Queen Hospital.

"Taken to Hospital" Bisbee Daily Review 8 November 1918 page 6

January 18, 1919, Lowell Mine

Around 10:30 pm, Charles R. Brandon was working at a chute when he heard a 200 lb. boulder roll. He moved, but the rock smashed his foot. He was taken to the Calumet and Arizona Hospital where two x-rays were taken. His foot was not broken.

"Injures Foot" Bisbee Daily Review 10 January 1919 page 8

March 7, 1923, Lowell Mine 1000 level

Frank Blackburn received minor injuries when he was struck by buried by ground. Miners nearby freed him quickly. He was treated at a hospital.

"Cave-in Catches Man at Lowell Shaft, Rescued" Bisbee Ore 7 March 1923 page 1

Manganese workings on the Twilight Claim

Manganese Workings

These are a number of small pits and underground workings that are scattered throughout the Warren Mining District. They were typically operated during the World Wars. The largest manganese mines were located on the Twilight and No.4 claims

August 11, 1917, Manganese workings of Calumet & Arizona Mining Company

Benito Garcia had his arm broken when a fly rock from a blast hit him. He stayed at the Calumet & Arizona Hospital until August 17, 1917.

"Calumet & Arizona Hospital Records." My Cochise.

http://www.mycochise.com/hospcalfl2go.php (June 2, 2012)

Office of State Mine Inspector. *Sixth Annual Report of the State Mine Inspector State of Arizona for the Year Ending November 30, 1917.*

August 6, 1918, Manganese workings above Cole Shaft

Juan Rodriguez had drilled a hole and the drill steel had become stuck. Unknown to him he had drilled into a missed hole from a couple of days previous, but it did not detonate. Reyes Somosa went to get a Stillson wrench to help get the drill steel out. While he was gone, Rodriguez kept trying to get the steel out, and the hole detonated. The blast cut up his chest and face, killing him. He was 37 years old and was survived by family in Tintown.

"Killed by Blast" Tombstone Epitaph 11 August 1918 page 2

Dugan Mortuary Records July 19, 1918 – March 27, 19206 Accession 2010.10.14 Bisbee Mining and Historical Museum, Bisbee.

Office of State Mine Inspector. *Seventh Annual Report of the State Mine Inspector State of Arizona for the Year Ending November 30, 1918.*

"Cochise County Coroner's Inquest No. 1346" Arizona State Archives Phoenix

Nighthawk Mine

Development of this mine largely occurred after the Nighthawk Leasing Company was formed on March 27, 1917. This company soon sank the 1 ½ compartment shaft to a depth of 380ft.* Early work, focused on the upper levels, since that is where the nearby White Tailed Deer mine had been successful. During 1919, work was mainly on the 450 level, but in March of 1920 the shaft was sunk from the 650 level to the 750 level. At this time the 650 level was the major ore producing level. The ores were generally oxides and in September a large orebody of azurite was hit 250 ft. east of the shaft on the 650 level. In May of 1921, an orebody of sulphide ore was struck on the Boras Leasing Company and Nighthawk Leasing Company sideline. The orebody was unexpectedly struck while the Nighthawk Company was sinking a winze on the 650 level to connect to the Boras 700 level for ventilation and as an escapeway. Mining continued until around 1930. During the mid-1930s the mine was reactivated, but was unsuccessful and the mine was finally closed around 1938. The shaft attained a final depth of 749 ft. with one and one half compartments.

June 7, 1923, Nighthawk Mine

Felipe Ybarra, a 46-year-old Mexican miner, was delivering blasting caps and fuse to miners, while he was waiting on a level and it is believed he decided to smoke. After he lit his pipe, hot ashes the fell into a tin of blasting caps. The resulting explosion blew off both of his hands and blinded him. The other miners were not initially concerned by the sound of the detonation. They were working close to the Boras Mine and often heard blasts from the Boras. As he was being transported Ybarra told Alberto Acosto *"I die with fire."** Ybarra died at the Copper Queen Hospital.*Note that Spanish was the language typically spoken at the Nighthawk Mine, and this is likely a translation

"Explosion Today Takes Hands off Mexican, Dies" Bisbee Ore 7 June 1923 page 1

"Original Certificate of Death." Arizona Department of Health Services. http://genealogy.az.gov/azdeath/027/10270502.pdf (October 25, 2012)

Office of State Mine Inspector. *Fourteenth Annual Report of the State Mine Inspector State of Arizona for the Year Ending November 30, 1923.* Tombstone Epitaph.

"Cochise County Coroner's Inquest No.1514" Arizona State Archives Phoenix

A tin containing blasting caps.

July 15, 1923, Nighthawk Mine

Miguel Esquibel was carrying a stoper (drill) in a stope. Manuel Gutierrez was working above him and saw some oxide boulders start to fall and yelled out *"Cuidado Abajo"* or look out below Esquibel was struck by a boulder. The rock broke his neck and crushed his chest. His left thigh was also broken. As he was taken to the hospital he commented that this was the first time he had been hurt in all of his years of mining. He died on July 16 in the hospital, and was survived by his father, Antonio Esquibel.

"Mexican Dies This Morning from Injuries, Dies" <u>Bisbee Ore</u> 16 July 1923 page 1
"Original Certificate of Death." <u>Arizona Department of Health Services.</u> http://genealogy.az.gov/azdeath/027/10270960.pdf (October 25, 2012)
Office of State Mine Inspector. *Fourteenth Annual Report of the State Mine Inspector State of Arizona for the Year Ending November 30, 1923*. Tombstone Epitaph.
"Cochise County Coroner's Inquest No.1521" Arizona State Archives Phoenix

July 5, 1924, Nighthawk mine

An unnamed miner had his finger cut by a saw.

Office of State Mine Inspector. *Thirteenth Annual Report of the State Mine Inspector State of Arizona for the Year Ending November 30, 1924*.

November 1, 1927, Nighthawk Mine

Sebastian Corona had spent one hour trying to bar down a four-ton boulder, and it would not fall. Giving up, he decided to start moving out ore, and the rock fell crushing him. He suffered a broken right tibia, a compound fracture of the left femur and cuts around the head. As he was transported to the hospital, he kept saying *"Idios Marita."* Corona died at the Calumet & Arizona Hospital at around 7:00 pm.

"Original Certificate of Death." Arizona Department of Health http://genealogy.az.gov/azdeath/035/10352495.pdf (May 31, 2012)

Office of State Mine Inspector. *Sixteenth Annual Report of the State Mine Inspector State of Arizona for the Year Ending November 30, 1927.*

Dugan Mortuary Records June 23, 1926 – September 9, 1928, Accession 2010.10.19 Bisbee Mining and Historical Museum, Bisbee.

"Cochise County Coroner's Inquest No.1663" Arizona State Archives Phoenix

Oliver Mine, c-1914

Oliver Mine

Often overshadowed by its nearby sister mine the Irish Mag, this important mine was started in 1903. By the end of the following year stations had been cut on the 850, 950, 1050, 1100 and 1150 levels. Abundant ore had been discovered during the first two years of operation, so in 1905 a steel headframe was erected over the shaft and a tunnel was driven to the shaft from the surface at the 20 ft. level. This adit was used to bring in timber and bring out waste rock. (Later, waste rock was hoisted directly out of the main shaft to the toplander's deck for dumping.) Cars of ore being hoisted were brought to the toplander's deck on the headframe and pushed across the trestle to the ore bins.

In 1910 the heavy and caving ground resulted in the mining of the main orebodies to be put on hold and only quickly mineable ore was removed. At this time it was also, necessary to retimber the shaft. Three crews worked to exchange the rotted timbers for new at a rate of seven sets every 24 hours. The retimbering was from the 950-750 levels and from the 400 level to the surface. Essential supplies and men for the Oliver were lowered down the Irish Mag for the two weeks while this was being accomplished. During the following year the 1200 level was driven over from the Hoatson Mine. After reaching a position under the Oliver Shaft, a raise was driven into the bottom of the Oliver Shaft deepening it to the 1600 level. Although, the company attempted to mine the fire zone between the 1050 and 1150 levels near the Irish Mag from the Oliver. The fire gasses prevented the mining of the fire zone.

By 1914, ore was becoming difficult to find in the Oliver and both electric locomotives were removed from the workings. For its remaining years of operation by the Calumet & Arizona Mining Company was limited to the Oliver's upper levels and areas near the Irish Mag. Generally, these last years were mining scraps of ore surrounding stopes that had been largely depleted. On February 5, 1919, the Oliver was shut down leaving only some reserves of low grade ore in place. The condition of the shaft was becoming problematic and by 1920 the hoist and headframe were badly out of level due to mining subsidence. The mine was later worked by lessees who mined intermittently until 1941, when the mine was permanently shut down. The shaft reached a final depth of 1,447 ft. and had four compartments.

April 18, 1904, Oliver Mine

Owen Murphy was struck by a falling rock. The impact broke his leg below the knee. John Bowen of the Palace Livery Stable was sent to take, Murphy to the Calumet & Arizona Hospital.

"Injured at Oliver" Bisbee Daily Review 19 April 1904 page 5

July 8, 1904, Oliver Mine

A resident of the Blair House, John Swanson was working cutting a new shaft station on the 1000 level. At the same time, E.A. Hodge was loading a full mine car onto the cage, and the landing chairs slipped. The dropped the cage about four inches. This caused ore to spill into the shaft. Hodge called down to warn the men. Swanson and his James Flannigan heard the call, and Swanson came up in a sinking bucket to the 900 level to see what was wrong. He saw the mine car and asked Hodge they could lift it up. They were unable to, so Swanson decided to use the cage to raise the car, which was half on and half off the cage. They had the hoistman raise the cage slowly. It appears that Swanson was on the cage and Hodge was on the station and as the cage rose it struck something. This knocked Swanson and some rock into the shaft. He fell to the 1000 level, which was the bottom of the shaft.* Swanson was buried in Evergreen Cemetery.

*The newspaper article and the inquest are poorly written this is an interpretation of the accident

"Swanson falls to Instant Death" Bisbee Daily Review 9 July 1904 page 5

"Cochise County Coroner's Inquest No.248" Arizona State Archives Phoenix

August 17, 1904, Oliver Mine

John L. Casey was smashed between a sinking bucket being raised and a column for mounting a drill. He was cut up and had his jaw broken. (It appears he was employed in sinking the shaft. or possibly sinking a winze.)

"Danger Considered Over" Bisbee Daily Review 19 August 1904 page 5

January 4, 1905, Oliver Mine

A new miner to Bisbee, William A. Queen was killed on his second day of work at the Oliver Mine. Queen and his partner were working in a stope. His partner left and then a slab fell pinning Queen to the ground. Joseph Scrugham nearby heard him moaning and found him trapped under the rock. He was unable to lift the boulder off of Queen. The injured miner told him to break up the soft rock with a pick. He was removed to the Calumet & Arizona Hospital* where he died at 3:00 am on January 5. The deceased was 40 years old and from Granite, Montana. He was buried in Evergreen Cemetery. He was survived by a brother in Queens Bridge, West Virginia and a wife. * The hospital records give his name as George Queen. Hospitals often had difficulty getting information from injured patients this would be likely if he arrived comatose and, of course, he was new to Bisbee.

"Death by Accident" Bisbee Daily Review 7 January 1904 page 5
"Bisbee-Lowell Evergreen Cemetery." My Cochise.
http://www.mycochise.com/cembisbeepq.php (May 22, 2012)
"Calumet & Arizona Hospital Records." My Cochise. http://www.mycochise.com/hospcaldied.php (May 22, 2012)
"Cochise County Coroner's Inquest No.246" Arizona State Archives Phoenix

January 21, 1905, Oliver Mine

Nicholas Vuckovich, Edward Walsh and Norman McKinsey were cleaning up muck on the west side of the shaft on the 1100 level. The shaft was undergoing repairs and the previous shift had been repairing shaft guides and the shaft was left open. Vuckovich went to get a pick and a shovel and tried to jump across the shaft and grab a guide and pull himself to the work area. He missed and fell to a bulkhead about five sets above the 1200 level. D. Eyster was on the 1200 level standing on a sinking bucket when he heard something falling in the shaft. He jumped for cover under timber with the other men and they saw the cable shake. Eyster rang one bell and sent the cage to the 1100 level and soon McKinsey came down and informed them a man had fallen into the shaft. Victor Johnson, D. Eyster and Norman McKinsey went to the bulkhead and recovered the body which they hoist to the 1000 level. At the 1000 level, they removed the body from the bucket and raised it to the surface on a cage. Vuckovich was 22 years old and was buried in Evergreen Cemetery.

"Death Due to Carelessness" Bisbee Daily Review 22 January 1905 page 1
"Bisbee-Lowell Evergreen Cemetery." My Cochise.
http://www.mycochise.com/cembisbeeuv.php (July 30, 2011)
"Cochise County Coroner's Inquest No.248" Arizona State Archives Phoenix

April 29, 1905, Oliver Mine

"Nelse" Zabrovich, a track tender was nearly killed in the Oliver Shaft. Zabrovich claims that he was lost in thought and stepped into the open shaft, thinking the cage was there. The cager told the story somewhat differently. He stated that the cage had been signaled to be lowered to the 1150 level from the surface. At this moment, Zabrovich ducked under the bar to get on the cage. The cage was already descending when Zabrovich came plunging in under the bar. A man grabbed by the collar and pulled him in. Zabrovich rode landed on the floor of the cage upside down with his body weight resting on his shoulders. He began kicking, and the other four men on the cage had to withstand the blows of his kicks without moving as any movement they made could have endangered themselves* The cager claimed that he had repeatedly warned Zabrovich not to hurry to the board the cage.

*Note, these cages had no gates and were open to the shaft. The men could not risk being caught by a passing timber or rock
"Frightful Experience of a Slavonian" Bisbee Daily Review 30 April 1905 page 5

October 20, 1905 Oliver Mine

Frank Imo was caught in a cave-in. He suffered only serious bruising.

"Caught in Cave-in" Bisbee Daily Review 21 October 1905 page 8

June 9, 1906, Oliver Mine

Twenty-year-old Harry Stanton, a mucker at the Oliver was caught by falling rock. His left leg received a compound fracture. He remained at the Calumet & Arizona Hospital until September 17, 1906.

"Cave-in at Oliver Catches Harry Stanton" Bisbee Daily Review 12 June 1906 page 3
"Calumet & Arizona Hospital Records." My Cochise. http://www.mycochise.com/hospcalsn2to.php (June 22, 2011)

September 12, 1906, Oliver Mine

On the night of September 10th, Joseph Zboray and George Love were working in a drift on the 1150 level. There was room for timber to be setup, but 17 car loads of muck were on the ground. Three muckers cleaned it up. Love and Zboray were told to drill. They drilled six holes. The shift boss told them to blast the bottom four holes. When Zboray and Love returned on the night of the 11th, Love noted that the area was 11 feet tall and there was room for installing timber. The pile of muck from the blast of the four holes was still on the ground. The area was problematic and had caved earlier. At this time stringers had been placed to catch the rock. The shift boss told them to set up and start drilling. While drilling with a bar and column set up, a small rock fell and hit Love on the head. The wound was bleeding profusely and he walked back to a pool of water and cleaned up the injury. They finished drilling and tore down the bar and column and began cleaning up to install timber. Suddenly a 700 lb. sulfide boulder fell about 2' X 2' and 14" thick struck Zboray. The boulder broke into four pieces. Love called to a young "Slavonian" to put jackets under Zboray's head, while he went to get help. He told two miners in a nearby drift to get a timber truck and Love went to the shaft station and told the station tender to inform the bosses. Zboray was still alive when he was brought to the shaft, but died soon afterward. The boulder had broken his back. Zboray was Canadian and his family lived at # 221 West 40th Street in New York City.

"Cochise County Coroner's Inquest No.364" Arizona State Archives Phoenix

December 25, 1906, Oliver Mine

Nicholas Johnson was working on a lower level when a small cave-in occurred. With dirt falling around him he jumped to safety. His only serious injury was caused by a rock hitting his right hand.

"Suffered Slight Injury" Bisbee Daily Review 27 December 1906 page 7

January 30, 1907, Oliver Mine

Victor Ritner was working on timber in the dinkey compartment of the shaft. The cage in the adjoining compartment was descending. A cage hanging from this cage stuck him in the face breaking his nose and sending him falling into the dinkey compartment. Luckily, he was only injured. Two sets below where he was a working there was a platform, which he landed on. The shaft continued a further 1,000-feet below the platform.

"Accident in Mine" Bisbee Daily Review 31 January 1907 page 7

May 14, 1907, Oliver Mine

Miner, William Costley and William Lloyd, a Cager were descending on a cage. As the passed a station the cage struck a landing chair*. The chair was thrown into the cage and dislocated Costley's right leg and Lloyd's left leg. Both men were taken to the Calumet& Arizona Hospital. Costly's injuries were minor, and he was released on May 17. Lloyd remained at the hospital until June 17.

*Landing chairs are braces that are extended underneath cages to provide extra support for the cage when loading heavy objects. When a heavy item such as loaded mine cars is loaded onto a cage the cable stretches and the cage drops a few inches. For example, this could cause the mine car to tip over spilling muck into the cage and shaft creating a hazardous situation and a difficult mess to clean up. To prevent this drop, the landing chairs are extended a support the cage preventing it from dropping down. Also, a stretched cable will cause the cage to jump when the weight is released.

"Injured in Mine" Bisbee Daily Review 15 May 1907 page 7

"Calumet & Arizona Hospital Records." My Cochise. http://www.mycochise.com/hospcalco2day.php (April 21, 2011)

"Calumet & Arizona Hospital Records." My Cochise. http://www.mycochise.com/hospcalkr2man.php (April 21, 2011)

July 1907, Oliver Mine

Fred Vangundy was struck by a piece of steel while working. At the end of the shift, his arm was still hurting, and he went to the Calumet & Arizona Hospital, where he learned his arm was broken.

"Did Not Know Arm is Broken" Bisbee Daily Review 9 July 1907 page 7

July 7, 1907, Oliver Mine

Electrician, James A. Masterson was working in the shaft, when the cage was raised he was smashed between the wall plates and the cage. Miraculously, he suffered only a broken nose and scratches.

"Miner has Narrow Escape from Death" Bisbee Daily Review 9 January 1907 page 8

"Calumet & Arizona Hospital Records." My Cochise. http://www.mycochise.com/hospcalmar2mc.php (May 28, 2012)

July 19, 1907, Oliver Mine

On the 1000 level, William Harrison was struck on the foot by boulders falling from the back (ceiling) of a drift.

"Miner is Slightly Injured" Bisbee Daily Review 20 July 1907, page 7

August 2, 1907, Oliver Mine

A Danish or Finnish miner named, John Keosker fell fifty feet down a manway. It was discovered that he was still alive and transported to the Calumet & Arizona Hospital. The doctors were unsure that he would live. One difficulty that the doctors struggled with was that Keosker's English was extremely limited, and they could not determine exactly where he was injured. He had serious injuries to his chest and spine. Keosker was released from the hospital on September 7, 1907, in an improved condition.

"Falls in Man Way of Oliver Shaft." Bisbee Daily Review 3 August 1907 page 3
"Calumet & Arizona Hospital Records." My Cochise. http://www.mycochise.com/hospcalje 2ko.php (April 2, 2011)

August 16, 1907, Oliver Mine

Austrian Miner, Samuel Dobovich was killed, when he tried to cross the Oliver Shaft rather than go around.

"Cochise County Coroner's Transcript of Inquest No. 003" Arizona State Archives Phoenix

August 22, 1907, Oliver Mine

Peter Powell was installing a timber in a stope on a lower level when his axe slipped. The axe cut through the flesh into his bone. Powell was able to walk to the Calumet & Arizona Dispensary, where he was treated.

"Is Hurt in Mine" Bisbee Daily Review 23 August 1907 page 7

October 29, 1907, Oliver Mine

Robert Furrovich and his partner Nicholas Angelvich were working on the 1050 level. Angelvich was barring down the back of a drift. He was working on a half-ton slab that appeared to be loose. After trying to drop the boulder for several minutes, Angelvich moved to stand underneath the slab. It broke loose and struck him on the left shoulder breaking his ribs from his sternum and crushing his heart. Furrovich was barely missed by the falling rock. Robert rolled the boulder off of Nicholas, but he was already dead. The deceased was 30 years old and of *"Slavonian"* descent. He was buried in the Evergreen Cemetery.

"Stone Crushes out Life in Mine" Bisbee Daily Review 30 October 1907 page 1
"Bisbee-Lowell Evergreen Cemetery." My Cochise.
http://www.mycochise.com/cemeteries.php (March 29, 2011)

January 31, 1908, Oliver Mine

Harmon Hill was caught in a cave-in and his head was seriously cut.

"Cut On Head" Bisbee Daily Review 31 January 1908 page 7

January 31, 1908, Oliver Mine

Ollie Brune was caught in a cave-in. The falling rock bruised his shoulders and cut his head.

"Rock Strikes Miner" Bisbee Daily Review 31 January 1908 page 7

September 29, 1908, Oliver Mine

Finnish, Powder Monkey, Jacob Ojola, along with Victor Ritner, Fred Ptoh, Sam Barish Mat Anderson with Rastus Weese as cager and two unnamed men were riding a cage from the 1050 level to the surface. Between the 950 and 850 levels there was a sudden jerk of the cage. Hoistman Mike Richards noticed a jerk on the bell wire. When the cage reached the surface Ojola was missing. His body was found at the 1250 level. Ritner believed Ojola was sick and had fainted, when he was caught on the shaft timber and dragged from the cage. (Note, Victor later married a red-light district madam, named May Gillis)

"Cochise County Coroner's Inquest No. 598" Arizona State Archives Phoenix

April 21, 1909, Oliver Mine

At the end of the shift, Elai Juraservich stepped on the top deck of a triple deck cage at the 1050 level. The cage stopped at the 950 level to let off a "Fire Bug" and then continued to the surface. At about 50 ft. above the 950 level, it appears that Juraservich dropped his lunch bucket. When he tried to pick it up his head and shoulders caught on the shaft timber. He was knocked out of the cage. His body fell passed the middle deck brushing George Middleton as it fell and landed on the bottom deck.

"Cage Killed One; Falling Rock Another" Bisbee Daily Review 22 April 1909 page 5
"Cochise County Coroner's Inquest No.641" Arizona State Archives Phoenix

April 21, 1909, Oliver Mine

Matt Arola was working on the 1150 level near Fred Jacobson and James McEnroe. Arola was clearing out for a corner set while Jacobson and McEnroe were setting up a drill. Jacobson heard some rock fall, when he turned around he saw Arola on his back covered with only about 30 lbs. of muck. The two men grabbed Arola's arms and lifted him up. The shift bosses were told a man was hurt. Initially, no one did not realize how serious Arola was hurt. He had been hit by only around, 200 lbs. of soft, muddy, rock. Soon, blood began seeping out of Arola's ears and within ten minutes died. Arola died about six hours after Elai Juroserovich. The young man was from the Aulu region of northern Finland. He was survived by an aunt in Vale, South Dakota

"Cage Killed One; Falling Rock another" Bisbee Daily Review 22 April 1909 page 5
"Cochise County Coroner's Inquest No.642" Arizona State Archives Phoenix

July 21or 22, 1909, Oliver Mine

Andrew Ganola was caught in a fall of rock around midnight. He received cuts on scalp and head. He was taken to the Calumet & Arizona Hospital and treated by Dr. Bledsoe.

"Oliver Employee (sic) is slightly injured" Bisbee Daily Review 22 July 1909 page 5

August 20, 1909, Oliver Mine

William. C. George, a 43-year-old miner and E.J. Hicks, had stayed overtime to put in a set of timber and blast in stope 55 on the 950 level. This was an oxide stope and Hicks had gone to get a block, while George was measuring the size they needed the ground fell. When Hicks returned, he found George on the ground. The falling rock broke legs, his collar bone and several ribs. One of the broken ribs penetrated a lung. He died at the Calumet & Arizona Hospital from shock. He was native to Aberdeen, Devonshire, England. A sister was notified about his death.

"Cave-in at Oliver Causes One Death" Bisbee Daily Review 23 August 1909 page 5
"William George Funeral" Bisbee Daily Review 24 August 1909 page 7
"Original Certificate of Death." Arizona Department of Health Services. http://genealogy.az.gov/azdeath/007/10070467.pdf (April 2, 2011)
"Calumet & Arizona Hospital Records." My Cochise. http://www.mycochise.com/hospcaldied.php (April 2, 2011)
"Cochise County Coroner's Inquest No.676" Arizona State Archives Phoenix

August 27, 1909, Oliver Mine

John Stijipcich,* a 32-year-old native of Austria was pushing a mine car, and his partner John Maki was pulling the car. A boulder fell striking Stijipcich. The back of his skull and the maxilla were fractured resulting in death. Two brothers, Krysto Stijipcich from Oakland, California and another unnamed brother from San Francisco came to Bisbee to handle the funeral. He was buried in Evergreen Cemetery. Stijipcich was from Bockdekattaro, Austria-Hungary.* In the mines he went by the name "John Stack."

"Ore Slip Kills John Stack, Miner" Bisbee Daily Review 28 August 1909 page 8
"Brothers of Miner Come for Funeral" Bisbee Daily Review 29 August 1909 page 5
"Funeral is Today" Bisbee Daily Review 31 August 1909 page 7
"Original Certificate of Death." Arizona Department of Health Services. http://genealogy.az.gov/azdeath/007/10070475.pdf
(April 3, 2011)
"Bisbee-Lowell Evergreen Cemetery." My Cochise. http://www.mycochise.com/cembisbees.php (April 3, 2011)
"Cochise County Coroner's Inquest No.679Arizona State Archives Phoenix

January 17, 1910, Oliver Mine

Martin Raill had a close call when he fell two sets and the six-shooter drill he was using landed on him, bruising his chest. His head suffered cuts as well.

"Miner is Hurt" Bisbee Daily Review 18 January 1910 page 7

February 22, 1910, Oliver Mine

T.F. Estrada fell one set in a manway and dislocated his hip. He was treated at the Calumet & Arizona Hospital.

"Dislocated Hip" Bisbee Daily Review 24 February 1910 page 7

March 11, 1910 Oliver Mine

John Juno was caught in a cave-in. As he jumped away a *"huge"* boulder fell and struck him on the back of the head. He was knocked unconscious. Juno was transported to the Calumet & Arizona Hospital by Palace Ambulance. It was determined he had a concussion at the base of the brain. His condition was critical. There is no death certificate so he most likely recovered.

"Juno Hurt by Falling Boulder" Bisbee Daily Review 11 March 1910 page 8

May 1910, Oliver Mine

Peter Bodina had his foot smashed by a falling rock. He was expected to be off work a few days.

"Foot is Crushed" Bisbee Daily Review 29 May 1910 page 7
"Calumet & Arizona Hospital Records." My Cochise. http://www.mycochise.com/hospcalb.u2cl.php (April 16, 2011)

May 10, 1910, Oliver Mine

Mule driver, James Krilly was driving a string of mine cars. One foot became caught between a timber and the airline. It appears that this caused him to be dragged onto the ground and a mine car ran over a leg. His leg was broken. After the accident, Krilly was able to free himself and unharness the mule, before help arrived.

"Has Broken Leg" Bisbee Daily Review 11 May 1910 page 5

May 14, 1910, Oliver Mine

At the sawmill, William "Billy" Speier and John Oliver Clement were preparing chute jaws* to be shipped underground. Clement was marking the boards, and Speier was cutting them with an electric saw. A board kicked back and hit Speier in the forehead. The force of the blow fractured his skull. He was survived by a wife, child and a brother working at the Denn Mine * The timber for chutes was precut and shipped underground in kits to be installed underground. Other mine timbers like posts and girts had the tenons precut in the sawmill before being sent underground.

"Sudden Death is Fate of Spier" Bisbee Daily Review 17 May 1910 page 1

"Miner Dies from Peculiar Accident" Daily Arizona Silver Belt 20 May 1910   page 6

Certificate of Death." Arizona Department of Health Services. http://genealogy.az.gov/azdeath/009/10090034.pdf (May 28, 2012)

"Cochise County Coroner's Inquest No.749" Arizona State Archives Phoenix

June 1910, Oliver Mine

T. Cucovich injured his right foot.

"Mexican Laborer Drops Dead of Heart Failure" El Paso Herald 13 June 1910 page 7

June-July 1910, Oliver Mine

Erick Ericson had a hand crushed between two mine cars. It was thought that one finger may need to be amputated.

"Work to Commence on New Bisbee-Douglas Roadway" El Paso Herald 18 July 1910 page 7

June 10, 1910, Oliver Mine

Sam Arnison was bruised up and injured his back in a cave-in.

"Suffers Severe Bruises" Bisbee Daily Review 10 June 1910 page 7

"Mexican Laborer Drops Dead of Heart Failure" El Paso Herald 13 June 1910 page 7

June 21, 1910, Oliver Mine

Steve Dabovich was struck by small rocks falling from the back (roof) of a drift and received a cut on the head.

"Falling Rocks Injure" Bisbee Daily Review 22 June 1910 page 5

July 8, 1910, Oliver Mine

Lee Vutovich was working in a stope when a timber block fell and barely missed killing him. The block impacted on his leg spraining his ankle and smashing his foot. He was taken to the Calumet & Arizona Dispensary.

"Sustains Painful Injuries" Bisbee Daily Review 8 July 1910 page 5

July 30, 1910, Oliver Mine

Shift Boss, J.W. Fisher slipped and fell from a ladder while making his rounds in the Oliver Mine. He fell twelve feet and sprained his ankle. He was expected to be off work a few days.

"Sprains his Ankle" Bisbee Daily Review 31 July 1910 page 5

August, 1910, Oliver Mine

Victor Ritner fell off a ladder on the 1350 level. He was cared for at the Calumet & Arizona Dispensary. (Note, Victor later married a red-light district madam, named May Gillis)

"Fell from Ladder" Bisbee Daily Review 7 August 1910 page 5

Timber just taken underground, Campbell Mine c-1935

August 2, 1910, Oliver Mine

Peter Locovich dislocated his left shoulder after falling around 22-1/2 ft. or three sets. He was treated at the Calumet & Arizona Dispensary.

"Left Shoulder Dislocated" Bisbee Daily Review 3 August 1910 page 5

August 5, 1910, Oliver Mine

Cager, Pete Kroker dislocated his wrist while loading a mine car onto a cage at the 1250 level station. He was treated at the Calumet & Arizona Dispensary.

"Dislocates his Wrist" Bisbee Daily Review 6 August 1910 page 5

August 5, 1910, Oliver Mine

Paul Sulander was cut on the forehead by a falling rock. He was taken to the Calumet & Arizona Dispensary.

"Rock Gashes Forehead" Bisbee Daily Review 6 August 1910 page 5

September 3, 1910, Oliver Mine

John Rico, a 20-year-old carman at the Oliver Mine, had a mine car turn over on top of him. His left leg was broken. He was taken to the Calumet & Arizona Hospital and released on November 25, 1910

"Miners are Injured in Bisbee Shafts" El Paso Herald 6 September 1910 page 8

"Calumet & Arizona Hospital Records." My Cochise. http://www.mycochise.com/hospcalpr2ry.php (July 22 2011)

Caved ground, c-1910
(Courtesy of the Bisbee Mining & Historical Museum)

September 20, 1910, Oliver Mine
Joe Pelusti, a thirty-year-old miner was caught in a cave-in. He was treated at the Calumet
& Arizona Hospital and released on September 22.

"Expenses Exceed Income of Board" El Paso Herald 12 December 1912 page 9
"Calumet & Arizona Hospital Records." My Cochise. http://www.mycochise.com/hospcalo2 po.php (June 22, 2011)

October 10, 1910, Oliver Mine

Moso Mihalevich* a 28-year-old miner from Montenegro and P. Lopez were working three floors up in a stope. Mihalevich was cutting a lagging above him to allow a boulder to fall. As he was cutting, both the lagging and the rock struck him. The impact of the timber punctured an intestine. He was taken to the Calumet and Arizona Hospital where he died at 7:05 am on October 12.

*given as actual name on death certificate other documents list him as Mike Milovich
"Blow Causes Death of Slavonian Miner" Bisbee Daily Review 13 October 1910 page 8
"Milovich Funeral Today" Bisbee Daily Review 14 October 1910 page 5
"Death Unavoidable" Bisbee Daily Review 14 October 1910 page 5
"Original Certificate of Death." Arizona Department of Health Services. http://genealogy.az.gov/azdeath/009/10091284.pdf (27 March 2011)
"Cochise County Coroner's Inquest No.789" Arizona State Archives Phoenix

January 14, 1911, Oliver Mine

O.F. Larson was caught in a cave-in. His jaw was broken, and head cut. He was taken to the Calumet & Arizona Hospital and remained there until April 11, 1910.

"Suffers Broken Jaw" Bisbee Daily Review 15 January 1910 page 7
"Calumet & Arizona Hospital Records." My Cochise. http://www.mycochise.com/hospcalkr2man.php (April 5, 2011)

January 23, 1911 Oliver Mine shaft collar

Santiago Ranteria a crippled miner was working as a cleaner at the collar of the Oliver Shaft. At 8:00 am, the cage in the center shaft compartment arrived at the surface with a mine car loaded on it. The mining company rules stated that the men on the headframe's toplander deck were supposed to come down and unload the cage. Ranteria needed an empty mine car for trash. He asked for the car and then noticed that the men were busy with other work and he decided to help them out and unload the car himself. As he got ready to enter the cage, men underground signaled the cage and the hoistman responded to the call. Santiago was caught by the cage and dragged through the six-inch space between the cage and the shaft timber. The mangled remains of Ranteria caused the cage to stop 40 feet below the shaft collar at the subway level. He was buried in Evergreen Cemetery and was survived by a mother in Mexico.

"Miner is Killed Instantly at Oliver Shaft." Bisbee Daily Review 24 June 1911 page 8
"Came to His Death by Own Carelessness" Bisbee Daily Review 25 June 1911 page 5
"Original Certificate of Death." Arizona Department of Health Services. http://genealogy.az.gov/azdeath/008/10080915.pdf (July 31, 2011)
"Cochise County Coroner's Inquest No.843" Arizona State Archives Phoenix

February 6, 1911, Oliver Mine

Patrick Cunningham, a native of Ireland and a mucker in the Oliver Mine, was caught in a cave-in. The falling debris ruptured his intestines and broke his right leg in two places one below and one above the knee. He late died from shock at the Calumet & Arizona Hospital.

"Man's Injuries Prove to be Fatal" Bisbee Daily Review 7 February 1911 1907 page 1
"Calumet & Arizona Hospital Records." My Cochise. http://www.mycochise.com/hospcaldied.php (March 31, 2011)

"Original Certificate of Death." <u>Arizona Department of Health Services.</u> http://genealogy.az.gov/azdeath/009/10092305.pdf (31 March 2011)

February 10, 1911, Oliver Mine

Victor Libla, a 23 -year-old miner fell four sets in 82 stope on the 1050 level. His skull was fractured at the base of the brain. It was originally, feared that he would die, but on March 21, 1911, the Finnish miner was released from the Calumet & Arizona Hospital in "improved" condition.

"Miner Falls in Oliver Mine; May Die" <u>Bisbee Daily Review</u> 11 February 1911 page 5
"Bisbee gets Rain and Raw Cold Wind" <u>El Paso Herald</u> 14 February 1911 page 6
"Calumet & Arizona Hospital Records." <u>My Cochise.</u> http://www.mycochise.com/hospcalkr2man.php (August 1, 2011)

March 6, 1911 Oliver Mine

Finnish Miner, Emil Linden was repairing a drift with Albert Drew. They need to change out a rotted drift set. The men had tried to bar down a boulder they suspected was loose, but it would not come down. Linden began shoveling muck from underneath the boulder into a mine car to get a solid footing to put in a stull supporting the rock. Suddenly the rock fell crushing Linden. The injured man was taken to the Calumet & Arizona Hospital, where he died on March 7. He was survived by his wife Martha and a child.

"Calumet & Arizona Hospital Records." <u>My Cochise.</u> http://www.mycochise.com/hospcaldied.php (July 22, 2015)
"Cochise County Coroner's Inquest No.816" Arizona State Archives Phoenix

May 9, 1911, Oliver Mine

Arthur Poquette*, his partner John Angius along with George Love* and G.E. Brown were working in 175 stope on the 1050 level. Joseph Horton, a timberman, came into the stope and told the men that the stope was shifting, and they needed to evacuate. Love, Brown and Angius left the stope, but Poquette remained. Angius called to his partner called back to Poquette to urge him to get out. Both times, Poquette responded, *"I'll be out in a minute."* Moments later, the stope collapsed in a massive cave-in. There was some hope that Poquette may have made it into a lower part of the stope where it was thought he could have survived the collapse and have enough air to breathe. After, nearly 24 hours of digging on double shifts the almost unrecognizable remains of Poquette were uncovered by the rescue crew. At around 40 years old, Arthur Poquette was French-Canadian and was survived by a wife, five children and a brother Charles Poquette, who worked in a Bisbee barbershop. The family left Bisbee for Michigan with the body to be interned there. They did not plan to return to Bisbee. (No coroner's inquest could be located)

*Also spelled Paquette in the Bisbee Daily Review articles
** George Love was later killed in the Czar on July 6, 1914
"Mangled remains of Poquette Found" <u>Bisbee Daily Review</u> 12 May 1911 page 5
"Tons of Earth on Miner at Oliver" <u>Bisbee Daily Review</u> 11 May 1911 page 5
"Paquette Warned in Ample Time" <u>Bisbee Daily Review</u> 13 May 1911 page 5
"Body to Michigan" <u>Bisbee Daily Review</u> 15 May 1911 page 5

May 9, 1911, Oliver Mine

James Crilly a 35-year-old mule-driver was driving a string of mine cars when his foot became caught between the airline pipe and a timber. He was knocked off, and a mine car ran over his leg. Even though, his leg was broken. James freed himself and was able to unharness the mule before help arrived. He was taken to the Calumet & Arizona hospital where he stayed until June 6, 1911.

"Has Broken Leg" Bisbee Daily Review 11 May 1911 page 5
"Calumet & Arizona Hospital Records." My Cochise. http://www.mycochise.com/hospcalco2day.php (June 20, 2011)

June 16, 1911 Oliver Mine

Italian Miner, Bartolo Rossi was mucking, in 8 stope on the 1350 level. Two miners had barred down the area he was working in and felt it was safe. The two miners began drilling down holes in the set next to him, when the ground collapsed and buried Rossi caught in a cave-in. It took over 1 hour for 12 men to dig him out. He was critically injured with his jaw bone exposed, one arm crushed, and a leg so badly smashed it had to be amputated. Although, the doctors at the Calumet & Arizona Hospital were optimistic, Rossi would survive, he died. Rossi was a veteran of the Italian Army and had been in Bisbee only five months. He was survived by his parents in Italy, five sisters and two brothers. His two cousins Joe Rossi and Bert Mozoni lived in Bisbee.

"Leg Amputated as Result of at Oliver Shaft. Cave-in" Bisbee Daily Review 17 June 1911 page 8
"Bert Rossi Dies of Injuries at C&A Hospital" Bisbee Daily Review 18 June 1911 page 8
"Cochise County Coroner's Inquest No.842" Arizona State Archives Phoenix

August 12, 1911, Oliver Mine

Nick Manovich was struck in the jaw by a falling rock. He was taken to his home in Dubacher Canyon.

"Man Hurt at Mine by Falling Rock" Bisbee Daily Review 13 August 1911 page 1

August 16, 1911, Oliver Mine

Mijailo "Miki" Benderach was working in 2 crosscut on the 1300 level with Jon Pach and Charles Jamar. Pach left to push a mine car to the shaft station while the others continued working. The face of the drift had caved, and they were working back from it a few feet when rocks fell hitting Benderach. A rock landed on his neck, one on his side and rocks and boards covered his feet. He was killed instantly. His body was removed from the mine and taken to the Palace Undertaker's Morgue before the coroner had viewed the body. This resulted in a dispute between the coroner's office and the Palace undertakers. Officer L.R. Bailey was ordered to give notice to the Palace to turn over the body. The undertakers did this. Baily who had not the foresight to bring a wagon to carry away the body, wittily responded *"I will be as generous as you are. I'll give it back to you."* So the remains of Benderach, although in legal possession of the coroner, remained at the Palace morgue. His was survived by his brother John Benderach, also an Oliver miner and his parents Sava and Zvana in Montenegro.

"Slav Killed at Oliver Yesterday" Bisbee Daily Review 17 August 1911 page 6
"Clash Occurs Over Remains" Bisbee Daily Review 18 August 1911 page 8
"Original Certificate of Death." Arizona Department of Health Services. http://genealogy.az.gov/azdeath/008/10081420.pdf (April 4, 2011)
"Cochise County Coroner's Inquest No.855" Arizona State Archives Phoenix

A safety photo showing a miner about to be caught
between a mine car and a timber. C-1917

September 4, 1911, Oliver Mine
 A 68 -year-old miner, James Fulmar received injuries in an undescribed accident. He was taken to the Calumet & Arizona Hospital and released on October 11.

"Two Slight Accidents" Bisbee Daily Review 5 September 1911 page 8
"Calumet & Arizona Hospital Records." My Cochise. http://www.mycochise.com/hospcalfl2go.php (May 19, 2012)

September 25, 1911, Oliver Mine

Chris Midzor, a 32-year-old timberman was caught between a mine car and timber. He was taken to the Calumet & Arizona Hospital where it was determined his pelvis was injured. He was released from the hospital on October 3, 1911.

"Miner Injured" Bisbee Daily Review 27 September 1911 page 5
"Calumet & Arizona Hospital Records." My Cochise. http://www.mycochise.com/hospcalme 2ny.php (April 2, 2011)

November 22, 1911, Oliver Mine

Polish Miner, Martin Zelinski smashed his foot.

"Miner is Injured" Bisbee Daily Review 23 November 1911 page 5

Timber truck at the 3rd Southwest station of the Copper Queen Incline Shaft

December 11, 1911, Oliver Mine

Gust Siltala, a 21-year-old Finnish miner and 27-year-old Arthur Wickerstrom were drilling in 25 crosscut on the 1350 level. During their work they drilled into a missed hole, which exploded. Both men were taken to the Calumet & Arizona Hospital for treatment. The blast inflicted Siltala with a skull fracture and other injuries. He died from shock on

December 12. Wickerstrom's injuries kept him in the hospital until December 24, 1911. It was noted that this type of accident was becoming rarer, now that the Calumet & Arizona Mining Company was posting notices of misfires in work areas.

"Missed Shot Hurts Two Miners Badly" Bisbee Daily Review 12 December 1911 page 5
"Victim of Explosion Dies of Injuries" Bisbee Daily Review 14 December 1911 page 3
"Calumet & Arizona Hospital Records." My Cochise. http://www.mycochise.com/hospcaldied.php (April5 2011)
"Calumet & Arizona Hospital Records." My Cochise. http://www.mycochise.com/hospcalwh2z.php (April5 2011)
"Original Certificate of Death." Arizona Department of Health Services. http://genealogy.az.gov/azdeath/008/10082324.pdf (April 4, 2011)
"Cochise County Coroner's Inquest No.882" Arizona State Archives Phoenix

February 8, 1912, Oliver Mine

Charles Fisher broke his leg slightly above the ankle in an accident at the Oliver Shaft. He was taken to the Calumet & Arizona Hospital and was released on February 15, 1912.

"Slight Mine Accident" Bisbee Daily Review 9 February 1912 page 6
"Calumet & Arizona Hospital Records." My Cochise. http://www.mycochise.com/hospcalde 2fi.php (March 29, 2011)

February 13, 1912 Oliver Mine

Joe Peccolo, a 21-year-old track cleaner at the Oliver was injured. He was taken to the Calumet & Arizona Hospital and released later the same day.

"Miners Injured" Bisbee Daily Review 14 February 1912 page 4

April 1, 1912, Oliver Mine

A 30-year-old miner, Charles Koik fell a distance of one and a half sets and was bruised. He was taken to the Calumet & Arizona Hospital where he remained until April 28, 1912

"Calumet & Arizona Hospital Records." My Cochise. http://www.mycochise.com/hospcalje 2ko.php (April4 2011)
"Miners Injured" Bisbee Daily Review 2 April 1912 page 6

April 24, 1912, Oliver Mine

Italian Miner, Bert Tomaroni was hit across the forehead by a falling timber during a cave-in at 40 stope on the 1200 level. Pat Guerin and Chris Mitzor were repairing timber that had been blasted out by the night shift, and Tomaroni was mucking into a chute a few feet away. They had just installed a post and were lifting up a cap. Rock began to fall. Guerin and Chris moved out of the way and then all, but one candle was blown out. They called for Tomaroni, but when they heard no response, they lighted a candle and looked for him. They discovered him buried by fallen timber. The blow of a timber fractured his skull and killed him. One of his cousins had been killed in a mine accident at Bisbee roughly ten months before. He was unmarried and around 23 years old.

"Miner is Killed at Oliver Shaft." Bisbee Daily Review 25 April 1912 page 8
"Original Certificate of Death." Arizona Department of Health Services. http://genealogy.az.gov/azdeath/010/10100391.pdf (August 1, 2011)
"Cochise County Inquest No. 910" Arizona State Archives Phoenix

May 6, 1912, Oliver Mine

A 26-year-old, Spaniard named, Benjamin Blanco* was on the 1150 level getting ready to drilling with a *"Waugh"* stoper in 137 raise. This raise was being mined through to the next level. It appears that he knocked out the staging he was working on with the drill. This probably happened when he set the machine down hard to let the stinger catch into the lagging. After his staging had failed Blanco and the stoper fell one set, then fell into the chute. Although, he was alive after the accident, Blanco died before he could be taken to the hospital. He was survived by four cousins in Bisbee, including Antonio Blanco. (Note, the inquest describes the accident differently than the newspaper reports.)

*The newspaper refers him as Benjamin Blanco

"Benjamin Blanco Killed in Shaft." Bisbee Daily Review7 May 1912 page 1

"Blanco Funeral" Bisbee Daily Review9 May 1912 page 8

"Original Certificate of Death." Arizona Department of Health Services. http://genealogy.az.gov/azdeath/010/10100631.pdf (30 March 2011)

"Cochise County Inquest No. 920" Arizona State Archives Phoenix

March 31, 1912, Oliver Shaft,

At 2:00 pm, W. L. Ballard suffered two broken ribs in an undescribed accident.

"Superstitious Say They are Vindicated" Bisbee Daily Review 2 June 1912 page 8

June 1, 1912, Oliver Shaft

George Ellis strained himself while lifting a heavy object. He was transported home by ambulance.

"Superstitious Say They are Vindicated" Bisbee Daily Review 2 June 1912 page 8

June 1, 1912, Oliver Shaft

At 12:00 pm, Sanfred Harlin crushed his foot in an undescribed accident.

"Superstitious Say They are Vindicated" Bisbee Daily Review 2 June 1912 page 8

June 6, 1912 Oliver Mine

John Wilson was overcome by gas. It is not clear whether these were gasses from a fire or powder gasses from a blast.

"Overcome by Gas" Bisbee Daily Review 6 June 1912 page 8

June 13, 1912, Oliver Mine

Robert Parker dislocated his shoulder in an undescribed accident.

"Miner Injured" Bisbee Daily Review 14 June 1912 page 6

August 17, 1912, Oliver Mine

B.T. Lake broke his jaw in a mine accident. He was treated at the Calumet & Arizona Hospital.

"Has Jaw Broken" Bisbee Daily Review 18 August 1912 page 6

October 4, 1912, Oliver Mine

Cliff Allred received minor injuries in the mine and was taken home.

"Personal Mention" Bisbee Daily Review 5 October 1912 page 5

January 10, 1913, Oliver Mine

G.H. Foster was taken to the hospital after receiving bruises and cuts in an undescribed accident. The newspaper reported that he was sent to the Copper Queen Hospital, but he does not appear in the records. It would have been more likely he was sent to the Calumet & Arizona Hospital under normal condition.

"Miner Injured" Bisbee Daily Review 21 January page 6

March 29, 1914, Oliver Mine

At 3:00 am, it was raining heavy and pitch black as night watchman, William Arndt approached the Oliver powder magazine. He discovered three men trying to break into magazine. He shouted at them to put their hands. The attempted robbers responded with gunfire. One bullet shot off one of Arndt's fingers. Another, bullet creased his leg. Law enforcement officers followed, buggy tracks near the magazine to the South Bisbee home of Billy Scrimpsher a Gardner Mine foreman. Also, arrested two other Gardener mine employees, H. Hendrick a miner and S.C. Smiley a powder monkey. The high reputation of the men quickly resulted in their release and no charges were pressed. It was suspected later, that the magazine was going to be looted and the dynamite sold to rebels in Naco, Sonora and other parts Northern Mexico. The Mexican Revolution was occurring at this time and significant battles had occurred at the nearby towns of Naco, Sonora, Mexico and Agua Prieta, Sonora, Mexico. Note, the Oliver Powder Magazine stored dynamite for all of the Calumet & Arizona Mines. It was distributed to the smaller powder magazines underground from here.

"Powder Magazine Objective of Near Robbers" Bisbee Daily Review 31March 1914 page 3

April 13, 1914, Oliver Mine

Mace Morris was working in a stope on the 1450 level. Mace was drilling with a "Waugh" machine to blast out room for timber. Lyman Fischer a mucker was working nearby and heard the rock fall and found Morris with his face bloody, but still alive. He went to get water out of both his and Morris's lunch buckets and washed his face to see if Morris could be revived. This did not work. His neck was broken, and he died soon after being brought down the manway. Morris was stuck by around a half ton of rock. He was survived by his parents and four sisters. The deceased was from Galena, Kansas.

"Body of Morris to be Shipped to Old Home This Evening" Bisbee Daily Review 10 January 1903 page 8
"Cochise County Inquest No. 1085" Arizona State Archives Phoenix

December 21, 1916, Oliver Mine

J. F. Branson suffered a cut on the head and a cut ankle after he fell through a grizzly. He spent two days in the hospital

"Calumet & Arizona Hospital Records." My Cochise. http://www.mycochise.com/hospcalb.e 2br.php (June 2, 2012)
Office of State Mine Inspector. *Sixth Annual Report of the State Mine Inspector State of Arizona for the Year Ending November 30, 1917.*

April 11, 1917, Oliver Mine

Mule Driver, James Vickers was badly bruised after he became caught between two mine cars. He was released from the Calumet and Arizona Hospital on May 1.

"Two are Injured" Bisbee Daily Review 12 April 1917 page 8

June 4, 1917, Oliver Mine

Trackman, Matthew Grigg hit his hand with an axe and his amputated left index finger. He was treated at the Calumet & Arizona Hospital. Matthew Grigg was later killed in the Cole Mine on October 3, 1921.

"Calumet & Arizona Hospital Records." My Cochise.
http://www.mycochise.com/hospcalgr2he.php (June 2, 2012)
Office of State Mine Inspector. *Sixth Annual Report of the State Mine Inspector State of Arizona for the Year Ending November 30, 1917.*

January 21, 1918, Oliver Mine

Brothers, Lee and Louis Hardt* were working in 230 raise on the 1050 level. They had almost finished their shift Louis had gone to get dynamite and capped fuses. After he had returned he handed the explosives to Lee, who loaded a single hole while, Louis waited below a the bulkhead. Lee needed someone to shine a carbide lamp so he could see and Louis climbed and sat on a timber. At that moment, a mass of dirt fell and struck Louis. Both of the carbide lamps were knocked out. After a short time Lee was able to get Louis in a place safe so he would not fall into the raise and called for help. Louis was taken to the Calumet & Arizona Hospital where he died on January 24th from a broken back. Louis was 27 years old and married.

*Death certificate gives the last name as "Horat". Carefully reading of the certificates reveals it is a poorly written "Hardt"
"Miner Killed by falling Ground" Tombstone Weekly Epitaph 27 January 1918 page 8
"Original Certificate of Death." Arizona Department of Health Services. http://genealogy.az.gov/azdeath/021/10211867.pdf (August 1 2011
"Cochise County Inquest No. 1311" Arizona State Archives

Louis Hardt, c-1916

July 9, 1918, Oliver Mine

Grady Vaughn and Bee Dobbins were injured when blasting caps exploded. Vaughn was injured in the face arm and shoulder. Dobbins was hurt in the legs and right arm. Both men were 24 years old and released from the hospital in the middle of July.

"Calumet & Arizona Hospital Records." My Cochise. http://www.mycochise.com/hospcalde 2fi.php (June 2, 2012)

"Calumet & Arizona Hospital Records." My Cochise. http://www.mycochise.com/hospcaltr2we.php (June 2, 2012)

Office of State Mine Inspector. *Seventh Annual Report of the State Mine Inspector State of Arizona for the Year Ending November 30, 1918.*

February 10, 1941, Oliver Mine

Eduardo A. Gomez was working to repair the 1050 level station with Pascal Salas. They were clearing the area for timber. The men began working near a large boulder, which began dribbling dust. Concerned the men moved away and worked in another area. An hour later they returned, and the area looked safer. They began working near the hanging slab again. The three-ton boulder fell striking a loaded mine car that had been left near the station and crushing Gomez. He was survived by a brother Frank Gomez. (Note Another miner, Michael R. Burgoss and felt the high ceiling and broad untimbered space had made the area dangerous.)

Original Certificate of Death." Arizona Department of Health Services. http://genealogy.az.gov/azdeath/064/10641782.pdf (May 28, 2014)

"Cochise County Coroner's Inquest No. 1791" Arizona State Archives Phoenix

Pittsburg and Hecla Mine (prospect)

Pittsburg & Hecla Shaft c- 1904

On June 22, 1903, sinking of the double compartment shaft began on a site *"surrounded by lofty ridged mountains"* by the Pittsburg & Hecla Development Company. The ground nearby was stained by malachite giving an indication of copper, but little clue to the presence of mineable ore. Under the direction of Superintendent Thomas A. Tate the shaft made incredible progress the shaft was almost 80ft. deep by July 26. It was felt that the shaft may break the shaft sinking record in the district. It is important to recognize this shaft was being hand drilled not machine drilled and the rock was being hoisted by a horse whim not a steam hoist. In August of 1903, a double drum steam hoist was being installed and a headframes was constructed. Around the mine a small community known as *"Tom's Camp"* developed. This consisted of five or six house including a bunkhouse and a baby blue mine office. By the summer of 190, specks of sulphides covered the dumps and a stringers of copper and lead sulphides had been intercepted in the shaft. The shaft was completed at 575 ft. deep and a diamond drill hole was drilled 1,000 ft. from the bottom of the shaft. 1905, was the end of work at the Pittsburg & Hecla in June the company was unable to make the last payment on the property and the claims reverted back to Thomas Tate the original owner. Mr. Tate reported, that no ore had been intercepted by the drill hole, but he did complete the assessment work on the claims.

September 6, 1903, Pittsburg & Hecla Mine

The Johnnie Jones, Paul Gireux and James Campbell were drilling blast holes in the bottom of the Pittsburg and Hecla Shaft. This double compartment shaft had been sunk to a depth just over 200 ft. They had been warned by the previous shift that a hole had misfired. As they began to work Johnnie reminded them again of the misfire. Johnnie Jones was drilling by the single jack method and began to work. Gireux and Campbell were a drilling as a double jack team. The missed hole was reported to be four feet deep and loaded with nine sticks of "Giant" powder. Ignoring the advice, they started with Gireux turning and Campbell striking. Campbell had hit the steel three times before the hole detonated. The full force of the explosion hit Campbell, who was directly over the hole. He was thrown into the air and then buried by the blasted muck. His skull was crushed, and nearly every one of his bones was broken. He was mutilated to such a point that the undertakers were ordered not to allow anyone to view the body. Gireux's left eye was blown out and drained of its fluid and his little finger the left hand was blown off, while the hand itself was mutilated beyond repair. His skin was peppered with small rocks. He was cared for at the Central Lodging house by F. J. Hart M.D. and by September 9th he seemed to be improving. Jones was on the other side of the shaft when the explosion occurred, was knocked unconscious and received minor cuts and bruises. The top carman hoisted Jones out in the sinking bucket before recovering Campbell and Gireux. James Campbell was 29 years old and from Nova Scotia He was survived by cousins Henry, Stewart and Sam Grant and a brother Robert Campbell* Oddly, his two sisters Sadie and Aldbert were not mentioned in his obituary. Evergreen Cemetery was his final resting place.

*Robert Campbell was later killed on July 17, 1908, in the Czar Shaft by a falling boulder.
"One Miner Killed and Two Injured by Powder Explosion" Bisbee Daily Review 8 September 1903 page 4
"The "Campbell Funeral" Bisbee Daily Review 8 September 1903 page 5
"Gireux's Condition" Bisbee Daily Review 9 September 1903 page 5
"Advertisement" Bisbee Daily Review 9 September 1903 page 3
"R.H. Campbell Popular Miner Killed by Rock" Bisbee Daily Review 18 July 1908 page 5
"Cochise County Coroner's Inquest No. 158" Arizona State Archives

July 27, 1904, Pittsburg and Hecla Mine

J.H. Goodwin, the diamond setter at the mine was in charge of all diamond drilling at the mine. He had hired an unidentified Mexican man that was described as well-educated and able to speak English. It was the Mexican man's first day on the job and his name was known only to Goodwin at the mine. These men were riding down the on a sinking bucket, when for an unknown reason at a depth of 250 ft., the sinking bucket they were riding down the shaft tipped. Both men plummeted down the shaft. S. M. Richter was working ten feet off the bottom of the shaft or 550 ft. down, when he saw something fall. The miner climbed down to the water-filled sump to investigate. As he did this, he was struck by another falling object. Richter took shelter in the pump station and waited to see if anything else was falling in the shaft. After a time, the high temperature at the pump station began to bother him and he climbed the shaft up 40 ft. He realized he had left candles burning below and had to climb back down to extinguish them. After the fire hazard was eliminated, he climbed to 200 level and met W. Ross the hoistman climbing down the shaft to investigate. Quickly, they realized that the men had likely fallen down the shaft and sent to the nearby Houghton Mine for help. The rescuing men soon found blood and brains on the shaft timber. Upon reaching the sump, they fished out the bodies with an iron hook. At the coroner's inquest, it was discover that one of the young men around the mine knew the name of the Mexican man, but in the inquest he was listed as *"John Doe."*

"Fatalities at Bisbee" The Arizona Republican 30 July 1904 page 4
"Cochise County Coroner's Inquest No.216" Arizona State Archives Phoenix

Portage Lake Mine, c-1903

Portage Lake Mine (prospect)

Portage Lake & Bisbee Development Company started work in April of 1903. It was a reorganization of the earlier the Portage Lake & Calumet Development Company. By June of the same year the shaft had reached a depth of a 120ft. At this depth about five gallons a minute of water was entering the shaft and work was temporarily suspended until a pump was installed. In 1904, the development work appeared to be largely diamond drilling and by July 1904 the operations became dormant. This shaft reached a final depth of 300 ft. with two compartment. At times it was called the Portage Kake & Bisbee Mine.

October 16, 1903, Portage Lake Mine
O.M. King, a champion hand driller and Bob Bowdish were getting ready to blast at the bottom of the Portage Lake Shaft. Bert Warner* was at the collar of the shaft awaiting the bell signal from the men below. Warner heard a single shot detonate and knew something was wrong. He then grabbed the hoisting cable and slid down a 150 ft. to a pump station. From the pump station he called to the men below. Not getting a response he again slid down the hoisting cable. On the bottom smoke and darkness prevented him from seeing the injured men. Fortunately, King was conscious and called to Warner to lift a rock off his shoulder. After the rock was moved King told Warner that seven shots still had not detonated. Carefully, Warner lifted King into the sinking bucket and rang him up to the surface. Once the bucket returned he gathered the unconscious Bowdish and sent him to the surface After Bowdish was safely on the surface, Warner climbed into the bucket and ascended to the surface. On his ascent, three of the remaining holes detonated. On the operating table, King told the story of Warner's heroism to Reverend Harvey M. Shields. The Bisbee Daily Review started a subscription to award Bert Warner a gold medal. The paper asked 250 of its readers to donate 50 cents apiece to pay for the award. Later, at the request of Bert Warner himself, all the money raised for the medal was given to O.M. King,

who was without money after getting out of the hospital. * Warner's father C.C. Warner was killed in the Holbrook Mine on June 13, 1904
"Drillers Will Remain Here" Bisbee Daily Review 7 July 1902
"Bert Warner the Hero" Bisbee Daily Review 18 October 1903 page 2
"King and Bowdish" Bisbee Daily Review 18 October 1903 page 8
"Medal for Warner" Bisbee Daily Review 21 October 1903 page 2
"Untitled" Bisbee Daily Review 22 October 1903 page 2
"They are Improving" Bisbee Daily Review 23 October 1903 page 7
"Warner's Fame Spreading" Bisbee Daily Review 6 November 1903 page 6
"Fund Being Raised for O.M. King" Bisbee Daily Review 6 March 1904 page 4

Prospect shaft of Frank Johnson

Little is known about this prospect other than it was a shallow shaft three miles east of Bisbee.

November 9, 1901, Prospect shaft

Fourteen year-old James McNalley and twelve year-old Charles Philbrick went hunting with a .22 caliber rifle three miles east of the Bisbee town site. The saw a mine and hiked over to the mine and climbed down the shaft and found a small box of *"Giant"* powder* The boys climbed up the shaft and McNalley hung his coat on the windlass. He said to Philbrick, *"Watch me shoot that little box of powder."* Philbrook climbed down the dump and McNalley fired at the box. It detonated sending timber and rocks flying. After it was safe Philbrook went to check on Johnnie and discovered his brains were completely blown out. Philbrook ran back to town. He found a partner of his father's and told him. Then went home and could not find his mother. Philbrook then went to the office of S.K. Williams the coroner.*Rather than the normal 50lb boxes dynamite is also sold in 10lb and 25lb boxes. Each stick weighs about 1 lb. Smaller boxes were commonly used by prospects and small mines. The term "Giant" powder became a slang term for all brands of dynamite, so the dynamite may have been any brand. Dynamite produced by Giant Powder Company, The California Powder Works (Hercules Powder) and likely, Safety-Nitro Powder Company were used at this period in Bisbee.

"Cochise County Coroner's Inquest No. 33" Arizona State Archives

Three sizes of powder (dynamite) boxes from left to right 50lb., 25 lb., & 10lbs. They are slightly newer than the accident mention above and were manufactured in 1904

Red Jacket Shaft c-1904

Red Jacket Mine (prospect)

Red Jacket & Bisbee Development Company was incorporated on May 18, 1903. The three compartment Red Jacket shaft was started using a horse whim as a hoist. In charge of the whim was Henry Tarr. He was renowned as one half of the champion double jack hand driller, the Tarr brothers. The shaft was 150 feet deep by December 1903, but little work was done after that. By 1906 the mine had shut down. Sometime, later the mine was reopened as the Contact shaft. Again the work on the property was short lived.

January 18, 1904, Red Jacket Mine

William M. Evans and his son Seth were about 160 feet down at the bottom of the Red Jacket Shaft. They were getting ready to blast and wanted to load a hole that already had powder in it, likely a misfire. William tried to remove the charge with a copper spoon and could not, so he began pounding on the spoon. The pounding detonated the hole. His left hand was blown off at the wrist. The rest of him was severely bruised. Fortunately, Seth was only bruised. Doctor Caven was called to the mine to care for the injured men. William's had need further amputation at the hospital to clean up the ragged tear.

"Left Hand Blown Off" Bisbee Daily Review 19 January 1904 page 1
"Hids Wife Arrives" Bisbee Daily Review 23January 1904 page 5

Sacramento Mine

Sacramento Mine

Copper Queen Consolidated Mining Company began preparing the shaft site on March 4, 1904. Early in its development the decision was made to use this new shaft as a main hoisting shaft for the Copper Queen Mines. The shaft had been sunk in porphyry and was securely out of the mining zone and was located near the El Paso and Southwestern Railroad tracks. The new mine plan allowed for the development of haulage levels. Even number levels like the 200, 400, and 600 would be provided with electric trolley locomotives that would pull gable-bottomed Koppel cars. Odd numbered levels would haul ore cars with mules or be pushed by men and dumped into transfer raises to the haulage levels. This aggressive plan required miles of drifts to be enlarged to handle locomotives to connect to all of the Copper Queen's Mines including the distant Uncle Sam and Czar Mines. This also meant miles of new drifts driven in solid ground would be driven. Before the shaft was even completed, connecting drifts were being driven from the Lowell Mine and the Gardner Mine. The development of this new hoisting shaft was painfully slow; delays resulted in the headframe not being erected until December 1907. In April of 1908 the Koppel cars arrived. Finally, in May the new Nordberg hoist was installed and made its trial run on June 16th. This hoist used round cable unlike, the older flat cable that most hoists in Bisbee used and pulled 3 ton skips. Up to this time ore had been hoist by placing loaded ore cars on the decks of cages. On the surface 150ft. conveyor from the shaft to the El Paso & Southwestern rail line with two conveyor belts had been installed that ran between four rails that held 36 rail cars. Each of these had dumping carriages that moved constantly to ensure that the ore in each car was mixed. The Koppel cars introduced in 1908 had proved a failure and began to be replaced with two ton rocker dump cars, locally known as "E" cars. The locomotives were pulling 24 of these at a time. These locomotives were not perfect and for a time the Copper Queen considered building their own.

357

In March of 1910, the decision was made to install a dinkey hoist from the Gardner Mine underneath the headframe of the Sacramento and convert the pipe compartment into a dinkey hoisting compartment. A shaft compartment was sealed with timber from top to 1700 level to prevent rock falling from fast moving skips from the entering the new compartment. Interestingly, creosoted timber was used for a large part of this work. Men and material were hoisted in this compartment. On the 1700 level, pumps that were taken from Courtland, Arizona were installed to handle water. As the mine workings grew further from the either the Lowell or Sacramento shafts it became necessary to sink another major winze, down from the 1600 level to explore the area. Driving the level from the Sacramento was uneconomical, so in 1912 a winze was sunk and fixed to serve as an interior shaft. On May 5 a hoisting record for the district was set with 3087 tons in under 16 hours (note, hoisting was typical done only 7 ½ hours per shift to allow for men to be hoisted.)

The Sacramento underwent massive changes during the following year. An adit was driven from the EL Paso & Southwestern Rail bed on the southwest side of the mountain to the Sacramento Shaft. This drift was gunited and was used to transport men and timber to the shaft. Men would walk from the change house through this drift to the shaft station. At the station they would wait to be lowered to their levels. A new change house was also constructed and the shaft was increased by two compartments raised from the 1700 level. The compartments were completed in February 1914 and brought the shaft up to a massive five compartments. In March 1915 at the 300 level experiments were completed to test to see if the shaft could be concreted while operating. This experiment was successful and by June 25th storage bins for sand and gravel had been erected at the mouth of the Sacramento Adit and concrete mixing area was built at the "Subway" station. The concrete would be dropped in a 4 inch pipe and blown into the forms with compressed air. This was the first shaft ever to be concreted, while in operation. During the concreting process men were hoisted at the Lowell Shaft. The mine maintained steady production during 1916. In 1919, another major winze was developed, known as 16-4. It was raised from the 1600 to the 1500 level and sunk to the 1800 level. It had two compartments, one for hoisting and the other for a manway and pipes. The hoist was located on the 1500 level. At this time, the Dallas was being considered as becoming the main hoisting shaft. This was to occur, if the Sacramento was going to be mined out by the Sacramento Pit.

During 1928, the Porphyry Division was created to handle the mining of the Southeast Extension, North Cave Block and the Sacramento Pit Gloryhole Operations. It was decided that the last remaining ores in the Sacramento Pit would be dumped down large raises or "Gloryholes" that had been raised up from the 400 level and then transferred to the 500 level to be hauled to the shaft for hoisting In 1929 to increase hoisting capacity, the manway/cage compartment was raised from 1800 level to the 1600 level and converted to a handling skips. The first signs that block caving was not going to be successful occurred when, the first block of north end of the East Orebody failed to collapse. Quickly, the block next to it was undercut hoping to force it to cave. One of the blocks that was cut and blasted during 1930 was actually still standing in 1950. On November 1, 1931 mining in the Sacramento was shut down and the station was cut on the 960 level of the Junction Shaft with the intention of mining the Southeast Orebody from the Junction to be used as smelter flux

On January 12, 1932, the Sacramento Shaft was shut down. In 1936 the Sacramento and Gardner mines reopened and were formally titled Division "E". Mining continued, but as square set stopes. In 1940 the Sacramento produced 119,835 not including ores from the Southeast Extension. Finally, 1946 the Sacramento Mine permanently ceased operations and by the late 1940s, its surface facilities were dismantled. This shaft reached a final depth of 1,795 ft. and had five compartments.

September 14, 1904, Sacramento Mine
A.J. Wadleton had his right foot caught between the sinking bucket and the shaft timber. He suffered two broken toes.
"Foot Injured" Bisbee Daily Review 15 September 1904 page 5

November 7, 1907 Sacramento Mine
At 5:30 pm, a timber from a shaft compartment being temporarily as a chute broke into the dinkey compartment. The Sacramento did not have a functioning main hoist at this time and miners would be lowered down the Gardner mine to the 1000 level. At the 1000

level miners would walk to the Sacramento Shaft then they would be raised in a dinkey cage with an underground hoist to the 400 level to work. The broken timber prevented the dinkey cage from moving through the shaft. After a few hours the shaft was repaired and the men could be lowered to the 1000 level. Rumors, flooded the town indicating that men had been killed. In fact no one was injured or was in significant danger from the incident.

"Exaggerated Rumor is Spread Around" Bisbee Daily Review 8 November 1907 page 5

April 8, 1909, Sacramento Mine

Conveyor tender, John Conley was working on surface at the conveyor that brought ore down to load into rail cars, when his arm became caught and dragged over a roller. The ore weighing hundreds of pounds crushed the bones and tore up his arm. He was alone and some distance from any other worker. Finally, his cries were heard, and the belt was shut down. Conley instructed his rescuers on how to help him. After the accident, he walked to the Copper Queen Hospital and requested that the doctors do not amputate his arm. He stated, *"Doctor if the limb must go, I want to go with it."* His fellow workers commented how much *"nerve"* Conley had. He was working his last shift, when the accident occurred. He was recently married to Miss Sadie Dyess and was planning to go to California on a trip. Later, Doctor felt they could save the arm, but it would not be usable.

"Man Prefers Death to the Loss of Arm" Bisbee Daily Review 10 April 1909 page 5
"Will Save Conley's Arm" Bisbee Daily Review 13 April 1909 page 7

February 8, 1910, Sacramento Mine

John "Scotty" D. Clark was working on repairing a cracked airline at the 600 level station with Charlie Marshall and Willard M. Brown. They had installed on a pipe clamps over the crack and were going to measure the pipe to have a new one cut. Both Marshall and Clark were standing on a spreader that suddenly slipped out. Charlie fell about one set and grabbed a four-inch pipe. But the spreader and Clark fell. Brown and Marshall descended on the cage looking for him on the levels. When they reached the 1400, they found the shaft had been bulkheaded, about 30 ft. above the station and a second hoist was being used to hoist from the 1400 to 1600 levels. The hoistman told them to climb a ladder up to the bulkhead. Under the bulkhead Marshall shifted a board and felt Clark's body. They found him badly mangled with the spreader on his head. They left the body as it was and it was later removed by other men. Clark fell about 770 ft. down to the bulkhead on the 1370 level. Clark was married with a son and daughter living in Magdalena, Mexico. His wife came to Bisbee to arrange the funeral.

"Falls 750 Feet to his Death down a Shaft." Bisbee Daily Review 9 February 1912 page 7
"Clark's Funeral" Bisbee Daily Review 12 February 1912 page 7
"Copper Queen" Bisbee Daily Review 13 February 1912 page 1
"Will return to Bisbee" Bisbee Daily Review 9 March 1917 page 8
"Cochise County Coroner's Inquest No. 723" Arizona State Archives Phoenix

September 16, 1910, Sacramento Mine

Skip tender, W.C. Green and his partner were working loading skips on the 400 level. They would draw ore out of a large transfer raise into a "cartridge". The cartridge is a small section of a chute that holds just enough ore to fill a skip. When a skip arrived on the 400 level, the men would open the chute door at the bottom of the cartridge and fill the skip. This method prevents large quantities of ore from being dump down the shaft area* accidently or if the chute door on the transfer would get hung open. As the men worked, they did not put in place a board that would prevent someone from falling into the cartridge. Green fell into the cartridge. He grabbed onto a scaling bar that was laying across cartridge and held onto the chute door. His partner became paralyzed with fear and was unable to help Green. With his partner unable to help him, Green finally asked his partner to open the chute door and he would try to save himself. When the chute door, opened approximately, ½ ton of ore fell and knocked Green into the shaft Green fell 1,100 ft. to his death.* The skip tender was a broken, bloody, brainless mass when he was brought to the surface. He was 28 years old and survived by a brother Harry Green and a sister. His body was sent to Warsaw Missouri for burial. Note this of one of four fatal accidents that occurred in a two week period.

* The skip compartments at the bottom of the shaft were converted into an ore bin. Spilled ore was drawn from this bin and hoisted to the 1600 level ore pocket. On average a skip could hold 8,117 lbs. of wet ore (60 cubic ft.). Under good operating condition, a skip was loaded every minute.

"Swept to his Doom in fall of 1100 feet" Bisbee Daily Review 17 September 1910 page 1

"Relatives Claim Greene's Remains" Bisbee Daily Review 18 September 1910 page 1

"Original Certificate of Death." Arizona Department of Health Services. http://genealogy.az.gov/azdeath/009/10091081.pdf (July 24, 2011

Gerald F. G. Sherman. "Tramming and Hoisting at the Copper Queen Mine." American Institute of Mining Engineers Transaction Volume LII 1916:

September 19, 1910, Sacramento Mine

An unknown miner was buried up to his knees in mud on the 400 level. This accident was a few feet away from where W.S. Greene was killed. As a result there was a rumor that a man had fallen to his death at the Sacramento Mine.

"Report was Exaggerated" Bisbee Daily Review 20 September page5

April 20, 1911, Sacramento Mine

Joseph H. Lamb was killed in the Sacramento Shaft at 1:15 in the morning. It was likely that Lamb was in a hurry, it was close to the end of shift and he wanted to take some drill steel from the 300 level to the surface. Lamb had chosen not to put the seven to eight drill steels he was carrying into boxes that were used to transport drill steel, scaling bars and the like, but rather carried them in his arms. His partner noticed had that he was carrying steel down in his arms. During the ascent, one of the steels became caught in the shaft and Lamb was thrown out of the cage. The dinkey hoist engineer, John Duncan Grant noticed the cable wobble and realized something was entangled in the shaft. He stopped the hoist and told the hoistman on the ore hoist there was a problem. Ed Taylor the skip tender was sent down with another man and went to the 300 level and found nothing. He rang three slow bells indicating he wanted to be raised up slowly. At five sets above the station, they found the dinkey hung up, but could not see because of the darkness. So they went up and got a lamp and with Mr. Kinney went down and removed the lagging between the compartments and discovered Lamb. His body was found twenty-five feet above the 300 level station wedged between the cage and the shaft wall. His neck was broken, and death was believed to be instantaneous. Mr. Lamb was 42 years old and single. Foreman Kahler stated that he was one of his best men. J.H. Lamb had worked at the Sacramento for about one year. Before working at the Sacramento, he had attended medical school. In Bisbee, he had been a bartender in saloons and excellent pastry cook at the English Kitchen.

"J.H. Lamb is Killed in Mine" Bisbee Daily Review 20 April 1911 page 1
"Came to Death by Own Carelessness" Bisbee Daily Review 21 April 1911 page 8
"Original Certificate of Death." Arizona Department of Health Services. http://genealogy.az.gov/azdeath/008/10080355.pdf (May 15, 2012)
"Cochise County Coroner's Inquest No. 826" Arizona State Archives

July 17, 1911, Sacramento Mine

John *"Wildman"* Weilderman was killed at 11:00 pm. A witness stated that he saw Weilderman carrying a keg of water on a mine car. The car stopped, and when he stood up to lift the keg, he fell over dead. It was initially felt that he died from electric shock but, later it was revealed that heart failure was the likely cause of death. The autopsy noted that his lungs were blackened probably from working in a coal mine. He was about 24 years old.

"Weilderman is Struck Dead" Bisbee Daily Review 18 July 1911 page 3
"Weilderman Died of Heart Failure" Bisbee Daily Review 19 July 1911 page 8
"Cochise County Coroner's Inquest No. 826" Arizona State Archives

September 23, 1911, Sacramento Mine surface

Antonio Espinosa had his arm caught in a conveyor belt. It was torn up and a piece of bone was broken off. There was fear that he may lose his arm. He spent 218 days at the Copper Queen Hospital. His arm was saved.

"Mexican Miner Injured" Bisbee Daily Review 26 September 1911 page 3
Copper Queen Hospital Patients Register Sept. 23, 1911 Bisbee Mining & Historical Museum Bisbee

October 18, 1911, Sacramento Mine

John Dennis received a minor injury underground. While examining this injury, it was discovered that he had fractured his skull year's earlier.* He was released from the Copper Queen Hospital on Nov. 13, 1911.

*The October 25, 1911 newspaper article describes this accident as the first fractured skull in a series of three. These were believed to be part of the mining superstition that mining accidents occurred in sequences of threes. The others were Ben Hurst on October 24 in the Gardner Shaft and Joe Hall on October 19, 1911, in the Uncle Sam Shaft. It is interesting to note that the fractured skull was discovered and had not been caused by this accident.
"Miner Injured by Falling Timber" Bisbee Daily Review 20 October 1911 page 3
"Skull Fractured by Falling Object" Bisbee Daily Review 25 October 1911 page 3
Copper Queen Hospital Patients Register Jan 1, 1913 – Mar 24, 1914 Bisbee Mining and Historical Museum, Bisbee.

April 6, 1912, Sacramento Mine

R.H. White was working alone as a loader at a transfer chute on the 1400 level. The chute was new and had just been completed two days before. This chute had become hung up, and White was trying to free it when rock fell into the manway and killed him. He was married with his wife and son in Ishpeming, Michigan and a brother in Iron River, Michigan.

"To Send Body Home" Bisbee Daily Review 9 April 1912 page 8
"Cochise County Coroner's Inquest No. 906" Arizona State Archives

August 16, 1912, Sacramento Mine

Lawrence Moinardi a miner from St. George, Italy had his left leg broken by falling rock. He had been in Bisbee only ten days. Moinardi remained in the Copper Queen Hospital 98 days.

"Casualties in Mines 1912" Bisbee Daily Review 12 January 1913, page 7
Copper Queen Hospital Patients Register August 16, 1912, Bisbee Mining and Historical Museum, Bisbee.

June 8, 1914, Sacramento Mine

W.F Cone* was struck by falling rock and his right leg was broken above the ankle. He was taken to the Copper Queen Hospital, where he remained 198 days.

* His name was given as John Coine in the Bisbee Daily Review.
Office of State Mine Inspector. *Fourteenth Annual Report of the State Mine Inspector State of Arizona for the Year Ending November 30, 1914.* Tombstone Epitaph.
"Has Leg Broken" Bisbee Daily Review 9 June 1914 page 8
Hospital Patients Copper Queen Bisbee Mining and Historical Register June 8, 1914 Museum, Bisbee.

December 18, 1914, Sacramento Mine

The lights on at least the 300 and 400 levels were out and Daniel Clarence *"Dennie"* Hiatt an electrician was on the 300 level, trying to get them back on. He climbed a ladder up into the shaft, and it appears he reached over to a switch box to change a fuse. After changing the fuse, he was struck by a cage being hoisted to the surface. Hiatt was knocked into the shaft and fell to about 40 ft. below the 1600 level. He was survived by a brother O.G. Hiatt from Grand Junction, Colorado and a six-year-old son. His funeral was delayed until his brother arrived in Bisbee, He was buried on December 24 in Evergreen Cemetery.

"Hiatt Funeral Postponed" Bisbee Daily Review 24 December 1914 page 6
"Original Certificate of Death." Arizona Department of Health Services. http://genealogy.az.gov/azdeath/013/10130332.pdf (May 15, 2012)
Office of State Mine Inspector. *Fourth Annual Report of the State Mine Inspector State of Arizona for the Year Ending November 30, 1915.* Tombstone Epitaph.
"Bisbee-Lowell Evergreen Cemetery." My Cochise.
http://www.mycochise.com/cembisbeeh.php (May 19, 2012)
"Cochise County Coroner's Inquest No. 1129" Arizona State Archives Phoenix

March 4, 1915, Sacramento Mine

William *"Sharky"* Horn was working with Bud Beem in a stope on the 1400 level. Horn, who had been off the previous day, began drilling. After about a minute, Beem saw a flash, when a missed hole exploded. The roar of the drill drowned out the sound of the explosion. Horn was caught in a blast that blew a hole into his throat. He was admitted to the Copper Queen Hospital. He died from shock on March 6th. The missed hole was the remnant of a small blast from the previous day. That round consisted of three holes that were drilled and loaded with one stick of 30% powder in each by Charles R. Kirk. Cracks in the rock were also loaded. Kirk had reported a misfire that Horn later drilled into and detonated. He was survived by a sister, Mrs. Mary Allie Sullivan of Manchester, New Hampshire

Certificate of Death." Arizona Department of Health Services. http://genealogy.az.gov/azdeath/013/10131196.pdf (May 28, 2012)

"Office of State Mine Inspector. *Seventh Annual Report of the State Mine Inspector State of Arizona for the Year Ending November 30, 1915.*

Inquest Held" <u>Bisbee Daily Review</u> 9 March 1915 page 8

"Cochise County Coroner's Inquest No. 1143" Arizona State Archives Phoenix

May 3, 1916, Sacramento Mine

English miner, Thomas Richard Williams was working in a stope with Leo Kelly. Williams was picking down the back in order to set up a drill, when a boulder fell from the top of a set of timber and crushed his skull. He was 39 years old and survived by a widow and two children living on Clawson Hill. His remains were taken to Ishpeming, Michigan. The Deputy State Mine Inspector felt that Williams had done everything he could to protect himself, but a crack behind the boulder was hidden behind a piece of timber.

Dugan Mortuary Records Aug. 26, 1914 – Dec 21, 1916 Accession 2010.10.9 Bisbee Mining and Historical Museum, Bisbee.

"Original Certificate of Death." <u>Arizona Department of Health Services.</u> http://genealogy.az.gov/azdeath/015/10150020.pdf (May 28, 2012)

Office of State Mine Inspector. *Fifth Annual Report of the State Mine Inspector State of Arizona for the Year Ending November 30, 1916.*

"Cochise County Coroner's Inquest No. 1215" Arizona State Archives

October 1916, Sacramento Mine

Hoistman, Dan Twomey fell in the pit under the hoist drum and was off work several days.

"Dan Twomey Hurt" <u>Bisbee Daily Review</u> 31 October 1916 page 8

Date unknown circa 1915-1917 Sacramento Mine

Cris (Chris) Kukich was struck in the head by a falling rock. According to Kukich after the accident, he began having epileptic fits and as a result permanently injured by the accident and unable to work. He filed a lawsuit against Phelps Dodge for $15,000. This suit was later dropped by Kukich.

"Brings Suit for Damages" <u>Bisbee Daily Review</u> 27 June 1917 page 6

"Was Dismissed" <u>Bisbee Daily Review</u> 6 November 1917 page 5

February 26, 1917, Sacramento Mine

English Miner, Hamilton Walton was working with Everett Brizee in a sulfide stope on the 1200 level*. They need to cut out about five inches of rock to fit in a set of timber. Initially, they tried to dig it out with a pick. After a while, they realized they need to drill a short hole and blast it. Walton began drilling, and a 300 lb. rock fell and hit his arm and landed on his legs. Brizee had called out a warning, but Walton could not hear him over the noise of the drill. He was killed at 7:45 pm. * The inquest states the 400 level, but I believe it actually occurred on the 1200 level.

"Walton Funeral Thursday" <u>Bisbee Daily Review</u> 28 February 1917 page 8

"Jury Investigates Death of Walton" <u>Bisbee Daily Review</u> 2 March 1917 page 3

"Original Certificate of Death." <u>Arizona Department of Health Services.</u> http://genealogy.az.gov/azdeath/086/10860570.pdf (May 28, 2012)

Office of State Mine Inspector. *Sixth Annual Report of the State Mine Inspector State of Arizona for the Year Ending November 30, 1917.*

"Cochise County Coroner's Inquest No. 1256" Arizona State Archives Phoenix

February 19, 1918, Sacramento Mine
Oscar Winn broke a toe on his right foot.
"Has Fractured Toe" Bisbee Daily Review 20 February 1918 page 8

June 24, 1918, Sacramento Mine
Joseph Thomas was given a *"premature burial"* during a cave-in. He suffered only bruises.
Although, initially it was thought his back may be broken.
"Injured in Mine" Bisbee Daily Review 25 June 1918 page 8
"Much improved" Bisbee Daily Review 27 June 1918 page 8

July, 1918, Sacramento Mine
R.E. Covington in juried his ankle in an undescribed accident.
"Slight Injury" Bisbee Daily Review 26 July 1918 page 6

August 1918, Sacramento Mine
E.S. Summers a resident of Laundry Hill injured his back putting a derailed mine car back
on track.
"Back is Sprained" Bisbee Daily Review 28 August 1918 page 8

September 18, 1918, Sacramento Mine
A rock fell and struck J. Bowles on the neck. He was taken to the Copper Queen Hospital.
"Bowles Injured at Sac" Bisbee Daily Review 20 September 1918 page 8

October 1, 1918, Sacramento Mine
Electrician's Helper, John Patche tripped over a rail and sprained his wrist.
"Wrist is Sprained" Bisbee Daily Review 3 October 1918 page 8

October 10, 1918, Sacramento Mine
Mucker, Bernard Connelly injured his back while lifting a derailed loaded mine car. He
was expected to be off work a few days.
"Back Is Sprained" Bisbee Daily Review 11 October 1918 page 6

January 8, 1919, Sacramento Mine
Bernard Conley was smashed between a mine car and a timber. His left side was bruised.
"Is Slightly injured" Bisbee Daily Review 9 January 1919 page 8

February 7, 1921, Sacramento Mine
Sam Woods was caught in a cave-in. His back was injured and he was taken to the
Copper Queen Hospital.
"S.B. Woods Hurt" Bisbee Daily Review 8 February 1921 page 6

April 30, 1921, Sacramento Mine
Shift Boss, Leonard Warmington climbed into 34 raise on the 1200 level, before the crew
arrived and located the two missed holes reported by the previous shift. One was in the
center, and the other was off in a corner. Both had fuses dangling from them. Alfred
Peterson climbed the raise and Warmington pointed out the two holes and ordered Peterson
to shoot them right away. Peterson argued stating that he had been gotten dizzy from

powder smoke the day before. The argument continued with his partner Carl Schondelmeir, who wanted to blast the holes. Schondelmeir sent up a stoper and a hose but continued to tell Peterson they needed to shoot the holes. Finally, Peterson called down and told Schondelmeir to get powder. At that moment the efficiency engineer, L.R. Jackson arrived to measure the raise. Schondelmeir told him to call up and let Peterson know he was climbing the raise. After he measured the raise he came down and told Schondelmeir it was 42 ft. to the back, Peterson started the drill, and before he could even get to full power the machine slipped into the bootleg in the corner of the raise, and it detonated. Jackson went and got Jack Rainy who was nearby, and Schondelmeir began bring Peterson down the manway. Peterson told Schondelmeir, *"I am a goner – But it don't make no difference, - I have to go one time or another, I am old enough to die. - Get me out of here- My stomach is paining me."* At the hospital, they determined he was cut up on the left arm, over the eye and there was hole in the wall of his abdomen with organs sticking through. They X-rayed him and discovered rocks had been shot into him on the left side and put him into surgery. They sewed up four holes in his intestines. At 4:00 pm he died. His family was from South Dakota, and Peterson was a Swedish-born naturalized citizen. He was survived by his wife Thelma and five children three daughters ranging from 24-34 years old and two son's ages 26 & 24.

"Dies from Injuries" Bisbee Daily Review 1 May 1921 page 7

"Original Certificate of Death." Arizona Department of Health Services. http://genealogy.az.gov/azdeath/023/10232162.pdf (May 30, 2012)

"Cochise County Coroner's Inquest No. 1150" Arizona State Archives

June 11, 1921, Sacramento Mine

On the 900 level, Henry Claude Sommers was hit by a falling rock while installing timber to support the same rock. He died before he could be taken to the hospital.

"H.C. Summers Dies after Mine Accident" Bisbee Daily Review 12 June 1921 page 1

"Original Certificate of Death." Arizona Department of Health Services. http://genealogy.az.gov/azdeath/023/10233054.pdf (May 30, 2012)

Office of State Mine Inspector. *Tenth Annual Report of the State Mine Inspector State of Arizona for the Year Ending November 30, 1921.*

September 30, 1921, Sacramento Mine

Motorman, Charles F. Pelot drove a locomotive into a timber truck and broke his leg.

"Breaks Leg" Bisbee Daily Review 1 October 1921 page 6

October 13, 1921, Sacramento Mine

Around 9:00 am, Taylor Bentley Sessions was clearing out a section on the 1000 level to install timber when he was killed A cave-in occurred tearing out the timber. A timber struck Sessions fracturing his neck. He was 37 years old and buried in Thatcher, Arizona.

(No coroner's inquest could be located)

"One Killed Three Injured in Peculiar Series of Accidents in Bisbee District Yesterday" Bisbee Daily Review 14 October 1921 page 4

"Original Certificate of Death." Arizona Department of Health Services. http://genealogy.az.gov/azdeath/024/10241239.pdf (May 30, 2012)

Office of State Mine Inspector. *Tenth Annual Report of the State Mine Inspector State of Arizona for the Year Ending November 30, 1921.*

October 19, 1922, Sacramento Mine

Isidor Straussnig and Chris Prenovich Vucedalich were working in a stope on the 1600 level. Straussnig dropped down the manway to get timber. While he was gone, Vucedalich started to make room to install a cap. In the manway, Straussnig heard the "black sulfide" collapse for about ten seconds. Straussnig ran to get a motorman and told him to get the foreman. Originally, it was hoped he was only trapped. The location was still caving heavily, and the tangled mass of timber only allowed two men to work, at a time. After hours of work his body was discovered, but it took over 24 hours to recover the body. He was about 37- years-old and from Montenegro and was survived by a widow in the old country.

"Rescue Crews Work at Top Speed; Hope to Find Miner Still Alive" Bisbee Daily Review 20 October 1922 page 8
"Cochise County Coroner's Inquest No. 1492" Arizona State Archives
"Hope to Recover Vucedalich Body Some Time Today" Bisbee Daily Review 21 October 1922 page 2
Office of State Mine Inspector. *Twelfth Annual Report of the State Mine Inspector State of Arizona for the Year Ending November 30, 1923.*
"Original Certificate of Death." Arizona Department of Health Services. http://genealogy.az.gov/azdeath/026/10260045.pdf (May 31, 2012)
Dugan Mortuary Records Aug 24, 1922 to June 5, 1924 Accession 2010.10.15 Bisbee Mining and Historical Museum, Bisbee

November 21, 1922, Sacramento Mine

Mike Hass had two fingers blown off his left hand when a blasting cap detonated.

"Fingers Blown Off" Bisbee Daily Review 23 November 1922 page 6

November 16, 1923, Sacramento Mine

On the 1200 level, H. Leon McNeil, a motorman and his swamper, Ed Wright were loading the last mine car on the last trip of the shift. No. 1230 chute had become hung up, and McNeil stood up to free it, and his head touched the trolley wire. He had forgotten to turn off the power to the trolley wire and was electrocuted. McNeil was born in Sonora, Mexico and buried in Douglas, Arizona.

Office of State Mine Inspector. *Twelfth Annual Report of the State Mine Inspector State of Arizona for the Year Ending November 30, 1923.*
"Original Certificate of Death." Arizona Department of Health Services. http://genealogy.az.gov/azdeath/027/10272587.pdf (May 30, 2012)
"Cochise County Coroner's Inquest No. 1534" Arizona State Archives Phoenix

April 11, 1924, Sacramento Mine

Around 10:30 pm, Cager C.W. Moore sent a timber truck loaded with gunite from the 1500 level to William A. Taylor another cager waiting on the 1700 of the Sacramento Winze. Both cages were stopped at the 1700 level, and a release signal was never given for either cage, so the hoistman could not move the cages. During this time, pumpman J.O. Barnett heard what he thought was a boulder falling in the winze, but since this often occurred he was not concerned. Two miners above thought a timber truck may have fallen into the shaft. Finally, Shift Boss Tom Stetson and Bassett Watkins climbed down the manway. Watkins remained on the 1600 level, but Stetson climbed to the 1700 level and found the cages unattended. Taylor's lamp was hanging on the 1700 station, but since cagers worked around brightly lit areas, they often used their carbide lamps largely for cigarette lighters more than lights. So this did not overly concern the men. Stetson went to the 1800 level and ordered Barnett to pump out the sump. At the sump they discovered a bulkhead that had been under four feet of water and cover with muck had two planks broken. Watkins had previously recovered a body from a sump andused a track spike puller to fish out Taylor's body. His neck and other bones were broken. It was felt that Taylor had tripped and fallen into the winze. He was survived by a married sister who lived in Texas and his father in Ardmore, Oklahoma.

"William A. Taylor Meets Death by Fall Winze" Bisbee Ore 12 April 1924 page 1
Dugan Mortuary Records Feb. 9, 1923 – Aug. 16, 1926, Accession 2010.10.17 Bisbee Mining and Historical Museum, Bisbee.
Office of State Mine Inspector. *Thirteenth Annual Report of the State Mine Inspector State of Arizona for the Year Ending November 30, 1924.*
"Original Certificate of Death." Arizona Department of Health Services. http://genealogy.az.gov/azdeath/028/10281962.pdf (May 31, 2012)
"Cochise County Coroner's Inquest No. 1543" Arizona State Archives Phoenix

May 24, 1924, Sacramento Mine

German Miner, Martin N. Miller and Columbus F. Hicks were killed on the 1700 level when an entire round of blast holes prematurely detonated around 3:00 pm. It was reported that the explosion blew off Miller's upper torso, head and one leg. Miller was survived by his wife, Josephine Miller.

"Two Killed On the Sac 1700 Level" Bisbee Ore 24 May 1924 page 1
Dugan Mortuary Records Feb. 9, 1923 – Aug. 16, 1926 Accession 2010.10.17 Bisbee Mining and Historical Museum, Bisbee.
Office of State Mine Inspector. *Thirteenth Annual Report of the State Mine Inspector State of Arizona for the Year Ending November 30, 1924.*
"Original Certificate of Death." Arizona Department of Health Services. http://genealogy.az.gov/azdeath/028/10282539.pdf (May 31, 2012)
Dugan Mortuary Records Feb. 9, 1923 – Aug. 16, 1926 Accession 2010.10.17 Bisbee Mining and Historical Museum, Bisbee.
Office of State Mine Inspector. *Thirteenth Annual Report of the State Mine Inspector State of Arizona for the Year Ending November 30, 1924.*
"Original Certificate of Death." Arizona Department of Health Services. http://genealogy.az.gov/azdeath/028/10282543.pdf (May 31, 2012)

September 22, 1927, Sacramento Mine

William David Orton and L.J. Wright had loaded 36 mine cars from a chute on the 800 level. They had pulled up another nine car train. The chute had become hung up, and Orton held open the door while Wright tried to free the clog with a blowpipe. Suddenly, 15 tons of mud poured out and buried Orton between a mine car and the chute platform. He was suffocated. His cousin was Cecil Orton was a shift boss at the Sacramento Mine.

He was survived by a widow Johnnie Ida Orton and was buried in Kentucky.

"Original Certificate of Death." Arizona Department of Health http://genealogy.az.gov/azdeath/035/10351582.pdf (May 31, 2012)
Office of State Mine Inspector. *Sixteenth Annual Report of the State Mine Inspector State of Arizona for the Year Ending November 30, 1927.*
Dugan Mortuary Records Aug. 29, 1926 – Jun4 1930 Accession 2010.10.20 Bisbee Mining and Historical Museum, Bisbee.
"Cochise County Coroner's Inquest No. 1660" Arizona State Archives Phoenix

February 9, 1928, Sacramento Mine

Perry M. Byerly was working with his brother J.R. Byerly at the 1400 level shaft pocket loading skips. While Perry was trying to load the cartridge, the chute hung up, and then suddenly mud poured out burying him. He was suffocated.

"Original Certificate of Death." http://genealogy.az.gov/azdeath/036/10361184.pdf Arizona Department of Health (May 31, 2012)
Office of State Mine Inspector. *Seventeenth Annual Report of the State Mine Inspector State of Arizona for the Year Ending November 30, 1928.*
Dugan Mortuary Records Aug. 29, 1926 – Jun 4, 1930, Accession 2010.10.20 Bisbee Mining and Historical Museum, Bisbee.
"Cochise County Coroner's Inquest No. 1667" Arizona State Archives Phoenix

September 9, 1930, Sacramento Mine

Swedish skiptender, Eric Erikson and Thomas Rascola had emptied the shaft pocket on the 1500 level. They needed to change levels, but the shaft bell rope had become caught on a skip the evening of the 8th and was torn out. The shaft bell rope could only be replaced on the weekend, so the men were using the call bells to signal the cage. The men would signal with the call bell, and the hoistman would give them 45 seconds to walk from the call bell onto the cage. Erikson rang the call bell and before he was completely on the cage it moved rolling him between the shaft timber and the cage. Rascola just kept ringing the call bell until the cage stopped, but Erikson was already dead. He was survived by his wife, Ida.

"Original Certificate of Death." Arizona Department of Health Services. http://genealogy.az.gov/azdeath/042/10421710.pdf (May 31, 2012)
Copper Queen Hospital Patients Register Nov 13 1929- March 25, 1931, Bisbee Mining and Historical Museum, Bisbee.
"Cochise County Coroner's Inquest No. 1701" Arizona State Archives Phoenix

May 15, 1939, Sacramento Mine

German Miner, George Basil Wollman was working on the 1700 level when he was caught in a cave-in. 50-tons of fine dirt buried and suffocated him. It took miners seven hours to uncover his body He was survived by his wife Martha, two sisters, two brothers and his mother Mrs. Max Wollman.

"Bisbee" Evening Courier 16 May 1939 page 1, Prescott Az.

September 21, 1940, Sacramento Mine

Leon P. Dage and George Maczygemba were on the 1000 level in 3-15 stope*. A.L. Ralph told the men that they needed to take to stull up a three-ton sulfide boulder hanging in the back of the stope. Dage decided to install the flooring first. The rock fell killing him.

*Can also be written 10-3-15 stope. The ten indicates the level. This often dropped if the level is known
"Cochise County Coroner's Inquest No. 1785" Arizona State Archives Phoenix

Sacramento Pit c-1927

Sacramento Pit

In 1909, exploration began on the Sacramento Porphyry afert an intensive search by underground workings and by churn drilling from the surface two separate orebodies were delineated, the East and West Ore Bodies. The West orebody was of higher grade, but the ores from both would be required to be processed by a concentrator regardless of the mining method chosen. To be profitable, the mining method would need to move large tonnages quickly at a low cost. The three alternatives considered were open pit mining with steam shovels, underground block caving and underground top slicing. The idea of block caving was quickly eliminated. The advantage of top slicing was that the waste rock covering the ore could remain and not have to be mined. On the other hand, underground mining would restrict the tonnages mined to available mine cars and hoisting capacity. Underground mining was considered more dangerous and skilled miners are always a challenge to acquire. The open pit would require mining millions of tons of waste for at least two years before any significant ore would be mined. Also, a heavy investment in machinery would be needed. Finally it was hoped that the mine would be safer than underground and for many of the positions less skilled labor could be hired. As the estimated cost were roughly the same, the difficulty in hiring skilled miners swayed the decision and it was decided to develop an open pit mine, Yet a just before this decision and area was being prepared to be stoped and was closed after the decision to start an open pit. The pit would use rail for haulage and with 20 and 25 -ton rail cars which would be loaded with steam shovels.

On April 5, 1917, stripping began with one steam shovel operating. On June 6, 1918 the peak was blasted from Sacramento Hill. Phelps Dodge had hired some experienced open pit miners largely from the Chino Pit at Santa Rita, New Mexico, but others had come from the Iron Range. Yet, with the United States being drawn in to World War I hiring quality staff was difficult. Blasting became a problem. At the time a Bisbee miner was reported at the time, as saying in reference to blasting on Sacramento Hill, *"Powder is the most uncertain thing in the world, except a woman"*. After the first three years of Sacramento Pit operating, he may have removed the exception. Fly rock from the blast initially, caused the most problems. The town of Jiggerville, roads and mine buildings were regularly pummeled by flying rocks People were warned by Phelps Dodge to keep off all roads and trails from west end of Sacramento Hill and Gardner Shaft. Also they wanted all people to keep clear of the area from the Copper Queen machine shop to the Sacramento Shaft unless, they were an employee or on urgent business. The company guarded area during large blasts. When the miners were blasting boulders in the pit the areas may not be guarded, but people should listen for blasting signals, locomotive whistles and shovel whistles, seven short blows. The company was particularly concerned about, visitors and sightseers in particular. In 1918, the Copper Queen Safety build had to be abandoned because it location was too dangerous. The building was too close to the pit. A new safety building was constructed at the Czar Mine. For the blast on May 31, 1917, Phelps Dodge asked residents of Naco road to evacuate, as the 6,000-7,000 lbs. of explosive were detonated. Windows were regular broken and plaster in building was knocked down, but this was more of an inconvenience and than a danger, unlike fly rock which injured residents and killed a miner. Great tragedies occurred with premature blasts. In 1918, eight men were killed from early detonations. With most of these accidents it remained unclear of the cause of the detonation, but conditions improved rapidly. During 1919, no one was killed working in the Sacramento Pit and only two more men were killed in premature explosions until the final closure of the pit. To help aid in blasting, the speed each blast hole was drilled was monitored. This gave the crews a better idea on how much explosive was needed in each hole. Small steel blasting shelters were soon placed around the mine site. A bilingual Mexican, was added to the safety department to ensure that the safety could be readily understood by Spanish speaking workers of Phelps Dodge.

The steam locomotives and shovels needed water. Originally water from Naco, Arizona was tried, but this water did not effectively soften. Instead the water for the Sacramento Pit was from the Junction Mine. A water softening plant was constructed and provided between 100,000 and 180,000 gallons of softened water per day. At the end of World War I, the copper market fell and compiled with delays in the construction of the concentrator, all stripping operations to be stopped in the pit in 1921. The main orebody was uncovered in June 1921 and soon all work was stopped in the pit except the mining of 4,000 tons a month to be used as a silica–rich flux at the Douglas Smelter. In 1922 the Calumet & Cochise Shaft finally, encountered enough clean water to provide water for the concentrator and the Sacramento Pit. During December, the steam shovels were being overhauled to begin mining again. From April 1922 until 1929, the Sacramento Pit mined continuously. Slowly, the rails spiraled on a gentle 2 ½ % grade towards the bottom.

The last 130-145 ft. of ore was mined through "Glory Holes." Eleven large ten foot by ten foot raises were driven into the bottom of the Sacramento pit from the 400 level of the Sacramento Mine. At the 400 level were the *"bulldozing"* chambers with grizzlies covering raises to the 500 level for haulage. Getting as close to the edge of the raises as was safe, churn drills drilled 60 foot holes that were blasted with 400-500 lbs. of explosive. An adit from the 200 level of the nearby Holbrook mine was used to deliver explosives and drill steel to the top of the glory holes. Once at the bottom of the pit burros (not mules) were used to deliver the supplies. Interestingly, water seeping down the pit was captured in a water ditch that was directed into this adit to be pumped from the Holbrook Shaft. Churn drills along with jackhammers and Leyner drills mounted on tripods carved out a conical pits that included the raises. The blasted rock would fall down the raise to the grizzlies in the bulldozing chamber. Boulders too large for the haulage level chutes would be caught on the grizzlies and were re-blasted or broken with a sledge hammer. From the grizzlies it would fall into storage chutes on the 500 level to await haulage. This ore was hauled in 4-ton gable bottom *"Koppel"* style mine cars to the ore pockets at the Sacramento Shaft. The glory hole mining continued until 1931 when the West Orebody was depleted.

The Sacramento Pit had mined from 5,665 ft. elevation down to 4,925 ft. elevation. It presented a hole at the 5,360 ft. elevation that was 1,400 ft. by 1,200 ft. The monstrous, mechanical, machines had moved 11,200,000 tons of waste rock, 12,600,000 tons of low grade leach material and including the gloryhole operation, 7,957,370 tons of ore. A total of 358,144,662 pounds of copper, 1,365,191 ounces of silver and 54,234 ounces of gold were directly produced from the operation. Leaching of the low grade ores produced a furth Heer 57,220,648 lbs. of copper, but this leaching continue off and on until 1944. This engineering marvel of the time became a popular site for area tourists to visit until the time it was backfilled by mining operations from the newer Lavender Pit. Then in 1965, it was decided to expand the Lavender Pit into the Holbrook Mine region. Operations from the Lavender pit mined through the older Sacramento Pit removing the back fill and nearly all of the Sacramento Pit. In the early years the Sacramento open pit was the West Orebody or called simply *"Sacramento Hill"* after a true pit began to develop when the benches dropped below the 5,360 elevation, it tended to be called the *"Sac"* Pit and during the last couple years it was referred to as the plural *"Glory Holes"* This should not be confused with the original open cut of the Copper Queen Mine which is called the singular *"Glory Hole."*

March 8, 1917, Sacramento Pit

A flying boulder from a blast at the Sacramento Pit smashed through the house Of Mr. and Mrs. Holland. It barely missed the Holland's and their baby. The destructive rock *"played havoc with their furniture."*

"Have Narrow Escape" Bisbee Daily Review 9 March 1917 page 8

October 7, 1917, Sacramento Pit

Switchman, Roy Lovick injured his back climbing from a rail car. He was taken to the Copper Queen Hospital.

"Is in Hospital" Bisbee Daily Review 9 October 1917, page 8

November 10, 1917, Sacramento Pit

F.O. Frost a powderman broke a small bone in the ankle. It was remarked that he was the first man in over seven days that an ambulance had been called for.

(Note he was killed on May 7, 1918 in the Sacramento Pit)
"Was Injured" Bisbee Daily Review 11 November1917 page 8

December 10, 1917, Sacramento Pit

A section of railroad track fell on the leg of Miguel Gonzales and bruised his left ankle.

Office of State Mine Inspector. *Seventh Annual Report of the State Mine Inspector State of Arizona for the Year Ending November 30, 1918.*

January 9, 1918, Sacramento Pit

It was a cold, miserable, windy, day, and the powder crew was loading three holes on the east end of the top bench. An engineering crew was also working in the area. Two holes were loaded and one hole containing 1,750 lbs. of explosives was two cases short of being loaded. The holes were loaded with both Trojan 40% bag powder, which was poured into the holes with a tin funnel. It had the consistency of oatmeal. Also, 40 % Trojan stick powder was used. Each stick was cut into three pieces and dropped into the holes. The blasting caps were electric. Powder man, J.D. McBride was wiring the primer for a hole containing 1,300 lbs. of explosive.* Suddenly, a detonation occurred. A locomotive on the second bench near the base holes was knocked over. The burning gases escaping from the blast burned men over 100 ft. from the blast. Sidney Drakenfield, a civil engineer, was holding the end of a surveying tape was killed instantly. Roger Pelton, the head of the engineering department was holding the other end of the tape was uninjured. Modesto Olibas Vastado was also killed instantly. Florenzo Vasquez** and Carlos Calderon, a Spanish miner, were fatally injured and died at the Copper Queen Hospital. Eight other men were injured Juan Nunez suffered a broken nose, jaw and an injured eye. The left eye of Francisco Valenzuela was destroyed. His leg was also injured. Jose Monarres had his front teeth broken and face burned. Nat Anderson survived with a broken nose and cuts. Juan Villeneda had his eyes injured and burns on the face. J.D. McBride suffered only cuts. Frederico Esquer had his face and eyes burned. Jose S. Martinez, luckily, only had bruised shoulders. All the injured men were taken to the Copper Queen Hospital. This accident was the largest mine accident to occur in Bisbee; four men were killed and eight were injured. The actual cause of the detonation was never determined. On the 3rd level of the Southwest Mine on April 24, 1923, the largest underground accident occurred. In that accident three men were killed and one was injured.

*At the time, it was thought both holes had exploded, but it appears that only the larger hole detonated. The smaller hole containing 1,300 lbs. of explosive would result on another fatal accident that happened on January 19, 1918.

**To the challenge of prosecution lawyers, Florencio Vasquez was the only eye witness in the murder of Pablo (Jose) Padilla. The case was tried on April 24 & 25, 1918 after his death. Vasquez saw Padilla's miner's candle stick on a table when Padilla and Miguel Alvarado began arguing. Padill supposedly, picked up the candlestick and attacked Alvarado tearing his shirt. Alvarado took the candlestick away from Padilla. They continued fighting and both grasping the candlestick Alvarado claimed, Padilla fell on the candlestick. Alvarado still carrying the candlestick left the house and dropped it on the street. Alvarado was later found guilty of manslaughter.

"Blast Takes Heavy Toll" Bisbee Daily Review 10 April 1918 page 1&8

"Was on Trial" Bisbee Daily Review 24 April 1918 page 3

Office of State Mine Inspector. Seventh Annual Report of the State Mine Inspector State of Arizona for the Year Ending November 30, 1918.

"Original Certificate of Death." Arizona Department of Health Services. http://genealogy.az.gov/azdeath/017/10170804.pdf (May 29, 2012)

"Original Certificate of Death." Arizona Department of Health Services. http://genealogy.az.gov/azdeath/017/10170805.pdf (May 29, 2012)

"Original Certificate of Death." Arizona Department of Health Services. http://genealogy.az.gov/azdeath/017/10170814.pdf (May 29, 2012)

"Original Certificate of Death." Arizona Department of Health Services. http://genealogy.az.gov/azdeath/017/10170803.pdf (May 29, 2012)

"Cochise County Coroner's Inquest No. 1309" Arizona State Archives Phoenix

"Cochise County Coroner's Inquest No. 1297" Arizona State Archives Phoenix

January 19, 1918, Sacramento Pit

Men working in the Sacramento Pit were removing the rock that was blasted out by the disastrous premature explosion on January 9, 1918. These men uncovered a hole that had failed to detonate on that fatal day. The wires to the blasting cap were discovered intact. It was decided to try to detonate the hole. A string of rail cars was left near the hole to protect the Sacramento Shaft from rocks flying from the blast. A warning whistle was blown to notify people to take cover. The hole containing 1,300 lbs. of explosive was then shot. It exploded with an unexpected great force. A rock was thrown 1,300 ft. to the conveyor at the Sacramento Shaft. This rock hit Ephraim Patrick Crump on the head and knocking him to the ground crushing his head and killing him. Another rock flew in the opposite direction towards Johnson Addition. It broke through the roof of R.A. Wood's barbershop and stuck the head of, Percy Rowland. His skull was fractured, and he was taken to the Copper Queen Hospital. He worked for the Calumet & Arizona Mining Company and was waiting to get a shave. W.E. Cobb was sitting next to Rowland was uninjured. Roofs of houses near the pit were *"riddled"* with rocks and a large number of windows were broken. The newspaper reported that the property damage from the blast was the most significant since the start of the pit. Crump had the reputation of being a devoted family man and was survived by his wife Evaline and six children, including little Orville Crump, who was just over a year old. Ephraim was 39-years-old and was buried in Bismarck, Missouri.

"E.R. Crump Killed by Flying Rocks Thrown by Blast" Bisbee Daily Review 20 January 1918 page 5
"Another Man Killed by Sacramento Blast" Tombstone Epitaph 27 January 1918 page 5

February 16, 1918 Sacramento Pit
Driller, A. Harvey was taken to the Copper Queen Hospital for undescribed injuries.

"Was Injured" Bisbee Daily Review 17 February 1918 page 8

February 19, 1918, Sacramento Pit
Sebastian Ruiz broke his thumb.

"Hurt on Sac Hill" Bisbee Daily Review 20 February 1918 page 8

March 25, 1918, Sacramento Pit
Juan Covarrvia and Francisco Castenada were trying to load a blast hole. The rock was broken, and rocks would shift down in the holes and prevent the powder from loading properly. Against company rules, they took a steel bar and began pounding on it, the pounding must have crushed a blasting cap and detonated the hole. Covarrvia* and Castenada were killed, and six men were injured. A nearby churn drill was knocked over, and Pedro Ureas was critically hurt. Also, Francisco Avidrez and Pablo Manrojo were admitted to the Copper Queen Hospital. Mike Hurley was one of the primary witnesses and was only 16 years old and had been also close to the explosion on January, 19. He had started working in the pit when he was 15. Although, both men had come to Bisbee from Santa Rita, New Mexico, Covarrvia was 26 years-old and originally from Zacatecas, Mexico. Castenada was 30 years old and also originally from Mexico.

*The reports spell his name as Covarribias
"Another Explosion at Sacramento Hill" Tombstone Epitaph 31 March 1918 page 4
Office of State Mine Inspector. *Seventh Annual Report of the State Mine Inspector State of Arizona for the Year Ending November 30, 1918.*
"Original Certificate of Death." Arizona Department of Health Services. http://genealogy.az.gov/azdeath/017/10171679.pdf (May 29, 2012)
"Original Certificate of Death." Arizona Department of Health Services. http://genealogy.az.gov/azdeath/017/10171678.pdf (May 29, 2012)
"Cochise County Inquest No.1318" Arizona State Archives

April 30, 1918, Sacramento Pit

Juan Salas had his hand caught the door of a steam shovel bucket. A finger was bruised and cut.

Office of State Mine Inspector. *Seventh Annual Report of the State Mine Inspector State of Arizona for the Year Ending November 30, 1918.*

May 7, 1918, Sacramento Pit

It was on the last day of work in the mine for Floyd. O. Frost. He had decided to head to Southern California and marry Miss Mayme Lamore, a girl from Bisbee. A few miners were joking with Frost about quitting the mines when he decided to sit down on a tool box with sacks of powder next to it and fill out his final time card so that he could get his last paycheck. Reynaldo Moreno believed he was smoking a cigarette. It was suspected he sat the burning cigarette on the tool box, and it rolled in and detonated the powder. He was killed in the explosion.

"Sacramento Hill Accident Claims F.D. Frost's Life" Bisbee Daily Review 8 May 1918 page 1

Office of State Mine Inspector. *Seventh Annual Report of the State Mine Inspector State of Arizona for the Year Ending November 30, 1918.*

"Bisbee-Lowell Evergreen Cemetery." My Cochise. http://www.mycochise.com/cembisbeeef.php (October 1, 2011)

"Cochise County Coroner's Inquest No. 1328" Arizona State Archives

June 10, 1918, Sacramento Pit

Jesus Flores dropped a section of railroad track and bruised his right foot.

Office of State Mine Inspector. *Seventh Annual Report of the State Mine Inspector State of Arizona for the Year Ending November 30, 1918.*

July 8, 1918, Sacramento Pit

Harry Anderson bruised his back and legs when he fell after pulling a rope for a water funnel and the rope broke.

Office of State Mine Inspector. *Seventh Annual Report of the State Mine Inspector State of Arizona for the Year Ending November 30, 1918.*

August 10, 1918, Sacramento Pit

Florentino Delgado broke his jaw and lost four teeth when a rock fell on him.

Office of State Mine Inspector. *Seventh Annual Report of the State Mine Inspector State of Arizona for the Year Ending November 30, 1918.*

Equipment and men working in the Sacramento pit. C-1925

August 28, 1918, Sacramento Pit

T.H. Chambers injured his back and bruised right hip while unloading a steam shovel bucket.

Office of State Mine Inspector. *Seventh Annual Report of the State Mine Inspector State of Arizona for the Year Ending November 30, 1918.*

September 3, 1918, Sacramento pit

Jose Nunez, a trackman, was buried by a dumping car on the Sacramento dump. He died from suffocation.

Office of State Mine Inspector. *Seventh Annual Report of the State Mine Inspector State of Arizona for the Year Ending November 30, 1918.*
"Original Certificate of Death." Arizona Department of Health Services. http://genealogy.az.gov/azdeath/018/10181232.pdf (May 29, 2012)

September 29, 1918, Sacramento Pit

Jose Gutierrez broke two toes when he dropped a track tie on his foot while unloading ties.

Office of State Mine Inspector. *Seventh Annual Report of the State Mine Inspector State of Arizona for the Year Ending November 30, 1918.*

October 23, 1918, Sacramento Pit

James Brooks sprained his left knee while climbing a bank.

Office of State Mine Inspector. *Seventh Annual Report of the State Mine Inspector State of Arizona for the Year Ending November 30, 1918.*

October 25, 1918, Sacramento Pit

W. H. Whitaker bruised and sprained his right ankle jumping off a moving locomotive.

Office of State Mine Inspector. *Seventh Annual Report of the State Mine Inspector State of Arizona for the Year Ending November 30, 1918.*

November 13, 1918, Sacramento Pit

Around 4:30 pm, Juan Salas needed to blast four boulders in front of No.4 steam shovel. Three of the rocks he plastered explosives on, but the fourth he drilled an 18-inch deep hole. About two minutes after he finished the hole he placed a ½ stick of Hercules 40% dynamite in the hole primed with a Hercules No. 8 blasting cap. The hole detonated and Salas fell to the feet of powder Foreman, William Kuehn and began yelling *"Mata me!"* It was suspected that the high temperature of the freshly drilled hole caused the detonation. He was taken to the Copper Queen Hospital where he died. Salas was survived by a wife, a brother and grown children.

"Killed in Blast" Bisbee Daily Review 15 November 1918 page 8

Office of State Mine Inspector. *Seventh Annual Report of the State Mine Inspector State of Arizona for the Year Ending November 30, 1918.*

"Original Certificate of Death." Arizona Department of Health Services. http://genealogy.az.gov/azdeath/019/10190130.pdf (May 28, 2012)

"Cochise County Coroner's Inquest No. 1352" Arizona State Archives Phoenix

November 20, 1918, Sacramento Pit

Locomotive Engineer, J. C. Cain pulled his train up to the dump. Brakeman, John Carretto jumped off the train to start dumping cars. He had noticed a large boulder in the last car and told Maximino Urrutia to get a chain to tie the car down before they dumped it. This was so the rock would not cause the car to fall off the waste dump. As Urrutia was placing the chain, the car dumped backwards onto him, crushing his skull. It was felt that leaking airline had caused the car to dump unexpectedly. It was believed, if safety chains to prevent dumping had been installed on these cars the accident would have been prevented. He was survived by his father, Luis Urrutia in Penjama Guanajuato, Mexico.

Dugan Mortuary Records July 19, 1918 – March 27, 1920 Accession 2010.10.14 Bisbee Mining and Historical Museum, Bisbee

Office of State Mine Inspector. *Seventh Annual Report of the State Mine Inspector State of Arizona for the Year Ending November 30, 1918.*

"Original Certificate of Death." Arizona Department of Health Services. http://genealogy.az.gov/azdeath/019/10190169.pdf (May 28, 2012)

"Cochise County Coroner's Inquest No. 1351" Arizona State Archives

November 23, 1918, Sacramento Pit

Phillip Minor received undescribed injuries in an accident. While recovering it was believed he suffered a *"rupture"*. The doctors operated and discovered the bladder had been forced out of its normal position.

"Was Operated On" Bisbee Daily Review 19 December 1918, page 8

December 13, 1918, Sacramento Pit

C.H. Williamson was working on track, when a steam shovel bucket hit him. The impact broke his pelvis.

Office of State Mine Inspector. *Eighth Annual Report of the State Mine Inspector State of Arizona for the Year Ending November 30, 1919.*

"Cast is Set" Bisbee Daily Review 17 December 1918 page 8

January 7, 1919 Sacramento Pit

A recently, built water tank slid down Sacramento Hill. It was felt snow and loosened the ground. No one was injured, it was expected to be expensive to repair the damage.

"Tank Slides Down" <u>Bisbee Daily Review</u> 8 January 1919, page 8

February 10, 1919, Sacramento Pit

Manuel Hernandez was removing the track and a rail fell amputating a finger.

Office of State Mine Inspector. *Eighth Annual Report of the State Mine Inspector State of Arizona for the Year Ending November 30, 1919.*

March 6, 1919, Sacramento Pit

Pablo Sanchez was hit by a rock flying from a blast. He was bruised on the side.

Office of State Mine Inspector. *Eighth Annual Report of the State Mine Inspector State of Arizona for the Year Ending November 30, 1919.*

May 3, 1919, Sacramento Pit

Ignacio Lara had his ribs bruised when he was struck by a fly rock from a blast.

Office of State Mine Inspector. *Eighth Annual Report of the State Mine Inspector State of Arizona for the Year Ending November 30, 1919.*

May 9, 1919, Sacramento Pit

A churn drill ran over the leg and foot of T.L. Reed. He was only bruised.

Office of State Mine Inspector. *Eighth Annual Report of the State Mine Inspector State of Arizona for the Year Ending November 30, 1919.*

A steam locomotive and steam shovel in the Sacramento pit.

June 16, 1919, Sacramento Pit

W.O. Steger suffered burns on his side and abdomen. He was working on a steam locomotive when hot water poured on him.

377

Office of State Mine Inspector. *Eighth Annual Report of the State Mine Inspector State of Arizona for the Year Ending November 30, 1919.*

June 25, 1919, Sacramento Pit

Dan Goins broke a rib when he fell against a churn drill.

Office of State Mine Inspector. *Eighth Annual Report of the State Mine Inspector State of Arizona for the Year Ending November 30, 1919.*

July 21, 1919, Sacramento Pit

B.L. Roberts sprained an ankle when he was thrown from a rail car that derailed.

Office of State Mine Inspector. *Eighth Annual Report of the State Mine Inspector State of Arizona for the Year Ending November 30, 1919.*

September 11, 1919, Sacramento Pit

Locomotive No. 107 was pulling a train load of waste on No.2 dump. According to the investigation *"synchronous vibrations"* of the rail cars caused the locomotive to derail and fall over the edge of the dump on its side. The engineer was thrown from the engine, but rushed back to the locomotive to shut off the steam. No one was injured.

"Cars Vibrating in Sympathy Upset Locomotive" Bisbee Daily Review 12 September 1919, page 1

October 3, 1919, Sacramento Pit

Ramon Acuna was hit by a boulder tumbling off an embankment.

Office of State Mine Inspector. *Eighth Annual Report of the State Mine Inspector State of Arizona for the Year Ending November 30, 1919.*

October 23, 1919, Sacramento Pit

Serberiano Hernandez was cut in the calf when he was struck by a bolt from a steam shovel.

Office of State Mine Inspector. *Eighth Annual Report of the State Mine Inspector State of Arizona for the Year Ending November 30, 1919.*

October 29, 1919 Sacramento Pit

Behind the Bisbee Daily Review Office on Main Street, a Sacramento Hill Locomotive with empty ore cars was struck and derailed by another locomotive. The impact derailed the locomotive. No one was injured. The site of this accident is on present day, Commerce Street.

"Engines Collide" Bisbee Daily Review 30 October1919, page 6

January 3, 1920, Sacramento Pit

Section Foreman, Parley Black injured his ankle in an undescribed accident. He was treated at the Copper Queen Hospital.

"Foreman Hurt" Bisbee Daily Review 4 January 1920, page 3

January 11, 1920, Sacramento Pit

Tom R. Warnock a locomotive engineer, Harry D. Miller a fireman, M. Brereton a timekeeper and Jack Englehart, a brakeman were using a "Dinkey locomotive to haul was to No. 4 dump above the Briggs Shaft, The locomotive sank in a soft section dump and Miller was fatally squeezed between an oil tank on the tender and the locomotive. As the locomotive derailed his body was released. The two men were uninjured, but Englehart suffered undescribed injuries. Miller was survived by bride of two years from Noblesville, Indiana. During World War I, Miller was a sergent in the Battalion of Death under Colonel Dan Morgan Smith and saw heavy action.

"Falling Train Kills Fireman on Mine Road" Bisbee Daily Review 13 January 1920, page 6

"Brakeman Hurt" Bisbee Daily Review 14 January 1920, page 6

"Original Certificate of Death." Arizona Department of Health Services. http://genealogy.az.gov/azdeath/021/10210782.pdf (May 30, 2012)

Office of State Mine Inspector. *Ninth Annual Report of the State Mine Inspector State of Arizona for the Year Ending November 30, 1920.*

January 28, 1920, Sacramento Pit

Juan Miranda, a miner from Durango, Mexico and Bert Clement, the owner of the Ozark Rooming House, were loading a blast hole close to the top of a bench. A premature explosion occurred and both men were caught in the slide of broken rock. Clement's arm was broken, but he was not buried. Miranda could not be located. It was hoped that he had been dazed by the blast and had wandered off. Late that night, most of the rock had been removed by steam shovel, and his body still had not been found. He also had not returned home. The next day his body was found buried at the bottom of the bench. He was 29 years old and buried in El Paso, Texas.

"Fail to Find Man Lost in Mine Accident Bisbee Daily Review 29 January 1920 page 6

"Original Certificate of Death." Arizona Department of Health Services. http://genealogy.az.gov/azdeath/021/10210806.pdf (May 30, 2012)

Office of State Mine Inspector. *Ninth Annual Report of the State Mine Inspector State of Arizona for the Year Ending November 30, 1920.*

February 27, 1920, Sacramento Pit

Francisco Caneles (sp?) had his ankle broken as a boulder rolled over his foot.

"Has Ankle Broken" Bisbee Daily Review 28 February 1920, page 6

March 23, 1920, Sacramento Pit

J.B. Burns was bruised after a railroad car collided with a steam locomotive.

Office of State Mine Inspector. *Ninth Annual Report of the State Mine Inspector State of Arizona for the Year Ending November 30, 1920.*

April 22, 1920, Sacramento Pit

Car Foreman, James D. Gresham was fatally injured by a rock falling out of a loaded car. Gresham and Roy Green were trying to unhook a safety chain from a waste car. The car slightly tilted and dumped rocks on top of the men. Green was bruised, but a large rock smashed Gresham's skull. He was taken to the hospital where he died from pneumonia on April 30th. His widow was the acting secretary at the Y.W.C.A. (No coroner's inquest could be located)

"Falling Boulder Injures a Foreman" Bisbee Daily Review 22 April 1920 page 6

"Original Certificate of Death." Arizona Department of Health Services. http://genealogy.az.gov/azdeath/021/10212449.pdf (May 30, 2012)

Office of State Mine Inspector. *Ninth Annual Report of the State Mine Inspector State of Arizona for the Year Ending November 30, 1920.*

April 27, 1920, Sacramento Pit

Jose Fuentez (Fuentes?) was injured after he was caught in a gasoline explosion after a lantern ignited the fuel.

Office of State Mine Inspector. *Ninth Annual Report of the State Mine Inspector State of Arizona for the Year Ending November 30, 1920*

April 29, 1920, Sacramento Pit

Locomotive Engineer, J.E. Jennings pulled up a train of five cars onto dump No. 9. The men began dumping the cars. Ricardo Reyes was dumping a car near Jose Munoz. Munoz was supposed to clean any spilled rock off the tracks after dumping. It is believed that after the car had dumped and began to right itself it caught Munoz on the chin, breaking his neck. He was buried in Bisbee.

"Cochise County Coroner's Inquest No. 1415" Arizona State Archives Phoenix

Sacramento Pit in 1927. The Holbrook mine area with Young and Charon shafts are in the foreground.

A lantern used in the Sacramento pit (marked C.Q.B.)

June 1920, Sacramento Pit
A pipe fell from a crane and struck William Costley on the head. His skull was fractured and there was concern the wound would be fatal.
"Costley will Live" Bisbee Daily Review 2 July 1920, page 6

June 2, 1920, Sacramento Pit
Antonio Yanez was burned by hot water from a steam shovel.
Office of State Mine Inspector. *Ninth Annual Report of the State Mine Inspector State of Arizona for the Year Ending November 30, 1920.*

July 14, 1920, Sacramento Pit

Powderman, Juan Villaneda was loading a toe-hole when a boulder began to fall. He tried to move out of the way, but the boulder rolled over him. His skull was fractured and he died at the Copper Queen Hospital on July 15. (Note, no inquest could be located. Also, it appears he was injured on January 9, 1918 at the Sacramento Pit)

"Falling Rock Crushes Miner" Bisbee Daily Review 15 July 1920, page 4

"Original Certificate of Death." Arizona Department of Health Services. http://genealogy.az.gov/azdeath/022/10220983.pdf (March 20, 2019)

August 28, 1920 Sacramento Pit

James Farrel who operated the oil station on Sacramento Hill was injured after he was struck by a "Jitney" bus operated by the Phelps Dodge.

"Auto Injures Man" Bisbee Daily Review 29 August 1920, page 10

September 3, 1920, Sacramento Pit

Fireman, Ray Dartee broke his ankle when he jumped from a locomotive No. 110 when it derailed on No. 7 dump.

"Fireman Breaks Leg" Bisbee Daily Review 5 September1920, page 8

Office of State Mine Inspector. *Ninth Annual Report of the State Mine Inspector State of Arizona for the Year Ending November 30, 1920.*

Two views of a derailed locomotive from the Sacramento pit.

September 13, 1920, Sacramento Pit

Rafael Cordova was struck by a steam shovel boom. He suffered a cut finger.

Office of State Mine Inspector. *Ninth Annual Report of the State Mine Inspector State of Arizona for the Year Ending November 30, 1920.*

October 29, 1920, Sacramento Pit

Victor Morales had his foot broken when it became caught under a steam shovel jack arm.

Office of State Mine Inspector. *Ninth Annual Report of the State Mine Inspector State of Arizona for the Year Ending November 30, 1920.*

November 13, 1920 Sacramento Pit

Locomotive 108 was pushing a train of loaded cars down No.7 dump. William Brown Engineer of Locomotive 106 thought the switchman had given him the go ahead signal. Brown was pulling a train of empty cars. Near the Calumet & Arizona Hospital the trains collided. Brown jumped from the engine and was bruised up. The Fireman, A.N. Chipman on No. 106 had his arm crushed between the locomotive cab and the cab door. It was thought it may need amputation. J. Goin a brakeman on Locomotive No. 108 was bruised and battered after he jumped from his engine.

"Three Injured as Ore Trains Crash on Hill" Bisbee Daily Review 15 November 1919, page 3

December 21, 1920, Sacramento Hill

B.R. Davis fell from a ladder. He suffered only minor injuries.

"Injured on Hill" Bisbee Daily Review 22 December 1920, page 8

January 26, 1921, Sacramento Pit

Narisco Arguello (sp?) had one arm and part of a foot cut off when he was run over by a train. There was confusion of how the accident occurred because the train was slowly moving. He was taken to the Copper Queen Hospital in a serious state of shock.

"Run Over by Train" Bisbee Daily Review 27 January 1921, page 6

June 7, 1922, Sacramento Pit

Rosendo Rodriquez was seriously bruised when a jack arm from a steam shovel dragged a boulder and caught him.

Office of State Mine Inspector. *Eleventh Annual Report of the State Mine Inspector State of Arizona for the Year Ending November 30, 1922.*

Boulders near a steam shovel jack arm

March 7, 1923, Sacramento Pit

C.K. Wood lost his small finger, and his arm was bruised when a "runaway" car hit a locomotive.

Office of State Mine Inspector. *Twelfth Annual Report of the State Mine Inspector State of Arizona for the Year Ending November 30, 1923.*

March 7, 1923, Sacramento Pit

Dewey G. Nowlin had his skull and right leg fractured when hit by a railroad car of ore. Nolan was admitted to the Copper Queen Hospital at 1:30 am and died at 3:25 pm the same day. He was survived by a brother De Witt Nowlin.

Office of State Mine Inspector. *Twelfth Annual Report of the State Mine Inspector State of Arizona for the Year Ending November 30, 1923.*

"Original Certificate of Death." Arizona Department of Health Services. http://genealogy.az.gov/azdeath/026/10262319.pdf (May 30, 2012)

Copper Queen Hospital Patients Register Dec 30, 1922 – Feb 26, 1924, Bisbee Mining and Historical Museum, Bisbee.

May 18, 1923, Sacramento Pit

Desiderio Valenzuela smashed his thumb in a track jack.

Office of State Mine Inspector. *Twelfth Annual Report of the State Mine Inspector State of Arizona for the Year Ending November 30, 1923.*

May 21, 1923, Sacramento Pit

Porfirio Coronado was working on 5315 bench near No.7 steam shovel. A 55 ft. deep blast hole had been loaded by Albert E. Deegan the powder foreman. This hole did not have a blasting cap inserted as it was planned to not detonate it until later. Francisco Silvas and

Coronado had prepare boulders to blast. After lunch, the No.7 shovel which was under repair gave the blasting signal. The small charges unexpectedly detonated and a bank fell crushing Coronado. He was taken to the Copper Queen Hospital, where Dr. H.J. French was informed there was a dying man in the elevator. By the time Dr. French came to him, he had already died.

Office of State Mine Inspector. *Twelfth Annual Report of the State Mine Inspector State of Arizona for the Year Ending November 30, 1923.*

"Original Certificate of Death." Arizona Department of Health Services. http://genealogy.az.gov/azdeath/027/10270038.pdf (May 30, 2012)

"Cochise County Coroner's Inquest No. 1512" Arizona State Archives Phoenix

July 28, 1923, Sacramento Pit

Earl A. Conway, a brakeman, was killed when the rail spread apart derailing an unknown number of cars. He died from a broken pelvis and other undescribed internal injuries.

Office of State Mine Inspector. *Twelfth Annual Report of the State Mine Inspector State of Arizona for the Year Ending November 30, 1923.*

"Original Certificate of Death." Arizona Department of Health Services. http://genealogy.az.gov/azdeath/027/10270976.pdf (May 30, 2012)

August 6, 1923, Sacramento Pit

Jose Gonzales cut up his fingers removing a drill steel.

Office of State Mine Inspector. *Twelfth Annual Report of the State Mine Inspector State of Arizona for the Year Ending November 30, 1923.*

September 1, 1923, Sacramento Pit

Alberto M. Mata bruised the back of his hand putting down a case of powder.

Office of State Mine Inspector. *Twelfth Annual Report of the State Mine Inspector State of Arizona for the Year Ending November 30, 1923.*

October 27, 1923, Sacramento Pit.

J.H. Atkinson lost fingers when they were caught in the gears of a churn drill.

Office of State Mine Inspector. *Twelfth Annual Report of the State Mine Inspector State of Arizona for the Year Ending November 30, 1923.*

February 14, 1924, Sacramento Pit

Pedro Cortez injured an eye while oiling a steam shovel.

Office of State Mine Inspector. *Thirteenth Annual Report of the State Mine Inspector State of Arizona for the Year Ending November 30, 1924.*

February 16, 1924, Sacramento Pit

C.H. Martin lost an arm when it was caught in the gear wheel of a steam shovel.

Office of State Mine Inspector. *Thirteenth Annual Report of the State Mine Inspector State of Arizona for the Year Ending November 30, 1924.*

June 9, 1924, Sacramento Pit

Henry May Byerly was killed when he fell on a chain cable for a steam shovel. He was 21 years-old and buried in Rising Star, Texas.

Office of State Mine Inspector. *Thirteenth Annual Report of the State Mine Inspector State of Arizona for the Year Ending November 30, 1924.*

"Original Certificate of Death." <u>Arizona Department of Health Services.</u> <u>http://genealogy.az.gov/azdeath/028/10282543.pdf</u> (May 31, 2012)

Tourists inside the still active Sacramento Pit C-1923

The Sacramento Concentrator and Diesel Power Plant

Sacramento Pit Concentrator

This was a processing plant to concentrate the amount of copper in the ore before being shipped to the smelter in Douglas, Arizona. For the time unusual choices were made in the design. Concrete was intensively used from motor mounts, stands and even the flotation tanks. Later, this would make the ruins of the mill visually intriguing and a popular place for kids to explore. A jaw crusher was chosen for the primary crusher rather than the gyratory crushers popular at the time. Gyratory and disc crushers provided secondary and tertiary crushing. Another feature was that each piece of equipment was provided with its own electrical power and switch. At the time it was common to have a single motor power multiple machines with a system of belts.

After crushing the ore was sent for grinding. Primary grinding was completed in Marcy rod mills and then sent to originally another set of rod mills for secondary grinding. After 1926, Ball Mills replaced rod mills for secondary grinding. The ore was ground to minus 200 mesh. Initially, the ore was processed with gravity and flotation. Although, most mines had stopped using gravity tables, they were used at Bisbee because extra pyrite was wanted to serve as smelter flux for the carbonate ores being mined at Bisbee. During 1925, the gravity recovery tables were put out of service and the mill depended on flotation to concentrate the copper. Callow pneumatic cells were used for flotation. As Callow cells were not ideal. Originally, this may have been to avoid the excessive royalties demanded by the patent holders of oil flotation, Mineral Separation Ltd. The royalties were about $.02 a ton. This was about four times the normal royalties demanded by most patented mineral processes. Also, Mineral Separation Ltd. claimed the rights to all discoveries and inventions made by users of their patented process. In 1926, Phelps Dodge made a deal with the proverbial devil of ore concentrating and the Mineral Separation and Forrester cells were installed in the concrete tanks that held the Callow Cells. An advantage of Forrester flotation cells is that they could produce a lower grade concentrate when needed. At times the mill would often receive higher grade ore which could be processed as a lower grade concentrate to ensure adequate copper recovery. Lime was added to the ground pulp from the mills to neutralize the acidity, steamed pine oil was added to .04 lbs. per ton and .10 lbs. per ton of potassium ethyl xanthate was added to the pulp. In the Forrester cells the pulp was violently agitated and 203 half inch pipes bubbled air through the ore pulp. The copper sulfide particles were now strongly hydrophobic and would cling to the air bubbles creating a copper rich floating froth. To create a higher grade concentrate less xanthate was added and more lime and to create a lower grade concentrate less lime and more xanthate would be added This froth was collected and sent to a thickener tank for dewatering. At the thickener the froth was added near the center of the tank and under water. The solid particles fall to the bottom of the tank the heavy, dense iron sulfide particles squeeze out the water as it becomes a thick sludge on the bottom of the tank. The water being less dense floats towards the top of the tank. A slow moving series of rakes move the sludge towards the center of the tank which has an exit pipe at the bottom. From this point it was loaded into rail cars for shipment to the Smelter at Douglas, Arizona. The concentrates were poor by modern standards and average from 4.79% copper in 1923 to as high as 6.58% in 1928. In comparison the later, Lavender Pit concentrator produced concentrates that ran 16-18% copper which was also not even considered ideal. Also, known as the Don Luis Mill and the Crawford Mill. Note, the available accident information on this mine site is presently limited.

August 10, 1918 Sacramento Concentrator
Carpenter, John Benhio fell in a five foot hole.
"Is Slightly Injured" <u>Bisbee Daily Review</u> 13 August1918, page 8

Saginaw Mine c-1963

Saginaw Mine

      Saginaw Development Company started sinking the Saginaw Shaft on April 12, 1904, after they purchased the World's Fair mine and group of claims. During, September of 1904 chalcocite samples from the Saginaw were being shown around Bisbee. Even though, the newspaper Iron Ore from Ishpeming, Michigan was critical of how slow the Saginaw shaft was being sunk, by March the following year the three compartment shaft was 747ft. deep. Also, the 350ft. level was being developed with the intent of connecting to the World's Fair Mine. In 1905 just at 776ft. water was hit and the company sank to 800 level. Sinking stopped at the time and the company discussed sinking a second shaft down in the "flats" to be used as a pumping shaft to drain the ground around the Saginaw shaft. Although, this was not done at the Saginaw, this technique was used at the Junction shaft to drain the Briggs and Hoatson mines.

      Early in March of 1906, the American Development Company Merged with the Saginaw Development Company to form The American-Saginaw Development Company. This new corporation continued to operate and was able to sink the shaft to the depth of 920 ft. The mine was sold to the Calumet & Arizona Mining Company in February of 1913. It was not until 1929, that the mine became active again. The hoist and steel headframe from the Irish Mag mine was moved and installed on the Saginaw. During the following year, the shaft was sunk 829ft., further to a total depth of 1,744ft. Importantly, during 1937 the collar of Saginaw shaft was concreted and two years later the shaft was retimbered and gunited. In 1943 the Saginaw hoist was removed and sent to the 2100 level of the Campbell Mine to aid in the sinking of the Campbell Shaft from the 2700 level to the 2966 level. An another used hoist purchased from Del Norte Leasing Company was installed at the Saginaw and a connection was made from the Campbell mine to the Saginaw to ventilate the 2700 level Campbell. The Saginaw continued to be used for ventilation until the mines closed in 1975. The Saginaw had a final depth of 1792 and consisted of three compartments.

August 27, 1904, Saginaw Mine

G. Clark Hudler* and Sam Mercier* were informed of a misfire and were told to reshoot the missed hole with the next round. When Hudler began to drill another hole next to the misfire, he accidently drilled into it. The force of the blasted impacted Hudler in the chest around his heart. Broken rock and dirt blasted up fell back on top of his body mutilating it. Sam Mercier was slightly injured and survived with only cuts and bruises. Three other men nearby were not injured. Mercier and Hudler were hoisted up in a sinking bucket and taken to the change house. Hudler died after 45 minutes. The other men at the Saginaw felt that Hudler had a premonition of his death, as he had told them to contact a friend in Nacozari, Mexico if anything had happened to him. His brother lived in Rockford, Illinois. Both men were contacted after Hudler's death.

*He is named Carl Hudley, Guy Hudley and Charles Hudler in different Bisbee Daily Review Articles.
*Sam is referred to as George Murphy and George Mercer in some Bisbee Daily Review Articles.
(This must have occurred while sinking the shaft around the 300 level. Thirteen days earlier the shaft had reached a depth of 280 ft.)
"Saginaw Development Co." Bisbee Daily Review 14 August 1905 page 3
"Hurt at Saginaw" Bisbee Daily Review 27 August 1905 page 5
"Tater" Bisbee Daily Review 27 August 1905 page 5
"Hudley's Tragic End Due to his Own Fault" Bisbee Daily Review 28 August 1905 page 5
"Funeral Services" Bisbee Daily Review 31 August 1905 page 5
"Saginaw is Doing Good Work Quick" Bisbee Daily Review 18 December 1905 page 9
"Cochise County Coroner's Inquest No. 224" Arizona State Archives Phoenix

July 17, 1906, Saginaw Mine

John T Hodges was working in a crosscut on the 350 level when a rock fell and fractured his skull. He was taken by Palace Ambulance to the Calumet & Arizona Hospital, where he died on July 19. (No coroner's inquest could be located)

"Miner Suffers Fractured Skull at the Shattuck <u>Bisbee Daily Review</u> 19 January 1906 page 8

"Original Certificate of Death." <u>Arizona Department of Health Services.</u> http://genealogy.az.gov/azdeath/007/10071430.pdf (June 19, 2015

The grave marker for Clark Hudler in Evergreen Cemetery

Shattuck Mine c-2010

Shattuck Mine

The Shattuck & Arizona Copper Company formed in March of 1904 and by August 1, 1904, they were sinking a two compartment shaft on the Iron Prince Claim. The original hoisting was done with a windlass, but preparations were being made for a regular hoist. By October 23 the shaft was already 110 ft. deep.

Typical of the time, the company's goal was to seek out buried ores with the thought of a deeper depth was better. By September 10, 1905, the shaft was 825 ft. deep and a station was being cut on the 800' level. By this time, ore had been hit on the 500' level and the 700' level. Soon, native copper was found in altered limestone on the 800' level, and an orebody of cuprite was discovered. With the discovery of significant ore and the challenging location of the mine inside a steep canyon, it was decided that an aerial tramway would need to be constructed to haul down the ore and the timber with supplies up to the mine. It was also determined that the shaft needed to be enlarged to three compartments. Before a tramway could be constructed, ore was hauled to the railroad by wagon. In August, the 3,200 ft. aerial tramway was completed. It had 14 towers varying from 12 to 40 ft. tall and could handle five tram cars (buckets) at a time. The cars traveled at 387 ft. per minute. At the terminus were 1,000-ton ore bins for loading into rail cars. A new steel headframe was erected, and a hoist was borrowed from the Junction mine until the ordered hoist arrived at the mine. It became evident that the aerial tramway was not going to be able to handle enough ore, so it was enlarged to handle ten cars. On November 20, after 12:00 am, James Nowlin a hoisting engineer noticed smoke coming up the Shattuck Shaft. He thought this was unusual and soon high billowing smoke and flames poured out the shaft. Two fire hoses were attached to a fire plug and lowered down the shaft. This method seemed to work as the smoke lessened. Men attempted to reach the fire from the 200' level Cuprite, but were driven back by smoke.

During 1910, the Shattuck & Arizona began looking towards the upper reaches of the mine. Stations were cut on the 400' and 500' levels. Production started to increase slowly and they were shipping 100-150 tons a day in August. In April, a crosscut on the 300' level intercepted the largest natural cave found in the local mines. It was well decorated with cave formations and for a few years became a favorite tourist site in Bisbee. Thousands of people came to visit this beautiful cavern. Initially, it was planned to close the cave to the public and in May 1913, the company began backfilling. However, it was known that visitors were occasionally taken to the cavern until 1915. As 1915 approached so did the demise of the Shattuck Cave. The company wanted to donate part of

390

the cave to the Smithsonian Institution, but instead specimens from the cave were given to the Michigan College of Mines in 1915. Shattuck, mine superintendent, Arthur Houle's, brother was a professor at this school.

Excitement was stirred up again when a cave containing cuprodesclozite was discovered on the 600' level. This vanadium oxide prompted the interest in the possibility of the mining for vanadium. Although, there was keen interest and an area 200 ft. long and 3 ft. wide was exposed, significant mining of vanadium never occurred. At this time, the new mineral species shattuckite was discovered on the 300' level. 18,500,000 lbs. of copper, over 4,000 ounces of gold, 260,000 ounces of silver and 16,000,000lbs of lead were produced at the Shattuck during 1916.

1919 began as a challenging year. On February 22 a fire broke out in a sulphide stope between the 700 and 800' levels and helmet crews were sent down to install bulkheads. Eventually, 25 million gallons of water was pumped into the mine to extinguish the fire. The fire was put out when the water reached 8 ft. below the 700' level.

The shaft was deepened from 900 ft. to the 1136 ft. in 1920 and a new level was developed at the 1100' level. On January 1, 1921, the mine was shut down, and only development work continued. Some ore was discovered on the 600 level, but in July the pumps were pulled, and the lower levels were allowed to flood. The Shattuck continued to operate off and on until 1925 when the mine was leased. Also during 1925, the Shattuck & Arizona Mining Company merged with the Denn & Arizona Mining Company and became the Shattuck Denn Mining Company. A miner was arrested at the Shattuck mine for "high grading" as he was taking from the mine, pieces of altered limestone that were *"thickly peppered"* with gold. At the time, it was felt a dynamite box full would have been worth hundreds of dollars. From 1942-1945, the mine was leased by James Maffeo and produced an average of 400 tons a month. Lessees continued to operate the mine until 1947 when operations ceased.

In 1952, children started a fire and the mine site burned all buildings and the aerial tramway leaving only the steel headframe. Phelps Dodge Corporation then purchased the Shattuck Mine in 1973. With the ending of mining in Bisbee, Phelps Dodge became interested in the possibility of opening the Shattuck for precious metals and to explore the sulphides in the Abrigo Limestone on the 1100' level. The original headframe from the Spray Mine was removed from the Calumet & Cochise Shaft and erected over the Shattuck Shaft. The main hoist was removed from the Denn Shaft and installed. A hoist house and a storage and shop building were also erected. The shaft was reopened relatively easy to 800 ft. below the surface, where the shaft was filled. It appeared that leasers may have dumped rock into the shaft. Eventually, the shaft was reopened to 30 ft below the 800' level. Water was struck at 780 ft. and initially the water was pumped along the 700' level to a point where it was hoped the water would drain into the Uncle Sam Mine. This unfortunately failed, probably due to caved ground and water and was then pumped to the surface. Shaft stations were cleared and repaired to the 700' level. Most of the development work occurred on the 200 & 300' levels. Low copper prices and a need to conserve money resulted in the project being shutdown on August 27, 1975, before the lower section of the shaft had been cleared.

The need for Phelps Dodge to diversify away from copper lead to the development of a small mines division. During November 1980, interest began in developing the 100 and 200 levels for precious metal mining. Air and waterlines were installed in December In 1981 a raise was driven from the 200 level to the 100 level. The mine worked two shifts. A small tonnage of high silver silica flux was discovered but no signicant tonnages were located. Phelps Dodge reported in June 1981, 64,000 ounces of silver and 1,500 ounces of gold had been mined from operations in Bisbee this would include Shattuck, Campbell and Cole Mines. During 1982 and 1983, an attempt to mine precious metals was initiated. The work was confined to the 200 and 300' levels near the Shattuck cave. The small scale mining operation hoisted mine cars full of ore instead of using skips, producing little ore. This mining venture ceased after only a few months.

December 3, 1905, Shattuck Mine

John Herrick was driving a loaded,ore wagon down the steep, Shattuck Mine Road. The break on the wagon failed. Initially, the rolling wagon of 3,000lbs. of ore forced the horses to trot, then to run and finally gallop to keep in front of the wagon. After close to a quarter mile , Herrick saw a curve in the road and realized it was impossible for the wagon and horses to make the turn. He jumped off and the wagon struck the embankment on the curve. The wagon and horses rolled over the embankment. Luckily, Herrick and one horse were uninjured. The second horse suffered a serious cut and the wagon suffered some damage.

"Frightfull Run of Loaded Wagon" Bisbee Daily Review 5 December 1905 page 5

Unknown date, 1906, Shattuck Mine

Thomas Callaghan had his leg broken in an undescribed accident. At the time, L.C. Shattuck gave Callaghan $400 and told him to find a doctor and have his leg set. In late April 1912, Callaghan returned to Bisbee and saw Shattuck and told him to make a give him $1, 1000 by Wednesday, May 1 at 9:00 or he would kill him. He was arrested at the Legal Tender Saloon in Lowell and held on $2,000 bail. Callaghan served six months in a Tombstone jail. The court investigated his sanity and declared him sane.

"Life of Banker Shattuck Threatened by Miner Who Demand Money for Injury" Bisbee Daily Review 3 May 1912 page 1
"Believes Shattuck Owes Him Damages" Bisbee Daily Review 4 May 1912 page 1&2
"Callahan Found to be Sane" Bisbee Daily Review 9 November 1912 page 8

March 13, 1906, Shattuck Mine

Bozo Vucurovich was at the 500 level with another miner, Michael C. Burke. It appears they were raising the third compartment to the main shaft. After reaching the 500 level they decided to ride a sinking bucket with a crosshead up to where they were working. They also needed to cross the shaft to get to their workplace. His partner heard the rattling of a descending cage and Vucurovich jumped across the shaft and landed in the corner, just as the cage passed. The cage struck him on the head and knocked him into the shaft.*. His body fell 300 ft. to the bottom of the shaft. Vucurovich's head was smashed, his left arm was almost torn off. He is believed to have been survived by a wife in Trebinga, Hercegovina, Austria-Hungary

* The information on this accident is confusing the men must have been working in the shaft itself. A third compartment was being raised at this time. In the Shattuck shaft unlike many shafts, the stations are cut only on one side shaft. There was a solid wall of rock on the other side shaft. The only reason to cross the shaft would be if they were working inside it.
"Careless Act is Cause of Death" Bisbee Daily Review 14 March 1906 page 8
"Jury Pronounces it Careless Act" Bisbee Daily Review 15 March 1906 page 8
"Bisbee-Lowell Evergreen Cemetery." My Cochise.
http://www.mycochise.com/cembisbeeuv.php (July 30, 2011)
"Cochise County Inquest No. 328" Arizona State Archives Phoenix

July 26, 1906, Shattuck Mine

Jake J. Rigler was working on top of a crosshead attached to a sinking bucket putting in bolts. Two other men were with him in the shaft on the 600 level, cutting bolts. They were installing pipe in the shaft. Suddenly, the clutch on the hoist slipped. The sinking bucket and Rigler fell the 200 feet to the bottom of the shaft. It is believed that Rigler's head impacted the shaft timber as the bucket fell. His head was badly fractured. The hoist was brand new and had been purchased from the Calumet & Arizona Mining Company. The hoistman felt that because the Shattuck was using two small hoists the vibration from the one he was operating caused the pin to fall out and release the clutch. Rigler's wife who was in the east at the time of the accident was initially informed that her husband had been only injured in the mine. It was felt that a friend of the family needed to tell her of her husband's death. Mrs. Hattie Rigler, his widow, left Bisbee in August 1906 to return to Parkersburg, West Virginia at that time she was not sure she would return to Bisbee. On October 20, 1906, she returned to Bisbee to live in the home, she had shared with Jake in Johnson Addition.

"Rigler is Killed in Fall Shattuck Mine" <u>Bisbee Daily Review</u> 27 July 1906 page 1
"Funeral Notice" <u>Bisbee Daily Review</u> 28 July 1906 page 1
"Widow Goes Home" <u>Bisbee Daily Review</u> 11 August 1906 page 3
"Returns from East" <u>Bisbee Daily Review</u> 21 October 1906 page 7
"Cochise County Inquest No. 365" Arizona State Archives Phoenix

October 13, 1906, Shattuck Mine
At 8:00 pm, a fire broke out in the newly constructed two-story engineer's office. The night shift blacksmith and the hoisting engineer discovered the fire and reported it to Foreman Joseph Walker. All men underground began to be hoisted to the surface. In Bisbee residents saw flames reaching above the mountain behind the Spray Mine and notified the fire department. The Bisbee fire department was unable to get the chemical fire engine up the Shattuck road. So the fireman continued without the engine and assisted the miners battling the fire. The flames quickly engulfed the blacksmith's shop. Bisbee, Fire Chief Henkel was severely injured, when a section of sheet metal fell and cut through his hat. The ore bins were ignited, but the miners were able to extinguish the flames. The shaft, hoist house, and oil tanks were saved. This fire although costly, did not significantly affect mine production. It was believed to have been caused by faulty wiring.

"Miners Fight Flames at the Shattuck" <u>Bisbee Daily Review</u> 14 October 1906 page 1

October 21, 1906, Shattuck Mine
Nick Zoricic and his brother John Zoricic* walked into No.2 crosscut, better known as the "Cuprite Drift." on the 800 level, when the ore in the back (roof) collapsed. The rock slightly hit Nick, but it completely buried John. Nick quickly, tried to unbury his brother. Soon he realized he could not do it alone and found William Kingston. The men could not remove a large boulder, but the attempted to dig a hole to provide air for John. Finally, men were able to uncover his body with digging and pry bars. (Note, the newspaper reports are highly dramatized and have only a slight resemblance to the coroner's inquest.) * In Bisbee the brothers adopted the last name "Zork".

"Buried Alive" <u>The Arizona Republican</u> 27 October 1906 page 10
"Cochise County Inquest No. 372" Arizona State Archives Phoenix

February 27, 1907, Shattuck Mine
Austrian, Louis Rossman struck a misfire while using a pick. The hole detonated, and the blast hit him in the face. There was concern he would lose an eye. He was treated at the Copper Queen Hospital, and he was able to regain partial sight. He was able to discern objects, but not clearly. He began to brood over his family in Austria and eventually tried to kill himself in the hospital with a pocket knife. He was taken to Tombstone, Arizona to

see if a judge would commit him to an insane asylum. Rossman was 44 years old and had only been in Bisbee three months. His wife Marta Rossman was in Austria.

Copper Queen Hospital Patients Register February 27, 1907, Bisbee Mining and Historical Museum, Bisbee.
"Is Doing Very Well" Bisbee Daily Review 1 March 1907 page 7
"Luis Rossman Violently Insane" Bisbee Daily Review 4 June 1907 page 1

August 5, 1907, Shattuck Mine

Around 2:00 pm, Robert Engle and John Cornish were timbering in a stope between the 700 and 800 levels, Engle went to lift a cap into place, when a boulder fell from the back of the stope struck his right leg and pinned him to the ground. The other miners working nearby freed him and rapidly transported him to the surface. Engle was still breathing, but unconscious on the surface. The Shattuck Mine doctor arrived at the mine in under a half hour, but Engle was already dead. He was old Bisbee resident who had come from Michigan. Two of his brothers lived in Cochise County one ran the Calumet and Arizona boarding house, and the other lived in Tombstone. Robert Engle was laid to rest in The Evergreen Cemetery.

"Old Time Miner is Killed at Shattuck" Bisbee Daily Review 6 August 1907 page 1
"Inquest is Held" Bisbee Daily Review 7 August 1907 page 7
"Funeral of Robert Engle" Bisbee Daily Review 11 August 1907 page 7
"Cochise County Inquest No. 477" Arizona State Archives Phoenix

Mid-October 1907, Shattuck Mine

Austrian, John Brajovich* was caught in a cave-in and severely injured on the 800 level. His ribs were broken and bladder punctured. Brajovich died at the Shattuck-Denn Hospital at 9:00 am on October 31. He had been in the Hospital about 10 days. Bray had been injured on the 800 level. After an operation it appeared he may live, but then he passed away. He was 23 years old and survived by a brother, who was working as an interpreter in New York and a cousin in Los Angeles. * In Bisbee he was better known as "John Bray." (No coroner's inquest could be located) (Note, the Shattuck & Arizona Mining Company had their own hospital for a short time. It is believed he was hospitalized at the Shattuck & Arizona Hospital)

"Injuries Finally Prove Fatal" Bisbee Daily Review 1 November 1907 page 5
"Dies from Injuries" Bisbee Evening Miner 31 October1907 page 5

December 11, 1909, Shattuck Mine

Robert Hunter Pattinson was working with his brother, John Pattinson, a Shattuck mine shift boss. They were just below the surface at the subway level. These men had unloaded a loaded mine car from the top deck of a cage and then pushed on an empty car. Then the cage was raised, and the cage rested about six inches below the station. The Pattinsons continued to load an empty mine car onto the cage and as the mine car dropped the few inches onto the cage it tipped over as the weight of the mine car caused the cage to fall even more. The car caught Robert under the chin, killing him. The Bisbee Daily Review reported *"When workmen found the body the mangled portion of his face rested upon his breast, while his brains were oozing out upon the floor."* This quote does not match the details of the inquest. He was survived by his brother and his parents in England.

"Descending Cage Breaks Mans Neck" <u>Bisbee Daily Review</u> 12 December 1909 page 5
"Cochise County Coroner's Inquest No. 709 Arizona State Archives Phoenix

December 27, 1909, Shattuck Mine

A 500 lb. boulder rolled through the Shattuck mine office. It continued rolling until it was half way thru the building. It stopped at a table, which held costly and delicate equipment (probably surveying instruments). Mr. Vantress and Harry Miller, bookkeepers, were luckily in the backroom at the time. Footprints were found, near where the boulder started its descent. This situation resulted in the belief the boulder was possibly intentionally rolled into the building. It was not determined if or for whom the boulder intended to harm.

"Huge Boulder Crashes Into Mine Office" <u>Bisbee Daily Review</u> 30 December 1909 page 8

December 31, 1909, Shattuck Mine

Michael Green was on the ore bins located at the terminal of the Shattuck mine aerial tramway when he fell into the bins and fractured his skull. He quickly died from his injuries. Green was buried in Patton, Pennsylvania.

"Green Verdict and Funeral" <u>Bisbee Daily Review</u> 4 January 1910 page 7
"Original Certificate of Death." <u>Arizona Department of Health Services.</u> http://genealogy.az.gov/azdeath/007/10071430.pdf (May 28, 2012)

May 4, 1911, Shattuck Mine

Hoisting Engineer *"Bat"* Leary leaned too far out a window in the Shattuck hoist house. As a result, he fell through and broke his right leg. He was taken to the Calumet & Arizona Hospital where he remained until May 18. At this time, he was sent home in a cast.

"With Broken Leg" <u>Bisbee Daily Review</u> 13 May 1911 page 5
"Calumet & Arizona Hospital Records." <u>My Cochise.</u> http://www.mycochise.com/hospcalkr2man.php (June 20 2011)

October 21, 1911, Shattuck Mine

At 9:30 am., a wagon carrying 8,000 lbs. ore from the Shattuck had its brakes fail and ran into an embankment. The driver* was struck in the head by the brake and one of the horses that was thrown against an exposed pipe and remained severely injured. Unfortunately, it was determined the horse was mortally injured and shot out of mercy. The contract of hauling ore to the railroad was operated by the Palace Livery Stables. * His surname was Clifford.

"Brake Gave Way Horse Killed" <u>Bisbee Daily Review</u> 22 October 1911 page 5

September 10, 1913, Shattuck Mine

28-year-old miner J.T. Blalock had his foot crushed by a falling rock. He remained at the Calumet & Arizona Hospital until September 30.

"Foot Crushed" <u>Bisbee Daily Review</u> 13 September 1913 page 6
"Calumet & Arizona Hospital Records." <u>My Cochise.</u> http://www.mycochise.com/hospcalb.e 2br.php (June 20 2011)

May 23, 1913, Shattuck Mine
J. Loweg was injured when a boulder crushed his foot.
"Foot Injured" Bisbee Daily Review 24 May 1913 page5

November, 22, 1913, Shattuck Mine
In the change house, James Gordon began bullying and picking a fight with a much smaller man, Horace Ravovich. At his locker, Ravovich warned Gordon to leave him alone. Gordon continued and Ravovich pulled out a .45 six shooter and shot him in the shoulder. Although, witnesses favored Ravovich, he went and immediately sought legal counsel. He sought advice from a saloon keeper who recommended a lawyer name Cleary, but through a mix up he ended at Assistant District Attorney Murray's office. Confused and thinking the Ravovich had been released on bond and was trying to influence him, Murray told him the law would settle his matter and he could not help him. Ravovich dissatisfied with the conversation fled Bisbee. The bullet grazed Gordon's collar bone and he was expected to be off a few days.
"Takes Shot in Change Room" Bisbee Daily Review 23 November page 5
"Ravovich is Yet at Large" Bisbee Daily Review 25 November page 5
"Ravovich Still at Large" Bisbee Daily Review 26 November page 2

January 17, 1914, Shattuck Mine
Lee Byich fell 20 ft. and broken three ribs. It was reported that he was taken to the Calumet & Arizona Hospital for treatment, but no records of his care were found. (Misspelled surname?)
"Had Ribs Broken" Bisbee Daily Review 18 January 1914 page 8

January 27, 1914, Shattuck Mine
J. R. Jones was working when around 2:00 pm he was struck by a boulder. The rock broke his right foot. He was treated at the Calumet & Arizona Hospital.
"Miner Injured" Bisbee Daily Review 28 January 1914 page 6

August 7, 1914, Shattuck Mine
Carman, Aaron Askew was overcome by gasses in a stope. He was taken to the Calumet & Arizona Hospital for treatment. Note, this was probably blasting gasses and not fire gasses.
"Overcome by Gas" Bisbee Daily Review 9, August 1914 page 6
"Calumet & Arizona Hospital Records." My Cochise. http://www.mycochise.com/hospcala2ba.php (June 20, 2011)

August 22, 1914, Shattuck Mine
On Friday, August 22, George Moore was working in a crosscut. He was working bent over, when a slab fell at struck him in the back of the head cutting an artery. He was transported to the Copper Queen Hospital after losing a lot of blood. It was expected that he could return to work on August 25th.
"Shattuck Miner was Seriously Injured" Bisbee Daily Review 23 August 1914 page 5

December 9, 1915, Shattuck Mine
George P. Medigovich a cage bar fell and bruised his left hand.

Office of State Mine Inspector. *Fifth Annual Report of the State Mine Inspector State of Arizona for the Year Ending November 30, 1916.*

August 16, 1916, Shattuck Mine

Michael Treyne,* a 26-year-old Irish miner and John Jackson were repairing a drift. The area they were working was considered relatively safe. It was thought that the work they were doing caused the ground to begin moving. Suddenly, a cave-in occurred, and Treyne was killed. His partner, Jackson received only minor injuries and went for assistance. Treyne's remains were taken to the O.K. Undertaking Parlor and later shipped to Philadelphia for burial. It was believed he had a sister there. (No coroner's inquest could be located)

"Repairman Killed by Cave-in at Shattuck" Bisbee Daily Review 17 August 1916
Dugan Mortuary Records 1914 – 1917 Accession 2010.10.8 Bisbee Mining and Historical Museum, Bisbee.
Office of State Mine Inspector. *Fifth Annual Report of the State Mine Inspector State of Arizona for the Year Ending November 30, 1916.*

August 18, 1916, Shattuck Mine

Charles Burgoon had set up a drill on a bar and column to drill in 134 drift on the 500 level. He decided to drill along a small *"vein"* of ore. Around 8:00 pm, when he was drilling his second hole a two-ton boulder fell on him breaking his neck. His partner Thomas Webb, who was working about 50 ft. away, found him, when he went to get a hammer from Burgoon. Webb a mucker, ran to his aid and summoned assistance to remove his body. It was believed that the actions of the drill he was using caused the boulder to fall. He had lived in Bisbee for 14 years and had the reputation as being one of the best Shattuck miners. He was survived by a brother Ross Burgoon of Bisbee, an unnamed brother in Hayden, Arizona and family in Pennsylvania. His remains were taken to Ashville, Pennsylvania for burial. (Note, the newspaper article describes the accident details different than the inquest.)

"Charles Burgoon Killed When Rock Falls in Shattuck working, Breaking his Neck." Bisbee Daily Review 19 August 1916 page 1
Dugan Mortuary Records Aug. 26, 1914 – Dec 21, 1916 Accession 2010.10.9 Bisbee Mining and Historical Museum, Bisbee.
Office of State Mine Inspector. *Fifth Annual Report of the State Mine Inspector State of Arizona for the Year Ending November 30, 1916.*
"Original Certificate of Death." Arizona Department of Health Services. http://genealogy.az.gov/azdeath/015/10151040.pdf (May 28, 2012)
"Cochise County Coroner's Inquest No. 1233 Arizona State Archives Phoenix

December 5, 1916, Shattuck Mine

A rock fell and bruised the left foot of John McCloskey.

Office of State Mine Inspector. *Sixth Annual Report of the State Mine Inspector State of Arizona for the Year Ending November 30, 1917.*

December 6, 1916, Shattuck Mine

William Daly was caught in a cave-in and bruised his side and back.

Office of State Mine Inspector. *Sixth Annual Report of the State Mine Inspector State of Arizona for the Year Ending November 30, 1917.*

May 3, 1917, Shattuck Mine

Irish Miner, Martin Mulroe was killed between the 300 and 400 levels in an intermediate drift. Mulroe was installing bridging above the sets. For some reason he had decided to climb above the sets and work between the top of the timber and the back of the workings He was using a scaling bar and a pick to make room when an 18-inch strip of siliceous ore slipped and pinned him to the timber. Sandy ore began to run and filled in the timbered sets. A rescue crew began working and after hours had almost released him from his entrapment. They talked to Mulroe and had given him water. Dr. N.C. Bledsoe felt that Mulroe was *"suffering unduly"* and climbed on top of the set and gave him a shot of anesthetic. They also tried to carry him out but one leg was caught firmly by the boulder. A second run of fine ore buried him, and the rescue workers could see his arms twitching as he suffocated. Before the accident, he had been talking about the Red-light District* with Domineck Chino. Chino went to load a wheelbarrow, and when he came back, he found that Mulroe had been buried. He was survived by a mother, three sisters and his brother Michael, who was also a Shattuck miner. *The presence of a U.S. Army camp in Lowell, Arizona was forcing the closure of the Red-Light District and it was a local news topic of the time.

"Shattuck Miner, Pinned Under Boulder Smothers to Death" Bisbee Daily Review 4 May 1917 pages4& 5
"Cochise County Coroner's Inquest No. 1275" Arizona State Archives Phoenix

May 15, 1917, Shattuck Mine

Alfredo Valenzuela was caught in a blast. His nose was broken, and one hand was cut.

Office of State Mine Inspector. *Sixth Annual Report of the State Mine Inspector State of Arizona for the Year Ending November 30, 1917.*

May 23, 1917, Shattuck Mine

On the night shift, Marko Draskovich and Archer E. Olsen were working in 8 stope on the 600 level. This stope was mining next to a stope that had been mined about eight years earlier. The ground was treacherous. The stope collapsed trapping Olsen and killing Draskovich. Trapped, Olsen could hear the other crews blasting as they went off shift. There was no man check system at the Shattuck Mine, and these men were not missed. After seven hours, at the beginning of day shift the next crew entered the area. Olsen heard one of the miners comment that it appeared someone was already working there, because of the lunch buckets hanging. The trapped miner called to the other men and was finally heard. After nine hours he was rescued. He was taken to the Calumet & Arizona Hospital for treatment and released from their care on May 28, 1917. It took several hours to recover the body of Draskovich. The deceased was 28 years old and from Austria-Hungary. Draskovich lived with his sister near Central School. (Note, the newspaper description varies distinctly from the information provided by witnesses at the inquest.)

"Bisbee Miner Killed in Cave-in" Tombstone Weekly Epitaph 27 May 1917 page 8
"Calumet & Arizona Hospital Records." My Cochise. http://www.mycochise.com/hospcalo2 po.php (August 2, 2011)
"Original Certificate of Death." Arizona Department of Health Services. http://genealogy.az.gov/azdeath/016/10160893.pdf (August 2, 2011
Office of State Mine Inspector. *Sixth Annual Report of the State Mine Inspector State of Arizona for the Year Ending November 30, 1917.*

"Cochise County Coroner's Inquest No. 1280" Arizona State Archives Phoenix

June 9, 1917, Shattuck Mine

Ed Coyne fell and bruised a leg. The 42 -year-old mucker, remained in the Calumet & Arizona Hospital until June 18.

"Calumet & Arizona Hospital Records." My Cochise.
http://www.mycochise.com/hospcalco2day.php (June 2, 2012)
Office of State Mine Inspector. *Sixth Annual Report of the State Mine Inspector State of Arizona for the Year Ending November 30, 1917.*

December 23, 1917, Shattuck Mine

Englishman, Robert Albert Ireland was working as a cager on the dinkey cage with W.H. Gohring as hoistman. Around 10:00 pm, Ireland was bringing up a broken ladder, a rope, and other items to the surface. He had stopped at the subway, a tunnel used to bring in supplies a short distance below the surface. Then he rang the bells to be brought to the collar. Gohring thought for a moment that the cage was on the 900 level and raised the cage expecting it to travel quite a distance. Quickly, the cage was on the surface, and the safety device failed to stop the cage, and it was pulled into the sheave wheel. Tracey Christo was the top lander and heard a crash. A gate was torn off the cage, and the ladder rope, and other things fell onto the hoist house roof. Christo caught a glimpse of something falling into the shaft. On the 200 level, Swing Foreman, John Gilmore was waiting for Ireland to bring him a rope when he heard something banging as it fell down the shaft. Ireland's hat fell onto the 200 level station, not realizing a man had fallen Gilmore called the surface to find out what happened. It was later learned Ireland had fallen to his death, down the Shattuck Shaft. After his death his name appeared on a list of men who had avoided the World War I draft. His niece, Mrs. Joe McGarry wanted to make it known her uncle had been killed and was not a *"slacker"* avoiding the war.

Office of State Mine Inspector. *Seventh Annual Report of the State Mine Inspector State of Arizona for the Year Ending November 30, 1918.*
"Original Certificate of Death." Arizona Department of Health Services. http://genealogy.az.gov/azdeath/017/10170405.pdf (May 28, 2012)
"Cochise County Coroner's Inquest No. 1306" Arizona State Archives Phoenix
"Ireland not Slacker Bisbee Daily Review23 February 1918 page 6

January 5, 1918, Shattuck Mine

John Mihelicia was barring down the back (ceiling) and a rock slid down the bar. It then fell off and hit his right foot. Rocks loosened by barring down often will slide down the bar after falling. In later years, a short piece of drill air hose would be wired onto scaling bars. This provided a bump to knock off rocks sliding down the bar.

Office of State Mine Inspector. *Seventh Annual Report of the State Mine Inspector State of Arizona for the Year Ending November 30, 1918.*

June 6, 1918, Shattuck Mine

Emil Haggblom broke a ladder rung while climbing and injured his back. He was injured again later in the Denn Mine on May 19, 1919

Office of State Mine Inspector. *Seventh Annual Report of the State Mine Inspector State of Arizona for the Year Ending November 30, 1918.*

August 18, 1918, Shattuck Mine

Earnest H. Foster sprained his wrist as he was dumping a mine car.

Office of State Mine Inspector. *Seventh Annual Report of the State Mine Inspector State of Arizona for the Year Ending November 30, 1918.*

September 7, 1918, Shattuck Mine

Chris Rafailovich was breaking a boulder with a double-jack and a rock fragment flew and abraded his left eye.

Office of State Mine Inspector. *Seventh Annual Report of the State Mine Inspector State of Arizona for the Year Ending November 30, 1918.*

December 21, 1918, Shattuck Mine

Tom Doherty was working in a stope when he was caught in a cave-in. His left leg was broken.

Office of State Mine Inspector. *Eighth Annual Report of the State Mine Inspector State of Arizona for the Year Ending November 30, 1919.*

January 31, 1919, Shattuck Mine

D.B. Cota dislocated his right arm at the elbow, when a mine car derailed and turned over smashing him against the drift.

Office of State Mine Inspector. *Eighth Annual Report of the State Mine Inspector State of Arizona for the Year Ending November 30, 1919.*

October 3, 1919, Shattuck Mine

Fernando Noriega was riding a mine car and was knocked off when it stopped.

Office of State Mine Inspector. *Eighth Annual Report of the State Mine Inspector State of Arizona for the Year Ending November 30, 1919.*

January 1, 1920, Shattuck Mine

Amado Lopez had his hand smashed in the door of a mine car.

Office of State Mine Inspector. *Ninth Annual Report of the State Mine Inspector State of Arizona for the Year Ending November 30, 1920.*

February 6, 1920, Shattuck Mine

John Vercellino fell *"through timber"* and injured the ribs on his left side.

Office of State Mine Inspector. *Ninth Annual Report of the State Mine Inspector State of Arizona for the Year Ending November 30, 1920.*

April 10, 1920, Shattuck Mine

E.B. Stephens, a mucker wrenched his back assisting a timberman to stand a post. He was taken to the Calumet & Arizona Hospital where he stayed until April 16, 1920.

"Calumet & Arizona Hospital Records." My Cochise.
http://www.mycochise.com/hospcalhi2ja.php (June 2, 2012)

Office of State Mine Inspector. *Ninth Annual Report of the State Mine Inspector State of Arizona for the Year Ending November 30, 1920.*

July 19, 1920, Shattuck Mine

George Gudlj and Pat Powers were installing a set of booms. One had been installed, and Powers left to get the other. While he was gone Gudlj was hit by a rock falling off the end of a boom (part of the temporary timber designed to protect miners before permanent timber is installed) His neck was broken. Gudlj was 27 years old and from Tebinje, Serbia. He was buried in Evergreen Cemetery.

"Original Certificate of Death." Arizona Department of Health Services. http://genealogy.az.gov/azdeath/022/10220991.pdf (May 30, 2012)

Office of State Mine Inspector. *Ninth Annual Report of the State Mine Inspector State of Arizona for the Year Ending November 30, 1920.*

"Cochise County Coroner's Inquest No.1423" Arizona State Archives Phoenix

September 24, 1920, Shattuck Mine

August Martinez injured his hand after he fell while emptying a can of carbide. (Note that cans of carbide normally weighed 50 lbs.)

Office of State Mine Inspector. *Ninth Annual Report of the State Mine Inspector State of Arizona for the Year Ending November 30, 1920.*

April 23, 1923, Shattuck Mine

A falling timber bruised the back of Jacob Hill's head.

Office of State Mine Inspector. *Twelfth Annual Report of the State Mine Inspector State of Arizona for the Year Ending November 30, 1923.*

May 8, 1923, Shattuck Mine

Jim Carpena hit his elbow on a pipe while moving a mine car on a turnsheet.

Office of State Mine Inspector. *Twelfth Annual Report of the State Mine Inspector State of Arizona for the Year Ending November 30, 1923.*

November 1, 1923, Shattuck Mine

E.R. Martinez broke his toe when he rolled a mine car over it.

Office of State Mine Inspector. *Twelfth Annual Report of the State Mine Inspector State of Arizona for the Year Ending November 30, 1923.*

April 19, 1924, Shattuck Mine

Vaso Martinovich injured an eye while breaking boulders.

Office of State Mine Inspector. *Thirteenth Annual Report of the State Mine Inspector State of Arizona for the Year Ending November 30, 1924.*

August 13, 1924, Shattuck Mine

A rock fell out of a chute and smashed a finger of Francisco Hernandez.

Office of State Mine Inspector. *Thirteenth Annual Report of the State Mine Inspector State of Arizona for the Year Ending November 30, 1924.*

October 3, 1924, Shattuck Mine

John Planinich wrenched his wrist pushing a mine car.

Office of State Mine Inspector. *Thirteenth Annual Report of the State Mine Inspector State of Arizona for the Year Ending November 30, 1924.*

January 13, 1925, Shattuck Mine

Around 2:20 pm, Fernando Gomez and Ezekial Atundo were working on the 600 level in a stope about 50 ft. from the station. Gomez needed to install two posts. He placed the first post when he was setting up the second, the area caved. Atundo was a set below him,   but protected by timber. His carbide lamp tried to go out, but stayed lit. The dust caused the light from his lamp to darken. He escaped from the caving stope. It took about four hours to recover Gomez's body. He was survived by a widow Rosario Gomez and five children. Gomez was from Sonora, Mexico.

"Original Certificate of Death." Arizona Department of Health Services http://genealogy.az.gov/azdeath/030/10300037.pdf (May 31, 2012)

Office of State Mine Inspector. *Fourteenth Annual Report of the State Mine Inspector State of Arizona for the Year Ending November 30, 1925.* Tombstone Epitaph.

"Cochise County Coroner's Inquest No. 1584" Arizona State Archives Phoenix

March 7, 1974 Shattuck Mine

As the road from the Junction Yard /Lavender Pit area was being extended to the Shattuck Mine. Pit shift boss, C. Hendricks was instructing S. Devilbiss how to build a berm on the road. Obviously, tensions were high and Devilbiss punched Hendricks in the mouth. Hendricks suffered a loose tooth and a bruised lip.

Phelps Dodge Corporation Copper Queen Branch Accident Report 3-7-74

October 15, 1974 Shattuck Mine

C.J. Riggs was installing corrugated metal on the Shattuck hoist house when something blew into his right eye.

Phelps Dodge Corporation Copper Queen Branch Accident Report 11-15-74 (original document misdated?)

July 3, 1975 Shattuck Mine

J.J. Stanford was working in the shaft at the 800 level. He was with D.C. Vincent. They were hoist muck from the shaft. According to the accident report, *"cable pulled board loose and fell on bucket"*. When this occurred Stanford somehow was cut on the hand and nose. The description of accident is vague, but the cable could have been the hoisting cable and the bucket a sinking bucket, but this not clear.

Phelps Dodge Corporation Copper Queen Branch Accident Report 7-3-75

July 15, 1975 Shattuck Mine

Boilermaker, H.T. Millican was cutting a roof bolt with a torch. The roof bolt fell and cut his hand between his thumb and forefinger.

Phelps Dodge Corporation Copper Queen Branch Accident Report 7-15-75

July 24, 1975 Shattuck Mine

Working with a jackhammer at the 800 level inside the shaft. A piece of something flew into R.F. Herrera's right eye. Note, the Shattuck Shaft had burned in 1952 and the shaft had become clogged with debris. This mix of rock timber and pipe had become lightly cemented by gypsum formed from mine water draining into the shaft. Below, the 600 level water rained into the shaft from seepage.

Phelps Dodge Corporation Copper Queen Branch Accident Report 8-1-75

August 27, 1975 Shattuck Mine
W.M Kasun fell off the steps going to the hoist house. He suffered bruised hip and a
scraped left shoulder.
Phelps Dodge Corporation Copper Queen Branch Accident Report 8-27-75

The abandoned 5ᵗʰ level adit of the Southwest Mine

Southwest Mine

This mine actually was developed as part of the Czar Mine. The orebodies that were mined
by the Southwest Mine likely would have been discovered early except, the focus of mining in the
district was deeper and eastward. In 1907, the Higgins was the only productive mine to the west and
it was actually mining Wolverine & Arizona Mining Company ore, thousands of feet from the mine
entrance and these ores were to the south-southwest of the Czar Mine. The Shattuck was an
immensely profitable mine to the south of the Czar. North of the Czar, the footwall of the Dividend
Fault was a geologic barrier to ore. At the beginning of the twentieth century the Calumet and
Arizona Mining Company had acquired the all valuable lands to the east. So the Copper Queen
Consolidated Mining Company was effectively encircled and limited with exploration opportunities.
They searched the porphyry to the East for low grade orebodies and from the Czar Mine they began
driving raises southwest from the shaft on the 200 level. Three of these raises were #2-27, #2-27-1 and
#2-27-2. According to a mine map 2-27 became the Southwest #1 interior shaft. Even though it is
noted on a map it was a single compartment raise and is not believed to have intercepted any level

403

above the 200. It seems this may actually have been a simple exploration raise. By 1910, #2-27-1 raise actually had become an interior shaft. Called the Southwest #2 Shaft it had three compartments and extended to the 4th level with stations at the 200, 100, "B", 3rd and 4th levels. The hoist was located on the 200 level. Raise #2-27-2, became the Southwest # 3 interior Shaft by 1911. This shaft had only two compartments and extended from the 200 level upwards to the 6th level. When the Southwest # 3 was complete the hoist was located on the 5th level station.

The location of the shaft was at the western end of the Atlanta Claim resulted for a time the shaft and related workings being referred to as the "West Atlanta" The actual West Atlanta shaft was sunk in the earliest days of mining by Dr. James Douglas following streaks of copper ore near the lead-silver ore of what was later known as the Hendricks mine. Another Atlanta Shaft located on the eastern end of the Atlanta Claim was sunk in 1884 and discovered the orebody that made Dr. Douglas famous. The Southwest #2 was operated only a few years before it suffered from a problem common with shafts, it was driven to close to a major orebody. As the orebody was mined the shaft began to take weight and the crosscuts around the shaft began caving.

Southwest # 3 initially fared better until it was raised about 50 ft. above the fourth level. At this point the ground became heavy and poor ground conditions continued to the top of the shaft at the 6th level. A massive orebody was discovered extending to above the 7th level. The ore was located in the relatively strong silica breccia and was mined with limited backfilling. This series of interconnected stopes left a vast empty chamber which was referred to as the *"Ballpark."* Even the strong silica breccia could not support this open space forever. After mining ceased the *"Ballpark"* collapsed. Boulders, often the size of small houses fell and created massive rubble piles in the stope. Crevices between boulders created passages that traveled hundreds of feet between boulders. One vertical crack extended from the track of the 7th level to down past the 6th level into a small 5th level stope, a vertical distance nearly 200 ft. The general outline of the stope is visible on satellite images. Distinctive subsidence cracks form a rough oval shape from the top Queen Hill and across Hendricks Gulch up the flank of the opposite hill. Of interest, was the hundreds of small caves and cave-like openings that were exposed by the collapses. Also hematite was abundant and was mirror polished along faults as slickened sides. These created boulders with mirror-like faces.

Until 1915, the Southwest Mine had no adits to the surface. This meant all supplies and miners were lowered to the 200 level of the Czar Mine and would travel to one of the Southwest Shafts to be hoisted to the working areas. The steepness of the hillsides did limit the value of adits, but in 1915 two major adits were driven. The Queen Tunnel was driven from the site of the old Copper Queen smelter back to the Southwest #2 & #3 shafts. Above at the 5,500 ft. elevation the Southwest Tunnel (adit) was driven to the Southwest # 3 shaft. In 1919, the 7th level of the Southwest Mine was extended to have an adit portal in Hendricks gulch. The 4th and 6th levels also had adits, but it is unclear when they were driven. In the case of the 6th level which had two portals side by side at least one of the adits likely predates the development of the Southwest Mine and is probably part of the Hendricks Mine. The 8th and 10th levels had adits but were isolated from other workings of the Southwest Mine. Although, the 8th level was intercepted by a raise from the 7th level.

The orebody continued to extend in a southwesterly direction and soon the Southwest Shafts were no longer suitable to supply the stopes. In 1919, the Sunrise Shaft was raised from the 3rd level or Queen Tunnel level. Supplies and men were brought through the Queen Tunnel to Sunrise Shaft at the 3rd level. The Sunrise had a single deck cage that filled two shaft compartments. This allowed for mules to be transferred to the levels above without using the difficult procedure of swinging a carefully bound mule under a cage. More importantly, it allowed for rapid hoisting of timber. Timber trucks loaded with timber could simply be rolled onto a cage without being unloaded (except stringers.) The headframe was unique. It was a four story building with a flat cabled hoist mounted immediately over the shaft and the cable was directly attached to the cage. No sheave wheel was used. Also, this was Bisbee first automated shaft and could be operated from the cage, like an elevator.

April 27, 1911, Czar Mine /Southwest Shaft.

John Brown loaded two holes about 25 ft. from the Southwest No.3 Shaft on the 4th level. He used a six-foot fuse. Around 3:25 pm, he ignited the fuse and caught the cage down to the third level. On the third level, he walked over to the Southwest No.2 Shaft. Dave R.

Riley* met up with him on the 3rd level and talked to him about his shift. Brown replied, *"Yes, I had a good shift, shot two holes."* Meanwhile, eight men going off shift boarded the third cage in the Southwest No. 3 Shaft to be lowered for the end of shift. F.J. "Steam Shovel" Wright tried to encourage his partner Davie to squeeze onto the cage, but Davie decided to wait for another cage. After the cage had descended 50 ft, rocks began falling into the shaft. Then after the cage passed the 3rd level, the second shot detonated and more rocks began to fall the shaft. The bonnets initially protected the men, but more rock fell. M.C. Benton remembers hearing a man shout that his arm was broken and all the men were trying to squeeze to the center of the cage. When the cage stopped on the 200 level (2nd level) Erick Sanberg fell over backward and landed with his head under the cage. Benton gave Erick water, but he died immediately. His skull was broken and part of the skull was pushing down on the brain. All of the other men were also injured. The two seriously injured were F.C. Webb and Dave Foster. Webb had his shoulder broken, cuts on his head and his right hand was injured. Foster's head had serious cuts on his head and shoulders. John Edmonds and H.E. Henderson both suffered a broken finger and cuts bout the head. Both "Steam Shovel" Wright and Hugh Shaw had a bruised arm and also cut on the head. M.C. Benton received only minor injuries, bruises, and an injured hand. On the surface, the injured men were either treated at the Czar Shaft for minor injuries or taken to the Copper Queen Hospital. Wright the miner who was next to Sanberg was drenched in blood from his head wounds insisted on showering in the change house instead of going to the hospital. Although, he was initially unable to give much detail about the accident, he later was able to provide some details including that if his partner Davie had got onto the cage he would have been killed. As news of the accident, a crowd assembled at the shaft. One miner discovered his wife had come to Czar to see if he had been in the accident *"as they met they embraced silently and went to their home."*** Shift Boss A.G. Watkins** along with, Superintendent Gerald Sherman and Mine Superintendent Woodman went underground to inspect the accident site. They found about *"a car and a half"* of broken rock on the cage and 200 level station. The shaft timber had scars from falling rock and two places in the shaft where rock had fallen into the shaft. One in the shaft close to the 4th level station and the other was 3 sets (of timber) below the 4th level. The general agreement was that the rock had fallen down the shaft was rock that fell from walls as a result of being disturbed by the explosion. One miner, M.C. Benton felt that the rock had possibly been shot into the cage by the blast. Erick Sanberg a Finnish miner was 25 years old and was survived by a wife and child in Finland. His only relative in Bisbee was a brother-in-law J. L. Johnson. He was buried at Evergreen Cemetery. F.C. Webb remained at the Copper Queen Hospital for 46 days.

*Dave Riley may have been Brown's partner he is quoted to have said *"We had orders to blast at 2:30."*
**A.G. Watkins was later killed in the Southwest mine on December 29, 1915
*** lack of punctuation sic
This accident predates the Queen and Southwest adits ("tunnels"). The orebodies that were later developed into the Southwest mine were still being mined from the Czar mine. Technically, this accident occurred in workings of the Czar Mine, although the accident actually occurred in the Southwest No. 3 Shaft. It is also important to recognize that in the Southwest shafts the levels are numbered

based on elevation above sea level. The 6th level is at 5,600ft. elevation, the 4th level at 5,400ft. elevation. This gives the impression that the levels are numbered backward to the 3rd level compared to most shafts in Bisbee. The 6th level is the top of the shaft, and the 3rd level is in the middle. Below the third level the numbers reverse and the shafts bottom out on the 2nd level which is equal to the 200 level Czar. It was important to number the levels differently, or the Copper Queen Consolidated Mining Company would have had two 600 levels, two 700 levels, two 1000 levels all at dramatically different elevations.

"One Killed 7 Others Injured in Czar Shaft." Bisbee Daily Review 28 April 1911 page 1

"Jury sits on Mine Let Go" Bisbee Daily Review 29 April 1911 page 1

"Jury sits on Mine Let Go" Bisbee Daily Review 29 April 1911 page 4

"Funeral of Erik Sanberg" Bisbee Daily Review 2 May 1911 page 5

"Original Certificate of Death" Arizona Department of Health Services http://genealogy.az.gov/azdeath/008/10080375.pdf   (May 2, 2012)

Copper Queen Hospital Patients Register Jan 1, 1910 – Aug. 30, 1911, Bisbee Mining and Historical Museum, Bisbee.

"Cochise County Coroner's Inquest No. 827" Arizona State Archives Phoenix

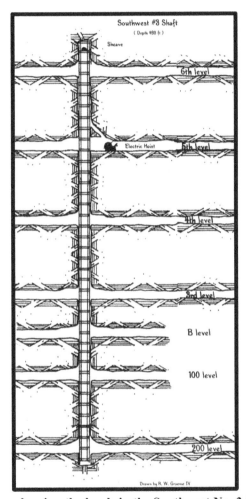

A section showing the levels in the Southwest No. 3 Shaft.

November 30, 1911, Southwest Mine

Steve Cole and his partner, Herbert McCutcheon were working in a raise extending from the 4th level up to the 5th level. There was limited room in the raise, so McCutcheon waited at the bottom of the raise, to turn the air off and on while Cole drilled out room for timber. After 15 minutes, Cole fell seven to eight feet with an 800 lb. boulder. The rock landed on Cole's leg pinning him to a cap. McCutcheon went up after Cole called him, but discovered that if they moved the boulder it would knock Cole down the raise or the boulder would roll onto him. Quickly, McCutcheon got Michael Hannon operator of the lease, Bob Tate and Southwest Mine Foreman, Albert G. Watkins*. They held up the boulder to keep it from rolling on Cole and cribbed it up with timber and were able to pry the boulder off him. He remained conscious as he told the men how to pry off the rock and remained so as he told friends to make sure his leg was not amputated. After the accident, Cole told that he had dreamed, he would die in the mine that day and had almost turned to go back home. Steve was better known as *"Whippie"* a nickname. He had received this nickname from a time he went to Mexico and left his horse in front of a store. When he came back out his whip was stolen He tried to explain it to a Mexican officer who responded *"No sabe, Senor,"* so Steve tried to explain it by saying *"Whippie, Whippie"* He later died from shock and blood loss.

*Watkins was later killed in the Southwest Mine on December 29, 1915
"Dreamed of Death the Night before He Turned Back" Bisbee Daily Review 2 December 1911 page 2
"Crushed by Rock Dies from Shock" Bisbee Daily Review 1 December 1911 page 2
"Dreamed of Death the Night before He Turned Back" Bisbee Daily Review 2 December 1911 page 2
"Cochise County Coroner's Inquest No.880" Arizona State Archives Phoenix

January 8, 1913, Southwest Mine*

Irish Miner, C.H. Gordon had his foot smashed and bruised. He was released from the Copper Queen Hospital on February 1.

*Newspaper states Czar Mine, Hospital records indicate Southwest Mine.
"Foot Injured" Bisbee Daily Review 9 January 1913 page 2
Copper Queen Hospital Patients Register Jan 1, 1913 – Mar 24, 1914 Bisbee Mining and Historical Museum, Bisbee.

September 27, 1913, Southwest Mine

Ed Tribolet fell into a 50 ft. raise. His unconscious form was taken to the Copper Queen Hospital. He suffered a concussion and was released from the hospital after 20 days.

"Bisbee Miner Slightly Injured by 50ft. Fall" El Paso Herald 1 October 1913 page 8
Copper Queen Hospital Patients Register Jan 1, 1913 – Mar 24, 1914 Bisbee Mining and Historical Museum, Bisbee.

April 2, 1915, Southwest mine

Ham Daniels was caught in a cave-in. His hip was dislocated, and both ankles were sprained. He stayed at the Copper Queen Hospital 19 days.

"Miner Badly Hurt" Bisbee Daily Review 3 April 1915 page 6
Copper Queen Hospital Patients Register April 2, 1915 Bisbee Mining and Historical Museum, Bisbee.

August 1, 1915, Southwest Mine

Fred Nicholas had his left leg crushed by a falling boulder. He was sent home.

"Nicholas Improving" Bisbee Daily Review 4 August 1915 page 8

December 29, 1915, Southwest Mine

Shift Boss Rasmussen and Mine Foreman Albert G. Watkins* went into to inspect a short incline raise being driven off a large transfer raise that was being driven from the 200 level Southwest Mine up to the 5th level Southwest Mine. To inspect the raise Watkins and

Ramussen had to cross over the waste filled transfer raise. Both men were aware of the danger and Ramussen warned Watkins that the motorman on the 200 level had been told to pull the chute. As Watkins and Ramussen were crossing the waste filled raise, F.N. Evans began loading ten "E" cars from the chute. It appears the chute hung up slightly then suddenly dropped 12 ft. Ramussen was buried up to his knees, and Watkins was buried completely. Ramussen had Mike L. Davis a miner in the raise above, drop him a rope so he could tie himself off on and then order Evans to order them to stop pulling cars on the 200 level and then climb the manway up from the 3rd level until he was to cut through the lagging on the side of the manway across from where Watkins was buried. Evans cut through the lagging and allowed the broken rock to flow into the manway. They recovered Watkins body still standing straight up with his hat on and one arm covering his eyes. Watkins was an important and long member of the Bisbee community and had served on the Bisbee School Board. He eventually became school board president. While on the school board he worked to build a new high school. This school still exists today on school hill, but now serves as Cochise County offices. Albert Watkins had come to Bisbee in 1899 and during his years there he became an expert on minerals *"Whose knowledge of various minerals and their occurrence is unsurpassed by anyone in this district."* One of his last important accomplishments was when he was assigned by the Copper Queen Consolidated Mining Company to prepare and exhibit of minerals and ores from the district for the 1915 Panama-Pacific International Exhibition in San Francisco. For this exhibit he displayed the specimens in the orientation in which they had formed. This exhibition closed only 25 days before his death. At the time of his death Watkins was 46 years old and survived by a widow, his daughters Florence and Barbara Watkins, his father Christopher Watkins and six brothers. Six months after his death, the miners of the Southwest Mine presented to Mrs. Watkins a gold plate set in ebony, engraved with *"To Mrs. Mary C. Watkins, in loving remembrance of Albert G. Watkins, from the boys of the Southwest Mine."* The money for this gift was paid for from donations of only regular miners, no supervisors.

* Albert Watkins was a shift boss for the Southwest area when Erick Sanberg was killed April 27, 1911, in the" Southwest country" of the Czar Shaft.

"A.G. Watkins Killed in Mine" Bisbee Daily Review 30 December 1915 page 1

"High School Graduates will pass through Commencement into the World" Bisbee Daily Review 30 may 1913 page 8

"In and About the Mines" Bisbee Daily Review 27 September 1914 page 1

"Mine Foreman is Smothered" El Paso Herald 31 December 1915 page 2

"Token of Esteem is sent Mrs. Watkins by Southwest Miners "Bisbee Daily Review 15 June 1916 page 2

"Original Certificate of Death" Arizona Department of Health Services http://genealogy.az.gov/azdeath/014/10140876.pdf (July 22, 2011

Dugan Mortuary Records Aug. 26, 1914 – Dec. 21, 1916, Accession 2010.10.9 Bisbee Mining and Historical Museum, Bisbee.

"Jury Sits on Mine Let Go" Bisbee Daily Review 29 April 1911 page 1

Cochise County Coroner's Inquest No.1184" Arizona State Archives Phoenix

July 24, 1916, Southwest Mine

Shift Boss, Andrew Finety was supervising Jake Jacobson installing a chute lining in a raise between the 100 and 200 levels. A collapse occurred, and Andrew Finety was trapped. Jacobson quickly alerted Assistant Mine Superintendent, Emmett Finety, Captain Hodgson, and others. After three hours of digging by hand, they freed the uninjured man.

"Entombed Three Hours in Mine" <u>Bisbee Daily Review</u> 25, July 1916 page 8

March 7, 1917, Southwest Mine

Mike Kline was caught in a premature explosion. His nose was broken.
"Miner is Injured" <u>Bisbee Daily Review</u> 8 March 1917 page 8
Copper Queen Hospital Patients Register Mar 7 1917Bisbee Mining and Historical Museum, Bisbee.

February 22, 1918, Southwest Mine

B. Boulden had his leg broken in an undescribed accident. He was treated at the Copper Queen Hospital.
"Miner Injured" <u>Bisbee Daily Review</u> 23 February 1918 page 6

August 17, 1918, Southwest Mine

At 11:30 pm, Walter Hall was working with J. W. Jones and Robert Fulton in a stope on "A" level* Hall was cleaning ore from around a four-foot diameter boulder in order to crib it up. While picking, it fell breaking his arm and the boulder pinned his broken leg next to a track tie. His nose was broken as well as several ribs. Jones rushed over to see what happened and called for help. Fulton, who was 15 ft. below saw Hall's lamp fall and went up to see what happened. Fulton went to get help and the shift boss. Miner, Pete Andrews called for a man basket and then went to call for a doctor and an ambulance. Unfortunately, the lights were out in the town of Bisbee and the telephone operator could not see where to put the plugs in for the connection. Andrews ask her if she had a lamp, but she replied *"No."* After a while, he sent men to get them, but finally, the operator reached the doctor and ambulance. They were unable to notify the mine officials. At the Copper Queen Hospital, Hall died at 7:00 am on August 18th. * The Southwest mine is not believed to have had an "A" level. Technically, this accident may have occurred in the Copper Queen or Uncle Sam mines or on a sublevel equal to "A" level.
Office of State Mine Inspector. *Seventh Annual Report of the State Mine Inspector State of Arizona for the Year Ending November 30, 1918.*
"Cochise County Coroner's Inquest No.1337" Arizona State Archives

September 15, 1918 Southwest Mine

Rock fell on the left foot of H.H. Hilton. He was expected to be off work a few days.
"Off of Work" <u>Bisbee Daily Review</u> 17 September 1918 page 6

September 21, 1918, Southwest Mine

A. Rzabel Johnson* had his hand smashed by falling rock. * This name is possibly a misspelling.
"Hand is Smashed" <u>Bisbee Daily Review</u> 22 September 1918 page 8

October 12, 1918, Southwest Mine

J.R. Ferrell had his fingers smashed in an undescribed accident.
"Is Slightly Injured" <u>Bisbee Daily Review</u> 13 October 1918 page 8

March 27, 1920 Southwest Mine

Perry Riley Byrd was better known as *"Pony,* "was working in 5-15-1 stope on the 6th level to start gobbing. The stope was taking weight and Byrd was told to access the stope from No.18 drift and not through No.19 drift like normal. While he was removing lagging, a multi-ton boulder broke free smashing the timber and released muck that nearly completely

409

buried Byrd. Over 100 tons fell. The rock and debris broke his back. His body was lowered and brought to the surface though the Queen Tunnel. He was 36 years old and survived by a wife and three children. Before coming to Bisbee, he had owned a ranch in Oklahoma. This ranch including the house, chickens, cattle and farm equipment had been destroyed by a tornado.

"Fall from Car Kills Worker" Bisbee Daily Review 30 March 1920 page 3
Dugan Mortuary Records Accession 2010.10.13 Bisbee Mining and Historical Museum, Bisbee
"Falling Soil Kills Miner" Tombstone Epitaph 4 April 1920 page 5
"Original Certificate of Death." Arizona Department of Health Services. http://genealogy.az.gov/azdeath/021/10211867.pdf (August 1, 2011
Cochise County Coroner's Inquest No.1408" Arizona State Archives Phoenix

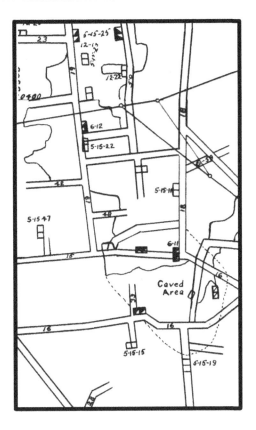

Map of area where Pony R. Byrd was killed on the 6th level Southwest Mine. The location marked caved is on the original map and possibly shows the exact area.

March 16, 1921, Southwest Mine
A boulder crushed and broke C. F. McGregor's leg.
"Rock Breaks Leg" Bisbee Daily Review 17 March page 8

May, 1921, Southwest Mine
Roy Smith was digging when his pick struck a misfire and it exploded. It was believed he may lose one eye.
"Smith loses Eye" Bisbee Daily Review 14 May 1921 page 6

June 3, 1921, Southwest Mine

At 12:45 am, V.H. Cass was working on the 3rd level when he was caught in a premature blast and was injured.

"Pioneer Miner Hurt in Premature Blast." Tombstone Epitaph 5 June 1921 page 4

A caved-in crosscut just off the 3rd level of the Southwest No.3 Shaft station. Note, the concrete frames of the fire door.

May 29, 1922 Southwest Mine

Montenegrin Miner, Ilia J. Vuksanovich and John L. Regan were in a stope on the 3rd level Southwest Mine. At 11:45 pm a massive cave-in occurred in the stope. The resulting concussion blew out the flames on the carbide lamps of *"scores of other miners"* After recovering from being suddenly blanketed by darkness miners located the source of the collapse. *"One old-time miner said the roar and concussion were the worst he had ever heard."* By 2:45 am the body of Regan had been located, but was still caught under fallen timber and rock. It appeared that the collapse had trapped him while he was running to safety. It was felt that if the cave-in had held off just a few seconds, Regan would have made it out safely. Crews of 15 men worked 8-hour shifts in an attempt to recover the body of Vuksanovich. Miners recovered Ilia's vest with a watch still running in a pocket hanging on a timber. Five days after the accident the body of Vuksanovich was found and early in the next morning June 3rd his body was removed from the mine. Little hope must have been given for his survival. The newspaper reported him as killed days before his body was recovered. Regan worked in the Southwest Mine only three weeks. He had returned to Bisbee around four months before the accident from service in the tank corps overseas. John was 25 years old and buried in Evergreen Cemetery with a military ceremony. Interestingly, Regan was listed as divorced. His brother and mother attended the funeral. Ilia Vuksanovich was a 49 -year-old widower his wife Ikee died March 21, 1917, when she was 30 years old. He was survived by three children who were all under 14 years old.

"Cave-in at 300 Foot Level in Southwest, Kills 2" Bisbee Daily Review 30 May 1922 page 1

"Unable to Find Body of Second Cave-in Victim" Bisbee Daily Review 31 May 1922 page 8

"Victim of Cave-In to be Buried with Military Ceremony" Bisbee Daily Review 2 June 1922 page 6

"Continue Search for Miner's Body in Southwest Stope" Bisbee Daily Review 1 June 1922 page 6

"Victim of Cave-In to be Buried with Military Ceremony" Bisbee Daily Review 2 June 1922 page 6

"Body of Southwest Victim Recovered after Long Search" Bisbee Daily Review 3 June 1922 page 6

"Card of Thanks" Bisbee Daily Review 6 June 1922 page 6

"Original Certificate of Death." Arizona Department of Health Services. http://genealogy.az.gov/azdeath/025/10251126.pdf (May 6, 2012)

"Original Certificate of Death." Arizona Department of Health Services. http://genealogy.az.gov/azdeath/025/10251124.pdf (May 6, 2012)

"Original Certificate of Death." Arizona Department of Health Services. http://genealogy.az.gov/azdeath/016/10160882.pdf (May 6, 2012)

Dugan Mortuary Records 1920-1923 Accession 2010.10.13 Bisbee Mining and Historical Museum, Bisbee

Cochise County Coroner's Inquest No.1479" Arizona State Archives Phoenix

Grave marker for John Regan.

Marker for Illia & Ikee Vuksanovich.

July 29, 1922, Southwest Mine*

Charles E. Johnson and his partner James Coughran were informed that there was a missed hole in their work area as they went on shift to the 7th level. Around 9 o'clock Johnson climbed into a raise to drill a thin section of rock. He began drilling and detonated the missed hole. The explosion punched a large hole in his chest and embedded a rock into his arm. His eyes were believed to be damaged. Johnson reported, that he thought one eye was ruined.

"Bisbee Miner Is Injured in Premature Blast" Tombstone Epitaph 30 July 1922 page 1

*The original article contained a couple of errors. It stated that the accident occurred on the 700 level of the Southwest Shaft. The Southwest Mine does not have a 700 level. It does have a 7th level, and 700 is a slang term referring to that level. Also, the Sunrise Shaft is the only shaft in the Southwest Mine that reaches the 7th level. Two 7th level tunnel entrances were also used to access the mine. One is in Uncle Sam Gulch and the other is in Hendricks Gulch. They are unusual that they form a tunnel and are not adits.

March 19, 1923, Southwest Mine /M.R. Gilman lease

On the 200 level, M.R. Gilman had his leg broken by a falling rock.

Office of State Mine Inspector. *Twelfth Annual Report of the State Mine Inspector State of Arizona for the Year Ending November 30, 1923.*

April 24, 1923, Southwest Mine

The largest fatal underground accident in Bisbee occurred, when Four Mexican miners were working on the Reese-Yutich lease on the 3rd level of the Southwest Mine. Around 8:00 am, Jose Lopez, Ramon Munoz, Victoriano Tanori, Blas Flores and Donaciano Casillas were working in an incline stope that reached the adit level. They were mining waste rock to be used in backfilling. Tanori and Flores were drilling. A boulder 20 ft. by 15ft. broke free and slid down the stope carrying rock and dirt. and Flores became completely buried by the flowing debris and killed. Ramon Munoz was working Casillas with cleaning up around a mine car. The car blocked Casillas' escape path and he was buried and killed, but Munoz was quickly rescued and sent to the Calumet & Arizona Hospital. Jose Lopez was mucking near the chute, but was protected from injury by the edge of the stope. Tanori suffered a tragic death as stated *"Another man was instantly killed when caught and crushed between a boulder and sidewall. His body is plainly visible according to reports pinned high up at one side of the stope."* The miners trying to uncover the two buried miners stated they could hear groaning until close to 11:00 am when they ceased. Although, a coroner's jury did not place blame for the accident, the deputy state mine inspector James Malley disagreed. He stated that he had inspected the same stope on February 26, 1923, and had instructed Robert Yutich to back fill part of the stope and on how to correctly timber it. Malley concluded that the miners were killed because the lease operators William Reese and Robert Yutich had failed to follow his recommendations. All three men were buried in Evergreen Cemetery. Donaciano was 26, Blas was 38 and Victoriano was 52 years old.

"Big Boulder Traps Four Men" The Bisbee Ore Tuesday Evening, 24 April 1923 page 1

"Mine Inspector Blames Leasers for Fatal Cave In" The Bisbee Ore Tuesday Evening, 28 April 1923 page 1

"Original Certificate of Death." Arizona Department of Health Services. http://genealogy.az.gov/azdeath/026/10262818.pdf (May 7, 2012,)

413

"Original Certificate of Death." <u>Arizona Department of Health Services.</u> http://genealogy.az.gov/azdeath/026/10262819.pdf (May 7, 2012,

"Original Certificate of Death." <u>Arizona Department of Health Services.</u> http://genealogy.az.gov/azdeath/026/10262817.pdf (May 7, 2012,)

"Bisbee-Lowell Evergreen Cemetery." <u>My Cochise.</u> http://www.mycochise.com/cembisbeeef.php (May 6, 2012)

"Bisbee-Lowell Evergreen Cemetery." <u>My Cochise.</u> http://www.mycochise.com/cembisbeet.php (May 6, 2012)

"Bisbee-Lowell Evergreen Cemetery." <u>My Cochise.</u> http://www.mycochise.com/cembisbeed.php (May 6, 2012

Dugan Mortuary Records Aug 24, 1922 to June 5th 1924 Accession 2010.10.15 Bisbee Mining and Historical Museum, Bisbee

Cochise County Coroner's Inquest No.1505 C" Arizona State Archives Phoenix

The concrete headstone of Donaciano Casillas.

May 26, 1923, Southwest Mine /M.R. Gilman lease

While working on the 200 level, a boulder fell on G.A. Edwards' foot bruising it.

Office of State Mine Inspector. *Twelfth Annual Report of the State Mine Inspector State of Arizona for the Year Ending November 30, 1923.*

June 1, 1923, Southwest Mine /M.R. Gilman lease

During his work on the 200 level, a timber fell on George Johns injuring his ribs.

Office of State Mine Inspector. *Twelfth Annual Report of the State Mine Inspector State of Arizona for the Year Ending November 30, 1923.*

August 25, 1923, Southwest mine /Gilman, Hargis & Wheeler Lease

While working on the 100 level, Theodora Castillo's hand was bruised after he was struck by a falling rock.

Office of State Mine Inspector. *Twelfth Annual Report of the State Mine Inspector State of Arizona for the Year Ending November 30, 1923.*

September 2, 1923, Southwest mine /Gilman, Hargis & Wheeler Lease

Juan Angel Luna had a rock roll on to his foot while working on the 100 level. His foot was only bruised.

Office of State Mine Inspector. *Twelfth Annual Report of the State Mine Inspector State of Arizona for the Year Ending November 30, 1923.*

October 26, 1923, Southwest Mine

Mark Stanley Hunter was working in a sill set and needed to cut out a piece of timber to lay rails. He borrowed a saw from Joe Knox and Joe McNelis. Hunter cut part of the way through the timber. Then he took a pick and began to pry on it to break it off the rest of the way. Suddenly, about one mine car load of rock fell and completely buried him. Gus Jaeger was nearby and began sawing timber in the next set to get to him. After a few minutes, other men arrived, and they chopped through the set and found his feet. He was already dead. Hunter had suffocated and suffered a broken neck in the cave-in. Records indicate this occurred in the Southwest Tunnel.* He was 27 years old and had lived in Bisbee 21 years. * The Bisbee Ore states the mine was the Czar. Funeral and Inquest records indicate the Southwest mine

Stanley Hunter Killed today in Mine Cave-in Bisbee Ore 26 October 1923 page 1
Dugan Mortuary Records Feb. 9, 1923 – Aug. 16, 1926 Accession 2010.10.17 Bisbee Mining and Historical Museum, Bisbee.
"Original Certificate of Death" Arizona Department of Health Services. http://genealogy.az.gov/azdeath/027/10272206.pdf (July 22, 2011
Cochise County Coroner's Inquest No.1530" Arizona State Archives Phoenix

August 5, 1924, Southwest 100 level (Gilman & Hargis Lease)

Juan Moreno injured his eyes when a carbide lamp "exploded". * Note, it is likely the gasket separating the water chamber and the carbide chamber failed. This would have resulted in the lamp bursting out in flames around the middle of the lamp. Some calcium hydroxide would likely splatter and potentially entered Moreno's eyes. The corrosive property of calcium hydroxide and the flames would have resulted in the injury. An alternative explanation is that less likely is that the acetylene reacted with copper present as brass parts lamp and formed copper(I) acetylide. When dry the resulting copper (I) acetylide is a shock sensitive high explosive. In the laboratory, copper (I) acetylide is created by bubbling acetylene through a solution of copper (II) chloride and ammonia. The copper chloride and ammonia react to form a tetraaminecopper (II)hydroxide complex and the addition of calcium carbide reacts to create acetylene, which reacts with tetraaminecopper (II)hydroxide to form copper(I) acetylide. Presently, it is a violation of Mine Safety and Health Administration's (MSHA) regulation, AP2004-M105 to allow acetylene to contact pure copper or high copper content alloys, except in a torch. This is due to the formation of copper (I) acetylide.

Office of State Mine Inspector. *Thirteenth Annual Report of the State Mine Inspector State of Arizona for the Year Ending November 30, 1924.*

July 11, 1925, Southwest Mine

A lessor in the Southwest Mine, George Washington Stewart had pulled a string of mine cars off onto a side track 300 hundred feet inside the Queen Tunnel he hung his carbide lamp at the *"lease hoist"* (Copper Queen Incline) then he went to throw the switch back to allow the trains to pass by. While he was bent down at the switch, a locomotive driven by Louis Voelkel went by and threw Stewart against the drift crushing the top of his skull. The trolley motor derailed and two of Stewart's cars were knocked off the track as well. The motor swamper, Mose Unsel broke his leg. He was 67 years old and survived by a widow.

"Geo. Stewart is Killed in Mine Accident" Bisbee Ore 11 July 1925 page 1
Dugan Mortuary Records Feb. 9, 1923 – Aug. 16, 1926 Accession 2010.10.17 Bisbee Mining and Historical Museum, Bisbee.

Office of State Mine Inspector. *Fourteenth Annual Report of the State Mine Inspector State of Arizona for the Year Ending November 30, 1925.* Tombstone Epitaph.
"Original Certificate of Death" <u>Arizona Department of Health Services.</u> http://genealogy.az.gov/azdeath/031/10310030.pdf (July 22, 2011
"Cochise County Coroner's Inquest No. 869" Arizona State Archives

The location where George Washington Stewart was killed. The switch and side rails have long since been removed.

May 18, 1926, Southwest Mine

On the 5th level, a 42-year-old Mormon miner named, Joseph Ben Jean was working 14 ft. above the track, pulling out cribbing and replacing it with lagging. The weight on top of the cribbing caused it to buckle, and Jean suffocated. He was survived by a wife and three daughters of six, four and one years of age.

Dugan Mortuary Records Feb. 9, 1923 – Aug. 16, 1926, Accession 2010.10.17 Bisbee Mining and Historical Museum, Bisbee.

Office of State Mine Inspector. *Fifteenth Annual Report of the State Mine Inspector State of Arizona for the Year Ending November 30, 1926.* Tombstone Epitaph.
"Original Certificate of Death" <u>Arizona Department of Health Services.</u> http://genealogy.az.gov/azdeath/032/10322279.pdf (July 22, 2011
"Cochise County Coroner's Inquest No. 1629" Arizona State Archives

Spray Shaft c-1908

Spray Mine

In April of 1899, The Copper Queen Consolidated Mining Company was developing what they wanted to be a *"model shaft"* It was located 100ft. above the Holbrook Mine and near the Silver Bear House. It was built on a solid rock foundation that allowed the future steel gallows frame to sit above the collar of the shaft. This would allow the construction of the headframe without interfering with the timbering of the shaft. In April the shaft was 30 ft. deep and two windlasses were used to hoist muck from the three compartment shaft. A pipe line was being sent from the Holbrook mine to provide water. By April 1900, the shaft was 550ft. deep and had struck ore. The company had hoped to sink the shaft outside the ore zone, so it would have limited ground movement caused by mining stopes.

On November 10, 1902, miners located a fire in No.40 stope. The stope had been backfilled with sulphides that did not meet ore grade (pyrite, chalcopyrite, bornite, etc.) The sulphides spontaneously ignited and miners began to smell the sulfur fumes and discovered the fire. Pipe fitters worked all night and were able to install a pipe line to flood the burning (smoldering) stope. A few months later, on March 25, 1903 another small fire was discovered burning in two sets.

The mine continued to a major producer of ore. In April 1914, the Spray mine was closed to reduce production. It was noted that when the Spray area was to be mined again, it would be mined through the Gardner and the Holbrook Mines. This action would eliminate the need for using the

417

surface facilities at the Spray. The headframe at the Spray was dismantled and erected at the Calumet and Cochise Shaft. Waste dumps from the Sacramento Pit covered the shaft in 1918. Before the shaft was covered it was bulkheaded to prevent the dumps from filling the shaft.

During the early 1930's, a lessee repaired the lower sections of the Spray shaft by accessing the area from the Holbrook Mine. Then the lessee impressively raised through the 80 ft. of Sacramento dump material covering the shaft. A dangerous and challenging feat. A small wooden headframe was erected over the shaft. The shaft was still accessible underground from the Holbrook Mine in the early 1960's and by climbing up the shaft a person could examine the part raised through the dump. In 1940, the Spray was closed for the last time and in 1968 the dumps from the Lavender Pit covered the site again. The shaft can be located on Google Earth images by a distinctive conical depression that formed after the Lavender pit dumps began subsiding and filling in the shaft. At the end of mining the shaft was 1,059 ft. deep and had three compartments. In the very early days, it was sometimes referred to as the Silver Spray Mine.

May 12, 1900, Spray Mine

Four miners were injured when they walked into a blast at ten o'clock on a Saturday night. The men had made an error when counting the shots and entered the workplace just as a delayed hole exploded. John Kronman was severely injured (possibly fatally) He was struck by a mass of blasted rock, and it was believed had internal injuries. Lee Borgstrom had his two front teeth knocked out and was cut up around the face. John Williams and Joe Ballinger escaped with only minor cuts.

"Four Miners Injured by a Blast at the Spray Shaft." Cochise Review and Arizona Daily Orb 14 May 1900 page 1

"Four Miners Injured by Blast at Spray Shaft." The Arizona Republican 18 May 1900

January 3, 1902, Spray Mine

Oscar Peters was injured, when he fell a chute. He was taken to the Copper Queen Hospital.

"Local Happenings in Brief" Bisbee Daily Review 4 January 1902 page 4

April-May 1902 Spray Mine

William O' Brien had worked at the Spray Mine for seven months when he was struck by a seven-pound rock falling in the main shaft as he was loading a mine car (onto cage). The rock broke two of O'Brien's ribs. On the way home, William fainted and was treated by Dr. Edmundson. He was expected to be okay in a few days.

"Mining Notes" The Arizona Republican 2 May 1902 page 3 (another article specifies the time as happening at ten o'clock at night)

March 5, 1902, Spray Mine

Sam French was clearing the ground to set up timber. He continued to work and dangerously exposing himself by working beyond the timber in place. While working in this area, he was struck on the back by falling muck. During the lunch break, that day it was discussed that they were working in a dangerous place. French at this time commented that if were pinned under a boulder he would rather be killed immediately, instead of suffering the remainder of his life. He survived the accident.

"Accident in Mine." Bisbee Daily Review 8 March 1902 page 1

July 6, 1902, Spray Mine

Between 8:00 pm and 9:00 pm, Neil M. Askel was working on the 200 level installing timber with J.H. Kane. Askel was described as a thin delicate man that had the appearance of a person with consumption. As they were working, Askel began spitting up blood. Kane

418

called to J.S. Stewart working three sets below to help him. Askel began spitting up as much blood as he could and within five minutes was unconscious. They got more men and raised Askel up four sets to the level and in about ten minutes were able to get him to the surface. Although Stewart remembered that Askel had mentioned he had been hurt on a wheelbarrow a few nights earlier and had even taken a day off work. It was determined a blood vessel ruptured in his lung. He died of natural causes n. Askel was from Canada.

"Miner Dies" Bisbee Daily Review 7 July 1902
"Cochise County Coroner's Inquest No. 80" Arizona State Archives

August 19, 1902, Spray Shaft.

James Critchley Sr. was working in a crosscut on the 600 level. He had shot seven holes, but one missed. After waiting awhile, he entered the smoke filled crosscut. When he reached the face, he discovered a burning fuse. James grabbed the fuse to yank it out, and the hole detonated. The blast injured his eyes, and it was initially thought he may lose one. This later proved not to be true. He was definitely one of the most experience miners in Bisbee. He had started working in mines when he was 11 and had approximately 50 years of experience at the time of the accident. On October 9, 1908, His son James Critchley Jr. was killed in a cave-in at the Czar Mine. He arrived at the Czar in time to see his dead son brought up. James Sr. had twelve children.

"Narrow Escape in The Mine" Bisbee Daily Review 20 August 1902 page 5
"Calumet & Arizona Hospital Records." My Cochise. http://www.mycochise.com/hospcalco2day.php (May 28, 2012)
Certificate of Death." Arizona Department of Health Services. http://genealogy.az.gov/azdeath/012/10120057.pdf (May 28, 2012) Office of State

August 25, 1902, Spray Mine

Working on the 600 level, W. H. Hines was caught in a collapse of soft muck that knocked him unconscious. Dr. Baum came to treat the victim of the cave-in and discovered his injuries were only bruises. Hines was able to walk to his room on Chihuahua Hill after the accident.

"A Slight Accident" Bisbee Daily Review August 26 1902 page 8

September 20, 1902, Spray Mine

At 7:30 in the evening, a carman named Page was barring down No. 4 chute on the 600 level when he slipped and fell a distance of two sets and hit a mine car. He was taken to the hospital and his injuries were determined to be slight.

"Accident at Spray" Bisbee Daily Review 21 September 1902 page 8

November 29, 1902, Spray Mine

S.J. Harris, a carman was on the 500 level station. He hooked his candlestick to a mine car and began pushing it and heard a noise. Harris saw Joseph Netherlands, a carpenter falling backward into the shaft, and the dinkey cage descended pass the station and jammed up. Netherlands landed partly on a lagging in the shaft and the station. Harris telephoned to the surface to have a main cage brought down to bring Netherlands to the hoist house. It is believed Netherlands was working on the 500 level, when he looked up the shaft. The cage hit Netherlands and knocked him back onto the station. He died at the hospital.

"Series of Accidents" Tombstone Epitaph 30, November 1902 page 1
"Cochise County Coroner's Inquest No. 100" Arizona State Archives Phoenix

November 1902 Spray Mine
Bob Campbell fell into a raise about 40 ft. He injured his head and shoulders.

"To Recuperate" Bisbee Daily Review 5, December 1902 page 8

January 1903, Spray Mine
Carl Lewis was struck in the arm by a rock that fell six sets.

"Copper Queen Accidents" Arizona Republican 21, January 1903 page 3

January 26, 1903, Spray Mine
Henry Tift slipped and fell two sets, breaking his arm.

"Tift Hurt" Bisbee Daily Review 27, January 1903 page 8

May 8, 1903, Spray Mine
Lewis Mons was being lowered on a cage when his arms were caught in the shaft. One arm was broken, and the other was injured.

"Hurt in Mine" Bisbee Daily Review 9, May 1903 page 5

April 2, 1903, Spray Mine
Charles Kline was working near a wall of a stope when a 200 lb. boulder moved about two feet and smashed his ankle and shin. He was taken to the Copper Queen Hospital where Dr. Sweet treated his bruises and his sprained ankle. The doctor kept him at the hospital for a few days.

"Slid Down a Slippery Trail" Bisbee Daily Review 4 April 1903 page 8

May 29, 1903, Spray Mine
Jake Preston was struck by a falling rock. His head was cut and required several stitches.

"Miner Injured" Bisbee Daily Review 31 May 1903 page 5

June 15, 1903 Spray Mine
Charles Flynn was installing timber, when a rock fell throwing him to the ground. His arm was broken and his head was cut. The broken arm was set at the hospital and he was sent home.

"Miner's Arm Broken" Bisbee Daily Review 16, June 1903 page 5

July 16, 1903, Spray Mine
Timberman, William Slattery was riding a cage down from the 700 level to the 800 level when he was struck on the head by an unknown object. He was knocked unconscious but was only bruised.

"Another Miner Injured" Bisbee Daily Review 17, July1903 page 5

August 1, 1903, Spray Mine
Two miners, Dan McDonald, and another named Fitzpatrick, had a disagreement that turned into a fight underground. Fitzpatrick a larger man than McDonald rushed at McDonald who put out his arm holding his candlestick.   The candleholder's point punctured Fitzpatrick's jaw. He was taken to the Copper Queen Dispensary and treated. It was expected that the man who started the fight would be fired after an investigation by the mine bosses.
"Fought Underground" Bisbee Daily Review 2 August 1903

August 25, 1903, Spray Mine
George E. Garver was working on the 500 level and noticed that the area was caving–in and tried to get to safety, but before he made it he was stuck by falling rock. The doctors felt he would recover, but told him to rest at home a few days.
"Miner Caught by Cave-in" Bisbee Daily Review 26 August 1903 page 3

September 2, 1903, Spray Mine
John W. Nelson was walking on the 500 level. From a turn sheet to the "Bear"* drift. A loaded mine car passed him and a boulder fell from the car. The rock pinned his left hand to the wall (rib) and broke his index finger. He was expected to be off work around three weeks.* Note, this could indicate the drift was headed towards or to the Silver Bear Shaft or Claim.
"Miner Fractures Hand" Bisbee Daily Review 3 September 1903 page 5

September 5, 1903, Spray Mine
Dan O'Connell was climbing the manway of 43 stope from the 500 level to the 400 level to get nails when he slipped. He fell 30 ft. and was knocked unconscious. O'Connell received bruises and a serious cut on the hip. The cut required eight stitches.
"Miner Fell Thirty Feet" Bisbee Daily Review 5, September 1903 page 5

October 19, 1903 Spray Mine
In No.45 stope, a rock rolled onto the left foot of N. Grimes. He suffered bruising.
"Hurt his Foot" Bisbee Daily Review 20 October 1903 page 4

October 26, 1903, Spray Mine
J.O. Gruell had a rock fall and lacerated his right hand.
"Brief City News" Bisbee Daily Review 29 October 1903 page 5

October 29, 1903, Spray Mine
George Morrissey was hit on the right hand with his partner's hammer. His index finger was possibly broken. (Note, Morrissey was likely part of a double jacking team.)
"Local Personal" Bisbee Daily Review 30 October 1903 page 5

November?, 1903, Spray Mine
C.D. Morrison twisted his knee. He was employed as a carman.
"Sprained his Knee" Bisbee Daily Review 24 November 1903 page 8

November 22, 1903, Spray Mine
Two carmen, broke into a fight the men with the surnames Benson and Graves continued the tussle until a shift boss discovered them. Both men were fired.
"Mules at Loggerheads" Bisbee Daily Review 24 November 1903 page 8

December 9, 1903, Spray Mine
G.G. Young was struck in the back by a boulder while working on the 600 level. He was seriously bruised.
"Personal Mention" Bisbee Daily Review 10 December 1903 page 8

March 7, 1904, Spray Mine
E.E. Mattinson was working on the 400 level when a boulder fell and landed on his left shoulder. He was badly bruised and expected to be off work.
"Had Shoulder Injured" Bisbee Daily Review 9 March 1904 page 5

June 25, 1904, Spray Mine
A timber fell and smashed the left foot of Cal Mesner.
"Had foot Crushed" Bisbee Daily Review 26 June 1904 page 5

August 27, 1904, Spray Mine
George Morres miraculously survived a cave-in. George and his partners were working in a sub-level drift. They had been informed by the Assistant Superintendent Taylor to begin installing timber as soon as the ground conditions required it. After examining the area the miners decided the area, was solid enough to hold its own. Unbeknownst, to the men a thin veneer of strong rock camouflaged the weak rock behind it. As George was pushing out a wheelbarrow load, when the ground collapsed. *"boulders the size of horses fell"* along with an *"avalanche of dirt"*. The wheelbarrow was crushed, and George found himself trapped, but alive. A stull had fallen and had become wedged at an angle between the rib of the drift and the floor. In this cramped protected hole with barely enough room to breathe and unable to move, George waited for four hours as a crew of miners dug him out. The rescuers were surprised to find him alive. They had expected only to recover a body.
"Marvelous Escape of Miner at Spray" Bisbee Daily Review 27 August 1905 page 5

September 1904, Spray Mine
W.R. Sharp had his arm caught between a mine car and a timber. He suffered bruising and cuts.
"W. R .Sharp" Bisbee Daily Review 15 September 1904 page 5

March 20, 1905, Spray Mine
Electrician, J.R. Wall was repairing a light in a stope, when he slipped and fell. He was found unconscious and was taken to the Copper Queen Hospital. Wall suffered back injuries and was expected to be off work three weeks

"Spinal Injuries" <u>Bisbee Daily Review</u> 21 March 1905 page 3

March 18, 1905, Spray Mine

John Erickson was working in No. 2 stope on the 800 level when a timber fell and hit him on the head and shoulder. He was able to walk to the Copper Queen Hospital, where it was determined his shoulder was dislocated.

"Spray Miner Hurt" <u>Bisbee Daily Review</u> 19 March 1905 page 1

August 10, 1905 Spray Mine

In the early morning hours under bright moonlight, a miner named Connors left his lunch bucket outside the change room. Connors heard a noise and when he stepped out, Connors saw a man running away with his lunch bucket. The moonlight enabled Connors to see the man and chase him. During the pursuit, the man just disappeared. The lunch box was found sitting on the path, but no sign of the man could be found. It was thought that the thief had fallen into one of the large subsidence cracks* (crevices) that had formed from mining. Later, Connors discovered that the thief had also taken a dollar from the pocket of his pants in the change room.

*Sometimes these subsidence cracks in Bisbee are well over one hundred feet deep and twenty feet across. Falling into one would likely be fatal. When the Holbrook Extension of the Lavender Pit was started a human skeleton was uncovered during mining and stored in the Phelps Dodge warehouse. This skeleton was most likely one of the very early residents that had been buried near a home and not the thief. This practice of burial was not uncommon during the early days of mining.

"Connors' Streak of Hard Luck" <u>Bisbee Daily Review</u> 11 August 1905 page 8
Richard W. Graeme III Personal communication February 3, 2019

December, 1905, Spray Mine

In the sawmill (surface) W.J. White tried to remove a block from a saw blade. The third finger from his right hand was cut in such a terrible manner that it was essential to amputate the finger.

"Lost a Finger" <u>Bisbee Daily Review</u> 16 December 1905 page 5

February 1, 1906, Spray Mine

William Wright was working in stope No. 3 between the 700 and 800 levels of the Spray mine. The stope was closely timbered. At around 9:00 pm, 50-tons of muck unexpectedly knocked out the timber and fell on top of him. The rock crushed the ribs on his left side. The men nearby immediately began to uncover him, but he was already dead. He was about 35 years old and was survived by brothers Jacob and Ernest Wright, and also a sister Mrs. Barkdoll of Bisbee. His brother Frank Wright lived in Douglas Arizona, and his brother Tom Wright was the mine superintendent at Minas Prietas, Sonora Mexico.

"Lost Life in Spray Mine" <u>Bisbee Daily Review</u> 2 February 1906 page 1
"Death was Caused by Falling Rock" <u>Bisbee Daily Review</u> 3 February 1906 page 5
"Funeral Held" <u>Bisbee Daily Review</u> 4 February 1906 page 7
"Cochise County Coroner's Inquest No.322" Arizona State Archives Phoenix

May 5, 1906, Spray Mine

Jack Shepard was working in the Spray mine when his partner struck him just above the eye with a pick. If the tool had hit him a half inch lower, Shepard would have been blinded.

"Eye is Injured Working in Mine" <u>Bisbee Daily Review</u> 6 May 1906 page 3

June 5, 1906, Spray Mine
Hugh Frazier, a foreman, slipped in a stope and twisted his wrist.
"Foreman Frazier Hurt by Fall in Stope" Bisbee Daily Review 7 June 1906 page 3

September 11, 1906, Spray Mine
Finlander, Lee Hanley was working on the 900 level when muck fell from the back of a drift. The miners nearby freed him, and he was transported to the Copper Queen Hospital. His back was broken and he was suffering from shock. He died from his injuries on October 27, 1906, and was survived by a wife and three children living on Opera Drive. (No coroner's inquest could be located)
"Hurt at Spray" Bisbee Daily Review 12 September 1906 page 5
"Old Time Miner Dies of his Injuries" Bisbee Daily Review 28, October 1906 page 5

October 6, 1906, Spray Mine
James Bell was struck by a boulder falling from the back of a drift. The impact of the rock almost severed his hand from the arm.
"Hurt in Mine" Bisbee Daily Review 7 October 1906 page 3

December 7, 1906, Spray Mine
Miner, John Cox was placing a set of timber, when an axe fell from the timber above and struck his right arm. The ax cut two tendons. He was treated at the Copper Queen Hospital.
"Axe Falls on Hand" Bisbee Daily Review 8, December 1906 page 7

September 4, 1907, Spray Mine
Greek Miner, Chris Peper was working in a six-post raise. He had placed lagging over the chute side of the raise and began picking down loose rock. A boulder fell and knocked out the lagging, and he fell 60 feet. His back and ribs were broken, and he had internal injuries. He died at the Copper Queen Hospital.
"Cochise County Coroner's Inquest No.491" Arizona State Archives Phoenix
Copper Queen Hospital Patients Register September 4, 1907 Bisbee Mining and Historical Museum, Bisbee.

January 12, 1907, Spray Mine
On Sunday morning, a hoistman noticed a bundle of clothes on a cage. He noticed this as being unusual and after a while when no one had claimed the clothes he reported it. It was determined a miner named Stephen Murich was missing, and a search was started that ended hours later when his gruesome corpse was discovered underwater in the shaft sump. The Bisbee Daily Review described it, *The body was horribly mangled, the top of the skull being cut clean off and the brains entirely gone. The back was broken and all the bones in both legs.* "It was felt at the time that Stephen had tried to board a moving cage, and his head had been caught between the steel cage floor and the station timber. It was also believed he had been dead about 24 hours before his body was discovered. He was survived by a brother at the Hoatson Mine.

March 24, 1907, Spray Mine

Jon Enright and J.C. Beals were cleaning debris* off the shaft timber from the surface to "B" level, then to the 100 level. They had built platforms across the shaft on the 100 level to catch the debris. Below them John Sanders and Pete Swanson were cleaning shaft timber on the 200 level. Dave Dagleish a Holbrook miner was working on the 300 level station blasting to make room for telephone boxes. James Henry Pellows and Heber Taylor were removing old timber from the 300 station. It was after dinner time and Beals had finished mucking off his platform and was putting the lagging from the platform on the dinkey cage. Suddenly, he heard a noise like a board tipping. Beal looked at Enright's platform and a lagging was missing. On the 200 level, John Sanders heard the noise of a timber falling down the shaft and called up to see if everyone was ok. Men from above and below the 200 called back that everyone was ok, but when Sanders picked up the shovel that had fallen with Enright, he discovered brains on the shaft timber. Swanson and Sanders realized a man had been killed. At the same time, Dagleish heard something falling down the shaft and found Enright's body. Taylor and Dagleish took the body out of the shaft and placed it on the 300 station. . Unusually, Taylor, Pellows and Dagleish had to wait 35 minutes before a cage was lowered to hoist the body. This was due to the fact that Foreman Kohler was at home and was sent for. This accident occurred during the first attempt of unionization of the mines in Bisbee. The mines were working with a reduced workforce and the Spray Shaft was shut down and repaired for seven weeks. Enright's missing board was found broken at a knot on the 200 level. There was concern at the inquest that the concussion from the blast on the 300 level station may have lifted the lagging and the board settled into an unsafe position. Others felt the lagging split at the knot. *The debris is believed to be from retimbering the shaft and wood have consisted of wood shaving and chips mixed with small rocks.
"Cochise County Coroner's Inquest No.424" Arizona State Archives Phoenix

July 17, 1907, Spray Mine

William Riley was struck in the chest by a falling pick. He was only bruised.
"Injured by a Pick" <u>Bisbee Daily Review</u> 18 July 1907 page 7

September 4, 1907, Spray Mine

Pete Tetter was working in No. 87 stope on the 500 level. He was on a staging in a raise hand drilling. It is believed that the striking of the hammer to the steel caused the platform to move and fall taking Tetter with it. Other miners quickly found him and transported him to the hospital where he died. (No coroner's inquest could be located)
"Falls to Death While at Work in Mine" <u>Bisbee Daily Review</u> 5 September 1907 page 5

December 16, 1908 Spray Mine

Henry Lauber was killed instantly. It appears he was working while standing on timber truck when he was shocked by the trolley wire causing him to slip and fall. His neck struck a rail and fractured a vertebrae killing him. Martin Gregory was the last man to see him alive and also the man to find him, Gregory stated that Lauber was working on top of a timber truck when he was last seen alive. No relatives of Lauber could be located. A sort of mystery man J.J. Horace a friend of the victim stated he thought Lauber was a German from New York. The deceased had two and a half dollars in his pocket and among his possessions was a letter from a friend Fred Auld of Victor, Colorado. (Note, this accident was considered important, because a new trolley locomotive haulage system had been recently installed and the Copper Queen Consolidated Mining Company was examining it whether it could be safely and economically be used.)

"Inquest reveals Nothing New" Bisbee Daily Review 18 December 1908 page 5

"Personal Mention" Bisbee Daily Review 20 December 1908 page 7

"Lauber's Funeral Yesterday" Bisbee Daily Review 22 December 1908 page 7

Gerald F. G. Sherman. "Tramming and Hoisting at the Copper Queen Mine." American Institute of Mining Engineers Transaction Volume LII 1916: Page 465.

March 14, 1908, Spray Mine

John Wetzel and A.W. Kerr were overwhelmed by powder gasses*. The men were quickly revived by one of the Copper Queen doctors.

*These noxious gasses are produced from the blasts underground

"Overcome by Gas" Bisbee Daily Review 15 March 1908 page 7

June 3, 1909, Spray Mine

James Henry Christian and Ernest Thomas were in a sulfide stope on the 600 level. The ground began to collapse, and both men detected this but, Christian moved in the wrong direction and was caught under 50 carloads of falling sulfide ore. Thomas escaped unhurt and gathered a rescue party. They began digging Christian out and at one point they thought they heard Christian moan. A second collapse buried the area again and at that moment they increased the size of the rescue party. A cousin of Christian, James Skillicorn was part of the rescue team. The body of James H. Christian was recovered, and the coroner determined that his death was caused by suffocation, and no bones were broken. They coroner's jury was divided on whether the accident could have been avoided. Thomas testified, that he felt the stope was not properly timbered, and four of the jurors agreed with this. Two other jurors disagreed and felt the accident was unavoidable. A shift boss testified but he stated that this was his second day that he was in charge of that stope. He commented further that even though the timbering had been done before, he was in charge of the stope that it looked safely timbered to him. Christian was 25 years old and native to the Isle of Man. He was buried in the Evergreen Cemetery.

"Miner is Buried Alive" Bisbee Daily Review 4 June 1909 page 8

"Coroner's Jury Divided" Bisbee Daily Review 5 June 1909 page 5

"Miner is Buried" Bisbee Daily Review 6 June 1909 page 7

"Cochise County Coroner's Inquest No.655" Arizona State Archives Phoenix

July 22, 1909, Spray Mine

John McGreary was holding the chain connecting two mine cars when the train of cars jerked. The movement amputate his index finger at the first joint.

"Loses First joint of One Finger" Bisbee Daily Review 25, July 1909 page 7

January 5, 1910, Spray Mine

Russian, Alex Laurinas a carman was coupling two loaded cars when one car rolled and pinned his head between the cars until he was released by other men. He was taken to the

Copper Queen Dispensary and later to the Copper Queen Hospital. It was feared that he was seriously injured and had fractured his skull. It was later revealed that he suffered only a bad cut on his scalp.

"Miner's Head is Caught between Cars" Bisbee Daily Review 7 January 1910 page 2
"Injuries were Slight" Bisbee Daily Review 8 January 1910 page 7
Copper Queen Hospital Patients Register Jan 5, 1910 Bisbee Mining and Historical Museum, Bisbee.

A safety photo showing a miner unsafely coupling two mine cars, c-1917

April 3, 1910, Spray Mine
Thomas Quigley had his arm broken by a falling rock. It was a compound fracture

"Boulder Breaks Arm" Bisbee Daily Review 5 April 1910 page 5

August 2, 1910, Spray Mine

Jodie C. M'Ewen a switcher/ swamper on an electric ore train was killed on the afternoon of August 2. Mr. M'Ewen was working on the 600 level of the Spray shaft in the haulage drift between the Spray and the Sacramento shaft. He had been working on motor trains for the Copper Queen for about a year and a half, but two days before he was killed he had been assigned to the 600 level. The exact cause of the accident was not determined, but it appears that after M'Ewen gave the motorman the *"High Ball"* (go ahead) signal, he either contacted the trolley wire and shocked or was jolted from the train when it started. He then fell to the track and was crushed by the moving train. The motorman stopped the train and discovered him badly smashed and gasping for breath. He lived for only a few minutes after the accident. When Dr. Ferguson of the Copper Queen Medical staff arrived, he had already expired. J.C. M'Ewen was survived by a wife and three children. The oldest child was nine years old. He was laid to rest in Evergreen Cemetery.

"Miner Killed on Ore Train in the Spray" Bisbee Daily Review 3 August 1910 page 1
"Funeral of J.C. M'Ewen" Bisbee Daily Review 5 August 1910 page 5
"Original Certificate of Death." Arizona Department of Health Services. http://genealogy.az.gov/azdeath/009/10090801.pdf (July 24, 2011
"Cochise County Coroner's Inquest No.771" Arizona State Archives Phoenix

January 13, 1911, Spray Mine

Joe McGeary was caught in a fall of muck. He was transported to the Copper Queen Hospital by the Palace Ambulance. McGeary was only bruised and spent four days in the hospital.

"Accident at Spray Shaft." Bisbee Daily Review 15 Jaunuary1911 page 5
Copper Queen Hospital Patients Register Jan 13, 1911 Bisbee Mining and Historical Museum Bisbee

January 31, 1911 Spray Mine

During night shift, Sam Cornette fell across a rail and was bruised up. He was expected to be ok in a few days.

"Miner Injured" Bisbee Daily Review 1 February page 5

September 4, 1911, Spray Mine

Pipe Fitter, E.B. Matthews was injured while riding a cage with timber. A timber became caught on the side of the shaft and as a result, Mathews was struck by the thrown timber in the leg and pelvis.

"Two Slight Accidents" Bisbee Daily Review 5 September 1911 page 8
Copper Queen Hospital Patients Register Sept 4, 1911 Bisbee Mining and Historical Museum Bisbee

January 7, 1912 Spray Mine

Frank Thomas, a miner from Lowell, Arizona, was caught in a cave-in. His back and both legs were broken by falling rock. He was taken to the Copper Queen Hospital. His condition was considered serious and potentially fatal. After three days his condition was still critical and had not improved. Thomas remained in the hospital 225 days He was thought to be the brother-in-law of Harvey Hughes, but this is unlikely, and he was probably confused for Frank Thompson.*

**At this time Harvey Hughes was on trial for the killing a miner named Ardley Mc Clymonds at the Hughes rooming house in Lowell. One of the primary witnesses of the killing, was Roy Jacobs, who was later killed in the Czar mine on October 8, 1912 (note do not to confuse with another, infamous Harvie Hughes a competitive hand driller, who held the record for boys drilling in 1906. At 16 years old he drilled 19 ½ inches. He died in the murder- suicide of Margaret Matheson, a chorus girl at the Orpheum Theater on May 2, 1910, in Bisbee.)

"Suffers Serious Injuries" Bisbee Daily Review 9 January 1912 page 3
"Harvey Hughes Tells His Story" Bisbee Daily Review 14 July 1911 page 8
"Harvey Hughes Tells Story of Killing M'Clymons" Bisbee Daily Review 14 July 1911 page 1
"Harvey Preliminary Hearing This Morning" Bisbee Daily Review 13 July 1911 page 8
"Harvie Hughes without a Doubt was Out of his Mind When he Committed the Awful Deed" Bisbee Daily Review 5 May 1910 page 5
"Sel Tar's Record" Bisbee Daily Review 18 August 1911 page 5
Copper Queen Hospital Patients Register Jan 7, 1912 Bisbee Mining and Historical Museum, Bisbee.

May 1, 1912, Spray Mine
Around 3:00 pm, a rock fell and knocked John D. Lowern unconscious. He had revived by the time a Copper Queen doctor had arrived at the Spray Mine.
"Miner is Injured" Bisbee Daily Review 1 May 1912 page 8

May 26, 1912, Spray Mine
At the water tank up behind the Spray Mine, Frank Gilbert Huber and fourteen other boys decided to swim in the tank. Frank was the only boy who could not swim and the water was 14 ft. deep. He was sitting on a pipe with others boys and it began to bend, then broke at a coupling. After swimming the boys noticed Frank's clothes still on the ground and could not find him. Unsure, whether he was hiding or drowned they went to the Spray Mine for help. Miner, C.A. Baily and a shift boss took iron hooks up to the tanks to see if they could get him out. This did not work in the muddy bottomed tank and the men stripped off and dived into the tank. Finally, they found him with a pole and a man named Fenwick recovered the body. Note, his brother Charles Huber was killed June 12, 1907 in the Holbrook Mine. Also, today this would be considered a mine accident, but at the time it was not.
"Cochise County Coroner's Inquest No.927" Arizona State Archives Phoenix
"Boy Drowned in Big Tank" Bisbee Daily Review 28 May 1912 page 8

June 13, 1912, Spray Mine
William Uren received injuries to his head in an undescribed accident.
"Miner Injured" Bisbee Daily Review 14 June 1912 page 6

October 9, 1912, Spray Mine
John Crowle received undescribed minor injuries.
"Personal Mention" Bisbee Daily Review 9 October 1912 page 3

November 10, 1913, Spray Mine
Albert Hall was struck by falling rock. He was taken to his home.
"Miners Hurt" Bisbee Daily Review 11 November 1913 page 8

June 18, 1913, Spray Mine
Cornish Miner, Thomas Martin was fatally injured while working on the 400 level. He was bent over digging when a rock fell severing his spine and breaking two vertebrae. Martin was taken to the Copper Queen Hospital where he lingered until July 2 when he died. The deceased was survived by a sister in Cornwall, England. (No coroner's inquest could be located)

"Thos. Martin is Badly Hurt" <u>Bisbee Daily Review</u> 20 June 1913 page 6

"Original Certificate of Death." <u>Arizona Department of Health Services</u> http://genealogy.az.gov/azdeath/011/10111804.pdf. (May 19, 2012)

February 15, 1913, Spray Mine

English Miner, Charles Lobb Jr was working with V.L. Murray on the 700 level. They saw a boulder that needed to be taken down. The men used a pick to try to bring it down and sounded it to see how loose it was. They decided it needed to be blasted down. After filling a mine car, Murray reached for his lunch bucket to get a drink, and he heard a crash and saw the boulder on Lobb. The rock fell from the back of a drift and pinned him to the ground. It was large enough that the rescuing men could not move it on their own and had to pry it off Lobb. He was 43 years old and buried in Evergreen Cemetery. Lobb was survived by his wife, Ada, two children and sisters Mrs. Edward Dickerson, John W. Fisher and Mrs. Thomas Maddern.

"Charles Lobb Loses Life" <u>Bisbee Daily Review</u> 16 February 1913 page 8

"Charles Lobb Funeral will be Held Today" <u>Bisbee Daily Review</u> 18 February 1913 page 5

"Card of Thanks" <u>Bisbee Daily Review</u> 20 February 1913 page 3

"Original Certificate of Death." <u>Arizona Department of Health Services.</u> http://genealogy.az.gov/azdeath/011/10110043.pdf (May 28, 2012)

"Cochise County Coroner's Inquest No.984" Arizona State Archives Phoenix

Uncle Sam Mine

The Neptune Mining Company was already working the Uncle Sam property by March 1881, but by 1885 the operations had shut down. In 1889 the property was foreclosed and was sold to Willis James & William Dodge of the Copper Queen Consolidated Mining Company. By 1895 the shaft was at least 150 ft. deep. In 1903 noted geologist, Fredrick Ransome reported that there was an inaccessible shaft and a tunnel on the property, but the waste dumps looked promising. At the same time the newspaper reported that the Uncle Sam was being considered for a new shaft. During 1905, a *"chlorider"* (lessee) mined the waste dumps and shipping them to a smelter.

Inspired by developments at the nearby Shattuck mine the Copper Queen started a new double compartment shaft in November 1907. At this time it was already decided that the Uncle Sam Shaft would provide ventilation and handle men and materials only, not ore. The necessary long haulage drifts on the 200, 400 and later 3rd level Southwest were foreseen by the engineers. By January 26, 1908 a hoist had been installed and the new shaft was 115 ft. deep. The first significant ore was discovered on "B" level in 1910. At this the company began considering building an ore pass to the 200 level. A small trolley locomotive was placed on the 200 level at this time to replace the *"spike team"*, a pair of mules that worked the long haul from the Uncle Sam to the ore pass at the Holbrook Shaft. This mine was chosen to test the first battery locomotives used in Bisbee. Unfortunately, the technology wasn't ready and the locomotives lack the necessary power to continuously pull ore trains. It would be another 12 years before battery locomotives would be adopted. A major sulphide orebody was developed on the 200 level.

The Reed brothers made a fortune on their lease in the Uncle Sam in 1911. They fortuitously struck a gold-silver-lead orebody in the term of the lease. They made $300,000. This is the second most profitable lease given in Bisbee. The most profitable was the Leedy, Stole and Berquist, Higgins Mine lease. Sinking of the shaft continued in 1912 and by 1913 the shaft was 822 ft. deep. In 1912, Gerald Sherman the mine superintendent decided to build a new style of change house based on the designs he had seen during his recent travels in Europe. Up to this time the miners at the Uncle Sam had been provided lockers and showers at the Czar Mine change house. The new change house was built in European style with abundant windows and a cement floor. No lockers were provided only benches. The miners were to hang their clothes on a hook and lift towards the ceiling on pulley to dry. This is common even now, but was new at the time. During the following years, all change houses in Bisbee were built on this style, except, lockers were added. During 1914, a new steel headframe and hoist were installed at the shaft. Both the headframe and hoist were identical to set ordered for the Czar shaft, which were also installed that year. Unfortunately, erecting the headframe and hoisting facilities was largely the only work done that year. Low copper prices forced the Copper Queen to shut down both the Uncle Sam and Spray mines, due to their high mining costs. Little work occurred in the mine over the next few years. A connection from the 400 level to the Uncle Sam was started in 1915, but was not completed until 1917. This expensively driven haulage crosscut was developed to haul ore for stopes that would eventually be mined below the 200 level. In 1916 it was decided to extended the Queen Tunnel of the 3rd level Southwest Mine from the Southwest #3 Shaft to the Cuprite, Uncle Sam and Shattuck mines (later the Sunrise Shaft was included) The Queen Tunnel intercepted the Uncle Sam Shaft 35ft. below "A" level. A short transfer raise close to the Uncle Sam Shaft delivered ore from the stopes on "A" level to the Queen Tunnel for haulage to the surface. In 1918, the shaft was retimbered and the mine was intensely mined until 1929. Heavy mining continued from the 3rd Southwest level *down to the 300 level. Serbian miners leased the upper level for mining in the1930s. During 1934, the shaft was repaired and mining by leases continued until 1942. At the end of mining the Uncle Sam was 923 ft. deep and had two compartments.

February 1, 1895, Uncle Sam Mine

The shaft continued down 150 ft. At this point there was a trap door in the shaft. Beyond the door the shaft continued down at an incline for about 70 ft. Dominick Munio was working with Pat Devens. The powder gasses overcame Devens and Munio called to Andrew Johnson who was working nearby to help him get Devens into a sinking bucket. While helping get Devens into the bucket Munios also succumbed to the gasses. A request for help was sent to the Holbrook Mine and Max Goodenstein was sent to assist. At the shaft, he descended the first 150 ft. After dropping below the trapdoor his light extinguished but he found Andrew Johnson on his back groaning. Fighting the effects of the gasses, Goodenstein put Johnson in the bucket and they went to the surface. Johnson later died from suffocation and powder smoke poisoning.

"Cochise County Coroner's Inquest No.298" Arizona State Archives Phoenix

October 19, 1911, Uncle Sam Mine

Joe Hall's skull was badly crushed leaving a wound several inches across when he was struck by a falling timber. The injury a compound depressed fracture was considered to be serious enough to be fatal.* Hall was released from the Copper Queen Hospital on November 23, 1911 after an operation.

*The October 25, 1911, newspaper article describes this accident as the second mining injury of a fractured skull in a series of three. These were believed to be part of the mining superstition that mining accidents occurred in sequences of threes. The others were Ben Hurst on October 24 in the Gardner Shaft and a man named Dennis in the Sacramento Shaft on October 18, 1911.

"Miner Injured by Falling Timber" Bisbee Daily Review 20 October 1911 page 3

"Skull Fractured by Falling Object" Bisbee Daily Review 25 October 1911 page 3

Copper Queen Hospital Patients Register Jan 1, 1913 – Mar 24, 1914 Bisbee Mining and Historical Museum, Bisbee.

February 11, 1912, Uncle Sam Mine

John Morris was received minor injuries while working.

"Miner Slightly Injured" Bisbee Daily Review 13 February 1912 page 8

October 8, 1912, Uncle Sam Mine*

Roy C. Jacobs went to the 500 level, which was the bottom of the shaft to ask, Frank McCabe for a chute bar. When Jacobs was being hoisted to the 400 level, the chute bar caught on the shaft timber. He was knocked out of the cage and fell to the bottom of the shaft. It was determined he had broken his right leg, crushed ribs and had suffered other internal injuries as well. The accident occurred early that night. He died from his injuries at the Copper Queen Hospital at 2:00 pm on October 9th. Jacobs was 28 years old and was married to Miss Nora Hanley around a year prior to the accident. His son had been born on September 14th a few weeks before his death. He was survived by his father and his brothers, Kirk and Harry of Lowell, Arizona. The chute bar was found sticking out of the timber 2-1/2 sets above the bottom and there was blood on the timber 60 ft. above the 500 level.

Note, 14 months before Jacobs had narrowly escaped death when he was walking with Miss Anna Hanley (Mrs.?)* In front of the Hughes rooming house on main St. Lowell, Arizona. A stray bullet fired by Harvey Hughes narrowly missed him. Mr. Hughes was busily shooting a miner, Ardley McClymonds ten times. * The newspaper states that the accident occurred in the Czar mine, but the men at inquest testified it was the Uncle Sam Mine.

*His Mother-In Law was Mrs. Anna Hanley.

"Harvey Hughes Tells His Story" Bisbee Daily Review 14 July 1911 page 8

"Harvey Hughes Tells Story of Killing M'Clymons" Bisbee Daily Review 14 July 1911 page 1

"Harvey Preliminary Hearing This Morning" Bisbee Daily Review 13 July 1911 page 8

"Son Born" Bisbee Daily Review 15 September 1912 page 6

"Roy Jacobs injured" Bisbee Daily Review 9 October 1912 page 8

"Roy Jacobs Dies" Bisbee Daily Review 10 October 1912 page 8

"Jacobs Funeral Today" Bisbee Daily Review 11 October 1912 page 8

"In the Superior Court in the County of Cochise, State of Arizona" Bisbee Daily Review 27 October 1912 page 13

February 22, 1913, Uncle Sam Mine

Ben H. Brooken was sitting on a mine car and had signaled the motor to couple to the car. When the motor impacted the mine car he was knocked off the car onto the rails. The car was then pushed on top of him. He was pinned under the wheels of the car. Brooken received severe bruises and cuts on the neck and head.

"Falls Beneath Ore Car Wheels" Bisbee Daily Review 23 February 1913 page 9

October 14, 1913, Uncle Sam Mine *

Charles Pelot was caught in a cave-in. One of his ribs was broken, and his left foot was smashed. He was taken to the Copper Queen Hospital.

*The El Paso Herald listed the mine as the Holbrook shaft.

"In the Hospitals" Bisbee Daily Review 19 October 1913 page 3

"Chas Pelot Badly Injured in Mine Cave-in at Bisbee" El Paso Herald 17 October 1913 page 7

October 29, 1913, Uncle Sam Mine

While installing timber, Vaugh Hunicke was struck by a timber and knocked unconscious. He was taken to the Copper Queen Hospital where he revived and was sent home.

"Struck by Timber" Bisbee Daily Review 30 October 1913 page 8

February 10, 1914, Uncle Sam Mine

Miner, John Ronchette fell onto a timber and broke a rib. He was taken to the Copper Queen Hospital and later released to go to his room at the Kinsey House.
"Miner Injured" Bisbee Daily Review 11 February 1914 page 8

The Kinsey House is large building with the double porch.

A small stope in the Hargis Lease of the Higgins Mine

Unspecified Mines owned by the Copper Queen Consolidated Mining Company

The name Copper Queen Mine was often used as a general term to represent any mine. Newspapers and other documents would refer to any mine operated by the Copper Queen Consolidated Mining Company as the "Copper Queen Mine". The actual Copper Queen Mine was short lived and was shut down by 1886 and thus had few recorded accidents.

1886-1887

Dan Hankins, a pioneer of Bisbee resident was working as a timberman and fell into a raise (ore chute) As a result he was crippled for the remainder of his life. As an invalid he was able to start the successful Malachite Cigar Store on Main Street which he operate until 1904. It was considered the *"Headquarters of all the miners and cattlemen of this part of the territory" "a mecca (sic) for young and old"* He was able to *"amass a large fortune which enable him to educate his children"* He died on July 11, 1907.

"Malachite Cigar Store Ad" <u>Cochise Review and Arizona Daily Orb</u> 9 May 1900 page 1

"Resort of the Past" <u>Bisbee Daily Review</u> 9 April 1904 page 5

"Death Angel has Called Dan Hankins" <u>Bisbee Daily Review</u> 12 July 1907 page 5

January 18-25 1890, Czar or Holbrook Mine

Fred Stone received injuries around the head and arms in an undescribed accident.

"Wholesale Accidents" <u>Arizona Weekly Citizen</u> 25, 1890 January page 4

January 18-25 1890, Czar or Holbrook Mine

An unnamed miner was carrying a group of picks when he fell and on pick point penetrated his ankle, and another entered near his heart. It was reported he almost bled to death from his injuries.

"Wholesale Accidents" <u>Arizona Weekly Citizen</u> 25, 1890 January page 4

June-July 1890 Czar or Holbrook Mine

An unnamed miner walked into a raise and fell 40-feet. It was unsure if he would survive.

"Local Notes" <u>Tombstone Daily Prospector</u> 2 July 1890 January page 4

May 12 1891, Czar or Holbrook Mine

Charles S. Nelson and John Torpey were spitting five fuses. The fifth fuse gave them difficulty and the men were caught at the site when the blast detonated. Nelson died from shock, but his partner Torpey recovered. The mines were shut down for Nelson's funeral. Nelson was said to have supposed to be married a short time after the explosion ended his life

"Blown Up" Tombstone Epitaph 17 May, 1891 page 3
"Death at Bisbee" The Arizona Republican 17 May 1891 page 2
"Original Certificate of Death." Arizona Department of Health Services. http://genealogy.az.gov/azdeath/001/10011880.pdf (June 6, 2012)

June 31, 1897

Angus Gillis was being hoisted in a cage when a mine car wheel fell from the surface and glanced off his arm breaking the bone.

"All over Arizona" The Arizona Republican 2 July 1897 page 4

August 12, 1899

A miner named Trevick had a foot smashed by a boulder. Doctors were not able to determine if any bones were broken.

"Useful Information" The Arizona Daily Orb 12 August 1899 page 4
"Arizona Day by Day The Arizona Republican 16 August 1899

May 29, 1900, (Rucker Division Copper Queen mine)

At 7:30 pm, while working in the Rucker division, Harvey Johnson was caught in a cave-in. His shoulders took the impact. The extents of his injuries were unknown.

"Painfully Injured" Cochise Review 30 May 1900 page 4

August 17, 1900

A cave-in during the afternoon left four men injured. The area was dangerous and was predicted to collapse. Superintendent Clawson had the foresight to have the lower set evacuated of men and the men working in the upper set were on the lookout for a collapse. The cave-in occurred suddenly catching the men in the upper set. Gibson was bruised around the hips. E.A. White had cuts on his face and back. C.M. Lee had his left leg broken above the knee and his right was temporarily paralyzed. The fourth man came from another workplace to rescue the men. While trying to throw them a rope he fell and dislocated his elbow.

"Cave In" Cochise Review 24 August 1900 page 1

October 14, 1903

A miner was working in 53 raise and dropped a chain. The falling chain struck Joseph LeDuc on the head. He was treated by Dr. Dysart.

"Dropped Chain on his Head" Bisbee Daily Review 16 October 1903 page 4

Around 1904

Martin Carter was killed underground He was survived by a widow and three small children Lote, Goldie, and Wadie. Interestingly the Copper Queen Consolidated Mining

Company cared for the family after Martin's death. His widow died about four years after the accident, and the children were placed in the custody of Jesse B. Curtis.
"Mrs. Carters Funeral Today" Bisbee Daily Review 7 November 1908   page 5

April 30, 1904
Frank Wright was killed in an undescribed mine accident. (No coroner's inquest could be located)
"Frank Wright Buried" Bisbee Daily Review 3 May 1904 page 5

December 25, 1904
Hector Smith fell 30 ft. down a stope. He was taken to the hospital and reported as bruised up.
"Out of Danger" Bisbee Daily Review 30 December 1904 page 5
"Miner Hurt" Bisbee Daily Review 27 December 1904 page 5

August 1905
Frank Miller broke his leg in an undescribed mine accident and taken to the Copper Queen Hospital. On September 13, 1904, in a maniac state he cut his throat from *"ear to ear"* in the surgical ward in the view of 15 patients. The nurse arrived within a minute, but it was already too late. He was 30 years old.
"Frank Miller Dead by His Own Hand" Bisbee Daily Review 14 September 1905 page 5

May, 1906
Miner, Dan Burns suffered acute copper poisoning from copper water. By May 11, his eyes were able to withstand light with glasses.
"Copper Water Causes Burns Much Suffering" Bisbee Daily Review 11 May 1906 page 3

February 8, 1911
C.A. Graves was injured in an undescribed cave-in.
"Miner Injured" Bisbee Daily Review 9 February 1911 page 5

September 2, 1912
Irish miner, Ed Riley fell down a manway and broke his clavicle.
"Casualties in Mines 1912" Bisbee Daily Review 12 January 1913, page 7
Copper Queen Hospital Patients Register September 2, 1912, Bisbee Mining and Historical Museum, Bisbee.

October 26, 1912
Swedish miner, Henry Johnson broke his ankle. He spent 101 days in the hospital.
"Casualties in Mines 1912" Bisbee Daily Review 12 January 1913, page 7
Copper Queen Hospital Patients Register October 26, 1912, Bisbee Mining and Historical Museum, Bisbee.

April, 1914
John Graves broke and smashed his toes while taking up three turnsheets. For a time, it was thought amputation would be necessary, but by April 11, he was doing much better.
"Will Not Amputate" Bisbee Daily Review 11 April 1914 page 8

November 17, 1916
Tom Decker burned his hand on a carbide lamp. The reaction of water and calcium carbide is an exothermic reaction, and the bottoms of lamps can become quite hot. Also carbide

lamps, often leak acetylene around the gasket between the top and bottom and can burst into flames.

Office of State Mine Inspector. *Fifth Annual Report of the State Mine Inspector State of Arizona for the Year Ending November 30, 1916.*

Unspecified Mines owned by Phelps Dodge Corporation

In 1917, the Copper Queen Consolidated Mining Company became part of the Phelps Dodge Corporation. At this time the term P.D. Mine or Phelps Dodge mine became popular general terms used to represent any mine in Bisbee operated by Phelps Dodge.

December 20, 1917

A division car loaded with steel (drill) fell on W.W. Aseltine. His chest, body, and right arm were bruised.

Office of State Mine Inspector. *Fifth Annual Report of the State Mine Inspector State of Arizona for the Year Ending November 30, 1918.*

January 24, 1918

Motorman, George Eoff had his leg broken in a compound fracture. He later died on February 14, 1918. (No coroner's inquest could be located)

Office of State Mine Inspector. *Seventh Annual Report of the State Mine Inspector State of Arizona for the Year Ending November 30, 1918.*

February 20, 1918

"Copper water" went into John R. Ryan's eye. His right- eye became inflamed.

Office of State Mine Inspector. *Seventh Annual Report of the State Mine Inspector State of Arizona for the Year Ending November 30, 1918.*

February 27, 1918

Ernest Hicks got sulfide ore into his eye. As a result, he lost vision in his left eye.

Office of State Mine Inspector. *Seventh Annual Report of the State Mine Inspector State of Arizona for the Year Ending November 30, 1918.*

April 9, 1918

C. C. Sharp was caught in a cave-in. Both his ankles and his right leg were broken.

Office of State Mine Inspector. *Seventh Annual Report of the State Mine Inspector State of Arizona for the Year Ending November 30, 1918.*

July 30, 1918, William Reese Lease from Phelps Dodge

Hoistman, Donaciano Cassias received three bells followed by one bell and began to hoist, Mine Foreman, Thomas Lee Thornberry. He was riding a sinking bucket, which was against mine rules. About 30ft. below the shaft collar, his head caught on a timber. Cassias stopped the hoist the moment it became hung. The impact fractured his vertebrae. He was taken to the Calumet & Arizona Hospital, where he died. He was survived by his wife, Gertrude. He was 34 years old and a native to Arizona.

Office of State Mine Inspector. *Seventh Annual Report of the State Mine Inspector State of Arizona for the Year Ending November 30, 1918.*

"Original Certificate of Death." <u>Arizona Department of Health Services.</u> http://genealogy.az.gov/azdeath/018/10180547.pdf (May 28, 2012)

"Cochise County Coroner's Inquest No. 1370" Arizona State Archives Phoenix

October-November 1918

O.E. Tomlinson crushed his right foot in a mine accident.

"Weekly News Letter of Young Men's Christian Association of Warren Mining District" Bisbee Daily Review 3 November 1918 page 7

November 12, 1919

While operating a motor Bert Pierce had a head on collision with another locomotive. His chest was bruised, and two ribs were broken.

Office of State Mine Inspector. *Ninth Annual Report of the State Mine Inspector State of Arizona for the Year Ending November 30, 1920.*

July 12, 1920

Robert P. Little was coupling two mine cars together and dropped his carbide lamp. When he reached to get it, he was caught between the cars and cut his ear.

Office of State Mine Inspector. *Ninth Annual Report of the State Mine Inspector State of Arizona for the Year Ending November 30, 1920.*

August 13, 1920

George Vasil decided to climb over an empty ore train. At the same time, the locomotive drive began to move the train. Vasil hit an overhead timber (cap) and injured his eye.

Office of State Mine Inspector. *Ninth Annual Report of the State Mine Inspector State of Arizona for the Year Ending November 30, 1920.*

February 6, 1920, Probably Sacramento Pit

Jose Valenzuela had a jack (probably a track jack) slip, and it broke his big toe.

Office of State Mine Inspector. *Ninth Annual Report of the State Mine Inspector State of Arizona for the Year Ending November 30, 1920.*

January 11, 1921

Richard George had his ribs bruised when he was squeezed between a mine car and a timber.

Office of State Mine Inspector. *Tenth Annual Report of the State Mine Inspector State of Arizona for the Year Ending November 30, 1921.*

January 11, 1921

A collar brace (4"X6"x5' timber) fell and broke the foot of Robert Maitland.

Office of State Mine Inspector. *Tenth Annual Report of the State Mine Inspector State of Arizona for the Year Ending November 30, 1921.*

March 17, 1922

Aaron Kennwaugh cut his fingers when a chute door fell onto the track. (The chute door was probably not installed, or the door was being transported to the location it was needed.)

Office of State Mine Inspector. *Eleventh Annual Report of the State Mine Inspector State of Arizona for the Year Ending November 30, 1922.*

A chute door laying at the side of a crosscut, 3rd level Southwest Mine.

November 22, 1922

William Haas lost the fingers and part of one hand in an explosion. (Probably caused by a blasting cap)

Office of State Mine Inspector. *Eleventh Annual Report of the State Mine Inspector State of Arizona for the Year Ending November 30, 1922.*

January 9, 1923

Ben Dear broke a finger when it was crushed by a trolley pole.

Twelfth Annual Report of the State Mine Inspector State of Arizona for the Year Ending November 30, 1923.

January 29, 1923

B.J. Mc Pherson broke his leg when he was caught in a blast.

Twelfth Annual Report of the State Mine Inspector State of Arizona for the Year Ending November 30, 1923.

April 24, 1923

Ben Dear broke a finger when a rock fell out of a chute. Note, that Dear had broken another finger three months earlier (Jan 9)

Twelfth Annual Report of the State Mine Inspector State of Arizona for the Year Ending November 30, 1923.

September 22, 1923

August Unwin bruised his eye taking an air hose off a drill. He most likely forgot to turn off or release the air from the hose, and the hose flung back at him as soon as he took it off.

Twelfth Annual Report of the State Mine Inspector State of Arizona for the Year Ending November 30, 1923.

October 23, 1923

James McElroy lost a hand when dynamite exploded.

Twelfth Annual Report of the State Mine Inspector State of Arizona for the Year Ending November 30, 1923.

November 16, 1923
R. Radigan broke his collar bone when he was caught between a mine car and chute timber.
Twelfth Annual Report of the State Mine Inspector State of Arizona for the Year Ending November 30, 1923.

February 3, 1924, Probably Sacramento Pit
Roberto Aguillar was struck by a boulder. His left leg was crushed and suffered internal injuries, including likely damage to his kidneys. He was taken to the Copper Queen Hospital where he died on February 4th. He was 21 years-old and from Cananea, Mexico.
(No coroner's inquest could be located)
Office of State Mine Inspector. *Thirteenth Annual Report of the State Mine Inspector State of Arizona for the Year Ending November 30, 1924.*
"Original Certificate of Death." Arizona Department of Health Services. http://genealogy.az.gov/azdeath/028/10280935.pdf (May 31, 2012)

July 25, 1924
Vaughan Banta was caught between a mine car and a drift wall. He was hospitalized for three days.
Copper Queen Hospital Patients Register July 25, 1924, Bisbee Mining and Historical Museum, Bisbee.

November 30, 1924, Hargis Lease probably 100 level Southwest Mine
Foreman, Jesus Romero picking down a drift and Francisco Pacheco Jr. was watching, when a rock fell striking him. Pacheco was rushed to the Calumet & Arizona Hospital. Initially, it was thought he was not seriously injured, but he died from shock the following morning. He was 19-years-old and from Mexico.
Office of State Mine Inspector. *Thirteenth Annual Report of the State Mine Inspector State of Arizona for the Year Ending November 30, 1924.*
"Original Certificate of Death." Arizona Department of Health Services. http://genealogy.az.gov/azdeath/029/10292184.pdf (May 31, 2012)
"Cochise County Coroner's Inquest No.1582" Arizona State Archives Phoenix

January 21, 1925, Hargis/ Wheeler Lease probably Czar Mine 100 level
Jose Moreno was mucking off an area to install a set of timber. This stope was being remined by the lessees and had been originally mined about 40 years earlier. He moved a 1,500 lb. boulder and a timber slipped. Both Moreno and the boulder fell seven feet. One of his legs was caught by the boulder, but he was largely on top of the rock. The fall ruptured his intestines. He died at 11:00 am on January 22 from the operation to repair them.
"Original Certificate of Death." Arizona Department of Health Services http://genealogy.az.gov/azdeath/030/10300056.pdf (May 31, 2012)
Office of State Mine Inspector. *Fourteenth Annual Report of the State Mine Inspector State of Arizona for the Year Ending November 30, 1925.* Tombstone Epitaph.
"Cochise County Coroner's Inquest No.1585" Arizona State Archives Phoenix

March 9, 1925 Hargis Lease probably Czar Mine 100 level
Jesus Acosta was caught in an undescribed blast and died from shock
"Original Certificate of Death." http://genealogy.az.gov/azdeath/030/10301142.pdf (May 31, 2012)

Office of State Mine Inspector. *Fourteenth Annual Report of the State Mine Inspector State of Arizona for the Year Ending November 30, 1925*. Tombstone Epitaph.

January 27, 1928

Jake Supancich was killed when he was crushed by two mine cars. His pelvis was broken, and he died of pneumonia on February 14th. He was 19 years-old.

"Original Certificate of Death." http://genealogy.az.gov/azdeath/036/10361192.pdf Arizona Department of Health (May 31, 2012)

Office of State Mine Inspector. *Seventeenth Annual Report of the State Mine Inspector State of Arizona for the Year Ending November 30, 1928*.

July 25, 1929, Mardon lease possibly Holbrook mine

Working on the Mardon Lease, Antonio Gutierrez was caught in a cave-in. His pelvis and back were broken. Suffering from shock, he died at 5:25 pm.

"Original Certificate of Death http://genealogy.az.gov/azdeath/039/10392646.pdf Arizona Department of Health (May 31, 2012)

Office of State Mine Inspector. *Annual Report of the State Mine Inspector State of Arizona for the Year Ending November 30, 1929*.

August 23, 1930

W.G. Inglas, a shift boss from Nova Scotia was hospitalized for bruised ribs.

Copper Queen Hospital Patients Register August 23, 1930 Bisbee Mining and Historical Museum, Bisbee.

December 3, 1930

Pumpman, John Yarcho spent four days at the Copper Queen Hospital for a cut cheek and bruising.

Copper Queen Hospital Patients Register December 3, 1930, Bisbee Mining and Historical Museum, Bisbee.

December 11, 1930

Clarence Hallstead lost a finger on his left hand.

Copper Queen Hospital Patients Register December 11, 1930, Bisbee Mining and Historical Museum, Bisbee.

February 21, 1931

English Miner, William Askew broke his jaw.

Copper Queen Hospital Patients Register February 21, 1931, Bisbee Mining and Historical Museum, Bisbee.

March 30, 1931

Cager, Walter Pierce bruised his pelvis and was taken to the Copper Queen Hospital.

Copper Queen Hospital Patients Register March 30, 1931, Bisbee Mining and Historical Museum, Bisbee.

April 21, 1931

E.J. Carnes, a miner, was hospitalized for a broken nose and cuts on his face.

Copper Queen Hospital Patients Register April 21, 1931, Bisbee Mining and Historical Museum, Bisbee.

May 4, 1931

Herman Schieffler, a miner from Texas suffered a broken ulna and abrasions.

Copper Queen Hospital Patients Register May 4, 1931, Bisbee Mining and Historical Museum, Bisbee.

May 29, 1931

Miner, Frank C. Reeves broke his 3rd vertebrae.

Copper Queen Hospital Patients Register May 29, 1931, Bisbee Mining and Historical Museum, Bisbee.

June 1, 1931

George Forrey, a miner from Iowa dislocated his left shoulder and bruised his back.

Copper Queen Hospital Patients Register June 1, 1931, Bisbee Mining and Historical Museum, Bisbee.

July 27, 1931

Swedish Miner, Ernest Bergman fractured a tibia.

Copper Queen Hospital Patients Register July 27, 1931, Bisbee Mining and Historical Museum, Bisbee.

October 19, 1931

Motorman, Haywood Cunningham cut his left leg.

Copper Queen Hospital Patients Register October 19, 1931, Bisbee Mining and Historical Museum, Bisbee.

March 22, 1932

John Foloy*, a motorman from South Wales was hospitalized for one day after receiving a cut eye and a concussion. (The spelling of his surname maybe incorrect.)

Copper Queen Hospital Patients Register March 22, 1932, Bisbee Mining and Historical Museum, Bisbee.

August 31, 1933

Cornish Miner, Edwin James was killed in a cave-in.

Original Certificate of Death." Arizona Department of Health Services. http://genealogy.az.gov/azdeath/048/10481191.pdf (May 27, 2014)

October 15, 1933

Autice Dickson, a miner was stuck by a loaded mine car. His lower back was severely bruised. He was released from Copper Queen Hospital after seven days.

Copper Queen Hospital Patients Register October 15, 1933, Bisbee Mining and Historical Museum, Bisbee.

January 6, 1934

Henry Stewart, a motorman had a foreign object enter an eye. He was hospitalized for four days.

Copper Queen Hospital Patients Register January 6, 1934, Bisbee Mining and Historical Museum, Bisbee.

January 18, 1934

Miner, W.B. Higgins was struck in the eye by a steel cable. He suffered bleeding into the anterior chamber of the cornea. Higgins remained at the Copper Queen Hospital for five days.

Copper Queen Hospital Patients Register February 14, 1934, Bisbee Mining and Historical Museum, Bisbee.

February 14, 1934

On St. Valentine's Day, Italian miner, George (Gervaso) Gardoni suffered a compound skull fracture. He remained in the Copper Queen Hospital 156 days.

Copper Queen Hospital Patients Register June1, 1931, Bisbee Mining and Historical Museum, Bisbee.
Elizabeth Lopez (Grandaughter) Personal communication 2024

December 12, 1934, McKenna Lease

Antonio Chavez spent 59 days in the hospital after being injured.

Copper Queen Hospital Patients Register December 12, 1934, Bisbee Mining and Historical Museum, Bisbee.

December 19, 1934

Fred Mesa, a miner from New Mexico was hospitalized for one day after being exposed to powder gasses after blasting a missed hole.

Copper Queen Hospital Patients Register December 19, 1934, Bisbee Mining and Historical Museum, Bisbee.

July 1, 1941

Jose Antonio Perez fell between cars on a moving ore train and was killed. He was survived by a wife and children in Tombstone, Arizona.

"Cochise County Coroner's Inquest No.1798" Arizona State Archives Phoenix

December 31, 1941 (42?)

Florian M. Pilarczyr had a mine accident that severed his spine. He died at the Copper Queen Hospital on May 26, 1943.

Original Certificate of Death." Arizona Department of Health Services http://genealogy.az.gov/azdeath/069/10692100.pdf (May 27, 2014)

March 15, 1943

Manuel Guzman was injured in a cave-in. The accident was undescribed, and he died on March 21st.

"Original Certificate of Death." Arizona Department of Health Services. http://genealogy.az.gov/azdeath/069/10690750.pdf (July 27, 2015)

February 9, 1963, Campbell Mine (probably)

Jose Valenzuela entered a drift filled with "bad air" and suffocated. The first men on the scene could see him lying on the track, but could not get close enough to help him.

Pete Olier Personal communication May 27, 2014

August 9, 1968

D.R. Bernal was killed while working with a machine.

Office of State Mine Inspector. *Seventh Annual Report of the State Mine Inspector State of Arizona for the Year Ending November 30, 1968.*

Date unknown, probably Campbell mine post World War II

Joe Machain fell into the top of a raise. The details of the accident are unclear, but the motorcrew kept finding coins mixed among the rock they drew out the chute. As a result they baptized Machain with the nickname *"Piggy Bank"*

Al Hirales Personal communication 1992

Date Unknown Possibly Campbell Mine mid-1930's to mid-1940's
Jay Howard need to use the bathroom and he found a toilet car. While he was sitting on the car he decided to clean out his carbide lamp. He opened up the lid on the seat next to him and dumped the old carbide into the toilet car. After this he decided to smoke a cigarette. While he was smoking the waste carbide reacted and filled the toilet car with acetylene gas. When he was done he lifted the lid and dropped his still burning cigarette into the toilet car. The resulting explosion blew Howard off the car. Although, his injuries are unknown he was likely lightly burned. In a way more seriously, the miners baptized him with the nickname *"Shit Car Howard."*

Al Hirales Personal communication 1992, Toby Valdez Personal Communication 1992   Richard W. Graeme III Personal Communication 1980

Unidentified Mine belonging to Calumet & Arizona Mining Company and related companies.

The Calumet & Arizona Mining Company was the second major mining company in Bisbee in the earlier years it was common to call the Irish Mag mine the C&A Mine. Later this term was applied to the Oliver and other mines. Related companies such as, the Pittsburgh and Duluth and the Superior and Pittsburgh often had mines that were called by the company name or initials and not the actual mine name. These accidents are those in which the mine the accident occurred could not be conclusively determined.

May 15, 1899, South Bisbee Mining Company
James McNeill was drilling in the center of the bottom of the shaft. Joseph O'Hara and Earl McCutcheon were drilling on either side of him, when McNeill drilled into and misfire that he was right above. The explosion blew off one arm and blasted out his eyes. A flying rock knocked out O, Hara. Earl McCutcheon was temporally stunned and soon had taken the body of McNeill to the sinking bucket. While holding O'Hara, he signaled James Williams the hoistman and brought his partners to the hoisted surface. Somewhat conscious, McNeill muttered unintelligibly about God and the Virgin Mary and was laid down on a cot and eventually into the bunkhouse to wait for a doctor. He died soon after the accident.

"Bisbee Miner's Pick Strikes Dynamite" The San Francisco Call 4 May 16, 1899 page 4
"Original Certificate of Birth." Arizona Department of Health Services. http://genealogy.az.gov/azbirth/421/4210049.pdf (June 21, 2012)
Office of State Mine Inspector. *Seventh Annual Report of the State Mine Inspector State of Arizona for the Year Ending November 30, 1918.*
"Original Certificate of Death." Arizona Department of Health Services. http://genealogy.az.gov/azdeath/017/10170833.pdf (May 29, 2012)
"Cochise County Coroner's Inquest No.399" Arizona State Archives Phoenix

Around December 27, 1901, South Bisbee Mine (LS&P No.3?)
R.E. Daly and his partners employed to sink the shaft. They were down close to 1000- feet and rang the bells to indicate they were ready to blast. They spit the fuses climbed into the

sinking bucket and rang the bells to be hoisted. There was a delay in the hoistman's response, and the bucket had been lifted only about twenty feet when the round detonated. A rock flew and struck Daley right arm and wrist, breaking them. In December 1902 Daley filed a suit against the mining company claiming that the bell system was not functioning and that the hoistman was not only incompetent was also hard of hearing. He was asking for $10,000 for damages since he claimed he could no longer work as a miner and $500 in medical expenses.

"Files Suit for Damages" Bisbee Daily Review 28 December 1902 page 4

August 21, 1903
An unnamed workman crushed his finger with a heavy plank.

"Crushed his Finger" Bisbee Daily Review 22 August 1903 page5

July 21, 1904, (Irish Mag* or Oliver Mine)
J. McCarthy was working with Rouland Livesey. J. McCarthy was working in over a chute on two lagging that were nailed down. One end of a lagging broke near the nails, and he fell into the chute, and fell breaking bones as he struck the timber. His partner had gone to get sharp drill steels and was not present at the time of the accident. After Livesey return he found McCarthy's candlestick and a shift boss looking for McCarthy. Finally, they lowered a man into the chute and he found McCarthy's body partially buried by rock with only his hands and head exposed. According to Livesey, the area above the chute had not caved, but rather the chute was hung up and when McCarthy fell his impact freed the jammed up muck, it fell burying him. He was survived by a brother in New York City, who was a letter carrier and another relation in Madison, Texas. * This accident most likely, occurred in the Irish Mag Mine.

"Three Fatal Accidents Occur" Bisbee Daily Review 22 July 1904 page 1
"Cochise County Coroner's Inquest No.218" Arizona State Archives Phoenix

August 31, 1904,
John Lyons was hit by a falling timber. He was considered lucky that it did not kill him. He suffered and bruised left leg.

"Got Off easy" Bisbee Daily Review 1 September 1904 page 5

February 8, 1905, (Irish Mag* or Oliver Mine)
Michael J. O' Sullivan was working on the 1100 intermediate level of a new double compartment interior shaft that extended from the 1050 to the 1150 level. On the intermediate level, O' Sullivan was loading ore into mine cars from a chute. The procedure was that he was to load a car at the chute and push it about 200ft. until he reached the shaft. At the shaft, a cage would be waiting with an empty car on it, while the second cage was at the bottom or 1150 level. He would take the empty mine car off the cage and push on the full car he had brought. Then he rang two bells and the cage would be lowered and the second cage would be raised with an empty car. The station was illuminated by a couple of candles, and the floor was covered with turnsheets, but the shaft did not have a safety

bar preventing anyone from falling into the shaft. It appeared that while pushing a loading car he forgot which shaft compartment had a cage waiting. He pushed the loaded mine car into the shaft and the car dragged him with it. The loaded mine car landed on a cage. His body was believed to have landed on the car and then slid down and rested against the empty mine car sitting on the cage. A gash in the side of his skull, running down to the jaw, leaked brains. The doctors hopelessly tried to save him, but after three and one half-hours he died. He was preceded in death by his wife and was survived by a son. Patrick Finn another miner had seen O'Sullivan pulling a mine car with his back to the shaft early that day. He had warned O'Sullivan never to do that, and O' Sullivan showed him a spot where he had stepped on a loose plank and had almost fallen in the shaft earlier that day. Finn believed that O'Sullivan had backed into the shaft rather being pulled. * This accident most likely, occurred in the Irish Mag Mine. The Oliver Mine was undergoing a renovation of the surface facilities and was used for limited work at this time.

"Miner Falls to Death" Bisbee Daily Review 9 February 1905 page 5

"Cochise County Coroner's Inquest No.253" Arizona State Archives Phoenix

February 12, 1905, (L.S. & P. No. 3 or Cole Shaft.)

George Nelson shook a tin of blasting caps to loosen them up to make them easier to remove and they detonated. The explosion destroyed both of his hands and one eye. It was thought the other eye might be saved. From the waist up peppered with bits of copper from the blasting caps. Nelson was a recent graduate of the Michigan School of Mines and had been working in Bisbee to develop first-hand knowledge of mining.

*A Michigan paper indicated that this occurred in the Junction Mine, but Bisbee records state the L.S&.P, which is either the Cole Mine or the L.S.P. No. 3 Mine.

"Calumet & Arizona Hospital Records". http://www.mycochise.com/hospcalme 2ny.php (May 28, 2012)

"A Frightful Accident" Bisbee Daily Review 14 February 1905 page 5

"Michigan Boy" Bisbee Daily Review 19 February 1905 page 2

July 10, 1905, Oliver or Irish Mag Mine

George Smith was caught in a cave-in on the 1050 level. A large quantity of soft dirt hit Smith flattening him to the ground. He suffered only bruising.

"Miner Slightly Injured" Bisbee Daily Review 11 July 1905 page 1

February 19, 1906

Mike Medigovich was standing under a chute when another miner dumped a wheelbarrow load of rock on top of him. He suffered cuts to the head.

"Injured in Mine" Bisbee Daily Review 20 February 1906 page 1

September 26, 1906, Irish Mag/ Oliver Mine #367

G.E. Ware better known as "Whiskers"* was killed when he picked into a missed hole in the Southwest "motor" drift. The bosses were confused by this accident, because Ware was working in the wrong drift. He was supposed to be working in the North Drift with Lou Medin. After learning Ware was in the Southwest Drift, Shift Boss W.J. Greenwood told Medin to get Ware and tell him to work in the North Drift. When Medin found Ware he was already dead and Medin went to the 1150 station and found Shift Foreman U.S.

Ratterree and told him of the accident. (* Medin knew him only as Whiskers and only learned his real name at the inquest.)

"Cochise County Coroner's Inquest No.367" Arizona State Archives Phoenix

Around March 28, 1907 (L. S & P. No. 3 or Cole Shaft.)

Cousin Jack, Ethelbert Hayes, and Frank Earl Allen were working in No. 2 sulfide stope on the 1000 level. A cave-in occurred killing Hayes and injuring Allen. (No coroner's inquest could be located)

"Territorial Items" Coconino Sun 28, March 1907 page 8

August 25, 1907, (L. S. & P. No. 3 or Cole Shaft.)

William Kranz, a timberman, was working on a new chute on the 900 level. While he was working a section of rock fell and knocked him to the ground breaking his leg just above the ankle. He was taken to the Calumet & Arizona Hospital where the 35-year-old Kranz stayed until September 13, 1907.

"Is Hurt in Mine" Bisbee Daily Review 27 August 1907 page 7
"Calumet & Arizona Hospital Records." My Cochise. http://www.mycochise.com/hospcalkr2man.php (April 2, 2011)

November 23, 1907, Superior & Pittsburg Mine

J.H. Lee was injured on the 900 level when timbers fell and hit cutting his hand. He was expected to be off work two weeks.

"Fingers Lacerated" Bisbee Daily Review 24 November 1907 page 3

February 12, (?) 1908, Superior & Pittsburg Mine

A.C. Carter was pushing a car on a lower level when it derailed violently and crushed his fingers of one hand against the timber.

"Fingers Crushed in Mine" Bisbee Daily Review 12 February 1908 page 7

March 3, 1908 (Irish Mag or Oliver Mine)

George Cook was taken to the Calumet & Arizona Hospital after timbers fell on top of him.

"Hurt by Timbers" Bisbee Daily Review 4 March 1908 page 7

July 2, 1909

On the 1200 level. A Greek miner named Papadopolis attacked Shift Boss, John Halliman with a rock. The rock broke ribs, punctured a lung and affected the operation of the Halliman's heart. Initially, he was expected to die, but he recovered.

"Case of Greek Goes Over" Bisbee Daily Review 11 July 1909 page 5

August 24, 1917

A blasting cap exploded in the right hand of Ben Critchley. The ends of his fingers were destroyed. He was 22 years old and was released from the Calumet & Arizona Hospital on September 6, 1917.

Office of State Mine Inspector. Sixth Annual Report of the State Mine Inspector State of Arizona for the Year Ending November 30, 1917.

December 24, 1918

Louie Franks broke two ribs when a machine (drill?) fell on him. He was released from the Calumet & Arizona Hospital around January 7, 1919.

"Leaves Hospital" Bisbee Daily Review 8 January 1919, page 8

December 31, 1917, Cole Mine (probably)

A blasting cap exploded injuring the right arm and left knee of George Corris.

Office of State Mine Inspector. *Seventh Annual Report of the State Mine Inspector State of Arizona for the Year Ending November 30, 1918.*

February 19, 1920

A pick fell on the head of Gus Jurich. The top of his head was cut.

Office of State Mine Inspector. *Seventh Annual Report of the State Mine Inspector State of Arizona for the Year Ending November 30, 1920.*

March 20, 1920

Timberman, Victor Ritner had his leg broken when a boulder fell on it.

Office of State Mine Inspector. *Seventh Annual Report of the State Mine Inspector State of Arizona for the Year Ending November 30, 1920.*

June 5, 1920 Junction Mine (probably)

George Bakota was drilling, and the steel broke cutting his hand.

Office of State Mine Inspector. *Seventh Annual Report of the State Mine Inspector State of Arizona for the Year Ending November 30, 1920.*

June 27, 1922

Joe Parvin was caught between to mine cars and suffered a bruised pelvis.

Office of State Mine Inspector. *Eleventh Annual Report of the State Mine Inspector State of Arizona for the Year Ending November 30, 1922.*

February 11, 1923

L.F. Haggard broke a finger when it became caught between a chute and a bar.

Twelfth Annual Report of the State Mine Inspector State of Arizona for the Year Ending November 30, 1923.

June 6, 1922

B.K. Gillespie broke an arm and was generally bruised up when he fell a 100ft. down a stope.

Twelfth Annual Report of the State Mine Inspector State of Arizona for the Year Ending November 30, 1923.

February 27, 1923

Vic Ritner was bruised up had an arm broken after being caught by falling rock.

Twelfth Annual Report of the State Mine Inspector State of Arizona for the Year Ending November 30, 1923.

August 25, 1923

Henry Williams broke his elbow stopping a group of mine cars.

Twelfth Annual Report of the State Mine Inspector State of Arizona for the Year Ending November 30, 1923.

August 29, 1923

Hilmer Hanson was too close to a face being blasted when it detonated. He suffered puncture wounds on his back and arms

September 8, 1923
H.C. Neely was hit by a rock while barring down. The rock broke his shoulder.
Twelfth Annual Report of the State Mine Inspector State of Arizona for the Year Ending November 30, 1923.

October 19, 1923
Cleofos Baron smashed his hand when a cage bar fell on it.
Twelfth Annual Report of the State Mine Inspector State of Arizona for the Year Ending November 30, 1923.

February 18, 1924
Sherman Fellers wrenched his back lifting a turnsheet.
Office of State Mine Inspector. *Thirteenth Annual Report of the State Mine Inspector State of Arizona for the Year Ending November 30, 1924.*

February 22, 1924
H.E. Neely broke a rib while lifting a box of powder (dynamite). At this time powder came in 50 lb. wooden boxes.
Office of State Mine Inspector. *Thirteenth Annual Report of the State Mine Inspector State of Arizona for the Year Ending November 30, 1924.*

May 11, 1924
J.A. Anderson broke his hand when a rock hit his hand while using a chute bar.
Office of State Mine Inspector. *Thirteenth Annual Report of the State Mine Inspector State of Arizona for the Year Ending November 30, 1924.*

June 20, 1924
John C. Perkins was gassed. The gasses could have been powder gasses left over from blasting or gasses from a mine fire that had leaked into active workings.
Office of State Mine Inspector. *Thirteenth Annual Report of the State Mine Inspector State of Arizona for the Year Ending November 30, 1924.*

September 6, 1924
Robert Grant broke his arm when a cage jolted when he was being hoisted.
Office of State Mine Inspector. *Thirteenth Annual Report of the State Mine Inspector State of Arizona for the Year Ending November 30, 1924.*

September 11, 1924
G.W. Bell broke two fingers when a drill steel broke while he was drilling.
Office of State Mine Inspector. *Thirteenth Annual Report of the State Mine Inspector State of Arizona for the Year Ending November 30, 1924.*

October 21, 1924
Joe Mandarich broke his toes when a rock landed on them while he was barring down.
Office of State Mine Inspector. *Thirteenth Annual Report of the State Mine Inspector State of Arizona for the Year Ending November 30, 1924.*

October 30, 1924
A.O. Smith was bruised and wrenched his hip when he fell while breaking a mule.
Office of State Mine Inspector. *Thirteenth Annual Report of the State Mine Inspector State of Arizona for the Year Ending November 30, 1924.*

A mine with a long, forgotten identity near the Holbrook mine.

Unidentified Mine

May 7, 1888, Unknown Mine probably a C.Q.C.M.Co. mine

John Waters fell 65 ft. down a manway. The back of his head was cut, and both ankles sprained.

"Territorial Topics" The Arizona Silver Belt 12 May 1888 *page 6*

July 28, 1902

Babes Estes broke his leg when rock fell.

"Leg Broken" Bisbee Daily Review 28 July, 1902 page8

January 9, 1903

W.R. Smith was struck in the head by a handle from a windlass.

"Slightly Injured" Bisbee Daily Review 10 January 1903 *page 8*

January 1904

T.D. Davis had his foot crushed in a mine.

"Still in Bed" Bisbee Daily Review 17 January 1904, page 5

Around 1905

O.S. *"Tex"* McCain had a piece of steel lodged into an eye while working at a mine. He was disabled and unable to work. After a few months, during which he spent considerable time at the Johnson Saloon on Naco road, he was accused of robbing the saloon on November 24th. Noel Thursday owner of the Saloon stated that McCain and another man wore handkerchiefs over their faces. McCain stood by the stove with his back facing the bar. The other man pointed a gun to Noel's head. He remove $47 from the cash register and took a gold watch from Noel's pocket and some change. The two men then backed out of the saloon pointing six-shooters. Later Constable Humm arrested McCain and found $2.00 in his pocket. This was the only money that McCain was known to have for some

time. The case was dismissed on November 27. Judge Hogan cited lack of evidence. McCain had accumulated a dozen witnesses that he was elsewhere at the time. Note, although this is not a mine accident, a mine accident indirectly caused the problem.
"Hold-up Men take Saloon's Coin" Bisbee Daily Review 25 November 1905 page5
"Gray's Sins are Severe on Family" Bisbee Daily Review 26 November 1905 page8
"Not Sufficient Evidence to Hold" Bisbee Daily Review 28 November 1905 page5

May 5, 1905
Mike O'Brien was dragged behind a mine car by a runaway mule. He was cut up and bruised
"Injured Yesterday" Bisbee Daily Review 6 May 1905 page 6

May, 1906
Dennis Twomey had his left forefinger crushed by a mine car. Soon after the finger had to be amputated in fear of blood poisoning. He became a Bisbee constable on January 2, 1907 and worked until 1911.
"Twomey Lost Finger by Amputation" Bisbee Daily Review 31, May 1906 page 3
"New Officers Begin Work" Bisbee Daily Review 2, January 1907 page 2
"Officers Surprise Two Opium Fiends" Bisbee Daily Review 29, May 1907 page 5
"Ex-policeman Henry Hall Shoots and Instantly Kills G. Langford" Bisbee Daily Review 19, September 1908 page

1908*
William Muir was struck on the head with a timber. In February 1905 he was removed to the Territorial Asylum for the Insane at Phoenix. He had spent time in a private sanatorium but without results. His condition was blamed on the mine accident.* Date is not clear on newspaper page could be 03, 05, 06 or 08
"Taken to Asylum" Bisbee Evening Miner 6 1908(?) page5

July 11, 1912, Unknown mine probably a C.Q.C.M.Co. mine
Irish Miner, Michael Maguire was injured and taken to the Copper Queen Hospital on July 7th 1912. He died from a ruptured artery. He was survived by a brother Patrick Maguire in Bisbee and a sister living in New York. His body was shipped to New York for burial.
"Michael Maguire Dies" Bisbee Daily Review 12 July 1912 page 2
"Original Certificate of Death." Arizona Department of Health Services. http://genealogy.az.gov/azdeath/010/10101196.pdf (July 22, 2011

February, 1916 Unknown Calumet & Arizona Mine
Jack O'Hara broke his leg in an undescribed accident. He was a well-known local tenor who had been part of Lew Dockstader's Minstrels.
"O'Hara Recovering" Bisbee Daily Review 15 February 1916 page 8

May? 1918
G.L. Conens broke his leg in an undescribed mine accident. Hobbling on crutches into a World War I, Red Cross Benefit he gave a gold and emerald ring to be sold. He had given all the money he could, but wanted to give more and decided to give the ring. The ring was

sold for $34.00 to Mrs. C.L. Thompson who offered to give it back to Mr. Conens, but he refused. The next night the ring was sold again at the Elks Bazaar for war stamps.

"Presents Ring to Red Cross to Boost Funds" <u>Bisbee Daily Review</u> 26, May 1918 page 3

May, 1919

George Buschampf broke several toes in an undescribed mine accident.

"Out on Crutches" <u>Bisbee Daily Review</u> 8, June 1919 page 8

Whitetail Deer Mine c-1965

Whitetail Deer Mine

By March 13, 1881, a forty foot shaft had already been developed on the claim. In November 1885 the Probate court ordered 1/2 of the Whitetail Deer Claim, be sold as part of the estate of Matthew Crooker. Two months later, on January 4, 1886 another probate sale was declared also, on ½ of the Whitetail Deer Claim this time as part of the estate of James A. Nolley. On December 3, 1886, the Tombstone newspaper reported, an unknown party offered $10,000 in cash and $20, 0000 in a bond for mine, but there was a problem that the claim over lapped the property owned by Charles Anshultz. It was hoped the buyers would acquire the Anshultz land as well.

In May 1887, the Copper Queen Consolidated Mining Company purchased the White Tail Deer Claim for $10,000 and on August 24 the company applied to patent the claim. During this time a short incline shaft was sunk around 50ft. in depth and some rich ore was mined, but the area soon became inactive. In 1903 Louis, Linol. Doma W. Birdno and Robert Boggs leased the property and began to clear out the old incline shaft of debris. After six months of work the lessees shipped 75 ton of ore running close to 25% copper. The ore was mined in a crosscut driven towards the Wolverine workings. The mine soon quieted down and it was not until 1910 when a Charles J. Lundvall took the leases and began sinking a shaft using a gasoline powered hoist. By July 10, 1910 the vertical shaft was 45ft. deep. Later in the year, drifting was done trying to intercept the older workings from the incline shaft. Work continued and 1,073 of crosscut was driven during 1911 and in 1912 a large orebody was discovered on the 100 level (sometimes called 150 level) on the Sweepstakes Claim.

The lease ended in 1915 and the Copper Queen began to develop the mine and sunk the shaft 161ft. deeper and purchased another gasoline hoist. Quickly, the mine was restored and in August 1916 ore was struck on the 200 level. To provide ventilation and a secondary exit a connection was made with the Wolverine mine workings (probably from the 200 level Whitetail Deer to the 400 level of the Wolverine#2 shaft by a raise). Mining continued until 1919, when low copper prices forced the operation to shut down even with ore in sight. After two years in 1921, the mine was reopened and the shaft was sunk 300ft. to the 500 level and a total depth of 602ft. The 200, 400 and 500 levels were developed and by 1922 the mine had 19,625 tons of copper ore as reserves. This mine continued to be operated through the 1920s often by lessees. The mine continued to operate off and on until 1941. Phelps Dodge resumed operations for the duration of World War II. The mine ceased operations around 1945. When mining ceased the shaft was 602 ft. deep with two compartments.

April 7, 1916, Whitetail Deer Mine
A fire destroyed the surface facilities at the mine burning the headframe, change room, and hoist house. The shaft timbers were partly burned and the hoist was damaged.
Mills C.E. (1958) Notations from annual reports (Copper Queen Consolidated Mining Company, Phelps Dodge & Company and Phelps Dodge Corporation) years 1909-1950. Unpublished, Phelps Dodge Corp. files, 12 p.

October 28, 1916, Whitetail Deer Mine
Mucker, Joseph Masima was working and a mine car freed itself and rolled onto his ankle. His ankle was badly crushed and he was crippled in the ankle. He remained at the Copper Queen Hospital for 109 days. Later, he sued Phelps Dodge for $15,000 as he was unable to work.
Copper Queen Hospital Patients Register October 28, 1916, Bisbee Mining and Historical Museum, Bisbee.
"Wants Damages" Bisbee Daily Review 28, 1917 page 4

February 14, 1918, Whitetail Deer Mine
Hoist engineer, S. E Beden was working when the flywheel came off the hoist and smashed through the side of the hoist house and went off 150 ft. into the desert. Flying lumber struck Beden breaking his leg in a compound fracture and breaking his hand in three places. He also was seriously cut on the hand in the area of a tendon. The hoist was badly damaged, and one side of the hoist house was torn out.
"Flywheel Flies Engineer Injured" Bisbee Daily Review 16 February 1918 page 6

July 13, 1921, Whitetail Deer Mine
Tom Moat, employed in sinking the shaft was injured when he was struck by a rock.
"Miner is Injured" Bisbee Daily Review 13 July 1921 page 6

December 13, 1941, White Tail Deer Mine
The White Tail Deer Shaft was used as ventilation and for the escapeway for the 600 level Cole Mine. It was maintained as an operative shaft and inspected monthly. During one of these inspections the manway was declared unsafe. The manway landings and ladders were not useable. Thomas Mason Jr. and Swedish, Jigger Boss Peter Harold Welander were working repairing the manway in the shaft 416 ft. below the collar. Both men fell from their staging into the shaft and fell 186 ft. Hoistman, B.J. Watkins thought he heard a problem and went to the shaft pulled on the cable to see if he could see them and then banged on the pipe hoping for a response. Dr. George Harry Hess and the rescue crew traveled underground from the Cole Shaft to the accident site. LeRoy L. Walton and Bill Crawford hiked over from the Cole Shaft to the White Tail Deer Mine. Once at the White Tail deer they went down the shaft and joined the rescue crew from the Cole. Mason died from a fractured skull and broken back. Welander's body. He died from a broken neck and skull was found mixed up with fallen timber. Another different version was told by Glenn O'Leary, who was working on the surface at the Whitetail Deer. He said that the men were retimbering the shaft and had taken the cage down to the 200 level. They got off the cage and were standing on the station, but the timber was rotted and gave way. The two men fell

453

into the shaft. Their bodies were found at the bottom of the shaft.*. Mason was survived by 14 month old daughter named Dorothy, his wife and his brother George. Welander was survived by his six children, Louise, Ruth, Arthur, Harold, Irene, Alice, and his wife.

* Note that the bottom of the Whitetail Deer shaft is the 500 level it is called the 500 level because it is equal to the 500 level in the other Copper Queen Mines, like the Spray. In this case the 500 level is actually 602 ft. from the surface.

"Two Dead in Fall at Mine" Bisbee Daily Review 14 December 19 41 page 3

"Thomas Mason Jr. Rites Today, 4:30" Bisbee Daily Review 16 December 19 41 page 1

"Original Certificate of Death." Arizona Department of Health Services. http://genealogy.az.gov/azdeath/066/10660566.pdf (October 25, 2012)

"Original Certificate of Death." Arizona Department of Health Services. http://genealogy.az.gov/azdeath/066/10660567.pdf (October 25, 2012)

"Cochise County Coroner's Inquest No. 1803" Arizona State Archives

Richard W. Graeme III personal communication 2011

Wolverine #1 Shaft C-1903

Wolverine Mine

  Wolverine & Arizona Development Company was incorporated on March 10, 1903 and they had brokered a deal to purchase the six claims of the Chicago group. This included the Broken Promise Claim. On April 21 the Wolverine #1 shaft was started on the Broken Promise Claim. Operations quickly advanced and by October, the three compartment shaft was hand drilled to a depth of 438ft., with stations cut on the 200, 300, and 400 levels. Boarding and bunk houses were also built on the property. At the end of 1904 the Wolverine & Arizona Development Company became the Wolverine & Arizona Mining Company.

  During 1906, arrangements were made to explore the Warren Claim. This claim was thousands of feet and on the opposite side of Escabrosa Ridge from the other Wolverine workings. It was decided to set up a diamond drill on the Claim. Oxide ore was struck by this drill hole at 410ft. The decision was made in 1907 to mine the orebody on the Warren Claim through the Higgins Mine, rather than extend Wolverine workings to the claim. On September 6, 1907, the orebody discovered by the diamond drilling was struck from the Higgins side. When they were still 125ft. from the hole. The miners drove the tunnel 40ft. through ore.

  For the next few years Wolverine operations focused on mining the Warren Claim The only surface opening on the Warren Claim was the Warren Raise, which dropped into the top of a sulphide stope. The discovery of theses ores resulted in the Uncle Sam, Shattuck and later Southwest mines exploring and mining ore right up to the Wolverine & Arizona property lines. This area was significant producer of fine crystalline azurite with stalactitic malachite specimens. Around 1908, to develop silver-lead- copper ores the Wolverine & Arizona sank two interior shafts; one was single compartment which extended from the Higgins Tunnel level down 100ft. to a level. A second double compartment shaft was sunk from the 100 level of the first interior shaft down another 100ft. to the 200 level. Both of these shafts were sunk on the Backbone Claim belonging to Thomas Higgins and not Wolverine & Arizona ground.

In 1909, the Wolverine #1 Shaft, which had been sunk to a depth of 665ft., was shut down completely and work was totally done through the Higgins tunnel. Production increased and the Wolverine and Arizona Mining Company became profitable. In 1911, all pipe and fittings were removed from the Wolverine #1 shaft and stored.

The years that followed were successful through the Higgins. Part of the Warren Claim was leased in 1913 to M. J. Cunningham and Allie Sowles. Pneumatic drills were introduced in 1914. All work previous to this had been accomplished by hand. With profitable years, the company financed exploration in 1916. The Georgia Tunnel was started on the Georgia claim. At the same time William White, Cliff Winters and Carol Thomas began sinking the Wolverine #2 Shaft on the Broken Promise Claim. Soon they had sunk and timbered a 240ft. shaft into an orebody. At the end of the lease in 1917, the Wolverine and Arizona took over the shaft. This shaft was sunk to the 400 level and shipped 1,000 tons a month from the 200 and 300 levels. The ore was located on the property line with the Whitetail Deer Mine. The ore also continued with ore into the Crescent Claim owned by the Calumet & Arizona Mining Company.

In 1920, the Wolverine #1 shaft was cleared and retimbered. During the following year ore was reported as blocked out on the 300 level of the #1 shaft, but no stopes are shown on Wolverine and Arizona maps. The Wolverines were a small, but consistent producers. The Kentucky Tunnel was cleaned out and a 150ft winze was sunk in 1925. It was eventually sunk to a depth of 200ft. and then around 400 ft. of drifting was completed at the bottom.

In 1931 the Higgins lease was given up and the mines shut down and the last entry in their reports is July, 24, 1940. On February 23, 1953, the property was purchased by Phelps Dodge for $12,500.00 At the end of operations the Wolverine workings consisted of the Georgia tunnel (adit), Kentucky Tunnel (adit), one single compartment interior shaft, one double compartment, interior shaft, The Wolverine #1 shaft with three compartments and 663 ft. deep, and the Wolverine #2 Shaft with two compartments and about 430 ft. deep.

August 27, 1903,* Wolverine No.1 Mine
Gilbert A. Phelps died from injuries received after a ten ft. fall. * Date of death, not of accident.
"Phelps is Dead" Arizona Republican 31 August 1903 page 6

February 17, 1904, Wolverine No.1 Mine
W.G. Mc Call was killed when he fell down the Wolverine Shaft. Three men and Mc Call were descending riding on a sinking bucket. When they reached the 500 level, McCall stepped off on the wrong side of the landing and fell through a trapdoor to the bottom of the shaft. eighty feet below. He appeared to have died instantly. His head was cut and bruised from striking the sides of the shaft. It was determined that even if he had survived the fall, he would have drowned since the shaft sump had several feet of water in it. The other men riding the bucket were Richard Nesbitt, Ed Botsford, and Arthur T. Bennetts
"Two Miners Killed Accident Last Night" Bisbee Daily Review 18 February 1904 page 1
"Cochise County Coroner's Inquest No.190" Arizona State Archives

September 21, 1907 Wolverine Mine
John Keating was working on the dump and stepped on a rusty nail. The nail penetrated his instep. Blood poisoning began take hold and he was taken to hospital.
"Blood Poisoning Threatens" Bisbee Daily Review 22 September 1907 page 7
"Taken to Asylum" Bisbee Evening Miner 6 1908(?) page5

February 13, 1908* (Probably Higgins Tunnel)
Four men entered a tunnel (adit) operated by the Wolverine and Arizona Mining Company. They were overcome by powder gasses from the previous shift's blast. They were brought

to the mouth of the tunnel and were treated by Dr. N.C. Bledsoe. * Date is not clear on newspaper page could be1903, 1905, 1906 or 1908

"Four Men Overcome in Wolverine Tunnel" Bisbee Evening Miner 6 1908(?) page5

September 6, 1918, Wolverine Mine

Charles A. Coburn was caught in a cave-in. His nose received a compound fracture, and he died from meningitis on September 10th. He was 53 years-old.

Office of State Mine Inspector. *Seventh Annual Report of the State Mine Inspector State of Arizona for the Year Ending November 30, 1918.*

"Calumet & Arizona Hospital Records." My Cochise. http://www.mycochise.com/hospcaldied.php (May 28, 2012)

July 25, 1921, Wolverine Mine

Enrique Terran and James Egan were being hoisted to the surface, riding a crosshead attached to a sinking bucket. At this time, a monsoon rain had started on the surface. The water flowed down the hillside and flooded the dump, then began to pour into the shaft. The water washed out a section of shaft. timber and released the muck it was holding When Terran and Egan were about 50 ft. from the surface the falling muck struck the bucket knocking the men to the bottom of the shaft. The cable jerked when the muck struck the bucket and hoistman, Harry Simmers stopped hoisting and reported this to Foreman James Malley. The foreman inspected the shaft and noted it was too badly damaged for hoisting. He went down the manway until he discovered the bodies of the two men at the bottom of the shaft. He placed the bodies on the station for the coroner to examine (most likely the 400 level station) (Note under most circumstances the bodies were supposed to be left. where they were killed for the coroner to examine. In this case Malley made the right decision and moved the bodies as the bottom of the shaft after an accident like this would be a dangerous place.)

"Two are Killed in Peculiar Accident" Bisbee Daily Review 26 July 1921 page 4

"Cloudburst at Bisbee Kills Mine Workers" Tombstone Epitaph 31 July 1921 page 4

Certificate of Death." Arizona Department of Health Services. http://genealogy.az.gov/azdeath/024/10240047.pdf (May 28, 2012) Office of State

Dugan Mortuary Records 1918/22 Accession 2010.10.12 Bisbee Mining and Historical Museum, Bisbee p447.

Dugan Mortuary Records 1918/22 Accession 2010.10.12 Bisbee Mining and Historical Museum, Bisbee p443.

General Bibliography

"Accidents on and Off Duty: Their Cause in 1913" Bisbee Daily Review. February 08, 1914, mining section, Page 2

"Activities of the District are Apparent in Increased and Constantly Expanding Work" Bisbee Daily Review. March 15, 1914, mining section,

"Advertisement" Bisbee daily review. October 18, 1913, Page 5,

Barbour, Percy E. "Explosives Used in War and Mining." Engineering and Mining Journal 100.3 (September 25, 1915): 507-10.

"Below is a list" Bisbee daily review. August 31, 1913, section two, page 9

"Big Warren Dance" Bisbee Daily Review 22 June 1916 page 8
"Controlling Mine Fires in Cananea" Bisbee Daily Review 25 July 1914 page 1

"Copper Queen" Weekly Arizona citizen. September 04, 1880, page 1

Cowperthwaite, Thomas. "Safety Organization and Method of Operating and Maintaining Interest among Shift Bosses and Foremen." National Safety Congress Tenth (1922): 459-62.

"Cowperthwaite on Safety First." Engineering and Mining Journal 105.12 (March 23, 1918): 566-67.
"Do You Have to Learn" Bisbee Daily Review., August 31, 1913, section 2

"First Smoker Dates" Bisbee Daily Review. December 10, 1913, Page 4

"Firefighters back from Cananea Mines" Bisbee Daily Review 8 August 1914 page 3

"Human Life is Sacred says Capt. Hodgson" Bisbee Daily Review 4 April1914 page 1

"Hundreds at Safety Smoker" Bisbee Daily Review 31 January 1914 page 3

McKeehan, Wallace. "Accident Prevention in Copper Mining." Safety Engineering Vol 29.1 (January 1915): 65-67.

McKeehan, Wallace. "A Feature of the Copper Queen Safety Methods." State Safety New 4th ser. (April 1, 1916): 13.

McKeehan, Wallace. "A Great Tunnel Disaster at El Cumbre." The Coal Industry Vol1.9 (September 1918): 333-34.

McKeehan, Wallace. "Report of the Secretary of the Committee on Safety and Sanitation." Bulletin of the American Institute of Mining Engineers 123 (March 1917): 419-24.

"Medical Examination Required for Men Desiring Work in C.Q. Mines" Bisbee Daily Review.
March 11, 1914, Page 6, Image 6

Mills C.E. (1958) Notations from annual reports (Copper Queen Consolidated Mining
Company, Phelps Dodge & Company and Phelps Dodge Corporation) years 1909-1950.
Unpublished, Phelps Dodge Corp. files, 72 p.

Mitke, Charles A. "A History of Mine Fires in the Southwest Part 1." Mining & Scientific
Press 121.5 (July 31, 1920): 155-60.

Mitke, Charles A. "Standardization of Mining Methods." Engineering and Mining Journal
106.19 (November 9, 1918): 814-19.

"National Gathering of Those Interested in Mines Safety" Bisbee daily review. August 03, 1913,
section 2, page 3

Phelps Dodge Corporation (1919) The Copper Queen Practical Mining Course. Bisbee
Publishing Company, Bisbee, Arizona,

Phelps Dodge Corporation (1955a) Code of Safe Practice for Raise Mining. Copper Queen
Branch Mines Division, Bisbee, Arizona,

Phelps Dodge Corporation (1955b) Code of Safe Practice for Drift. Mining. Copper Queen
Branch Mines Division, Bisbee, Arizona,

Phelps Dodge Corporation (1956) Code of Safe Practice for Underground Haulage. Copper
Queen Branch Mines Division, Bisbee, Arizona,

Phelps Dodge Corporation (1962) Code of Safe Practice for Stope Mining. Copper Queen
Branch Mines Division, Bisbee, Arizona,

Phelps Dodge Corporation (1971) Code of Safe Practice for Stope Mining. Copper Queen
Branch Mines Division, Bisbee, Arizona,

"Says Safety First Methods Succeed in Bisbee Mine Work" Bisbee Daily Review 29 July1914
page 2
"Safety in the Mines"Bisbee daily review. June 29, 1913, section 2 page 2

"Safety First Is Subject of Talk to Bisbee Scholars" Bisbee Daily Review. March 27, 1914, Page
5,
"Safety First on Your Cigar" Bisbee daily review. August 31, 1913, section two, page

"Safety First Is Subject of Talk to Bisbee Scholars" Bisbee Daily Review. March 27, 1914, Page
5,
"Safety First" is the Effort" Bisbee daily review. April 10, 1913, Page 8
Russell, S. R. "More "Kick" in Blasting Caps and Why." DuPont Magazine Vol.13.1 (July
1920): 13.
"The Important Recent" Bisbee daily review. July 06, 1913, section 2, page 1

Unknown. "Accidents in Metal Mines." Mines and Methods (January 1910): 185-94.

Unknown. "Misfires." Mining and Scientific Press Vol115 (July 21, 1917): 77-78.

"Untitled" <u>Bisbee Daily Review</u> 3 May1914 Sporting Section page 4

Willis, Charles F. "Physical Examination Previous to Employment." Safety Engineering 38.3 (September 1919): 155-56.

Young, George J. "Practical Mining Course at Copper Queen." Engineering and Mining Journal 112.25 (December 18, 1920): 1171-174.

1st level station of the Hargis Incline.

459

30 crosscut, 3rd level Southwest Mine

Accidents

Listed by Mine

Holbrook No. 1 Buildings, Holbrook No.2 mine, Spray Mine Irish Mag Mine
(foreground to background)

= Underground Miner

= Surface Miner

= Smelter Employee

= Child (not employed by a mining company)

Bisbee Queen Mine
Period of Operation/Maintained: 1903-1904, 1926-1928
Fatal Accidents
1 Fall of Object (bolt)
Total 1

Bisbee West Mine
Period of Operation/Maintained: 1899-1907
Fatal Accidents
2 Shaft Accident
1 Fall of Object (timber)
Total 2

Boras Mine
Period of Operation/Maintained: 1919-1975
Fatal Accidents
None
Total 0

Briggs Mine
Period of Operation/Maintained: 1902-1948
Fatal Accidents
3 Shaft Accident
2 Haulage
1 Blasting delayed leaving
1 Blasting Misfire
1 fall
Total 8

Campbell Mine
Period of Operation/Maintained: 1917-
1980
Fatal Accidents
2 Shaft Accident
8 Fall of Ground
3 Blasting Premature detonation
1 Fall
2 Haulage
Total 14

Charon Mine
Period of Operation/Maintained: 1914
-1935
Fatal Accidents
1 Fall of Ground
Total 1

Cochise Mine
Period of Operation/Maintained: 1898-
1907
Fatal Accidents
1 Shaft Accident
Total 1

Cochise & Calumet Mine
Period of Operation/Maintained: 1903-
1905, 1917-1975
Fatal Accidents
1 Blasting Premature Detonation
2 Blasting Misfire
Total 3

Cole Mine
Period of Operation/Maintained: 1902-1929, 1934-1944, 1947-1975
Fatal Accidents
3 fall
3 Blasting Misfire
1 Haulage
1 Haulage chute failure
2 Shaft Accident
10 Fall of Ground
1 Electrocution
1 Stabbing
1 Fall of Timber
1 unknown
Total 21

Congdon Mine
Period of Operation/Maintained: 1903-1906
Fatal Accidents
2 fire
Total 2

Copper Queen Mine
Period of Operation/Maintained: 1880-1895
Fatal Accidents
1 Blasting Misfire
Total 1

Copper Queen Smelters
Period of Operation/Maintained: 1880-1904
Fatal Accidents
2 Burns
2 Cinders
3 Falls
2 Machinery
Total 9

Cuprite Mine
Period of Operation/Maintained: 1905-1944
Fatal Accidents
1 Fall of Object (sheave wheel)
2 Blasting Misfire
Total 3

🚶🚶🚶

Czar Mine
Period of Operation/Maintained: 1885-1947
Fatal Accidents
9 Fall of Ground
1 Collapse of Backfill
4 Fall
2 Haulage
2 Haulage chute failure
3 Electrocution
Total 21

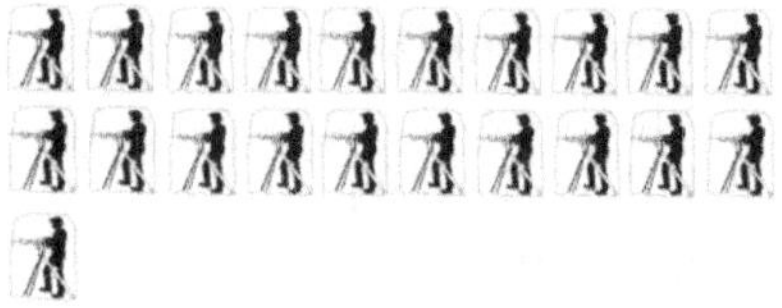

🚶🚶🚶🚶🚶🚶🚶🚶🚶🚶
🚶🚶🚶🚶🚶🚶🚶🚶🚶🚶
🚶

Dallas Mine
Period of Operation/Maintained: 1911-1929, 1940-1975
Fatal Accidents
2 Shaft Accident
1 Fall of Ground
1 Haulage
Total 4

🚶🚶🚶🚶

Denn Mine
Period of Operation/Maintained: 1907-1975
Fatal Accidents
1 Shaft Accident
2 Fall of Ground
4 Fall
2 Blasting delayed leaving
1 Falling Object (Timber)
1 Electrocution
1 Machinery
Total 12

🚶🚶🚶🚶🚶🚶🚶🚶🚶🚶
🚶🚶

Gardner Mine
Period of Operation/Maintained: 1902-
1944
Fatal Accidents
1 Shaft Accident
9 Fall of Ground
2 Electrocution
2 Blasting Misfire
2 Fall
Total 16

Hendricks Mine
Period of Operation/Maintained: 1881-
1904
Fatal Accidents
2 Fall of Ground
Total 2

Higgins Mine
Period of Operation/Maintained: 1903-
1944
Fatal Accidents
1 Fall of Ground
3 Blasting Misfire
Total 4

Hoatson Mine
Period of Operation/Maintained: 1905-
1919
Fatal Accidents
5 Fall of Ground
1 Fall of Object (timber)
1 Fall
1 Machinery (hoist drum)
Total 8

Holbrook Mine
Period of Operation/Maintained: 1881-
1944
Fatal Accidents
13 Fall of Ground
6 Shaft Accidents
2 Blasting Misfire
1 Blasting Returning to Detonation
1 Blasting Premature Detonation
5 Fall
4 Electrocution
Total 32

Irish Mag Mine
Period of Operation/Maintained: 1899-
1928
Fatal Accidents
2 Shaft Accidents
2 Fall of Ground
1 Fall
Total 5

Junction Mine
Period of Operation/Maintained: 1903-
1980
Fatal Accidents
9 Shaft Accidents
17 Fall of Ground
3 Fall
5 Haulage
4 Electrocution
2 Blasting Powder gasses
2 Blasting
1 Fire gasses
1 Machinery (forklift.)
1 Drowning
Total 43

Lake Superior & Pittsburg No.3 Mine
Period of Operation/Maintained: 1900-
1922
Fatal Accidents
1 Shaft Accident
1 Fall of Ground
Total 2

Lavender Pit Mine
Period of Operation/Maintained: 1950-
1974
Fatal Accidents
1 Fall of Ground
Total 1

Lowell Mine
Period of Operation/Maintained: 1903-
1940
Fatal Accidents
2 Shaft Accident
3 Fall of Ground
1 Blasting Premature Detonation
1 Tool
1 Electrocution
Total 8

🚶🚶🚶🚶🚶🚶🚶🚶
🚶🚶🚶🚶

**Manganese Workings near Cole
Mine**
Period of Operation/Maintained :
1914-1918, 1940-1945
Fatal Accidents
1 Blasting Misfire
Total 1

Nighthawk Mine
Period of Operation/Maintained: 1917-
1938
Fatal Accidents
1 Blasting Premature Detonation
2 Fall of Ground
Total 3

🚶🚶🚶

Pittsburg & Hecla Mine
Period of Operation/Maintained: 1903-
1905
Fatal Accidents
2 Shaft Accident
1 Blasting Misfire
Total 3

Portage Lake Mine
Period of Operation/Maintained: 1903-
1904
Fatal Accidents
Total 0

Prospect of Frank Johnson
Period of Operation/Maintained: 1901
Fatal Accidents
1 Blasting, shot explosives with rifle
Total 1

Oliver Mine
Period of Operation/Maintained: 1903-
1941
Fatal Accidents
6 Shaft Accident
16 Fall of Ground
1 Blasting Misfire
1 Machinery (saw)
1 Fall
Total 25

Sacramento Mine (underground)
Period of Operation/Maintained: 1904-
1946
Fatal Accidents
7 Shaft Accident
7 Fall of Ground
2 Haulage Chute failure
4 Blasting Misfire
1 Electrocution
Total 21

🚶🚶🚶🚶🚶🚶🚶🚶🚶🚶
🚶

Sacramento Open Pit Mine
Period of Operation/Maintained:
1917-1929
Fatal Accidents
10 Blasting Premature Detonation
1 Blasting Fly rock
4 Dumping Rail Car
1 Derailment
1 Machinery (Fell onto Steam Shovel
cable)
1 Machinery (Caught between
Locomotive and Oil Tank)
1 Machinery (Hit by Rail car)
Total 19

Sacramento Concentrator
Period of Operation 1920-1931
Fatal Accidents
Total 0

🚶 🚶

Saginaw Mine
Period of Operation/Maintained: 1904-
1913, 1929-1975
Fatal Accidents
1 Fall of Ground
1 Blasting Misfire
Total 2

🚶 🚶

Shattuck Mine
Period of Operation/Maintained: 1904-1947
Fatal Accidents
4 Shaft Accident
9 Fall of Ground
1 Fall
Total 14

Southwest Mine
Period of Operation/Maintained: 1911-1944
Fatal Accidents
1 Shaft Accident
10 Fall of Ground
1 Haulage (chute)
1 Haulage
Total 13

Spray Mine
Period of Operation/Maintained: 1889-1940
Fatal Accidents
3 Shaft Accident
7 Fall of Ground
1 Fall
1 Electrocution
1 Haulage
1 Drowning
Total 14

Uncle Sam Mine
Period of Operation/Maintained: 1881-1905, 1907-1944
Fatal Accidents
1 Blasting Powder Gasses
1 Shaft Accident
Total 2

Unknown Mine owned by C.Q.CM.Co.
Period of Operation: 1880-1917
Fatal Accidents
2 Unknown cause
Total 2

Unknown Mine owned by Phelps Dodge
Period of Operation: 1917-1980
Fatal Accidents
1 Shaft Accident
8 Falling Ground
1 Fall
2 Haulage
1 Blasting unknown
1 Suffocation
6 Unknown cause
Total 20

Unknown Mine owned by Calumet & Arizona and related companies.
Period of Operation 1899-1931
Fatal Accidents
1 Shaft Accident
1 Fall of Ground
2 Blasting Misfire
1 Fall
Total 5

Unknown Mine
Period of Operation: 1880-1980
Fatal Accidents
1 Blasting Misfire
1 Unknown Cause
Total 2

Whitetail Deer Mine
Period of Operation/Maintained: 1910-
1945
Fatal Accidents
2 Shaft Accident
Total 2

Wolverine Mine
Period of Operation/Maintained: 1903-
1931
Fatal Accidents
3 Shaft Accident
1 Fall
Total 4

ARIZONA STATE CODE OF MINE BELL
SIGNALS

1 BELL ___ STOP *IMMEDIATELY IF IN MOTION.*
1 " ___ HOIST MUCK.
1 " ___ RELEASE *CAGE, SKIP OR BUCKET.*
2 BELLS, LOWER.
3·1 " ___ HOIST MEN, *IF BELLS RUNG SLOWLY*
3·2 " ___ LOWER MEN, *MOVE SLOWLY.*
4 " ___ STEAM ON OR OFF.
5 " ___ BLASTING *OR READY TO SHOOT.*
*THIS IS A CAUTION SIGNAL AND IF THE ENGINEER IS
PREPARED TO ACCEPT IT HE MUST ACKNOWLEDGE BY
RAISING BUCKET OR CAGE A FEW FEET THEN LOWERING
IT AGAIN. AFTER ACCEPTING THIS SIGNAL ENGINEER
MUST BE PREPARED TO HOIST MEN AWAY FROM BLAST
AS SOON AS SIGNAL "1 BELL" IS GIVEN AND
MUST ACCEPT NO OTHER SIGNAL IN THE MEANTIME.*
6 BELLS, AIR ON OR OFF.
7 " ___ DANGER SIGNAL, *FOLLOWED*
*BY STATION SIGNAL CALLS CAGE TO THAT STATION
THIS SIGNAL TAKES PRECEDENCE OVER ALL OTHERS
EXCEPT AN ACCEPTED BLASTING SIGNAL.*

STATION SIGNALS
1·2 BELLS, COLLAR OF SHAFT.

1·3 BELLS, 1ST LEVEL		2·1·2 BELLS, 20TH LEVEL	
1·4	2D	2·1·3 " 21 ST
1·5	3D	2·1·4 " 22ND
2·1	4TH	2·1·5 " 23RD
2·2	5TH	2·2·1 " 24TH
2·3	6TH	2·2·2 " 25TH
2·4	7TH	2·2·3 " 26TH
2·5	8TH	2·2·4 " 27TH
4·1	9TH	2·2·5 " 28TH
4·2	10TH	2·4·1 " 29TH
4·3	11TH	2·4·2 " 30TH
4·4	12TH	2·4·3 " 31 ST
4·5	13TH	2·4·4 " 32ND
5·1 "	14TH	2·4·5 " 33RD
5·2 "	15TH	2·5·1 " 34TH
5·3 "	16TH	2·5·2 " 35TH
5·4 "	17TH	2·5·3 " 36TH
5·5 "	18TH "	2·5·4 " 37TH
6·1 "	19TH "	2·5·5 " 38TH
		2·6·1 " 39TH

*STATION SIGNAL MUST BE GIVEN BEFORE HOISTING OR LOWERING
SIGNAL – THE ENGINEER SHALL NOT MOVE A CAGE, SKIP OR
BUCKET UNLESS HE UNDERSTANDS THE SIGNAL – ONE COPY
OF THIS SIGNAL CODE SHALL BE POSTED ON THE GALLOWS
FRAME, ONE AT EACH STATION & ONE BEFORE THE ENGINEER.
SPECIAL SIGNALS MAY BE USED PROVIDED THEY ARE EASILY
DISTINGUISHED BY THEIR SOUND, OR OTHERWISE, FROM THE
FOREGOING CODE, AND DO NOT INTERFERE WITH IT IN ANY WAY.*

STATE MINE INSPECTOR

STONEHOUSE SIGNS, Inc., DENVER COLO.

Shift of the Junction Mine Circa 1924

Name	Location	Date	
Acosta, Jesus	Hargis Lease probably Czar Mine 100 level	9-Mar-25	
Aguillar, Roberto	Probably Sacramento Pit	3-Feb-24	
Allen, Eugene	Junction Mine	7-Jul-19	
Angelvich, Nicholas	Oliver Mine	29-Oct-07	
Anshutz, Charles	Holbrook #1 Mine "B" level	Nov 9, 1899	
Anstess, Percy	Junction Mine	26-Oct-17	
Arksey, Wesley S.	Briggs Mine	7-Jan-15	
Arnold, William H.	Higgins Mine	4-Dec-15	
Arola, Matt	Oliver Mine	21-Apr-09	
Atkins, Charles	Cuprite Mine 500 level	10-Oct-24	
Badich, Peter Popvich	Denn Mine 1600 level 6xc	8-Nov-18	
Baker, John	Campbell Mine	1-Feb-44	
Balma, Frank	Junction Mine 1500 level 127 stope	27-Apr-19	
Barrett, C.T.	Briggs Mine	29-Apr-22	
Beecroft, R.F.	Cole Mine	16-Jun-61	
Beers, Joseph	Cole Mine 1000 level	31-Mar-08	
Benderach, Miki	Oliver Mine	16-Aug-11	
Benny, Thomas	Denn Mine	10-Jul-35	
Bernal, D.R.	Phelps Dodge mines surface facilities	9-Aug-68	
Besil, Joseph	Czar Mine 200 level	16-Dec-21	
Billing, Frank E.	Lowell Mine	18-Dec-06	
Blanco, Benjamin	Oliver Mine 1150 level 137 raise	6-May-12	
Blozevich, Frank	Gardner Mine	5-Oct-11	
Bowman, Frank	Bisbee West Mine	13-Dec-01	
Boyd, George	Holbrook Mine /Holbrook #1 Shaft	3-Sep-08	
Boyd, Spencer B	Junction Mine	2-Feb-06	
Boyle, John P.	Lowell Mine	12-Jan-11	
Brajovich, John	Shattuck Mine 800 level	31-Oct-07	

Branson, Albert A.	Holbrook #1 Mine	24-Dec-05	
Breen, Mike	Hoatson	16-Apr-15	
Brooks, Shelby Clay	Campbell Mine 1800 level 23 xc	19-Dec-36	
Brunas, Dominic	Congdon Mine	13-Feb-04	
Burgoon, Charles	Shattuck Mine 500 level 134 xc	18-Aug-16	
Burgos, Frank R.	Campbell Mine 2700 level	28-Feb-67	
Burks, S.D.	Campbell Mine 2833 level	2-Jan-45	
Byerly Henry May	Sacramento Pit	9-Jun-24	
Byerly, Perry, M.	Sacramento Mine	9-Feb-28	
Byrd, Perry Riley	Southwest Mine 6th level 5-15-1 stope	27-Mar-20	
Caine, John	Junction Mine 900 level	3-Mar-06	
Calderon, Carlos	Sacramento Pit	9-Jan-18	
Campbell, Frank	Junction Mine 1800 level	8-Sep-23	
Campbell, James	Pittsburg and Hecla Mine	6-Sep-03	
Campbell, Robert H.	Czar Mine	17-Jul-08	
Carbajal, Richard	Campbell Mine 2966 level 42 A stope	11-Nov-68	
Carter, Martin	Unknown Mine	Around 1902	
Carver, Edward Stanley	Cole Mine	24-Feb-47	
Casillas, Donaciano	Southwest Mine 3rd level	24-Apr-23	
Castenada, Francisco	Sacramento Pit	25-Mar-18	
Christian, James Henry	Spray Mine 600 level	3-Jun-09	
Clark Edward C.	Holbrook Mine	Feb 4, 1898	
Clark, John D.	Sacramento Mine 600 level	8-Feb-10	
Coburn, Charles A.	Wolverine Mine	6-Sep-18	
Cole, Steve	Southwest Mine	4-Nov-11	
Compton, Thomas J,	Lowell Mine	8-Sep-18	
Conklin, U	Holbrook#1 Mine 500 level 21 stope	7-Mar-01	

Conway, Earl A.	Sacramento Pit	28-Jul-23	
Conway, James F.	Gardner Mine	14-Sep-14	
Cook, Harry F.	Junction Mine Compressor House	4-Feb-11	
Corona, Sebastian	Nighthawk Mine	1-Nov-27	
Coronado, Porfirio	Sacramento Pit 5315 bench	21-May-23	
Cota, Antonio M.	Irish Mag Mine surface	30-Jan-25	
Coughran, R.	Holbrook Mine 500 level # 21 stope	Mar 1901	
Covarrvia, Juan	Sacramento Pit	25-Mar-18	
Coyne, Martin	Cole Mine	21-Oct-13	
Crawford Vere Monroe	Junction Mine 2000 level	8-Jan-28	
Critchley, James jr.	Czar Mine 400 level	8-Oct-09	
Crump, Ephraim Patrick	Sacramento Pit	19-Jan-18	
Cunningham, P.A.	Holbrook #1 Mine 100 level	28-Jun-1899	
Cunningham, Patrick	Oliver Mine	6-Feb-11	
Dage, Leon P.	Sacramento Mine 1000 level 3-15 stope	21-Sep-40	
Daoust, Usaii	Holbrook Mine stope #29	May 22, 1899	
Davidovich, Nick	Briggs Mine	9-Sep-13	
Dean, John Henry	Junction Mine	5-Apr-28	
Deck, John	Holbrook Mine	10-Feb-05	
Denne, Michael	Junction Mine 1300 Level	7-Apr-16	
Dexter, Walter	Cochise and Calumet Mine	30-Jun-27	
Di Paolo, Armando	Junction Mine	27-May-29	
Dickey, Sam	Cole Mine	17-Mar-05	
Dobovich, Samuel	Oliver Mine	16-Aug-07	
Dolan, John	Holbrook Mine		Apr 5, 1898
Drakenfield, Sidney	Sacramento Pit	9-Jan-18	

Draskovich, Marko	Shattuck Mine 600 level 8 stope	23-May-17	
Drew, Albert	Cole Mine	6-May-15	
Drury, William	Junction Mine 1500 level 19 stope	26-Jun-14	
Duder, Alex	Bisbee West Mine	13-Dec-01	
Dugie, Timothy S.	Campbell Mine 2700 Level	29-May-58	
Dykeman, Walter F.	Lowell Mine	14-Mar-09	
Earthal, Daniel George	Junction Mine 1100 level	10-Oct-06	
Egan, James	Wolverine Mine	26-Jul-21	
Engle, Robert	Shattuck Mine	5-Aug-07	
Enright, Jon	Spray Mine 100 level	24-Mar-07	
Eoff, George	Unknown Mine	24-Jan-18	
Erikson, Eric	Sacramento Mine 1500 level	9-Sep-30	
Esquibel, Miguel	Nighthawk Mine	16-Jul-23	
Fairclough, Charles	Hoatson Mine Hoist House	15-Feb-15	
Farrier, Price	Holbrook Mine	December 14, 1898	
Figueroa, Antonio	Dallas Mine	7-Jun-71	
Fling, F.L.	Campbell Mine 2833 level	2-Jan-45	
Flores, Blas	Southwest Mine 3rd level	24-Apr-23	
Flores, David Soliz	Denn Mine 2800 level 10 stope	7-Jan-46	
Fogelson, Lester Henry jr.	Junction Mine Yard	1955	
Frodin, John R.	Gardner Mine	7-Mar-12	
Frost O. Floyd	Sacramento Pit	7-May-18	
Gallagher, John	Czar Mine	3-Sep-10	
Garcia, Manuel	Junction Mine 2000 level 135xc	29-Jan-34	
Garcia, Tomas	Van Horn Shaft (lease)	9-Oct-20	
Garner, William Melvin	Campbell Mine	15-Nov-42	
George, William C.	Oliver Mine	20-Aug-09	
Gerdes, Henry R.	Denn Mine (surface)	29-Dec-40	
Gidley, Edward A.	Czar Mine 300 level	7-Jan-14	

Gill, Kenneth Noble	Cole Mine 1100 level caylyx raise	29-Mar-68	
Gomez, A.	Phelps Dodge lease by Hunt & Zananoria	1-Nov-18	
Gomez, Eduardo A.	Oliver Mine 1050 level (lease)	10-Feb-41	
Gomez, Fernando	Shattuck Mine 600 level	13-Jan-25	
Goodenstein, Sam	Czar Mine 300 level	4-Mar-08	
Goodwin, J.H.	Pittsburg and Hecla Mine	July 27, 1904	
Green, John Alexander	Holbrook # 2 Mine	30-Nov-11	
Green, Michael	Shattuck Mine Tramway Terminal	31-Dec-09	
Green, W.C.	Sacramento Mine 400 level	16-Sep-10	
Greer, Bill H.	Campbell Mine 2100 level 25 stope	3-Nov-38	
Gresham, James D.	Sacramento Pit	22-Apr-20	
Grier, Wison Percy	Junction Mine	8-Jul-05	
Griffith, Albert Frank	Campbell Mine 1700 level 229A stope	28-Aug-47	
Griggs, Matthew C.	Cole Mine	3-Oct-21	
Grossklaus, William	Czar Mine 100 level	9-Apr-06	
Gudlj, George	Shattuck Mine	19-Jul-20	
Gupton, W.R.	Cole Shaft	12-Aug-07	
Gutierrez, Antonio	Mardon lease possibly Holbrook mine	25-Jul-29	
Guzman, Manuel	Unknown	15-Mar-43	
Hairston, Oscar Evans	Campbell Mine	5-May-41	
Hall George C.	Holbrook # 2 Mine	25-Apr-06	
Hall, Walter	Southwest Mine	17-Aug-18	
Ham, Frank Alfred	Junction Mine	27-Feb-48	
Hamilton, Charles A.	Junction Mine 1800 level 231xc	18-Apr-36	
Hanley, Lee	Spray Mine	September 11, 1906 accident, died October 27, 1906	

Hansen, Robert	Czar Mine 200 level	23-Aug-02	
Hardt, Louis	Oliver Mine	21-Jan-18	
Harris, Albert	Gardner Mine 900 level 9-3-1 stope	5-May-08	
Harris, Dallas A.	Cochise and Calumet Mine	30-Jun-27	
Hatten, Floyd Elmo	Junction Mine	6-Oct-52	
Hayes, Ethelbert	Lake Superior & Pittsburg Mine # 2 or #3	28-Mar-07	
Heebee, Alvin	Holbrook # 2 Mine	13-Jun-07	
Helberg, Dick/Rinehart, Frank	Czar Mine	18-Feb-11	
Henderson, Austin	Holbrook #2 Mine 500 level	6-Jan-12	
Herr, Casper	Junction Shaft 1600 level	28-Sep-26	
Hiatt, Daniel Clarence	Sacramento Mine	18-Dec-14	
Hicks, Columbus, F.	Sacramento Mine 1700 level	24-May-24	
Hodge, Albert	Czar Mine 200 level	6-Jun-13	
Hodges, John T.	Saginaw Mine 350 Level	17-Jul-06	
Hoffman, Erick	Junction Mine 1500 level 66xc	25-Jul-14	
Holguin, Guillermo	Higgins Mine	21-Sep-20	
Holland, Harry	Holbrook Mine 300 level	18-Jan-01	
Hollister, Frank	Congdon Mine	13-Feb-04	
Horn, William	Sacramento Mine	4-Mar-15	
Howser, Henry	Briggs Mine 1200 level 121 XC	29-Jan-14	
Huber, Charles	Holbrook # 2 Mine	12-Jun-07	
Hudler, Carl	Saginaw Mine	27-Aug-04	
Huff J.B.	Gardner Mine 800 level	6-Mar-14	
Hunter, Mark Stanley	Southwest Mine	26-Oct-23	
Ireland, Robert	Shattuck Mine	23-Dec-17	
Jacobs, Roy C.	Uncle Sam Mine	8-Oct-12	
Jacques, Simon.	Czar Mine	23-Nov-12	
James, Edwin	Unknown Mine	31-Aug-33	
James, John H	Junction Mine	26-Oct-20	
Jean Joseph Ben	Southwest Mine 5th level	18-May-26	

Johnson , Andrew John	Denn Mine 1600 level 6xc	8-Nov-18	
Johnson, Edward	Briggs Mine	27-Dec-13	
Johnson, Edward	Cole Mine 1000 level 33 raise	17-Aug-12	
Johnson, Edward	Lowell Mine 1400 level 14-9 stope	17-Jun-12	
Johnson, Emil F.	Hoatson Mine	28-Jan-10	
Johnson, William T.	Gardner Mine	27-Sep-08	
Jones, Hugh	Lowell Mine 1300 level	4-Jun-10	
Jones, James L	Copper Queen Mine	November 7, 1890	
Juliff, Frank Melville	Junction Mine 1500 level 19 stope	26-Jun-14	
Juraservich, Elai	Oliver Mine 1050 level	21-Apr-09	
Kaneaster, Arthur	Denn Mine	20-May-36	
Keton, John	Holbrook#2 Mine 500 level	6-Aug-09	
Kewely, William Henry	Czar Mine 400 level	30-Aug-10	
Klinger, Hiram E.	Holbrook # 2 Mine	14-Jun-07	
Knucky C.L.	Holbrook # 2 Mine	15-Sep-08	
Krahn, Hugo	Czar Mine	15-Sep-05	
Krumlin, John C.	Higgins Tunnel	18-Sep-07	
Kultanen, Joseph	Lowell Mine 1300 level 13-1-3 stope	17-Jun-10	
La More, Richard	Denn Mine	17-Jan-27	
Lamb, Joseph H.	Sacramento Mine	20-Apr-11	
Lampi, Robert S.	Denn Mine	16-Nov-28	
Larned, Mitchel	Campbell Mine 3100 level	5-May-67	
Lauber, Henry	Spray Mine	16-Dec-08	
Lean, James	Cole Mine	17-Jan-06	
Lerwell, Thomas	Junction Mine	20-Nov-14	
Lewis, Oscar	Bisbee Queen Mine	7-Jun-27	
Lifman, Fred	Junction Mine 2000 level 21 stope	12-Jul-29	
Liggett, William	Junction Mine	18-Jul-17	
Linden, Emil	Oliver Mine	9-Mar-11	
Lobb, Charles jr.	Spray Mine 700 level	15-Feb-13	

Long, William P.	Holbrook Mine 300 level 32 stope	November 25, 1899	
Lorang, John	Denn Mine	24-Jul-18	
Love, George A.	Czar Mine 400 level	6-Jul-14	
Luke, Paul	Cole Mine, timber yard	1-Nov-09	
Maak, John	Holbrook #2 Mine 200 level	4-May-12	
Maquire, Michael	Unknown mine probably a CQCMCO mine	11-Jul-12	
Martin, Thomas	Spray Mine	18-Jun-13	
Martino, Cima	Czar Mine	Nov 1888	
Mason, Thomas jr.	White Tail Deer Mine 200 level	13-Dec-42	
Matson, James	Holbrook Mine 300 level	6-Nov-04	
McBurney, Thomas C.	Czar Mine	3-Sep-14	
McCall, W.G.	Wolverine Shaft	17-Feb-04	
McCarthy, J.	Undetermined C&A Mine	21-Jul-04	
McDonald, James H.	Junction Mine 2500 level	23-Jun-23	
McDougal, William	Junction Mine	26-Nov-09	
McEnroe, Michael	Gardner Mine	19-Mar-17	
McFarland, Albert	Cole Mine, Hoist Room	17-Oct-03	
McIntosh, H.B.	Dallas Mine	1-Mar-13	
McNeil, H. Leon	Sacramento Mine	26-Nov-23	
McNeill, James	South Bisbee Mine	15-May-99	
McOsker, Paul H.	Dallas Mine	9-Jun-20	
Means, Lyle Floyd.	Campbell Mine 2700 Level	26-Apr-65	
Menear, William T.	Czar Mine 200 level	6-Jun-13	
Merrill, Chester Henry	Denn Mine 2800 level 3 raise	1-Sep-44	
M'Ewen, Jodie C.	Spray Mine 600 level	2-Aug-10	
Midzor, Mike J.	Cole Mine 1000 level station	17-Jul-14	
Mihalevich, Moso	Oliver Mine 950 level	10-Oct-10	

Milam, Barney O.	Unknown Mine	27-Sep-39	
Miller, Charles A.	Holbrook # 2 Mine	8-Aug-07	
Miller, Chris (Millerkervich)	Irish Mag Mine	16-May-07	
Miller, Harry D.	Sacramento Pit	11-Jan-20	
Miller, Martin N.	Sacramento Mine 1700 level	24-May-24	
Miller, Percy	Cole Mine	25-May-48	
Miranda, Juan	Sacramento Pit	28-Jan-20	
Molander, Otto	Congdon Mine	13-Feb-04	
Monaghan, James P. jr	Campbell Mine 1800 level	6-Sep-35	
Morales, Ramon	Unknown Mine	4-Aug-27	
Moreno, Jose	Hargis Lease probably Czar Mine 100 level	21-Jan-25	
Morris, Mace	Oliver Mine	13-Apr-14	
Moyer, Lester R.	Junction Mine	13-Sep-19	
Mukavoc, John	Lowell Mine 1000 level	20-Nov-11	
Mulroe, Martin	Shattuck Mine 400 level	3-May-17	
Munoz, Jose	Sacramento Pit dump no.9	29-Apr-20	
Murich, Stephen	Spray Mine	11-Jan-07	
Murphy, Patrick	Junction Mine 1600 level	26-Oct-28	
Murray, James	Junction Mine	8-Mar-18	
Narche, Claude William	Calumet & Cochise Mine	7-Jun-21	
Netherlands, Joseph	Spray Mine 500 level Station	29-Nov-02	
Newton, William or Ruegg, E.	Czar Mine	14-Nov-06	
Nichols, Dave	Cuprite Mine shaft collar	16-Apr-07	
Norton, E.M.	Gardner Mine bottom of shaft	25-Nov-02	
Nowlin, Dewey G.	Sacramento Pit	7-Mar-23	
Nunez, Jose	Sacramento Pit	3-Sep-18	
Obertaxer, John	Gardner Mine 1000 level	11-May-08	
Ojala, Jacob	Oliver Mine	30-Sep-08	
Orton, William David	Sacramento Mine 800 level	22-Sep-27	
O'Sullivan, Michael J.	Undetermined C&A Mine	8-Feb-05	

Pacheco, Francisco jr.	Hargis Lease Probably 100 level Southwest Mine	30-Nov-24	
Page, George Andrew	Denn Mine 2200 level	13-Jan-42	
Pasnenan, Tovio	Irish Mag Mine	24-Sep-10	
Pattinson, Robert	Shattuck Mine	11-Dec-09	
Pavlicich, Leopold P.	Gardner Mine	22-Oct-14	
Pawlowski, Joseph	Gardner Mine 600 level	30-May-17	
Peper, Chris	Spray Mine	4-Sep-07	
Perez, Jose Antonio	Unknown Mine	1-Jul-41	
Perez, Luciano	Cole Mine 700 level of Interior Shaft	15-Nov-61	
Pesikan, Theodore	Junction Mine 1500 level 211 stope	27-May-19	
Peterson, Alfred	Sacramento Mine 1200 level	30-Apr-21	
Petrovich, George	Lake Superior & Pittsburg #3 Shaft 1000 level #73 stope	26-Jul-07	
Phelps, Gilbert A.	Wolverine #1 Mine	27-Aug-03	
Pierce, Charles Whitney	Campbell Mine	1-Sep-39	
Pilarczyr, Florian M.	Unknown Mine	December 3, 1941 (died May 26, 1943)	
Poole, George	Junction Mine 2200 level	27-Mar-33	
Pope, William	Hoatson Mine	11-Jun-05	
Popovich, Peter	Irish Mag Mine	21-Dec-06	
Poquette, Arthur	Oliver Mine	9-May-11	
Queen, William A.	Oliver Mine	4-Jan-05	
Rajhala John	Briggs Mine	11-Jul-16	
Ramsen, Alfred	Junction Mine 1600 level	28-Feb-27	
Ranteria, Santiago	Oliver Mine shaft collar	23-Jan-11	
Rawley, Robert A.	Junction Mine 1800 level 231xc	18-Apr-36	
Reed, William B.	Hoatson Mine	17-Jul-08	
Regan, John L.	Southwest Mine 3rd level	29-May-22	
Regnier, John	Lowell Mine	30-Nov-09	

Reibuffo, Joseph	Gardner Mine 700 level	22-Feb-13	
Richardson, Raymond Lee	Campbell Mine 2566 level	11-Mar-47	
Rigler, Jake J.	Shattuck Mine	26-Jul-06	
Rivera, Peter	Cole Mine	19-Nov-54	
Roberts, William	Junction Mine 1300 Level	27-Nov-15	
Rodriguez, Juan	Manganese workings near Cole Shaft	6-Aug-18	
Rogers, James	Holbrook # 2 Mine	5-Apr-10	
Romero, Domincio	Czar Mine waste dump	December 14, 1896	
Romero, Jesus	Hargis Lease probably 100 level Southwest Mine	30-Nov-24	
Rossi, Bartolo	Oliver Mine 1350 level 8 stope	16-Jun-09	
Sakota, Stojan	Briggs Mine	7-Jan-15	
Salas, Juan	Sacramento Pit	13-Nov-18	
Sanberg, Erick	Czar Mine /Southwest Shaft	28-Apr-11	
Sandoval, Manuel A.	Cole Mine	1956	
Sessions, Taylor Bentley	Sacramento Mine 1100 level	13-Oct-21	
Shea, James	Hoatson Mine 1100 level	20-Aug-08	
Short, Phillip Arthur	Junction Mine 1800 level	14-Jun-29	
Siltala, Gust	Oliver Mine 1350 level, 25 xc	11-Dec-11	
Simpson, Frank Silas	Holbrook #2 Mine 200 level 3-81 stope	4-May-12	
Skinner, David	Lavender Pit	22-Oct-54	
Sloutz, Matt	Junction Mine	29-Dec-18	
Smith, Charles N.	Junction Mine 1600 level 317 stope	13-Oct-26	
Sommers, Henry Claude		11-Jun-21	
Speier, william	Oliver Mine sawmill	14-May-10	
Springer, Urias W.	Gardner Mine	14-Nov-09	
Stalley, George L.	Lake Superior& Pittsburg #3 Mine	17-May-22	
Sterberg, Andy	Cole Mine	23-Sep-14	
Stewart, George Washington	Southwest Mine 3rd level	11-Jul-25	

Stewart, Henry	Campbell Mine 1600 level 478 Stope	6-Jan-34	
Stijipcich, John	Oliver Mine 850 level 74xc	27-Aug-09	
Stone, George	Holbrook Mine 400 level	5-Jan-00	
Stringer, Donald Eugene	Lavender Pit	22-Oct-54	
Supancich, Jake	Unknown Mine	27-Jan-28	
Sutherland, George	Czar Mine 400 level	22-Nov-20	
Swanson, Gust Lailola	Cole Mine	26-May-12	
Swanson, John	Oliver Mine 650 level	8-Jul-04	
Switzer, Jacob C.	Briggs Mine near 1200 level	2-Jul-10	
Tanori,Victoriano	Southwest Mine 3rd level	24-Apr-23	
Taylor, Thomas	Lowell Mine	3-Sep-10	
Taylor, William A.	Sacramento Mine 1700 – 1800 levels Sacramento Winze	11-Apr-24	
Teel, Charles William	Czar Mine (Surface)	14-Aug-52	
Terran, Enrique	Wolverine Mine	26-Jul-21	
Tetter, Pete	Spray mine 500 level 87 stope	4-Sep-07	
Thayer, Daniel T.	Junction Mine 1600 level	7-Aug-18	
Thornberry, Thomas	William Reese lease	30-Jul-18	
Tomasoni, Bert	Oliver Mine	24-Apr-12	
Tonkyro, Paul John	Dallas Mine 1000 level 424 xc 193 raise	16-Dec-53	
Tramp, Charles	Czar Mine	31-Dec-11	
Tremain, Frank	Holbrook #1 Shaft	17-Feb-04	
Trengove, Thomas H.	Gardner Mine 700 level 8-11-10 stope	22-Sep-09	
Treyne, Michael	Shattuck Mine	16-Aug-16	
Unknown Mexican man	Pittsburg and Hecla Mine	July 27,1904	
Unknown Miner	Bisbee West Mine	January- February 1902	
Urrutia, Maximino	Sacramento Pit	20-Nov-18	
Vaernerijk , Rene	Cole Mine 1000 level	5-May-16	

Valenzuela, Jose	Campbell Mine (probably)	9-Feb-63	
Vasquez, Florenzo	Sacramento Pit	9-Jan-18	
Vastado,Modesto Olibas	Sacramento Pit	9-Jan-18	
Vershay, Joe	Holbrook # 2 Mine	28-Nov-08	
Villaneda, Juan	Unknown Mine	14-Jul-20	
Vlacis, William	Gardner Mine 900 level 8-23 stope	23-Jan-13	
Vucedalich, Chris Prenovich	Sacramento Shaft 1600 level	19-Oct-22	
Vuckovich, Nicholas	Oliver Mine 1000 level	21-Jan-05	
Vucurovich, Bozo	Shattuck Mine 500 level	13-Mar-06	
Vujacich, Sam	Hoatson Mine 1200 level	24-Jun-14	
Vuksanovich,Ilia	Southwest Mine 3rd level	29-May-22	
Wacek, John	Cole Mine	1-Jul-12	
Walton, Hamilton	Sacramento Mine 1200 level	26-Feb-17	
Ware, G.E.	Irish Mag /Oliver Mine 1150 Level	29-Sep-06	
Warne, John	Holbrook # 2 Mine 300 level	3-Jan-12	
Warner, Charles C.	Holbrook #1 Mine	15-Jun-04	
Wasby, Matt	Cochise Mine 900 level	22-Mar-07	
Watkins, Albert G.	Southwest Mine	29-Dec-15	
Welander, Peter Harold	White Tail Deer Mine 200 level	13-Dec-42	
Welch, Michael	Gardner Mine	27-Sep-08	
Whisand, James E.	Czar Mine 400 level	28-Mar-20	
White, Elwin J.	Higgins Mine 200 level	29-Jul-20	
White, R.H.	Sacramento Mine 1400 level	6-Apr-12	
Whitfield, Herman F.	Cole Mine 1200 level	6-Mar-50	
Williams, Marvin F.	Cole Mine 900 level	20-Jul-17	
Williams, Thomas Richard	Sacramento Mine 1500 level	3-May-16	
Williamson, John E.	Junction Mine	19-Jan-26	

Wollman, George Basil	Sacramento Mine 1700 level	15-May-39	
Wood, F.W.	Holbrook#2 mine 400 level	20-Nov-07	
Wright, Frank	Unknown Mine	30-Apr-04	
Wright, Thomas Wade	Junction Mine 1600 level 16 stope	19-Jul-19	
Wright, William	Spray Mine stope #3 between the 700 and 800 levels	1-Feb-06	
Wycoff, William P.	Junction Mine	26-Nov-09	
Ybarra, Felipe	Nighthawk Mine	7-Jun-23	
Yokinen, Tsak	Irish Mag Mine 850 level 25 raise	23-Mar-11	
Young, W.S.	Holbrook Mine	February 4, 1898	
Zboray, Joseph	Oliver Mine 1150 Level	12-Sep-06	
Zoricic, John	Shattuck Mine 800 level 2 xc	21-Oct-06	

Site of the Vucedalich accident 1600 level Sacramento Mine

County of Cochise, ss.

The Territory of Arizona
In
The matter of the Inquisition } Before S K Williams
upon the body of U. Doust, } Coroner ex officio
deceased

Territory of Arizona } ss.
County of Cochise

402

R. Poulglaze being by me first
duly sworn deposes & says:—
What is your name?
R. Polglaze.
Where do you reside?
In Bisbee Cochise Co., Arizona
What is your occupation?
I am a miner.
Are you so employed at present?
Yes Sir.
By Whom?
By the Copper Queen Con. Mining Co.,
Did you know U. Doust during
his life time.
Yes Sir.
Was he employed by said Company?
yes Sir.
Did you & the deceased work together
as partners, in the mine of the
Copper Queen Company?
Yes. Sir.

onto a truck and ran him
to the station, and from the
station he was taken to the surface.
Was he still alive?
Yes, the last I saw of him he was
breathing.
I did not go to the surface with
him.
I went back to where we were
working & picked up his clothes,
and I took them to the changeroom on the surface.
When I reached the surface the
other men had taken him
to the Company Hospital.
Is this all that you know about
this matter.
Yes Sir.
Was ~~this rock~~ the falling of this
rock due to any carelessness or neglegence
of any person under the employ of
the Companys?
No Sir, It was purely an accident,
~~I am unavoidable~~
The only cause that I can see, is
due to the jar of his Ax which he
was driving the wedge with.
This is certainly the only way that
I can account for it.

2

Were you working together as partners, to-day, May 22 - 1899?

Yes Sir.

What if anything happened to-day which you would term unusual?

Well, we started to work, in what what is commonly known as Slope No 29, of the, Holbrook, we put in what is known as a Cap-Sill & Tie, for the timbers to rest on, and our timbers were brought to us, by Isaac Oberg (the timberman) at about fifteen minutes to 2 o'clock A.M. and Mr Doust & myself. put up the timbers, After we stood up the posts, we make a platform, to stand on, we then put up our cap & tie, I handed him the blocks & wedges & he wedged the set. and after the set was wedged he told me "to go & get him a tenant-block" I brought him a tenant-block & he told me to cut it just six inches long as it was too long." & while I was cutting him the tenant-block

491

he took the pick up & commenced
to trim down the roof or rock
over heads, and after I had the
tenant-block cut, I gave it
to him, & he said "It is all right"
& told me to give him a wedge
to go between the block & the
ground, so I gave him a wedge
and while he was driving the
wedge in, the there was a large
rock, which I should judge would
weigh 300 lbs, came down,
and the jar of the rock falling
put out our lights,—I went just
one set back to where we had a
candle burning & got a light from
it, and when I came back,
I found the platform which we
had built, with one side broken
down—, Mr. Doust was lying on
the ground, with this large rock
lying on his face, I immediately
call pulled the rock off from
him & called, to an Italian
who we call "Joe" & Aug Wetterau
to come down, that old Doust
was killed. They came immediately,
and we lifted him and put him

We both examined the rock over head, when we came on this morning, I put my light on the end of my measuring stick, and held the light up to the ground, and decided that it was safe to work under.

R. Polglaze

Subscribed & sworn to before me this 22nd day of May 1899.

S. K. Williams

Coroner ex officio

In Coroner's Office of Precinct No 2,

County of Cochise, Territory of Arizona.

The Territory of Arizona)
)
              In   )
)
The matter of the Inquisition)
upon the body of W. Daoust,)
)
         deceased   )
)
              Territory of Arizona)
              County of Cochise   ) ss.

....

  We, the jury summoned to appear before S. K. Williams
Coroner ex officio of the town of Bisbee, County of Cochise, Territory, at
his office this 22nd day of May A. D. 1899, to inquire into the cause of
the death of U. Daoust, deceased, who was killed by a cave in the Mines of
the Copper Queen Consolidated Mining Company, in Bisbee, in said County and
Territory, having been duly summoned, sworn and qualified according to law,
and having made such Inquisition, after first inspecting the body, and hearing all testimony adduced in said action, upon our oaths each and all do say
That we find the deceased was named _Ulson Daoust_ was a
native of _Canada_, aged about _50_ years, that he
came to his death on this 22nd day of May A. D. 1899, in the Mines of the
Copper Queen Consolidated Mining Company, in Bisbee, in said County and
Territory, and that his death was caused from the effects of _injuries_
received from falling rock in a cave
in the Stope No. 29 of the Mines of the Copper
Queen Consolidated Mining Company
which was accidental as aforesaid. &c.
And we hereby fully exonorate said Company
and all other persons from any Criminal
or negligent prosecution.

All of which we do hereby duly certify to, by this Inquisition, in writing,
by us signed, this 22nd day of May A. D. 1899.

        H. C. Crydass..........(seal)
        Wm M Loggett..........(seal)
        Geo H Lee..........(seal)
        Peter C Hansen..........(seal)
        Oliver P Hunt..........(seal)
        Jeff Hollman..........(seal)
        George Bedick..........(seal)
        Lewis Tupple..........(seal)

In the Matter of the Inquisition
Into the Cause of the Death of

CHRIS VUCEDALICH,   *1492*

Deceased.

MR. DUGAN,

called as a witness herein, having been first duly sworn,
was examined by Coroner Ex-Officio, W. P. Craig, and testified as follows:

CORONER:

Q.   What are your initials, Mr. Dugan?

A.   John B.

Q.   Just state here for the Jury, how you come to get the
      body, and the time, and where, and all about it.

A.   Well, the body of the deceased, Chris Primevich was
      taken from the Sacramento shaft, - that was on Satur-
      day morning, and taken to the Morgue; examination show-
      ed that the body was very badly decomposed, likewise,
      very badly swollen, - probably about at least twice
      the normal size.   The face and head were badly crush-
      ed, likewise the chest.   There was no close examina-
      tion made, on account of the greatly decomposed condi-
      tion of the body, and the swollen condition also, but
      it was very apparent at the first glance, what caused
      the man's death.   The body was in such shape that no
      close examination was given, but the man's body and
      face and head were just crushed beyond recognition, -
      impossible to recognize him.

Q.   By what means did you get his name; what did you under-
      stand his name was?

A.   His name was given to us on the death certificate, as
      Chris Primevich Vucedalich; both names were given to
      us.

Q.   The reason I asked that question, is, there seems to
      have been two different names used by the deceased here

by the two Companies, and to clear it up to the Jury, I wanted it brought out, if you knew.   And, both names now are used on the deceased at your Undertaking Parlors?

A.   Yes sir.

Q.   And they were filled in on the death certificate?

A.   Yes sir.

Q.   Then, in your opinion, the condition of the body when you got it at the Sacramento shaft, was that of a man who had been suffocated by some means, - smothered?

A.   Yes; the body showed that he not only suffocated, but life had just been squeezed completely out; the tongue and eyes were just squeezed out of position.

Q.   (To the Jury)

Any other questions, gentlemen?

JUROR:

Q.   Say, Mr. Dugan, did you examine the body close enough to know whether the legs were broken, or not?

A.   Why, no, I did not; the hips were crushed, -

Q.   That would extend one leg longer than the other, would it not?

A.   The body was crushed, you know, pretty hard, - out of its natural shape.

Q.   That is what I thought, in viewing the body.

A.   The kind of position he was in when decomposition took place, - -

Q.   The reason I asked the question, - he was described to me as 5 foot 6 inches; the position of the body in the basket looked like a taller man.

JUROR:

Q.   You think he was suffocated or crushed?

-3-

A.   Well, he was crushed, - life was crushed immediately,
       you know, crushed out immediately, no question; no
       suffocation, I don't think; life was extinct right
       in the moment.

CORONER:

Q.   The purpose of asking those questions formerly by me,
       was to get the immediate cause of his death. He would
       suffocate, though he might not have been instantly kill-
       ed by the concussion on his head and body anyway. It
       is a matter simply to get before the Jurors here, in
       your opinion, what would be the immediate cause of
       death.
A.   Well, it would not be suffocation, because life was
       completely out of him before he had a chance to suffo-
       cate.

JUROR:

Q.   As far as I am concerned, I am satisfied as to who it
       was, - this man. I think that is what you are trying
       to do, Judge?
A.   Yes, simply trying to establish who it was, and how he
       met his death.

CORONER:

Q.   Any further questions from the Jury? That is all,
       Mr. Dugan.

                                        Witness Excused.

ISIDOR STRAUSSNIG,

called as a witness herein, having been first duly sworn,
was examined by Coroner Ex-Officio, W. P. Craig, and testified as follows:

CORONER:

Q.   Now, you can state here, for the benefit of the Jury,
      just what took place there at the time this man met
      his death.

A.   Why, when we came on down, he had not room on the bot-
      tom, so he was digging out on the bottom, and then I
      was working in my place, about fifteen feet apart from
      him, and he was, - had not room for his timber. I was
      not quite finished for my room, so he went down to the
      manway to get his timber, and then he come up and told
      me I should go down and hoist his timber up, and then
      I come up, and I heard him set up the post, and he had
      not quite room for the cap, - and we fixed the staging, -
      platform; he was working, and then he said I can go down
      and get my timber ready, - he make room for the cap, so
      I went down, got my timber to the manway, and got the
      stuff about half way in, then I hear a cave; last about
      ten seconds, - not longer. Then I went up, and it quit
      right away. I called his name, - I see big muck pile
      where he was working, and I went down right away and get
      the motorman; I guess he run right away to see about it.
      In a very short time, Mr. foreman was there, and lots
      of men were there to start rescue work. That is about
      all I know.

JUROR:

Q.   Was he stoping or drifting?

-5-

A.   Stoping.   He was working three days in the set; was
        blasting about thirty holes, - hard ground there where
        he was working, and it was not looking bad.   We was
        not expecting at all that anything would happen.

JUROR:

Q.   You did not think the ground was dangerous then, at all?

A.   It was not open so much; not quite three-quarters of a
        set was open.

Q.   Are you a miner?

A.   Yes.

Q.   Was he a miner?

A.   Yes.

Q.   Able to protect himself?

A.   Oh, yes, he was working good.

Q.   Both getting miner's wages?

A.   Yes sir.

Q.   You was working in a stope, were you?

A.   Yes; five sets off from the floor, - from the bottom,
        about five sets.

Q.   And you had the post and sill up, did you?

A.   We had the post standing, and platform, and he was only
        working for a cap, - not much ground to take out.

Q.   Did you have your tie up?

A.   No, we was not working for a tie, only for post and cap.

Q.   The post and cap was up?

A.   No, not the cap, - making room for the cap; had the post
        standing.

Q.   The back seemed to be alright, did it?

A.   Was looking not so bad.

Q.   That is all.

-6-

CORONER:

Q.   I think that is all.

Witness Excused.

LEONARD WARMINGTON,

called as a witness herein, having been first duly sworn,
was examined by Coroner Ex-Officio, W. P. Craig, and testified as follows:

CORONER:

Q.   Now, Mr. Warmington, if you will tell the Jury just
       what you know about this affair, when your attention
       was called to it, etc.

A.   The last time I was in this place was Wednesday night,
       Wednesday evening, - probably eight o'clock, between
       seven and eight, - I just don't know, - -

Q.   On the 18th?

A.   Yes sir, Wednesday night.   Thursday evening, I got
       there about five minutes to eight, - that was, I start-
       ed in, in the thirteenth, and just got down to this
       place, - this was the next place I would go into, and
       the motorman, Ericksen, was there by the chute.   He
       said, "I think this place caved in."   I started up the
       ladder, - met Mr. Straussnig coming down.   He said, "My
       partner is sure caved en", and Osler was around the cor-
       ner making out his time book, so I run around and get

-7-

Jack. We went up and saw the situation. Osler walked over the pile on the inside, where Straussnig was
working, - it was alright. Then we rustled some men
and started to rescue him. The dirt apparently had
came from his own set. We worked there until, - I
stayed until 7:30 in the morning; came back again 3:30
that afternoon, stayed until 7:30 next morning. Then
he was released from where he was caught. He was working for a post and cap; this was to be the left side of
lead set, I believe, the right hand side was waste. He
was cutting out for a post and cap, intending to turn a
lead to the left. There was black, hard sulphide there,
and this was a top slice. All the way down, over where
this fellow was working, had been iron waste; on this
floor it made ore. This Chris Vucedalich, he was working in this place.

Q. At what time now, would you place it, that the cave in
took place?

A. Eight o'clock.

Q. On what date?

A. Friday night.

Q. Friday?

A. Thursday night, the 18th, - Thursday night.

Q. Not the 18th then, - Wednesday was the 18th.

A. Thursday, on the 19th.

Q. On the 19th?

A. Yes sir, Thursday.

Q. About what hour?

A. Eight o'clock.

Q. This all occurred in Bisbee, Arizona?

A. Yes sir; Sacramento Mine.

-8-

Q.   I think that is all.

JUROR:

Q.   What position do you hold there?

A.   Night foreman.

Q.   This ground was not considered extra dangerous, or any-
     thing of the kind, was it?

A.   No sir, considered a good place, - very much surprised
     to find out that it had caved.

Q.   In your opinion, what was the cause of this, - just a
     big boulder broke loose, or something of the kind?

A.   The boulder we found when the body was first discovered,
     looked like nearly the width of the set.   The boys told
     me when they came to break it up, it was not so thick as
     they thought it might be, - long and narrow.   I had known
     this fellow about two and a half years.

Q.   Good miner?

A.   Yes, good miner.

Q.   Able to protect himself?

A.   Yes, he worked for me over at the Lowell.   I worked at
     the Lowell two years ago last April.

Q.   (To the Jury)   Any other questions?
     That is all.

                                        Witness Excused.

J. B. RILEY,

called as a witness herein, having been first duly sworn,
was examined by Coroner Ex-Officio, W. P. Craig, and testified as follows:

CORONER:

Q.   Mr. Riley, you can make a statement, if you will,
      here, for the benefit of the Jury, just what you know
      about this matter.

A.   Well, I was at work in what is known as 16-6 D stope,
      right in the immediate vicinity, and I was called down
      by the Shifter, and told to bring my partner. When I
      got down on the level, he told me there was a man bur-
      ied. Well, I went up, and we commenced to lag over to
      keep the rock from going down the manway, first thing,
      so that we could get inside and lace the cave, so as to
      get in to the man that was covered. We worked there un-
      til 7:30 in the morning, until relief came; worked from
      eleven the following day, on the 20th, until seven o'-
      clock Saturday, - -

Q.   Seven o'clock Saturday morning?

A.   Yes sir. We had him free when I left there, all except
      his right foot, -

Q.   Alright, go ahead.

A.   Well, that is all I know, - - as far as I know.

Q.   Were you acquainted with the deceased during his life
      time?

A.   I saw him the night previous to his death, first time.
      I had seen him before, but not in the Sacramento.

Q.   You recognized him as this party mentioned here in the
      Inquisition?

                        -10-

A.   Knowing he had worked there, I came to the conclusion
       he was the same man. The night previous to his death
       he told me he worked there, - I met him down on the
       level.

Q.   I think that is all, unless there is some question from
       some member of the Jury.
       That is all, Mr. Riley.

                                           Witness Excused.

                   LEONARD WARMINGTON RE-CALLED,

JUROR:

Q.   Say, was the Mine Inspector, or his Deputy, - did he
       come to the place of the accident and examine it?

A.   Yes, he was notified right away; he stayed all night.

Q.   (To the Coroner)
       Judge, I would like to have him subpoenaed as a witness
       here.

A.   Very well, that is your privilege.

       RECESS TAKEN FOR TWENTY MINUTES UNTIL THE DEPUTY MINE
       INSPECTOR ARRIVED.

                          -11-

ED. MYERS,

called as a witness herein, having been first duly sworn,
was examined by Coroner Ex-Officio, W. P. Craig, and testified as follows:

CORONER:

Q. What official capacity do you hold?

A. Why, I am Deputy State Mine Inspector, by appointment.

Q. Now, you can answer any questions that the Jury may
    wish to ask, Mr. Myers.

A. Yes sir.

JUROR:

Q. Say, Mr. Myers, you was called to the place where this
    accident occurred?

A. I was, yes.

Q. Please state just exactly what you found?

A. Well, when I got there, - - I was down at the Political
    Meeting when I got word; I got up home, and got there as
    quick as I could, - I presume it was about 9:30, - -

CORONER:

Q. What date do you refer to?

A. The 19th. When I got there, why, I don't know, - there
    was about eight or ten men working around there, getting
    everything ready to find out the extent of the accident,
    to see if they could find the man, - it was presumed at
    first they could get him alive. It was a very narrow
    place, - thought they could get him through the timbers.
    The ground had broken from above. Where the accident
    occurred, it was just in a narrow space, you know, right
    going off of the chute, presumably one set to work, and

-12-

they were trimming it down, - lacing it down to keep
the ground from running, which is proper. When they
got that done and cleaned out, about five o'clock in
the morning, - had not found him yet. They were fixing up to see if they could find him underneath, -dir-
ectly underneath. I left at five o'clock in the morning, - it was a question when they would get him; the
place was so small only two men could work at a time, -
just a mass of tangled timbers. After they would locate him, it would take some time to get him out. I
did not see the nature of the ground before the accident happened, but it was good solid land all around
the timber, - never moved a particle while I was there.

Q.   You would consider that it was properly handled?

A.   I would, yes; one of those accidents that you would consider safe, until it happens. I would call it a trade
risk myself. Further than that, I know nothing about
the ground. It wasn't looking bad, and even the post
the man was standing at the time of the accident, was
standing erect at the time they got it cleaned out.

Q.   He was standing erect?

A.   The post was. I understand he was getting ready to
place the cap over the post; his partner started back
to get something, - while he was out, the roof come in.
That is the way I understand it.

Q.   Mr. Myers, in your experience as a miner, you would consider it probably one of the unavoidable, - one of those
things which occur, - -

A.   Yes, one you couldn't explain, nor look out for, - cannot guard against it; everything looks alright, - you go
ahead and do this work, and, in this case, it came in on
them.

-13-

507

Q.   Treacherous, you would call it?

A.   Yes, treacherous is as good a word as you could use
     for it.

Q.   The only reason you was not here on time, was a mis-
     understanding as to the time?

A.   Yes, absolutely; I understood it was four o'clock.
     I intended to be here then.

Q.   That is all.

CORONER:

     Any further questions from the Jury?
     That is all, Mr. Myers.

                                        Witness Excused.

-14-

508

IN THE JUSTICE COURT OF PRECINCT NO. 2

COUNTY OF COCHISE, STATE OF ARIZONA.

In the Matter of the Inquisition)
)
Into the Cause of the Death of)
)
CHRIS VUCEDALICH,) VERDICT OF CORONER'S JURY.
)
Deceased.)
)

We, the undersigned, having been duly summoned and sworn
by W. P. Craig, Ex-Officio Coroner of Cochise County, Arizona,
to act as Jurors in the matter of inquisition into the cause of
the death of CHRIS VUCEDALICH, having viewed the remains and considered all the evidence presented, and being fully informed in
the premises, upon our oaths do say that from the evidence before
us we find the facts to be as follows:

That the name of the Deceased was CHRIS VUCEDALICH; that

he was of the age of about 39 years, at the time of his death;

that he came to his death in Bisbee, County of Cochise, State

of Arizona, at about the hour of 8:00 o'clock P.M., on the 19th

day of October, A. D. 1922, From, "AN UNAVOIDABLE CAVE IN, IN

THE SACRAMENTO MINE, WHILE EMPLOYED AT STOPING."

To all of which we certify by attaching our signatures

hereto this 23rd day of October, A. D. 1922.

Isaac Jacobson,

Otho Fowler,

F. Van Voast,

G. S. Routh,

Ed. Barnett,

O. D. Piper.

Examples of Phelps Dodge-Copper Queen Branch Accident Reports

R.V. Encinas jr. & J.D. Pursley

Queen rocker & a timber truck, 6th level Southwest Mine.

Form 532 D. Rev.

PHELPS DODGE CORPORATION—Copper Queen Branch
ACCIDENT REPORT

Answer All Questions Fully   Date ___1-9___ 19_25_

Date of Accident ___1-8___, 19_25_   Hours ___10:00___ A.M

LOCATION—Department or Division ___Cole___

Mine Level ___1100___   Is this a lost-time injury? ___Yes___

Working Place ___315 XC___   Was blue card issued? ___Yes___

Name of Injured Employee ___R. V. Encinas Jr.___   Payroll. ___1735___

Residing at ___Bisbee arizona___   Married ___X___ Single ___

Occupation ___motor swamper___   Wage Rate ___11___

What was employee doing at time of accident? ___Putting wrecked H car back on track___

Had he passed an examination on the procedure for this work? ___yes___

Was this his regular job? ___yes___   Was employee experienced? ___yes___

Was accident caused by violation of any rule or instruction? ___no___

What instructions were given employee by boss concerning work being done? ___They He was told to service 339 XC___

Injured employee's statement as to how accident occurred ___was told that a H car came off track and when he was putting it back on his foot slipped and he sprained his back___

Was injury caused by fellow employee? ___no___   If so, give name ___

Names of eye-witnesses to accident ___none___

Nature of reported injury ___sprained Back___

Bosses statement regarding accident ___I think he may had other things on his mind and wasn't paying attention to what he was doing___

State fully how accident could have been prevented ___By getting Help and using a bar to lift car with___

Accident investigated by ___A. L. Renteria #620 R. V. Encinas jr. #1735___

___J. E. Williams___

Shift Boss ___R. V. McC___ Foreman

The Following Data Is to be Furnished by the Saftey Inspector

Exact nature and extent of injury ___STRAINED LOWER BACK MUSCLE___

Classification as to,

Fault:—Injured Employee ___I-E___ Fellow Employee ___ Faulty Equipment ___ Direct Supervisor ___

Cause:— ___20 HAULAGE - 3 LIFTING CAR___

I. Agency ___10 - MINE CAR___   II. Type ___13 - HAULAGE___

III. Supervisory ___5 - UNSAFE PRACTICE___   IV. Physical ___NONE___

___2 - EMPLOYEE___
___d - WORKING METHOD___

___J. C. Ramsey___ Safety Inspector

(One Copy Each to:—Mine Superintendent, Safety Department, Foreman)

511

Form 532 B. Rev.

PHELPS DODGE CORPORATION—Copper Queen Branch
ACCIDENT REPORT

<u>Answer All Questions Fully</u> Date 1-18-, 19 75

Date of Accident .... 1-16-, 19 75 Hours .... 1:15 A_M

LOCATION—Department or Division .... Cole #3

Mine Level .... 1100 Is this a lost-time injury? NO

Working Place .... 339XC Was blue card issued? yes

Name of Injured Employee .... J.D. Pursley Payroll 952

Residing at .... Bisbee, Arizona Married ✓ Single ....

Occupation .... Miner Wage Rate 6

What was employee doing at time of accident? .... BARRING DOWN

Had he passed an examination on the procedure for this work? .... Yes

Was this his regular job? .... Yes Was employee experienced? .... yes

Was accident caused by violation of any rule or instruction? .... NO

What instructions were given employee by boss concerning work being done? To BAR DOWN Then Boom out

Injured employee's statement as to how accident occurred WAS BARING DOWN, Stuck Head out AGAST Timber To see The BACK & A small Rock Fell & Hit Front Tooth

Was injury caused by fellow employee? NO If so, give name ....

Names of eye-witnesses to accident .... B.F. Stewart # 1798

Nature of reported injury .... Chiped upper Front Tooth

Bosses statement regarding accident .... They Had Blasted At Lunch Time & Was Just Starting To BAR Down

State fully how accident could have been prevented By Not Putting Head out From under Timber

Accident investigated by J.D. Pursley #952 - B.F. Stewart #1798 - C.L. Havercamp
C.L. Havercamp

.... Shift Boss .... R.R. McCollester .... Foreman

The Following Data is to be Furnished by the Safety Inspector

Exact nature and extent of injury Chipped upper FRONT Tooth - Right Side

Classification as to,

Fault: — Injured Employee J.E. Fellow Employee .... Faulty Equipment .... Direct Supervisor ....

Cause: — 9 Fall of Ground A DRIFTS

I. Agency 2 Falling object II. Type FALL OF GROUND

III. Supervisory 4 Lack of Concentration IV. Physical 13 Improper working Conditions
B - Inattention 1 - Miscellaneous C.L. Ramsey

.... Safety Inspector

(One Copy Each to: — Mine Superintendent, Safety Department, Foreman)

Train hauling decayed timber on the 3rd level Southwest mine.

PHELPS DODGE CORPORATION
COPPER QUEEN BRANCH
- - -

Discussion of a Lost Time Accident Occurring in June, 1968

Report No. 1

Underground Department - Div. "C" Cole

D. E. Altamirano, payroll no. 1549, motor swamper, was injured in 80-crosscut at 69 general chute on the 800-foot level at 11:00 P.M. on June 6, 1968.

Nature of Injuries: Fractured right collar bone; right 1, 2, 3 and 4th ribs; punctured right lung.

Estimated Period of Disability: 6 to 8 weeks.

How Accident Occurred: Altamirano was caught between a Granby car and drift post, rolled and pushed against the protruding end of the chute load-stand floor. R. Salazar, motorman, was pushing the car with Baldwin trolley motor no. 45 when he saw Altamirano caught between the car and timbers.

Investigation was held at the scene by the following committee: Unit Secretaries R. E. Brandt, Timberman, S. L. Butler and M. C. Martinez, Miners; G. H. Leonard, Division Night Foreman, M. M. Arias, Shift Boss, and C. J. Wright, Safety Inspector. Salazar assisted.

Salazar and Altamirano were doing routine work when this accident occurred. They had already pulled two 9-"G" car trains of ore from 69 general chute and had started loading the 3rd train. Salazar, operating the motor, pushed eight cars of the train past the chute and spotted the car next to the motor under the chute. Altamirano got on the loading stand and had filled approximately half of the car when according to Salazar, he called from the motor and told him they would not have time to finish loading the train, and take it out and dump it before the end of shift. Altamirano then turned off the air at the cylinder which opens and closes the chute door, cleaned muck off the loadstand floor and got down off the loadstand. He uncoupled the first car from the second car and signalled Salazar to pull down so he could clean the track under the chute. Salazar stated that after pulling the car down three or four feet from the chute he got off the motor and was helping clean the track when he noticed the chute door was not completely closed. He told the committee he instructed Altamirano to get back on the loadstand and that he would push the car back under the chute to avoid spilling muck when Altamirano closed the door with the cylinder. Salazar stated that he went back the motor, heard Altamirano pounding on the chute door with a sledge hammer,

and then, without having received a signal, started backing the car under the
chute. He had pushed approximately half of the 11-foot car under the chute
when he saw Altamirano caught between the car and timber. Altamirano's
statements in regard to details leading up to the accident were contrary to
Salazar's. According to Altamirano Salazar did not leave the cab of the motor
while the track was being cleaned and that he told Salazar he was going upon
the loadstand to close the chute door. He stated he had climbed upon the
loadstand, hammered on the chute door to close it and climbed off the loadstand. While he was squeezing between posts of the chute set of timber and
the car Salazar started backing the car toward the chute. The side of the
car caught his left shoulder and shoved his right side up against the ends
of some lagging nailed onto and below the loadstand floor to deflect muck into
cars being loaded. Measurements taken during investigation showed that the
space between the car and timbers was eleven inches. The moving car rolled
Altamirano in this space, jamming his right side against the timbers. Salazar
became aware of what had happened when his attention was attracted by a red
shirt Altamirano had on. He stopped the motor and tried to release the
injured man. Being unable to do so he got back on the motor and pulled the
car back, freeing him.

The committee investigating this accident decided that Salazar violated
haulage safety rules by moving the motor and car without having received a
signal to do so. Had he been paying attention and waited for a signal the
accident would not have occurred. Recommendations were:

(1) Strict compliance with safety procedures regarding movement of
    trains.

(2) Attention to work being done.

This accident is classified as follows:

20. Haulage (Undg.)
    A. Caught between train and wall

I. Agency
   10. Mine Cars

II. Type
    13. Haulage

III. Supervisory
     3. Poor Discipline
        a. Disobedience

IV. Physical   C. F. Wright
    None   Safety Inspector

Bisbee, Arizona
June 23, 1965

PHELPS DODGE CORPORATION
COPPER QUEEN BRANCH
- - -

DISCUSSION OF A LOST TIME ACCIDENT OCCURRING IN MARCH, 1973

Report No. 1

UNDERGROUND DEPARTMENT "Div. "C" DALLAS

L. A. Patscheck, payroll #928, miner, was injured in 279-E stope on the 2000 level at 6:20 p.m. on March 21, 1973.

Nature of Injury: Fractured right ankle.

Estimated Period of Disability: 6 to 8 weeks.

How Accident Occurred: Patscheck was standing in a shallow trench, making adjustments on a slusher mucking pole, when some ground fell from the back in a newly blasted corner set. A sulphide lime boulder approximately 16" in diameter rolled down the muck pile, striking his ankle. B. J. Oller, miner, was standing in a set nearby when the accident occurred.

Investigation was held by a committee of the following:

        C. L. Hostetler and J. F. Shaffer, miners
        C. W. Welles, Shift Boss
        R. J. Whelan, Night Foreman
        C. J. Wright, Safety Engineer
        B. J. Oller assisted.

Preliminary investigation was held shortly after the accident occurred by Whelan, Welles and Oller and the following morning by M. H. Imus, General Mine Foreman, J. W. Melton, Division Foreman and Wright.

A square set section, consisting of 8 X 8 timbers was being mined in sulphide ore on the stope floor level above the Dallas 1800 foot level, terminating at the waste contact in the back and on the right side. A row of corner sets were being driven along the right side of the section. The preceeding day shift had blasted for the third corner set. At start of shift on date of accident Welles instructed Patscheck and Oller to do the preliminary work of barring down and installing booms. When the men arrived at the stope Patscheck went down into the stope, wet down, hooked up the slusher and started mucking. Oller remained on the mine level and rustled timber. After he entered the stope the slusher cable hook-up was changed and the mucking continued until it was decided to install a mucking pole at the top of the pile outside of the sets. Accordingly Oller climbed the muck-pile and Patscheck carried the collapsible mucking pole to the bottom of the muck pile. He was using an axe to loosen the extension when the back started dribbling. As Oller was returning to the safety of the square sets an estimated ton of ground crumbled off the back. Patscheck was moving toward the adjacent set and stumbled on the bank of the shallow trench. He stated that the boulder struck him as he was falling down.

The committee was of opinion that Patscheck should have made adjustments on the mucking pole before taking it up to the muck pile. Had he done so the accident would not have occurred.

This accident is classified as follows:

        9. Fall of Ground
            C. Stopes

516

Discussion of a Lost Time Accident
March 21, 1973

I. Agency
   2. Falling objects

II. Type
   5. Fall of ground

III. Supervisory
   2. Inability of Employees
      d. Poor judgement

IV. Physical
   13. Improper Working Conditions
      f. Back not barred down

C. J. Wright
Safety Engineer

Bisbee, Arizona
3/26/73
CJW:fc

B. J. Otter here when accident occurred to Patscheck.

Day Shift Blasted.

Trench

Patscheck here when boulder hit his rt. ankle.

Slusher

Manway

Accident Scene 3-21-73.   L.A. Patscheck, Miner.

279 E stope 2000 Dallas.

Square set section one floor level high.

Sulphide ore. Waste on rt. side & in back.

Pancho Yguado and 1300 Calyx Raise

By Richard W. Graeme III, May 27, 2014

The calyx system was a mechanically driven series of interconnected raises from the 1300 level to the surface at the Cole mine. It principle use was to bring in mine waste rock from the surface and various level in between to use as gob in stopes during the normal mining process.

While the raise was one long opening, transfer points were placed on all of the levels it intercepted to allow for the control of the flow of rock as well as to allow for waste rock developed on the individual levels to be introduced into the system. When there was no need for rock waste, the material dumped into the waste system on the various levels was pulled on the 1300 level and loaded into typically H-cars and transported to a waste system that fed into slusher scrams on the 1400 level for loading by slusher into Granby cars and then hauled to the Dallas waste pocket for hoisting to the surface.

Even though the calyx raises were smooth-walled, waste with a high content of clay or claylike materials and few rocks was difficult to get through the system. Much of the time, it was possible to get it moving using a long blow-pipe, but not always. Blasting the hung up muck using loading sticks wired together to reach the plug was the next resort, which was often successful. Lastly and though it was the forbidden, but occasionally used was the practice of running water on top of the hung muck to somewhat liquefy it and make it move. The danger here was that liquefied muck could move suddenly and was unstoppable. Ken Gill was killed on the 1100 at the calyx raise when liquefied muck flowed over the chute door and buried him, causing him to suffocate. This was caused by accumulated water during a long strike and was not intentionally introduced.

One graveyard shift, I was working as a motor swamper with Pancho Yguado as motorman on the 1300 Cole; trying to pull very sticky waste from the calyx. It was our first train of the shift and I had worked a blowpipe for several hours to fill the first seven of the nine car train, when Pancho said he would spell me. I should have been suspicious as it was not in his nature to work, much less take on such an arduous task or to cut me any kind of a break. As using the blowpipe for such a long time filled the air with mist, I had not seen the tiny light in the distance; our boss Harim Wright was coming and Pancho knew it. We changed places and Pancho was working the blowpipe, I was seated on the motor at the far end of the train when Harim arrive. The first thing he did was to chastise me for making "poor ol" Pancho do the dirty work; me covered from head to toe with mud blown back by the blowpipe. I said nothing. He then climbed on the loading platform, which was quite long in case of runaway muck, and talked to Pancho for a bit. I have always suspected he told Pancho that he had put a good bit of water into the raise from the 1200 level, as he knew it was difficult muck from the nightshift reports. Harim then left, but not before reminding me that loading cars was my job.

Moments later there was an air blast as the muck dropped, not uncommon, but Pancho's scream could be heard over the running blow pipe and flowing mud. The dropping muck had blown out the chute door and flowed onto the loading stand; first covering Pancho's feet and lower legs so he could not run, then washing him onto the track five feet below between the crosscut rib and mine cars, totally burying him.

I ran through the knee-deep, still flowing mud to his hardhat, now floating on the watery mass, but the cap-lamp was not burning, suggesting a broken cord, so I pushed on, now waist deep in mud and began a frantic search in another spot for my fat friend. Why I chose to dig where I did, I will never know, but within seconds I uncovered his face a foot or so down and struggled to keep it free of the flowing muck. I took off my Army field coat and encircled his head, forming a dam of sorts, while digging with my hands to take some of the weight off of his ample chest so that he could breath. Fortunately the flow of the muck had slowed substantially.

Once I had some of this chest uncovered and was sure that muck would not again cover his face I said I would go for help and he begin to plead with me not to go. He was terrified that the more mud would flow and cover him again. However, I knew that to delay could be fatal, as I had no idea of how badly he might be hurt. I ran the half-mile or so to the shaft., sounded the seven bell emergency signal followed by the level bell code, called the cager on the mine phone and told him where I was, what happened and that medical help was needed immediately. I then ran back to Pancho, reassured him and uncoupled the cars behind of him and pulled the train completely out of the crosscut so the basket/stretcher could be brought in. I began to wash the mud from his eyes with water I had put into my hardhat, then slowly freed his arms. He was delusional with pain by this time and fought me as I attempted to uncover him.

Soon help arrived and we very carefully removed the mountain of mud several feet high from his lower body while supporting him as the very liquid mass, which was slowly flowing from underneath his body as he fought and squirmed; a great concern of mine if he had spinal injuries I wanted his back supported. Before we had completely freed him a doctor arrived and gave him something to calm him down. One leg was bent 90° to the right, clearly broken, and blood was oozing through his pant leg. Still, we had no idea what all might be broken or badly hurt.

Four of us slid him into the basket, along with copious amounts of mud, covered him with blankets, strapped him in and then placed him on the motor for the trip to the shaft, where the cagers and the doctor took over. Except for a badly splintered leg and assorted bumps and bruises, Pancho was OK. He would miss most of a year's work recuperating.

The accident investigation revealed that substantial water had entered the raise – somehow – and when the muck fell, knocking out the chute door, it pinned Pancho's feet and he could not run along the long loading stand built for just such an incident. The force of the flowing muck against his ample torso twisted his body while his feet were stuck in the thick mud, causing a rotational fracture to his one leg before completely washing him off of the loading stand to the space between the loaded mine cars and the stand. Had I not quickly uncovered and protected his face, he would have suffocated like Ken did on the 1100.

While Pancho was off, I worked the graveyard shift, swamping for his temporary replacement, a crazy, but likable Mexican called Indian Joe", we got along very well. During this time, I would often stop and see Pancho as he sunned himself in the park at the old General Office. He never mentioned the accident and neither did I, but his slight limp said it still hurt a bit.

Foolishly, I figured that when Pancho came back to work he would be a changed man, a grateful person for being saved. Wrong! He was meaner to me than ever - abusive to the point that I cursed him on occasion, something I seldom did. Then reality set in as I realized that here he was – now with a limp and pain – forever to be the graveyard motorman, while for me, this was just a passing, but necessary phase, as I spent most every day in school, preparing for a future that he never had. It wasn't me he hated, it was the dead end he had built for himself that made him angry, something I saw in more than a few of my fellow miners as I worked nights to shape my tomorrows. Still, I was a little miffed that he failed to show any kindness. Years later he would thank me.

A train load of waste rock, 3rd level Southwest Mine.

Stopes

The rich ores in Bisbee were not mined in tunnels. (drifts & crosscuts) Stopes are where the copper, lead zinc and other metals were removed. Tunnels are the service passages used to bring men and supplies into the stopes. They also served as the routes that trains brought the broken ore to the hoisting shafts that lifted it to the surface. To understand many accidents it is essential to have a basic understanding of stoping. Stopes can be different sizes. Small stopes may be 20 ft. x 20 ft., larger ones are massive and can leave an opening over a 1,000 ft. across and 200 ft. tall. Different methods were used to mine stopes and many of these methods can be confusing. The following is a brief explanation of the two most common stoping methods, Square-set and Cut & Fill.

Stope in Higgins Mine, tunnel level

Copper Queen Style, Square-sets (after J.W. Toland)

Square-set stoping was used in Bisbee from the beginning until the closure in 1975. This method was invented by Philip Deidsheimer at the Ophir Mine in the Comstock Lode of Nevada. The method uses rectangular timber sets that interlock creating a honeycomb-like structure. Ores in heavy ground conditions are mined with this method. Although, the massive timbers do support the walls and ceiling of the mine workings, it is considered a temporary solution. Timber alone cannot support the weight of the caving rock. After sets are mined they are carefully filled with waste rock. As a result, when the stope is mined out it is also completely filled. As a result there is limited space left for the ground to cave. Some compaction of the waste rock does happen and a few feet of open space develops at the top of the stope. A limited amount of collapsing does occur, but the collapse is small and does not affect other mine workings. In contrast when a stope is left open the collapses are massive and mine workings within a couple hundred feet in any direction are destroyed. A square sets are typically modified to meet the needs of the mining company. At Bisbee

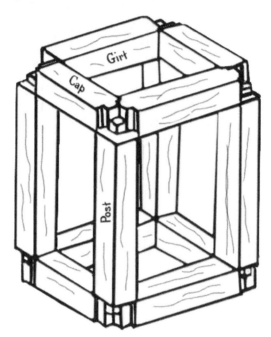

the sets were made of three types of 10" X 10" or 8"X8" timber, posts, caps and girts. Each of these has a unique style of tenon or horn cut on each end. Posts have a 5" X 5" X 5" cube on each end. These are the vertical supports. Caps are the main horizontal supports. When the square- sets are built they are oriented with the caps perpendicular to the direction that the greatest weight is expected. They have a 1-1/2" thick, 5" X 10" rectangle fashioned on each end. Girts often serve as spreaders and their main purpose is to keep the posts vertical and locked in position. On each end a 2-1/2" in thick 8" X 10" tenon is cut.

Square Set Tenons

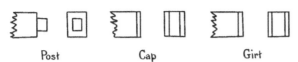

Post   Cap   Girt

Square Set Joint

Cap   Girt

Post

Normally, when an orebody is discovered the ground conditions are examined to determine the method in which to mine it. The square set method is timber intensive and expensive method to mine ore. Other methods such as Cut & Fill are preferred. If the decision is made to square set an orebody. The edges of the ore are determined and the stope is divided into blocks. These blocks are five sets by five sets and will extended vertically 100 feet. Extra sets may be added as needed to ensure all the ore is mined. A two compartment raise is driven from the starting level completely through to the level above. If the orebody is large other raises will be driven to be used as chutes. Waste rock for backfill is essential. In some cases a drift will be driven from the wall of the stope into waste rock. This is dumped into empty sets. Generally, a small raise centrally located in the stope a driven to the level above and cars of waste rock are dumped into it from tunnels and raises being driven for mine development. At times waste rock was scarce and raises were driven from the underground haulage drifts to the surface. This allowed for rock from the waste dumps to be sent underground to be distributed as backfill. Larger stopes may require several gob raises. Square sets stopes are often mined on multiple floors at the same time. In sturdy ground conditions permit 60-70 sets may be open at a given time. In heavy ground fewer than 25 sets may be open during mining. The largest orebodies mined in Bisbee exceeded a million tons. In this case the orebody was mined by a series of small stopes. Any pillars of ore left between these stopes would later be mined by a modified method of square-set mining called Mitchell Slicing. Timber that was used in square sets was generally not salvaged. After mining the wood is in poor condition. The timber is peppered with embedded rocks from blast and has splinter edges from work damage. Tenons can be deformed or broken. As a result it is not cost effective to salvage.

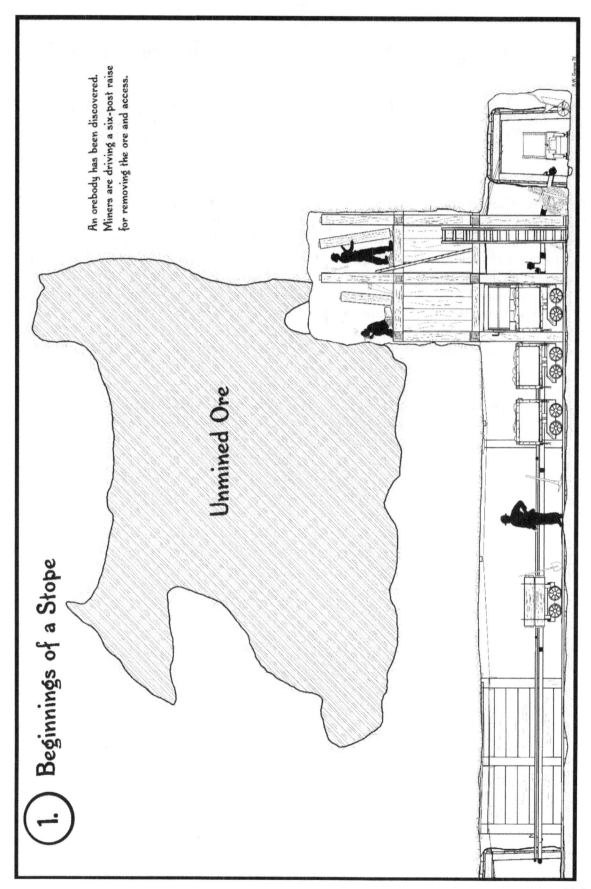

1. Beginnings of a Stope

An orebody has been discovered. Miners are driving a six-post raise for removing the ore and access.

Unmined Ore

R.W. Greene IV

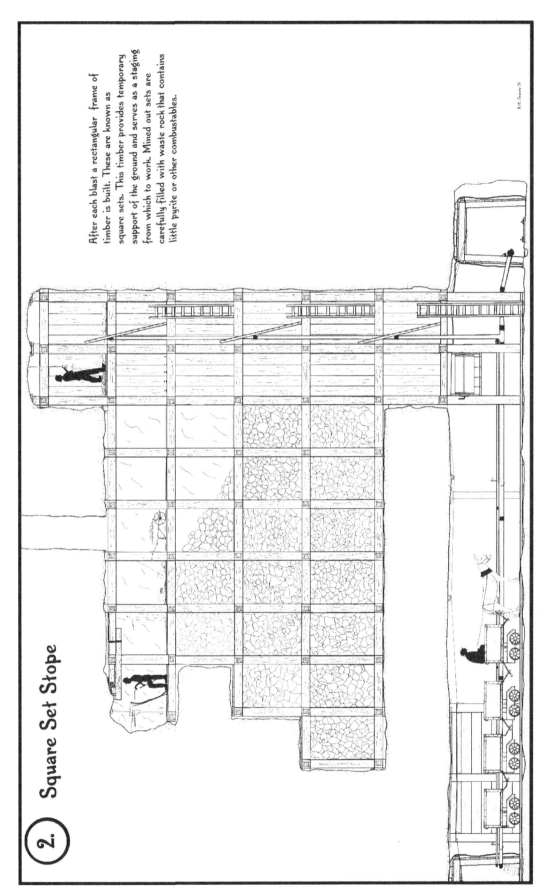

2. Square Set Stope

After each blast a rectangular frame of timber is built. These are known as square sets. This timber provides temporary support of the ground and serves as a staging from which to work. Mined out sets are carefully filled with waste rock that contains little pyrite or other combustables.

R.W. Greene IV

527

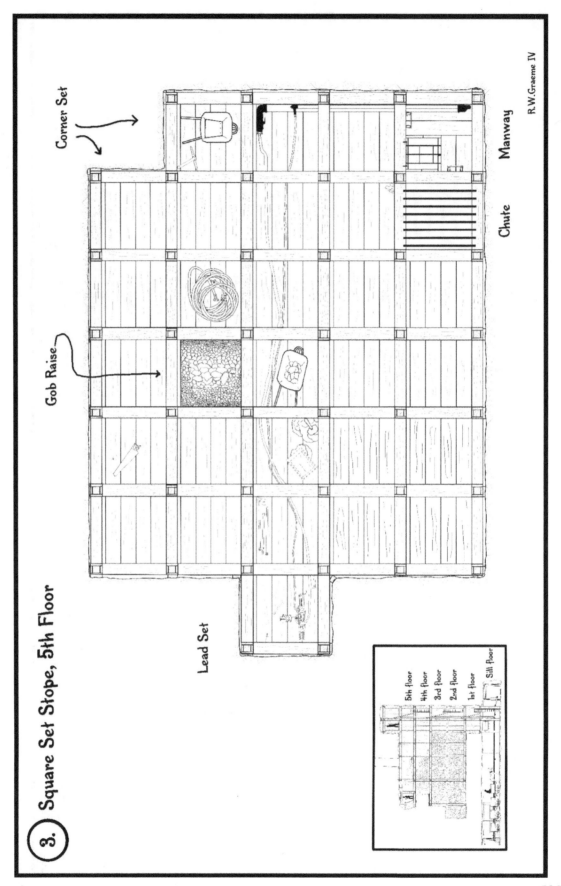

3. Square Set Stope, 5th Floor

Corner Set

Gob Raise

Lead Set

Chute

Manway

R.W.Graeme IV

5th floor
4th floor
3rd floor
2nd floor
1st floor
Sill floor

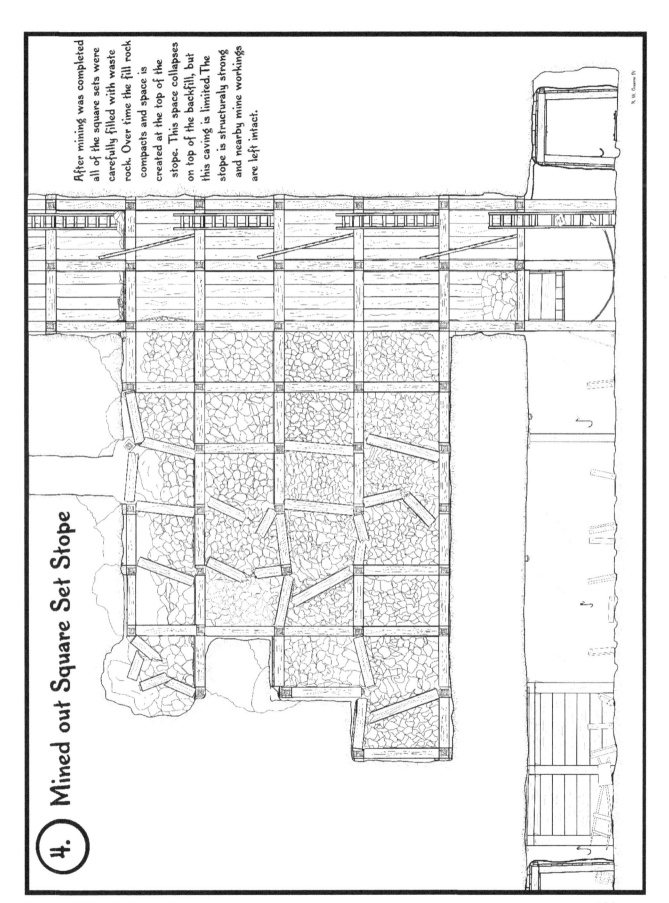

4. Mined out Square Set Stope

After mining was completed all of the square sets were carefully filled with waste rock. Over time the fill rock compacts and space is created at the top of the stope. This space collapses on top of the backfill, but this caving is limited. The stope is structurally strong and nearby mine workings are left intact.

R. W. Gruene IV

A square-set stope that has not been backfilled, c-1905

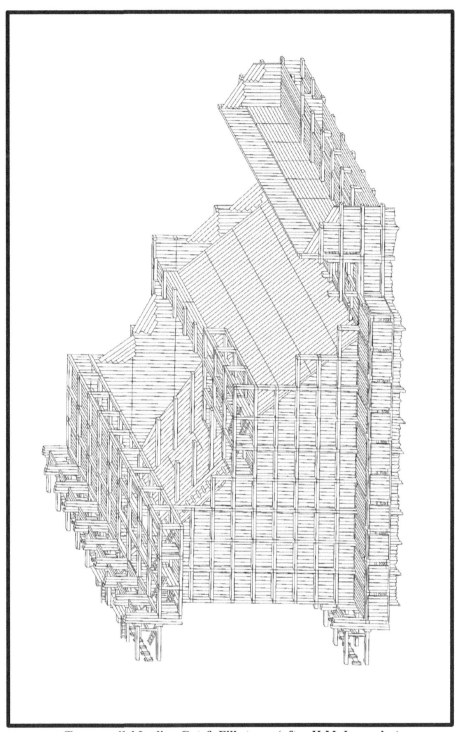

Two parallel Incline Cut & Fill stopes (after H.M. Lavender)

Another popular method of stoping in Bisbee was Cut & Fill. Although, the principles of this method were developed in the 1880's it was not until the twentieth century that it became in common use. This techniques was introduced at the Junction Mine at Bisbee in 1915, by Mine Foreman, Oscar Gilman. For a time it was known as "Gilman Cut & Fill stoping.

After an orebody was discovered and its boundaries determined the engineers divided it into stope sections and support pillars. A stope section was 45-50ft. wide and extended a length of 75ft. or if less to the end of the ore. Pillar sections were 45ft. wide and extended to the ore boundary. The orebody was mined with two 45-50ft. stope sections followed by a 45ft. pillar then two more stope sections followed by another pillar and so on. The remaining pillars were later mined with the Mitchell Slice method.

While the first floor was cut, a backfill (gob) raise would be driven to the level above. When the bottom floor was finished the bottom was covered with a mat of scrap timber. This timber mattress would allow miners to develop another stope directly underneath the first stope. Mining would continue upward at a 37 degree angle. The backfill would naturally form a slope at this angle. After an area was cut, the stope would be gobbed within two or three feet of the ceiling. This backfill would be covered with lagging and the next cut would begin. The lagging would prevent ore from mixing with the waste rock. The backfill also served as a staging and eliminated any significant timber used as scaffolding.

Chute underneath a Cut & Fill Stope, Campbell Mine, c-1940

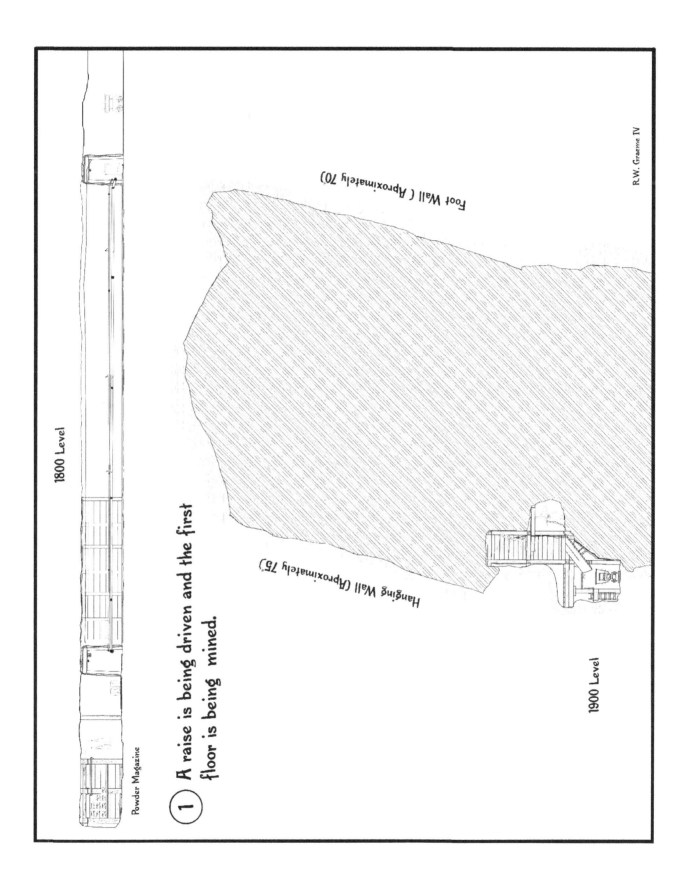

1800 Level

Powder Magazine

R.W. Graeme IV

Foot Wall (Aproximately 70')

Hanging Wall (Aproximately 75')

(1) A raise is being driven and the first floor is being mined.

1900 Level

533

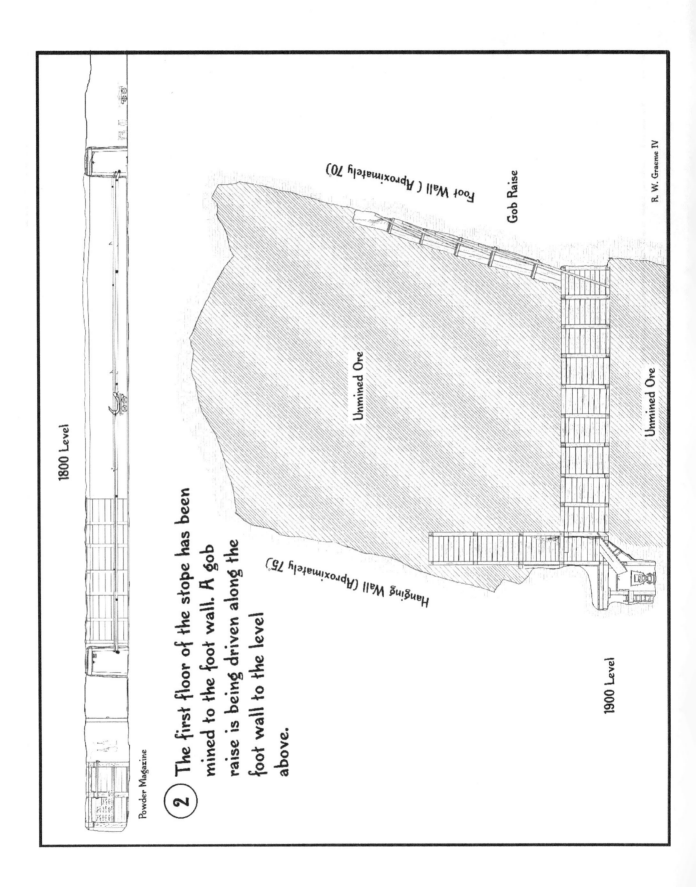

1800 Level

Powder Magazine

(2) The first floor of the stope has been mined to the foot wall. A gob raise is being driven along the foot wall to the level above.

Hanging Wall (Aproximately 75°)

Foot Wall (Aproximately 70°)

Gob Raise

Unmined Ore

Unmined Ore

1900 Level

R. W. Graeme IV

534

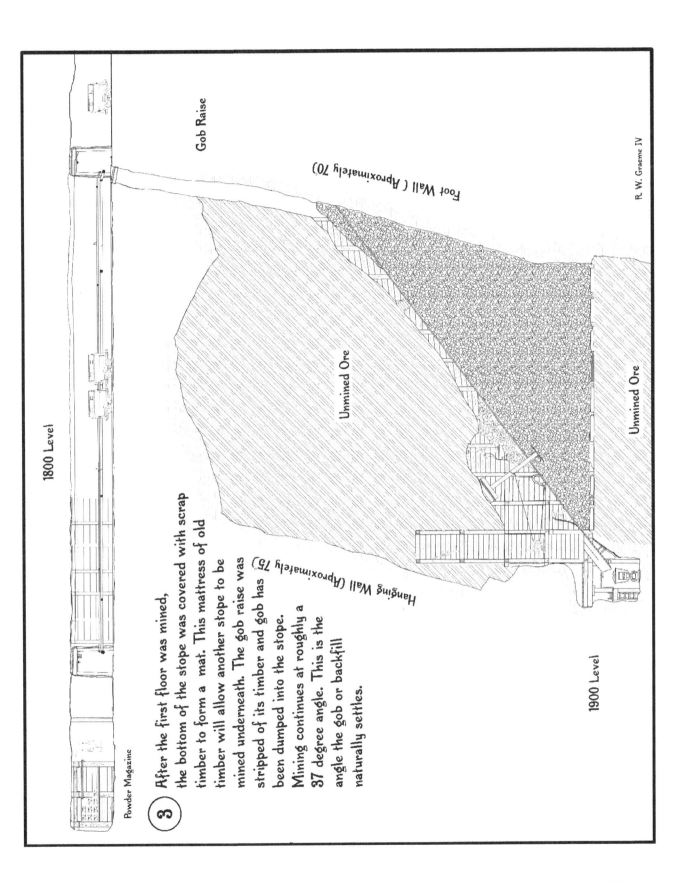

1800 Level

Powder Magazine

Gob Raise

Foot Wall (Aproximately 70)

Unmined Ore

R. W. Graeme IV

Hanging Wall (Aproximately 75)

Unmined Ore

1900 Level

③ After the first floor was mined, the bottom of the stope was covered with scrap timber to form a mat. This mattress of old timber will allow another stope to be mined underneath. The gob raise was stripped of its timber and gob has been dumped into the stope. Mining continues at roughly a 37 degree angle. This is the angle the gob or backfill naturally settles.

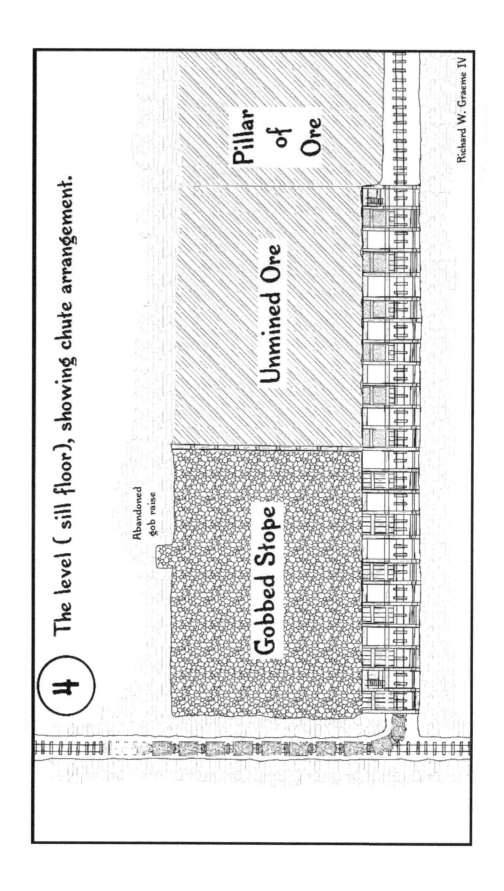

4 The level (sill floor), showing chute arrangement.

Pillar of Ore

Unmined Ore

Gobbed Stope

Abandoned gob raise

Richard W. Graeme IV

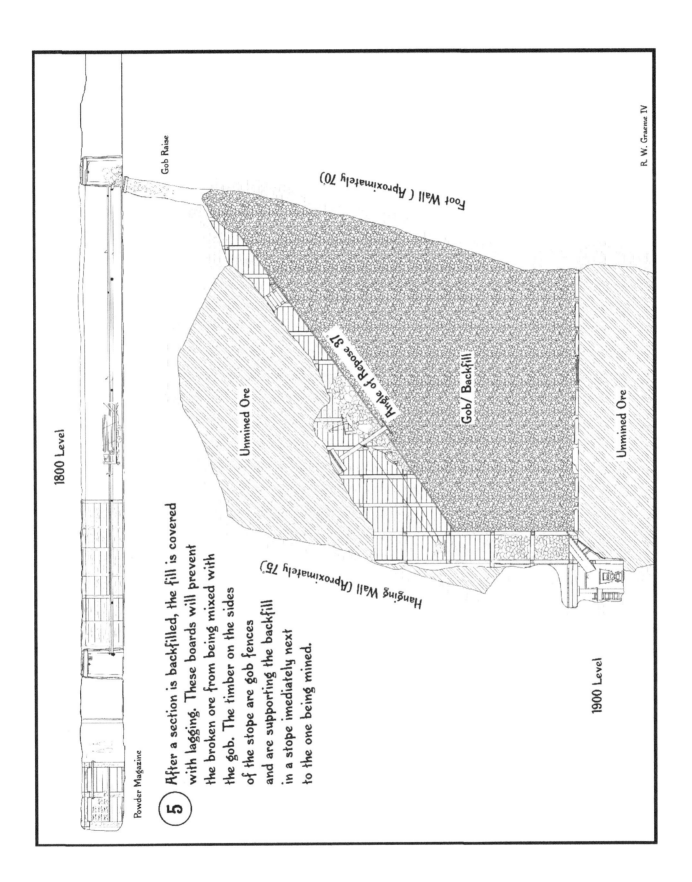

1800 Level

Powder Magazine

⑤ After a section is backfilled, the fill is covered with lagging. These boards will prevent the broken ore from being mixed with the gob. The timber on the sides of the stope are gob fences and are supporting the backfill in a stope imediately next to the one being mined.

Gob Raise

Foot Wall (Aproximately 70°)

Angle of Repose 37°

Unmined Ore

Gob/ Backfill

Unmined Ore

Hanging Wall (Aproximately 75°)

1900 Level

R. W. Graeme IV

537

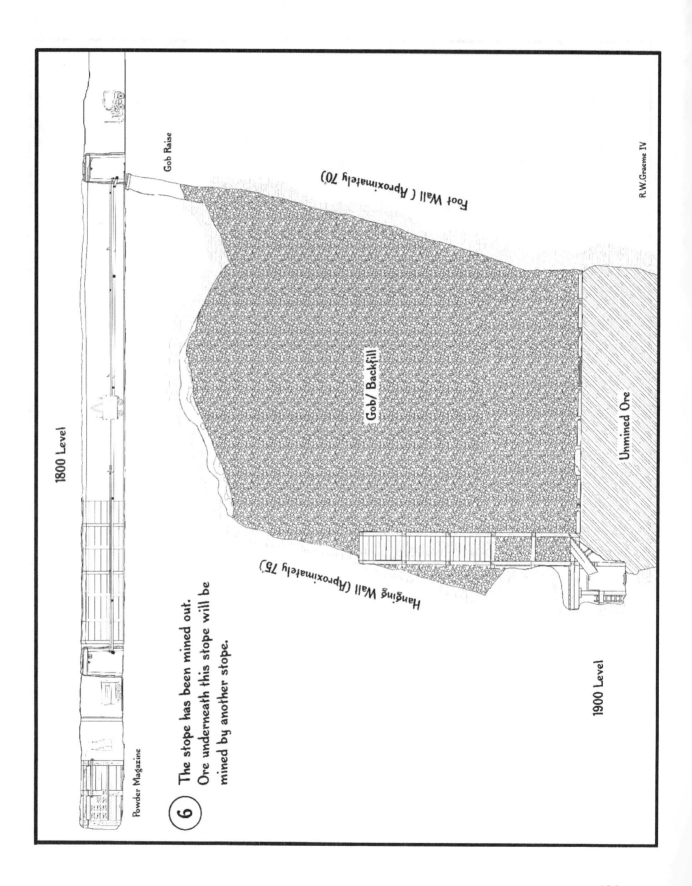

Powder Magazine

1800 Level

Gob Raise

Foot Wall (Aproximately 70')

Gob/ Backfill

Hanging Wall (Aproximately 75')

Unmined Ore

R.W. Graeme IV

1900 Level

6 The stope has been mined out. Ore underneath this stope will be mined by another stope.

Drilling in an Incline Cut & Fill Stope, Campbell Mine, c-1940

Loading blast holes in an Incline Cut & Fill Stope, Campbell Mine, c-1940

539

Brief Glossary of Mining Terms

The following is a quick reference guide and the definitions focus on how the terms are used in the previous text. For a complete dictionary acquire the *Glossary of Mining and Related Terms as used at Bisbee, Arizona* by Richard W. Graeme III, Douglas L. Graeme & Richard W. Graeme IV.

Air Door: These are doors built across the tunnels (crosscut or drift) to prevent air flowing through a particular section of the mine. They are often built in pairs to form a simple airlock. The distance between doors is longer than a full train of cars, so that only one door is opened at a time. The driver of the train will pull a lever attached to a pneumatic cylinder to open the door. He will pull on another lever to shut the door. At least three men were killed when they crashed through closed air doors.

Backfill: Waste rock that has been used to fill in abandoned mine workings. Backfill was essential part of the mine support system when it was used to fill in stopes. When there was an excess of waste rock other mine workings, such as tunnels were backfilled. Gob is a more common term used for backfill.

Bar: A long, pointed steel bar, usually with a 3" piece of air or water hose attached to the middle. They were used to pry down loose rocks. The piece of hose prevented rocks from rolling down the bar and striking the miner.

Bar & Column: A drill mount consisting of a vertical pipe called a column and a horizontal piece with a clamp called the arm. The column was secured to the ceiling or walls of the mine by large screws. Often drills were mounted on the arm when drilling in tunnels. This arrangement is sometimes called a machine bar & column.

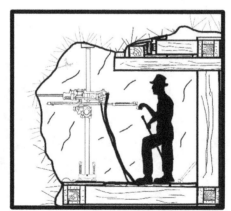

A drill mounted on a bar and column

Cage: These are the elevators used to transport men and supplies into the mine. In contrast to building elevators these cages can be completely open or are partially enclosed. An occupant has a view of the shaft timber and stations as it moves up or down the shaft. Also unlike, building elevators they often have multiple decks. Cages of one, two and three decks were used at Bisbee. They are controlled underground by ringing bells. Each number of bells tells the hoistman how to move the cage. If a miner rings 1—2 bells (to collar) followed by 3—2 bells (hoist men) the hoistman would know he was taking the cage to the surface and was hoisting a cage containing people. The Calumet & Arizona Mining company used flashes of light rather than bells, but used the same signals.

Cap: A horizontal piece of timber and are often located at the top of a set. They give support for ground movement from the side. (see set)

Chute: Typically, these are raises that rock is being dropped into to transfer the broken material to a lower area of the mine. They have steel or wooden doors mounted at the top of a short wooden trough. This allows mine cars to be loaded directly from the chute.

Chute

Crib: Timber that has been stacked in the shape of a hollow square. These timbers are loose and are held in place by shallow notches. The center of a crib set is often filled with broken waste rock. Crib sets are strong, but can buckle if they are built overly tall.

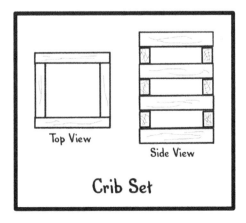

Crosscut: These are what layman refer to as tunnels. In Bisbee the terms drift and crosscuts were used interchangeably. At mines (not Bisbee) where veins are being mined these are tunnels that are driven at 90 degrees to the vein and crosscut the vein.

Drift: These are what layman refer to as tunnels. In Bisbee the terms drift and crosscuts were used interchangeably. At mines (not Bisbee) where veins are being mined these are tunnels that are driven following the vein and drift with the vein.

Drifter: Massive 125-250 lb. pneumatic drills. These are too heavy to be hand-held by miners and are either mounted on a bar and column or mounted on a drill rig called a Jumbo. These were replaced by jackleg drills in the 1960s.

Finlay: A pneumatic overshot mucking machine. These machines would move foreward and scoop up broken rock. Then the operater would lift the bucket over the machine's body and dump the bucket full of muck in a waiting mine car. They are also called mucking machines (see picture page 92)

Finlay loading an "A" car

Girt: These are horizontally placed timbers in square-sets. They keep posts locked in position and vertical. (see set)

Gob (see backfill)

Grizzly: These are rails that are placed at equal distances across a raise. This is to prevent large boulders falling into a chute, but allows smaller rocks and dirt to fall through. The boulders would be caught on the rails and broken with a double jack (sledge hammer).

Headframe: A tall tower structure over the top of a shaft. Located at the pinnacle of the tower are sheave wheels. These are spoked steel wheels that serve as pulley wheels. The cable comes from the hoist and passes over the sheave wheel and then down to attach to a skip, cage or sinking bucket. Most headframes in Bisbee were 60-100 ft. tall. Just below the middle of the tower and about 30 ft. above the ground was often a toplander's deck. These are often partially enclosed with sheet to protect the workmen called toplanders from the weather. At the toplander's deck mine cars loaded with rock would be unloaded and pushed to either and dumped into an ore bin or on the waste dump. At ground level is the shaft collar. This is where men and supplies were loaded on caged to enter the mine.

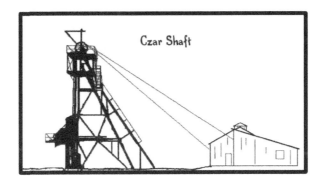

Headframe

Lagging: These are wide relatively thin boards. They came in two common sizes 2" X 12" and 3" X 12". They were cut to needed lengths. To save on lumber the lagging was often split in two pieces. This was called split lagging.

Machine Bar & Column: (see bar & column)

Manway: Ladder way in a shaft, winze or raise. Often one compartment of these type of workings was devoted to ladders for men to climb, pipes and electrical lines. Early manways were built as a single long ladder made of shorter ladders scabbed together. This was dangerous. A man who fell went completely to the bottom. In main shafts this could be over 2,000 ft. As one of the first safety changes, ladders in manways were offset with landings. This limited the distance a man could fall to less than 10 ft.

Manway

Mine car: A small rail car designed to haul broken rock. Many different designs were used and the cars were classified by a letter. An "H" car was a rocker dump style and held roughly one ton of rock. The "K" were cars shipped to Bisbee after the mines at Jerome, Arizona closed. These had a two ton capacity and were a rocker type dumping car.

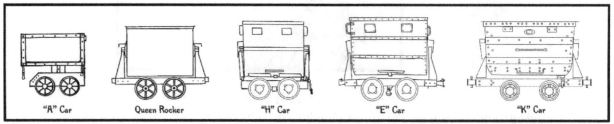

"A" Car   Queen Rocker   "H" Car   "E" Car   "K" Car

Types of Mine Cars

Motor: a common term meaning locomotive. Three basic types of electric locomotives were used. Trolley locomotives were larger and used in main haulage areas with a 250v DC bare copper trolley wire providing the necessary power. Battery powered locomotive were used for lighter service. A few combination motors which could use battery or trolley power were used.

Mucking Machine: (see Finlay)

Plugger: 40-65 lb. drills that were could be hand held or at times were suspended from a rope attached to a side rod on the drill. (see picture page 39)

Post: Vertical or nearly vertically placed timbers used to support downward ground movement. (see set)

Powder: A term that refers to dynamite or in 1960s or later to ANFO (ammonium nitrate fuel oil)

Powder Box

Raise: A mine opening that is started from the bottom and drilled and blasted upward. Raises provided access to stopes and other mine workings. Other raises, called gob holes were used to dump waste rock. This provided essential rock fill to support stopes. Raises with chutes at the bottom were used to drop ore from a higher area to a level for haulage to the surface. Raises were divided into compartments. The two compartment raise was the most common with one compartment devoted to a manway, pipes and a timber slide. The second had a chute door at the bottom and was for handling rock. One, two & three compartment raise are often used. Larger raises may have four compartments and rarely as many as six. Raises are easier and cheaper to build than winzes.

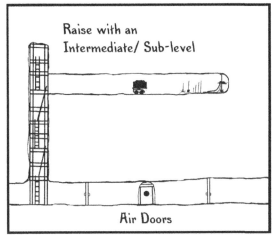

Side view of a raise

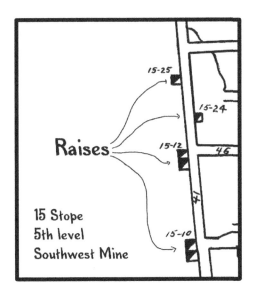

A map showing the location of raises

545

Set: a complete unit of timber. (see Crib)

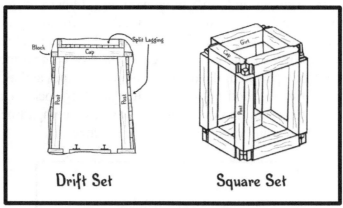

Two different types of sets

Shaft: An inclined or vertical mine working that is used to provide ventilation and / or hoisting of rock, supplies and men. At intervals horizontal levels branch out, much like floors in a building.

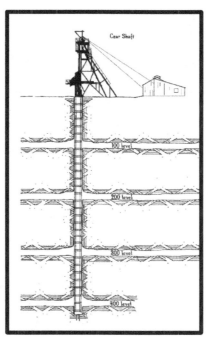

Shaft

Shaft Timber: This timber provides support from ground movement from the shaft walls. It also is used to attach the shaft guides which allows for a smooth traveling of cages and skips. It consists of wall plates, end plates, dividers and bearers. The bearers or bearing timber are hitched into the walls of the shaft. The other timbers can hang from the bearing timber, although generally the shaft timbers are wedged in tight enough to support themselves.

Shaft Timber

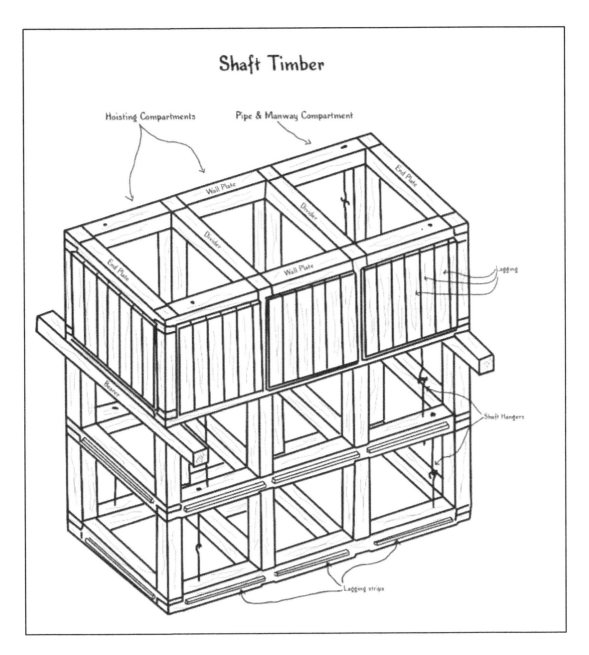

Shaft Timber

Sinking Bucket: Steel buckets with heavy bails. During shaft sinking they were attached to the hoisting cable. At the bottom of the shaft the broken rock would be shoveled into the bucket and hoisted to the surface. On the bottom of the bucket there was a steel chain with a steel ball or a thick plate attached. At the surface this ball or plate will catch on the dumping mechanism when the bucket is lowered slightly. The bucket tilts over and pours its contents into an ore bin. Smaller buckets are used to sink winzes. To ride a bucket, miners would stand on the edge of the bucket and hold onto the cable. This practice was exceeding dangerous, but was regularly done.

547

Skip: A bucket-like device to hoist broken rock out of a shaft. Unlike sinking buckets they were designed to use shaft guides for a smooth journey through the shaft. They were first used in Bisbee at the Sacramento Shaft in 1908.

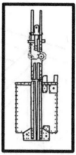

Side view of a skip

Stope: This is location were ore is being mined. These are irregularly shaped chambers vary in size. The largest stopes extended over 2,000 ft. across and extended vertically over 200 ft. Three major methods for mining stopes were used in Bisbee. Square-set, Cut & Fill and Stull.

Stoper: A pneumatic drill that is designed to drill vertical or near vertical holes. The drill is attached to a pneumatic cylinder that extends and pushed the drill upwards.

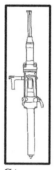

Stoper

Timber Truck: Small flat cars for use on the underground rails. They are often used to haul timber through the mine, but not exclusively. Rock drills, rail and other equipment are moved underground on timber trucks. When a man was injured a timber truck was found and boards (lagging) placed across it to transport them to the surface. Miners often referred to them simply as "trucks"

Timber truck

Wall plates: Long, heavy timbers used in shafts that are fashioned have end plates and dividers attached. They are used on the long sides of a shaft. (See shaft timber)

548

Winze: These workings are drilled and blasted from the top down. They are more difficult and expensive to build than raises. Winzes are typically developed to explore areas underground below the main mining areas and do not have other mine workings nearby at the lower elevation.

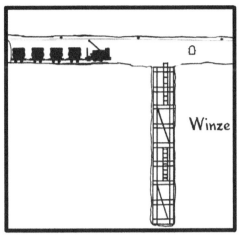

Side view of a winze

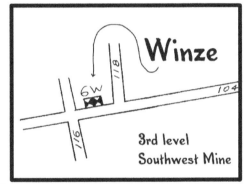

A map showing the location of a winze

Index

A

Jesse B., 435

D

E

H

Edward, 277

Kahler
    Foreman, 360
Kahrs
    Henry, 199, 214
Kalastro
    M.E., 286
Kane
    J.H., 417
Kaneaster
    Arthur, 177
Kangas
    E.W., 58
Kankaala
    Charlie, 254
Kasun
    W.M, 114
Kauffman
    August, 324
Keating
    John, 454
Keckman
    Victor, 210
Keefe
    Mike, 148
Keenan
    Thomas, 241
Keiler
    John, 219
Keller
    Charles, 242
Kelly
    J.W., 227
    John R., 251
    Leo, 362
    William, 120
Kempton
    ?, 177
Kennwaugh
    Aaron, 437
Keosker
    John, 334
Kerr
    A.W., 425
Keton
    John, 236
    Matt, 236
Kewley
    William Henry, 143
Kickham
    John, 198, 199
King

Charles C., 194
    O.M., 353
    Sam, 123
Kingston
    William, 392
Kirk
    Charles R., 361
Kirkland
    George, 127
Kirschwing
    M., 125
Kiser
    George, 185
Klag
    George, 262
Kline
    Charles, 419
    Mike, 408
Klinger
    A.R., 231
    Hiram E., 231
Kneale
    Robert, 133
Knox
    Joe, 414
Knucky
    C.L., 235
Koff
    Anton, 219
Kohler
    Foreman, 424
Kohlmeyer
    Harry J., 146
Koik
    Charles, 346
Koscielniak
    L., 98, 99
Kovach
    George, 77
Krahn
    Hugo, 136
Kraker
    Pete, 176
Kranz
    William, 446
Kren
    Frank, 175
Krieger
    John, 259
Krilly
    James, 337
Kroker
    Pete, 339
Kronman
    John, 417
Krumlin
    Charles, 201
    J.H., 201
    John C., 201

M

Maitland
    Robert, 437
Maki
    John, 80, 336
Malcovich
    Sam, 251
Malley
    C.O., 107, 306
    James, 412, 455
Mallory
    Robert, 319
Mandarich
    Joe, 448
Manix
    M.D., 195
Manje
    J., 108
Mankin
    Frank L., 236
Manovich
    Nick, 343
Manrojo
    Pablo, 372
manway, 9, 26, 32, 34, 58, 59, 73, 76, 80, 81, 100,
    119, 133, 139, 140, 141, 142, 143, 144, 159, 162,
    178, 186, 187, 192, 216, 218, 219, 229, 230, 234,
    235, 254, 266, 315, 334, 337, 348, 357, 360, 364,
    365, 366, 407, 420, 435, 449, 452, 455, 523, 526,
    527, 553
Marenez
    W.P., 88
Marinez
    W.P., 114
Marrujo
    C.D., 107
    P., 157
Marshal
    Tom, 148
Marshall
    Charlie, 358
    Chris, 325
Martin
    C.H., 384
    H.M., 99
    L.H., 84
    T.A., 170
    T.P., 63, 288, 289
    Thomas, 428
    William H., 80
Martinez
    Andrew, 400
    C.L., 163
    C.T., 54
    E.F., 96, 110
    E.R., 400
    F.Q., 101
    Gilberto, 197
    J.E., 63, 287
    J.M., 111, 114

Jose S., 371
Martino
    Cima, 132
Martinovich
    Vaso, 400
Marusich
    M.I., 99, 109, 165
Masgrove
    A.R., 59
Masima
    Joseph, 452
Mason
    G.A., 307
    Tom, 280
Mass
    William, 259
Massey
    Charles, 271
Masterson
    James A., 334
Mata
    Alberto M., 384
Mathews
    Thomas, 280
Matson
    Ben, 319
    James, 225
Matta
    William, 177
Matthews
    ?, 320
    D.A., 299
    E.B., 427
Mattingly
    Ron, 302
Mattinson
    E.E., 421
Mattson
    Theodore, 175
Matzmacher
    A., 192
Mauser
    John L., 230
Mauzy
    Kim, 307
Maybry
    G.P., 196
Mayers
    George, 61
Mc Allister
    J.W., 125
Mc Call
    W.G., 454
Mc Pherson
    B.J., 438
McAguire
    Jose, 247
McBride
    J.D., 371
McBurney

Najara
    Julian, 85
Narce
    Claude N., 72
Navarrete
    J.A., 62
Naylor
    Lewis B., 291
Neely
    H.C., 448
    H.E., 448
Neenan
    Jack, 263
Neff
    Mary L. Dr., 316
Nelson
    Charles S., 434
    Eric, 67
    George, 445
    Jack, 228
    John W., 420
Nemie
    Oscar, 39
Neonan
    Andy, 194
Nesbitt
    Richard, 454
Netherlands
    Joseph, 418
Newton
    William, 138
Nicholas
    Fred, 406
Nichols
    Dave, 130
    R.G., 291
Nicolson
    R., 179
Niemi
    A.E., 288
Nieta
    F.T., 95
Nieto
    F.L., 108
    F.T., 112
Niglayson
    Alex, 183
Nolan
    M.J., 221
    Martin, 214
Nolley
    James A., 451

Noriega
    Fernando, 399
Norris
    Harold, 289
    N., 305
Norton
    Edward M., 181
Norwegian, 218
Nova Scotia, 140, 142, 317, 352, 440
Nowlin
    De Witt, 383
    Dewey G., 383
Nunez
    A.R., 295
    Jose, 374
    Juan, 371
Nuquest
    Charles, 182

O' Brien
    William, 417
O' Sullivan
    Michael J., 444
O'Brien
    Mike, 450
O'Connell
    Dan, 420
O'Donald
    John, 234
O'Donnelly
    Pat, 322
O'Hara
    Jack, 450
    Joseph, 443
O'Neill
    Michael Thomas, 223
    Patrick J., 223
Obermiller
    Frank, 74, 75
Obertaxer
    John, 184
Oddo
    A., 321
Oder
    Jack, 218
Ojang
    ?, 296
Ojola
    Jacob, 335
Oleary
    C.C., 100

Oliver
   Frank, 187
Olney
   Lizzie, 202
Olsen
   Archer E., 397
Olson
   L., 82
Olvera
   M.P., 103, 107
Oquita
   R., 109
Ordonyon
   George, 326
ore, 12, 15, 17, 18, 19, 21, 28, 32, 33, 34, 35, 43, 44,
   53, 54, 57, 63, 71, 73, 77, 85, 88, 90, 96, 100, 101,
   103, 109, 112, 116, 119, 122, 123, 131, 132, 149,
   151, 154, 155, 158, 160, 161, 163, 164, 165, 171,
   180, 193, 194, 195, 198, 199, 200, 202, 205, 208,
   213, 219, 224, 228, 248, 249, 250, 257, 258, 263,
   273, 277, 278, 280, 290, 295, 296, 297, 298, 303,
   304, 305, 306, 313, 328, 330, 331, 351, 356, 358,
   359, 368, 369, 370, 377, 383, 385, 389, 390, 392,
   394, 396, 397, 402, 403, 408, 416, 425, 427, 429,
   430, 433, 436, 437, 442, 444, 451, 453, 454, 517,
   526, 529, 533, 540, 550, 553, 555, 556
Orice, 123
Orize, 123
Orozco
   B.R., 110
   R.J., 100
Orton
   August, 280
   Cecil, 366
   H., 50
   Johnnie Ida, 366
   William David, 366
Osborn
   John, 40

Pach
   Jon, 343
Pacheco
   Francisco jr, 439
Paco
   Manuel, 250
Padilla
   O.E., 167
Page
   ?, 418
   George Andrew, 178
Paken
   Roy M., 275

Palebro
   Gabriel, 250
Palmer
   A.E., 236
   Harry, 137
Palomino
   John, 53
   Julio M., 157, 161
Panovich
   M., 310
Papadopolis
   ?, 446
Papas
   Dominic, 192
Paprika
   George, 149
Parker
   Robert, 347
Parra
   B.C., 95, 98
Parrish
   F.C., 306
   George, 130
Parten
   J.L., 156
Parvin
   Joe, 447
Pascoe
   Bert, 84
   Norman, 84
Pasnenan
   Tovio, 255
Patche
   John, 363
Patscheck
   L.A., 503
Patterson
   G.M., 272
   Supeintendent, 172
Pattinson
   John, 393
   Robert Hunter, 393
Pavlicich
   Leopold P., 194
Pawlowski
   Joseph, 196
Peccolo
   Joe, 346
Peck
   N.S., 221
Peeler
   J.E., 307
Pellows
   James Henry, 424
Pelot
   Charles, 245, 431
   Charles F., 364
Pelton
   Roger, 371
Pelusti

Vaernervijk
  Rene, 85
Valdez
  Reyes, 281
  Toby, 18, 49
Valence
  Bentero, 247
Valenzuela
  Desiderio, 383
  Francisco, 371
  J.P., 57
  Jose, 437, 442
Valley
  Joseph, 127
Vangundy
  Fred, 334
Vanhulen
  M.D., 210
Vantress
  Mr., 394
Vargas
  J.B., 104
  J.M., 303
Vasil
  George, 437
Vasquez
  A.D., 101, 105
  Florenzo, 371
  J.Y., 48
  Jose, 127
Vastado
  Modesto Olibas, 371
Vaughn
  Grady, 350
Vega
  A.A., 105
Velarde
  J.G., 100
  Newton J., 279
Velardo
  Francisco, 150
Veliz
  Ramon, 177
Vercellino
  John, 399
Vernagus
  T.H. jr, 57
Vershay
  Joe, 235
Vian
  L.W., 112, 114

Vickers
  James, 349
Villa
  F.Q., 157
Villaneda
  Juan, 381
Vincent
  D.C., 401
Vinson
  E.C., 304
Vlacis
  William, 191, 475
Voelkel
  Louis, 414
Vorin*
  Al, 114
Vucedalic
  Chris Prenovich, 365
Vucedalich
  Chris, 478
Vuckovich
  Nicholas, 332
Vucotich
  Andrew, 125
Vucovitch
  Charles, 278
Vucurevich
  D., 169
Vucurivich
  Dan, 179
Vucurovich
  Bozo, 391
Vujacich
  John, 211
  Sam, 211
Vukic
  Sam, 118
Vuksanovich
  Ikee, 411
  Ilia J., 410
Vulich
  Nicholas, 252
Vutovich
  Lee, 338

W

J.S., 127
Ned, 193
R.H., 360
Robert, 263
S.S., 321
Sherriff Bill, 77
W.A., 269
W.J., 422
Whitehead
William, 275
Whitfield
Herman F., 87, 467
Whitford
William, 259
Wickerstrom
Arthur, 345
Wickman
Julius, 203
Wickstrom
Jack, 214
Widmer
Mrs., 84
Wildgrube
W., 79
Williams
Barney, 155
Charles, 250
D.C., 247
E.J., 268
F. Marvin, 86
Henry, 447
James, 443
Joe, 77, 226
John, 417
S.K., 354
Thomas Richard, 362
Williamson
C.H., 375
John E., 279
T., 279
Wilmoth
Jay Officer, 229
Wilmuth
Jay, 220
Wilson
Blondy, 326
John, 347
Lew, 142
Windsor
L., 103
L.C., 299
L.G., 99, 109
W.D., 100, 112
Winn
Oscar, 363
Winsley
Joseph, 234
Winters
Joe, 32

winze, 27, 181, 186, 202, 203, 214, 296, 328, 331, 357, 365, 454, 520, 526, 551, 557
Wise
A.L., 278
Wittig
Albert, 317
Charles, 229
E.H., 215, 225
Wollman
Basil, 280
George Basil, 367
Max Mrs., 367
Wood
C.K., 383
F.W., 233
J., 90
James Mrs., 140
John, 234
R.A., 372
Woodbury
John Edward, 130
Woodman
Parker, 153, 314, 404
Woods
I., 102
Sam, 363
Tommy, 133
Woosley
John, 282
Woron
William, 197
Wright
D.M., 302
Ernest, 422
F.J., 404
Frank, 422, 435
Harim, 509
Hiram, 93
Jacob, 422
L.J., 366
Thomas Wade, 275
William, 422
Wyatt
Lee, 172
Wycoff
Earl, 265
William P., 264

Y

Yanez
    Antonio, 380
Yarbrough
    R.P., 151
Yarcho
    John, 440
Ybarra
    Felipe, 328
Yeach
    Samuel, 173
Yguado
    Pancho, 93, 158, 509
Yokinen
    Tsak, 256
Young
    G.G., 421
    W.S., 214
Youtz
    C. Ralph, 277
Yungaray
    E., 62

Yutich
    Robert, 412

Z

Zabrovich
    Nelse, 332
Zannoria
    Dominic, 199
Zapf
    Oscar, 79
Zboray
    Joseph, 333
Zelinski
    Martin, 345
Zepeda
    E.C., 106
Zoricic
    John, 392
    Nick, 392

Main haulage drift, 3rd level Southwest Mine

Made in the USA
Las Vegas, NV
01 March 2025

18902905R00326